Agricultural Law

NEWTON RIGG COLLEGE

Agricultural Law

Christopher P. Rodgers

LLM (Cantab) LLB (Wales)
Solicitor of the Supreme Court,
Senior Lecturer in Law
Centre for Law in Rural Areas,
The University College of Wales,
Aberystwyth

Chapter 10 on Taxation by
C. V. Margrave-Jones LLM (Cantab)
Solicitor of the Supreme Court,
Lecturer in Law,
The University College of Wales,
Aberystwyth

Butterworths
London, Dublin, Edinburgh
1991

United Kingdom	Butterworth & Co (Publishers) Ltd, 88 Kingsway, LONDON WC2B 6AB and 4 Hill Street, EDINBURGH EH2 3JZ
Australia	Butterworths Pty Ltd, SYDNEY, MELBOURNE, BRISBANE, ADELAIDE, PERTH, CANBERRA and HOBART
Canada	Butterworths Canada Ltd, TORONTO and VANCOUVER
Ireland	Butterworth (Ireland) Ltd, DUBLIN
Malaysia	Malayan Law Journal Sdn Bhd, KUALA LUMPUR
New Zealand	Butterworths of New Zealand Ltd, WELLINGTON and AUCKLAND
Puerto Rico	Equity de Puerto Rico, Inc, HATO REY
Singapore	Malayan Law Journal Pte Ltd, SINGAPORE
USA	Butterworth Legal Publishers, AUSTIN, Texas; BOSTON, Massachusetts; CLEARWATER, Florida (D & S Publishers); ORFORD, New Hampshire (Equity Publishing); ST PAUL, Minnesota; and SEATTLE, Washington

A CIP Catalogue record for this book is available from the British Library.

ISBN 0 406 11269 X

Typeset by Phoenix Photosetting, Chatham, Kent
Printed and bound in Great Britain by Mackays of Chatham PLC, Chatham, Kent

Preface

This is primarily a book about agricultural land – about the law governing its tenure, its use, and ancillary related matters. Hitherto the concern of agricultural lawyers has been primarily with the Agricultural Holdings legislation and its not inconsiderable complexities. The advent of the common agricultural policy of the European Economic Community, and increased concern for environmental protection, have in recent years, however, led to a significant increase in the volume of legislation regulating the use of agricultural land. Although the law of agricultural holdings is dealt with in some depth in the text, additional chapters have therefore been included dealing with Quotas, Planning and Conservation, Set Aside and Diversification, and Tied Agricultural Accommodation. I am grateful to the publishers for allowing considerable revision of the introduction at a late stage to take in discussion of the Ministry of Agriculture's consultation paper on agricultural tenancy law reform. Whether the Ministry's radical proposals will be implemented depends, of course, on the outcome of the consultation process and the vagaries of the British electoral system, as parliamentary time is unlikely to be available prior to a general election. Nevertheless, it was felt that inclusion of some discussion of the proposals was necessary, if only to put into perspective the discussion of the existing law of agricultural holdings in Chapters 2 to 9 of the main text.

I owe a debt of gratitude to a number of friends and colleagues who have helped in the preparation of the text. Colleagues in the Law Faculty at Aberystwyth who assisted by reading draft chapters include Ann Barlow and Letitia Crabb. Clive Margrave-Jones contributed the chapter on Taxation of Agricultural Property. David Clarke, of Bristol University, read the chapter on Rent Reviews in draft and contributed a number of helpful suggestions. Professor Jill Martin, of King's College London, kindly agreed to read and comment on the Security of Tenure chapters. Allan Lennon somehow found time in a busy schedule to read the chapter on Set Aside and Diversification. Michael Gregory, latterly chief legal adviser at the CLA, brought his not inconsiderable experience and learning to bear on the chapter on Succession to Agricultural Holdings. I am also indebted to his successor at the CLA, Angela Sydenham, for reading the material on tied cottages in Chapter 11. This chapter also benefited from comment and analysis by Peter Williams, of Burges Salmon. No book is perfect, however, and such imperfections as remain are attributable to the author.

I am indebted to the Royal Institution of Chartered Surveyors for kindly permitting the inclusion of their very helpful *Guidance Notes* for arbitrators in rent arbitrations in the Appendix. The Ministry of Agriculture very kindly allowed the reproduction of their guidance notes on short term lettings with Ministry consent. Inclusion of both texts would, it was felt, be of assistance to the non specialist without ready access to Ministry of RICS material. This is not, however, intended as a reference book – rather as a general guide to what is rapidly becoming a highly complex and specialised area of law. For this reason we have eschewed including additional appendix material readily available in the specialist literature on (for instance) agricultural holdings or dairy quotas. Similarly, the security of tenure and succession provisions of the agricultural holdings legislation have generated a considerable body of agricultural land tribunal decisions. Discussion of the detailed tribunal jurisprudence has been omitted, and the chapters on security of tenure seek instead to give a guide to the statutory provisions, as interpreted by the courts, and the context within which they operate – a topic of sufficient complexity in itself. Transcripts of agricultural land tribunal decisions are available from the Agricultural Law Association c/o the secretary, Nunton Cottage, Nunton, Salisbury, Wilts. Tribunal succession decisions, with commentary, are also available in a collection by RND Hamilton, published by the Royal Institution of Chartered Surveyors (2nd edn, 1991).

The law stands still for no man, least of all legal authors and their publishers. A number of measures affecting agricultural land and its use came into force while the text was in proof. Chief among these are the following:

– *The Control of Pollution (Silage, Slurry and Agricultural Fuel Oil) Regulations 1991, SI 1991/324.* These regulations make detailed provision for the conditions in which silage and slurry may be stored, and lay down detailed specifications and requirements to be met by storage facilities. The regulations are made under powers contained in section 110 of the Water Act 1989.

– The Ministry of Agriculture issued, in January 1991, a draft revision of the *Code of Good Agricultural Practice for the Protection of Water*. If implemented, this will take effect under section 116 of the Water Act 1989. Under the 1989 Act, however, the legal status of the code has changed – compliance will not necessarily provide a defence to a pollution offence (principally section 107 of the 1989 Act). Instead, the National Rivers Authority must take it into account when exercising its powers to issue prohibition notices, or exercising other of its pollution control functions.

– *The Dairy Produce Quotas (Amendment) Regulations 1991, SI 1991/832.* Discussion of the three amending SI's introduced in 1990 has been included in the text. The latest amendments arrived too late to be incorporated, however.

– Several important cases discussed in the text have now been reported in full. *Rous v Mitchell* and *Crawford v Elliott*, in which the construction of notices to quit was examined in depth, have now been reported at (respectively) [1991] 1 All ER 677 and [1991] 13 EG 163. The rent review decision in *Mann v Garner* is now reported in full at [1991] 11 EG 107. In addition, several decisions were reported while the text was in proof, and are not discussed in the text. Of these, the decision in *Divall v Harrison* [1991] 14 EG 108 is of interest, in that it discusses the construction of notices to quit given by executors. The Scottish case of *Cambusmore Estate Trust v Little* [1991] SLT 33 is of interest in that the Scottish land court there examined the content of the rules of good husbandry, albeit in the context of the Agricultural Holdings (Scotland) Act 1949. Although the statutory context is different, the relevance of the discussion to the interpretation of the parallel English legislation is self evident.

– Discussion of the *Nitrate Sensitive Areas (Designation) Order 1990, SI 1990/1013* has been included in a separate Appendix, to which the reader is referred when using chapter 12.

My aim throughout has been to provide a basic guide to the complexities of the agricultural holdings legislation, and the law regulating agricultural land use and tied cottage lettings. If it is some modest assistance to those (be they valuers, land agents, legal practitioners or students) who have to deal in agricultural law it will have achieved its aim. I owe a considerable debt of gratitude to Christine Davies, Carol Parry, Ann Gee and Ann Watkin-Jones for producing a clearly typed script from considerable disorder. Any imperfections that remain are mine, however.

Chris Rodgers
Temple Chambers
Llandrindod Wells

April 1991

Contents

Table of statutes

References in this Table to *Statutes* are to Halsbury's Statutes of England (Fourth Edition) showing the volume and page at which the annotated text of the Act will be found.

Table of cases

M

Chapter 1
Introduction

This is principally a book about agricultural land, and the law governing its tenure and use. Lawyers and agriculturalists have hitherto been primarily concerned with the complexities of the Agricultural Holdings legislation and its impact on the landlord and tenant relationship. In recent years, however, the volume of legislation affecting agricultural land, and restricting its use, has grown considerably. The advent of the European Economic Community and the Common Agricultural Policy has led to an increase in legislation restricting agricultural land use on conservation and environmental protection grounds, and to the introduction of effective controls on production (especially in the dairying sector via the introduction of milk quotas). In addition, the social legislation embodied in the Rent (Agriculture) Act 1976 and (now) the Housing Act 1988 affords considerable legal protection to occupiers of tied agricultural accommodation, both in terms of security of tenure and control of rents.

A   Agricultural tenure and protective legislation

Although the landlord/tenant sector has been in decline for at least the last 70 years, the Agricultural Holdings legislation retains a central position in any consideration of the law as it applies to agricultural land. The last comprehensive survey of agricultural tenure in England and Wales was conducted by the Committee of Inquiry into the Acquisition and Occupancy of Agriculture Land (the Northfield Committee).[1]

They found that the area of agricultural land subject to tenancies had fallen from approximately 88% in 1908 to a position where only 35–40% of agricultural land was subject to commercial agricultural tenancies by 1979.[2]

The proportion of tenanted land subject to the direct application of the legislation has steadily decreased, although it remains significant. The importance of the Agricultural Holdings Acts cannot, however, be measured solely by reference to the decline of the landlord/tenant sector. The very existence of the security of tenure, rent control and compensation provisions contained in successive Agricultural Holdings Acts is important to an

---

1 Report to the Committee of Inquiry into the Acquisition and Occupancy of Agricultural Land (1979) Cmnd 7599.
2 See Cmnd 7599 Table 5 at p 42. The figure for tenanted land has more recently been put at 36% by MAFF; *Agricultural Tenancy Law – Proposals for Reform* (Joint Announcement by the Agriculture Departments, 12 Feburuary 1991), para 2.

understanding of the various arrangements by which land is held *outside* the landlord/tenant relationship. Although the tenanted sector itself has declined, much land is held under arrangements designed specifically to avoid the creation of a tenancy subject to the protective provisions of the Acts, eg partnerships, share farming and other forms of joint venture. These are, therefore, considered in Chapter 2 alongside the categories of tenancy and licence protected by the legislation.

1.   Development of statutory intervention

Before 1875, the relations of the parties to a tenancy of agricultural land were governed principally by common law. In the best traditions of the common law, this meant that effect was given to the terms of the tenancy agreement itself, with the law stepping in only to fill the gaps (often by reference to local custom) and to supply overriding obligations as to the manner of cultivation and certain other basic duties of the tenant.[3] Most agricultural tenancies were terminable by six months notice to quit at common law and there was, of course, no security of tenure, with the result that the tenant's occupation of land was at best precarious.

Improving the land and farming profitably require forward planning, and the insecurity of tenants at common law was clearly a disincentive to long term improvement of buildings and land, as a tenant could find his interest terminated at any time without any prospect of reaping the reward of his labours.

Statutory intervention to improve the legal position of the agricultural tenant began with the Agricultural Holdings (England) Act 1875, which conferred qualified rights to the payment of compensation for improvements, and gave tenants the right to remove fixtures erected at their own expense. The Agricultural Holdings (England) Act 1883 prohibited contracting out,[4] thus making payment of compensation for improvements obligatory. It also extended the period required for notices to quit to 12 months.[5] The list of improvements for which compensation could be claimed was extended by the Agricultural Holdings Act 1906, which gave tenants for the first time the right to claim compensation for damage done by game, enhanced rights to compensation for improvements and the right to claim compensation for disturbance.[6] The extant legislation was consolidated in the Agricultural Holdings Act 1908, and then the Agricultural Holdings Act 1923.

The next major landmark was the Agriculture Act 1947, which completed the modern statutory framework by introducing security of tenure. Part V of

---

3 See *Powley v Walker* (1793) 5 Term Rep 373; *Onslow v —* (1809) 16 Ves 173; *Horsefall v Mather* (1815) Holt NP 7 (Tenants duty of good & husbandlike cultivation). Also *Auworth v Johnson* (1832) 5 C & P 239 (duty to keep buildings wind and watertight).

4 Section 55 of the 1883 Act. Section 54 of the 1875 Act had previously entitled the parties to enter into and carry into effect 'any such agreement as they think fit'.

5 Ibid s 33. At common law an annual tenancy of agricultural land would, previously, have been terminable on six months' notice to quit.

6 Sections 2, 3 and 4 of the 1906 Act. Ibid s 1 made arbitration by a single arbitrator compulsory.

the 1947 Act also established for the first time Agricultural Land Tribunals to adjudicate in disputes as to security of tenure. These are an important feature of the modern law. The 1947 Act was soon superseded and replaced by the Agricultural Holdings Act 1948. This replaced and consolidated the previous legislation and set out a detailed code of rights to compensation and security of tenure, as well as providing a system of arbitration for the settlement of disputes as to rent, compensation and the terms of tenancy agreements.

Security of tenure for agricultural tenants was significantly extended by Part II of the Agriculture (Miscellaneous Provisions) Act 1976. This provided that certain close relatives of a deceased tenant could succeed to his tenancy, subject to the requirements that they prove themselves 'eligible' and 'suitable' to take on the tenancy. Two successions are possible under tenancies subject to the 1976 Act.

2. The Northfield Report

Growing concern about the large-scale purchase of agricultural land by the financial institutions prompted the appointment in 1977 of a Committee of Inquiry, under Lord Northfield, to examine trends in the Acquisition and Occupancy of Agricultural Land. The Northfield Report,[7] published in 1979, is of major importance for two reasons – it made a detailed survey of the structure of agricultural landowning and tenure, and its recommendations for reform of the tenure legislation subsequently formed the basis of Agricultural Holdings Act 1984.

The Northfield Committee found that the area of agricultural land subject to tenancies had fallen from approximately 88% in 1908, to about 43% (according to official statistics) in 1978. Because of the development of some forms of tenancy not at arm's length they estimated that the proportion of land let under commercial agricultural tenancies was probably in the region of 35–40%.[8] The introduction of security of tenure in the 1948 Act undoubtedly hastened this trend. Looking into the future, the Northfield Committee estimated that the likely size of the tenanted sector by the year 2020 would be about 20–25%, although if all tenanted land falling in was farmed in hand, and not re-let, the tenanted sector could shrink to a minimum size of between 7% and 19% by that date.[9] With these projections in mind they suggested a number of reforms to improve the operation of the Agricultural Holdings legislation. These aimed to hold the tenanted sector at around 20–25% by the year 2020.

(a) Succession rights

The introduction of succession rights in the Agriculture (Miscellaneous Provisions) Act 1976 had proved a further disincentive to landlords to let land. While not advocating the removal of succession rights altogether, the Northfield Committee recommended that the succession scheme be

---

7 Cmnd 7599, above note 1.
8 See note 2 above.
9 Cmnd 7599 paras 111 and 113.

reformed to remove some of its more glaring anomalies. They recommended that a limit should also be placed on the amount of land to which an applicant could succeed, so that succession would only be possible to land aggregating one commercial unit from one landlord.[10] Stricter rules to assess the eligibility and suitability of successors should also be introduced to ensure that successors were experienced in husbandry and business management.[11]

(b)   Lifetime succession[12]

In order to encourage efficient farming, it was recommended that a tenant should have the right, when he reached the age of 65, to nominate a successor to succeed to the tenancy. Retirement would be voluntary, compulsory retirement for tenants having been rejected as impractical.

(c)   Lettings without security of tenure

Some members of the Committee of Inquiry were in favour of introducing fixed term tenancies without security of tenure, but only subject to the safeguard of prior tribunal or ministry consent to the letting.[13] They were unanimous, however, in advising that a code of guidelines for agricultural landlords should be drawn up and published.[14] This could for instance, indicate desirable features for inclusion in tenancies and partnership arrangements, and replace the existing rules of Good Husbandry and Estate Management currently outlined in sections 10 and 11 of the Agriculture Act 1947.

3.   The Agricultural Holdings Act 1984

The Northfield Committee recommended that the required amendments to the existing legislation should be agreed between government and the organisations involved in the agriculture industry – notably the Country Landowners Association and the National Farmers Union.[15] The 1984 Act was subsequently based on a package of measures agreed by the CLA and NFU, although a number of technical legal amendments were also incorporated. The Act, which received the Royal Assent on 12th July 1984, implemented many of the Northfield Committee's recommendations.

The central feature of the CLA/NFU package was the removal of succession rights for all tenancies granted after the passage of the Act. As a *quid pro quo* for the abolition of succession, a new rent formula was introduced to break the link between rent valuations and the free market rental demanded on first lettings.[16] The Act made a number of alterations,

---

10 See Cmnd 7599 paras 627, 629 and 630.
11 Cmnd 7599 para 631.
12 Ibid para 633 ff.
13 Ibid para 637 ff.
14 Ibid para 651 ff.
15 Ibid para 642.
16 Agricultural Holdings Act 1984, ss 1 and 2. The Act went further in this respect than the Northfield Committee suggested, the latter having drawn back from advocating the withdrawal of succession rights altogether.

along the lines suggested by the Northfield Report, to the succession scheme itself. The amount of land to which a successor can succeed has, for instance, now been limited to one 'commercial unit'. Schedule 2 to the 1984 Act also provided for voluntary retirement for tenants at 65, and lifetime succession by their 'nominated' successors. This implemented one of the Northfield Committee's major recommendations, although the scheme only applies to tenancies to which succession rights on death still accrue.[17] The Act also made detailed amendments to the provisions governing notices to quit and other aspects of the security of tenure provisions. It did, however, omit some of the measures recommended by the Northfield Committee, and the opportunity was not taken to institute a thoroughgoing review of all aspects of the operation of the legislation. As a result, some major anomalies remain, eg the fact that sub-tenants, and tenants holding under tenancies of between one and two years, have no security of tenure at all under the Acts.

4. The Agricultural Holdings Act 1986

(a) Consolidation and amendment

The 1984 Act was the last in a series of amending statutes passed since the last consolidating Act in 1948. The major reforms introduced by the 1984 Act were grafted onto the principal provisions in the earlier legislation, causing considerable problems of cross-referencing and interpretation when handling the primary legislation applicable to agricultural holdings. Further consolidation was long overdue. The Law Commission, having reviewed the operation of the legislation *in toto*, subsequently suggested a major reorganisation of the statutory material.[18] This was effected by the Agricultural Holdings Act 1986, which came into force on 18th June 1986.[19] Although principally a consolidating measure, the 1986 Act contained a number of minor alterations of substance, suggested by the Law Commission, which had remained untouched by the 1984 Act:

(i) It had previously been uncertain whether agreements contemplating both grazing *and* mowing for a period less than a year were outside the protection of the Act, as are grazing agreements and mowing agreements *simpliciter*. It is clear that all seasonal lettings of grassland were intended to be outside the security of tenure provisions, and section 2 of the Act has been amended accordingly.[20]

(ii) A futher anomaly arose where a sub-tenant carried out works of provision or alteration of fixed equipment. The mesne landlord is

---

17 See Chapter 8 below p 169 ff.
18 See Law Com No 153 'Report on the Consolidation of Certain Enactments relating to Agricultural Holdings' Cmnd 9665 (Dec 1985).
19 Agricultural Holdings Act 1986, s 102(2).
20 See section 2(3)(a) of the 1986 Act ('grazing or mowing (*or both*)'). Under the original provision, agreements 'for grazing *or* mowing during some specified period of the year' were exempted, leading to the argument that grazing only, and mowing only, were the situations envisaged.

liable to repay the cost of the work less any grant aid received by the sub-tenant. The same requirements did not formerly apply, however, between the mesne landlord and freehold owner, so that the latter may have been liable to pay compensation on termination of the mesne tenancy without such aid being taken into account. The 1986 Act therefore introduced an amendment to ensure that grants made toward such work were taken into account between a tenant's immediate and superior landlord.[1]

(iii)   It was also previously unclear whether sums *agreed* to be paid on termination of tenancy could be recovered in the same way as those awarded by an arbitrator. The legislation has now been modified to ensure that both agreed sums and arbitration awards can be recovered by County Court Order, and the holding charged with payment if the landlord is a trustee.[2]

(iv)   Provisions were also introduced to ensure that the power of limited owners extend to all matters covered by the Act, and that the special rules as to service of notices cover all notices required under the legislation.[3]

(v)   Despite the thorough review initiated by the Law Commission, a number of anomalies in the legislation remain. So, for instance, a fixed term granted for more than one but less than two years is *not* converted by the Act into a protected tenancy.[4] It is by no means clear, however, whether such a tenancy is outside the 1986 Act altogether (ie, is not an 'agricultural holding') or is merely outside the security of tenure provisions. Similarly, although the Act gives a tenant the statutory right to remove fixtures and fittings,[5] it is by no means clear whether contracting out of this right is permissible.[6] In the same way, it remains unclear whether a tenant can contract out of his right to claim compensation for long-term improvements made to the holding.[7] It is to be regretted that these long-standing anomalies were not addressed by either the 1984 legislation or the Law Commission's study prior to consolidation.

The process of statutory development did not stop with the 1986 consolidation, masterly though the latter was. Already, further amending legislation has proved necessary. The Agricultural Holdings (Amendment) Act 1990,[8] a private measure sponsored by the NFU, was introduced to protect the security of tenure of tenants diversifying into non-agricultural activities. This proved necessary after the Court of Appeal had ruled in *Bell*

---

1   See ibid s 68(2)(b).
2   Ibid s 85(1) and (3) (previously ss 71 and 73 of the 1948 Act).
3   Ibid ss 88 and 93.
4   *Gladstone v Bower* [1960] 2 QB 384, CA. See below p 37 ff.
5   Section 10(1) of the 1986 Act.
6   For doubts as to the effectiveness of contracting out see Lord Hailsham in *Johnson v Moreton* [1980] AC 37 at 59–60, HL. Note also that contracting out of the right to freedom of cropping and disposal of produce, conferred by s 14, is expressly banned (s 15(1)).
7   See the ambiguous phrasing of s 67(2), providing for the landlord's consent to improvements to be given unconditionally 'or upon such terms as to compensation *or otherwise* as may be agreed upon in writing' between the parties. (Italics added).
8   The 1990 Act came into force on 29th July 1990.

v McCubbin[9] that a landlord could serve an effective notice to quit if he wanted to put the land to the same non-agricultural use himself – as no change of use was involved this would be a proposed non-agricultural user not requiring planning permission, and within Case B to Sch 3 of the 1986 Act. The 1990 Act has remodelled Case B to remove this anomaly and clarify the law governing re-possession of farmland for non-agricultural user.[10]

(b) Protective legislation – principles of protection

In policy and approach the agricultural holdings legislation differs from other statutory codes of protection (such as the Rent Act 1977 and Landlord and Tenant Act 1954) in significant respects. The 1986 Act puts in place a comprehensive framework providing for security of tenure, regulation of the terms and conditions of the tenancy (eg, as to maintenance of fixed equipment) and for the payment of compensation to tenants for improvements and disturbance. The following distinguishing features should be noted:

(I) OBLIGATIONS OF LANDLORD AND TENANT

With a few exceptions, the legislation does *not* intervene *directly* to modify the agreement reached between landlord and tenant. The 1986 Act only overrides the terms of the tenancy if the latter abrogates certain basic rights – principally to allow a tenant to vary permanent pasture, and giving him freedom to dispose of the crops and produce of the holding.[11] The 1986 Act puts in place a comprehensive framework of rights and liabilities as to fixed equipment (the 'model clauses') and Sch 1 lists basic terms which can be incorporated into the tenancy. Incorporation is not automatic, however, as either party must request an agreement in the Sch 1 terms and then invoke the arbitration machinery to compel 'incorporation'.[12] Similarly, the 'model clauses' as to fixed equipment do not apply if the tenancy makes contrary provision – although the arbitration machinery can be invoked to bring the tenancy into harmony with the statutory standards in appropriate circumstances.[13] In like vein, although s 12 and Sch 2 provide a comprehensive framework for the regulation of agricultural rents, control on statutory lines can only be achieved by one of the parties invoking the rent arbitration machinery by serving an appropriate demand for arbitration.

(II) SECURITY OF TENURE

The 1986 Act also differs from other protective legislation in that security of tenure is *not* conferred irrespective of the tenant's own volition. The Act places extensive control on a landlord's ability to re-possess tenanted land,

9 [1990] 1 QB 976, CA.
10 See Agricultural Holdings (Amendment) Act 1990, s 1, and further Chapter 7 p 126 ff below.
11 Agricultural Holdings Act 1986, ss 15 and 16.
12 See ibid s 6 and Sch 1, and Chapter 3 p 51 ff below. Incorporation by arbitration is, even then, not automatic; it must be 'reasonable and just' between the parties (s 6(2)(b)).
13 See ibid s 8.

but this protection will only apply if the tenant invokes it by serving the appropriate counter-notice after receiving a notice to quit.[14] If he chooses not to do so, the landlord can re-possess unhindered by the requirement to prove compliance with the Cases for Possession, or the other requirements of the Act – in this the legislation differs markedly from the Rent Act 1977 and Housing Act 1988.[15]

If anything, the legislative technique adopted by the 1986 Act is most similar to that employed by the Landlord and Tenant Act 1954, applicable to business tenancies. Like the latter, the 1986 Act statutorily continues a tenancy on expiry, in this case as a tenancy from year to year.[16] This is a contractual tenancy conferring rights *in rem*, unlike the Rent Act statutory tenancy, and as such it can be assigned or sub-let as a whole, can be devised by will, and will vest in personal representatives on intestacy. Likewise it will vest in a trustee on bankruptcy. To avoid the undesirable consequences of this approach, the Act contains provisions limiting security of tenure to the tenant's lifetime (subject to succession rights) and removing security where the tenant is declared bankrupt.[17] Unlike the Rent Act statutory tenancy, mere cesser of occupation will not *per se* bring a protected annual tenancy to an end. The 1986 Act differs from the business tenancy code in one important respect, however. The Landlord and Tenant Act 1954 prescribes a statutory mode of terminating business tenancies.[18] The Agricultural Holdings Act, on the other hand, leaves intact the landlord's common law right to serve notice to quit. Security of tenure is then provided by Part III of the Act, which places restrictions on the *operation* of notices to quit – principally by requiring the landlord to obtain the consent of an agricultural land tribunal or (where the Cases for Possession are applicable) an arbitrator's award upholding the notice to quit. These restrictions only apply, however, if the tenant challenges a notice to quit by serving the appropriate counter notice.

(III)   COMPENSATION ON TERMINATION OF TENANCY

The 1986 Act also gives the tenant important rights to claim compensation for long- and short-term improvements made to the holding, and for disturbance. The voluntary approach is maintained here also, however, in that these claims are only available if the tenant serves notice of claim on the landlord, within the statutory time limits following termination.

The provisions of the 1986 Act are therefore mostly *facilitative* in nature, and not regulatory – the Act confers extensive rights on both landlord and tenant, and puts in place a statutory framework within which the relationship

---

14 See ibid s 26 as to service of notices claiming security of tenure, and Chapter 6 p 101 ff below. *Cf* Rent Act protection, which accrues (even after expiry of the contractual tenancy) while, and so long as, a residential occupier occupies a dwelling as a residence (Rent Act 1977, ss 1 and 2, Housing Act 1988, s 1(1)).

15 Protection under the Rent Act legislation is based on the *status* of the residential occupier, without the need for service of notices claiming statutory protection; Rent Act 1977, ss 1 and 2 Housing Act 1988, s 1.

16 Agricultural Holdings Act 1986, s 2. *Cf* Landlord and Tenant Act 1954, s 24.

17 See Agricultural Holdings Act 1986, Sch 3, Cases F and G. *Cf* the Rent Act statutory tenancy, which confers merely a personal right of occupation (a 'status of irremoveability'), and not a contract of tenancy vesting *in rem*; Rent Act 1977, s 2, *Jessamine Investment Co v Schwartz* [1978] QB 264 at 277, CA; *Lloyd v Sadler* [1978] 2 All ER 529 at 537, CA.

18 See Landlord and Tenant Act 1954, s 25.

of landlord and tenant can be regulated. These rights can only be invoked, however, by the parties serving notices to trigger application of the statutory provisions. This factor, together with the rigour of the applicable time limits for the service of various kinds of notice, gives the law of agricultural holdings a procedural quality absent in other areas of the law of landlord and tenant.

(c) Perspectives for Reform

The *corpus* of legislative regulation affecting agricultural holdings is considerable. Perceived as a continuing disincentive to a revival of the tenanted sector, its reform to encourage new lettings (particularly for new entrants to the industry) has for some time been under discussion between the various organisations within the agriculture industry. The Ministry of Agriculture have now produced proposals of a far reaching nature which, if implemented, would represent the most radical revision of the agricultural legislation since 1948.[19]

The Ministry proposals are prefaced by three guiding principles – to deregulate and simplify the legislation, to encourage letting of land, and to provide a framework which can accommodate change and enable the industry to respond to changes in policy and market conditions.[20] To promote these objectives it is proposed to introduce a market-led approach in which landlord and tenant would be free to negotiate terms which best suit their needs and circumstances. The extension of the business tenancy legislation[1] to agricultural holdings was considered inappropriate eg because a closer relationship frequently exists between agricultural landlord and tenant than is common in commercial lettings. Instead, the following proposals have been put forward for consultation:

– The parties should be free to negotiate the length of the tenancy. Although short term arrangements are appropriate for grazing and mowing agreements, and some other special circumstances,[2] and may not be considered appropriate for full tenancies, it is not proposed that there should be a statutory minimum term of tenancy. Similarly, it is not proposed that there be a statutory right to renewal.[3] In this respect the proposals differ markedly from the legislation currently applicable to business tenancies *simpliciter*.

– It is not proposed to include any statutory provision regulating notices to quit.[4] The parties should be free to agree what notice provision should be included in the tenancy.

19 Agricultural Tenancy Law – Proposals for Reform (Joint Announcement by the Agricultural Departments, 12 February 1991), MAAF Release 45/91, and appended Consultation Paper on Reform of Agricultural Tenancy Law.
20 Agricultural Tenancy Law – Proposals for Reform, *ibid*, para 4.
 1 Ie Part II of the Landlord and Tenant Act 1954.
 2 Those specifically referred to in the Ministry consultation paper also include lettings for specialist cropping requiring clean land, imminent estate reorganisation, impending development of the land let, and short term lettings before the owner's successor takes over a holding (Agricultural Tenancy Law, Proposals for Reform, *ibid*, para 8). These are situations in which Ministry consent to a letting outside the ambit of the Agricultural Holdings Act 1986 is already available under ss 2 and 5 of the 1986 Act (see Ch 2, p 34 ff. below).
 3 Agricultural Tenancy Law – Proposals for Reform *ibid*, para 9.
 4 *Ibid*, para 11. Cf. regulation of the operation of notices to quit is the mechanism by which statutory protection is currently conferred on agricultural tenants by the 1986 Act.

– Compensation on termination of a tenancy is one area in which it is envisaged that regulation should be retained. It is here envisaged that fallback provisions be retained to cover the case where a tenancy makes no provision for compensation for improvements etc made by the tenant. Compensation for long term improvements should continue to be regulated by the code in the Agricultural Holdings Act 1986, as should compensation for dilapidations and game damage.[5] Compensation for short term improvements and tenant right should be based on their value to an incoming tenant. There should, however, be no right to compensation for disturbance. Clearly, the proposals for statutory compensation will require careful examination, particularly in the context of the tenant's ability to raise finance for long term agricultural improvements. It is also proposed that the parties be free to negotiate terms as to the removal of fixtures and buildings, in lieu of which 'fallback' provisions based on the existing rights of removal in the 1986 Act should be retained. The ability of the parties to 'contract out' of this right, as proposed, could involve serious implications for farm tenants.[6]

– To provide greater flexibility in rent levels, it is proposed to include *no* statutory regulation of rent levels or rent review.[7]

– *Disputes procedures.* It is proposed that there should be no statutory arbitration code applicable to agricultural holdings, and no special disputes procedures. The parties should be free to decide to have disputes referred to arbitration if they wish to do so, but not otherwise.[8] Arbitration under the 1986 Act is now often a lengthy and expensive mode of resolving agricultural disputes, especially if interlocutory legal points are raised necessitating references to the county court. Its demise would probably, therefore, not provoke an adverse response from agriculturalists and their advisers.

The Ministry's proposals, if implemented, would apply to new lettings after the introduction of legislative reform. Existing tenancies would be unaffected, and would continue to be regulated by the code in the Agricultural Holdings Act 1986.

B   Conservation, planning and land use

1.   Agriculture and conservation; controls on land use

Agricultural practices and land use have, in recent years, been subjected to increasing controls by a growing volume of conservation legislation. Much of the primary legislation, restricting agricultural operations on conservation

5 *Ibid*, para 12.
6 Agricultural fixtures are not trade fixtures at common law, and were not removable by a tenant: *Elwes v Maw* (1802) 3 East 38. The statutory right of removal (now s 10 of the 1986 Act) was introduced to reverse this harsh rule. The omission of statutory removal rights from future legislation would, it is suggested, take tenants back to the position obtaining in the early nineteenth century under the *Elwes v Maw* doctrine. Clearly, this is one aspect of the Ministry proposals which will require careful consideration.
7 Agricultural Tenancy Law – Proposals for Reform, *ibid*, para 13.
8 *Ibid*, para 14.

grounds, originates in European Community requirements. Legal policy has, in the UK, always favoured a voluntary approach to conservation and the control of land use in the countryside. The modern legislation seeks to encourage farmers and landowners to participate voluntarily in conservation measures. The legislative provisions fall into several different groups:

(I) DESIGNATION OF AREAS OF PROTECTION

Land considered by the relevant Nature Conservancy Council to be of environmental importance can be designated a 'site of special scientific interest' under the Wildlife and Countryside Act 1981.[9] The detailed effects of designation in restricting use of the land are considered in Chapter 12. Broadly, designation has the effect of restricting certain agricultural operations, prescribed in the designation order, until the conclusion of a management agreement with the owner. The National Parks and Access to the Countryside Act 1949 also makes provision for management agreements where land has been designated a 'nature reserve' under the 1949 Act. A further step was taken by the Agriculture Act 1986,[10] which gave the Minister of Agriculture power to designate areas as 'Environmentally Sensitive Areas'. Following designation the Minister has powers to enter into voluntary management agreements with landowners and farmers, so as to secure the long-term conservation and preservation of extensive tracts of the countryside. To date, 14 designation orders have been made under the 1986 Act.

It should be added that local authorities also have general powers to conclude management agreements relating to land within their area, under the Wildlife and Countryside Act 1981[11] – a power which they are actively encouraged to use.[12] The use of management agreements, particularly under the Wildlife and Countryside Act 1981, has become widespread, and emphasises the voluntary nature of conservation and environmental protection.

(II) SUPPLEMENTARY PLANNING CONTROL

Although management agreements provide the primary mode of regulating agricultural operations, they are supplemented in certain situations by subjecting agricultural operations to planning control. The use of compulsion is reserved primarily for the control of agricultural operations in areas considered to be of national significance. Additional planning controls apply to land within National Parks,[13] and similar controls apply where an area has been designated an area of Outstanding Natural Beauty under the

---

9 Wildlife and Countryside Act 1981, ss 28 and 29, Environmental Protection Act 1990, ss 131–4, Sch 9.
10 Agriculture Act 1986, s 18(1).
11 Wildlife and Countryside Act 1981, s 39.
12 See DOE Circular No 27/1987, 'Nature Conservation' paras 38–40.
13 Designation is by the Countryside Commission under National Parks and Access to the Countryside Act 1949, s 5. For limitation of permitted development rights see Town and Country Planning General Development Order 1988, Sch 2, Part 6, Article 2(2), below Chapter 12 p 260 ff.

1949 Act.[14] Designation in both instances is by the Countryside Commission.

The voluntary principle is also evident in the increasing use of grant aid to encourage the adoption of conservation measures by farmers and landowners. So, for instance, financial subsidies have been introduced to encourage farmers to take arable land out of production altogether under the set aside scheme, implemented in UK law by the Set Aside Regulations 1988.[15] These have now been amended to emphasise the environmental protection features of the scheme, most notably by the introduction from 1990 of new conditions on grant aid.[16] Similarly, the Farm and Conservation Grant Scheme,[17] introduced in 1989, provides subsidies to enable farmers to introduce fixed equipment and improvements specifically aimed at preventing pollution and conserving the environment. The Minister is also now under a statutory duty[18] to consider conservation objectives when making capital grant schemes under section 29 of the Agriculture Act 1970.[19]

While not altering the substantive law greatly, the Environmental Protection Act 1990[20] provides for the division of the Nature Conservancy Council into three new bodies, to whom its designation powers (above) are to be transferred: these are the Nature Conservancy Council for Scotland, the Nature Conservancy Council for England, and the Countryside Council for Wales, The Welsh Council (but not, note, its English or Scottish counterparts) also assumed many of the previous functions of the Countryside Council in Wales.

2.   Town and country planning: development rights

The use of land or buildings for agriculture has traditionally been a matter outside the control of the Town and Country Planning legislation. This policy is perpetuated in the Town and Country Planning Act 1990, s 55 (2)(e) of which exempts from the definition of 'development' the use of land or buildings for agriculture, or a change of use to agricultural use. This exemption covers the use of land and existing buildings. It is supplemented by

---

14 Designation is by the Countryside Commission under section 87 of the 1949 Act. For restrictions on development rights see the Town and Country Planning General Development Order 1988, Art 1(5).
15 SI 1988/1352, as amended by SI 1989/1042 and SI 1990/1716.
16 Set Aside (Amendment) Regulations 1990, SI 1990/1716. These require the cutting of foliage cover, on land set aside to fallow, to be increased to twice a year, and introduce a limited 'grazed fallow' option. They also extend the list of environmental features, such as vernacular buildings and unimproved grassland, that participants will be expected to maintain. See further Chapter 13 p 294 ff below.
17 SI 1989/128.
18 Agriculture Act 1986, s 17(1).
19 For instance the Farm Diversification Grant Scheme 1987 (SI 1987/1949), made under ss 28 and 29. The Farm Business Non-Capital Grant Scheme 1988, SI 1988/1125, which complements this by providing non-capital grants for diversification, was made under the Farm Land and Rural Development Act 1988, s 1.
20 See in particular Part VII Environmental Protection Act 1990 ss 131 ff and Sch 9.

the Town and Country Planning General Development Order 1988,[1] Sch 2, Part 6, which gives planning permission for a wide range of building and other operations on agricultural land, including the erection and modification of buildings, excavation work and engineering operations. These 'permitted' agricultural development rights are, however, subject to numerous exceptions and (even where applicable) are subjected to conditions as to their exercise, eg restricting agricultural building near other dwellings or public roads. The terms of the General Development Order are considered below in Chapter 12.

The long-standing exemption of agricultural operations from planning control has, of course, led to controversy and demands for greater control, on environmental grounds, of agricultural development. A limited degree of environmental control has now been introduced as a consequence of European Council Directive 85/337/EEC of 27th June 1985 (the Environment Assessment Directive). This directs Member States to ensure, before consent to certain types of development is given, that projects likely to have a 'significant' effect on the environment are made subject to an assessment of their environmental effects. Annex 2 to the directive specifies certain agricultural operations which must be subjected to environmental assessment, but only where Member States consider a development's characteristics so require, eg projects for restructuring rural land holdings, and projects for the use of uncultivated land for intensive agricultural purposes.

The EEC Directive has been implemented in UK domestic law by the Town and Country Planning (Assessment of Environmental Effects) Regulations 1988.[2] The latter subject planning applications for certain kinds of agricultural operation, such as poultry or pig rearing, to the requirement of environmental assessment. This will necessitate the submission of an Environmental Statement with the application, giving details of the likely effects of the proposed operation on the physical and human environment. Not all applications will require environmental assessment; only those having a 'significant' effect on the environment are subjected to assessment. Official guidelines for the application of the 1988 Regulations[3] indicate that in most cases this will be limited to operations of considerable size, such as the installation of large scale poultry and pig rearing facilities, and new drainage works. Quite apart from their limited scope, the 1988 Regulations are open to the obvious objection that they only require environmental assessment of agricultural development when planning permission is actually required. As planning permission is either not needed, or is given automatically by the General Development Order, for many kinds of agricultural operation, the scope for environmental assessment of agricultural operations is considerably limited.

---

1 SI 1988/1813.
2 SI 1988/1199. See below, Chapter 12 p 268 ff.
3 See SI 1988/1199, Sch 3, para 2 and DOE Circular 15/1988 para 20, and (generally) paras 22–29.

C   Controls on production: quotas

1.   Control of structural surpluses in European law

Controls on the production of certain kinds of agricultural produce (eg hops, potatoes) has for some time existed under marketing schemes made pursuant to the Agricultural Marketing Act 1958.[4] Quotas under the domestic marketing schemes are personal to each affected producer, however, and do not attach to land (or a holding) *per se*. The introduction of dairy quotas in 1984 introduced a new species of quota to English law, and one that has proved far more effective in limiting surplus agricultural production. Like much of the modern conservation and set-aside legislation, dairy quotas are a product of European Law.

Implementation of the Common Agricultural Policy of the European Economic Community has resulted in quantitative controls having to be placed on the production of milk and other dairy products. The common organisation of the market in milk was established in 1968, and is regulated by Council Regulation (EEC) No 804 of 1968.[5] This provides for a target price for milk to be fixed annually. In a first attempt at controlling structural surpluses in the dairy sector, a guarantee 'threshold' was introduced in 1982.[6] This threshold having been passed, production quotas were subsequently introduced in 1984, based on a 'super levy' of a confiscatory nature payable on deliveries and sales of milk. Community law[7] entitles each Member State to produce milk and dairy products up to a fixed threshold (or 'reference quantity') based originally on actual production in 1981 plus one per cent. If this figure is exceeded additional levy becomes payable on the Member State's over-production. This will in turn be recouped from individual producers, and at present stands at 100% of the target price for milk, having been fixed at this level by Council Regulation (EEC) No 857 of 1984.[8] The quota system was originally expressed to operate for five years from 1st April 1984. This has now, however, been extended to eight years.[9]

---

4 Quotas apply under the Potato Marketing Scheme 1955, SI 1955/690, as amended, (especially Sch, para 84), made under Agricultural Marketing Act 1958, ss 1–32. The Hops Marketing Scheme was discontinued by the Hops Marketing Act 1982, in order to comply with European Community requirements. The other extant schemes under the Agricultural Marketing Act 1958 are the British Wool Marketing Scheme 1950, SI 1950/1326, as amended and the Milk Marketing Scheme 1933, SR and O 1933 No 767 as amended. Quotas do not operate under the wool marketing scheme. Milk Quotas, on the other hand, are a product of European Community law and are provided for separately in the Dairy Produce Quota Regulations 1989 SI 1989/380, SI 1990/380.
5 OJ L 148, 28.6.1968, p 13.
6 See Council Regulations (EEC) No 1183/82, OJ 1982 L 140 p.l.
7 Ie Council Regulations (EEC) No 857/84, introducing a new Art 5c to Council Reg 804/68 (above).
8 Art 1.1. Council Regulations (EEC) No 857/84, OJ 1984 L 90, 1.4.84, p 10.
9 Council Regulations (EEC) No 1109/88, OJ 1988, L 110, p 27.

2. Implementation of dairy quotas in domestic law

The European requirements were initially implemented in domestic law by the Dairy Produce Quota Regulations 1984.[10] These were amended and replaced in 1986 and (again) in 1989. The currently applicable provisions are the Dairy Produce Quota Regulations 1989 (as amended).[11] The introduction of dairy quotas into domestic law has given rise to unique problems. In the first place, the regulations fall to be interpreted according to European Law canons of construction, which are somewhat wider than the domestic rules of interpretation familiar to English lawyers. Additionally, the European provisions make little allowance for the peculiarities of land tenure in the UK, and for the existing framework of protective legislation in the Agricultural Holdings Acts. This has caused difficulty, for instance, in interpreting the rules governing transfers of quota, especially those concerned with licences to occupy land – most of which will be converted by the Agricultural Holdings Act into yearly tenancies with security of tenure.[12] The very nature of quota itself is, arguably, alien to the accepted tenets of English property law. Quota attaches to land (or to be precise to a 'holding'[13]) and can only be transferred when a change of occupation of that land occurs.[14] It is not, however, an incorporeal hereditament within the meaning of English law – it attaches to land in a peculiar way, but is not an interest in land within the meaning of the Law of Property Act 1925.[15] The law governing transfer and apportionment of milk quotas is, then, a subject of considerable complexity.

Registration of quota will considerably enhance the value of a holding and (if let) its letting value. The Agriculture Act 1986[16] introduced provisions entitling the tenant of an agricultural holding to claim compensation, on quitting, for the added letting value accruing as a consequence of the registration of quota. The rules for valuing quota compensation, set out in Sch 1 of the 1986 Act, are complex in the extreme, and tie compensation to the value of dairy improvements made to the holding by the tenant. To avoid confusion with the compensation provisions of the Agricultural Holdings Act 1986, these are considered in Chapter 13 alongside the general law applicable to milk quotas. Special provision was also made by the 1986 Act for the effect of registered milk quota on rent reviews.[17]

10 SI 1984/1047 as amended (and replaced) by SI 1986/470.

11 SI 1989/380. These have now been amended by SI 1990/132, SI 1990/664 and SI 1990/784.

12 See Agricultural Holdings Act 1986, s 2(2)(b) and further Chapter 2 p 27 ff below. As a consequence, few licences remain which can fall within the projected exception to the quota transfer rules.

13 See SI 1989/380, reg 2(1), Council Regulations (EEC) No 857/84 Art 12(d), for the definition of a 'holding' in this sense. It encompasses *all* production units of the producer located within the community.

14 The transfer rules are now contained in reg 9 of SI 1989/380.

15 See Law of Property Act 1925, s 205(1)(ix).

16 Agriculture Act 1986, s 13 and Sch 1.

17 See ibid s 15. The rent provisions are considered in Chapter 5 p 96 ff alongside the general law on rent review.

Chapter 2
Scope of the Agricultural Holdings Act

To come within the code of protection contained in the Agricultural Holdings Act 1986, a tenancy must be of an 'agricultural holding' as statutorily defined. The occupier's legal interest must, moreover, be of a type to which the 1986 Act extends protection and not, for instance, a gratuitous or non-exclusive licence.

A   'Agricultural holding' defined

By virtue of section 1(1) of the 1986 Act, an 'agricultural holding' is defined to mean the 'aggregate of the land (whether agricultural land or not) comprised in a contract of tenancy which is a contract for an agricultural tenancy'. Whether a contract is that of an agricultural tenancy is to be determined by reference to the terms of the tenancy, the actual or contemplated user of the land (both *ab initio* and subsequently) and 'any other relevant circumstances'.[1] This is subject to an important caveat, however, in that the tenancy will be agricultural *only* if the whole of the land comprised in the contract of tenancy, 'subject to such exceptions only as do not *substantially* affect the character of the tenancy', is let for use as agricultural land.[2] The correct question is whether the substantial user of the whole is agricultural or not.[3]

1.   Aggregate of agricultural land

If the substantial user is agricultural, no severance of the contract of tenancy into agricultural and non-agricultural land is possible, and the whole will be within the 1986 Act. This clearly follows from the reference in s 1(1) to the 'aggregate' of land let under the contract of tenancy, and to the inclusion of non-agricultural land within a holding ('whether agricultural or not').

'A Contract of Tenancy'

Section 1 envisages a single contract of tenancy. So in *Blackmore v Butler*[4] where land was let on the understanding that a cottage would be let later when it fell vacant, there were two contracts of tenancy, each of which had to

1 1986 Act, s 1(2).
2 Ibid, italics added.
3 See *Howkins v Jardine* [1951] 1 KB 614, CA. *Lord Monson v Bound* [1954] 3 All ER 228.
4 [1954] 2 QB 171, CA.

be looked at separately to see whether it qualified for protection as an agricultural holding. There is a possible exception where a second agreement expresses itself to be supplemental to the first, and applies the latter's provisions to the additional land or buildings subsequently let, thus allowing the court to read the two documents as one tenancy for the purposes of s 1.[5] Where land is let under a single contract of tenancy, the subsequent partition and assignment of the tenant's leasehold interest does not create separate holdings. To determine whether the partitioned parts are comprised in an agricultural holding, the land comprised in the original contract of tenancy has to be looked at as a whole.[6] Similarly a severance of the landlord's reversionary interest, and its assignment in part to a third party, does not create separate tenancies of the severed parts.[7] The latter will still be comprised in an agricultural holding, and protected as such, if the substantial user of the whole remains agricultural.

2. 'Agriculture' defined

Land can only qualify as 'agricultural land', protected by the 1986 Act, if it is used for agriculture, and so used for the purposes of a trade or business.[8] 'Agriculture' is defined by s 96(1), which states that it 'includes horticulture, fruit growing, seed growing, dairy farming and livestock breeding and keeping, the use of land as grazing land, meadow land, osier land, market gardens and nursery grounds, and the use of land for woodlands where that use is ancillary to the farming of land for other agricultural purposes'. The following points should be noted:

'Agriculture includes . . .'

The statutory definition is *inclusive*, and not exhaustive. Land used for purposes not enumerated in s 96 may still constitute an agricultural holding, provided the user thereof may properly be termed agricultural. Decisions on the analogous definitions found in the Rent (Agriculture) Act 1976, the General Rate Act 1967, the Rating Act 1971, and the Town and Country Planning legislation will also be of assistance (if not authority). In the context of the 1976 Act a similarly inclusive definition has been held to include all operations involved in the farming of land for commercial purposes, but not every rural activity.[9] So, for instance, arable farming (an obvious omission) *would* be included – although not, it would seem, the growing of weeds for the purpose of testing weedkillers.[10] It was said in *Hemens v Whitsbury Farm and Stud Ltd*[11] that an 'inclusive' definition, such as the present, does not extend the definition of agriculture without limit. Rather, the definition must be construed in the agricultural context in which it occurs, and by reference to those matters expressly admitted to qualify as 'agriculture' by the terms of s 96 itself.

5 Ibid [1954] 2 QB 171, 177 and 178 per Romer and Somervill LJJ.
6 *Lester v Ridd* [1989] 1 All ER 1111, CA.
7 *Jelley v Buckman* [1973] 3 All ER 853, CA.
8 1986 Act, s 1(4)(a).
9 *Lord Glendyne v Rapley* [1978] 1 WLR 601, CA.
10 Cf *McClinton v McFall* (1974) 232 EG 295.
11 [1988] 1 All ER 74, 78, HL.

'*Livestock keeping and breeding*'

'Livestock' is defined to include 'any creature kept for the production of food, wool, skins or fur or for the purpose of its use in the farming of land or the carrying on in relation to land of any agricultural activity'.[12] Animals reared for sport or entertainment, or their decorative qualities, are not livestock, and are not to be be regarded as reared in the course of agriculture.[13] So, pheasants reared for sport are not livestock, with the consequence that gamekeepers employed in their production are not employed in 'agriculture', properly defined.[14] Similarly, racehorses cannot be livestock within the definition, and land used simply for keeping (but not grazing) horses cannot comprise an agricultural holding – unless horses are kept for the production of meat or for use in farming the land.[15] It should also be noted that the definition in s 96 is wider than that in the Rent (Agriculture) Act 1976, applicable to tied cottages. The latter defines livestock by reference to 'animals', and while including birds, expressly *excludes* fish. Section 96 refers instead to 'creatures' reared for the production of food, wool, etc, which phrase would clearly encompass fish, mink, and possibly other less common forms of stock.[16]

'*Use of land as grazing land*'

Grazing is *per se* an agricultural use, as defined by s 96(1), irrespective of whether the animals grazed are themselves 'livestock' (above). Thus land used for *grazing* horses will be used for 'agriculture', even if land used for keeping or exercising horses is not. If the substantial user is predominantly for grazing, it follows that the land can qualify as an agricultural holding within the 1986 Act.[17] The land must be used for grazing in connection with a trade or business to qualify as an agricultural holding, but the business need not itself be agricultural in nature.[18] Land let for private grazing on a non-commercial basis is not, however, agricultural land within the meaning of the 1986 Act.

'*Grazing*': although it does not have to be by 'livestock', it should be appreciated that 'grazing', properly defined, describes the use of land for *feeding* animals. It will not suffice if horses are fed elsewhere and turned onto the land occasionally.[19]

---

12 1986 Act, s 96(1).
13 See *Forth Stud Ltd v East Lothian Assessor* [1969] RA 35, 46.
14 *Lord Glendyne v Rapley* [1978] 1 WLR 601, CA; *Earl of Normanton v Giles* (1978) 248 EG 869, CA.
15 *Belmont Farm Ltd v Minister of Housing and Local Government* (1962) 13 P & CR 417; *Hemens v Whitsbury Farm Ltd* (above).
16 For instance, snails. Cf *Jones v Bateman* (1974) 232 EG 1392, CA; *Wallace v Perth and Kinross Assessor* 1975 SLT 118; *Gunter v Newtown Oyster Fishery Co Ltd* (1977) 244 EG 140; *Cresswell v British Oxygen Co Ltd* [1980] 3 All ER 443, CA and other rating decisions.
17 See *Rutherford v Maurer* [1962] 1 QB 16, CA and *McClinton v McFall* (1974) 232 EG 707 – grazing land used occasionally to break in horses held an agricultural holding.
18 *McClinton v McFall* (above).
19 *Sykes v Secretary of State for the Environment* (1981) 42 P & CR 19, 23, per Donaldson LJ.

3. Agricultural land

By virtue of s 1(4), agricultural land is defined to mean, 'land used for agriculture which is so used for the purposes of a trade or business' or land designated by the minister as such pursuant to section 109 of the Agriculture Act 1947. The 1947 Act gives the Minister power to designate land which would otherwise not qualify as 'agricultural land', and so bring it within (for instance) the protection of the 1986 Act; he cannot however, make designations in respect of land used as private gardens, allotments or for recreational activities.

'Land'

This phrase includes not only the land let, but also buildings on it. In appropriate circumstances a letting of buildings without land can constitute an agricultural holding. When considering whether a building can constitute 'agricultural land' one must take into account the situation of the property, its history, and the purpose for which it was let. The parties must intend, at the time of letting, that the property is to be used for agricultural purposes and form part of an integrated agricultural holding. It will not suffice if, for instance, the tenant separately leases a house near the holding for reasons of convenience, but it is not intended to be let as a farmhouse for the holding.[20] On the other hand, a cottage let for housing farmworkers has been held to constitute an 'agricultural holding',[1] as can in principle the farmhouse itself.[2] There is no minimum size for an agricultural holding, the only criteria being whether land and buildings are let for agricultural purposes. So, for instance, a half acre allotment used to produce vegetables for sale has been held to be an agricultural holding,[3] as has a smithy let with an orchard and garden.[4]

4. 'Substantial' agricultural user

Section 1(1) of the 1986 Act expressly envisages both non-agricultural and agricultural land being included in an agricultural holding. The central issue, then, is whether, having regard to the terms of the tenancy, the actual or contemplated use of the land and 'any other relevant circumstances', the *whole* of the land comprised in the tenancy, subject to such exceptions as do not *substantially* affect the agricultural character of the tenancy, is let for use as agricultural land. The formulation now found in s 1(2) expresses in negative form the 'substantial user' test previously formulated by the courts. One must look at the letting as a whole and ascertain whether the parties intended the predominant user to be agricultural:

> 'One must look at the substance of the matter and see whether as a matter of substance the land comprised in the tenancy, taken as a whole, is an agricultural

20 *Godfrey v Waite* (1951) 157 EG 582, CA.
1 *Blackmore v Butler* [1954] 2 QB 171, CA.
2 Cf *Hasell v McAulay* [1952] 2 All ER 825, decided under the Agriculture Act 1947.
3 *Stevens v Sedgeman* [1951] 2 All ER 33, CA.
4 *Adsetts v Heath* (1951) 95 Sol J 620, 633.

holding. If it is, then the whole of it is entitled to the protection of the Act. If it is not, then none of it is so entitled.'[5]

Despite early doubts[6] it is now clearly established that the 1986 Act does not effect a severance of non-agricultural land where the predominant user is agricultural.[7] It follows there can be no severance of a notice to quit, which latter must comply with the requirements of the 1986 Act if the substantial user is agricultural, and will terminate the tenancy of both agricultural and non-agricultural land included in the holding.

5.   Unlawful use

Section 1(2) of the 1986 Act refers to land 'let for use as agricultural land'. If, therefore, the tenant carries on agricultural activity in breach of the terms of the tenancy agreement the land will not be an agricultural holding. So, for example, where a house was let with nine and a half acres of rough pasture under an agreement which prohibited use 'otherwise than as a private dwelling house', the subsequent use of the land to keep poultry and cattle did not make it an agricultural holding.[8] However, where 15 acres of land were let together with a farmhouse under an agreement which prohibited the carrying on of any 'profession, trade or business' at the property, the Court of Appeal held that the land *was* an agricultural holding, as the parties clearly intended that it should be used for the business of farming. The prohibition was construed as one on the use of the land for any profession, trade or business 'other than agricultural business'. There was therefore no breach of covenant, and the landlord's notice to quit was invalid as it did not comply with the Agricultural Holdings legislation.[9] Whether an existing agricultural user is in breach of the terms of the tenancy agreement will depend on the construction of the agreement itself, and the intention of the parties at the time of making it. Where the intended user was clearly agricultural the courts will (in so far as is possible) construe the agreement accordingly. Where there has been a breach of the tenancy agreement, receipt of rent by the landlord with actual knowledge of the breach (i.e. the agricultural user) may constitute a waiver of the breach of covenant, even though the tenancy does not thereby become one of an agricultural holding (see below).

6.   Change of user

Can property move in and out of the Agricultural Holdings code if the user by the tenant changes from agriculture to some other user, and vice versa? Similarly, if property ceases to be an agricultural holding, does it then come automatically within the protection of the Rent Act 1977 or the Landlord and Tenant Act 1954 if the new user is residential, or for business purposes? The principles applied by the Courts to solve this problem differ where the

---

5 *Howkins v Jardine* [1951] 1 KB 614, 628, CA, per Jenkins LJ.
6 See *Dunn v Fidoe* [1950] 2 All ER 685, CA.
7 See *Howkins v Jardine*, above; *Lord Monson v Bound* [1954] 3 All ER 228.
8 *Kempe v Dillon-Tranchard* [1951] EGD 13.
9 *Iredell v Brocklehurst* (1950) 155 EG 268, CA.

change is from a non-agricultural to agricultural user, and where an initial agricultural use is subsequently abandoned. It is therefore convenient to consider them separately.

(a)   Abandonment of agricultural use

It was decided by the Court of Appeal in *Hickson and Welch Ltd v Cann*[10] that if agricultural use is abandoned by the tenant, either with or without the consent of the landlord, then notwithstanding the terms of the tenancy the land will cease to be an agricultural holding. A tenant can, in other words, unilaterally abandon the protection of the Agricultural Holdings Acts, although given the serious consequences which follow for the tenant the criteria required for effective abandonment clearly need to be closely defined. The issue was examined more closely by the Court of Appeal in *Wetherall v Smith*,[11] from which the following principles emerge:

1. The period to which attention must be drawn when deciding whether a tenancy has ceased to be agricultural is, where a notice to quit has been served, the period leading up to the service of the notice to quit.
2. The change in the legal status of the property cannot be brought about by abandonment of agricultural user for a matter of days or weeks. Evidence of a serious intention to abandon is required, and the Court suggested that abandonment of agricultural user for a period of at least two years prior to service of the notice to quit would be required.[12]
3. The consent of the landlord to cesser of agricultural use is not necessary for the tenancy to cease to be that of an agricultural holding.

   'It is in my judgement right that the protection of the statute should be lost if agricultural activity is wholly or substantially abandoned during the course of the tenancy, even without the consent of the landlord. The object of the legislature is to maintain continuity in the conduct of farming and horticultural operations rather than to put people who have at some time in the past acquired a particular type of tenancy in a privileged position'.[13]

4. An agricultural holding can cease to be within the protection of the Act if it is still used for 'agricultural' purposes, but it is not used as such in connection with a trade or business in the period leading up to service of a notice to quit. This follows, of course, from the fact that use for a trade or business is an integral part of the statutory definition.
5. Conversely, an agricultural holding can cease to be within the protection of the Act if it is still used for the purpose of a trade or business, but the character of the business itself ceases to be substantially 'agricultural', viz. the activities generating the income of the business cease to be agricultural. This is the most problematic situation. In *Short v Greeves*[14] the Court of Appeal endorsed the presumption, derived from the principles in *Wetherall v Smith*,

10 (1977) 40 P & CR 218n.
11 [1980] 2 All ER 530, per Sir David Cairns at 536–7.
12 And see now *Short v Greeves* [1988] 1 EGLR 1, CA.
13 [1980] 2 All ER 530, per Sir David Cairns, at 537.
14 [1988] 1 EGLR 1, CA.

against a holding which is clearly agricultural at the outset ceasing to be such, without clear evidence of its substantial user ceasing to be agricultural. It was there held that the proportion of business turnover derived from agricultural, as opposed to non-agricultural, activities was relevant to determine whether a tenancy was an agricultural holding. Notwithstanding, in *Short v Greeves* the development of a 60% non-agricultural turnover was not sufficient to deprive a tenancy of its *existing* status as an agricultural holding. In *Lord Monson v Bound*[15], on the other hand, it was held that a tenancy of a florists shop was not an agricultural holding where only 10% of horticultural sales from the premises were of flowers grown on the holding. To outweigh actual agricultural user on the land demised, therefore, it would appear that turnover from non-agricultural sources must be high. In borderline cases, moreover, the terms of the tenancy may also reinforce the presumption that it is an agricultural holding eg in *Short* itself the tenancy contained the usual terms as to good husbandry commonly found in agricultural leases. Ultimately, whether agricultural use is the *substantial* or predominant user, taking the land demised as a whole, is a question of fact, not law. Where cesser of a pre-existing agricultural user is claimed, one obvious anomaly arises from the approach endorsed in *Wetherall v Smith* and *Short v Greeves*; a tenancy which was once an agricultural holding may still qualify as such under the cesser rules even if, on the facts as found, it would *not* have qualified as such *ab initio*.[16] Where the character of the tenant's business user has changed it will, therefore, be necessary to show on the facts that a sufficiently high proportion of turnover is derived from non-agricultural sources for a considerable period (of probably two years or more) prior to notice to quit.[17]

(b)   Change to agricultural use

The position where the tenant adopts an agricultural user at some time subsequent to the commencement of the tenancy is more problematical. Dicta in *Godfrey v Waite*[18] and *Wetherall v Smith*[19] indicate clearly that land that was not an agricultural holding at the outset can only become such if there has been consent by the landlord to the change of use. The problem is to ascertain *when* and *how* such consent needs to be given.

Different considerations will apply according to whether or not the tenancy agreement itself specifies the intended user.

---

15 [1954] 3 All ER 228.
16 Indeed, this may be true of *Short v Greeves* itself – had the agricultural land there been in disuse and 60% of turnover derived from non-agricultural sources at the outset, it would, it is suggested, have been open at first instance to hold that the letting was a business tenancy simpliciter and not an agricultural holding at all.
17 On cesser and change of use generally see [1983] Conv 390–397 (Martin), and on *Short v Greeves* [1988] 138 NLJ 329 (Wilkinson), (1988) 14 EG 51 (Muir Watt), (1988) Conv 430 (Rodgers).
18 (1951) 157 EG 582, CA.
19 [1980] 2 All ER 530, CA.

'The first place to ascertain [the parties] intention is in the lease itself. If that does not provide an answer you look at all the surrounding circumstances to see what must have been in the contemplation of the parties; if that yields no solution, you must look to the nature of the premises and the actual user at the relevant time.'[20]

The terms of the tenancy agreement itself are the primary consideration, and if they clearly express the intended use of the property to be non-agricultural (for instance, as a dwelling) then this is conclusive. Moreover, the normal rules of construction will apply, with the result that oral evidence will be inadmissible to add to or vary the terms of the lease. In this situation the tenant must establish that there is a new contract of tenancy providing for the changed use, or that the original agreement has been validly varied.

'The user prescribed in the terms of the lease is what counts. If it is departed from through the parties making a new contract or varying the existing contract so as to permit or provide for a changed user, then the new user may . . . be treated as the material one; but nothing short of a new contract or variation of the contract will suffice.'[1]

For a variation to take place it is settled law that the landlord must have actual knowledge of the change of use, and have consented to the new user. Mere acceptance of rent with knowledge of the changed use will have no effect 'unless it can be inferred, as a matter of fact, that the landlord has affirmatively assented to the change of user.'[2]

It is now expressly provided by section 1(3) of the 1986 Act that any change in user which involves a breach of the terms of the tenancy must be disregarded, when determining whether a contract which was not originally an agricultural tenancy has subsequently become one, 'unless it is effected with the landlord's permission, consent or acquiescence'.[3]

If there is no express provision in the lease then one can look at the circumstances of the letting to ascertain the intention of the parties. If this gives no indication then one can look to the actual user at the material time.[4]

The principles of the general law were reformulated into five specific propositions in relation to the law of agricultural holdings by Slade LJ in *Russell v Booker*:[5]

1   Where the terms of the tenancy agreement provide for the use of premises for some particular purpose (for instance as a dwelling or for agricultural use) then that purpose is the essential factor in deciding whether it has been let 'as a separate dwelling' (within the Rent Act 1977) or as an agricultural holding.

2   Nevertheless, where the agreement provides for the use of the premises for some particular purpose, but that agreement is superseded by a subsequent contract providing for a different user, that subsequent contract can be looked at.

20 Upjohn J in *British Land Co Ltd v Herbert Silver (Menswear) Ltd* [1958] 1 QB 530, 539, CA.
1   Per Asquith LJ in *Court v Robinson* [1951] 2 KB 60, 70, CA.
2   *Wolfe v Hogan* [1949] 2 KB 194, 206, CA per Denning LJ.
3   This provision derives from Agricultural Holdings Act 1984, Sch 3, para 1(3).
4   *Wolfe v Hogan*, supra, at 206.
5   (1982) 5 HLR 10.

3   If the tenant changes the user of the premises, and this fact is fully known to and accepted by the landlord, it may be possible for the Court to infer a subsequent contract to let the premises for the new purpose, even though this would be a contract different in essentials to the original tenancy. Constructive knowledge of the change of use is not sufficient for this purpose, however.

4   Unless a contract of this nature can be made out, a merely unilateral change of user will not enable the tenant to claim the protection of the Agricultural Holdings legislation in a case where the terms of the tenancy agreement itself provide for, and contemplate, the use of the premises for some other purpose, eg a shop or dwelling.

5   Where a tenancy agreement does *not* provide for or contemplate the use of the premises for any particular purpose, actual subsequent user has to be looked at to determine whether the property was let as an agricultural holding, as a dwelling within the Rent Act 1977, or as business premises.

The combined effect of the decisions in *Wetherall v Smith* and *Russell v Booker* is that a tenant may lose his protection under one statutory code by unilateral abandonment, without being able to prove the existence of a new contract which would bring him within one of the other schemes of protection. *Russell v Booker* itself provides an example. Land and a house were there let under a tenancy which explicitly contemplated agricultural use. The tenant ran a bed and breakfast business and also kept poultry and cows on the land, but both business and agricultural activities ceased when he reached old age. His successor claimed the tenancy had become that of a dwelling protected by the Rent Act 1977. The Court of Appeal held that the property was not an agricultural holding because agricultural user had been unilaterally abandoned. A new tenancy protected by the Rent Acts had not, however, come into being because the landlord had no knowledge of the change of use. The only relevant agreement was the original tenancy, and as agricultural use had been abandoned it was no longer protected by the Agricultural Holdings Acts. Moreover, while the original tenancy subsisted the tenant had no protection under either statutory code. Similarly, where property let as a dwelling is adapted to agricultural use it may lose its Rent Act status without acquiring the status of an agricultural holding.

7.   Use in connection with a trade or business

To constitute an agricultural holding, agricultural land must be let 'for the purposes of a trade or business'.[6] The user must be commercial in nature, so that fields let for pleasure use (such as private horse jumping), or as private pasture for horses, will not constitute an agricultural holding. The trade or business itself need not be agricultural, however, so long as the land itself is used for agriculture. Thus, a tenancy of a field let for grazing horses belonging to a riding school has been held of an agricultural holding within the Act.[7] Where the business is of a non-agricultural nature, however, any turnover derived from non-agricultural activities carried out on the demised land will

6   1986 Act, s 1(4)(a).
7   *Rutherford v Maurer* [1962] 1 QB 16, CA.

have to be considered alongside the agricultural user itself, and the terms of the tenancy, to decide whether it is substantially 'let for use as agricultural land'.[8]

B   Legal interests protected

1.   The protected annual tenancy

For agricultural land to qualify as an 'agricultural holding', so coming within the protection of the legislation, it must be let under a 'contract of tenancy' as defined by section 1(5) of the 1986 Act, viz. a letting of land, or agreement for letting land, for a term of years or from year to year. Many agricultural tenancies are yearly tenancies, and the legislation provides that such tenancies can only be terminated by a minimum of twelve months' notice to quit expiring on a term date of the tenancy.[9] The Agricultural Holdings Act 1986 also converts into a yearly tenancy with protection any letting of land for an interest less than a yearly tenancy and many contractual licences to occupy agricultural land. Provision is also made for the continuation of fixed term lettings of two years or more as yearly tenancies following termination. The scheme of protection is therefore based on the (deemed or actual) yearly tenancy of agricultural land, and security is given to the tenant by providing that such tenancies can only be brought to an end in accordance with the notice to quit provisions of Part III of the 1986 Act.[10] The contract of tenancy must not be a contract under which the land is let to the tenant during his continuance in any office, appointment or employment held under the landlord.[11] To prove the existence of a tenancy, writing is not essential – although the tenancy will, of course, commonly be in writing. If a landowner allows someone to occupy land in return for an annual, or other regular, payment, the inference is that he is granting an agricultural tenancy or licence and the Agricultural Holdings Acts will apply accordingly. Entering into occupation in response to an oral offer of tenancy may also give rise to an oral tenancy to which the provisions of the 1986 Act will apply.[12]

2.   Statutory extension of tenure

The Agricultural Holdings Act 1986 converts the following types of tenancy and licence into yearly tenancies, thus bringing them within the protection of the security of tenure, compensation and other provisions of the Act.

(i)   Conversion of short term lettings into yearly tenancies

Section 2(2)(a) of the 1986 Act provides that where under any agreement agricultural land is let to a person for an interest less than a tenancy from year to year, then unless prior Ministry approval has been obtained, the agreement

8 Section 1(2), *Short v Greeves* [1988] 1 EGLR 1, CA.
9 Agricultural Holdings Act 1986, s 25.
10 See Chapters 6 and 7 below.
11 1986 Act, s 1(1).
12 See, eg *Epps v Ledger* (1972) 225 EG 1373.

will take effect, with necessary modifications, as a letting of the land for a tenancy from year to year. Thus, a tenancy for six months, or for 364 days, will be converted into a yearly tenancy with full protection. A tenancy for one year exactly is also an interest less than a tenancy from year to year, and as such will be converted by section 2 into a yearly tenancy. A yearly tenancy is something more than a fixed term of one year, because unless a notice to quit has been given the tenant has the right to stay on from year to year, whereas under a fixed tenancy for one year exactly he does not.[13] Consequently, in the latter case, at least 12 months' notice to quit must be given, ending on a term date, and the security of tenure provisions will apply. A grant for a term certain exceeding one year but less than two is not, however, caught by the section, and does not create a protected yearly tenancy.[14] For the purposes of the section the 'interest' referred to is the interest which as a matter of law the agreement gives rise to. It is irrelevant that the parties think they are creating some other type of agreement (eg one of the exempt classes of agreement, discussed below); the section is mandatory in that, once facts to which it applies exist, the parties cannot vary or exclude its operation by agreement or conduct. No issue of estoppel, taking the tenancy outside the operation of Section 2, can arise. 'Interest' within the meaning of Section 2 means 'interest as a matter of law', and 'the parties can not take that actual interest out of the ambit of Section 2 by agreeing to treat it as an interest of some other length or type'.[15]

The section does not apply where the Minister (the Minister of Agriculture, or in Wales the Welsh Office Agriculture Department) has approved the agreement prior to its being created, and neither does it apply where the tenancy or licence was made in contemplation of the use of the land only for grazing or mowing during some specified part of the year. Its application is also excluded in the case of agreements made before 1st March 1948, and in cases where the tenancy was granted by a person 'whose interest in the land is less than a tenancy from year to year'.[16]

The overall result of the operation of section 2 is to convert many informal or short term agreements, which were never intended to have security of tenure, into yearly tenancies with full protection. The Court of Appeal have held in *Keen v Holland*[17] that no issue of estoppel can arise, so that the section will also act to confer protection even where the parties expressly intended that the agreement should be outside the protection of the Agricultural Holdings Acts altogether. It therefore presents a trap when letting land, and care should be taken to avoid creating an interest less than a tenancy from year to year, especially where an agreement is informal and/or oral, eg a trial tenancy,[18] a weekly tenancy,[19] or a backdated tenancy executed when less than one year of its term is left to run.[20]

---

13 *Bernays v Prosser* [1963] 2 QB 592, CA, especially at 599; tenancy 'for a period of one year to 31st March 1962' protected.
14 *Gladstone v Bower* [1960] 2 QB 384, CA; see further below.
15 *Keen v Holland* [1984] 1 All ER 75, 80, CA, per Oliver LJ.
16 Ss 2(1) and (3). These exceptions are discussed further below at p 32 ff.
17 [1984] 1 All ER 75, CA.
18 *Verrall v Farnes* [1966] 2 All ER 808.
19 *Harrison v Moss* (1952) 102 L Jo 305.
20 *Keen v Holland* [1984] 1 All ER 75, CA.

(ii)   Conversion of certain licences into yearly tenancies

Section 2 also operates to convert licences to occupy agricultural land into yearly tenancies 'where the circumstances are such that if [the licensees] interest were a tenancy from year to year he would in respect of that land be the tenant of an agricultural holding.'[1]

The courts have formulated two principles which govern conversion under this provision. A licence to occupy agricultural land will only be converted by s 2(2)(b) if it confers exclusive occupation on the grantee, and (secondly) if such occupation is granted pursuant to an agreement which is contractually enforceable. These are, in fact, manifestations of one guiding principle; to be converted into a tenancy from year to year, a licence must be capable of subsisting as a tenancy at law, and (moreover) must not thereby be converted into something radically different to the transaction entered into.[2] Quite apart from the requirements of exclusivity and contractual enforceability, discussed below, it follows that s 2 cannot operate where the necessary intention to create legal relations is absent[3] or where a grant of exclusive possession is referable to some legal relationship other than landlord/tenant, eg vendor and purchaser.[4] And see generally *Street v Mountford*.[5]

(A)   CONTRACTUAL ENFORCEABILITY

The Court of Appeal held in *Goldsack v Shore*[6] that, as the section refers to occupation under an agreement, it only operates where there is an agreement enforceable in law, ie. a contract supported by valuable consideration. The section only operates to convert contractual licences to occupy agricultural land, and will not convert a purely gratuitous licence into a yearly tenancy.[7] Normally consideration, if present, will be in the form of payment of rent. It is clear, however, that a licence to occupy rent-free will also be converted, provided it is supported by valuable consideration and enforceable at law. Thus in *Verrall v Farnes*[8] a landowner installed the defendant for a 12 month rent free 'trial period', with a view on its expiration to granting a full agricultural tenancy. The defendant was to keep crops, and to sell any livestock he did not wish to keep, paying the proceeds of sale over to the landlord. It was held that although the defendant was not paying rent, his position was not that of a mere gratuitous licensee. The landlord was clearly obliged to allow him to remain on the land for the probation period while, on the other hand, the defendant could not simply

---

1 See s 2(2)(b).
2 See *Goldsack v Shore* [1950] 1 All ER 276 at 278, CA, per Evershed MR; *Harrison-Broadley v Smith* [1964] 1 All ER 867 at 874, CA, per Pearson LJ: 'this section is not applicable to an agreement which is not capable of taking effect, with the necessary modifications, as an agreement for the letting of the land for a tenancy from year to year.'
3 See *Errington v Errington and Woods* [1952] 1 KB 290, CA.
4 See *Walters v Roberts* (1980) 41 P & CR 210.
5 [1985] 2 All ER 289 at 300, per Lord Templeman.
6 [1950] 1 KB 708.
7 *Avon County Council v Clothier* (1977) 75 LGR 344, CA; *King v Turner* [1954] EGD 7.
8 [1966] 2 All ER 808.

abandon the stock and the farm without giving reasonable notice. It was therefore a contractually enforceable agreement, and as such was converted into an annual tenancy with security of tenure. Similarly, if the Court detects consideration in the form of any benefit to the landlord, even where no rent is payable, this will render the agreement contractual and within s 2. So in one case a licensee who occupied land rent free, on condition he reclaimed and cleared it, was held to be holding under a contractual licence, and hence a yearly tenancy.[9] Any other benefit to the landlord – such as manuring or reseeding land or (for instance) erecting fences or buildings – will also clothe a licence with enforceability, and thus lead to the statutory creation of a protected yearly tenancy.

Previously, an act of part performance by a licensee, pursuant to an offer of tenancy, would similarly have rendered an agreement enforceable and within the section, even if the rent were not agreed, eg dissolving an existing partnership pursuant to a condition of the offer, and purchasing fencing materials to improve the holding.[10] Section 2(1) of the Law of Property (Miscellaneous Provisions) Act 1989 now requires, however, that a contract for the disposition of an interest in land can only be made in writing, signed by or on behalf of each party to the contract. The doctrine of part performance has, moreover, been abolished in so far as it previously applied to contracts for the sale or disposition of interests in land.[11] The question arises therefore, whether the operation of section 2 of the 1986 Act will be affected, especially as the principle in *Goldsack v Shore* limits the operation of s 2(2)(b) to the conversion of contractually enforceable licences. If the licensee goes into occupation, and pays a monetary consideration, a common law periodic tenancy may be inferred. The problem is more acute where no money payment is evident, but a licence is clothed with enforceability by some other valuable consideration. A licence granting rights of occupation is not *per se* a disposition of an interest in land[12] and should, therefore, be exempt from the requirements of section 2 of the 1989 Act. If caught by section 2(2) of the Agricultural Holdings Act, however, a yearly tenancy will arise by statutory operation. In this event, it is thought, the leasehold estate thus created will arise by operation of law, and not by a 'disposition' properly defined, thus excluding the operation of the 1989 Act.[13] In any event, following the decision in *Street v Mountford*,[14] many licences caught by section 2 of the 1986 Act may in fact constitute tenancies *ab initio*.[15] Section 2(4) of the 1989 Act exempts from its operation short term leases granted by parol and taking effect in possession for a term not exceeding three years.[16] This exemption only applies, however, if the lease is granted 'at the best rent which can be reasonably obtained without taking a fine'.[17]

9 *Mitton v Farrow* (1980) 255 EG 449, CA.
10 *Epps v Ledger* (1972) 225 EG 1373.
11 1989 Act, s 2(8) *ibid*.
12 See Law of Property Act 1925, s 205(i), (ii).
13 *Sed Quaere*, the Law of Property Act 1925 defines both 'conveyance' and 'disposition' to include, inter alia, the grant of a lease. It might be argued that the creation of a lease, albeit inadvertently, is within the definition.
14 [1985] 2 All ER 289, HL.
15 See below p 31 ff.
16 Ie, leases within the Law of Property Act 1925, s 54(2).
17 Ibid. Section 54(2).

(B)   EXCLUSIVITY OF POSSESSION

Section 2 refers to licences to 'occupy' agricultural land. Consequently, the licence must give the licensee the right to exclusive possession if s 2(2)(b) is to operate to convert it into a yearly tenancy. This is the principle in *Harrison-Broadley v Smith*[18] and *Bahamas International Trust Co Ltd v Threadgold*.[19] An agreement whereby the owner of land enters into partnership with a manager does not, therefore, confer a tenancy on the 'partner' or 'manager' – provided the partnership is one of substance and not merely a 'sham' or device for avoiding security of tenure.[20] Any other licence of a non-exclusive nature will, likewise, fail to confer a tenancy on the grantee – for instance, a right merely to keep animals on the land during a limited part of the year.[1] Similarly, a licence which is not a licence to occupy the land, but merely to take the produce of the holding, will also fail to confer a tenancy on the grantee.[2] A licence to remain in possession on expiry of a tenancy to harvest crops will not, therefore, be within s 2.[3]

Licences of any duration are converted into yearly tenancies by s 2. Provided it gives exclusive possession and is enforceable in law, a licence will be converted into a protected yearly tenancy even if it is of uncertain duration[4] or (for instance) if it is a licence to occupy for life. Whereas a tenancy for a fixed term of between one and two years is exempt from the protection of the legislation[5] a licence of this duration will be converted into a protected yearly tenancy by section 2.

3.   Tenancies for two years or more

By virtue of s 3 a tenancy for a fixed term of two years or more continues, after the date on which its fixed term expires, as a tenancy from year to year. Statutory extension of a fixed term, into an annual tenancy, does not take place where either party gives written notice of his intention to determine the tenancy not less than one year and not more than two years before the expiry of the tenancy. A notice in this form is, however, deemed to be a notice to quit[6] and will be subject to the restrictions in Part III of the 1986 Act. The section does not apply to leases for life converted by section 149(6) of the Law of Property Act 1925 into fixed terms of ninety years.[7]

In the case of tenancies granted on or after 12th September 1984, special provisions deal with the situation where a tenant with a fixed term dies prior to the end of the term. By section 4 of the 1986 Act,[8] where the tenant dies one year or more before the term date, the tenancy does not continue as a yearly tenancy, and terminates on the date fixed for expiry of the fixed term.

---

18 [1964] 1 All ER 867, CA.
19 [1974] 3 All ER 881, HL.
20 *Harrison-Broadley v Smith* [1964] 1 All ER 647 CA. *Cf*. Padbury v York [1990] 41 EG 65.
1 *Bahamas International Trust Co Ltd v Threadgold*. [1974] 3 All ER and ER 881 HL.
2 *Wyatt v King* (1951) 157 EG 124, CA.
3 Milton (Peterborough) Estates Co v Harris [1989] 2 EGLR 229.
4 See *Snell v Snell* (1964) 191 EG 361.
5 *Gladstone v Bower* [1960] 2 QB 384, CA. See further below p 37 ff.
6 Section 3(2). Agricultural Holdings Act 1986.
7 Section 3(3) ibid.
8 Introduced by Agricultural Holdings Act 1984, Sch 3, para 21.

By virtue of s 4(2)(b), however, if the tenant dies within the last year of tenancy, and no valid notice to quit has been given, then the tenancy shall continue for 12 months and expire on the first anniversary of the term date. For the purpose of claims for compensation under the 1986 Act, tenancies terminated in accordance with section 4 are treated as having been terminated by landlord's notice to quit.

The combined effect of sections 2 and 3 of the 1986 Act is therefore that all agricultural tenancies to which they apply automatically continue on the expiry of their term as tenancies from year to year, except fixed term tenancies where the tenant dies before the date fixed for expiry.

4.   Extension in lieu of claim for emblements

The 1986 Act contains an unusual provision (s 21) under the heading 'Extension of tenancies in lieu of claims to emblements.' Section 21 provides in subsection (1): 'Where the tenancy of an agricultural holding held by a tenant at a rackrent determines by the death or cesser of the estate of any landlord entitled for life, or for any other uncertain interest, instead of claims to emblements the tenant shall continue to hold and occupy the holding until the occupation is determined by a 12 months' notice to quit expiring at the end of a year of the tenancy, and shall then quit upon the terms of his tenancy in the same manner as if the tenancy were then determined by effluxion of time or other lawful means during the continuance of the landlord's estate.' This provision is aimed at the situation where the landlord granting the tenancy has only a life interest, or some other uncertain interest, which is determined either by his death or cesser. At common law the tenancy automatically terminated with the landlord's estate, subject to the tenant's right to re-enter to claim emblements, ie to harvest crops which come to maturity within a year of sowing. The right to emblements was unsatisfactory in a number of respects, and the 1986 Act now provides that where the landlord's interest terminates in these circumstances, the tenancy shall continue until terminated by 12 months' notice to quit given in the normal manner. The tenant, moreover, will be able to serve a counter notice invoking the security of tenure provisions of Part III of the 1986 Act.

The section only applies where the landlord has an interest for life or some other uncertain interest. It therefore applies where the landlord is in a position analogous to a tenant for life, and as such it will rarely be met with in practice. Tenants for life under a strict settlement normally have power to create leases for up to fifty years, and such tenancies will bind their successors.[9] Tenancies created by a life tenant within the Settled Land Act 1925 may, however, be covered by s 21 where the statutory formalities for their creation have not been complied with, and the tenancy thereby created is consequently for an uncertain term. The section also previously applied where a tenancy was created by a clergyman whose benefice enjoys glebeland, for a vicar or rector is 'a landlord . . . for an uncertain interest'.[10] An interest

---

9 Settled Land Act 1925, s 41. For formal requirements required for the creation of leases by a tenant for life, see ibid ss 41–48.
10 *Stephens v Balls* [1957] CLY 1154.

created by an incumbent in these circumstances would therefore continue until terminated by notice to quit. Incumbents no longer, however, enjoy powers of leasing. The provisions now found in s 21 are therefore of little practical significance in a modern context.[11]

5. Arbitration as to terms of tenancy

Where section 2 of the 1986 Act operates to convert a short-term letting or licence into a yearly tenancy, s 2(4) provides that 'any dispute arising as to the operation' of the Section in relation to any agreement is to be determined by arbitration under the Act. In *Goldsack v Shore*[12] the Court of Appeal held that any question as to the applicability of the section, and whether an agricultural holding had been created, fell instead within the jurisdiction of the Courts. The section provides, however, that any agreement converted into an agricultural holding is to continue 'with the necessary modifications' as if it were a yearly tenancy. Any dispute as to the required modifications to the agreement must, therefore, be decided by reference to arbitration.

6. *Street v Mountford* and agricultural tenure

The House of Lords ruling in *Street v Mountford*[13] has potentially major implications for agricultural tenure. It undoubtedly reinforces the importance of exclusivity of possession as the hallmark of a protected tenancy, and the necessity to avoid any implication that a short-term letting is 'sham'. Per Lord Templeton, if an agreement by which land is occupied manifests an intention to grant exclusive possession to the occupier for a term at a rent, then a tenancy arises and not a licence, whatever the parties choose to call their relationship.[14] It is now clear that the payment of a monetary rent is not necessary for a tenancy to arise, exclusive possession for a term under an enforceable agreement alone being sufficient.[15] Many agreements previously thought to create mere licenses may now, in fact, be found to create tenancies.

In one sense, *Street v Mountford* merely reaffirms a requirement already existing in agricultural law, viz. that section 2(2)(b) of the 1986 Act only operates on licences which confer exclusive occupation of agricultural land.[16] In this sense, it might be said that an interest taking effect as a tenancy by virtue of *Street v Mountford* would, in any event, have taken effect as a tenancy by statutory conversion, ie under section 2(2) of the 1986 Act. Although its import in the agricultural context has yet to be judicially decided, the redefinition of the lease/licence distinction in *Street* could have unforeseen consequences on the structure of statutory protection under the 1986 Act. So, for instance:

11 See further *Scammell & Densham's Law of Agricultural Holdings* (7th Ed) esp at p 33.
12 [1950] 1 KB 708.
13 [1985] 2 All ER 289.
14 [1985] 2 All ER 289 at 300.
15 *Ashburn Anstalt v Arnold* [1989] Ch 1, CA.
16 *Bahamas International Trust Co Ltd v Threadgold* [1974] 3 All ER 881, HL.

(i)   A licence to use agricultural land limited to a period of between one and two years may now create a tenancy, if exclusive possession is conferred. Such an interest will not, however, confer security of tenure, as lettings for between one and two years are outside the security provisions of the 1986 Act.[17] Viewed as a licence, however, such an interest would be caught by s 2, and an annual tenancy with protection would arise.

(ii)   Similarly, a licence for a fixed period of (for instance) two years or more would, by virtue of s 2, take effect as a periodic yearly tenancy. Under the rule in *Street v Mountford*, however, it would take effect as a tenancy for the period of grant, viz a *tenancy* for a term of years which would continue on expiry as an annual tenancy (under s 3 of the 1986 Act). This could have consequences for the application of other statutory rights, eg the availability, and timing, of rent reviews under s 12. The dicta in *Street v Mountford* go to the common law distinction between leasehold and lesser interests, and as such should in principle override earlier case law under the agricultural holdings legislation.[18] The decision could, therefore, render s 2(2)(b) of the 1986 Act largely redundant. The impact of *Street v Mountford* on the operation of s 2 was judicially considered in *McCarthy v Bence*[19] where it was tentatively suggested that the residual scope of s 2(2)(b) may be that it is intended to catch licences to use land for grazing or mowing (or both) which are not, by being limited to some specified period of the year, excluded from s 2 by s 2(3).[20] Alternatively, it was posited that the wording of s 2 goes back to the Agriculture Holdings Act 1948 and has simply not been updated in the light of *Street v Mountford*.[1]

C   Exceptions to statutory protection

A number of classes of tenancy and licence fall outside the protection of the 1986 Act, and will not take effect as protected annual tenancies. Some of the exclusions are expressly provided for in the 1986 Act, others being derived from the common law requirement of exclusive possession for the operation of s 2. Express exclusions from protection cover the following:

1.   Grazing and Mowing Agreements

By virtue of s 2(3)(a) a tenancy or licence to occupy agricultural land does not take effect as an annual tenancy, if it is 'made (whether or not it expressly so provides) in contemplation of the use of the land only for grazing or mowing (or both) during some specified period of the year'. The two essentials of a security-free letting for grazing are, firstly, that the period of

17 *Gladstone v Bower* [1960] 2 QB 384, CA.
18 Eg *Bahamas International Trust Co Ltd v Threadgold* [1974] 3 All ER 881 HL.
19 [1990] 17 EG 78, CA.
20 As to the exemption of grazing and mowing agreements generally see below.
 1 *McCarthy v Bence* [1990] 17 EG 78 at 82 per Dillon LJ.

let must be for a specified period of less than one year and, secondly, that the contemplated use of the land must be for grazing and/or mowing only (or both). Problems frequently arise where informal and/or oral arrangements are entered into. Not only is the onus of proof on the landlord to bring himself within the section; where the agreement is oral, evidence of what was actually done on the land will be relevant to establish the nature of the letting. If the agreement is in writing, however, the parol evidence rule dictates that the only admissible extraneous evidence will be evidence that the transaction is a 'sham'.[2]

(a) Period of Let

The period of let must be for no longer than 364 days, although it has been held that a period of 364 days exactly *will*, for these purposes, be a specified period of less than a year.[3] An agreement for 365 days will not, however, and will be caught by s 2(1). Note that an agreement 'from 1 April to 31 March' will constitute a 365 day let caught by the Act,[4] as will an oral agreement evidenced by the payment of a full year's rent.[5] Similarly, an agreement for 'six months periods' in fact gives the right to graze for at least two successive periods, and is therefore outside s 2(3).[6] Although the period of let should be clearly expressed, failure to do so need not be fatal, provided the period contemplated by the parties can be ascertained with reasonable certainty, and when ascertained is less than a year. So, if it is only possible to graze the land for part of the year, and this is customary in the locality, the implication will be that it was the contemplation of the parties that the grazier should have exclusive use of the land only during the period when it could provide food for his stock.[7] The period must be 'specified', not exactly defined. Custom and usage will often be important in ascertaining the period of let. In *Watts v Yeend*[8] a let of seasonal 'grass keep' was held to be within the exception. It was there held that the court is entitled to take account of Ministry returns made by the landlord, indicating the use of the land for seasonal grazing as evidence that an oral arrangement constituted a seasonal grazing licence. On the same basis, agreements for 'seasonal lets', 'summer grasskeeping' and 'grass keep' have been held to be within the exception in s 2(3).[9]

(b) Contemplated User

The agreement must contemplate the use of the land for grazing and/or mowing *only*, and not some other agricultural purpose. If the agreement contemplates the carrying out of additional acts of husbandry, other than those which are strictly ancillary to the use of the land for *grazing for less than a year*, this will take the agreement outside s 2(3). So, in *Lory v London Borough of Brent*[10] a grazing agreement pursuant to which the grazier was to

---

2 *Watts v Yeend* [1987] 1 All ER 744, 752, CA, Kerr LJ.
3 *Reid v Dawson* [1955] 1 QB 214, CA.
4 See *Cox v Husk* (1976) 239 EG 123.
5 *Lampard v Barker* (1984) 272 EG 783, CA.
6 *Rutherford v Maurer* [1962] 1 QB 16, CA.
7 *Stone v Whitcombe* (1980) 40 P & CR 296, CA.
8 [1987] 1 All ER 744, CA.
9 See *Mackenzie v Laird* 1959 SLT 268, applied in *Watts v Yeend* (above); *Butterfield v Burniston* (1961) 111 L Jo 696; *Luton v Tinsey* (1978) 249 EG 239, CA.
10 [1971] 1 All ER 1042

plough the land in the interests of good husbandry, on a crop rotation basis, was held to create a protected annual tenancy, for ploughing and growing of cereal crops over this period could not be said to be ancillary to the use of the land for grazing for less than one year (even if it might put it in good heart for grazing over a longer period). The inclusion of buildings will, similarly, take the agreement outside s 2(3), *unless* the contemplated use of the latter is strictly incidental to grazing or mowing, eg for stabling of ponies grazing the land.[11] Provided, however, the contemplated user at the outset is exclusively for grazing and/or mowing, the fact that the occupier subsequently ploughs the land, and does other acts not contemplated by the agreement, is irrelevant. Provided the parties' intention at the time of contract is to permit grazing only, subsequent acts cannot alter the nature of the agreement and take it outside the grazing proviso.[12]

(c)   Series of grazing lets

An exempt grazing agreement can be renewed on successive occasions, provided there is no express or implied understanding that it will be renewed.[13] If, however, the parties purport to create an exempt grazing agreement but agree that the grazier can remain in occupation for several years, the correct inference is that the latter will receive a series of agreements totalling several years. In this event, s 3 will apply to continue the agreement on expiry as a protected annual tenancy.[14] In reality the parties will have in contemplation grazing for a period greater than a specified period of one year, thus disapplying s 2(3). The parties' contemplation must be ascertained at the time of contract. If the agreement is in writing, it is only permissible to go outside its terms for the purpose of showing it is 'sham', viz. that the parties contemplated a different period of let to that expressed, and that allowed by s 2(3).[15] Where a grazier is granted a tenancy, as opposed to a mere licence, note however the possible exclusion protection if the period of use contemplated is for a fixed period of between one and two years.[16] In the absence of any implication of 'sham', it is only permissible to go outside the written terms of the agreement, and admit extrinsic evidence, where the agreement is silent.[17]

2.   Ministry consents

An agreement which was the subject of approval from the Ministry, prior to grant, does not take effect as a tenancy from year on year on expiry. Approval can be granted either under s 2(1) or s 5 of the 1986 Act.

11 *Avon County Council v Clothier* (1977) 75 LGR 344, CA.
12 See *Boyce v Rendells* (1983) 268 EG 268, CA; *Midgley v Scott* (1977) 244 EG 883.
13 *Scene Estate Ltd v Amos* [1957] 2 All ER 325, CA; grazing agreement for three months renewed 21 times without creating a protected tenancy.
14 See *Short Bros (Plant) Ltd v Edwards* (1978) 249 EG 539, CA.
15 *Scene Estate Ltd v Amos, ibid* at 328 Denning LJ; *South West Water Authority v Palmer* (1983) 268 EG 357, CA; *Watts v Yeend* [1987] 1 All ER 744, CA.
16 *Gladstone v Bower* [1960] 2 QB 384, CA, and see on this point *Cox v Husk* (1976) 239 EG 123.
17 *Lampard v Barker* (1984) 272 EG 783, CA, (no mention of limited period in correspondence, but rent paid for a full year and stock kept outside grazing season. Held, a protected tenancy had been created.)

(a)   Consent under section 2

By virtue of s 2(1), an agreement will not take effect as a tenancy from year to year under that provision if it was approved by the Minister before it was entered into. Section 2 consent is available for any grant by way of a *tenancy* less than from year to year, and for the grant of a *licence* of any duration. The Ministry's consent need not be to the particular agreement in question – it can be granted to named local authorities or government departments,[18] or named landlords, or limited to the subsequent letting of identified parcels of agricultural land. The Minister need not concern himself with the particular terms of the proposed tenancy, or even the manner of its creation. Consent can also apply to an implied tenancy, eg where a tenant holds over in possession and pays rent.[19] Note that a consent obtained under s 2(1) is effective from the moment of signature by the Minister, and that, once obtained, it cannot act retrospectively to validate an agreement already entered into. The letting must be approved prior to grant, the onus being on the landlord to prove that any conditions on approval have been met. So, in *Bedfordshire County Council v Clarke*[20] a protected tenancy arose where Ministry approval and the tenant's signed acceptance of the tenancy both bore the same date. The landlord was unable to prove that the Minister's consent pre-dated the tenant's acceptance in point of time, and so the consent could not apply to exclude the operation of section 2 of the 1986 Act.

(b)   Consent under section 5

Section 5 provides for Ministry approval to be available for fixed term *tenancies* of between two and five years. If consent is obtained, the tenancy will not then continue on expiry under s 3 as a tenancy from year to year. The formalities for obtaining consent differ from those applicable under s 2(1) (above), and are in some respects more stringent:

(i)   the parties must agree that s 3 is not to apply to the tenancy.

(ii)   landlord and tenant must make a *joint* application to the Ministry for approval of the agreement. *cf* under s 2(1) application can be made by either party, the participation of the other being unnecessary.

(iii)   the consent takes effect upon its being notified to both parties. *cf.* under s 2(1) consent takes effect upon grant, irrespective of notification to the parties themselves.

(iv)   the tenancy must be in writing, and contain a statement (or carry an endorsement) indicating clearly that s 3 does not apply to the tenancy. *Cf* s 2(1) consent, which applies to implied as well as express tenancies.[1]

These provisions were introduced by the Agricultural Holdings Act 1984[2]

---

18 *Finbow v Air Ministry* [1963] 2 All ER 647.
19 See *Epsom and Ewell Borough Council v Bell (Tadworth) Ltd* [1983] 2 All ER 59 (tenant holding over without signing formal tenancy agreement, Minister having consented to letting of specified *land* in general terms. Implied tenancy held exempted from s 2 by virtue of the prior consent.)
20 (1974) 230 EG 1587.
 1 *Epsom and Ewell Borough Council v Bell* [1983] 2 All ER 59.
 2 See Sch 3, para 2(4) of the 1989 Act.

with the aim of introducing flexibility into agricultural tenure by allowing for fixed term tenancies, without security, in appropriate cases.[3]

(c)   Availability of Ministry consent

The policy guidelines used by the Ministry when granting consent are contained in a joint announcement of the Agriculture Departments, made on 10th August 1989, on 'Approval of Short Term Lettings and Licences'. This replaced an earlier announcement, made on 19th July 1984, the main change being the Ministry's willingness to grant consent for tenancies of up to five years where a holding (or estate) is being reorganised. Previously tenancies for no more than three years were sanctioned in such circumstances.

Ministry consent will, in principle, be available in the following circumstances, the governing principle being that it will only be granted where it would be unreasonable to expect the landlord to let his land on a full agricultural tenancy. The situations contemplated are mostly temporary, but there are longer term instances where a tenancy is not appropriate because the predominant user of the land is non-agricultural:

(i)   *Redevelopment.* Where land is likely to go out of agricultural use within five to seven years approval of a short-term letting or licence would be justified. In such a case, the amount of compensation payable to the tenant would, otherwise, exceed the rent received by the landlord during the tenancy.[4]

(ii)   *Reorganisation and Transitional Arrangements.* Approval may be available for a short-term letting or licence for up to five years –
• if the owner is planning the amalgamation or regrouping of the holding;
• if he wishes to allow a purchaser into possession before completion;
• if the owner wishes to make temporary arrangements pending a final decision as to the land's future use.
• if he wishes to give a 'trial' tenancy to a prospective tenant prior to concluding a full tenancy. If entered into without consent, such an arrangement will normally result in the creation of a protected tenancy by s 2, even if no (or a nominal) rent is paid.[5]
• if the landlord's son or daughter are to take over a vacant holding within five years.

(iii)   *Specialist Cropping.* Approval may be given where land is to be let for the cultivation of a specialist crop which requires 'clean land', eg potatoes or carrots. Consent will normally, here, be limited to a tenancy or licence for one year only.

(iv)   *Allotments.* If allotments are temporarily surplus to requirements, Ministry approval may be given to a short-term letting or licence.

(v)   *Government Departments.* Approval may be given to government departments, typically the Ministry of Defence, where the operational requirements affecting the use of government land rule out the grant of a full agricultural tenancy.

3 And see further M Slatter (1985) 135 NLJ 771, *Report of the Committee of Enquiry into the Acquisition and Occupancy of Agricultural Land* (1979) Cmnd 7599 pars 627, 637 and 641.
4 See further Chapter 9 below.
5 See *Verrall v Farnes* [1966] 2 All ER 808.

The above are guidelines only, and consent may be given in individual cases where a temporary arrangement is necessary, especially if the area of land involved is small. There is no appeal against the Ministry's decision.[6]

3. Agreements made before 1st March, 1948

Section 2(1) only operates to convert lettings less than from year to year where they are made on or after 1st March, 1948. Short-term periodic tenancies entered into before that date are therefore exempt from the operation of the section and are not converted into yearly tenancies. A small number of monthly or weekly tenancies falling within this exception may still exist. Fixed-term lettings granted before 1st March, 1948 fall within section 3 of the 1986 Act, unless granted before 1st January 1921 (see Sch 12, para 2 of the 1986 Act).

4. Tenancies or licences granted by persons with limited interests

Section 2 expressly exempts from its operation any short-term letting or licence granted by a person whose interest in the land concerned is itself less than a tenancy from year to year, and which has not taken effect as a yearly tenancy by virtue of the section. This is very rarely encountered in practice.

5. Lettings for fixed periods of between one and two years

As we have seen, lettings for fixed periods of less than one year, or for one year exactly, are caught by s 2 and take effect as tenancies from year to year. Similarly, tenancies for a term of two years or more continue after expiry as yearly tenancies. In *Gladstone v Bower*[7] the Court of Appeal held that there is a lacuna in the 1986 Act in that a fixed term tenancy for a period of more than 12 months but less than two years is not converted into a yearly tenancy, and therefore falls outside the security of tenure provisions of the legislation. It is consequently very common for landlords to grant fixed term tenancies of between one and two years (for instance for eighteen months) as the tenant under such an agreement enjoys no security of tenure whatsoever. This is a rather surprising gap in the legislation, and one which the Northfield Committee (amongst others) have recommended should be closed.[8] None of the legislation subsequent to 1948 has taken the opportunity to do so, however, and the loophole in the security of tenure provisions remains.

Although a *Gladstone v Bower* tenancy will confer no security of tenure, it is by no means clear whether such tenancies are outside the scope of the 1986 Act altogether, or simply outside the security of tenure provisions. The question arises whether a *Gladstone v Bower* tenancy is one of an agricultural holding *at all*? The uncertainty arises because s 1(5) defines a contract of tenancy (an essential ingredient of the definition of an

6 For the text of the Ministry's Announcement of 10 August 1989 see Appendix 2 p 382 ff *infra*.
7 [1960] 2 QB 384.
8 Report of the Committee of Enquiry into the Acquisition and Occupancy of Agricultural Land (1979) Cmnd 7599 paras 627, 637 and 641.

agricultural holding) to mean a letting of land 'for a term of years' or from year to year. There is respectable authority for the proposition that a 'term of years' means a term of two years or more, a view which would exclude *Gladstone v Bower* lettings altogether from the 1986 Act. If such a tenancy is completely outside the 1986 Act, it may fall within the protection of the Landlord and Tenant Act 1954. The issue principally goes to the question of compensation on quitting – if such a letting is *not* one of an agricultural holding *at all*, the tenant will be unable to make claims for improvements or tenant right.[9] Notwithstanding these doubts the balance of argument favours the view that a *Gladstone v Bower* letting will constitute a tenancy of an agricultural holding, albeit without security of tenure. In the first place, they appear to have been assumed to be such by the drafters of the 1986 Act itself, eg s 36(2)(b) specifically excludes from statutory succession rights a 'holding' which was held by a deceased tenant for a fixed term of more than one but less than two years. More persuasively, the view that such a tenancy *is* indeed an agricultural holding has been assumed to be correct by the judiciary on at least two occasions (see observations of Diplock J at first instance in *Gladstone v Bower* itself,[10] and Oliver LJ in *Keen v Holland*.[11]) It would indeed be strange were such arrangements, so common in the agricultural industry, to be removed from the Agricultural Holdings Act altogether and consigned to the business tenancy legislation.[12]

6.   Gratuitous licences

It has already been noted that s 2 converts into a yearly tenancy a licence of any duration, provided that it is a contractual licence (ie, supported by valuable consideration) or is otherwise enforceable at law. A licence which is purely gratuitous will not, therefore, be converted into a protected yearly tenancy and will escape the operation of the Agricultural Holdings legislation. The agreement must be completely gratuitous and unenforceable at law, as the Courts are astute at finding consideration in the form of any benefit to the landlord in lieu of rent, and this will then render the licence contractual.

7.   Tenancies granted to office holders

Section 1(1) of the 1986 Act excludes from the definition of an 'agricultural holding' any contract of tenancy 'under which the . . . land is let to the tenant during his continuation in any office, appointment or employment held under the landlord'. An agricultural holding will not be created,

---

9 In this event compensation will be governed by the Landlord and Tenant Act 1927. For criticism of the uncertainty see Law Commission WP No 102 'Landlord and Tenant: Compensation for Tenants Improvements' (1987) pp 12–13.

10 [1960] 1 QB 170, 180.

11 [1984] 1 All ER 75, 79, CA 'it must therefore be assumed that the legislature was content to permit such tenancies to be created free from the restrictions on termination *applicable to other agricultural tenancies*' (italics added).

12 Further arguments in favour of the competing interpretations of the decision in *Gladstone v Bower* are admirably marshalled, in some detail, by Muir Watt, '*Agricultural Holdings*' (13th Ed) at pp 21–22.

therefore, where a landlord appoints a manager to run his farm for him and pays him a salary or a proportion of the profits of the business. The relationship must in substance be that of employer/employee, however. If the 'manager' is in reality bearing all the financial risks of the business and taking the farming profits, while paying a fixed sum to the landlord, the relationship will in substance be that of landlord and tenant, in which case a yearly tenancy may well have been created.

D Alternative modes of tenure

A number of legitimate avoidance techniques are commonly encountered, the aim of which is to avoid the creation of a full tenancy with security of tenure. These mostly exploit the common law requirement that a license to occupy agricultural land must, if it is to be converted into a protected tenancy, confer on the grantee exclusive possession of the land concerned (the principle in *Harrison-Broadley v Smith*[13] and *Bahamas International Trust Co Ltd v Threadgold*).[14]

1. Joint ventures and share farming

'Share' farming is the phrase commonly used to denote an arrangement whereby the owner of land enters into a contract with a working farmer (or 'share' farmer), under which the latter carries on the day-to-day management of the farming enterprise, but without obtaining exclusive possession of the land (and hence a tenancy). The twin objects of most share farming arrangements are to avoid the creation of a tenancy, on the one hand, while also precluding any implication of a partnership arising between landowner and share farmer. Where a partnership exists, the parties will be jointly and severally liable for all debts incurred, or tortious wrongs committed, by a partner acting in the course of the farming business. To achieve both objectives requires careful draftsmanship.

Where the business involves livestock farming, the agreement will usually provide for ownership of the whole or part of the stock to be retained by the landowner. The physical presence on the holding of machinery and/or stock belonging to the landowner will prevent any implication that the 'sharer' has exclusive possession of land or buildings. The landowner contributes to the venture the land, buildings and fixed equipment on the holding, plus all or some of the stock; the share farmer puts in his expertise and labour, working machinery, and agrees to pay a share of input costs. The share farmer may also agree to pay a headage charge for the use of the fixed equipment on the holding. If arable farming is involved, more difficult considerations arise. Here it is common for growing crops expressly to remain the property of the landowner until severance, so as to defeat any claim that exclusive possession has been conferred. The harvested crop, or its proceeds, will then be shared in an agreed proportion. The agreement will commonly provide for the sharing of input costs such as seeds and fertilisers. Whether the venture

13 [1964] 1 All ER 867, CA.
14 [1974] 3 All ER 881, HL.

involves arable or livestock farming, provision may be made for a management charge to be paid to the share farmer, to cover his day-to-day management of the owner's crops or livestock.

Different considerations apply if a partnership is to be avoided. It must be clear from the agreement that the joint venture is between two separate and distinct businesses. To this end the payment of all inputs should be expressly allocated and provided for, and the allocation of other costs between the parties expressed. Most important of all, receipts must be allocated gross, in the proportion agreed, and *not* net of payments for inputs and/or expenses of the business. By virtue of section 1 of the Partnership Act 1890 a partnership will exist, whether the agreement provides otherwise or not, whenever two or more persons are carrying on a business 'in common' with a view to profit. The 1890 Act also provides, in s 2(3), that a sharing of *net* profits raises an implication of partnership. This latter must, therefore, be carefully avoided.

Short-term ventures can be mounted using the exceptions to protection arising under the 1986 Act itself, eg the exception for grazing lets and *Gladstone v Bower* tenancies. Share farming constitutes a legimate mode of arranging *longer* term joint ventures, without raising the possibility of unwittingly creating a protected tenancy.[15] Perhaps the greatest danger inherent in such arrangements is that exclusive possession may, in fact, be granted to a share farmer. Although most agreements give the 'sharer' a licence to enter for the limited purposes of the business, if exclusive possession is in fact granted section 2 of the 1986 Act will operate to elevate the licence into an annual tenancy. Following *Street v Mountford*[16] it is clear that a grant of exclusive possession will give rise to a tenancy – whatever the parties themselves intend, and whatever the agreement itself says. It is primarily a question of finding the true intention of the parties at the time of contract. If the parties to a purported share farming contract intended the sharer to have exclusive occupation, then notwithstanding the terms of the agreement a tenancy will have been created. Terms found not to express the true intention of the parties (eg, a denial of exclusive possession) will then be disregarded as 'sham'.[17] In construing an agreement to ascertain whether it is a 'sham' the House of Lords have now decided, in *Antoniades v Villiers*,[18] that the court is entitled to have regard to all the circumstances including, inter alia, the relationship between the parties and the subsequent conduct of the occupation.[19] If a share farmer is allowed exclusive possession, there may be a difficulty in substantiating terms in the agreement to the contrary. The parties must be advised, therefore, that the sharing of occupation pursuant to the agreement must be carefully adhered to, and its terms fully carried out. The possibility of exclusive possession being unwittingly conferred arises, chiefly, where livestock are involved, eg if the owner does not retain stock of his own on the land. Where arable cropping is in issue the whole crop normally remains vested in the owner prior to severance, thus

---

15 For a share milking arrangement which validly achieved this object see *McCarthy v Bence* [1990] 17 EG 78, CA.
16 [1985] 2 All ER 289, HL.
17 See *Duke v Wynne* [1989] 3 All ER 130, CA.
18 [1988] 3 All ER 1058, HL.
19 See *McCarthy v Bence* [1990] 17 EG 78 esp at 82.

precluding the possibility of exclusive possession being given the share farmer.[20]

2. Partnerships

As we have seen, to be converted into a yearly tenancy by s 2, a licence must confer on the licensee an exclusive right of occupation as against the licensor and any other person claiming under him. In *Harrison-Broadley v Smith*[1] the Court of Appeal held that, where a landowner enters into a partnership and allows the partner to share occupation with him, no licence conferring exclusive possession is created and hence no yearly tenancy can arise. The partner will normally have, by implication, merely a licence to go onto the farm for the purposes of the partnership business. Because of the advantages to the landlord in avoiding the creation of a full agricultural tenancy, the use of partnerships as a medium for running farming businesses is common. The disadvantages of such arrangements include personal unlimited liability for all partnership debts, and the necessity of being involved in running the partnership's affairs. Because of these disadvantages, some may enter into 'sham' partnerships whereby, under the guise of a partnership deed, land is let to a working farmer (described as a partner) who undertakes all financial liability and agrees to pay a fixed or fluctuating return to the owner. Such an arrangement does not constitute a 'business carried on in common with a view to profit' within the meaning of s 1 of the Partnership Act 1890, and is in substance merely a tenancy disguised as a partnership. As such it will be converted by s 2 into a protected yearly tenancy of an agricultural holding.

The vast majority of partnership arrangements are, however, bona fide and represent a useful vehicle whereby a land owner who does not wish to farm himself can provide capital, and give responsibility to a farmer, without creating an agricultural holding. The Northfield Committee's survey of the structure of the agricultural industry found that approximately 20% of agricultural occupiers were partnerships of varying types[2], while their share of the total income from tenanted agricultural land had risen to over 55% by 1975/6.[3] The types of partnership encountered in practice, and the degree of security they offer the farmer, vary enormously. In a general farming partnership the owner will enter into partnership with a farmer, both parties providing working capital, and the profits will be split accordingly, taking account of the distribution of management responsibilities to each partner. The non-landowning partner will have either an express or implied licence to enter the land for the purposes of the partnership business. A variant of this

20 Share farming is a flexible concept, and individual contracts will vary greatly to suit different cases. For useful precedents see inter alia, *Share Farming – The Practice* by Stratton, Gregory & Williams (CLA), especially Appendices A and B; *Encyclopaedia of Forms and Precedents Vol 2*, paras [181]–[212] (Densham, Laws, Porter and Williams); *Precedents for the Conveyancer* 1–24 (Crops) and 1–25 (Livestock) (HAC Densham and J N Porter). Note in particular the editor's notes, and warning, as to 'sham', in the latter instance. There is also now a useful discussion in Scammell & Densham's *Law of Agricultural Holdings* (7th Ed) at pp 53–4.
1 [1964] 1 All ER 867 (above).
2 See Cmnd 7599 Pt 3, Ch 3, Table 8. For precedents, with explanatory notes, see *inter alia* *Encyclopaedia of Forms and Precedents, Vol 2*, paras [151]–[180] (Densham, Laws, Porter and Williams).
3 Ibid Table 9 (p 53).

arrangement, favoured by some institutional landowners, is to let land at a full rent to a partnership between a wholly owned subsidiary and a working farmer. The degree of security enjoyed by the farmer is written into the partnership deed itself, which usually provides that the termination of the partnership with the subsidiary terminates the tenancy. The partnership deed may include provision for compensation for the farmer in the event of termination. Yet another common form of partnership is the family farming partnership; (typically) the farmer's son becomes a partner in the family business and sometimes the partnership will take a tenancy of the farm. This type of partnership can cause problems with regard to statutory succession rights, and security of tenure generally, especially if the landowner is himself a partner/tenant. The son will often then play an increasing role in the business prior to the father's death. To avoid problems with future succession rights, where these apply, the partnership deed should expressly negative the creation of a licence to enter the land in members of the partnership other than the tenant.[4] All these forms of partnership are perfectly legitimate and will fall within the rule in *Harrison-Broadley v Smith* so that they do not create an agricultural holding. Perhaps the one form of partnership most likely to create a protected tenancy, depending on the individual circumstances, is the so-called 'management partnership'. This sort of arrangement will often be made between an owner and an experienced farmer, with the owner paying for seed, fertilizers, etc, and the farmer providing labour and machinery. This arrangement will confer no security of tenure on the farmer, but if the owner contributes only land and buildings to the partnership assets, and does little else except receive payments in lieu of rent, the transaction may well be a 'sham', and in reality a tenancy, with the result that a protected yearly tenancy with security of tenure will be created.

It is fairly common for a farmer to lease land to a partnership consisting of himself and his co-partners, especially where the business is a family partnership. This arrangement gives rise to difficult legal problems, for at common law it is clearly established that a person cannot let land to himself alone, and neither can he enter into a covenant with himself. In *Rye v Rye*[5] the House of Lords reaffirmed this position, but left open the question whether a person could let land to himself and others. In the context of the agricultural holdings legislation the issue is complicated by the fact that various notices must be served to claim security of tenure and other rights under the Acts,[6] with the result that a recalcitrant landlord could, in his capacity as partner, effectively block the service of the requisite notices. It is now clear, however, that a tenant can in limited circumstances compel his landlord/partner to join in the service of an effective counter notice to claim security of tenure,[7] with the result that the landlord/partner will not be able to block the claiming of statutory rights by the partnership. In other cases the tenants will have partnership authority to serve notices on behalf of the whole partnership.[8] There can therefore no longer be any practical objection to the legal validity of partnership arrangements of this sort.

4 See *Brooks v Brown* (1985) Conv 320 and further Chapter 8, p 161 ff.
5 [1962] AC 496.
6 See Chapters 6 and 7 below.
7 *Sykes v Land* (1984) 271 EG 1264, CA, *Harris v Black* (1983) 46 P & CR 366.
8 *Featherstone v Staples* [1986] 2 All ER 461, CA. These issues are explored in some detail below, Chapter 6 p 114 ff.

E Agricultural holdings and other protective codes

1. Agricultural Holdings and the Landlord and Tenant Act 1954

In some cases, as we have seen, it may not be immediately apparent whether a tenancy is properly an agricultural holding within the meaning of the 1986 Act, or whether it constitutes a business tenancy falling within the scope of Part II of the Landlord and Tenant Act 1954. Section 43(1)(a) of the 1954 Act, as amended by the Agriculture Act 1958, excludes from the protection of the business tenancy code all tenancies of agricultural holdings, including those tenancies (principally grazing/mowing agreements and tenancies with Ministry consent) which are not technically tenancies of 'agricultural holdings' because they are outside the scope of Section 2 of the 1986 Act.[9] It should be noted that the 1986 Act itself does not exclude from its scope a tenancy which would otherwise qualify as a business letting within the Landlord and Tenant Act 1954 (the provisions consolidated into the 1986 Act pre-date the latter). If a tenancy qualifies under both codes, therefore, the Agricultural Holdings Act prevails – a logical conclusion, in that an agricultural holding simply involves a more specialised form of business user than those otherwise protected under the 1954 Act. Agricultural land only qualifies for protection under the 1986 Act if used for the purpose of a trade or business[10] – all tenancies covered by the 1986 Act would, therefore, be within the 1954 Act in the absence of the special protection afforded by the Agricultural Holdings legislation.

Whether a tenancy is in law an agricultural holding, as opposed to a business tenancy *simpliciter*, is of importance for a number of reasons:

(i) Tenancies at will

A tenancy at will of agricultural land is a letting 'for an interest less than a tenancy from year to year'. As such it is caught by s 2 of the 1986 Act and will be converted into a fully protected annual tenancy.[11] *Cf* a tenancy at will of business premises *simpliciter* is *not* within the protection of the Landlord and Tenant Act 1954.[12] More generally, the 1954 Act does not apply to licences, and has no provision corresponding to s 2 of the Agricultural Holdings Act 1986.[13] There is a correspondingly greater risk of statutory protection having been inadvertently conferred, therefore, if property comprises an agricultural holding.

(ii) Compensation for improvements and disturbance

If a tenancy is of business premises, compensation for improvements will be governed by Part I of the Landlord and Tenant Act 1927. Agricultural holdings are excluded from the scope of the 1927 Act[14] and compensation

---

9 See above p 32 ff.
10 See above p 24 ff.
11 *Keen v Holland* [1984] 1 All ER 75, CA.
12 See *Cardiothoracic Institute v Shrewdcrest Ltd* [1986] 1 WLR 368; *Uzun v Ramadan* [1986] 2 EGLR 255.
13 See Landlord and Tenant Act 1954, s 23.
14 See Landlord and Tenant Act 1927, s 17.

falls to be determined in accordance with the special rules in Part V of the Agricultural Holdings Act 1986.[15] The distinction between the two codes is of importance as the consent procedures applicable to obtain permission prior to carrying out works of improvement (and so to lay the basis for a subsequent compensation claim) differ in material respects.[16] The procedures for making a claim on termination are also markedly different.[17] The compensation for disturbance provisions also differ in marked respects: in the case of business lettings it will be calculated by reference to the rateable value of the premises multiplied by the appropriate multiplier (see Landlord and Tenant Act 1954, s 37). In the case of agricultural holdings compensation is calculated by reference to the annual rent payable at termination.[18]

(iii)   Recovering possession

It should also be noted that the grounds for recovery of business premises are considerably more favourable to a landlord than those applicable under the Agricultural Holdings Act. In particular, Sch 3 of the latter has no provision corresponding to s 30(1)(f) and (g) of the Landlord and Tenant Act 1954, which allows for repossession of business premises where a landlord wishes to carry out works of reconstruction or demolition, or wishes to occupy the premises himself for business purposes.

(iv)   Change of user

The principles applicable where agricultural use ceases have already been considered.[19] One issue merits further discussion. If an effective abandonment of agricultural user is established, does it necessarily follow that the tenancy moves automatically into the protection of the Landlord and Tenant Act 1954? This will clearly be the result if the landlord acquiesces in the change of use, with knowledge, and in a manner which enables the court to infer a variation in the terms of the tenancy.[20] Section 23 of the 1954 Act requires occupation merely 'for the purpose of a business', and not (unlike the 1986 Act) that the business user be substantial. So if business user is not *de minimis* the business tenancy code will, in principle, apply. Thus, had an effective abandonment of agricultural user been established in *Short v Greeves*[1] the tenancy there would have fallen to be determined under the 1954 Act. This situation does, however, give rise to anomalies. Firstly, if the landowner is unaware of the change of use, or refuses to recognise it, Agricultural Holdings Act protection will be lost unilaterally by abandonment. The tenancy will not, however, move *into* the

---

15 See s 64 ff of the 1986 Act, below Chapter 9.
16 See section 3 of the 1927 Act, which enables the tenant to apply to the court if permission is refused by the landlord. *Cf* the arbitration and tribunal procedures outlined in s 67 of the 1986 Act, and the latter's differentiation between different types of improvement.
17 See section 47(1) and (2) of the Landlord and Tenant Act 1954, which in general requires notice within three months of notice to quit or statutory notice of termination under s 25. *Cf* the notice requirements of the 1986 Act, discussed below Chapter 9 at pp 179–182 ff.
18 See Chapter 9 below p 191 ff.
19 Above p 21 ff.
20 *Russell v Booker* (1982) 5 HLR 10 per Slade LJ.
 1 [1988] 1 EGLR 1, CA (above p 21–2).

1954 Act, thus leaving the tenant with no security of tenure.[2] Further anomalies arise where the tenancy ceases to be an agricultural holding, not because the substantial user has changed, but because agricultural activities have ceased to be carried out *in connection with a trade or business* (the land would then cease to be 'agricultural land' within section 1(4)(a) of the 1986 Act). Could the 1954 Act come in to protect such a tenancy in these circumstances? If the tenancy is vested in individuals it clearly cannot, for the 1954 Act here requires business user in the form of a 'trade, profession or employment'. However, where the tenant is a body of persons (whether a company or unincorporated association) business user is defined differently to include any 'activity' which is an occupation as opposed to a pleasure.[3] The latter has been held to be wider than merely a trade, profession or employment, and can cover purely charitable activities by unincorporated associations.[4] Where the tenancy is held by a body of persons, such as a farming company, it follows that the 1954 Act may well apply where land is converted from agricultural use to some non-commercial activity – but not in other cases, and not (anomalously) if the tenancy is vested in an individual.

2. Agricultural Holdings and the Rent Acts

If a farmhouse or cottage is let with land in circumstances where the letting of the whole is of an agricultural holding, then the relationship between landlord and tenant will be governed by the Agricultural Holdings Acts.[5] Rent Act protection for the occupant of a farmhouse is excluded[6] where a dwelling-house is comprised in an agricultural holding and is occupied by the person responsible for the control (whether as tenant, or as a servant or agent of the tenant) of the farming of the holding. Similarly, tenancies under which agricultural land exceeding two acres is let with the dwelling are excluded from Rent Act protection.[7] Such lettings may, of course, be protected under the Agricultural Holdings Act 1986 if the qualifying conditions are satisfied.[8]

The position is somewhat more complex where the tenant sublets a cottage or farmhouse, either to an agricultural employee or a third party. Agricultural employees occupying tied accommodation at low rents are now covered by the codes of protection in the Rent (Agriculture) Act 1976[9] and the Housing Act 1988,[10] which will apply as between the tenant of the holding and his sub-tenant if the latter is his employee. If, however, the

---

2 Eg *Russell v Booker* (above n 20) is such an example.
3 See section 23(2) of the 1954 Act and the well-known formulation by Lord Lindley MR in *Rolls v Miller* (1884) 27 Ch D 71, 88, CA.
4 See *Abernethie v Kleiman* [1969] 2 All ER 790, CA; *Lewis v Weldcrest Ltd* [1978] 3 All ER 1226, CA. For application to non-commercial activities see inter alia *Addiscombe Garden Estates Ltd v Crabbe* [1958] 1 QB 513, CA; *Hills (Patents) Ltd v University College Hospital* [1956] 1 QB 90, CA; *Groveside Properties Ltd v Westminster Medical School* (1983) 47 P & CR 507, CA.
5 Eg *Blackmore v Butler* [1954] 2 QB 171, CA where a cottage constituted an agricultural holding in itself.
6 See Section 10 of the Rent Act 1977 and Sch 1 para 7 of the Housing Act 1988.
7 Rent Act 1977, ss 6 and 26; Housing Act 1988, Sch 1, para 6.
8 Above p 16 ff.
9 As to which see Chapter 11 below.
10 See Sections 24–26. Housing Act 1988.

mesne tenancy is terminated, then at common law the sub-tenancy falls with it unless the termination was by surrender or other voluntary act of the tenant.[11] The sub-tenant is therefore in a potentially vulnerable position.

The Rent (Agriculture) Act 1976, the Rent Act 1977 and the Housing Act 1988 therefore make special provision to protect certain categories of subtenant:

(i) Tied agricultural accommodation

If the mesne tenancy is of an agricultural holding, and the tenant sublet dwellings to agricultural employees at a low rent before 15th January 1989, the applicable provision is the Rent (Agriculture) Act 1976, s 9(3). This provides that where a dwelling-house forms part of premises let on a superior tenancy which is not a statutorily protected tenancy, and is itself subject to a protected occupancy or statutory tenancy, then

'from the coming to an end of the superior tenancy this Act shall apply in relation to the dwelling-house as if, in lieu of the superior tenancy there had been separate tenancies of the dwelling-house and the remainder of the premises, for the like purposes as under the superior tenancy and at rents equal to the just proportion of the rent under the superior tenancy'.

This protection expressly applies where the superior 'premises' comprise an agricultural holding, part of which is then let as tied accommodation. As a consequence of s 9(3) there will be notional head leases of the dwelling and the remainder of the holding. If the head lease of the former is terminated the employee will therefore be entitled to rely on s 9(2), which provides that the sub-tenant will become the tenant of the landlord on the same terms as if the mesne tenant's statutorily protected tenancy had continued. Note that protection will only accrue if the subtenancy is itself lawful, and if the mesne tenancy is itself a 'statutorily protected tenancy', viz. a tenancy of an agricultural holding within the meaning of the Agricultural Holdings Act 1986.[12] Note also that the 1976 Act applies only to sub-tenancies granted prior to 15th January 1989. If granted on or after that date the employee will have an assured agricultural occupancy to which the Housing Act 1988 will apply. The rules in the 1988 are altogether more straightforward.[13]

(ii) Subtenant of non-tied accommodation

Similar provision to that contained in s 9 is made by section 137(3) of the Rent Act 1977. This applies to subtenants who are not themselves workers occupying tied accommodation at a low rent.[14] Like section 9 of the 1976 Act, s 137(3) provides that where the mesne tenancy is of 'premises' which do not themselves constitute a dwelling-house let on a statutorily protected or statutory Rent Act tenancy, then on termination of the mesne tenancy there will be deemed to be notional separate lettings of the dwelling-house and the remainder of the premises. The subtenant can claim the protection

11 The rule in *Bendall v McWhirter* [1952] 2 QB 466, CA.
12 See s 9(4) Rent (Agriculture) Act 1976.
13 See below (iii), p 47.
14 Section 137(3) reverses the earlier decision in *Cow v Casey* [1949] 1 KB 474, CA, where it was held that the forerunner of s 137 only applied where the mesne tenancy was *itself* a tenancy to which the Rent Act applied. This would, of course, have excluded protection where the mesne tenancy was of an agricultural holding.

of s 137(2) if the notional separate letting of the accommodation would itself have been protected. The subtenant will, as a result of s 137(2), become the tenant of the landlord 'on the same terms as if the tenant's statutorily protected tenancy had continued'.

In *Maunsell v Olins*[15] it was held that the phrase 'premises' in s 137(3), referring to the mesne tenancy, did *not* include an agricultural holding. The result there was that a protected subtenant of a cottage on a farm was unable to invoke the subsection against the head landlord. The phrase 'premises' was said by the House of Lords to be limited to a dwelling-house and could not include a farm. This awkward decision was partially reversed by the Rent (Agriculture) Act 1976, the latter adding an express proviso to s 137(3) that 'premises' includes an agricultural holding within the 1986 Act. It was further provided, however, that protection will only accrue to the subtenant 'if the subtenancy in question is a protected or statutory tenancy to which section 99 of the [Rent Act 1977] applies'. A subtenant will, therefore, only be protected if he is an agricultural worker and the circumstances are such that, if the subtenancy were at a low rent, it would have been a protected occupany or statutory tenancy within the Rent (Agriculture) Act 1976.[16] In other cases the rationale in *Maunsell v Olins* continues to apply – a fact now emphasised by the decision in *Pittalis v Grant*[17] that 'premises' cannot include a business tenancy within the Landlord and Tenant Act 1954, and that the residential subtenant of part of business premises is unprotected by s 137(3).

(iii) Housing Act 1988

Where a subtenancy (for instance, of a dwelling-house comprised in an agricultural holding) is created on or after 15th January 1989, the Housing Act 1988 will apply, and not the Rent (Agriculture) Act 1976 or Rent Act 1977.[18] The applicable rules under the 1988 Act are altogether more straightforward than those in s 137(3) of the Rent Act 1977.

Section 18(1) of the 1988 Act protects a subtenant whose interest, as between himself and the mesne tenant, constitutes an assured tenancy within the meaning of Part I of the 1988 Act. Section 18(1) provides that if a dwelling is lawfully let on an assured tenancy and the mesne tenant is himself a tenant under a superior tenancy which comes to an end, then the assured tenancy will continue to exist as a tenancy held of 'the person whose interest would, apart from the continuance of the assured tenancy, entitle him to actual possession of the dwelling-house at that time'. This provision will apply both to a subtenant with an assured tenancy *simpliciter* and to an agricultural employee occupying tied accommodation as an assured agricultural occupant – an 'assured' occupant of tied accommodation will either have an assured tenancy, or a licence which is deemed to be an assured tenancy for the purposes of the 1988 Act.[19] The following points should be noted:

1. The dwelling must be lawfully sublet for s 18(1) to apply, and not sublet in breach of a covenant against alienation. If the headlease does

---

15 [1975] AC 373.
16 See Rent Act 1977, s 99(1).
17 [1989] 2 All ER 622, CA.
18 Housing Act 1988, s 34.
19 See Housing Act 1988, s 24(3).

not contain a covenant against subletting without the landlord's consent, the new rules reinforce the importance of invoking the machinery in s 6 and Sch 1, para 9 of the Agricultural Holdings Act 1986 to secure a covenant against assignment or subletting without consent.

2. The mesne tenancy which is terminated need not itself be an assured tenancy. Section 18(1) will apply where the mesne tenancy is of an agricultural holding or (indeed) a business tenancy.[20] It will not apply, however, where the interest of the landlord is one which, by virtue of Sch 1 to the 1988 Act, precludes assured tenancy status, eg if the headlease was granted by the Crown or by a local authority, and the dwelling was then sublet on an assured tenancy to the subtenant claiming protection.[1]

3. It is clear from the terms of s 18(1) that the subtenant continues to hold the tenancy under the sublease originally granted to him, the only import of the section being as to the identity of his immediate landlord. The terms and conditions of the sublease remain in force and will be enforceable by and against the head landlord.[2] Although there is no express provision dealing with the question, it would appear that notices given, for the purposes of the mandatory grounds for possession, by tenant to subtenant would retain their validity and be available to the landlord.[3] This implication is reinforced by the fact that such notices can clearly be relied upon by successor landlords.[4]

4. It will be apparent from the foregoing that the protection afforded to subtenants by the 1988 Act is considerably greater than that under the Rent Act 1977. Provided a subtenant has either an assured tenancy *simpliciter* or an assured agricultural occupancy he will be entitled to protection vis-à-vis the ultimate landlord. The only control the latter can exercise over the creation of protected subtenancies is through refusal of consent to sublet, pursuant to a covenant against alienation in the head lease. The covenant against alienation implied into agricultural leases is absolute,[5] and a landlord may be well advised, therefore, to insist that subletting be by way of assured shorthold tenancy. Note also that the protection of s 18(1) will extend to all assured subtenants, and not simply agricultural workers. *Cf* Rent Act 1977, s 137(3), the protection of which was only available to agricultural workers with a protected or statutory tenancy which *would* have been within the Rent (Agriculture) Act 1976 if at low rent.[6] This restriction does not appear in s 18(1) of the 1988 Act.

20 Cf *Maunsell v Olins* [1975] AC 373, HL; *Pittalis v Grant* [1989] 2 All ER 622, CA and s 137(3) Rent Act.
1 Section 18(2) Housing Act 1988.
2 *Cf* the difficulties under Rent Act 1977, s 137(3).
3 See Sch 2, Grounds 1 to 5 of the Housing Act 1988. This would enable the landlord to invoke Ground 1 and repossess for his own use, for instance, if the tenant had served a notice under Ground 1 at the time of the sub-letting.
4 See Sch 1, Ground 1, para (b) of the Housing Act 1988.
5 See Chapter 3 p 53 ff.
6 See the proviso to s 137(3) (above) and Rent Act 1977, s 99(1).

If a cottage is let separately and by a different tenancy agreement to agricultural land,[7] then the tenancy will be governed by either the Rent Act 1977 or the Housing Act 1988 – provided of course that the premises have been let 'as a separate dwelling' within the meaning of those Acts and have the appropriate rateable value. If sublet by the occupant, the subtenant is protected by s *137(1)* of the 1977 Act, or s 18 of the 1988 Act,[8] if the mesne tenancy is terminated, as the latter is itself a tenancy to which the Rent Acts apply. The landlord will only be able to claim possession by satisfying one of the conditions set out in Sch 15 parts 1 or 2 of the 1977 Act, or Sch 2 of the 1988 Act. Of these, particular reference might be made in the present context to Sch 15 cases 17 and 18 of the 1977 Act, which provide that the landlord can recover possession if the dwelling is required for an agricultural worker, or if it is a farmhouse made redundant by an amalgamation of farms, or other circumstances, and which is required for an agricultural worker. There are no equivalent provisions in the Housing Act 1988.

Whether the dwelling is part of an agricultural holding, a protected tenancy under the 1977 Act or covered by the Rent (Agriculture) Act 1976, the basic protection afforded by the Protection from Eviction Act 1977 will apply. Provided the occupant is occupying the premises as his residence, the Act makes it a criminal offence to unlawfully deprive him of possession or to harrass him by 'doing acts calculated to interfere with [his] peace or comfort'. All notices to quit must be in writing and give at least four weeks notice of termination.[9] Note in particular that section 4 of the 1977 Act confers on the Court power to suspend the execution of a possession order made against an agricultural employee occupying hired accommodation, but whose tenancy is not protected by the Rent (Agricultural) Act 1976. The Court *must* grant suspension if the order is made within six months of the former tenancy coming to an end. The Housing Act 1988[10] extended the power of suspension to licences granted to agricultural employees.

7 As in *Darby v Williams* (1972) 232 EG 579 CA.
8 Above p 46 ff.
9 See Protection from Eviction Act 1977, ss 1 and 5, as amended by Housing Act 1988 ss 25–32.
10 See ss 30(3) Housing Act 1988.

Chapter 3
The tenancy agreement; obligations and form

The obligations of landlord and tenant will be drawn from several sources: the tenancy agreement itself, 'model clauses' as to maintenance and repair of fixed equipment implied by statute, and the statutory standards of good estate management and good husbandry. The parties obligations as to fixed equipment are dealt with separately in the next chapter.

The tenancy agreement need not be in writing, although this is desirable. The requirements of sections 52 and 54 of the Law of Property Act 1925 must be adhered to, so that a term of three years or more must be by deed if to create a legal lease. No formality is required for the creation of a lease which takes affect in possession for a term not exceeding 3 years, at the best rent obtainable without taking a fine[1]. An informal lease, though of no effect in itself, may by implication of common law lead to the creation of a yearly tenancy if the tenant goes into possession and pays rent quantified on an annual basis. Similarly, an oral lease may be enforceable in equity as an agreement for a lease under the *Walsh v Lonsdale*[2] principle. Note, however, that a contract to grant a lease must now be made in writing, incorporating all the terms agreed by the parties and signed by each.[3] An equitable lease cannot be enforced relying merely on acts of part performance, the equitable doctrine of part performance having now been abolished.[4]

A contract to grant a lease taking effect in possession for a term not exceeding three years is, however, exempt from these requirements of formality, and can be made orally.[5]

The policy of the law is, however, to encourage certainty, and the 1986 Act contains provisions enabling either party to have the tenancy agreement reduced into writing by arbitration, and to secure the inclusion of certain basic terms listed in Sch 1 to the 1986 Act.

1 S 54(2) Law of Property Act 1925.
2 (1882) 21 Ch D 9, CA.
3 S 2(1) Law of Property (Miscellaneous Provisions) Act 1989.
4 S 2(8). Ibid.
5 S 2(5)(a) of the 1989 Act exempts from the application of s 2(1) *ibid* a contract to grant a short lease of the kind mentioned in s 54(2) Law of Property Act 1925. This would include a contract to grant an annual periodic tenancy of agricultural land.

A   The written tenancy agreement

1.   Right to a written tenancy

By virtue of section 6 of the 1986 Act, where there is not in force a written agreement embodying all the terms of the tenancy (including the model clauses), or such written agreement does not contain all the matters enumerated in Sch 1 of the Act, then either landlord or tenant can request the other to enter into an agreement in writing specifying *all* the terms of the tenancy and containing provision for *all* the Sch 1 matters. The request does not have to be in writing. It must, however, demand inclusion of all, and not merely some, of the Sch 1 matters. *Quaere* whether a notice demanding the inclusion of (for instance) only a covenant against assignment (Sch 1, para 9) would be valid if the existing agreement made no provision for other Sch 1 matters. If no agreement is entered into following the request, then the party making the latter can refer the terms of the tenancy to arbitration under the Act. No time limit for doing so is prescribed, though clearly the parties should first attempt (unsuccessfully) to reach agreement on the terms of the tenancy. Provided a request within the meaning of s 6(1) has been made, however, subsequent negotiatons are not a condition precedent to a reference to arbitration; all that is required is that 'no such agreement has been concluded'.[6]

2.   Schedule 1 terms

The terms specified by Sch 1, the absence of which can be used to trigger the statutory machinery, and for which provision must be made on arbitration, are the following:

1) The names of the parties.
2) Particulars of the holding with a sufficient description (by reference to a map or plan) of fields and parcels of land to enable its extent to be identified.
3) The term or terms for which the holding or different parts of it are agreed to be let.
4) The rent reserved and dates on which payable.
5) Incidence of liability for rates and drainage rates.
6) A covenant by the tenant to return to the holding the full equivalent manurial value of crops destroyed, should harvested crops grown for consumption on the holding be destroyed by fire. The covenant should only require this so far as it is necessary to fulfill the tenant's obligations to farm in accordance with the rules of good husbandry.
7) A covenant by the tenant to insure against damage by fire all dead stock on the holding and all harvested crops grown on the holding for consumption on it.
8) A power for the landlord to re-enter on the holding in the event of the

6 Agricultural Holdings Act 1986, s 6(1).

tenant not performing his obligations under the agreement (ie a forfeiture clause).

9) A covenant by the tenant not to assign, sublet or part with possession of the holding or any part of it without the landlord's consent in writing.

3.   Arbitration as to terms

(a)   Jurisdiction of Arbitrator

If no agreement is reached, the party serving the request under Section 6 can apply to the President of the RICS for the appointment of an arbitrator. The arbitration will then proceed under the 1986 Act, Sch 11.[7]

The arbitrator's jurisdiction is circumscribed. By virtue of s 6(2) his function is three fold:

(a)   his primary function is to find and specify the *existing* terms of the tenancy, subject to any variation agreed between landlord and tenant.

(b)   then, in so far as the existing tenancy (as varied) *neither* makes provision for *nor* makes provision inconsistent with the matters specified in Sch 1, he must make provision for all those matters having such effect as may be agreed between the parties or, in default of agreement, as appears to the arbitrator to be 'reasonable and just between them'. Note that the Sch 1 matters are only incorporated if the tenancy itself is silent or makes no inconsietent provision. If the agreement, as found by the arbitrator, makes contrary provision to the Sch 1 terms then the agreement prevails: the arbitrator cannot substitute the Sch 1 clauses for those agreed by the parties. Note also that even where the lease is silent, incorporation is not automatic. The arbitrator must only incorporate Sch 1 matters in so far as this is 'reasonable and just' between the parties concerned. This will be a question of fact for the arbitrator. The policy of the Act is not to standardise lease terms, but to encourage certainty by ensuring that *some* provision is made in agricultural leases for the matters listed in Sch 1.

(c)   the arbitrator can also include any further provisions relating to the tenancy which may be agreed between landlord and tenant.

Rent: if the arbitrator considers that, because of any provision made in his award, it is equitable that the rent should be varied, section 6(3) entitles him to vary it accordingly.

(b)   The arbitrator's award

By virtue of s 6(4) the arbitrator's award as to terms takes effect *as if* the terms and provisions specified in the award were contained in a written agreement between the parties. They take effect by way of *variation* of the tenancy agreement previously in force, as from the making of the award or such later date as may be specified in it.[8] The making of an award, being merely a variation of the existing lease, will not invalidate a prior notice to quit served by the landlord.

---

7 As to which see Ch XV below. Note that arbitration can only be requested by the party who served the request for a written agreement, and *not* by either party.

8 Cf s 8(4) *ibid*; Cf *Hollings v Swindle* (1950) 155 EG 269, which is no longer sound law.

4. Covenant against alienation

Unless restricted by the terms of the lease, it is a basic incident of the tenant's leasehold interest that he has the right to assign or sub-let without reference to the landlord[9]. Where the lease is in writing, this right will commonly be restrained by the inclusion of either an absolute, a fully qualified, or a qualified covenant against assignment and sub-letting. The tenant's common law right to assign furnishes a strong incentive to use the statutory machinery and have the lease reduced into writing. While the tenancy remains oral it can be freely assigned, and assignment to (for instance) a limited company has the effect of perpetuating security of tenure beyond the lifetime of the original tenant, and sidestepping the restrictions on succession to tenancies contained in Part IV of the 1986 Act.[10] Where the statutory machinery is used to reduce the tenancy to writing, the 1986 Act affords the landlord protection by considerably restricting the tenant's right of alienation.

(a) Statutory bar pending arbitration

Where the tenancy contains no non-assignment clause the landlord can request the tenant to enter into a written agreement containing all the Sch 1 matters. If he does so, section 6(5) provides that the tenant may not, without the landlord's consent in writing, assign, sub-let or part with possession of the holding or any part of it during the period while the determination of the terms of the tenancy is pending. The intent is to prevent avoidance of the statute by a tenant assigning his interest after service of a request and before the arbitration.

(I) DURATION OF BAR

The statutory bar on assignment commences with the date of service of the landlord's request for a written tenancy, and ends with the date on which an agreement is concluded or the arbitrator's award is made[11]. Although the landlord's initial request for a written agreement, pursuant to section 6(1), need not itself be made in writing, clearly a written request is preferable to furnish proof of commencement of the statutory bar on assignment.

(II) EFFECT OF CONTRAVENTION

Section 6(5) expressly provides that any transaction which breaches the statutory bar shall be *void*. It will have no effect, therefore, on the leasehold relationship between landlord and tenant, the latter remaining in law liable on the covenants in the lease and for rent. Conversely, assignment in breach of the statutory bar will not in itself constitute a breach of tenancy entitling the landlord to forfeit – at this stage the written lease, including the Sch 1, para 9 clause, will not yet have been settled. The terms of any sublease or assignment made in breach of section 6(5) will accordingly be unenforceable in law, so that (for instance) the tenant may not be able to enforce payment of rent from a 'subtenant'. In declaring a transaction in contravention of the

9 *Church v Brown* (1808) 15 Ves 258.
10 As to which see Chapter 8 below.
11 Agricultural Holdings Act 1986, s 6(6).

statutory bar to be *void*, this provision negatives the common law rule that, though a breach of tenancy by the assignor, assignment in breach of covenant *does* vest a leasehold interest in the assignee (or sublessee where appropriate): *cf Old Grovebury Manor Farm Ltd v W Seymour Plant Sales and Hire Ltd (No 2)*.[12]

(b)   Inclusion of statutory covenant

If the parties cannot agree a clause the arbitrator must include in his award the Sch 1, para 9 covenant *viz.* a 'covenant by the tenant not to assign, sub-let or part with possession of the holding or any part of it without the landlord's consent in writing'. Incorporation in this form is not automatic. While the arbitrator must make provision for a covenant against alienation, it must have such effect 'as appears to the arbitrator to be reasonable and just' between the parties. Although in most cases the statutory clause will be incorporated without modification, there may be a case for modifying it where the justice of the case so requires eg by making the covenant fully qualified.

Section 19 of the Landlord and Tenant Act 1927 does not apply to agricultural holdings[13]. The landlord's consent to assignment can therefore be withheld for any reason, and is not subjected to the requirement of reasonableness. Where the statutory covenant is included, either by agreement or arbitration, it follows that the lease is for all practical purposes non-assignable. *Semble*, however, if the parties agree the inclusion of a fully qualified covenant ('such consent not to be unreasonably withheld') the guidelines approved in *International Drilling Fluids Ltd v Louisville Investments (Uxbridge) Ltd*[14] will become relevant to assess the reasonableness of any refusal of licence to assign. The rigour of the statutory covenant, however, makes variation of its terms inadvisable.

(c)   Content of obligation

The covenant in statutory form prevents the tenant assigning, sub-letting or parting with possession of the *whole* or *any part* of the holding. Assignment in contravention will be an irremediable breach of tenancy entitling the landlord to take possession proceedings under Case E to the Act.[15] Note, however, that the landlord can in appropriate circumstances be estopped by convention from relying on the covenant. So, in *Troop v Gibson*[16], the landlord failed where the lease containing the alienation clause had been lost. The parties had subsequently acted on the common assumption that no restraint on assignment existed, and engaged in rent arbitration proceedings on this basis. The landlord could not enforce the covenant because both parties at all material times did not believe it existed, and this common assumption was to the detriment of the tenant – for absence of a restriction

---

12 [1979] 3 All ER 504, CA.
13 Landlord and Tenant Act 1927, s 19(4).
14 [1986] Ch 513, CA.
15 See *Scala House and District Property Co Ltd v Forbes* [1974] QB 575, CA; *Troop v Gibson* [1986] 1 EGLR 1, CA.
16 [1986] 1 EGLR 1, CA.

on alienation would increase the holding's rental value.[17] Note, conversely, that a tenant will be estopped from denying the existence of a contract of sale or assignment if he allows the assignee to act to his detriment in reliance thereon (for instance by selling his own farm), even if the contract was entered into by an agent acting without authority.[18]

The statutory covenant prevents the tenant parting with possession of any part of the demised property. It does not, however, prevent him *sharing* possession (for instance pursuant to a share farming contract) with another, although many agreed covenants in fact seek to do so. Note that if the parties include a covenant (not in statutory form) not to assign or sublet the *whole* of the demised property, this will not be breached by an assignment or sublease of part[19]. If, however, by express covenant the tenant agrees 'not to assign or underlet *any part* of the premises', the covenant on its true construction will prohibit the tenant assigning etc the whole *or* any part of the property. A covenant against assigning or underletting 'any part' of the premises embraces the assignment or underletting of every part[20]. Allowing a licensee or contractor to share occupation does not, however, breach the covenant as long as the tenant retains exclusive possession.

B   Obligations as to cultivation

1.   Husbandry and estate management: statutory standards

Sections 10 and 11 of the Agriculture Act 1947 lay down statutory standards of 'Good Husbandry' and 'Good Estate Management'. The sanctions for breach of the 1947 Act were repealed by the Agriculture Act 1958.[1] The rules of good estate management are consequently unenforceable by a tenant, unless incorporated by agreement into the tenancy itself. The rules of good husbandry, however, are of considerable importance and remain enforceable against a tenant by both direct and indirect means:

    (i)   The rules of good husbandry are *directly* enforceable in that breach of the 1947 Act standard gives the landlord a right to apply for a certificate of bad husbandry and invoke Case C in Sch 3 to the 1986 Act by serving notice to quit. The tenancy itself may incorporate the rules, thereby also making Case D available to remedy breach.

    (ii)   The rules have *indirect* relevance in that many of the statutory rights and duties of landlord and tenant are qualified by reference to them. So, for instance, in repossession proceedings under both Case D and Case E, the breach of tenancy complained of must be one which is

17 See generally *Amalgamated Investment and Property Co Ltd v Texas Commerce International Bank Ltd* [1982] QB 84.
18 *Worboys v Carter* [1987] 2 EGLR 1, CA.
19 *Cook v Shoesmith* [1951] 1 KB 752, CA.
20 *Field v Barkworth* [1986] 1 All ER 362, approved obiter in *Troop v Gibson* [1986] 1 EGLR 1, 3, CA.
1 S 10(1) and Sch 2 Part I, Agriculture Act 1958.

not inconsistent with the tenants responsibilities to farm in accordance with the rules of good husbandry[2]. Similarly, in order to compel the provision of fixed equipment by the landlord, a tenant must satisfy the agricultural land tribunal that this is reasonable *having regard to his responsibilities to farm according to the rules of good husbandry*[3]. And, even if the Cases for Possession in Sch 3 are *not* relied on, a tribunal can consent to the operation of a notice to quit if termination of the tenancy is in the interests of good husbandry (see s 27(3)(a)).

It might be added that, although not directly enforceable by a tenant *per se*, the landlord can rely on the statutory standards of Good Estate Management to seek tribunal consent to a notice to quit under s 27(3)(b) ibid.

(a)   'Good Estate Management'

The rules of good estate management require management to be such as to be reasonably adequate, having regard to the character and situation of the land and other relevant circumstances, to enable an occupier reasonably skilled in husbandry to maintain efficient production as regards both the kind of produce and the quantity and quality of produce[4]. The landlord must provide such fixed equipment as is necessary to enable a reasonably skilled occupier to maintain efficient production. The rules also require that the landlord carry out his legal obligations with regard to maintenance and repair of such equipment once provided. The landlord's obligations in this respect will be governed by the tenancy agreement or the 'model clauses' set out in the Agriculture (Maintenance, Repair and Insurance of Fixed Equipment) Regulations 1973.[5]

(b)   'Good husbandry'

A tenant will be fulfilling his duty to farm in accordance with the rules of good husbandry if he is maintaining a reasonable standard of efficient production, having regard to the character and situation of the holding, the standard of management by the owner and 'other relevant circumstances'.[6] He must, moreover, keep the holding in a condition to enable such a standard to be maintained in the future. In this respect the duty imposed by section 11 is more onerous than the tenant's common law duty, for at common law the tenant is under no duty to leave the land in good heart and condition, eg where it was in poor condition when he took the tenancy[7]. Section 11(2) sets out a number of factors to which regard must be had when considering whether the tenant is complying with the rules of good husbandry, *viz*:

- whether permanent pasture is being properly mown or grazed and maintained in a good state of cultivation and fertility;
- arable land must be cropped in a way which maintains the land in a clean and good state of cultivation and fertility;

2 See Sch 3 Part I of the 1986 Act.
3 See s 11(1) of the 1986 Act.
4 Section 10 Agriculture Act 1947.
5 SI 1973/1473, discussed below Chapter 4 p 70 ff.
6 Agriculture Act 1947 s 11.
7 *Williams v Lewis* [1915] 3 KB 493.

– if the farm is a livestock farm it must be properly stocked and an efficient standard of management of livestock maintained;
– steps must be taken to keep crops and livestock free from disease and infestation by pests and insects;
– harvested and lifted crops must be adequately protected;
– 'necessary' work of maintenance must be carried out, where the obligation to do so is the tenant's.

2. Implied covenant at common law

The common law imposes on a tenant of agricultural land a minimal duty to cultivate according to the custom of the country in a good and husbandlike manner. There is no corresponding obligation at common law, however, as to the manner in which the estate is managed. The duty on a tenant to farm in a good and husbandlike manner was stated by the Court of Appeal in *Wedd v Porter*[8] in these terms:

> 'A tenant from year to year of a farm and buildings at a fixed rent, who has not entered into any other express covenant with the landlord than as to the amount of rent, is under an obligation implied by law to use and cultivate the lands in a husbandlike manner according to the custom of the country . . . and to keep the buildings wind and water tight.'

The tenant is not, however, under any duty to 'sustain and uphold the premises'[9]. The minimal nature of this obligation means that there is no duty, as such, to deliver up the land on termination of the tenancy in a clean and proper condition; neither is the tenant under any obligation to leave the land in as good a condition on quitting as when he came into possession. Provided he farms the land properly his implied obligation will be satisfied, and the fact that the land was at the outset in very good condition does not imply an obligation to keep it so. Conversely, where the land is in poor heart on commencement of the tenancy, the tenant is under no obligation to leave it in a clean, and good condition on quitting, provided he has farmed properly throughout the tenancy.

The implied covenant to cultivate according to the 'custom of the country', or an express covenant in these terms, renders a usage obligatory on the tenant if it is univerally obligatory in that part of the country where the farm is situated, and is a general usage applying to all farms of that description. The usage, to be applicable, does not need to have been practised from time immemorial. 'An agricultural custom need not have subsisted from time immemorial, but it must have subsisted for a reasonable length of time and be adequately proved. . . . The custom must therefore be collected not from what witnesses say they think the custom is, but from what has publicly gone throughout the district'.[10] The custom must be 'reasonable' in the eyes of the law, but once it has been established as the ordinary custom of the country there must be very strong grounds for holding it to be unreasonable. Once proved, the custom of the country can only be excluded if the terms of a written tenancy agreement either expressly

8 [1916] 2 KB 91, 100.
9 *Auworth v Johnson* (1832) 5 C & P 239.
10 *Tucker v Linger* (1882) 21 Ch D 18, 34.

or impliedly indicate that the parties did not intend to be governed by it. The custom will therefore be excluded where there are express terms in the tenancy agreement which are inconsistent with it. Where the tenancy is silent, however, the custom of the country will operate to fill out the obligations of the parties at common law.[11]

The landlord's remedy lies in damages to recover the monetary equivalent of the injury to the reversion occasioned by the breach[12]. This will normally be the diminution in the rent the landlord will be able to demand on reletting, or the allowance he will have to make to an incoming tenant because of the poor condition of the holding. In practice the common law obligations are of little practical significance. Where the condition of the holding is particularly bad, however, the landlord will have the supplementary remedy of suing to recover the diminution in the value of his reversion.

3.   Express covenants: statutory variation

Covenants are commonly taken to prevent the tenant ploughing permanent pasture, restricting the mode of farming the holding, and restricting the tenant's right to dispose of crops and produce. To protect the tenant, Sections 14 and 15 of the 1986 Act override agreed clauses in this form in some circumstances.

(a)   Variation of terms as to permanent pasture

Section 14 of the 1986 Act gives either party the right, where the tenancy provides for the maintenance of specified land or a proportion of the holding as permanent pasture, to demand arbitration as to whether the amount of land required to be maintained as pasture should be reduced. The arbitrator is directed to consider whether a reduction would be 'expedient in order to secure the full and efficient farming of the holding'[13]. His award may specify that the contract of tenancy should be modified as to the land which is to be maintained as permanent pasture, or treated as arable land, and as to cropping in the manner stipulated in the tenancy. If the award reduces the area of land which under the contract of tenancy was to be maintained as permanent pasture, then he may specify that on quitting the tenant should leave as permanent or temporary pasture an additional specified area of land, but only in so far as the total area of permanent pasture provided for does not exceed that originally provided for in the tenancy[14] *viz.* he can order reinstatement of the reduction on termination of the tenancy.

(b)   Freedom of cropping and disposal of produce

Section 15 of the 1986 Act confers on the tenant the full right, without incurring 'any penalty, forfeiture or liablity', and notwithstanding the terms of the tenancy or custom:

---

11 See *Hutton v Warren* (1836) 1 M & W 466. Also *Wigglesworth v Dallison* (1779) 1 Doug KB 201; *Senior v Armytage* (1816) Holt NP 197.
12 See *Williams v Lewis* [1915] 3 KB 493.
13 S 14(2) Agricultural Holdings Act 1986.
14 Section 14(4) and (5) ibid.

(a) to dispose of the produce of the holding (other than manure) and
(b) to practise any system of cropping of the arable land on the holding.

The tenant must make 'suitable and adequate' provision to return to the holding the full equivalent manurial value of all crops sold off or removed from the holding in contravention of custom or the tenancy agreement. In the case of cropping he must protect the holding from injury or deterioration. If the tenant does not make suitable and adequate provision to return the manurial value of crops, or exercises his rights under section 15 so as to injure or deteriorate the holding, then the landlord is entitled to seek an injunction to restrain the exercise of those rights, and on the tenant quitting can claim compensation for any deterioration in the holding.[15] Where proceedings are brought for an injunction, the issue of whether the tenant has, or is likely, to exercise his rights in such a way as to cause injury or deterioration to the holding must be determined by arbitration under the Act. The arbitrator's award is to be conclusive proof of the facts alleged for the purposes of injunction proceedings.[16] It will also be conclusive in a subsequent arbitration on termination of the tenancy, although an arbitrator's award is not a prerequisite for an arbitration on quitting, as it is under section 15(5) for injunction proceedings.

The tenant's rights under s 15 do not apply (see s 15(2)):
  (i)   In the case of a yearly tenancy, in the year before the tenant quits the holding, or during any period after he has received notice to quit. As notice to quit will normally be of at least 12 months' duration ending on a term date, the freedom will be excluded for the whole of the notice period, ie potentially for up to 23 months. If short notice is validly given, the freedom will be excluded for the 12 months prior to the end of the tenancy.
  (ii) In the case of any other tenancy, eg a fixed term, s 15 is excluded for the year before its termination.
  (iii) Section 15(1) does not apply to a tenancy of land let as a smallholding pursuant to a scheme for the farming of smallholdings on a co-operative basis, or a scheme which provides for the disposal of the produce of such holdings, or provides other centralised services for such smallholding tenants. The scheme must be approved by the Ministry.[17]
  (iv) In the case of cropping s 15(1) only confers rights in respect of arable land. The phrase 'arable land' does not include land in grass which by the terms of the tenancy is to be retained in the same condition throughout the tenancy.[18]

Where it applies, s 15(1) overrides any contrary provision in the contract of tenancy.

---

15 S 15(5) ibid.
16 S 15(6) ibid.
17 See s 82(1) of the 1986 Act.
18 See s 15(7) ibid.

(c)   Prohibition of removal of manure

The disposal of manure produced on the holding is expressly excluded from the scope of s 15(1).[19] A covenant preventing its disposal will be enforceable notwithstanding the general freedom of cropping conferred on the tenant. Section 15(3) of the 1986 Act provides, in any event, that once a notice to quit has been given, the tenant shall not, subject to any agreement *in writing* to the contrary, at any time after that date, sell or remove any manure, compost, hay, straw or roots grown on the holding in the last year of the tenancy. Unlike s 15(1), this provision can be varied or excluded by the tenancy agreement, provided the latter is in writing. 'Roots' included in the prohibition are further defined by s 15(7) to mean the produce of any root crop normally grown for consumption on the holding.

(d)   Penal rents

It was not uncommon in the past for tenancies to include a provision providing for the payment of an additional ('penal') rental in the event of the tenant committing a breach of one of the terms of the tenancy. Such covenants were enforceable at law. Moreover, a covenant of this nature was treated in equity as an agreed provision for liquidated damages for breach of the agreement, and not a penalty. Consequently, to protect the tenant section 24 of the 1986 Act provides that, notwithstanding any provision in the contract of tenancy making the tenant liable to pay a higher rent or liquidated damages in the event of breach of the agreement, the landlord shall not be able to recover for a breach any sum in excess of the damage actually suffered by him in consequence thereof. Section 24 applies to *all* breaches of tenancy (and not just breaches of covenants as to cultivation or repairs) and limits the landlord's right to recover damages to his actual loss. It cannot be excluded or varied by agreement of the parties.

4.   Miscellaneous statutory rights

(a)   Damage by game

Section 20 gives the tenant the right to claim compensation where his crops have been damaged by wild animals or game, where the right to kill and take the latter is vested in the landlord or a third party (eg a sporting tenant). This right does not apply if the tenant himself has permission in writing to kill the animals or game in question. The tenant must give notice in writing to the landlord within one month of becoming aware of the occurrence of damage, and give him a reasonable opportunity to inspect it before the crop in question is reaped or consumed. If damage is to crops already reaped or raised, the landlord must have an opportunity to inspect it before the crop is begun to be removed from the land. The tenant must then give notice of his intention to claim compensation within one month of the expiry of the year in respect of which the claim is made.[20] In default of agreement, the agricultural 'year' for the purpose of compensation claims means the 12

---

19 See s 15(1)(a) ibid.
20 S 20(2) ibid.

months ending on 29 September.[1] Compensation is quantifiable by arbitration if agreement cannot be reached. By virtue of s 20(5) the landlord has a right of indemnity where the damage is caused by a sporting tenant, and not by himself.

(b) Record of condition of the holding

Section 22 of the 1986 Act provides for either the landlord or tenant, at any time during the tenancy, to require the making of a record of the condition of the buildings, fences, gates, roads, drains and ditches on the holding, and of any other fixed equipment, and of the state of the holding itself (including any parts not under cultivation). Additionally, the tenant can require the making of a record of improvements made by him, or in respect of which he paid compensation to an outgoing tenant, and of any fixtures and buildings which he is entitled to remove. The parties can agree on a third party to draw up the record, but in default of agreement application can be made to the President of the RICS for the appointment of a suitable person to do so. The costs of making the record fall to be shared between landlord and tenant in equal shares in default of agreement.[2] The person appointed to make the record is entitled, on production of evidence of his appointment, to enter the holding at all reasonable times for the purpose of making the record.[3]

(c) Landlord's power of entry

In the absence of statutory or contractual authority to enter the holding the landlord has no right to do so. Section 23 of the 1986 Act gives the landlord a statutory power to enter for certain purposes *viz*:

(a)   to view the state of the holding;
(b)   to fulfil his responsibilities to manage the holding in accordance with the rules of good estate management; and
(c)   to provide or improve fixed equipment on the holding otherwise than in fulfilment of those responsibilities.

Note, also, that the model clauses implied into contracts of tenancy by s 7 and SI 1973/1473 give the landlord a power of entry to carry out repairs where the tenant has not started work on them within two months, or has not completed them within three months, of receiving written notice to do so.[4] Tenancy agreements will, of course, frequently contain powers of entry for additional purposes, eg to take game.

C Common leasehold covenants

Certain covenants will commonly be encountered in agricultural leases. The following considerations are of relevance in considering the legal effect of common leasehold covenants.

1 S 20(3) ibid.
2 S 22(3) ibid.
3 S 22(2) ibid.
4 See Sch para 4(2), SI 1973/1473.

1.   Good husbandry clause

The lease may include a covenant whereby the tenant expressly agrees to observe the rules of good husbandry, as set out in Agriculture Act 1947, s 11.[5] Observance of the latter will thereby become a term of the tenancy itself. The chief significance of a clause in this form is to make Case D (breach of tenancy) available to the landlord, should he wish to take subsequent possession proceedings for bad husbandry. In the absence of a clause incorporating the rules into the tenancy, the landlord's only remedy is Case C *viz.* to obtain a certificate of bad husbandry from the agricultural land tribunal, and then to take Case C proceedings based upon it.

2.   Short notice clause

Sch 3 Case B to the 1986 Act entitles the landlord to repossess a holding (or part) where land is required for a non-agricultural use for which planning permission has been obtained, or is not needed. By virtue of s 25(2)(b) ibid, notice to quit of less than the statutory minimum period can be given in such cases, *but only* if the notice is given in pursuance of a provision in the contract of tenancy authorising the resumption of possession of the holding for a specified non-agricultural use. A 'specified' non-agricultural purpose has. been held to include a power to repossess for *all* non-agricultural purposes.[6]

A short notice clause should allow for at least one month's notice of repossession. The tenant has a statutory right to claim additional compensation for disturbance and high farming (as well as improvements), but in both cases it is a prerequisite that he serve notice of intention to claim at least one month prior to the termination of the tenancy.[7] In *Coates v Diment*[8] and *Re Disraeli's Agreement*[9] it was held that a short notice clause which enables the landlord to resume possession without giving at least one month's notice to the tenant will be void, as it prevents the latter serving notice to claim compensation, and thus infringes the rule against 'contracting-out' of compensation under the Act.[10]

3.   Proviso for re-entry

The landlord has a statutory right to 'forfeit' for breach of tenancy, by serving notice to quit under Cases D or E to Sch 3 of the 1986 Act. The latter are, however, subject to challenge by arbitration under the 1986 Act and (in the case of Case D) the possible requirement of tribunal consent. The 1986 Act in no way limits the landlord's right to forfeit a lease under the general law, pursuant to a proviso for re-entry. The landlord's remedies under the 1986 Act exist alongside the general law governing forfeiture for breach of

5 This is discussed above p 55 ff.
6 *Dow Agrochemicals Ltd v E A Lane (North Lynn) Ltd* (1965) 192 EG 737, CCA; *Paddock Investments Ltd v Lory* [1978] EGD 37.
7 See Agricultural Holdings Act 1986, s 60(6), and s 70(2).
8 [1951] 1 All ER 890.
9 [1939] Ch 382.
10 For the latter see now s 78(1) of the 1986 Act.

covenant. Because of the procedural complexities associated with Case D, it may prove beneficial in some cases to proceed instead by way of forfeiture proceedings based upon a proviso for re-entry in the lease. The *quid pro quo*, of course, is that the tenant's right to relief from forfeiture under the general law [11] is not available if proceedings are based instead on Cases D or E to the 1986 Act.

For a forfeiture clause in an agricultural lease to be valid, it is essential that it should include provision for the right to forfeit to be exerciseable on the expiry of some period of notice of more than one month. In *Parry v Million Pigs Ltd*[12] it was held that a forfeiture clause which provides for no notice of re-entry, or notice of less than one month, will be void as in breach of the principle in *Coates v Diment* (above) ie it will prevent the tenant serving notice to claim compensation under ss 60(6) and 70(2), and will therefore infringe the contracting out rule (now section 78(1) of the 1986 Act).[13]

4. Conservation covenant

The pursuit of conservation objectives, for instance pursuant to a management agreement, could result in a tenant being in breach of the rules of Good Husbandry (above). By virtue of Sch 3, para 9(2) to the 1986 Act the tenant will be protected in proceedings for a certificate of bad husbandry if the practice complained of is adopted pursuant to a provision in the tenancy, or any other agreement with the landlord, which indicates (in whatever form) that its object is the furtherance of one or more stated conservation objectives *viz*. the conservation of flora or fauna, the protection of buildings of archeological/historical interest, and the conservation or enhancement of the natural beauty of the countryside. The tribunal must disregard the practice alleged *only* if it is sanctioned by a provision in the tenancy. It follows that a suitably drafted conservation covenant should be inserted if the tenant and/or landlord envisage entering into management agreements,[14] or otherwise wish to temper efficient farming methods with conservation objectives. *Semble*, also, if the rules of good husbandry have themselves been incorporated as a term of the tenancy, the inclusion of a conservation covenant will similarly remove the possibility of proceedings under Case D or Case E.[15] Without a conservation clause, however, proceedings under Case D (as well as Case C) would otherwise be available to the landlord to enforce the rules of good husbandry.

---

11 Section 146(4) of the Law of Property Act 1925.
12 (1980) 260 EG 281.
13 Per Ewbank J at (1980) 260 EG 281, 283, adopting Scammell and Densham's *Law of Agricultural Holdings (6th ed)* at p 132 to the effect that it would be illogical were the same rule not to apply to both short notice and forfeiture clauses.
14 For instance if the holding has been designated a Site of Special Scientific Interest under the Wildlife and Countryside Act 1981, or is in an Environmentally Sensitive Area designated under the Agriculture Act 1986.
15 See Sch 3 para 10(1)(d), para 11(2), Agricultural Holdings Act 1986.

5.   Residence clause

Modern agricultural leases commonly include a covenant by the tenant to reside constantly at the farmhouse on the holding. The object of this clause is to procure such continuity of personal residence as will enable the tenant to supervise personally the farming operation on the holding, and to prevent the farming of the holding by an absentee tenant who lives elsewhere and farms through someone else.[16] It creates an obligation not simply to make the farmhouse the usual place of residence of the tenant, but to live at the farmhouse with sufficient continuity to supervise personally the performance of all the tenant's leasehold obligations, and particularly those relating to good husbandry.[17] The obligation does not require unbroken residence at the farmhouse, eg it is assumed to be in the contemplation of the parties that the tenant may die, and suspension of personal occupation for a reasonable period consequent upon the death of the tenant will not be a breach of covenant.[18] Absence for more than a temporary period will, however, constitute a breach eg where the tenant is in prison.[19] Note, however, that breach of a residence covenant is remediable, and not an irremediable breach entitling the landlord to invoke Case E. The proper remedy therefore lies in service of a notice to remedy and proceedings under Case D.[20]

6.   Fixed equipment: repair and maintenance

'Model clauses' specifying in detail the parties' obligations with regard to fixed equipment are implied into the tenancy agreement, in so far as it does not provide to the contrary, by section 7 of the 1986 Act. The clauses currently in force are prescribed by the Agriculture (Maintenance and Repair etc) of Fixed Equipment Regs 1973 (SI 1973/1473), as amended. These are discussed in Chapter 4, infra. The process of implication is by no means, however, straightforward.[1] The parties may wish, for the avoidance of doubt, to expressly incorporate the model clauses by the inclusion of an appropriate covenant. Their obligations as to fixed equipment will then be covered *in toto* by the statutory code, and not by a mixture of express leasehold covenants and statutory model clauses (with attendant problems of interpretation). Note, however, that the model clauses are from time to time modified and reissued, eg those in force prior to 1973 were the Agriculture (Maintenance Repair and Insurance of Fixed Equipment) Regs 1948.[2] If the parties wish to have the benefit of subsequent upgrading of the regulations, the lease should provide for incorporation of the regulations in force from time to time, and any subsequent modification and/or variation thereof. Without this qualification, the clause will incorporate those regulations in force at the date of the lease without modification. This could

16 See generally *Lloyds Bank Ltd v Jones* [1955] 2 QB 298, CA.
17 *Sumnal v Statt* (1984) 49 P & CR 367, 375, CA per Cumming-Bruce LJ.
18 *Lloyds Bank Ltd v Jones* [1955] 2 QB 298, 324, CA per Jenkins LJ.
19 *Sumnal v Statt* (1984) 49 Pd CR 367 CA.
20 *Sumnal v Statt* (1984) 49 P & CR 367, 377, CA.
 1 See *Burden v Hannaford* [1956] 1 QB 142, CA.
 2 SI 1948/184.

be of significance, in the exceptional case, were later regulations to vary the obligations of the parties as to maintenance of certain items of fixed equipment, or where (as is more common) the allowances claimable by the tenant or landlord towards the cost of repair have been up-graded.[3] It should also be remembered that if the lease contains 'substantial modifications' to the model clauses currently in force it can be challenged by the tenant under section 8 of the 1986 Act. In this event, if he finds the terms are not justifiable, the arbitrator can vary the terms of the tenancy in such manner as appears just and reasonable between landlord and tenant (a question of fact).

7. Quota clauses

The presence or absence of dairy quota registered for a holding will substantially influence the value of the landlord's reversion. Quota is registered in the name of the registered producer (often the tenant), and its presence can give rise to acute problems where the lease contains no provision prohibiting dealings in quota by the tenant or requiring the keeping of adequate records. This will commonly be the case in pre-1984 leases. Quota attaches to 'areas of land used for dairy production' within a holding, which phrase has been given a wide interpretation by the English courts.[4] Its transfer is governed by reg 9 of the Dairy Produce Quotas Regs 1989[5], which provides for transfer and re-registration where there is a change of occupation of a holding (or part), other than one pursuant to a variety of short term arrangements eg a grazing let for less than 10 months or a licence. Any transfer by way of a *Gladstone v Bower* let, subtenancy, grazing let for 10 months or more, or assignment, could carry with it quota if the land concerned has been used for dairy production in the past 5 years.[6]

If the lease contains the statutory non-assignment clause, transfer by means of any of the methods recognised by reg 9 will constitute an irremediable breach of tenancy. This would entitle the landlord to serve a notice to quit invoking Case E. A more subtle problem arises, however, where the 'holding' (defined for these purposes in the European law sense) contains both leasehold and freehold land. The tenant could, over a period of years, switch dairy production to freehold land within his agricultural unit, the effect of which would be to 'move' registered quota onto freehold land over which the landlord has no control. Its subsequent disposition by the tenant would not then be restrained. To prevent this, and to ensure the tenant retains registered quota on leased land to which it was originally allocated, the lease should contain suitably drafted clauses restraining the tenant from selling, leasing, or otherwise dealing in quota without the landlord's consent, and obliging him to retain dairy production at an agreed level. The lease should also identify areas used for dairy production, and prohibit the tenant from either ceasing dairy production on the land in

---

3 For discussion of the substantive changes introduced by the 1973 regulations, for instance, see (1974) 118 So Jo 266 (Muir Watt).
4 See *Puncknowle Farms Ltd v Kane* [1985] 3 All ER 790.
5 SI 1989/380.
6 See reg 9(1) and (7), and Sch 3, SI 1989/380.

question or moving production to other land. For the avoidance of doubt it may also be advisable to oblige the tenant to keep detailed records of inputs to the dairy unit, of land used for grazing or production of silage etc, and other usages related to the dairy herd. Detailed records will avoid dispute should an apportionment of quota be called for under Sch 3 to the 1989 regulations. The quota clause must be taken *ab initio* in the tenancy agreement itself: it is not a matter obtainable by arbitration pursuant to s 5 and Sch 1 to the 1986 Act. Neither will cessation of dairy production amount, normally, to bad husbandry within the meaning of the latter. An express clause, however, will be enforceable by notice to quit pursuant to Cases D or E to Sch 3 of the 1986 Act. There is a question whether covenants taken to prevent dealings in quota under established agricultural marketing schemes (eg under the potato marketing scheme) are effective to prevent dealings in dairy quota. In *Lee v Heaton*[7] it was held that a covenant 'not to dispose of the whole or any part of any basic quota under a marketing scheme' did not apply to prevent disposition of milk quota. The Dairy Produce Quota Regs, it was held, do not establish a scheme for regulating the marketing of milk, but impose a levy on disposals of milk products to curb the growth of milk production within the EEC.[8] Even where a clause covering marketing quota is included, therefore, it is advisable to take an express clause restricting dealings in milk quota. Reference to the specialist literature on milk quotas is also advisable.[9]

7 [1987] 2 EGLR 12 (Dairy Produce Quota Trib).
8 [1987] 2 EGLR 12, 14.
9 See eg *Milk Quotas Law and Practice*, by Wood, Priday, Moss & Carter (1986), esp Chapter 7.

Chapter 4

Landlord and tenant: fixed equipment

Farming being capital intensive in nature, it is of central importance that the rights and liabilities of landlord and tenant as to the provision, repair, maintenance and removal of fixed equipment be clearly defined. Agricultural leases will commonly deal expressly with fixed equipment liabilities, but notwithstanding express agreement Part II of the 1986 Act makes provision for three contingencies. Firstly, the tenant is given a right to apply to an agricultural land tribunal in limited circumstances for an order directing the landlord to *provide* fixed equipment.[1] Secondly, by virtue of s 7 the Minister is empowered, after consultation with bodies representing the interests of agricultural landlords and tenants, to make regulations prescribing terms as to the maintenance, repair and insurance of fixed equipment (known as the 'model clauses') which are incorporated into every tenancy agreement (with some exceptions). And finally, special provision is made by s 10 for the removal of fixtures and buildings provided by the tenant at the end of the tenancy. Deference to principles of freedom of contract is maintained, however, in that contracting out of s 10 is not expressly prohibited, and by the fact that the model clauses only apply if no express contrary provision is made in the lease (although arbitration can be invoked to bring the lease into conformity with the model clauses where this is just and reasonable between the parties – Section 8). These provisions are not, therefore, strictly directive in nature *cf* the repairing code applied to residential lettings, from which contracting out is expressly prohibited.[2]

A   Fixed equipment – statutory definition

By virtue of section 96(1) of the 1986 Act 'Fixed Equipment' is defined to include 'any building or structure affixed to land and any works on, in, over or under land, and also includes anything grown on land for a purpose other than use after severance from the land, consumption of the thing grown or of its produce, or amenity'.

This is a wide definition and clearly includes, in addition to obvious items such as farm buildings and fencing, hedges and trees planted as wind breaks and shields.

1 Agricultural Holdings Act 1986, s 11.
2 See Landlord and Tenant Act 1985, s 11.

B   Direction to provide or alter fixed equipment

1.   Tribunal jurisdiction

By virtue of section 11(1) of the 1986 Act, the tenant of an agricultural holding is entitled to apply to an agricultural land tribunal for an order directing the landlord to carry out, within a specified period, such work for the provision or alteration/repair of fixed equipment as is necessary to enable the tenant to comply with statutory requirements eg as to disposal of waste under the Public Health legislation. The tribunal jurisdiction can be invoked in either of two situations:

(a)   where the tenant, in carrying on the agricultural activity specified in his application, would contravene requirements imposed by statute unless fixed equipment were provided, or

(b)   where fixed equipment is already provided at the holding, and it is reasonable that the tenant should use it for purposes connected with the proposed agricultural activity, it may be necessary for the equipment to be repaired or replaced if breach of statutory requirements is to be avoided.

Before making a direction, the tribunal must satisfy itself that the carrying on of the agricultural activity proposed by the tenant is reasonable, having regard to the latter's duty to farm the holding in accordance with the rules of good husbandry (as to which see Chapter 3 *supra*).

2.   Conditions to be satisfied

The jurisdiction under s 11 can only be invoked against a landlord if a number of clearly defined requirements have been met. These make the remedy unattractive in practice in many situations:

(a)   The tribunal cannot direct the landlord to carry out work in connection with a proposed agricultural activity unless satisfied that the starting of the activity did not (or will not) constitute or form part of 'a substantial alteration of the type of farming carried on on the holding'.[3] The substantiality or otherwise of the change in farming is, it is suggested, a question of fact for the tribunal. The statutory bar clearly looks to a change in the intrinsic nature of the farming activities previously practised, and now proposed by the tenant, and not simply the intensity or scale of farming on the holding – this would follow from the requirement that the change must be to the *type* of farming carried on eg from beef to dairying or arable farming. It should be noted that, even if a substantial alteration in the type of farming practiced *has* occurred, the tribunal's jurisdiction is preserved if the activity specified in the tenant's application has been carried on *continuously* for a period of

3 S 11(2) ibid.

at least *three years* preceding the date of application.[4] The rationale here would appear to be that in such cases the landlord's knowledge and consent to the change of user must be presumed. If the activity has *not* been practised for three years prior to the application, and amounts to a change in the type of farming on the holding, the tenant can provide fixed equipment at his own expense and (if he obtains the landlord's written consent to its provision) claim compensation for its unexhausted value on later termination of the tenancy. He cannot, however, compel its provision at the landlord's expense.

(b) Additionally, the tribunal cannot direct the landlord to carry out work unless satisfied that it is reasonable to do so 'having regard to the landlord's responsibilities to manage the land comprised in the holding in accordance with the rules of good estate management'. They are also to have regard to the period for which the holding may be expected to remain a separate holding 'and to any other material consideration'.[5]

This requirement gives the landlord considerable latitude to resist an application. Clearly it would be unreasonable to direct the provision of equipment at considerable expense if plans to merge the holding with others in an estate were far advanced.

(c) The landlord must be served with a written request to do the work concerned by the tenant. A tribunal application can only be made if he has failed to carry out the work within a reasonable time or has refused to do so.[6] No strict time limits for service of request and the landlord's response are imposed by the Act.

(d) The tribunal jurisdiction under s 11 is a measure of last resort. Accordingly, it cannot be invoked to compel the landlord to carry out work if he is *already* under a duty to carry out the work in order to comply with a requirement imposed by statute, or if provision is made in the tenancy agreement, 'or by any other agreement between the landlord and tenant' for the carrying out of the work by one of them.[7]

If the tenancy, or indeed some other binding agreement between the parties, imposes an obligation on the landlord to provide fixed equipment, then the tenant is left to his general remedies, eg an action for damages or an injunction. It also follows from s 11(4) that the parties can 'contract out' of the tribunal jurisdiction, and the obligations imposed by the Act, by providing in the lease for provision of fixed equipment by the tenant. Section 11 is supplementary, not directive in nature, imposing obligations only where the lease is silent and no collateral agreement allocates obligations as to the provision of fixed equipment between the parties.

4 See s 11(2) ibid.
5 S 11(3)(a) ibid.
6 S 11(3)(b) ibid.
7 S 11(4) ibid.

3. Remedies and enforcement

The general rule (see s 11(5)) is that if the landlord fails to comply with a tribunal direction the tenant has the same remedies as if the contract of tenancy had itself contained an undertaking to carry out the work within the period specified by the tribunal. The tenant can therefore claim damages and/or an injunction in the normal way – the tribunal itself does not, however, enjoy enforcement powers. Additionally, the Act specifically empowers the tenant to carry out the work himself and recover the reasonable cost of doing so from the landlord – this even though the tenancy may contain a term restricting the tenant from carrying out alterations.[8] Curiously, there is no provision for the reasonableness or otherwise of work to be referred to arbitration, and it therefore falls (in case of dispute) to the civil courts for determination. This would, it is suggested appear contrary to the general policy of the 1986 Act, which allocates most valuation matters to expert arbitrators. In valuing the reasonable cost of carrying out work, any grant aid received by the tenant must be taken into account to reduce the claim.[9]

In suitable cases the landlord can apply for an extension of time, for instance where the period specified by the tribunal has not proved sufficient to enable grant applications to be made and processed.[10]

4. Significance of Tribunal jurisdiction

The rigour of the qualifying conditions (above) means that the jurisdiction is not over-utilised in practice. The tenant (with the landlord's consent) may instead choose to provide fixed equipment at his own expense, and later claim its unexhausted value on termination of the tenancy in the form of compensation for improvements under Sch 7.[11] In the case of fixtures (as opposed to buildings) also, the Act permits removal on termination if certain conditions are met. The chief significance of s 11 would appear to be, there-fore, that it provides an avenue whereby the tenant can oblige the provision of equipment at the landlords expense *ab initio*, rather than postponing the compensation issue to termination of the tenancy. Against this, the provision of equipment under s 11 will entitle the landlord to an increase in rent under s 13, whereas the provision of equipment or improvements effected by the tenant will normally not influence rental value, being valued out of account unless provided pursuant to an obligation imposed on the tenant by the lease.[12]

C   Maintenance and repair – the Model Clauses

The Agricultural Holdings Act differs from other protective legislation in that it lays down standard terms as to the repair, maintenance and insurance of fixed equipment (including buildings) which apply unless the parties have

8 S 11(6) ibid.
9 S 11(8) ibid.
10 See s 11(7) ibid.
11 Especially Part II of Sch 7 ibid.
12 See Sch 2, para 2(1) ibid.

otherwise agreed. Although not without its difficulties, this approach may provide a useful model for reform in other areas of tenant protection legislation, where standardisation of repairing obligations is noticeably absent.[13] The regulations currently in force are the Agriculture (Maintenance, Repair and Insurance of Fixed Equipment) Regulations 1973[14] made under section 7(1) of the (now) 1986 Act, as amended by the Agriculture (Maintenance, Repair and Insurance of Fixed Equipment) (Amendment) Regulations 1988.[15]

1. Principles of incorporation

(a)   It must be appreciated that the 'model clauses' are not incorporated into every tenancy irrespective of its terms, and are of a supplementary not directive nature. By virtue of s 7(3) they are deemed to be incorporated into every contract of tenancy of an agricultural holding 'except in so far as they would impose on one of the parties to an agreement in writing a liability which under the agreement is *imposed* on the other' (emphasis added). Legislative policy here is aimed at promoting certainty by ensuring that, given the importance of fixed equipment, the obligations of the parties in respect of it are clearly expressed *either* in the lease or the regulations. The proviso to s 7(3) preserves the principle of freedom of contract by excluding the model clauses where the lease makes contrary provision. Notwithstanding this, however, the 1986 Act also seeks to promote standardisation of repairing obligations by providing (in Section 8) that where the terms of a tenancy agreement *substantially* modify the operation of the model clauses either party can request a variation so as to bring the tenancy into conformity with the latter, and then, (if agreement is not arrived at) refer the terms concerned to arbitration under the Act. The arbitrator's duty[16] is then to consider whether the terms concerned are justifiable having regard to the circumstances of the holding, and the circumstances of both landlord and tenant (but not the rent). If satisfied that the terms concerned are not justifiable, he can vary them 'in such a manner as appears to him to be reasonable and just as between the landlord and tenant'. This might involve varying the lease to bring it into conformity with the model clauses, or varying its terms in a way which reflects special circumstances. In so doing he can vary the rent if appropriate. Where an award has been made, no further reference under s 8 can be made for three years from the date of the award.[17]

(b)   Where an arbitration (or agreement) pursuant to ss 6 or 8 shifts liability for repair and maintenance from one party to the other, s 9 enables any dispute as to *prior* failure to carry out repairing obligations to be decided at the date of the variation of the tenancy (and not later on termination), by reference to arbitration. So if liability has been shifted to the landlord he can claim compensation for dilapidations in respect of any failure by the tenant to discharge his liability to repair prior to

13 See e.g. *Landlord and Tenant: Reform of the Law* (1987) Cm 145 para 3.24.
14 SI 1973/1473.
15 SI 1988/281, effective from 24 March 1988.
16 See Agricultural Holdings Act 1986, s 8(3).
17 S 8(6) ibid.

its transfer.[18] Where a variation is effected by the issue of new regulations, Section 9(4) empowers an arbitrator, for a prescribed period, to disregard the variation when settling the terms of the tenancy on a reference under s 6.[19] By virtue of the Agriculture (Time Limit) Regs. 1988[20] the prescribed period during which an arbitrator could ignore the amendments made to the model clauses by SI 1988/281 was the three months following their commencement on 24 March 1988. Clearly, Section 9(4) is of sporadic importance, remaining dormant in the intervals between the issue of fresh regulations (itself an infrequent occurrence).

(c)   The rule in *Burden v Hannaford*. The model clauses, it has been observed, are not incorporated in every case and are excepted (see s 7(3)) where 'they would impose on one of the parties to an agreement in writing a liability which under the agreement is *imposed* on the other'. This phraseology is not without its difficulties, and fell to be considered in *Burden v Hannaford*.[1] The tenancy agreement in this case expressly *relieved* the tenant of liability to repair hedges and fences – an obligation the regulations otherwise impose on tenants. The Court of Appeal there held that any inconsistency between the lease and model clauses must be resolved by giving effect to the contractual term (not the model clauses). The model clauses were incorporated, as there was no *positive* obligation to fence at variance with the regulations, but reading the contract of tenancy and model clauses together the former prevailed – with the (surprising) result that neither party was liable to repair hedges and fences. It follows that there may be cases in which no liability to repair items of fixed equipment exists, where the lease expressly *relieves* one party of the obligation, without imposing it on the other, so as to exclude the model clause. This is a possibility of which landlord and tenant should be aware, and care taken to avoid this form of wording when drafting repairing covenants.

Allowing for the rule in *Burden v Hannaford*, the model clauses will be incorporated in two situations: firstly, where the tenancy agreement is oral (s 7(3) talks of their exclusion by contrary provision *in writing)*, and secondly, where there is a written tenancy which *does not* impose a positive obligation on one party which the regulations impose on the other or expressly *relieve* the parties of liability eg where the lease is simply silent on the matter.[2]

2.   Structural and exterior repairs and replacements

Part I of the Schedule to the 1973 Regulations places liability for most repair and replacements of a structural nature on the landlord, and contains detailed clauses to govern the liabilities of the latter where the lease is silent. The general repairing covenant imposed on many landlords by Section 11 of the Landlord and Tenant Act 1985 does *not* apply to agricultural holdings.[3]

---

18 Ss 9(2) and 71 ibid.
19 See Chapter 3 supra.
20 SI 1988/2821.
 1 [1956] 1 QB 142, CA.
 2 For a helpful note on *Burden v Hannaford* and the difficulties it engenders see further (1956) JPL 15 (J Muir Watt).
 3 See Landlord and Tenant Act 1985, s 14(3).

Under the model clauses the landlord is obliged to execute all repairs and replacements to both main and exterior walls and roofs of farmhouses, cottages and farm buildings, including walls and fences of open and covered yards. This obligation extends to interior decoration and repair made necessary by structural defects to floors, walls, roofs, ceiling joists and timbers. Liability is also placed on the landlord for repair of items such as exterior and interior staircases and ladders, doors, windows and skylights (excepting glass). The obligation is qualified in that, in the case of repair to floorboards, staircases, ladders and windows, and guttering, the landlord can recover one half of the reasonable cost of the work from the tenant (Sch, para 1(1) of the 1973 Regs). The landlord is placed under an additional obligation[4] to paint and/or treat with preservatives all outside wood and ironwork of the farmhouse and other buildings at least once every five years.

In addition to the farm buildings, the landlord is under a duty to execute repairs/replacement to any underground water pipes, wells, bore holes and reservoirs, together with ancillary underground installations. This also extends to sewage disposal systems on the holding.[5] The landlord's obligations under the model clauses do *not* extend, however, to the execution of repairs or replacement to property belonging to the tenant, or to repairs rendered necessary by the wilful negligence of the latter or his family.[6]

3. Non structural repairs

The primary obligation imposed by the model clauses on the tenant is to 'repair and keep and leave clean and in good repair, order and condition' the farmhouse, cottages and farm buildings together with any fixtures and fittings on land or buildings, except in so far as structural repairs are imposed by the regulations on the landlord.[7] This obligation is extended to replacement and repair of *all* items of fixed equipment if this is rendered necessary by his own wilful negligence or his failure to repair it.[8] Because the tenant's general liability is to keep and *leave* in good tenantable repair buildings and fixed equipment, it has been held that it will not suffice to leave buildings or equipment in as good a condition as they were at the beginning of the tenancy.[9] However, it was there indicated, also, that when considering whether the obligation with regard to any particular item has been discharged regard should be had to its age and character, and its condition at the commencement of the tenancy. The time available to the tenant to effect repairs will also be relevant.[10]

The tenant's general obligation to repair the interior of the farmhouse and farm buildings is supplemented by para 7 of the Schedule to the 1973 Regs which requires him to clean, paint and/or treat with preservatives at least every seven years the inside of the farmhouse, cottages and farm buildings,

4 Sch, para 3 SI 1973/1473.
5 Sch, para 1(2) ibid.
6 Sch, para 4 ibid.
7 Sch, para 5 of the 1973 Regs.
8 See Sch, paras 6(1) and (2) ibid.
9 *Evans v Jones* [1955] 2 All ER 118, CA.
10 [1955] 2 All ER 118, 123, per Evershed MR.

including doors and windows. He is also liable to replace slipped and cracked tiles and slates, but only in so far as the cost doing so does not exceed £100 in any one year of tenancy (Sch, para 8, amended by SI 1988/281). On termination of the tenancy, the tenant must pay a proportion of the cost of painting in accordance with para 7, calculated by reference to the period since it was last effected, or alternatively the reasonable cost of effecting the work, whichever is less.[11]

The above is of necessity only an outline of the content of the 1973 Regulations, reference to the Schedule of which should be made for further information.[12]

4. Repair content of the obligation

Whether construing express terms in the lease *or* the applicability of the model repairing clauses, the general law on the construction of lease covenants will be of relevance.[13] The courts no longer draw a distinction between lack of repair and inherent defects, and it is now clear that damage/deterioration to buildings caused by inherent design defects can engage the landlord's liability for structural disrepair (for instance under the model clauses, above). For breach of the model repairing clauses, or of an express covenant, it is necessary that the structure of the farmhouse or buildings have deteriorated from some previously existing state or condition. In *Post Office v Aquarius Properties Ltd*[14] it was held that disrepair 'connotes a deterioration from some previous physical condition'. It is not sufficient to prove loss of amenity or utility, so that if a building becomes unusable because of damp resulting from a defect in construction, there is no remedy if the structure has not deteriorated in any way.[15]

If deterioration in the buildings *has* occurred, then it is a question of degree whether what needs to be done is properly to be called a 'repair', or whether it would involve the landlord receiving back something wholly different to that demised.[16] As a general rule the cost of the proposed work, as a proportion of the value or cost of the premises, can be used as a guide. So inserting a new damp course to replace a defective course placed below ground level will constitute repair, not improvement,[17] as will the replacement of piles supporting a building.[18] Inserting new foundations may not, however, be merely a 'repair'.[19] The imposition by the model clauses of an obligation on the landlord to execute both repairs and *replacements* of a structural nature, means that the distinction in the general law between repairs and improvements is of diminished significance where the model clauses are incorporated. In construing express covenants it will retain considerable importance however.

11 Sch, para 11(1) ibid.
12 And see articles at (1973) 227 Estates Gazette 767 and (1974) 118 Sol J 266 (Muir Watt).
13 *Evans v Jones* [1955] 2 All ER 118, CA.
14 [1987] 1 All ER 1055, 1065, CA.
15 Cf *Anstruther – Gough – Calthorpe v McOscar* [1924] 1 KB 716, CA; *Quick v Taff-Ely Borough Council* [1985] 3 All ER 321, CA.
16 *Ravenseft Properties Ltd v Davstone (Holdings) Ltd* [1979] 1 All ER 929.
17 See *Elmcroft Developments Ltd v Tankersley-Sawyer* (1984) 15 HLR 63, CA and *Quick v Taff-Ely Borough Council* supra.
18 *Smedley v Chumley and Hawke Ltd* (1981) 126 Sol Jo 33, CA.
19 *Lister v Lane and Nesham* [1893] 2 QB 212, CA; *Sotheby v Grundy* [1947] 2 All ER 761.

By virtue of the rule in *Proudfoot v Hart*[20] a covenant by the tenant to *keep* premises in tenantable repair (for instance *para 5* of the model clauses) imposes an obligation to put them *into* tenantable repair and deliver them up in such a condition. In *Post Office v Aquarius Properties Ltd*[1] it was indicated that this only applies to property the condition of which has deteriorated from a (former) better condition in which they existed prior to letting.

5. Remedies and enforcement

Landlord and tenant can exercise the normal remedies for breach of covenant under the general law, whether repairing obligations are express or incorporated by the model clauses. Thus under the rule in *Lee-Parker v Izzet*[2] the tenant can deduct the reasonable cost of landlord's repairs from rent prior to payment, provided notice of disrepair has been given. Likewise, an order for specific performance of landlord's repairing covenants can be made in extreme cases, provided there is a clear breach of the repairing obligation and the court is of no doubt as to what needs to be done to remedy it.

Additionally, where the breach is of an obligation incorporated into the lease by the model clauses, the 1973 regulations provide a special remedy – whether the breach complained of is of an implied obligation to repair, to replace or to carry out other works directed by the incorporated clause. Paragraphs 4 and 12 to the Schedule to the 1973 Regulations enable the landlord or tenant (whichever applies) to carry out works of repair and/or replacement, and then recover the reasonable cost of having done so from the other party. Recovery is limited in any one year to sums quantified by the regulations. These provisions are the sole source of the parties' right to *recover* costs of repairs and replacement, previously incurred, exclusive of their rights at common law.[3] The utility of the remedy under the model clauses has been considerably enhanced by SI 1988/281, which greatly increases the sums recoverable by means of the statutory remedy.

The model clauses oblige the *tenant* to start work on repairs which are his obligation, thereunder, within two months of the need for repair arising.[4] The landlord can serve notice under the regulations specifying the required repairs and replacements and calling on the tenant to execute them. If the tenant then fails to complete the repairs within three months of receiving notice the landlord is empowered to enter and execute the repairs himself and recover the reasonable cost of doing so from the tenant. The tenant can, however, dispute liability by serving counter notice within one month referring the matter to arbitration under the 1986 Act. If, on the other hand, the *landlord* is in breach of model clauses incorporated into the lease, the regulations enable the tenant to serve notice specifying the disrepair complained of and requiring its remedy.[5] If the landlord then fails to do so within three months the tenant can execute repairs and/or replacements and

20 (1890) 25 QBD 42, CA.
 1 [1987] 1 All ER 1055, 1063, CA.
 2 [1971] 3 All ER 1099.
 3 See *Grayless v Watkinson* [1990] 21 EG 163, 167.
 4 Sch, paras 4(2) and (3) of the 1973 Regulations.
 5 Sch, para 12(1) ibid.

recover the reasonable cost thereof from the landlord. The amount recoverable by way of *replacement* is limited in any year of the tenancy to £2,000 or one year's rent, whichever is less.[6] It has now been held[7] that this provision entitles the tenant to recover up to £2,000 or one year's rent in successive years to cover the cost of replacements. The effect of para 12(4), thus interpreted, is to enable the landlord to spread the cost of replacements so that it cannot in any one year exceed the rent of the holding in that year, and may well be less. It also enables the tenant to carry out replacements when required, rather than staging the work over successive years to ensure the recovery of the cost of doing so. This problem does not arise with work of repair, as the tenant can there recover the reasonable cost of repairs without financial limit.[8] The landlord can contest liability by serving notice within one month of referring the matter to arbitration, in which event the tenant's notice is suspended while arbitration is pending.

6.   Redundant equipment

Part III of the Schedule to the 1973 Regulations puts in place an arbitration procedure whereby buildings or fixed equipment can be declared redundant to the needs of the holding. In this eventuality the parties are relieved from repairing obligations in respect of the items concerned under the model clauses, and from any prior breach of obligation. The procedure is initiated by either party serving two months' notice requiring arbitration as to the redundancy of the equipment, in default of agreement. The arbitrator's remit here is broad, the regulations directing him to have regard to the landlord's responsibility to manage the holding in accordance with the rules of sound estate management, the length of time for which the holding may reasonably expect to remain separate, and both the character and situation of the holding and the needs of a tenant reasonably skilled in husbandry. The equipment must be redundant to the needs of the holding, and not simply aged or obsolete.

D   Tenant's right to remove fixtures and buildings

1.   The common law

Most buildings and items of fixed equipment will in law constitute fixtures. At common law the general rule has always been that fixtures annexed to the land become the property of the freehold owner, with the result that a farmer would be liable in damages for removing buildings, fencing and other

6   Sch, para 12(4) of the 1973 Regulations, as amended by SI 1988/281 – the upper limit was previously £500.
7   See *Grayless v Watkinson* [1990] 1 EGLR 6, CA.
8   Sch, para 12(1). Note however, that *Grayless v Watkinson* [1990] 1 EGLR 6, CA was decided upon the wording of the unamended para 12(2). SI 1988/281 has substituted a new para 12(2) with similar, but not identical, phraseology which may give rise to its own problems of interpretation – a point not unnoticed in the Court of Appeal; see [1990] 21 EG 163, 168 per Dillon LJ.

equipment provided at his own expense. This somewhat harsh rule was relaxed in the case of trade fixtures to allow removal of fixtures affixed solely for the purpose of the tenant's trade[9], provided removal occurred during continuance of the tenancy. Likewise, ornamental fixtures can be removed by the tenant by way of exception to the general rule. However, by virtue of the rule in *Elwes v Maw*[10] the exception in favour of trade fixtures did *not* extend to general agricultural fixtures, unless the latter were of a specialist nature appropriate to certain agricultural activities such as market gardening (in which case they would qualify as 'trade' fixtures; see *Wardell v Usher*[11] and *Mears v Callender*[12]). To rectify the common law rule, tenants have since 1851 had a statutory right to remove agricultural fixtures and buildings. The relevant provisions are now contained in section 10 of the 1986 Act.

2. Statutory right of removal

Section 10(1) gives the tenant the right to remove, at any time during the tenancy or before the expiry of two months from its termination, any building erected by him on the holding and also 'any engine, machinery, fencing, or other fixture (of whatever description) affixed, whether for the purpose of agriculture or not' to the holding.

The statutory right was extended to non-agricultural fixtures by the Agricultural Holdings Act 1984.[13] In the case of trade or ornamental fixtures, however, the common law right of removal subsists and can be exercised if (for instance) the strict criteria for exercise of the statutory right are not fulfilled.[14] The statutory right of removal does *not* extend to four classes of agricultural fixture,[15] *viz*:

(i) fixtures and buildings provided by the tenant in pursuance of some obligation (eg under public health legislation or pursuant to the contract of tenancy)

(ii) a fixture or buildings erected as a mere replacement for a fixture or building belonging to the landlord

(iii) a building in respect of which the tenant is entitled to compensation under the 1986 Act, ie where the building constitutes an improvement to which the landlord has consented and for which compensation is available under s 64 and Sch 7. Where the landlord has not consented to the building's erection the tenant's only recourse is to remove it under s 10.

(iv) fixtures affixed, and buildings erected, before 1 January 1884 (a rare class today).

9 See *Poole's Case* (1703) 1 Salk 368.
10 (1802) 3 East 38.
11 (1841) 3 Scott NR 508.
12 [1901] 2 Ch 388.
13 Agricultural Holdings Act 1984, Sch 3, para 6.
14 Agricultural Holdings Act 1986, s 10(8).
15 See s 10(2) ibid.

3.   Conditions for exercise of right of removal

Section 10(3) imposes two conditions which must be satisfied by the tenant before the statutory right of removal can be validly exercised. The tenant must, firstly, have paid all rent owing by him, and performed or satisfied all his other obligations to the landlord in respect of the holding. Rent must be fully paid up to date and all repairing obligations satisfied. Clearly this would be a difficult requirement to comply with if enforced to the letter. Secondly, the tenant *must* at least one month before *both* the exercise of the right and the termination of the tenancy, give notice in writing to the landlord of his intention to remove the fixture or building.[16] The notice requirement must be scrupulously adhered to if the statutory right of removal is to be preserved. By 'not less than' one month is meant a period including the date on which notice is served and ending on the corresponding date one month hence (the so-called 'corresponding date rule').[17]

   If these conditions are met the tenant can remove the building or fixture at any time up to two months after termination of the tenancy. In doing so, however, he is under a duty not to do any avoidable damage to any other building or part of the holding.[18]

   At common law, property in 'tenant's fixtures' (ie those, such as trade fixtures, removable by the tenant) vests in the landlord notwithstanding the tenant's right to remove them. Section 10 abrogates this rule in respect of both agricultural and non-agricultural fixtures affixed to an agricultural holding, and expressly provides that they remain the tenant's property so long as he has a right of removal conferred by the 1986 Act. As soon as that right is lost, however, for instance if notice of removal is not served in time, property in the fixtures concerned will vest at common law in the landlord. This will be the case even if the tenant has a residual right of removal conferred by the common law exceptions for trade and ornamental fixtures. One consequence of this rule is that distress can be levied on fixtures to which the Act applies, as they remain the tenant's property, but not on fixtures removable only at common law in which he has no interest pending exercise of his right of removal.

4.   Landlord's right of purchase

Where the tenant serves notice of removal, the landlord can, at his option, elect to purchase the buildings and/or fixtures at issue by serving a counter notice in writing to that effect.[19] No time limit for service is laid down, save that it be served before expiry of the tenant's notice of removal. If the landlord elects to purchase, the tenant's right to remove ceases to be effective. The landlord must, however, pay the tenant the fair value of the building or fixture to an incoming tenant. This is determinable by arbitration in the absence of agreement.

16 S 10(3)(b) ibid.
17 See *Dodds v Walker* [1981] 1 WLR 1027, HL; *E J Riley Investments Ltd v Eurostile Holdings Ltd* [1985] 1 WLR 1139, CA (decided on the similar wording of section 25 of the Landlord & Tenant Act 1954).
18 See s 10(5) of the 1986 Act.
19 S 10(4) ibid.

5.   Contracting Out

It has been observed that the other statutory obligations as to fixed equipment laid down by the 1986 Act are supplementary (and not directive) in that they allow contracting out by the parties – either expressly or by contrary provision in the lease. The right of removal conferred by s 10 is one of a number of provisions in the 1986 Act which neither expressly permits *nor* prohibits contracting out. In *Premier Dairies Ltd v Garlick*[20] a covenant obliging the tenant to deliver up a farm with all buildings and fixtures was held to have the effect of excluding the tenant's statutory right to remove fixtures.[1] In *Johnson v Moreton*[2] the applicability of the principle that this right could be renounced, being merely a right conferred on the tenant solely for his *private* benefit, was doubted. Clearly it might be argued that the policy underlying the provision is (at least partly) to encourage investment by tenants in fixed equipment at their own expense, and hence the promotion of efficient agriculture (a public interest). Similarly, it was strongly argued in *Johnson v Moreton* (and accepted, for instance, by Lord Hailsham) that the general scheme of the legislation in 1920 was considerably different, no security of tenure being then conferred on tenants.[3] The observations in the latter were clearly *obitier*, however, and in the absence of decisive authority *Premier Dairies v Garlick* must, it is suggested, be treated as sound law. Until overruled, then, it appears that contracting out of s 10 remains possible.

E   Record of condition of fixed equipment and holding

Section 22 of the 1986 Act entitles either party to require the making of a record of the condition of the fixed equipment on the holding and of the general condition of the holding itself. The tenant can, additionally, require the making of a record of any fixtures or buildings which he is entitled to remove by virtue of s 10 (above). In default of agreement the record is to be made by a person appointed by the Royal Institution of Chartered Surveyors, the cost being borne equally by both landlord and tenant. The making of a formal record will be of considerable evidential value, particularly (for instance) in assessing the condition of fixed equipment at the commencement of a tenancy so that liability under repairing covenants or the model clauses can be properly assessed.

20 [1920] 2 Ch 17.
 1 *Cf* also *Mears v Callender* [1901] 2 Ch 388.
 2 [1980] AC 37, 58 B-D per Lord Hailsham.
 3 See [1980] AC 37 at 44–5, 58.

Chapter 5
Agricultural rents

A   Introduction

Prior to 1984, agricultural arbitrators were required to assess the rent payable for an agricultural holding by reference simply to free market rent levels and tenders. Section 8 of the Agricultural Holdings Act 1948 (as amended by the Agriculture Act 1958) required the rent to be fixed as that at which the holding 'might reasonably be expected to be let on the open market by a willing landlord to a willing tenant', discounting the tenant's occupation. As a consequence of EEC agricultural policy, and the continuing dearth of land available for letting, tenders on first letting were by 1984 being made at inflated levels, although the free market rental thus established was not normally reflected in subsequent statutory rent reviews. Indeed, in some cases an inflated tender, including a hidden premium, would be made on the presupposition that the rent on later reviews would be valued at a lower level, discounting inflated tenders so as to reflect a more stable market valuation. Reflecting concern at the level of rents being tendered on first letting, section 1 of the Agricultural Holdings Act 1984 signalled a change in legislative policy by introducing detailed guidelines to arbitrators as to those factors to be taken into account, and those disregarded. Regrettably, however, the precise policy underlying these provisions is in some respects unclear. They ostensibly aim to break the link between rent reviews and the free market, and to tie the rent more closely to the productive and earning capacity of the individual holding. Under the 'package' agreement between the NFU and CLA, on which the 1984 Act was based, the latter agreed to proposals to remove scarcity value from the rent formula in return for the agreed abolition of succession rights for new tenancies. While parliamentary proceedings cannot be a reliable guide to the interpretation of the new provisions, it is apparent that the official view was that the new rent formula merely expressed in statutory form the current practice of arbitrators, and did not represent a radical change in the basis of valuation.[1]

The detailed provisions governing procedure on rent review and valuation are now contained in (respectively) section 12 and Schedule 2 of the Agricultural Holdings Act 1986. The influence of milk quotas on rent is dealt with separately by the Agriculture Act 1986.[2]

1 See inter alia Parl Debs (HL) Vol 444, Col 781 ff and Parl Debs (HC) Vol 55, Col 859 ff.
2 Agriculture Act 1986, discussed below p 96 ff s 15.

B Statutory rent reviews

By virtue of section 12(1) of the 1986 Act, both landlord and tenant are given the right to initiate a review of rent by serving notice in writing on the other demanding that 'the rent to be payable in respect of the holding as from the next termination date shall be referred to arbitration under [the 1986] Act'. No form of demand is prescribed.

1. 'Next termination date'

The date specified in the demand, from which the reviewed rent is to be payable, must be the next termination date following the date of the demand ie the date on which the tenancy could have been determined by notice to quit given at the date of the demand.[3] This will be the next ensuing contractual term date following the expiry of twelve months from the date of demand. So in the case of an annual Lady Day tenancy, a demand for arbitration seeking review from 25 March 1990 would have to be served (at the very latest) on 24 March 1989 – this is the last date on which a valid notice to quit could have been given terminating the tenancy at Lady Day 1990.[4] The 1986 Act provides for reviews at three yearly intervals, and so in practice a demand for arbitration must be made during the second year of the review period if the rent is be increased at the end of the third year. The requirements of s 12 will be met by a demand which simply refers to the next date on which the tenancy could have been validly determined by notice to quit, without specifying the date itself. If the termination date itself *is* specified in the notice, however, this must be done accurately on pain of invalidity. It may be advisable, if in doubt, to adopt the statutory formulation when making the initial demand.

The statutory review procedure applies principally to periodic tenancies. The requirement that review take place from the next termination date of the tenancy[5] means that the statutory procedure *prima facie* has no application to fixed term tenancies. The latter have one (fixed) termination date, on which the term will expire by effluxion of time, and following which the tenancy may continue as a yearly tenancy by virtue of s 3. It follows that a statutory review could be obtained on effluxion of a fixed term by serving a demand at least twelve months prior to the contractually agreed termination date, but not otherwise during the currency of the term. The majority of agricultural tenancies are periodic annual tenancies. Any attempt to exclude the statutory review procedure in a periodic tenancy would, it is suggested, be of no effect; the arbitration procedure remains available to both parties if agreement proves impossible. Although the statutory provisions are inapplicable where the tenancy is for a fixed term *simpliciter*, the question arises whether it is available to vary the rent under a lease making provision for either party to 'break' the term during its currency by service of notice. On its true construction, s 12 enables rent to be varied from a date on which the tenancy *might* have been terminated – it is not necessary that this in fact

3 Agricultural Holdings Act 1986, s 12(4).
4 See s 25 as to the length of notice to quit.
5 S 12(4) ibid.

happen.[6] It would follow that the date specified in a break clause for early termination by notice *is* a 'termination date' for these purposes *viz* a date on which the tenancy *could* have been ended by notice, although this may not have occurred. A further question arises whether rent can be reviewed if the 'break' clause allows for one party alone (eg the landlord) to determine the lease – can a review be sought at the break by both parties (if at all) or by the competent party alone? Applying the statutory provision in this context, it would appear a review could be sought by *either* party; (i) if a break clause provides for termination by notice, this is a 'termination date' of the tenancy within the meaning of s 12 (above), (ii) this being so s 12(1) itself gives *either* landlord or tenant the right (by demand) to seek a review using the statutory review procedure. The terms of a break clause, it is suggested, may be determinative of which party can *terminate* the tenancy during its currency, but cannot influence the entirely separate question of the parties' entitlement to a review of rent. This latter is a statutory right expressly conferred on both parties; it may be triggered by the presence of the break clause, but is entirely independent of the mode of termination of the lease.

One further problem arises concerning reviews during a fixed term. In *Edell v Dulieu*[7] it was held that the statutory period of notice to quit applies, and not any shorter period provided for in a break clause. So here a rent review could not be obtained where the landlord served notice of six months' duration, in accordance with the lease, which latter allowed for 'breaks' at seven and fourteen years in a fixed term of twenty one years. It follows that to seek a review the notice demanding arbitration, and seeking a review from the 'break', must be served at least twelve months prior to the termination date specified in the break clause. *Semble* a notice complying with the Act's requirements as to length will be valid, irrespective of contrary provision in the lease, and irrespective also of the period of notice therein agreed. So, for example, if a lease for 21 years contains a break clause permitting termination by notice at the end of seven and fourteen years, a review of rent under s 12 can be sought at the end of the seventh year *provided* a notice demanding arbitration is served during the sixth year of tenancy. If this is not done until the seventh year has commenced, it will have now become impossible to serve notice of requisite length before the next 'termination date', and the right to a review will be lost altogether until the end of the fourteenth year of tenancy. Furthermore, even if the demand for arbitration is served in good time, the 'break' in the lease must be accurately specified, on pain of invalidity (see above).

Although s 12 has no application during the currency of a fixed term – save one containing a break clause – the parties may include a rent review clause providing for periodic revision of rent. Section 12 has no application in this instance, and the review clause can specify its own procedure for initiating review. *Cf* for principles of construction the not inconsiderable case law on construction of review clauses in business leases. Careful drafting is required if problems of interpretation are to be avoided. In *Million Pigs Ltd v Parry*[8] an agricultural lease provided for three-yearly reviews, no time limit for the

6 See *Wallingford Estates Ltd v Tench* [1954] EGD 22, where a review was permitted although a simultaneously served notice to quit was held inoperative.
7 [1924] AC 38, HL.
8 (1983) 46 P & CR 333.

appointment of an arbitrator being specified. It was here held that if a review clause is silent as to the time within which the steps under it are to be taken, then reasonable delay in initiating the review procedure will not invalidate it. Where reasonable delay occurs, moreover, the review will be lost only if prejudice to the tenant would result from its going ahead.[9] So here a review was allowed, even though the landlord's application for an arbitrator was delayed until the three year period *after* that for which a review was sought had already commenced. It is now clear, furthermore, from the Court of Appeal's ruling in *Amherst v James Walker (Goldsmith and Silversmith) Ltd*[10] that a landlord's right to initiate a rent review will *not* be lost even by unreasonable delay, unless the latter amounts to an estoppel. The landlord's contractual right to initiate a review, depending on the true construction of the contract, will continue to exist unless and until it is abrogated by mutual agreement, or the contract is discharged by breach, or the landlord's delay raises an estoppel.[11] Delay in initiating a rent review, even if coupled with hardship to the tenant, cannot *of itself* preclude the landlord from exercising his contractual right to a review – delay cannot, in other words, act as a unilateral abandonment of the landlord's contractual rights, unless the combined circumstances evidence a promissory or equitable estoppel.

Note that where the clause lays down time-limits for steps in the review procedure, such as the service of a 'trigger' notice or appointment of an arbitrator, the principles enunciated in *United Scientific Holdings v Burnley Borough Council*[12] will apply, *viz* time will not be of the essence of the review procedure, unless the circumstances or the interrelation of the review and other lease clauses indicate otherwise, and that reasonable delay is permissible. Given the problems to which express review clauses can give rise, it may be preferable to incorporate expressly the statutory review procedure, which, for all its deficiencies, at least provides a clearly prescribed procedure for obtaining a review.

Occasionally the parties may agree that a favourable level of rent be payable, on the understanding that no increase of rent will be sought for an agreed period. The question arises whether such agreement excludes the landlord's right to a review under s 12 at three-yearly intervals. It appears from the decision in *Plumb Bros v Dolmac (Agriculture) Ltd*[13] that a collateral agreement not to increase rent will be binding, even if not under seal, if the lease and agreement as to rent are part of a single composite transaction. In this event, consideration supporting the landlords undertaking as to rent may be found in the tenant's promise to perform the obligations in the lease. In each case, however, it is a question to be decided according to whether the lease is to be read alongside other documents containing the undertaking in question. In *Plumb Bros (supra)* the modern process of construction, relying on examination of the 'factual matrix' in which the documents were drawn up, was criticised for placing emphasis on the subjective intention of the parties. The true approach is to determine objectively the intent of the parties from the documents themselves, in the light of the

9 See Goulding J, (1983) 46 P & CR 333 at 345–6.
10 [1983] 2 All ER 1067.
11 [1983] 2 All ER 1067, 1074 per Oliver LJ.
12 [1978] AC 904, HL.
13 (1984) 271 EG 373, CA.

circumstances surrounding the conclusion of the composite transaction.[14] If a promise to defer any rent increase is unsupported by consideration, it will be unenforceable if not under seal.

2.   Withdrawal of demand for arbitration

If either party serves a demand for arbitration, thus setting in motion the statutory review procedure, the other party cannot be denied a review by the later withdrawal of the demand. In *Buckinghamshire County Council v Gordon*[15] it was held[16] that a notice, once given, acts as a 'trigger' which starts the statutory procedure, and an arbitrator has jurisdiction unless the procedure is ended either by agreement, or by failure to apply for the appointment of an arbitrator in good time (see below). It cannot be withdrawn unilaterally. This must be the better view, for otherwise a tenant seeking a reduction in rent could be prejudiced, eg by the landlord withdrawing his demand once the next termination date had passed, as it would then be too late for the tenant to serve notice himself seeking a review on the date originally proposed.

3.   Severance of reversionary estate

By virtue of the rule in *Jelley v Buckman*[17] the severance of the landlord's reversionary estate does not bring separate tenancies of the severed parts into being. The original lease subsists, the only difference being that the reversion expectant on its determination is divided and vested in different persons. This has implications for rent reviews. It is now clear, similarly, that partition and severance of the tenant's leasehold interest does not create separate holdings with separate tenants for each: *Lester v Ridd*.[18]

Following severance, the rent payable for the holding may have been apportioned among the various reversioners. Unless the tenant expressly recognises (for instance as party to the apportionment) the creation of new tenancies of parts of the holding, mere apportionment of rent will not create a new tenancy of any severed part of the holding.[19] In *Stiles v Farrow*[20] it was held that the holding must be regarded as still subject to one contract of tenancy, and that the rent could only be reviewed as to the whole holding. Separate demands for arbitration of the apportioned rent, payable to the purchasers of part of the reversionary estate, were there, held invalid. It follows that to obtain a rent review under s 12 all reversionary owners must join together in demanding arbitration in accordance with the Act. The anomalous result is that while landlords must act jointly to obtain a rent review, they have a separate statutory right to serve notice to quit their severed portions of the original holding (conferred by section 140 of the Law of

14 See per May LJ, (1984) 271 EG 373.
15 [1986] 2 EGLR 8.
16 Albeit at first instance, per Judge Barr.
17 [1974] QB 488, CA.
18 [1989] 1 All ER 1111, CA.
19 See *Jenkin R Lewis & Son Ltd v Kerman* [1971] Ch 477.
20 (1977) 241 EG 623.

Property Act 1925).[1] Section 140 of the 1925 Act does not assist the landlord on rent review, as it merely apportions contractual rights among owners of severed parts of the reversion, whereas the right to seek a rent review is a statutory incident of ownership conferred by section 12 of the 1986 Act.[2]

If arbitration is required, it follows from the above that reversionary owners must also act together in taking subsequent steps, eg in applying to the RICS for the appointment of an arbitrator. It follows from *Lester v Ridd*[3], that tenants of severed parts of the original leasehold interest must also act together in seeking a review by arbitration.

4. Lapse of demand for arbitration

In *Sclater v Horton*[4] it was held that the arbitrator's appointment had to be 'perfected' prior to the next termination date of the tenancy specified in the demand for arbitration *viz*. if the ministry had not made an appointment, and the nominated arbitrator had not accepted appointment, before this date, then the demand for arbitration lapsed. This rule had serious implications for the landlord, who would have to start the review process afresh and (in so doing) could lose up to two years' increase of rent. The rigour of the rule in *Sclater v Horton* was somewhat relaxed by the 1984 Act. Section 12(3) of the 1986 Act now provides that a demand for arbitration will cease to be effective on the next termination date of the tenancy unless, before that date, either:

    (a)   an arbitrator has been appointed by agreement between the parties; *or*

    (b)   an application has been made to the President of the Royal Institution of Chartered Surveyors for the appointment of an arbitrator.

If the rent has not been agreed as the next termination date approaches it is therefore essential to preserve the right to a review by making application to the RICS for the appointment of an arbitrator. The 1986 Act does not require the application to be made by the party who served the demand for arbitration. *Semble*, therefore, either landlord or tenant can preserve the right to arbitration by making application under s 12(3). Note that there is now no necessity for the arbitrator to accept appointment, or for the parties to be notified of appointment, prior to the termination date.[5]

5. Date of reference for valuation purposes

The arbitrator is directed by s 12(2) to determine what rent should be payable for the holding *at the date of reference* and not (for instance) at the next termination date from which the reviewed rent takes effect. The valuation provisions (see below) must therefore be applied by the arbitrator in

1 And see *Persey v Bazley* (1983) 47 P & CR 37, CA.
2 See *Stiles v Farrow* (1977) 241 EG 623.
3 [1989] 1 All ER 1111.
4 [1954] 2 QB 1, CA.
5 *Cf Sclater v Horton* (supra), and see *University College, Oxford v Durdy* [1982] 1 All ER 1108.

accordance with the facts obtaining at the date of reference. For these purposes, Sch 11, para 31 of the 1986 Act provides that an arbitrator is to be taken as appointed at the time when the President of the RICS executes his instrument of appointment. In *University College, Oxford v Durd*[6] it was held that the arbitrator's appointment is perfected once the instrument of appointment is sealed, to which extent the decision has now been given statutory force. The additional suggestion there made, that time only begins to run for the purposes of time limits once the parties have been *notified* of appointment, is not now good law in the light of Sch 11, para 31 of the 1986 Act.[7] Where an arbitrator resigns or is replaced by another appointed by the President, the date of the reference for valuation purposes is the date on which the original arbitrator was appointed: Sch 11, para 3 *ibid*.

6.   Subsequent arbitration proceedings

It will be immediately apparent that the date of reference to arbitration (the valuation date) and the date from which the varied rent is to take effect (the next termination date) may differ. In order to achieve as near a correlation as possible, Sch 11, para 1(3) provides that any appointment must be made as soon as possible after the President of the RICS receives the application, but in rent arbitrations *not earlier* than four months before the next termination date of the tenancy ie the date on which the new rent will take effect.

Once an arbitrator has been appointed, the parties must within 35 days deliver to him their statements of case, the contents of which cannot be varied or supplemented without the arbitrator's consent.[8] The arbitrator's award must be made within 56 days of appointment.[9] For these purposes time begins to run from the date on which the appointment is sealed by the President of the RICS.[10] *Cf* where the parties are proceeding by way of arbitration other than under the 1986 Act, notification of appointment is necessary before time starts to run.[11]

C   Frequency of review

1.   Three-yearly reviews

The general rule is that statutory rent reviews can only take place once every three years. Supplementing s 12, Sch 2 para 4 of the 1986 Act provides that a demand for arbitration shall not be effective if the next termination

---

6 [1982] 1 All ER 1108.
7 And see *Richards v Allinson* (1978) 249 EG 59, the decision in which is no longer of good authority.
8 Agricultural Holdings Act 1986, Sch 11, para 7.
9 Sch 11, para 14 ibid.
10 Sch 11, para 31, above.
11 See *Tew v Harris* (1847) 11 QB 7 and observations of Lord Denning MR in *Tradax Export SA v Volkswagenwerk AG* [1970] 1 QB 537, CA,

date following the date of the demand falls earlier than the end of three years from either:

(a) the commencement of the tenancy
(b) the date on which there took effect a previous increase or reduction of rent (whether pursuant to arbitration or not) or
(c) the date as from which there took effect a previous direction of an arbitrator under section 12 that the rent should continue unchanged.

It follows from (b) and (c) (above), that an *agreed* increase or reduction in rent will trigger the three year cycle and prevent further review for three years thereafter. Where no increase or reduction is made, and a standstill rent agreed, the three-year bar will only be triggered if it is incorporated in an arbitrator's award (and not if simply negotiated and agreed without recourse to arbitration).

2. Exceptions to the rule

For the purposes of the three-yearly review principle, certain minor adjustments to the rent and/or other terms of the tenancy will not trigger the three year bar. In these cases the three-year bar will operate from the last prior rent review or agreed variation in rent. The following do not invoke the three-year rule:[12]

(a) An increase or reduction in rent under sections 6(3) or 8(4) of the 1986 Act *viz.* where an arbitrator settles the written terms of the tenancy under section 6, and directs that the rent be adjusted to reflect his award, and similarly where he does so on a reference under section 8 (arbitration where tenancy agreement is inconsistent with the 'model' clauses' provided for in SI 1973/1473).

(b) An increase in rent following completion of landlord's improvements, whether obtained by arbitration or by agreement within six months of the work's completion.[13] Similarly, a reduction in rent agreed by the parties, in consequence of a change in the fixed equipment provided on the holding by the landlord, will not activate the three-year bar. By a 'change' in the fixed equipment provided on the holding, is meant a change in the equipment provided itself, ie its removal or (in the case of a building or other structure) its removal or demolition, but one which leaves the holding otherwise unaffected. An agreed reduction in rent consequent upon the surrender of a dwelling or other building to the landlord is therefore not strictly a 'change' in the fixed equipment provided, and will activate the three-year bar on further reviews provided for in Sch 2, para 4(1)(b).[14]

(c) A decrease in rent following repossession by the landlord of part of

12 See Sch 2, para 4(2) ibid.
13 As to which see section 13(1) and (3) ibid.
14 *Mann v Gardner* [1990] EGCS 79, CA. A reduction of £100 in a total rental of £21,650, in consideration of the surrender of a farmhouse, was here held not to constitute a change in fixed equipment within the meaning of Sch 2, para 4(2)(b) – with the result that a rent review for the whole holding was precluded for three years thereafter. This even though a review had been demanded by the landlord, who subsequently wished to withdraw from review in a falling market.

the holding (whether obtained pursuant to Section 31 or a resumption clause in the tenancy) – see section 33 of the 1986 Act.

(d) *New tenancy of severed part*   Severance of the landlord's reversion does not of itself create new tenancies of the severed parts, neither does partition of the tenant's leasehold interest[15]. Following severance, however, the tenant may enter into fresh contracts of tenancy with the owners of the severed portions of the reversionary estate. To prevent this triggering the three-year review cycle, Sch 2, para 5 provides that the period of review shall be calculated by reference to the commencement date of the original tenancy and its subsequent rent reviews, *but only* (note) when the rent payable in respect of the new holding represents merely the 'appropriate portion of the rent payable in respect of the original holding'. The appropriate portion, which is not defined, falls to be determined by reference to the size of the new holding compared with the old, and its relative productive capacity compared to that of the original holding.

(e) *Adjustment of boundaries or terms of tenancy*   Sch 2, para 6 provides that any agreement whereby the boundaries of the holding are adjusted, or which provides for any other variation of the terms of the tenancy (exclusive of those relating to rent), shall not be treated as giving rise to a new contract of tenancy, and so will not start the three year cycle afresh. By an adjustment of boundaries is meant 'an arrangement, putting in order, harmonisation or adoption of the boundaries between the holding and some other property'[16] It will not include the surrender of part of the holding.

This provision ensures that minor alterations to the terms of the tenancy do not inadvertently trigger the review period, thus barring a rent review for three years. Note, however, that alterations in the terms of the tenancy are simply to be *treated* for rent review purposes as not terminating the tenancy. They may in fact create a new tenancy at common law, as for instance where additional land is added to the holding and an enlarged rent agreed to reflect this, rather than a separate letting of the new land being entered into.[17] Note also that the saving provision in Sch 2, para 6 does not apply if the agreed variation is expressed to take effect as a new contract between the parties.

D   Valuation of rent

The valuation principles applicable to farm rents were completely recast by the Agricultural Holdings Act 1984, which laid down detailed guidelines as to the *evidence* to be taken into account when assessing the rent 'properly payable' for a holding. Regrettably, however, the new rent formula

---

15 See *Jelley v Buckman* [1974] QB 488, CA; *Lester v Ridd* [1989] 1 All ER 1111.
16 *Mann v Gardner* [1990] EGCS 79, CA per Nourse LJ.
17 See generally *Jenkin R Lewis & Son Ltd v Kerman* [1971] Ch 477.

contains a number of omissions and obscurities which have aroused controversy. The Law Commission has expressed dissatisfaction with the operation of the present rent formula, and clarifying legislation is arguably needed.[18] The detailed provisions are now consolidated in Sch 2 of the 1986 Act.

1.   The rent properly payable

Free market rental value remains the starting point when calculating the 'rent properly payable' for a holding under s 12. Sch 2, para 1(1) defines the rent properly payable to be 'the rent at which the holding might reasonably be expected to be let by a prudent and willing landlord to a prudent and willing tenant'. The arbitrator is directed to take into account 'all relevant factors' *including*, in every case, the terms of the tenancy, the character and situation of the holding, its productive and related earning capacities, and the current level of rents for comparable lettings. The arbitrator must assume the land is being let substantially for use as agricultural land, but the direction to consider 'all relevant factors' clearly means that income derived from incidental non-agricultural sources (eg caravans) can be taken into account. *Semble*, also, income from grant payments under (for instance) conservation legislation could also be a 'relevant factor' to be taken into account. The arbitrator can consider all relevant factors which appertain to the potential profitability of the farming enterprise, and not simply those set out in further detail in the following provisions of Sch 2.

The valuation process envisaged by Sch 2 involves assessing the rent a reasonably competent tenant would expect to pay for the holding with whatever fixed equipment is *in situ*. The rent is that which 'a prudent and willing tenant' would expect to pay, ie a reasonably competent tenant, who must be assumed to act free from financial exigency or other constraints. The landlord, also, must be assumed to act free from financial or other pressures. The 1984 Act added the word 'prudent' to the previous statutory formula, which referred simply to the 'willing' landlord and tenant. It is not thought, however, that this makes any difference of substance to the content of the formula. On the notion of the 'willing' lessor or lessee see, further, observations in *F R Evans (Leeds) Ltd v English Electric Co Ltd*.[19] It was there held that, for purposes of valuing rent, a 'willing lessor' must be an abstraction and not the landlord himself – in other words a hypothetical person with the right to demise the premises on a yearly lease, but unafflicted by personal ills such as cash flow problems or importunate mortgages. He cannot, however, be assumed to be in the fortunate position of someone to whom it is a matter of indifference whether he lets on the review date or waits for the market to improve. He is a hypothetical lessor who wants to let the holding at a rent which is appropriate to all the factors which affect the marketability of the holding as an agricultural holding, including the market rent for competitive premises. The 'willing lessee' is also an abstraction; a hypothetical person actively seeking a holding which will fulfil needs which the demised premises could fulfil, and who must similarly be assumed to be

18 See *Landlord and Tenant: Reform of the Law* (1987) Cm para 4.64.
19 (1977) 36 P & CR 185 (esp at 189–90 per Donaldson J).

unaffected by liquidity problems, governmental or other pressures etc. In
Dennis & Robinson Ltd v Kiossos Establishment[20] it was further suggested
that the existence of a market, and of willing lessees prepared to tender, must
be assumed. It is for the valuer or arbitrator, however, to determine the
strength of the market using his skill and judgement. The prudent landlord
will clearly have regard to the long-term condition of the land, and not be
influenced by tenders of rent which the holding itself will not be able to
sustain in the long term. The arbitrator must assess, in other words, the rent
at which a well informed landlord, taking account of the long-term condition
of the holding and the number of potential tenants offering tenders, would
reasonably expect the holding to be let.

2.   Specific factors for consideration

The free market rental value of the holding is a question to be decided taking
account of *all* relevant factors. Having obtained a free market rental value,
however, the arbitrator is directed by Sch 2, para 1 to take into account *in
every case* the terms of the tenancy (including those relating to rent), the
character and situation of the holding (including its locality), its 'productive
capacity' and 'related earning capacity', and the current level of rents for
comparable lettings. The objective is to tie the rent more closely to the
productive capacity of the individual holding, and break the link with free
market rentals on rent review.

(a)   Terms of the tenancy/character etc of holding

These are matters which an experienced arbitrator would take into account,
in any event, when initially assessing the market rental value of the holding
(above). All the terms of the tenancy must be considered including, for
instance, repairing obligations. The injunction to consider those terms of the
tenancy 'relating to rent' means that special terms providing for adjustment
of rent, or suspension of payment, must be considered, eg a term making
payment conditional upon the carrying out of repairs.[1] *Quaere*, however,
whether the *amount* of the existing rent itself can be taken into account. The
reference to terms 'relating to rent' was added by the 1984 Act. The
previously applicable formula, laid down by the Agriculture Act 1958,
expressly required the arbitrator to discount the existing rent and terms
relating thereto. This was the case, no doubt, as the rent would otherwise be
distorted by special factors in each case, and the rent formula would not be
uniformly applied. Similarly, the formula now contained in section 12 of the
1986 Act requires the arbitrator, it is suggested, to assess the rent properly
payable *without* special reference to the existing rent; certainly, the latter
cannot be used as a point of reference, requiring the landlord to
affirmatively prove his case for an increase, or *vice-versa*. If this were the
case it would undermine the effectiveness of the rent formula, quite apart
from penalising the landlord who, on a previous review, agreed a
preferential rent. Some guidance can be ascertained from the authorities on
the general law of rent review, which stress that a provision requiring a
new rent to be assessed on the basis of a hypothetical lease containing the

20 [1987] 1 EGLR 133, CA.
  1 As to which see *Burton v Timmis* [1987] 1 EGLR 1, CA.

same provisions as the subject lease 'other than those relating to rent' requires the arbitrator to assume the hypothetical letting was on the same terms, *excluding* only the rent quantified and payable before the review date.[2] The arbitrator must, however, make allowance for the statutory provision for further rent reviews. Although the *quantum* of rent cannot, then, have a significant role in the review formula, the injunction in Sch 2, para 1 to have regard to 'all relevant factors' when assessing the rent properly payable would probably entitle the arbitrator to have regard to the existing rent as *one* factor, alongside productive and related earning capacity etc.[2a] but no greater weight can be given to it than this, – with this one *caveat*, peculiar to agricultural rent reviews, it is now clear from *Basingstoke and Deane Borough Council v Host Group*[3] that a rent review will normally be a valuation of a letting on the same terms other than as to the quantum of rent ('in general . . . the parties are to be taken as having intended that the notional letting postulated by their rent review clause is to be a letting on the same terms (other than as to quantum of rent) as those still subsisting between the parties in the actual existing lease. The parties are to be taken as having so intended, because that would accord with, and give effect to, the general intention underlying the incorporation by them of a rent review clause in their lease').[4]

There is also a question whether the accrual of succession rights to the holding can be a factor affecting rental value under this head. Succession rights continue to apply to tenancies granted after 12 July 1984 only if the tenancy agreement is in writing and contains words 'indicating (in whatever terms)' that the succession scheme is to apply.[5] It is by no means clear whether an 'indication' in this form is to be regarded as a term of the tenancy affecting rental value, or whether succession is to be regarded as deriving collaterally from the statutory provisions (in which case it need not affect rental value). *Semble*, however, the enhanced security enjoyed by a tenant with succession rights would in any event be a 'relevant factor' to be taken into account under the general clause.

(b) 'Productive Capacity' and 'Related Earning Capacity'

The arbitrator must in every case have regard to the productive capacity of the holding and its 'related earning capacity'. These concepts were initially introduced in the 1984 Act and are closely defined in Sch 2, para 1(2).

'*Productive Capacity*': this means 'the productive capacity of the holding (taking into account fixed equipment and any other facilities on the holding) on the assumption that it is in the occupation of a competent tenant practising a system of farming suitable to the holding'. The hypothetical nature of the valuation is here made explicit. The arbitrator must look not at the production actually achieved by the sitting tenant, but at that level of production which a reasonably competent tenant *would* achieve, making use of the existing fixed equipment on the holding.

---

2 See the principles laid down in *British Gas Corpn v Universities Superannuation Scheme Ltd* [1986] 1 All ER 978.
2a See now *Enfield London Borough Council v Pott* [1990] 34 EG 60 (CC) confirming, albeit at first instance, the relevance of the existing rent as 'a relevant factor', within Sch 2, para 1.
3 [1988] 1 All ER 824, CA.
4 [1988] 1 All ER 824, 829 per Nicholls LJ. The same rationale applies, it is suggested, to the review formula in Sch 2 of the 1986 Act.
5 See s 34(b)(ii) of the 1986 Act.

'Related Earning Capacity': the arbitrator must consider here 'the extent to which, in the light of [the holding's] productive capacity, a competent tenant practising such a system of farming could reasonably be expected to profit from farming the holding'. The arbitrator must consider under this head that level of income and profits which would be generated by agricultural production, the definition of 'related earning capacity' clearly being subsidiary (and linked) to that of 'productive capacity' (above). Income from non-agricultural activities (caravans, ponytrekking etc), grant payments not directly connected to agricultural production, and external factors such as marketing quotas, would not affect rental value under this head. *Semble*, however, these would be 'relevant factors' for consideration under the general clause if they affect the potential profitability of the farming enterprise taken as a whole.[5a]

It has not escaped comment that the linking of rent to profit in this way causes considerable problems, principally because rent is normally calculated *before* assessing the profitability (or otherwise) of the enterprise.[6] Certainly, ascertaining the holding's 'earning capacity' under the present statutory formulation seems to require a circular calculation; rent must of necessity be deducted to assess profitability, yet the latter must then be used to value the rent itself. In practice productive capacity and related earning capacity are reflected in gross margin budgets prepared by the parties' respective valuers, which will then form the basis of any subsequent arbitration.[7]

(c)   Current level of rents for comparable lettings

The final additional factor to be taken into account is the level of rents obtaining for comparable holdings. In determining the current level of rents for comparables, Sch 2, para 1(3) directs the arbitrator to have regard to any available evidence of rents which are, or (in view of rents currently being tendered) are likely to become, payable in respect of tenancies of comparable agricultural holdings on terms (other than terms fixing the rent payable) similar to the tenancy under consideration. The arbitrator can, therefore, consider rents arrived at either by agreement or arbitration, as well as current tenders for comparable holdings. Calculating the *likely* level of rents for comparable holdings to some extent involves the arbitrator in attempting to calculate the likely *future* level of comparable rents. Existing tenders will provide a basic guide, but this will inevitably involve arbitrators relying on their professional skill and intuition to gauge the future movement of rent levels. It appears that an arbitrator, in doing so, is entitled to rely upon his own professional opinion, provided it is based on experience acquired from transactions in which he has been involved, and from other sources within his range of competence, and direct evidence can be elicited to support it.[8] When relying on his professional skill in this manner, the

---

5a See now *Enfield London Borough Council v Pott* [1990] 34 EG 60 (CC) (income from farm shop held 'a relevant factor' within Sch 2, para 1). It was here indicated, further, that the arbitrator has to make a clear and separate assessment of both 'productive capacity' and 'related earning capacity', and that failure to do so in his award would constitute an error of law.

6 See for instance Muir Watt, *Agricultural Holdings* (13th ed) at 497–498.

7 As to which see the RICS 'Guidance Notes for Valuers Acting in Reviews of Rent at Arbitration under the Agricultural Holdings Act 1986', which contain detailed guidance on the preparation of gross margin budgets. These are set out in Appendix 2, p 384 ff.

8 See the observations of Megarry J in *English Exporters (London) Ltd v Eldonwall Ltd* [1973] Ch 415 at 420.

arbitrator should make his views known to the parties so that they may comment on them. Failure to do so may amount to technical misconduct.[9] When relying on factual evidence, however, both arbitrator and parties must avoid reliance on hearsay evidence of which they have no direct knowledge, and must be prepared to elicit proper evidence as to the identity and features of the holdings concerned, the terms of the tenancies and other relevant factors.

Guidance on the use of comparables is given in the RICS *Guidance Notes for Valuers Acting in Reviews of Rent* .[10]

(d)   Comparable lettings: factors to disregard

The objective of using comparables is to compare the subject holding with a 'true' comparable, in the rent of which any element attributable to peculiarities in the tenancy or holding have been valued out. When assessing comparable holdings, Sch 2, para 1(3) therefore directs the arbitrator to disregard:

  (i)   any element of the rents in question which is due to an 'appreciable scarcity of comparable holdings available for letting' on similar terms to the subject holding, comparable with the number of persons seeking to become tenants of such holdings (ie 'scarcity value'); *and*

  (ii)   any element in rents of comparable holdings which is due to the fact that the tenant of, or the person tendering for, any comparable holding is in occupation of other land in the vicinity of that holding that may be conveniently occupied together with that holding (ie 'marriage value'); *and*

  (iii)   any distortion or reduction in comparable rents made in consideration of the payment of a premium.

The statutory disregard of both scarcity value and marriage values has given rise to problems, and not a little controversy.

(I)   SCARCITY VALUE IN SUBJECT HOLDING

The discounting of scarcity value attaching to the subject holding is, of course, central to the policy underlying the rent review provisions of the 1986 Act *viz* to break the link between the free market rent obtainable on first lettings, and valuation on subsequent reviews. Curiously, however, Sch 2, para 1(3)(a) requires scarcity value to be valued out of the rent of comparable holdings, but is silent as to whether it is also to be disregarded if accruing to the subject holding itself. The balance of argument favours the view, it is thought, that scarcity value must be disregarded in the subject holding itself, even if this is not expressly required by the Act. The objective in using comparables is to arrive at a true (or undistorted) comparator with the subject holding. This being so, there seems little point in valuing scarcity value out of the rental of comparable holdings if the objective is not to arrive

---

9 See *Fox v Wellfair Ltd* [1981] 2 Lloyds Rep 514, CA; *Top Shop Estates Ltd v Danino* [1985] 1 EGLR 9 and *Zermatt Holdings SA v Nu-Life Upholstery Repairs Ltd* [1985] 2 EGLR 14, decided under ss 22 and 23 Arbitration Act 1979. There is no reason to suppose the same principle should not also apply in agricultural arbitrations.
10 *Supra* n. 7 and Appendix 2, p 386 ff.

at an undistorted rental value for the subject holding.[11] Although there is no direct judicial guidance to which reference might be made, some support for this view can be adduced from decisions in related areas. The Scottish courts, in construing similar (though not, it should be noted, identical) provisions in the Agricultural Holdings (Scotland) Act 1948[12] have indicated that scarcity value should be discounted in the subject holding, a view which must command persuasive force (if not authority) given the similar objectives of the Scottish and English legislation.[13] Comparison might also be made with the similar provisions of section 70(2) of the Rent Act 1977 and section 42(2) of the Rent (Scotland) Act 1971, which require that in determining the 'fair' rent for a residential dwelling it must be assumed that the number of persons seeking to become tenants is not substantially greater than the number of dwellings available for letting. In *Western Heritable Investment Co v Husband*[14] the House of Lords ruled that this required the rent to be determined on the hypothetical basis that the market was in a state of equilibrium, in that the number of *comparable* houses available for letting does not exceed the supply, *viz.* any element of scarcity value must be notionally valued out of the rent. Given the central role of comparables in assessing rent under Sch 2 to the 1986 Act, as under the Rent Act 1977, it is difficult to see how a different interpretation could be put on the agricultural provisions.[15]

(II)   MARRIAGE VALUES

'Marriage value' (ie the additional benefit arising because the tenant occupies other land in the vicinity of the holding which can be conveniently farmed with it) is to be discounted when assessing comparables. There is, however, no express direction to discount 'tenant's marriage value' in the subject holding itself. There are fewer policy reasons for discounting marriage value as well as scarcity in the subject holding. The Scottish courts have, interestingly, assumed that the discounting of 'tenant's marriage value' *is* required by the English provisions, but there is as yet no authoritative judicial guidance on the issue.[16] The better view, it is suggested, is that any particular benefit accruing to the tenant from potential 'marriage' of the holding with other land *should* be taken to affect rental value. This was certainly the view expressed during the passage of the 1984 Act, when government spokesmen indicated that marriage value in the subject should *not* be discounted.[17] This can be supported by reference to the possible use of the subject holding itself as a comparator in future rent arbitrations. If marriage value has already been 'valued out' of the rent of

11 See, for instance, dicta in *99 Bishopsgate Ltd v Prudential Assurance Co Ltd* (1984) 270 EG 950 (Lloyd 5); affd [1985] 1 EGLR 72, CA.
12 Agricultural Holdings (Scotland) Act 1948, s 7.
13 See *Aberdeen Endowments Trust v Will* 1985 SLT (Land Ct) 23.
14 [1983] 2 AC 849.
15 See especially per Lord Keith at [1983] 2 AC 849, 856 and Lord Brightman *ibid* at 860. In the absence of clear judicial guidance, the question cannot be regarded as entirely free of doubt. Further arguments favouring the discounting of scarcity value are persuasively put in Muir Watt, *Agricultural Holdings* (13th ed) at 50–2. For the contrary view see (1984) 269 EG 25 (Gregory). And see (1985) CSW 682 (Denyer-Green).
16 See *Aberdeen Endowments Trust v Will* 1985 SLT (Land Ct) 23 at 26.
17 See, eg Parl Debs (HL) Vol 447 Col 1010.

the former subject holding, the direction to discount marriage value in comparable rents (including that of our previous subject holding) becomes meaningless – there will be no such marriage value, it having previously been valued out on rent review. For these reasons it is suggested that scarcity value should be discounted in the subject holding, but that marriage value should not. In any event, any appreciable increase in productivity attributable to the proximity of the holding to other land in the vicinity could be taken into account as a 'relevant factor' influencing rental value under the general clause in Sch 2, para 1, and may even influence the 'productive capacity' of the holding under Sch 2, para 1(2).

(III)   'APPRECIABLE' SCARCITY

It should be noted that Sch 2, para 1(3)(a) requires the discounting only of rental value attributable to any 'appreciable' scarcity of comparable holdings available for letting. Schedule 2 clearly requires the discounting of any element of scarcity having a significant distorting effect on the rent of comparables, so as to arrive at a hypothetical rental for the holding on the assumption that the market is in a state of equilibrium. *Semble*, however, an arbitrator would not appear to be in error if some residual element of scarcity remains, attributable to special factors related to the nature of the individual holding.

3.   Factors to be disregarded

The following factors must be disregarded in *all* cases (and not just when assessing comparables).

(a)   Tenant's improvements or fixed equipment

Schedule 2, para 2(1)(a) requires an arbitrator to disregard any tenant's improvements or fixed equipment, *other than* equipment provided pursuant to an obligation imposed on the tenant by the contract of tenancy. By 'tenant's improvements' are meant any improvements executed on the holding in so far as they were executed wholly or partly at the expense of the tenant, without any 'equivalent allowance or benefit' given by the landlord in consideration of their execution (Sch 2, para 2(2)). If the terms of the tenancy (for instance as to rent) have been varied as a *quid pro quo* for an improvement executed by the tenant, this disregard does not apply. 'Tenant's fixed equipment' means fixed equipment provided by the tenant. Tenant's improvements must be discounted whether or not they are executed with the aid of grant monies provided by central or local government. Moreover, it was held in *Tummon v Barclays Bank Trust Co Ltd*[18] that improvements of both an agricultural and non-agricultural nature must be disregarded (the creation of a caravan park was there disregarded as a tenant's improvement under the 1948 Act provisions).

If the tenant has held a previous tenancy of the holding, the arbitrator

---

18 (1979) 39 P & CR 300.

must now also disregard any increase in rental value due to tenant's improvements or fixed equipment provided during that prior tenancy – provided, however, that the tenant did not receive compensation for the improvement on termination of the earlier tenancy.[19] This provision was introduced by the 1984 Act, with the aim of protecting the tenant in cases of surrender and re-grant.

(b)   Adoption of special system of farming

The adoption by the tenant of a system of farming ('high farming') more beneficial to the holding than that required by the tenancy or, if there is no such requirement, than that normally practised on comparable holdings, is to be treated as an improvement carried out at the tenant's expense.[20] Any increase in rental value attributable to high farming must, therefore, be disregarded.

(c)   Landlord's improvements

Schedule 2, para 2(1)(b) directs the arbitrator to disregard any increase in rental value attributable to landlord's improvements, but *only* insofar as the landlord has received central or local government grant aid to execute the improvements concerned. Improvements made at the landlord's own expense need not be discounted.

(d)   Tenant's occupation

By virtue of Sch 2, para 3(a) the arbitrator must disregard any effect on the rent attributable to the fact that the tenant who is a party to the arbitration is in occupation of the holding. This serves to emphasise the hypothetical nature of the valuation. The arbitrator must disregard any lowering of rental value attributable to the presence of a sitting tenant with security of tenure. *Semble*, also, any enhancement of rental value accruing as a result of good husbandry by the tenant, falling short of 'high farming', must also be disregarded.

(e)   Dilapidations by tenant

Similarly, the arbitrator must disregard any detrimental effect on rental value attributable to dilapidation or deterioration of, or damage to, buildings or land caused or permitted by the tenant.[1] Rental value must be assessed by reference to the potential of the holding if farmed by a reasonably competent tenant practising a suitable system of husbandry.

4.   Milk quotas: special provisions

The general law concerning milk quotas, and the Dairy Produce Regulations 1989, are considered separately in Chapter 13. Special provision is made, however, by section 15 of the Agriculture Act 1986, for any distorting effect that certain types of quota may have on the rental value of a holding.

19 Agricultural Holdings Act 1986, Sch 2, para 2(3).
20 Ibid, Sch 2, para 2(4).
 1 Ibid, Sch 2, para 3(b).

Clearly, the presence of registered quota attaching to the holding can be taken into account in an arbitration under section 12 of the Agricultural Holdings Act 1986; it must be considered a 'relevant factor' influencing rental value, and has a direct bearing on the productive and (in particular) 'related earning capacity' of the holding, as defined in Sch 2, para 1(2) (above). The problem addressed by s 15 of the Agriculture Act 1986 is that of 'transferred quota' *viz.* additional quota purchased by the tenant at his own expense.

Section 15(1) requires an arbitrator to disregard any increase in rental value due to quota which is registered under the Dairy Produce Quotas Regulations 1989 for the holding, or for land of which the holding forms part, and which was 'transferred to the tenant by virtue of a transaction the cost of which was born wholly or partly by him'. It should be appreciated that quota is registered in respect of a 'holding' as defined in the Dairy Produce Quotas Regulations and the European legislation *viz.* land used for dairy production. This is not coterminous with the definition of a holding, in the sense of land subject to tenancy, in the Agricultural Holdings Act 1986. The holding subject to rent arbitration proceedings may therefore be part of a larger agricultural unit constituting a 'holding' for the purposes of the European regulations. In this case, s 15 requires the disregard of that increased value which is due to so much of that quota which would fall to be apportioned to the land comprised in the tenancy, under the Dairy Produce Quotas Regulations, on a change of occupation of the land. Apportionment under the quota regulations is thus a pre-requisite to ascertainment of that quota which is to be discounted for present purposes.[2]

TRANSACTIONS TRIGGERING DISREGARD

Transferred quota (or, rather, the increase in rental value attributable to it) is only to be disregarded if acquired as a result of a transaction, the cost of which is born by the tenant. *Semble*, therefore, the disregard does not apply if quota is acquired in a gratuitous transaction. Similarly, problems could arise if the cost of transfer is born, not by the tenant himself, but by a farming company or partnership in which he has an interest. A further apportionment of any increased rental value may be required, also, if the tenant bears only part of the cost of transfer. Special rules apply to payments for transferred quota on the grant or assignment of a tenancy. Section 15(2) disallows the disregard where the payment for quota was in the form of consideration for the grant or assignment to him of the tenancy or any previous tenancy. The disregard *is*, however, available to any person who would be treated under Sch 1, paras 2, 3 or 4 of the Agriculture Act 1986 as having had quota transferred to him *viz.* close relatives taking by way of succession to the holding, assignees taking by way of assignment after 2 April 1984 where quota has been allocated or transferred to the assignor, and tenants who have sub-let where the subtenancy has subsequently terminated. In the latter instance, quota allocated or transferred to the subtenant is to be treated as allocated or transferred to the tenant.

---

2 As to which see Chapter 13 below.

E   Distress for unpaid rent

Where rent lawfully due remains unpaid, the landlord can at common law enter upon the premises or land and seize goods to the value of the amount outstanding in satisfaction of the debt. Distress for unpaid rent is a complex (even archaic) subject, a full consideration of which is outside the scope of this chapter.[3] At common law some goods are 'privileged' against distress – so perishables cannot be seized, and trade implements only if no other sufficient distress is available. Distress can, under the general law, be levied for up to six years' arrears of rent.[4] Protective legislation further restricts the landlord's right to levy distress for unpaid rent. So, for instance, no distress at all can be levied for unpaid rent of a dwelling let on a protected or assured residential tenancy, without prior County Court approval.[5] The Agricultural Holdings Act 1986 adopts a more liberal approach, but nevertheless restricts the amount of rent for which distress can be levied to one year's unpaid rent, and places restrictions on the distraint of goods and stock in which a third party has an interest.

1.   Limitation on rent recoverable by distress

By virtue of section 16(1) of the 1986 Act, the landlord of an agricultural holding is not entitled to distrain for rent which became due more than one year before the making of the distress. This limitation is relaxed where the ordinary course of dealing between the landlord and tenant of a holding indicates that the payment of rent has, as a matter of course, been deferred until the expiry of a quarter or half year after the date on which the rent legally became due. In this event the rent in question shall be deemed to have become due on the expiry of that quarter or half year, and *not* on the date on which it legally became due. Where rental payment is deferred in this way, the landlord may be entitled to distrain for more than one year's rent, eg for the year's rent unpaid *and* the quarter or half year's rent accrued due during the customary period allowed for payment (whichever applies). Note that if *more* than a year's rent is unpaid, the landlord's remedies at law to recover the balance remain unaffected, subject to the general limitation that no rent accruing due more than six years previously can be recovered (above). Ultimately, the landlord could invoke Case D to Sch 3 of the 1986 Act and institute proceedings for possession.

Where the amount of any compensation due the tenant has been ascertained prior to the landlord levying distress, whether under the 1986 Act or by custom or agreement, the amount of that compensation can be set off against unpaid rent. In this event the landlord is not entitled to distrain for more than the balance.[6] This would apply, for instance, if the parties have agreed the compensation to be payable on imminent termination of the tenancy.

---

3 For detailed consideration see, inter alia, *Woodfall's Law of Landlord and Tenant* (28th ed) Vol 1 pp 317–404 and *Hill and Redman's Law of Landlord and Tenant* (18th ed) Vol 1, A781–A889.
4 Limitation Act 1980, s 19.
5 See s 147 Rent Act 1977, s 19 Housing Act 1988.
6 Agricultural Holdings Act 1986, s 17.

2. Property and Livestock subject to third party interest

Section 18(1) of the 1986 Act places additional restrictions on distress where property or livestock present on the holding is owned by a third party.

(a) Absolute bar on distress

No distress can be levied on property which is agricultural or other machinery, and which is on the holding under an agreement with the tenant for its use or hire in the conduct of his business. *Semble* this would apply also to machinery taken by the tenant on hire purchase terms, property in which remains in the hirer until the last instalment under the agreement is paid. It would also apply, of course, to leased equipment. Where livestock belonging to a third party is on the holding, it cannot be distrained upon *at all* if present 'solely for breeding purposes',[7] eg rams or bulls on hire to the tenant. 'Livestock' is widely defined for this purpose to include 'any animal capable of being distrained'.[8] The restriction on distress therefore encompasses animals (such as horses) not generally regarded as 'livestock' for the purposes of the 1986 Act.

(b) Agisted stock – special rules

Special rules apply where livestock is present on the holding under a contract of agistment, *viz*. a contract by which stock has been taken in by the tenant to be fed at a fair price. By virtue of s 18(2) agisted livestock *cannot* be distrained for rent where there is other sufficient distress to be found on the holding, and if distrained (no other sufficient distress being available) the landlord cannot recover by that distress any sum exceeding the amount of the unpaid price agreed for feeding the stock, or any part of that price which remains unpaid. Section 18(3) gives the owner of the stock the right to redeem it prior to sale by paying the landlord an amount equal to the price agreed for feeding it. Payment by the owner of the sum agreed for feeding under the contract of agistment acts as a full discharge, as against the tenant, of any sum owing under the contract. Section 18(4) provides, however, that any *portion* of the agisted livestock remaining present on the holding shall continue to be distrainable for the amount for which the whole of that livestock could be distrainable. The wide definition of 'livestock' adopted for present purposes (above) means that animals not normally considered livestock in other contexts (*cf* section 96(1) of the 1986 Act) will be subject to distress if agisted. Stock cannot be distrained, however, if present under a legal arrangement other than a contract of agistment *simpliciter*, eg if a valid grazing agreement of part of the holding has been granted by the tenant.

3. Disputes as to distress

Where a dispute arises between landlord and tenant as to distress, s 19 confers jurisidiction on the county court, or a court of summary jurisdiction, to determine the matter. This jurisdiction specifically covers any dispute as

---

7 Section 18(1)(b) ibid.
8 Section 18(5) ibid.

to the legality of the distress levied, the ownership of stock distrained, or the fair price agreed for feeding agisted stock, and (generally) 'any other matter or thing relating to a distress on an agricultural holding'. The tenant's other remedies in the general law – for instance as to trespass to goods – remain unaffected. The court has jurisdiction under s 19 to order restoration of livestock or goods unlawfully detained, can declare the price to be paid for feeding agisted stock, and can make any other order it deems necessary. Appeal lies from the County Court to the Court of Appeal on a point of law[9] and to the Crown Court from a decision of a summary jurisdiction.[10]

9 County Courts Act 1984, s 77.
10 See section 19(2) of the 1986 Act.

Chapter 6
Agricultural Holdings: security of tenure

A   Restrictions on notices to quit

1.   General

The Agricultural Holdings legislation differs from other protective legislation[1] in that, rather than prescribing a statutory mode of termination for protected tenancies, it operates by placing restrictions on the operation of any notice to quit given by the landlord. No formal distinction is made by the 1986 Act between different kinds of notice to quit. Nevertheless notices to quit fall into at least four distinct categories, characterised by the nature and extent of the restrictions placed on their operation. Two distinctions must be clearly made.

(i)   The first is between notices to quit given in unqualified terms, and those given in reliance on one (or more) of the Cases for Possession set out in Sch 3 to the 1986 Act. The most extensive restrictions apply to unqualified notices to quit; such a notice cannot take effect unless the landlord obtains the consent of an agricultural land tribunal to its so doing. Protection is not conferred automatically, however, irrespective of the tenant's volition – the notice to quit will take effect unless the tenant elects to claim protection by serving a counter notice within one month, requiring the landlord to obtain tribunal consent. Where notice to quit is given pursuant to one of the Cases for Possession, however, the tenant's right to serve a counter notice is excluded.[2] In this event the notice to quit can only be challenged (if at all) by arbitration under the Act, or for ambiguity at common law.

(ii)   A second distinction is between those notices given pursuant to the Cases for Possession which can be challenged by arbitration, and those which cannot. If notice to quit is given relying on Cases A, B, D or E to Sch 3 of the 1986 Act, the tenant can challenge the facts on which it is based by referring the notice to arbitration. If one of the other Cases is relied on the arbitration procedure is not available. In this event a notice to quit can only be challenged on common law grounds, eg for ambiguity, uncertainty, or fraud. The least onerous restrictions, then, apply to notices to quit given under Cases C, F, G and H.

(iii)   Notices to quit served under Case G, following the death of the sole remaining tenant, fall into a further distinct category. If succession rights

1 Eg the Landlord and Tenant Act 1954.
2 Agricultural Holdings Act 1986, s 26(2), and see Chapter 7, p 120 ff below.

attach to the tenancy, any notice to quit is suspended once an application for succession has been made.[3] It can only take effect if no application for succession is made, if the succession application is rejected, or if consent to its operation is granted by the tribunal during the succession proceedings.[4]

2. Requirements of valid notice to quit

(a) Certainty and Unambiguity

Common law rules of construction apply, although the designation of different types of notice to quit as appropriate in different cases means that in agricultural cases the courts have had to develop additional principles of construction. To be valid, a notice to quit must contain 'plain, unambiguous words claiming to determine the existing tenancy at a certain time'.[5] It must be expressed sufficiently clearly that a reasonable person of ordinary capacity could not mistake its nature,[6] nor would be left in doubt as to when possession is demanded.[7] Although the notice can be coupled with the offer of a new tenancy, the notice to quit itself must not be ambiguous or optional.[8] Notice to 'vacate' by a given date has been held good, but notice to quit 'at the earliest possible moment' will be void for ambiguity.[9] A notice to quit 'on or before' a given date is valid and will take effect as an irrevocable notice to terminate the tenancy on the date specified.[10]

Although a notice to quit under s 26(1) must be accurate as to the termination date of the tenancy, and be unambiguous in intent, minor inaccuracies will be overlooked if a reasonably intelligent tenant would have understood the notice correctly. An unqualified notice will not, for instance, be invalid if the name of either landlord or tenant is inaccurately stated, provided the identity of the person giving the notice and its intended recipient are beyond reasonable doubt.[11] Different considerations apply where the notice to quit invokes one of the Cases for Possession in Sch 3. Because the procedure here is akin to forfeiture, the courts have developed strict rules of construction applicable to both the notice to quit itself and any preliminary notice to remedy or to pay rent on which it is based. These are discussed below.[12]

Note that although an unqualified notice to quit (under s 26(1)) need state no reasons[12a], it is advisable to do so to exclude any claim for 'additional' compensation for disturbance (four years' rent). Additional compensation will be excluded where the reason stated falls within paras (a)–(c) of s 27(3),

---

3 S 43(1) ibid.
4 See further Chapter 8 below.
5 Per Lord Coleridge CJ in *Gardner v Ingram* (1889) 61 LT 729, 730.
6 *Bury v Thompson* [1895] 1 QB 696, 697, CA; *Carradine Properties v Aslam* [1976] 1 WLR· 442; *Land v Sykes* [1990] EGCS 116.
7 *Phipps & Co Ltd v Rogers* [1924] 2 KB 45.
8 *Ahearn v Bellman* (1879) 4 Ex D 201, CA.
9 Cf, *Eastaugh v Macpherson* [1954] 3 All ER 214, CA and *Phipps & Co Ltd v Rogers* [1924] 2 KB 45; *Addis v Burrows* [1948] 1 KB 444, CA.
10 See *Dagger v Shepherd* [1946] KB 215, CA. And on the construction of notices to quit at common law see now, generally, *Manorlike Ltd v Le Vitas Travel Agency and Consultancy Services Ltd* [1986] 1 All ER 573, CA.
11 Cf *Frankland v Capstick* [1959] 1 All ER 209, CA; *Harmond Properties Ltd v Gajdzis* [1968] 3 All ER 263, CA.
12 See p 120 ff below.
12a See now *Crawford v Elliott* (1990) Times, 11 November CA, confirming the absence of any need to give reasons when serving notice to quit under s 26(1) ibid.

or is that hardship will be suffered by the landlord if the notice takes effect.[13] Where reasons *are* given, a notice to quit will be void at common law for fraud of the landlord had no genuine belief in the accuracy or truth of the reasons stated, at the time the notice to quit was served.[13a]

(b) Length of notice: statutory requirements

At common law, in the absence of express provision in the contract of tenancy, a yearly agricultural tenancy will be terminable on six months' notice. Agricultural holdings are, however, subject to special statutory provisions. By virtue of section 25(1) of the 1986 Act, a notice to quit an agricultural holding, or part of a holding, will be invalid if it purports to terminate the tenancy before the expiry of 12 months from the end of the then current year of tenancy. Any provision to the contrary in the contract of tenancy is to be disregarded – contracting out is expressly forbidden. The basic rule, then, is that at least 12 months' notice to quit must be given, ending on a contractual term date of the tenancy. The latter must be accurately specified in the notice to quit. For the purpose of calculating the 12 month period, the date on which the notice was served is included but the date of its expiry is not.[14] The requirement applies not only to yearly periodic tenancies, but to fixed term tenancies of agricultural holdings, and will also apply to the exercise of a 'break' clause by notice during the subsistence of such term.[15]

Although the parties cannot agree in advance that notice shorter than the statutory minimum be given, if invalid short notice has been given the parties are free to *agree* that it should nevertheless take effect as a valid notice to quit. Such agreement takes effect as a waiver by the tenant of his strict rights under the Act.[16] Where the parties agree to accept an invalid notice as effective, however, the period of notice agreed must not be less than is necessary to enable the tenant to make claims for additional disturbance compensation, or high farming, on termination of the tenancy. An agreement to waive the statutory notice period and substitute notice of less than one month would, it is suggested, be voided by s 78(1). In this event no valid notice to quit will have been given.[17]

Section 25(1) is subject to a number of statutory exceptions, allowing for less than 12 months' notice to quit to be given. In these excepted cases the appropriate period of notice will be that specified in the contract of tenancy or (if none) six months' notice to quit at common law. The exceptions are:

(a) Where the tenant is insolvent.[18] The tenant is 'insolvent' for this purpose if he has become bankrupt or has made a composition with his creditors, or where a receiving order has been made against him. A company is 'insolvent' if a winding-up order has been made or a resolution for voluntary winding-up has been passed.[19]

---

13 See s 60(3) ibid.

13a See *Earl of Stradbroke v Mitchell* [1989] 48 EG 59, 50 EG 45 (Aldous J.), [1990] EGCS 109, CA. And see further Chapter 7, p 122 below. Fraud is more likely to be relevant where notice to quit is given for the reasons enumerated in the Cases for Possession in Sch 3.

14 *Schnabel v Allard* [1967] 1 QB 627, CA.

15 See *Edell v Dulieu* [1924] AC 38, HL.

16 *Elsden v Pick* [1980] 1 WLR 898, CA.

17 And see *Coates v Diment* [1951] 1 All ER 890; *Re Disraeli's Agreement* [1939] Ch 382 and *Parry v Million Pigs Ltd* (1980) 260 EG 281, the rationale of which would, it is suggested, apply.

18 Agricultural Holdings Act 1986, s 25(2)(a).

19 Section 96(2) ibid.

(b)   Where a notice to quit is given pursuant to a provision in the tenancy agreement allowing for the resumption of possession for some specified purpose other than the use of the land for agriculture.[20]

(c)   Where a notice to quit is given by a tenant to his sub-tenant.[1] This exception is not restricted to cases where the tenant himself has received notice to quit from the landlord, and it therefore means that sub-tenancies can always be terminated on short notice, subject to the applicability of the security of tenure provisions (see below).

(d)   Where the tenancy subsists under an agreement made before 25 March 1947 and *either* the notice is given by the Ministry of Defence pursuant to the agreement because the property is required for naval, military or air force purposes *or* where the notice is given by a corporation carrying on a statutory undertaking, by a government department or local authority, where possession is required for a non-agricultural purpose for which the land was acquired or appropriated.[2]

(e)   Where the tenancy is a tenancy for life or lives which, by virtue of section 149(6) of the Law of Property Act 1925, takes effect as a fixed term of 90 years, determinable on the death of the tenant by one month's notice expiring on the appropriate quarter day.[3]

(f)   Where an arbitrator specifies a date for termination of the tenancy on the tenant's failing to comply with a notice to remedy, or where there has been an extension of time under a notice to remedy following notice to quit.[4]

(g)   Where following a rent review the arbitrator determines that the rent payable should be increased, the *tenant* can serve notice to quit of at least six months' duration, provided it purports to end the tenancy at the end of the first year of tenancy following the increase.[5] The practical effect is to enable the tenant to serve notice to quit within the first six months following an increase in rent, terminating the tenancy at the end of the first year of tenancy following the increase (instead of the second as under the basic rule in section 25(1) above, otherwise applicable). Note that this right may be lost if the arbitrator's award is not delivered prior to the expiry of six months from the review date from which it is to take effect eg where the arbitrator's appointment is delayed (or the giving of this award is delayed) by agreement, in order to facilitate negotiations.

(h)   Where a tribunal grants a Certificate of Bad Husbandry, they can specify a minimum period of notice of at least two months for termination of the tenancy, and direct that that period shall apply instead of the 12 months' notice otherwise required.[6] The landlord can then serve a notice to quit giving the minimum notice prescribed by the tribunal. The notice must state that it is given pursuant to the tribunal order. The object is to enable the landlord to regain possession quickly in extreme cases of bad husbandry by giving two

20 Section 25(2)(b) ibid. See further Chapter 3 p 62 above.
1 Section 25(2)(c) ibid.
2 Sch 12, para 4 ibid.
3 Section 25(2)(d) ibid.
4 Articles 7 and 15 of the Agricultural Holdings (Arbitration on Notices) Order 1987, SI 1987/710.
5 Agricultural Holdings Act 1986, s 25(3).
6 Section 25(4) ibid.

months' notice, instead of the minimum of 12 months' notice. The notice does not have to end at the end of a year of tenancy.[7]

In the case of exceptions (g) and (h), the notice to quit will not be rendered invalid by virtue of any term of the contract requiring a longer period of notice to terminate the tenancy.

3. Unqualified notice to quit: counter notice

Where the landlord serves an unqualified notice to quit, s 26(1) provides that the tenant can, not later than one month from the giving of the notice to quit, serve on the landlord a written counter-notice requiring that section to apply to it. In this event the notice to quit cannot have effect unless the landlord applies for, and obtains, tribunal consent to its operation. The notice to quit can be given in the alternative, ie pursuant to one of the cases in Sch 3 or (if that fails) as a general notice to quit subject to s 26. To be valid, however, it must be clear on the face of the notice that it is given under both provisions, or two notices must be given.[8] If the tenant challenges the notice by arbitration (eg if Case D or E is relied on), but is unsuccessful, and the notice is one to which s 26(1) applies in the alternative, then the time limit for serving a counter notice is extended to one month from the termination of the arbitration (see the Agricultural Holdings (Arbitration on Notices) Order 1987, Art 11). For the purpose of calculating the one month time limit for service of counter notice, the 'corresponding date' rule is applied.[9] The period for service of counter notice is inflexible; there is no provision for extension, whatever the merits.

If a counter notice is validly served, the landlord must apply to the agricultural land tribunal, within one month of its receipt, for consent to the operation of the notice to quit.[10] The tribunal can only grant consent on the limited grounds set out in s 27(3) (see below).

The 1986 Act does not expressly prevent the parties from contracting out of the protection of s 26. In *Johnson v Moreton*[11] it was held, nevertheless, that the provision is mandatory ('the notice to quit *shall not* have effect'), and that on grounds of public policy contracting out should not be permitted. It was here held that a clause in the contract of tenancy by which the tenant covenanted *not* to serve a counter notice claiming security was void, and that its breach could not ground possession proceedings under Case E. Similarly, in *Featherstone v Staples*[12] a clause contained in a partnership deed, and limiting the right to serve counter notice without the consent of the landlord's nominee, was held to be void. Where the tenancy is held by joint tenants, all must otherwise concur in the giving of a counter notice if it is to be effective.[13] If the lease is held on trust for sale, however, a tenant refusing to join in serving counter notice will be putting the trust assets at risk, and can in some circumstances be compelled in equity to join in its service.[14] He can also be compelled to concur

7 Section 25(4) ibid.
8 See *Cowan v Wrayford* [1953] 2 All ER 1138, 1141, CA.
9 See *Dodds v Walker* [1981] 1 WLR 1027, HL; *E J Riley Investments Ltd v Eurostile Holdings Ltd* [1985] 3 All ER 181, CA.
10 Rule 2, Agricultural Land Tribunals (Rules) Order 1978, SI 1978/259.
11 [1978] 3 All ER 37, HL.
12 [1986] 2 All ER 461, CA.
13 *Newman v Keedwell* (1977) 244 EG 469.
14 *Harris v Black* (1983) 46 P & CR 366, CA.

in service if his co-tenant has elected to purchase his share of the partnership assets, thus removing him from the legal title.[15] *Semble*, also, if application is made under section 30 of the Law of Property Act 1925 to remove him from the legal title. Note, finally, that a sub-tenant's right to serve counter notice is expressly excluded if he has received notice to quit from the tenant, and the notice to quit states that the latter has received notice to quit from the landlord.[16]

4.   Tribunal consent to operation of notice to quit

To obtain tribunal consent to the operation of a notice to quit, the landlord must establish two things:

1) the tribunal must, in all cases, withhold consent if it is satisfied that 'a fair and reasonable landlord would not insist on possession' (s 27(2)). This is a prerequisite to an order for possession in all cases.

and

2) the tribunal must withhold consent unless they are satisfied that one or more of the grounds for consent specified in s 27(3) is made out. The ground(s) on which the landlord is relying must be specified in his application for tribunal consent.[17] The tribunal cannot go outside the grounds therein stated, and grant consent on other grounds contained in s 27(3).

The consideration of the grounds for consent and the 'fair and reasonable landlord' requirement are separate matters and must be considered separately.[18] In particular, when considering whether one of the grounds for possession is made out the tribunal must put out of mind any hardship which might be caused to the tenant if possession is ordered, as this can only be considered at the discretionary stage as a relevant factor influencing the 'fair and reasonable landlord' requirement.[19]

(a)   The grounds for consent

These are contained in s 27(3) of the 1986 Act.

(I)   GOOD HUSBANDRY

'that the carrying out of the purpose for which the landlord proposes to terminate the tenancy is desirable in the interests of good husbandry as respects the land to which the notice relates, treated as a separate unit.'

This provision directs the tribunal to make a comparison between the efficiency of the regime obtaining under the tenant with that which will obtain if the tenancy is terminated. It is not sufficient to prove that the existing tenant is farming badly.[20] The landlord must prove affirmatively that the land will be better farmed if possession is granted, and he will for this

---

15 *Sykes v Land* (1984) 271 EG 1264, CA.
16 Art 16, Agricultural Holdings (Arbitration on Notices) Order 1987.
17 Agricultural Holdings Act 1986, s 27(1).
18 *R v Agricultural Land Tribunal for Eastern Province of England, ex Grant* [1956] 1 WLR 1240, 1244, CA per Singleton LJ.
19 See *Evans v Roper* [1960] 2 All ER 507.
20 *Davies v Price* [1951] 1 All ER 671, CA.

purpose have to produce a scheme or plan to show how he intends to improve the efficiency of the holding, farmed as a separate unit.[1] The land must, however, be treated as a separate unit, and the tribunal cannot consider the desirability of amalgamation with other of the landlord's land when assessing the landlord's proposals for the disputed property.[2]

(II) SOUND MANAGEMENT

'that the carrying out of the purpose is desirable in the interests of sound management of the estate of which the land to which the notice relates forms part or which that land constitutes.'

In considering sound management, the tribunal is entitled to look not only at the land to which the notice to quit relates, but also other land making up the landlord's estate.[3] The phrase 'sound management' is not defined in the 1986 Act, and clearly envisages something wider than 'good' estate management (as defined by section 11 of the Agriculture Act 1947), which latter is largely concerned with the landlord/tenant relationship. It involves a consideration, essentially, of the way the land itself is managed, and a comparison with the way it would be managed under the landlord's proposals. It is, therefore, not sound estate management to put forward a plan to eliminate onerous financial terms in the lease by obtaining possession and reletting the land to the same (or another) tenant under a lease omitting the offending clauses.[4] The landlord must put forward a concrete plan to prove that the land would be better managed and more efficiently farmed if amalgamated with the remainder of his estate. It will not be sufficient to seek possession in order to sell with vacant possession, for there will be no basis for the tribunal to assess the regime that will eventually replace the existing one at the property.[5] A proposal to sell part of the land may suffice, however, where this is necessary to finance improvements in the management of the estate as a whole. It is clear from the wording of s 27(3)(b) ('or which that land constitutes') that the estate referred to and the holding may be coterminous. If the 'estate' comprises only the land subject to the notice to quit, good husbandry and the standard of farming likely if the landlord resumes possession will be the only considerations relevant to the issue of sound management.[6] In this sort of case 'good husbandry' and 'sound management' are difficult to distinguish in practice, and in effect coincide.

(III) AGRICULTURAL RESEARCH

'that the carrying out of the purpose is desirable for the purpose of agricultural research, education, experiment or demonstration, or for the purposes of the enactments relating to smallholdings.'

This ground enables the repossession of land for the establishment of public (or private) agricultural colleges or other research institutions, or to facilitate re-letting as a smallholding by a smallholdings authority, eg to entrants into agriculture.

1 *Cf Lewis v Moss* (1961) 181 EG 685.
2 *Cf R v Agricultural Land Tribunal for Eastern Province of England ex p Grant* [1956] 3 All ER 321, CA.
3 *Evans v Roper* [1960] 2 All ER 507.
4 *National Coal Board v Naylor* [1972] 1 All ER 1153.
5 *Cf Burnett v Smith* (1951) 159 EG 3 and *Trustees of A Merchant v Sterry* (1954) 163 EG 655.
6 See *Greaves v Mitchell* (1971) 222 EG 1395.

(IV)   ALLOTMENTS

'that the carrying out of the purpose is desirable for the purposes of the enactments relating to allotments.[7]

(V)   GREATER HARDSHIP

'that greater hardship would be caused by withholding than by giving consent to the operation of the notice.'

The issue here is at large, and the tribunal can consider a wide variety of matters, provided always that they bear a causal relationship with the giving or refusing of tribunal consent.[8] 'Greater hardship' can also be relevant in proceedings to recover possession of residential dwellings under the Rent Act 1977.[9] In *Purser v Bailey*[10] it was indicated that the tribunal should interpret 'greater hardship' in the same way as established Rent Act jurisprudence. Hardship not only to the landlord, but to 'all those concerned on the landlord's side' will therefore be relevant.[11] The correct approach in Rent Act cases, and also it is suggested in the present context, was laid down in *Harte v Frampton*:[12]

'the [tribunal] should take into account hardship to all who may be affected by the grant or refusal of an order for possession – relatives, dependants, lodgers, guests and the stranger within the gates – but should weigh such hardship with due regard to the status of the persons affected and their proximity to the landlord or tenant, and the extent to which consequently hardship to them would be hardship to him.'

Hardship to third parties can, then, be taken into account, provided they are in a close personal or family relationship to landlord or tenant. Hardship to the wife or child of either party will be of importance (as in *Purser v Bailey*, above).[13] Hardship to a parent has also been held relevant,[14] but hardship to more distant relatives will carry little weight unless the circumstances are exceptional.[15] The effect of a decision to give or refuse consent on the *health* of either party has been held a relevant factor in Rent Act cases, although medical evidence as to the likely effect of the tribunal's decision will require close scrutiny.[16] In all cases the tribunal must weigh any perceived hardship against the closeness of the relationship of the person suffering it with landlord or tenant. The proximity of relationship with either party will determine to what extent the hardship can truly be said to be *caused* by the tribunal's decision to give or withhold consent.

Although Rent Act jurisprudence is of assistance (if not strictly authority), the context dictates that in agricultural cases the *financial* consequences of giving or refusing possession will have much greater prominence than under the Rent Acts. The land in dispute may be of

---

7 As to which see further Chapter 15, below.
8 See *Cooke v Talbot* (1977) 243 EG 831.
9 See Sch 15, Case 9 Rent Act 1977.
10 [1967] 2 QB 500, 508, CA.
11 Ibid at 508, per Lord Denning MR.
12 [1948] 1 KB 73, 79, CA.
13 And see *Rhodes v Cornford* [1947] 2 All ER 601, CA.
14 See *Addington v Sims* [1952] EGD 1.
15 See *R v Agricultural Land Tribunal for the South Eastern Area, ex p Parslow* (1979) 251 EG 667 – hardship to nieces/nephews of either party not relevant unless close personal relationship proven.
16 See *Thomas v Fryer* [1970] 2 All ER 1, CA.

importance to the viability of the tenant's business, or the landlord's financial plight; the question is therefore wider than simply a consideration of hardship arising from the loss of one's residence. Thus in *Purser v Bailey* (above) consent was given where the landlord had died leaving an insolvent estate, and sale with vacant possession was the only means of clearing its indebtedness. Hardship to the son (who had guaranteed the debts) and widow (who would receive no legacy) would ensue, and were relevant considerations dictating the giving of consent. It would appear, however, that the landlord's ability to sell with vacant possession will only be decisive if there are strong grounds to suppose hardship will otherwise ensue (as here). Financial hardship to the tenant must also be considered, and will often outweigh that to the landlord eg because the loss of the holding may render the tenant's agricultural enterprise, viewed as a whole, uneconomic. The availability of other land to the tenant will be an important factor, for if he has alternative land which in itself will support a viable agricultural business, he will have difficulty establishing that hardship will flow from the giving of tribunal consent.[17]

The exercise at issue involves balancing the *relative* hardship attributable to landlord and tenant from the giving or withholding of consent. Clearly, the underlying factors influencing issues of hardship will be subject to rapid change eg the parties' respective financial positions. Accordingly, the landlord is at liberty to seek consent to successive notices to quit on the same ground, even though earlier applications have been refused. Each application will be dealt with on its merits, and is not confined to material changes of circumstance which have intervened. The landlord runs the risk, however, of being penalised in costs if he alienates the tribunal by asking for what is, in substance, the same thing on successive occasions.[18]

Where the tenant has negotiated for the surrender of his interest, this may prejudice any claim that he would suffer hardship were possession to be given. *Semble*, negotiations will act to the tenant's detriment even if conducted on a 'without prejudice' basis.[19]

It should be noted, finally, that even if the tribunal consider the balance of hardship to be in the landlord's favour, they are entitled to refuse consent if satisfied that a 'fair and reasonable' landlord would not demand possession. They may still refuse consent if, for instance, they consider that the farming of the land would suffer if possession were granted.[20]

(VI) NON-AGRICULTURAL USE

'that the landlord proposes to terminate the tenancy for the purpose of the land's being used for a use, other than for agriculture, not falling within Case B.'

Sch 3, Case B relates to development for which planning permission is required, or for which *otherwise* than by virtue of the town and country planning legislation, no permission is required (see Sch 3, Part I, Case B para (b)). The present provision, consequently, is confined to cases where the landlord's proposals are exempted from planning permission by the

17 Compare *Purser v Bailey* (above); *Kinson v Swinnerton* (1961) 179 EG 691; *Sims v Wilson* [1946] 2 All ER 261, CA. *Cf* the Scottish case of *Clamp v Sharp* 1986 SLT (Land Ct) 2.
18 See generally *Wickington v Bonney* (1982) 47 P & CR 655 per Stephen Brown J.
19 See *R v Agricultural Land Tribunal for South Eastern Area, ex p Bracey* [1960] 2 All ER 518.
20 As in *Jones v Burgoyne* (1963) 188 EG 497.

terms of the Town and Country Planning Acts themselves, and are of a non-agriculural nature.[1]

(b)   The 'fair and reasonable landlord'

Even if one of the grounds for consent is made out, the tribunal *must* still refuse consent if they are satisfied, in all the circumstances, that a fair and reasonable landlord would not insist on possession. The question is at large, and the tribunal here comes into its own as a specialist arbiter of fact. The tribunal can consider issues of relative hardship to each party, irrespective of whether the 'greater hardship' ground (above) has been relied on. They can, moreover, look to hardship factors of a wider kind than those permitted by s 27(3)(e), ie those not causally connected with the giving or withholding of consent. The long term benefit of the land, and its productivity, will also be important factors for consideration. The tribunal may refuse consent if the long-term productivity of the land is likely to suffer, even if to do so would cause hardship to the landlord.[2] On the other hand, the tribunal may refuse possession where the landlord has established grounds (a) or (b), if to do so would cause hardship to an otherwise competent tenant.[3]

(c)   Conditions on tribunal consent

Section 27(4) gives the tribunal power to impose appropriate conditions when granting consent, to ensure 'that the land to which the notice to quit relates will be used for the purpose for which the landlord proposes to terminate the tenancy.' If the landlord contravenes, or fails to comply with, a condition imposed by the tribunal, it can impose a penalty of not more than 2 years' rent on the landlord.[4] Action to enforce the condition, by way of tribunal application, can only be taken by the Crown. Any penalty levied on the landlord is treated as a debt due to the Crown, and is payable into the Consolidated Fund.[5] The Tribunal can award costs in an application under s 27.[6]

B   Repossession of part of a holding

1.   Notice to quit part

In the absence of a clause in the tenancy, authorising resumption of possession of part of the holding, a notice to quit part of the land demised is bad at common law.[7] This restrictive rule is relaxed by statute, however, in several instances.

The contract of tenancy may itself authorise resumption of part of the

1 And see further Chapter 7 p 126 ff below.
2 See *Jones v Burgoyne* (1963) 188 EG 497.
3 *Evans v Roper* [1960] 2 All ER 507.
4 Agricultural Holdings Act 1986, s 27(6).
5 See s 27(8) ibid.
6 See s 27(7) ibid.
7 *Re Bebington's Tenancy* [1921] 1 Ch 559. The decision in this case has been superseded by statute, in the form of s 140(2), LPA 1925. The principle, however, still stands.

holding. Moreover, if it authorises resumption for the purpose of facilitating a non-agricultural use of the land, the landlord will not have to give the statutory period of notice to quit. The clause will only be good, however, if it provides for sufficient notice of resumption to enable the tenant to make claims for 'additional' compensation for disturbance and high farming, should he wish to do so.[8]

Additionally, section 31 of the 1986 Act authorises notice to quit part of a holding where possession is sought to facilitate the use of the land for 'objects' enumerated in s 31(2). Section 31(1)(a) also allows notice to quit part of it is given for the 'purpose' of adjusting the boundaries between agricultural units or amalgamating agricultural units (or parts of such units). The legislative policy manifested in s 31(2) is somewhat restrictive, allowing notice to quit part of a holding for specific, narrowly defined, objects of a public or social character. The 'objects' specified are:

(i) the erection of cottages or other houses for farm labourers with or without gardens;
(ii) the provision of gardens for cottages or other houses for farm labourers;
(iii) the provision of allotments;
(iv) the letting of the land as a smallholding under Part III of the Agriculture Act 1970;[9]
(v) the planting of trees;
(vi) the opening or working of a deposit of coal, ironstone, limestone, brick-earth, or other mineral, or a stone quarry or a clay, sand or gravel pit, or the construction of any building to be used in connection therewith;
(vii) the making of a watercourse or reservoir;
(viii) the making of a road, railway, tramroad, siding, canal or basin, or a wharf, pier, or other work connected there with.

The notice must state that it is given for the purpose or object in question. Most notices to quit served under s 31 will also be within Case B, in that many of the 'objects' (above) are non-agricultural and require planning permission. The security provisions apply, and the tenant can invoke the arbitration procedure to challenge the notice to quit in appropriate circumstances. If the notice to quit is unqualified, it can be challenged by a counter notice requiring its reference to the agricultural land tribunal for consent.

Finally, notice to quit part of a holding can also be served where there has been severance of the landlord's reversionary estate. Section 140 of the Law of Property Act 1925 provides that wherever there has been a severance 'by conveyance, surrender or otherwise' of any land comprised in a lease, then any right of re-entry (including a right to serve notice to quit) is apportioned and remains annexed to the severed parts of the reversionary estate. The tenant, however, continues to hold under one contract of tenancy, notwithstanding severance.[10] Note, however, that s 140 only applies where there is a 'severance' of the reversion, *viz* a 'real' conveyance from the

---

8 *Coates v Diment* [1951] 1 All ER 890; *Re Disraeli's Agreement* [1939] Ch 382.
9 As to which see further Chapter 15 below.
10 *Jelley v Buckman* [1974] QB 488, CA.

original reversioner. So, in *Persey v Bazley*,[11] it was held that the conveyance of the reversion on development land to bare trustees, to enable a notice to quit to be served as to that part only, was invalid and failed to effect a 'severance' in the required sense. The conveyance to the trustees was revocable at any time, and though not a 'sham' in the legal sense, was a device aimed solely at facilitating the service of notice to quit part by nominee trustees.[12] The decision has been criticised, not least because a tenant is not entitled to go 'behind the curtain' and seek information about any transaction affecting the beneficial interest in the reversion. He is obliged, on accepted principles, to deal with the holder of the legal estate, and him only. In *Persey* the fact that the conveyance was to bare trustees was evident on the fact of the deeds. In many cases it will not be. In the latter situation, the anomalous result will be that the tenant will not be able to challenge a severance, having insufficient information as to the nature of the trust and the equitable interests in the reversion. Neither has he the right to obtain such information. Whatever its merits, however, *Persey v Bazley* is undoubtedly in line with other decisions on s 140, in which the courts have consistently sought to protect the tenant.[13] It also accords with the more restrictive legislative policy reflected in section 31 of the 1986 Act.[14]

2.   Enlargement of notice to quit

Where notice to quit part is given by a person entitled to a severed part of the reversionary estate, or where it is validated by s 31 (above), s 32 gives the tenant the right to 'treat' the notice as notice to quit the whole holding. To do so he must give a written counter notice within 28 days to the landlord, or to the several owners of the reversionary estate, stating that he accepts the notice to quit as a notice to quit the entire holding, to take effect at the same time as the original notice. This right does not apply, however, if notice to quit part is given pursuant to a power contained in the contract of tenancy.

3.   Reduction in rent

Section 33 entitles the tenant to a reduction in rent where part of the holding is repossessed either by virtue of s 31, or under a power contained in the tenancy. Where the reversion has merely been severed the need for provisions to enforce a reduction does not arise. The tenant is entitled under s 33 to a reduction proportionate to that part of the holding which has been repossessed, and 'in respect of any depreciation of the value to him of the residue of the holding caused by the severance or by the use to be made of the part severed.'[15] If the land is repossessed pursuant to a power in the

---

11 (1983) 47 P & CR 37, CA.
12 See (1983) 47 P & CR 37, 44 per May LJ.
13 See *Re Clayton's Deed Poll* [1980] Ch 99; *Nevill Long & Co (Boards) Ltd v Firmenich & Co* (1983) 47 P & CR 59, CA.
14 And see further (1985) 49 Conv 292 (J Martin), and a helpful article at (1984) 8 CSW 175 (A Densham).
15 Agricultural Holdings Act 1986, s 33(1).

contract of tenancy, any relief or benefit allowed to the tenant under the tenancy in respect of the land, possession of which is resumed by the land-lord, must be taken into account.[16] The reduction is determinable by arbitration under the 1986 Act in default of agreement.

C   Joint and derivative interests: some problems

1.   Joint tenancies: some problems defined

Most agricultural tenancies are periodic yearly tenancies. It is therefore necessary to consider the position where the property has been let to joint lessees, or the reversionary estate is held by joint tenants under a trust for sale, and the effect of the common law rules of joint tenancy in this situation.

The doctrine of joint tenancy was stated in the following terms by Lord Tenterden CJ in *Doe d Aslin v Summersett.*[17]

> 'Upon a joint demise by Joint Tenants, upon a joint tenancy from year to year, the true character of the tenancy is this . . . that [each tenant] holds the whole of all so long as he and each shall please, and as soon as any one of the joint tenants gives a notice to quit he effectively puts an end to that tenancy.'

A periodic agricultural tenancy can therefore only be continued into the next period if all holders of a joint interest in the reversion or in the tenancy so desire, and if one such joint tenant does not agree he can unilaterally determine the tenancy. The position is complicated by the requirements of the Agricultural Holdings legislation as to the giving of notices to quit and counter notices:

(a)   Notice to quit by tenant

A notice to quit given by one of several joint lessees is effective to terminate the tenancy of all, as the consent of all is required to continue the tenancy into another period.[18]

(b)   Surrender of tenancy

To surrender a tenancy *before* its expiry date, *all* joint lessees must concur, with the result that no single joint lessee can validly surrender the tenancy before the contractual term date.[19] This principle was reaffirmed by the Court of Appeal in *Greenwich London Borough Council v McGrady*:[20]

> 'It is clear law that if there is to be a surrender of a joint tenancy, ie a surrender before the natural termination date, then all must agree to the surrender. If there is to be a renewal, which is the position at the end of each period of a periodic tenancy, then again all must concur.'

---

16 S 33(3) ibid.
17 (1830) 1 B & Ad 135.
18 *Greenwich London Borough Council v McGrady* (1982) 81 LGR 288, CA.
19 *Leek and Moorlands Building Society v Clark* [1952] 2 QB 788, CA.
20 (1982) 81 LGR 288, 290.

(c)   Notice to quit by landlord

Where the freehold reversion is held by joint tenants on trust for sale, a notice to quit served *by* one such joint tenant is effective to terminate the tenancy.[1] Note, however, that if service of notice to quit by one of several joint trustees results in expense which is greater than the benefit accruing, the trustee responsible may be liable for breach of trust.

Service by the landlord on one of the joint lessees of the property is effective provided it is addressed to all.[2]

(d)   Tenant's counter-notice

Section 26(1) of the 1986 Act requires that a counter-notice claiming reference of the landlord's notice to quit to an agricultural land tribunal must be served by 'the tenant'. Until recently it was considered that a counter-notice would only be good if served by (or on behalf of) *all* joint lessees, for all must (according to the joint tenancy rule) agree if the tenancy is to continue beyond the termination date in the notice to quit.[3] The issue is of some importance as a landlord will commonly let land to a partnership of himself and others (either a third party or other members of his family). It was previously thought that partnership tenancies could provide a means of avoiding conferring security of tenure; having served notice to quit, the landlord *qua* partner and lessee could refuse to join with his co-lessees in serving a counter-notice claiming the protection of the 1986 Act. Decisions of the Court of Appeal in *Sykes v Land*[4] and in *Featherstone v Staples*[5] mean that this assumption can no longer be maintained. Two related problems call for examination:

   (i)   In what circumstances will the concurrence of a joint tenant in the service of counter-notice be dispensed with?
   (ii)   In situations where the concurrence of all joint tenants *is* required, will the refusal of a tenant to join in serving counter-notice under s 26(1) engage liability for breach of trust? Can he, moreover, be compelled in equity to join in serving the appropriate counter-notice?

(i)   This problem was raised squarely in *Featherstone v Staples* itself, a case of statutory avoidance. Here land was let to a partnership comprising the tenants, who managed the holding, and a company controlled by the landlord. Under the collateral partnership agreement the tenancies were to comprise partnership property, and the Company to take a small share of partnership profits. The partnership agreement also provided that no partners would serve a counter-notice[6] without the consent of the Company 'nominee' tenant. Upon the landlord later serving notice to quit the latter duly refused to join in serving counter-notice, raising squarely the question whether the other tenants could claim the protection of the 1986 Act by serving notice without its concurrence. At first instance, Nourse J resolved

1 *Parsons v Parsons* [1983] 1 WLR 1390 (and see (1984) Conv 166).
2 *Jones v Lewis* (1973) 117 Sol Jo 373, CA.
3 *Newman v Keedwell* (1977) 35 P & CR 393.
4 (1984) 271 EG 1264.
5 [1986] 2 All ER 461.
6 Under what is now Agricultural Holdings Act 1986, s 26(1).

the issue in the tenant's favour by dispensing with the joint tenancy rule altogether.[7] The Court of Appeal, eschewing this radical approach, reaffirmed the strict application of the joint tenancy rule. As a matter of statutory interpretation the phrase 'the tenant' in s 26(1), in relation to any joint tenancy, must mean 'the joint tenants' and not 'the joint tenants or any one or more of them'. [8] This is in line with the trend of recent decisions in other areas of the law of landlord and tenant, which have stressed that the renewal of a periodic tenancy requires the concurrence of *all* joint tenants.[9] In most cases the concurrence of all joint lessees will, therefore, still be necessary. In *Featherstone*, however, the issue of statutory avoidance was dealt with by applying principles of the law of partnership. The principle in *Johnson v Moreton*[10] – that any restrictive clause in the lease preventing service of counter-notice is void as against public policy – applied here to void the clause in the partnership agreement. Being void, it could not limit the scope of the actual or usual authority of partners to bind the firm. Applying the wider rationale of *Johnson v Moreton* it was therefore held that (per Shaw LJ):

> 'if a landowner chooses to grant other persons a tenancy of agricultural land (whether or not including himself as a tenant) public policy affirmatively requires that those other tenants should have authority, or be treated as having authority, to serve an effective counter-notice under [section 26(1) of the 1986 Act] on behalf of all the tenants without his concurrence.[11]

In other words, those tenants not connected with the landlord are clothed with partnership authority to serve valid counter-notices on behalf of the whole partnership. The use of a 'nominee' co-owner to defeat the tenant's security of tenure will no longer be effective. Note, however, that problems could still arise where a lease is vested in co-owners who have, in law no partnership relationship *inter se*. The Partnership Act 1890 imposes a partnership wherever parties are carrying on a business in common with a view to profit, and participation in net profits of the farming business will be prima facie evidence of the existence of a partnership.[12] Where there is a joint tenancy whose members do *not* share net farming profits, *Featherstone v Staples* may not be of assistance, and no question of partnership authority will arise. In this event reliance may have to be placed on equitable principles if the tenancy is to be preserved (below). Problems may also arise if a partner is a limited partner under the terms of the Limited Partnerships Act 1907. Quite apart from implied partnership authority, however, a valid counter-notice *can* be given by one joint tenant, provided the person(s) giving the notice otherwise have the authority of the other joint tenants to do so. Such authority would not normally be found, for instance, if the other joint tenant(s) has been ordered to assign his whole interest in the tenancy to the

7 (1985) 273 EG 193, especially at 197.
8 [1986] 2 All ER 461, 473.
9 Eg *Greenwich London Borough Council v McGrady* (1982) 81 LGR 288.
10 [1980] AC 37.
11 [1986] 2 All ER 461 at 477.
12 See ss 1 and 2(3) to the 1890 Act.

person giving the notice, but assignment has not taken place; it may arise, however, if the order gives full power to conduct the farming business to the tenant (*Combey v Gumbrill*[13]).

(ii)   *Breach of trust: further problems.* Difficult issues of liability for breach of trust also arise. The partners hold the partnership assets (ie the tenancy) on trust for sale, and owe their co-partners an equitable duty to preserve those assets. The fact that the landlord is also a joint lessee cannot fetter his right to claim possession, and the courts will not generally interfere with his ability to do so.[14] They can in some cases, however, exercise their equitable jurisdiction to *compel* the landlord to join with his co-lessees in serving a counter-notice, in order to preserve the tenancy eg. where the tenancy is being held for third party beneficiaries.[15] Where the landlord is himself a joint lessee and partner, *Featherstone v Staples* indicates that his compliance will be dispensed with altogether so that no issue of breach of trust can arise. When the joint tenancy rule *does* apply, so that all lessees must join in serving a counter-notice, equity can in appropriate circumstances intervene to compel compliance by a reluctant joint lessee. The Court of Appeal have held, in *Harris v Black*,[16] that where joint lessees hold the tenancy for themselves alone then the equitable jurisdiction will not normally be exercised so as to compel a reluctant lessee to assume continuing obligations. It can be invoked, however, where the lease is on special terms, for instance as to how the partnership is to be dissolved. In *Sykes v Land*[17] agricultural land was let by the landlord to a partnership of himself and S, the partnership agreement providing that on dissolution of the partnership S should have the right to purchase the landlord's share of the partnership assets. The Court of Appeal accepted that on the facts any counter-notice would have to be served by both joint lessees, but exercised its equitable jurisdiction to compel the landlord to join with S in serving a counter-notice so as to preserve the tenancy (the main trust asset). Section 26(3) of the Law of Property Act 1925 requires that trustees for sale must consult those beneficially entitled to trust property and, consistent with the trust, give effect to their wishes. S, having exercised his option to acquire the partnership assets, could require the landlord to join in serving a counter-notice to preserve the tenancy.

Even where equity will not intervene to compel compliance, a joint lessee who fails to serve a counter-notice will in principle be liable for breach of trust – a point recognised in *Harris v Black*. As Fox LJ commented in *Sykes v Land*, 'in general it must be the duty of the trustees to preserve the trust property for the benefit of the ultimate beneficiaires and not let it be destroyed.'[18] The recalcitrant lessee will prima facie incur a pecuniary

13 [1990] 27 EG 85. (Final order in matrimonial proceedings ordering husband to assign tenancy, which was jointly held, into wife's sole name, and giving her sole authority to conduct the farming business. Authority to conduct the business, pursuant to the order, there held to include authority to serve notices under the agricultural holdings legislation, and counter notice served by the wife alone valid).

     For further discussion, and criticism, see (1986) EG (Muir Watt), (1985) 48 MLR 460 and (1986) 50 Conv 429 (Rodgers). And on problems of joint tenure see generally: Martin, (1978) 42 Conv 436; Webb (1983) 47 Conv 194, Landlord and Tenant: Reform of the Law (Cm 145, 1987) paras 4.20–4.26.

14 See *Bevan v Webb* [1905] 1 Ch 620; *Brenner v Rose* [1973] 1 WLR 443.
15 *Re Biss* [1903] 2 Ch 40, CA.
16 (1983) 46 P & CR 366.
17 (1984) 271 EG 1264.
18 (1984) 271 EG 1264 at 1266.

liability to make good the lost value of the tenancy to the partnership. As agricultural tenancies invariably include an absolute bar on assignment, this will be the surrender value of the tenancy. The trust assets include not only the lease itself, however, but also the statutory rights to security of tenure and continuation of the lease (a point accepted, *arguendo*, in *Harris v Black*).[19] Liability for breach of trust could therefore, in principle, extend to future loss of profits, as the tenancy will usually be the chief asset of the partnership, without which it cannot continue. Where the recalcitrant lessee is bone fide, therefore, and simply wants the tenancy to end, *Featherstone v Staples* indicates that continuing obligations under the tenancy will not be imposed – but at the expense of a potential pecuniary liability for breach of trust.

2. Sub-tenancies of agricultural land

The position of sub-tenants is a subject of some considerable complexity. Their legal position depends upon the manner in which the interest of the mesne tenant is determined, and whether (and in what form) they have received notice to quit from the latter.

(i) At common law, if the landlord terminates the tenancy of a mesne tenant by serving notice to quit, any sub-tenancy carved out of it also falls by operation of law.[20] If the tenant fails to serve a counter notice under s 26(1), therefore, the sub-tenant has no security of tenure. Not himself having received notice to quit he cannot serve a counter notice, and this would not in any event avail him against the ultimate landlord.[1] Note, however, that if the mesne tenant fails to serve a counter notice as a result of a collusive agreement with the landlord, the latter will be bound by the constructive trust arising out of his collusive part in the breach of trust by the tenant.[2] His notice to quit will be void. If, the notice to quit being valid, the tenant serves a counter-notice and tribunal proceedings ensue, rule 13 of the Agricultural Land Tribunals (Rules) Order 1978 gives the sub-tenant the right to be heard in those proceedings. Where the sub-tenant's interest falls at common law, no counter-notice having been served, his right to claim compensation for disturbance is preserved by s 63(1). He is, for compensation purposes, treated as if he had quitted in reliance on a notice to quit from the mesne tenant. Where the mesne tenant pays compensation to a subtenant, having himself given no notice to quit to the latter, his own claim for disturbance compensation against the landlord is preserved by s 63(2).

(ii) If the tenant gives notice to quit to his sub-tenant, not himself having received notice to quit from his landlord, the position between mesne tenant and sub-tenant is the same as between landlord and tenant. The sub-tenant can serve a counter-notice invoking

---

19 (1983) 46 P & CR 366, 372.
20 The rule in *Bendall v McWhirter* [1952] 2 QB 466, CA.
 1 See for instance *Harrison v Wing* (1988) 56 P & CR 358, CA.
 2 *Sparkes v Smart* [1990] EGCS 52, CA.

the tribunal consent provisions (or arbitration procedure if appropriate), and is protected vis-a-vis the tenant in the normal way.

(iii)   If the tenant has received notice to quit, and in turn serves notice to quit on his sub-tenant, the position turns on whether the tenant's own notice to quit recites the fact that he has himself received notice to quit from the landlord. If the notice to quit recites this fact then Art 16 of the Agricultural Holdings (Arbitration on Notices) Order 1987 expressly disapplies s 26(1), with the result that the sub-tenant is precluded from serving a counter-notice invoking the protection of the 1986 Act. If the landlord's notice to quit takes effect – either because no counter-notice is served by the tenant, or the tribunal gives consent – the sub-tenant's interest will terminate ·on expiration of the notice to quit. Art 16(2) provides, however, that the notice to quit given by tenant to sub-tenant shall only have effect if that given by the landlord has effect. Note, also, that the requirement of 12 months' notice does not apply to the notice to quit given by tenant to subtenant.[3] The Lord Chancellor has power, by order, to introduce provisions safeguarding the interests of sub-tenants, but this has never been done.[4] If the tenant's notice to quit fails to state that the tenant has himself received a notice to quit, the sub-tenant can serve a counter notice and, vis-a-vis the tenant, claim the protection of the 1986 Act. Even if successful, however, this will not avail him if the landlords notice to quit takes effect to terminate the tenants interest, as the common law rule will operate to destroy any sub-tenancy carved out of the tenancy.[5]

(iv)   A tenant cannot derogate from his grant by himself giving notice to quit to his landlord, or surrendering his tenancy, and in so doing destroying a sub-tenancy he has himself granted. So, by virtue of the rule in *Mellor v Watkins*,[6] a tenant cannot by *surrendering* his interest to his superior landlord destroy the interest of a sub-tenant. Section 139 of the Law of Property Act 1925 promotes the sub-tenant to hold directly of the landlord, against whom he will subsequently enjoy the protection of the 1986 Act. Neither can he destroy the sub-tenant's interest by serving notice to quit on his landlord.[7] *Semble*, in this event, also, the sub-tenant will have the protection of the 1986 Act vis-a-vis the landlord thenceforth. Note, however, that the principle does not apply where the tenant, acting in a different capacity, is also one of the landlords serving notice to quit.[8]

(v)   If the tenant's interest is forfeited, pursuant to a proviso for re-entry in the head lease, the sub-tenant's interest will fall by operation of law. He will, however, have the right to apply for relief against forfeiture pursuant to s 146(4) of the Law of Property Act 1925.

---

3   Agricultural Holdings Act 1986, s 25(2)(c).
4   See s 27 and Sch 4, para 7 of the 1986 Act.
5   See *Baron Sherwood v Moody* [1952] 1 All ER 389.
6   (1874) LR 9 QB 400.
7   *Brown v Wilson* (1949) 208 LT 144.
8   *Harrison v Wing* (1988) 56 P & CR 358, CA (tenant also executor of landlord estate).

(vi) It will be immediately apparent that the position of a sub-tenant is somewhat insecure. It has not been unknown for landlords to seek to exploit the interaction of common law and statutory rules, to defeat the tenant's security of tenure, by creating *ab initio* a 'sub' tenancy, the mesne tenancy being vested in a third party who could be relied upon not to serve a counter notice under s 26(1). If, following notice to quit, the nominal mesne tenant fails to serve a counter-notice, the sub-tenants interest would fall automatically without his being able to invoke the security of tenure provisions of the 1986 Act. Applying the rationale of *Baron Sherwood v Moody*[9] this result would ensue whether or not the tenant served notice to quit on his subtenant, provided he had not himself served a counter-notice invoking s 26(1) on his immediate landlord.

The position was reviewed by the Court of Appeal in *Gisborne v Burton*,[10] and the efficacy of the sub-tenancy as a means of avoiding security of tenure effectively destroyed. Here the landlord had granted a lease of an agricultural holding to his wife, who simultaneously granted a sub-tenancy to the 'sub' tenant. Some 20 years later the landlord's personal representatives sought possession in order to sell with vacant possession. By a majority the Court of Appeal effectively exploded the sub-tenancy scheme, applying for the first time the anti-avoidance principles enunciated in the tax cases of *W T Ramsay Ltd v IRC*[11] and *Furniss v Dawson*[12] in the landlord and tenant context. The *Ramsay* principle dictates that the fiscal consequences of a pre-ordained series of transactions should be ascertained by considering the result of the series as a whole, and not by dissecting the scheme and considering each transaction separately. According to Dillon LJ in *Gisborne* a similar principle must be applied wherever there is a pre-ordained series of tranactions which is intended to avoid some mandatory statutory provision, even if not of a fiscal nature.[13] The scheme here being of a preordained nature, the sub-tenancy having been created contemporaneously with the head tenancy, the mesne tenant was in law a mere nominee or agent of the landlord in the grant of a full tenancy to the 'sub tenant' – albeit the mesne and sub-tenancies could not individually be impugned as 'sham'. The sub-tenant's right to serve a counter-notice and invoke the security of the 1986 Act was therefore unimpaired. The precise scope of the *Gisborne* principle, if subsequently adopted, is uncertain. It will clearly apply where the grant of a sub-tenancy is 'pre-ordained', which latter will involve an investigation of the subjective intent of the parties at the time of grant. Where the interests of tenant and sub-tenant are created contemporaneously this implication will, it is suggested, be irresistable. The decision does not, however, affect the position of a true 'sub' tenant whose interest is not created as part of a pre-ordained series of transactions. The reasoning of Ralph Gibson LJ, in a powerful dissenting judgment, should also be noted and has much to commend it.[14]

---

9 [1952] 1 All ER 389.
10 [1988] 3 All ER 760.
11 [1982] AC 300, HL.
12 [1984] AC 474.
13 [1988] 3 All ER 759, 765.
14 And see further (1988) 138 NLJ 792 (J. Martin), (1988) 48 EG 64 (Muir Watt), (1989) Conv 196 (Rodgers).

Chapter 7

Removal of security: the cases for possession

A   Introduction

1.   Notice to quit and preliminary notices

Having received a notice to quit, a tenant's right to serve a counter notice, and invoke the tribunal consent procedure, is excluded where the notice to quit is given in reliance on one (or more) of the Cases for possession in Sch 3 to the 1986 Act (s 26(2) ibid).

Schedule 3 involves a procedure akin to statutory forfeiture. Accordingly, the courts have refined the common law principles of construction applicable to notices to quit, to reflect the differentiation between different types of notice by the Agricultural Holdings Act 1986. The more stringent rules applied in agricultural cases flow from the general principle that, being a species of statutory forfeiture, the provisions of s 26(2) and Sch 3 must be construed strictly so as to require landlords to fulfil their terms to the letter.[1] The general requirements as to certainty and unambiguity have already been discussed.[2] In agricultural cases the following additional requirements are insisted on by the courts:

(a)   Certainty as to type of notice

The terms of the notice to quit must be such that no reasonable tenant would be left in any reasonable doubt as to whether it is an unqualified notice (under s 26(1)), or a notice served for any of the reasons specified in Cases A–H of Sch 3 to the 1986 Act).[3] If it fails to make this clear it will be void for ambiguity. If the notice is served under Sch 3, but the ground relied on is not substantiated, it cannot take effect instead as an unqualified notice under s 26(1).[4] Despite dicta in both *Cowan v Wrayford* and *Mills v Edwards*, suggesting that notices should either give reasons appropriate to Sch 3 or *no* reasons at all, most landlords serving notice under s 26(1) will wish to give reasons so as to exclude a claim for 'additional' disturbance compensation. There is nothing to prevent an unqualified notice stating reasons as long as this would not raise doubts in the mind of the reasonable tenant, eg where

---

1 *Pickard v Bishop* (1975) 31 P & CR 108, 112, CA per Lord Denning MR.
2 Above p 102 ff.
3 *Mills v Edwards* [1971] 1 All ER 922, CA.
4 *Cowan v Wrayford* [1953] 2 All ER 1138, CA.

the landlord served an unqualified notice and stated 'as a matter of courtesy' the reasons for which it was given.[5] It must be clear on the face of an unqualified notice to quit, on pain of invalidity, that the reasons given are those in s 27(3), and not any of the reasons (breach of tenancy, etc) provided for by Sch 3. The question can be of practical importance; if the notice to quit is void a fresh one will have to be served. The requirement of at least 12 months' notice[6] means that possession could be lost for between a further one and two years.

Where notice is given under Sch 3 two further rules also apply:

(b)   Preliminary notice: certainty as to source of obligations breached

The preliminary requirements laid down in Sch 3 – particularly those relating to forfeiture for non-payment of rent, or other breach of tenancy, under Cases D and E – must be strictly complied with, or a subsequent notice to quit will be void.[7] Notices to pay rent, and to remedy breaches of tenancy, will be strictly construed against the landlord. They must strictly comply with the requirements of the Act, and must be accurate if a subsequent notice to quit is to be valid. So, for instance, a notice to pay rent must accurately identify the landlord on whose behalf it is given,[8] and if the rent demanded is specified it must be stated accurately.[9] Not every minor inaccuracy will be fatal, however. If the error is *de minimis*, of no material significance, and bears no direct relevance to the substance of the breach complained of, it will be excused. The notice must, nevertheless, correctly identify the source of the obligation whose breach is complained of.[10] It will not, however, suffice merely to say that a reasonable tenant would not have been misled by the notice.

(c)   Certainty as to case relied upon

Although Sch 3 need not be expressly referred to, a notice to quit given pursuant to one of the Cases therein contained will be void for ambiguity unless it is clear on the face of the notice *which* case for possession the landlord is relying on.[11] This is insisted upon because the tenant's remedies vary according to which Case is invoked, eg arbitration is available to challenge a Case A, B, D or E notice to quit, but not one under Cases C or F. The procedure where breach of tenancy is complained of will also vary depending upon whether it is a remediable breach (Case D) or irremediable breach (Case E), and the notice must therefore make it clear which the landlord is invoking.

5 *Hammon v Fairbrother* [1956] 2 All ER 108. And see *Harley v Moss* (1962) 181 EG 707, doubted in *Mills v Edwards* [1971] 1 All ER 922, 929, CA.
6 Section 25(1) Agricultural Holdings Act 1986.
7 *Pickard v Bishop* (1975) 31 P & CR 108, CA.
8 *Pickard v Bishop*, ibid.
9 See *Dickinson v Boucher* (1983) 269 EG 1159, CA (£650 demanded instead of £625, rendering subsequent notice to quit void.)
10 *Official Solicitor v Thomas* (1986) 279 EG 407, 414, CA (description of supplemental agreements in singular rather than plural held not to be invalid notice to remedy.)
11 *Budge v Hicks* [1951] 2 KB 335, CA.

2.   Arbitration on notices to quit

By virtue of Article 9 of the Agricultural Holdings (Arbitration on Notices) Order 1987[12] arbitration is available to challenge a notice to quit which is given for one or more of the reasons specified in Cases A, B, D or E to Sch 3. Legislative policy is to channel purely 'agricultural' disputes away from the courts, to be decided by expert arbitrators with specialist skill and knowledge. The tenant can by arbitration contest 'any question arising under the provisions of s 26(2) of, and Sch 3 to, the 1986 Act relating to any of the reasons so started', eg whether rent demanded is owing, whether there has been a breach of tenancy as alleged, or any other facts upon which the notice to quit is based. This phraseology ('any question arising . . . relating to any of the reasons so stated') is not sufficiently clear to exclude the jurisdiction of the Court to consider the validity of the notice at common law, eg whether a statement contained in it is fraudulent, rendering the notice to quit invalid and of no effect.[13] To invoke the arbitration procedure, however, the tenant must serve a written notice demanding arbitration within one month after service of notice to quit. This period is inflexible, the court having no jurisdiction to extend the time limit, whatever the merits. Note, also, that in the case of a joint vacancy all joint tenants must join in serving the demand.[14] There is no prescribed form for the tenant's demand for arbitration. Arbitration is not available to challenge notices to quit under Cases C, F, G or H. The tribunal consent and arbitration procedures being inapplicable, the only mode of challenge open to the tenant in this instance is to challenge the notice at common law, eg on grounds of ambiguity or fraud.

Where the arbitration provisions apply, arbitration is the *only* avenue available to the tenant to contest the facts on which the notice to quit is based.[15] If the tenant fails to challenge the notice by demanding arbitration within the month allowed, he cannot raise matters justiciable by arbitration under Article 9 in later possession proceedings.[16] Neither has the court jurisdiction to grant relief against forfeiture if either no arbitration was demanded, or the arbitrator upheld the notice to quit.[17]

3.   Lapse of demand for arbitration

By virtue of Article 10 of the 1987 Order, a notice demanding arbitration will cease to be effective three months after the date of its service unless, within that time, either an arbitrator has been appointed by agreement or, in default, an application has been made to the President of the RICS for the appointment of an arbitrator. If the demand lapses, the facts on which the

12 SI 1987/710.
13 *Stradbroke v Mitchell* [1990] EGCS 109, CA.
14 *Newman v Keedweel* (1977) 35 P & CR 393, *Combey v Gumbrill* [1990] 27 EG 85.
15 *Harding v Marshall* (1983) 267 EG 161, CA; *Parrish v Kinsey* (1983) 268 EG 1113, CA. For this reason notices served under Sch 3 to the 1986 Act are commonly referred to as 'incontestable' notices to quit; see *Scammell and Densham's Law of Agricultural Holdings (7th ed)* p 136 and (generally) Ch 11.
16 *Milton (Peterborough) Estates v Harris* [1989] 2 EGLR 229.
17 See *Parrish v Kinsey* (1983) 268 EG 1113 CA, a hard case where the tenant, who had poor sight, failed to realise the significance of the notice to quit served on him, and so failed to serve a demand for arbitration on the facts alleged.

notice to quit are based will be put beyond challenge, as if no demand had been served at all.[18] Clearly, it is a counsel of caution to make application for an appointment, within the three months allowed, even if an agreed appointment is likely.

4. Notice to quit in alternative

Where a notice to quit is expressed to be given in the alternative, *viz*. it is capable of taking effect either under s 26(1) or under s 26(2), then if the landlord subsequently fails to make out the facts alleged on arbitration, the notice to quit will take effect under s 26(1). In this event the time within which a counter notice under the latter provision can be served, to invoke the tribunal consent procedure, is extended to one month from the termination of the arbitration.[19] Where arbitration on such a notice takes place, it is clear from the wording of the Arbitration Order (ibid) that a counter notice invoking s 26(1) must be served within one month of its termination, even if a counter notice has already been served at some stage prior to the arbitration taking place.[20]

5. Postponement of notice to quit

Where a tenant invokes Art 9, requiring any question arising out of a notice to quit to be determined by arbitration, the operation of the notice to quit is suspended:

(i) *in all cases*, for the three-month period allowed by Art 10 for an application for the appointment of an arbitrator, and

(ii) if an appointment, or an application for such to the RICS, is made within that period, the notice to quit is further postponed until the termination of the subsequent arbitration.

If the arbitrator upholds the notice to quit, and the latter would come into effect within six months of the termination of the arbitration, the arbitrator can further postpone the operation of the notice to quit. Termination of the tenancy can be postponed in this way for a period not exceeding 12 months.[1] The postponement can be made by the arbitrator on his own motion, or on the application of the tenant, which latter must be made within 14 days after service on the tenant of the arbitrator's award.

6. Arbitration on notices to remedy

Arbitration is also available, where Case D (remediable breach of tenancy) is invoked, at the earlier stage following service of a Notice to Remedy the

---

18 See *Cawley v Pratt* [1988] 2 EGLR 6, CA.
19 Art 11, SI 1987/710.
20 '. . . the time within which a counter notice may be served by the tenant on the landlord under s 26(1) . . . *shall be* one month from the termination of the arbitration.' (italics added)
 1 Art 13(1) SI 1987/780.

breach complained of. Detailed provisions as to demands for arbitration and postponement of notices to quit are contained in Arts 3, 14 and 15 of the 1987 Order. These are discussed below in relation to Case D proceedings, as they have no relevance to proceedings under the other Cases for Possession.

B   The cases for possession

1.   Case A: retirement of statutory smallholders

The Agricultural Holdings Act 1984, following recommendations of the Northfield Committee, introduced compulsory retirement for tenants of statutory smallholdings. This was achieved by introducing what is now Case A to Sch 3 of the 1986 Act, enabling a smallholdings authority to serve a notice to quit upon the tenant attaining the age of 65. The following points should be noted:

(a)   if the result of the notice to quit would be to deprive the tenant of living accommodation occupied by him under the tenancy, then suitable alternative accommodation must be available for him, or must be available at the date the notice takes effect;

(b)   the tenancy agreement itself must contain an acknowledgement, signed by the tenant, stating that the tenancy is subject to Case A (or its predecessor, Case I to s 2(3) of the Agricultural Holdings (Notices to Quit) Act 1977;

(c)   the tenancy must have been granted on or after 12th September 1984 (ie on or after the commencement of the 1984 Act);

(d)   the right to serve notice to quit under Case A arises where the tenant has attained the age of 65; Sch 3, Case A(a). Notice to quit of at least 12 months' duration expiring on a term date will have to be given. It follows that the tenant may be 67 years of age (or older) before retirement actually takes place;

(e)   for Case A to apply the tenancy must be granted by a smallholdings authority or the minister in pursuance of Part III of the Agriculture Act 1970;[2]

(f)   the notice to quit must clearly state that it is given pursuant to Case A, or by reason of the matters contained therein.

Criteria for assessing the suitability of alternative accommodation are contained in Schedule 3, Part II, paras 1–7. These provisions are modelled on Schedule 15, Part IV of the Rent Act 1977, and are similar to the equivalent provisions in the Rent (Agriculture) Act 1976, and the Housing Act 1988 applicable to domestic and tied accommodation. The case law on the parallel Rent Act provisions, while not of authority, is of assistance in interpreting Schedule 3, Part II.

The burden of proof is on the landlord, who must discharge it as at the date of the order for possession.[3] The existence of suitable alternative accommodation can be established in one of two ways:

2 See further Chapter 15 below.
3 See *Selwyn v Hamill* [1948] 1 All ER 70, CA.

(a)   A certificate of the housing authority for the district in which the living accommodation is situated, certifying that the authority will provide suitable alternative accommodation by a specified date, is conclusive evidence that suitable alternative accommodation will be available on that date.[4]

(b)   If no housing authority certificate is obtained, accommodation is deemed to be suitable for the purposes of Case A if the premises concerned are such that the letting will be a protected tenancy under the Rent Act 1977 or an assured tenancy under the Housing Act 1988. Alternatively, the premises must be available to let to the tenant on terms that will afford him security of tenure 'reasonably equivalent' to that of a protected tenancy under the Rent Act 1977 or an assured tenancy under the Housing Act 1988.[5] If a housing Authority certificate is not available the accommodation must, additionally, be reasonably suitable to the needs of the tenant's family as regards proximity to place of work, and either similar as regards rental or accommodation to other accommodation provided by the authority to tenants with similar needs, or reasonably suitable to the means of the tenant and the needs of him and his family as regards extent and character.[6] The reference to proximity to the tenant's place of work will be superfluous in most Case A cases, as this will be the smallholding from which the tenant is retiring. It may be relevant where the tenant has other full- or part-time employment, however. The tenant's 'place of work' for these purposes will not be restricted to a particular establishment, but can, if the facts allow, be an area or a number of places of work within an area.[7] The time taken to travel from the proposed alternative accommodation to the tenant's place of work, and the means of transport available to him, can be relevant as can the physical proximity of the place of work to the alternative accommodation suggested. *Semble* the tenant's 'family' for these purposes will fall to be interpreted as in the equivalent Rent Act provisions, and may therefore include all those related to the tenant by marriage, to children and to those to whom he is in *loco parentis*. It will include those related to the tenant in any of these ways *de facto* as well as *de jure*, eg a common law wife.[8] The question whether accommodation is 'suitable' to the needs of the tenant or members of his family must be decided by reference to their housing needs, and not the relative advantages of the two properties.[9] The accommodation must be such that the tenant and the members of his family can live there in reasonably comfortable conditions, discounting any particular advantages their previous home enjoyed.[10]

The housing authority's certificate as to the accommodation it provides for tenants with similar family needs, and the rentals charged, is conclusive evidence of the facts stated in it.[11] If furniture was provided under the original smallholding tenancy, then similar furniture reasonably suitable to the tenant's needs must be provided at the alternative accommodation offered.[12] Alternative accommodation will prima facie not be suitable if it would, when occupied by the tenant and his family, be overcrowded within the meaning of

---

4 Sch 3, Part II, para 2 Agricultural Holdings Act 1986.
5 See Housing Act 1988, Sch 17, para 69.
6 Sch 3, para 3 Agricultural Holdings Act 1986.
7 *Yewbright Properties Ltd v Stone* (1980) 40 P & CR 402.
8 See *Dyson Holdings Ltd v Fox* [1976] QB 503, CA for a general discussion.
9 *Hill v Rochard* [1983] 1 WLR 478, CA.
10 *Redspring Ltd v Francis* [1973] 1 All ER 640, CA; *Hill v Rochard*, above.
11 Sch 3, para 4(2) Agricultural Holdings Act 1986.
12 Sch 3, para 4(3) ibid.

the Housing Act 1957.[13] The tenant can challenge a notice to quit by demanding arbitration within one month of its service.[14] If he does so, he can challenge any of the reasons stated in the notice, and on which it purports to be based, eg he may deny that he had attained 65 years of age at the date of the notice, or deny that the alternative accommodation offered is suitable to the needs and requirements of himself and his family. The notice to quit cannot be referred to an agricultural land tribunal if it is upheld on arbitration.

2.   Case B: non-agricultural use

The landlord can recover possession if his notice to quit is given expressly on the ground that the land is required for a use other than agriculture:

(a)   for which planning permission has been granted on an application made under the Town and Country Planning legislation, or

(b)   for which, otherwise than by virtue of any provision of the Town and Country Planning legislation, other legislation, or by virtue of Crown immunity, planning permission is not required. The fact that it is given on these grounds must be stated in the notice.

The Act confers protection on the tenant so long as the land is being used as agricultural land, but if it is no longer to be so used the parties once more have the rights given to them by the common law and the tenancy agreement.[15] The policy underlying Case B, in other words, is that as the owner of a capital asset (land) an agricultural landlord should (like any other property owner) be entitled to any increase in value that may accrue from possible development. Note also that if the contract of tenancy authorises the resumption of possession for some specified use of the land other than agriculture, on service of short notice, then the landlord can also serve notice to quit shorter than the usual 12 months' notice.[16]

Case B allows for repossession in two distinct situations: where planning permission has been obtained for non-agricultural development or use, and where such permission is not required for the development envisaged.

Land 'required' for non-agricultural use

The landlord must establish that there is a *present* intention to develop the land, and so (for instance) a mere intention to sell to an unidentified prospective developer will not suffice.[17] The land does not have to be 'required', however, for the use of the landlord himself; the requirement of any person obtaining planning permission is included, whether he be the landlord, a prospective purchaser of the landlord's reversion, or even a body intending to compulsorily purchase the latter.[18] If, however, the landlord is intending to sell to a third party developer, the latter must be identified and

13 Sch 3, para 5 ibid.
14 Art 9, SI 1987/710.
15 See *Rugby Joint Water Board v Foottit* [1972] 1 All ER 1057, HL per Lord Cross.
16 Section 25(2)(b) Agricultural Holdings Act 1986.
17 *Jones v Gates* [1954] 1 All ER 158, CA.
18 See *Rugby Joint Water Board v Foottit* [1972] 1 All ER 1057, HL.

establish a bona fide intention to develop the land with a reasonable prospect of doing so.[19] This will be a question of fact in each case.

(I) NON-AGRICULTURAL USE WITH PLANNING PERMISSION

Where Case B is invoked to facilitate redevelopment with planning permission, note that the latter must have been obtained after the lease was granted. Case B will not apply where planning permission was already in hand prior to the grant of the lease.[20] *Semble*, however, assignment following a grant of planning permission will have no effect on the availability of Case B. Note also that permission must have been applied for and obtained; it will not suffice if the proposed user is sanctioned by the implied permission of the General Development Order currently in force, or by the Use Classes Order.[1]

Special considerations apply where planning permission is obtained by the National Coal Board to carry out opencast mining operations on what has hitherto been agricultural land. Case B does not apply where the Board obtained such planning permission subject to a restoration or aftercase condition in which the use specified is use for agriculture or forestry.

(II) NON-AGRICULTURAL USE – NOT REQUIRING PLANNING PERMISSION

Most notices served under Case B will follow the obtaining of planning permission for non-agricultural use. The second limb of Case B was hitherto of use chiefly to the Crown and government departments, who are exempt from planning control by reason of their identity, and not by virtue of the Town and Country Planning legislation itself.[2] In *Bell v McCubbin*[3], however, it was held that a landlord was able to invoke Case B to serve notice to quit the farmhouse on a holding, in circumstances where he proposed to continue its residential user by letting it himself. There being no envisaged change in the non-agricultural user of the property, planning permission was not required, thus bringing the case within the second limb of Case B. The loophole in the security of tenure provisions exposed by *Bell v McCubbin* was potentially large. Whenever land or buildings were put to a non-agricultural use, the landlord would be able to repossess using Case B – *provided*, of course, that he proposed to put it to the same use himself, or to some use sufficiently similar not to constitute a 'material' change of use requiring planning permission. The decision undoubtedly undermined the position of tenants taking advantage of grant aid under the Farm Diversification or Set Aside schemes, particularly if conversion of land or buildings to some non-agricultural use was proposed. The Set Aside regulations themselves require that, before entering the scheme on the

---

19 *Paddock Investments Ltd v Lory* [1978] EGD 37, 46 per Goff LJ.
20 *Paddock Investments Ltd v Lory* [1978] EGD 37.
 1 *Ministry of Agriculture, Fisheries and Food v Jenkins* [1963] 2 QB 317, 324, CA *per* Lord Denning MR. The current order is the Town and Country Planning General Development Order 1988, SI 1988/1813, as to which see below, Chapter 12 p 261 ff.
 2 See *Ministry of Agriculture, Fisheries and Food v Jenkins* [1963] 2 QB 317, CA (application to convert grazing land to forestry). Note that, had the applicant here been a private individual, rather than a government department, s 27(3) would have applied (and not Case B) as the exemption from planning control for private forestry is contained in s 55(2)(f) of the (now) Town and Country Planning Act 1990.
 3 [1990] 1 All ER 54, CA.

non-agricultural use option, a tenant must obtain his landlord's written consent to do so.[4] Even so, a tenant diversifying in this way would be open to notice to quit under Case B – irrespective of his landlord's previous consent to the changed user. Not only therefore, did *Bell v McCubbin* undermine the security of tenure provisions of the 1986 Act itself – it was also contrary to public policy as reflected in both European Community and domestic legislation, which latter now encourages farmers to take land out of production and to diversify into alternative business uses.

For these reasons the decision has now been reversed by the Agricultural Holdings (Amendment) Act 1990.[5] The 1990 Act satisfies two objectives. Case B has been recast to reverse the decision in *Bell v McCubbin* and restrict its availability to that previously supposed. A number of new provisions have been added, however, to clarify the operation of Case B by providing for 'the various ways in which Parliament may in Acts or Parliamentary orders *not* forming part of the general town and country planning legislation, remove the need for a planning application'.[6]

The following amendments were introduced by s 1 of the 1990 Act. The new Case B provides that, in addition to the situation where planning permission has been granted on application (above p 127), a landlord can also serve notice to quit using Case B in the following circumstances:

- Where land is required for a non-agricultural use for which planning permission is granted by a general development order *by reason only* of the fact that the use is authorised by either a private or local Act, an order approved by both Houses of Parliament, or an order made under Sections 14 or 16 of the Harbours Act 1964. The provision to which this refers is currently Part II of Sch 2 to the 1988 General Development Order (SI 1988/1813). Part II gives what is, in essence, outline planning permission for development specifically authorised by a local or private Act, by a special procedure order, or by a harbour revision order made under Sections 14 or 16 of the 1964 Act. The Part II permission does not authorise any building works, or the formation of means of access, unless the prior approval of detailed plans and specifications by the local planning authority has been obtained. The approval required is limited, however, to the siting of the development and the design and/or external appearance of buildings and other structures.

- Where land is required for a non-agricultural use which is deemed to have planning permission by any provision contained in an Act of Parliament, but which does *not* form part of the enactments relating to town and country planning.[7]

- Where, similarly, land is required for a non-agricultural purpose which an Act, other than one forming part of the Town and Country Planning legislation, deems not to constitute 'development' and so does not require planning permission.

---

4 SI 1988/1352 para 6(i).
5 The 1990 Act came into force on 29th July 1990: Agricultural Holdings (Amendments) Act 1990, s 3(2).
6 See Parl. Debs. (HC) Vol 167 No 53 Col 614.
7 An example would be the Channel Tunnel Act 1987, Section 9 of which grants planning permission for development by the Tunnel Concessionaries and Kent County Council.

- Where land is required for a non-agricultural use for which permission is not required under the town and country planning legislation, 'by reason only of Crown immunity'. This provision is a redrafted version of the old Case B(b), limited to put it beyond doubt that Case B is only available where planning permission is not required because of the exemption of the Crown, and government departments, from planning control. It is therefore considerably narrower than the old formula. Where the landlord wishes to repossess in order to perpetuate a non-agricultural use *already* being practised by the tenant, as in *Bell v McCubbin*, he will no longer be able to use Case B. He will, instead, have to serve an unqualified notice to quit and (if required) seek tribunal consent to its operation – an altogether more difficult proposition, as a tribunal cannot give consent if it appears to them that a fair and reasonable landlord would not, in the circumstances, insist on possession.[8] This provision therefore restores the *status quo ante*, limits Case B to its previously understood scope, *viz.* the situation epitomised by *Ministry of Agriculture, Fisheries and Food v Jenkins*, and reverses *Bell v McCubbin*.

(III) TENANT'S CHALLENGE

The tenant can challenge a notice to quit given under Case B by serving a written notice within one month of service of the notice to quit, requiring any of the reasons stated in the notice to quit to be submitted to arbitration.[9] In this way, for instance, he can challenge whether the land concerned is really required for the non-agricultural use proposed. If (a) he fails to require arbitration within one month or (b) if an arbitrator is not appointed, or an application for the appointment of an arbitrator is not made, within three months after the date of service of his notice requiring arbitration, then the tenant will lose his right to challenge the grounds on which the notice is given.[10]

3. Case C: certificate of bad husbandry

The landlord can recover possession where an agricultural land tribunal has issued a certificate to the effect that the tenant is not fulfilling his responsibilities to farm in accordance with the rules of good husbandry. To this end the landlord can apply to the tribunal for a certificate of bad husbandry, and if satisfied that the tenant is failing to fulfil his obligation the tribunal *must* issue a certificate.[11] When deciding whether to grant a certificate they must, however, disregard any practice adopted by the tenant, the object of which is either:

(a) the conservation of flora or fauna, or of geological or physiological features of special interest, or

(b) the protection of buildings or other objects of archaeological, architectural or historical interest, or

8 See s 27(2) of the 1986 Act.
9 Art 9, SI 1987/710. See above, p 122.
10 See *Cawley v Pratt* [1988] 2 EGLR 6, CA.
11 Sch 3, para 9(1) of the 1986 Act.

(c)   the conservation or enhancement of the natural beauty or amenity of the countryside, or the promotion of its enjoyment by the public.

This disregard *only* applies, however, if conservation objectives are pursued pursuant to a term of the tenancy or other agreement with the landlord.[12]

Notice to quit must be served within six months of the grant of the certificate. When granting its certificate the tribunal can specify a minimum period of notice for termination of the tenancy of not less than two months. They can direct that this shorter period shall apply instead of the normal statutory notice period (ie 12 months expiring on a term date of the tenancy). Short notice given in accordance with the terms of a certificate of bad husbandry need not itself expire on a term date of the tenancy.

Arbitration is not available to challenge notice to quit under Case C.

4.   Case D: remediable breach of tenancy

Case D enables the landlord to serve notice to quit in two separate situations where the tenant has failed to comply with a written notice requiring him to remedy breaches of tenancy. The first is where the tenant fails to comply with a notice to pay rent, the second being where he fails to comply with a notice requiring him to remedy some other breach of tenancy, whether by doing work or otherwise.

(i)   Non-payment of rent

Case D paragraph (a) enables the landlord to serve notice to quit where the tenant has failed to comply with a written notice requiring him, within two months from the service of the notice, to pay any rent due in respect of the holding to which the notice to quit relates. The preliminary notice to pay rent must be given in Form 1, prescribed by the Agricultural Holdings (Forms of Notice to Pay Rent or to Remedy) Regulations 1987.[13]

Because failure to comply may lead to forfeiture of the tenant's interest, the statutory requirements are construed strictly against the landlord. The notice to pay must therefore demand payment expressly within the period of two months from the date of its service.[14] It must also correctly state the amount of any rent due and owing, the payment of which is demanded.[15] Moreover, the rent demanded must be actually due and owing at the date of service of the notice to pay.[16] The notice must be served by or on behalf of the person who is at the time of service the landlord. Thus in *Pickard v Bishop*[17] a notice to pay (and subsequent notice to quit) were invalid where the 'landlord' had previously transferred his reversionary estate to trustees under a discretionary trust, for the notice should have been served by the latter as landlords for the time being. The notice to pay must also accurately specify the tenants at the date of service, and if the holding is held on a joint

12 Sch 3, para 9(2).
13 SI 1987/711.
14 *Magdalen College, Oxford v Heritage* [1974] 1 All ER 1065, CA.
15 *Dickinson v Boucher* (1983) 269 EG 1159, CA.
16 *Urwick v Taylor* [1969] EGD 1106.
17 (1975) 31 P & CR 108, CA.

tenancy all joint tenants must be served.[18] Note, however, that the tenant's only mode of challenge is to demand arbitration within one month of service of notice to quit. If he fails to do so he will not be able to impugn the validity of the preliminary Notice to Pay, on which the notice to quit is based.[19] Indeed, whether the tenant has received notice to pay *at all* is a matter exclusively justiciable by arbitration under Art 9, and similarly cannot be raised in subsequent possession proceedings.[20]

A tenant purporting to exercise an option to purchase remains in occupation as a tenant until the exercise of the option is validly completed. He remains in occupation until then in the capacity of tenant, not purchaser, and his continuing liability for rent can be enforced by Notice to Pay and proceedings under Case D.[1]

The tenant must pay the rent demanded in full within the two months allowed. Substantial compliance will not suffice.[2] If he fails to do so the landlord acquires an indefeasible right to serve notice to quit, such that even if the tenant pays rent owing *after* the expiry of the two-month period, but before service of a notice to quit, this will not avail him.[3] It follows that common law rules governing the tender, appropriation and mode of payment can have an important role in deciding whether rent demanded has been paid within the statutory period.

MODE OF PAYMENT

Payment must be made in legal tender before expiry of the two-month period, unless the parties have agreed an alternative form of payment. Agreement to accept payment by cheque can be express or implied. An implied agreement to accept payment by cheque will be inferred from long usage showing this has become the accepted mode of payment by the parties – this inference will not be readily drawn, however, and must be clearly and emphatically supported by the facts.[4] Where payment by cheque is the accepted mode of payment, payment is deemed to be made when the cheque is posted.[5] So, in *Beevers v Mason*, notice to quit was bad where a cheque had been posted two days before expiry of the notice to pay, but arrived after its expiry. Moreover, although a cheque sent by post is normally at the tenant's risk, the latter passes to the landlord if he has impliedly authorised this mode of payment.[6] Payment may be deemed made, even if a cheque is lost in transit.

TENDER OF PAYMENT

Tender of payment by cheque, even if unconditional, does not discharge a debt at common law. It will, however, provide the tenant with a defence (and entitlement to costs) in subsequent possession proceedings. To plead the

---

18 *Jones v Lewis* (1973) 25 P & CR 375, CA.
19 *Magdelen College, Oxford v Heritage* [1974] 1 All ER 1065, CA (notice to pay invalid by reason of failing to give 2 months for payment, subsequent notice to quit nevertheless valid.)
20 Ibid [1974] 1 All ER 1065, 1070 per Megaw LJ.
 1 *Dockerill v Fitzpatrick* [1989] 1 EGLR 1, CA.
 2 See *Price v Romilly* [1960] 3 All ER 429.
 3 *Stoneman v Brown* [1973] 2 All ER 225, CA especially at 227 per Lord Denning MR.
 4 *Beevers v Mason* (1978) 37 P & CR 452, 459, CA.
 5 *Norman v Ricketts* (1886) 3 TLR 182, CA.
 6 *Pennington v Crossley & Son* (1897) 13 TLR 513, CA; *Luttges v Sherwood* (1895) 11 TLR 233.

defence of tender, the tenant must establish that he is still ready to make payment and must offer a *profert in curiam* of the money tendered.[7] Pleading tender does not bar the debt, rather it prevents the landlord taking advantage of his own act in failing to present cheques for payment. Payment by cheque is conditional, the debt being retrospectively satisfied on the cheque being honoured. So, if the cheque is dishonoured on presentation, and re-presented for payment *after* the two months allowed following notice to pay, Case D(a) will be available.[8] The defence of tender is only available as long as the landlord refuses to accept payment. So, for instance, it will cease to apply when a fresh cheque has been requested, provided the tenant has been given a reasonable period in which to produce one.[9] Note also that once the post has been accepted as a mode of tender, an express request for payment to be made in an alternative manner (eg to the landlord's agent) does no more than provide the tenant with an alternative destination for the payment.[10]

APPROPRIATION OF PAYMENTS

Where several instalments of rent are in arrears, the appropriation or otherwise of payments made by the tenant can have an important impact on the validity of any subsequent notice to quit. At common law the tenant, when making payment, is entitled to appropriate it to outstanding debts as he chooses. If he fails to do so, however, the initiative passes to the landlord, who may appropriate the payment to outstanding rental instalments as he chooses.[11] So, in *Official Solicitor v Thomas*[12]; by demanding payment of one half yearly instalment due, the landlord was held to have expressly appropriated £3,800 paid into court to two earlier unpaid rent instalments. Appropriation can also be *implied*, as where there is an intention to do so which is communicated to the landlord, or impliedly to be gathered from facts known to both parties.[13] It was held in *Official Solicitor v Thomas*, however, that the fact that distress cannot be levied for some rent owing does *not* have the effect of impliedly appropriating payments to later instalments accruing due.[14] Where recovery is statute-barred by the Limitation Acts payments are impliedly appropriated to debts not so barred.[15] In *Thomas* itself, the landlord was thus able to appropriate payments to unpaid Michaelmas 1980 and Ladyday 1981 rentals, which could not be distrained for, and serve notice to pay the Michaelmas 1981 rent, which could. Express appropriation of payment is clearly desirable.

NOTICE TO QUIT

If the tenant fails to pay within the time limit in the Notice to Pay, the landlord can serve notice to quit, and subsequent payment will not avail the tenant. It has been held that a notice to quit posted on the last day allowed for payment, but

---

7 *Dixon v Clark* (1848) 5 CB 365.
8 *Milton (Peterborough) Estates v Harris* [1989] 2 EGLR 229.
9 *Official Solicitor v Thomas* [1986] 2 EGLR 1, CA.
10 *Beevers v Mason* (1978) 37 P & CR 452, 460, CA.
11 See *The Mecca* [1897] AC 286, 293, HL.
12 [1986] 2 EGLR 1, CA.
13 *Leeson v Leeson* [1936] 2 KB 156, CA.
14 See section 16 of the 1986 Act, which prevents distress for rent due more than one year previously. Above chapter 3 p 98 ff.
15 *Nash v Hodgson* (1855) 6 De GM & G 474.

received on the following day, will be treated as being served on receipt. If payment has not been made by midnight on the last day of the two month period such notice to quit will be good, for the landlord will have brought himself within Case D at the date of service, notwithstanding that the notice to quit was posted earlier, during the two month time limit.[16]

The only avenue of challenge available to the tenant receiving a notice to quit is to serve notice within one month demanding arbitration.[17] He can challenge the veracity of any of the reasons stated in the notice to quit, eg (i) that the Notice to Pay was bad, demanded rent not owing, or the wrong amount, or (ii) that the notice to quit is bad as the rent was paid within the two months allowed. If he fails to demand arbitration, or his demand lapses,[18] he will not be able to challenge either the notice to pay or notice to quit, except (in the latter case) on common law grounds for ambiguity or fraud, etc.

(ii) Failure to remedy other breach of tenancy

Case D(b) enables a landlord to serve notice to quit where the tenant has failed to comply with a notice requiring him, within a reasonable time, to remedy any breach of the tenancy which is capable of being remedied.

Two distinctions must be made. The first is between those breaches which are remediable by the tenant, in respect of which proceedings under Case D will be appropriate, and those 'irremediable' breaches of tenancy to which Case E (below) is applicable. This distinction is encountered also in relation to forefeiture proceedings at common law, and the jurisprudence on the interpretation of section 146 Law of the Property Act 1925 may be of assistance (if not authority) in interpreting Cases D and E.[19] The distinction is based on the nature of the breach itself, and not on the tenant's ability to remedy it. Where the obligation concerned is a continuing one, it is remediable by a resumption of observance. If the obligation is not a continuing one, however, a single breach will normally be irremediable. Breach of a negative user covenant will normally be irremediable; breach of a positive covenant is remediable, even if of a once and for all nature. The following have been held to fall, respectively, into each category:

(a) *Remediable breaches.* Failure to repair, or to cultivate in accordance with the rules of good husbandry; failure to keep the property adequately insured;[20] failure to reside permanently in the farmhouse at the holding, contrary to a residency condition in the lease.[1]

(b) *Irremediable breaches.* Breach of covenant not to assign, sublet or part with possession;[2] breach of a covenant to lay out insurance moneys in reinstating the property following damage.[3]

16 See *French v Elliott* [1959] 3 All ER 866.
17 Art 9, SI 1987/710.
18 Art 10 *ibid.*
19 *Troop v Gibson* [1986] 1 EGLR 1, CA.
20 *Farimani v Gates* (1984) 271 EG 887, CA.
 1 *Sumnal v Statt* (1984) 271 EG 628, CA; *Lloyds Bank Ltd v Jones* [1955] 2 QB 298, CA.
 2 *Scala House and District Property Co Ltd v Forbes* [1974] QB 575, CA; *Troop v Gibson* [1986] 1 EGLR 1, CA; *Lord Stradbroke v Mitchell* [1989] 2 EGLR 5, [1990] EGCS 109, CA.
 3 *Farimani v Gates* (above).

Notice to quit under Case D(b) is only appropriate where the breach complained of is of a remediable nature.

A second distinction must be made, however, between those remediable breaches which require the tenant to do some work in order to remedy the breach complained of, and those which do not require work to effect a remedy. The procedure to be followed by the landlord under Case D(b) is different in each case. Examples of breaches, the remedy of which will involve no work of repair by the tenant, include a failure to insure, or causing the property to be used in a manner amounting to a nuisance. Failure to keep the property in a tenant-like state of repair, or breach of a term obliging the tenant to farm in accordance with the rules of good husbandry, will on the other hand be breaches requiring works of repair or maintenance by the tenant.

(A)   Form 2: Notice to do works of repair, maintenance or replacement

If the tenant is failing to keep the property in good repair or is failing to farm in accordance with the rules of good husbandry, the landlord must first serve a notice to do work in Form 2, prescribed by the Agricultural Holdings (Forms of Notice to Pay Rent or to Remedy) Regulations 1987.[4] The notice must comply with the prescribed form if it is to be valid and effective, or be 'in a form substantially to the same effect'.[5]

The notice must specify the works of repair, maintenance or replacement required to remedy the breach complained of. It must also state a reasonable period within which the tenant can carry out that work, such period to be not less than six months.[6] Once notice is served, any further notice requiring the doing of any work which is served on the tenant less than 12 months after the earlier notice shall be disregarded, unless the earlier notice was withdrawn with the written agreement of the tenant.[7]

(I) ARBITRATION ON NOTICE TO DO WORK

The procedure to be followed following service of Notice to Remedy in Form 2 is somewhat complex. The tenant can first challenge a notice in Form 2 by serving written notice requiring the matters specified in it to be referred to arbitration under the 1986 Act. If he wishes:

(a)   to contest his liability to do the work, or any part of the work, required by the notice to do work; or

(b)   to request the deletion from the notice of any item of work on the ground that it is unnecessary or unjustified; or

(c)   to request the substitution, in the case of any item of work, of a different method or material for the method or material required to be used by the notice,

then he *must*, within *one month* after service of the notice to do work,[8] serve written notice on the landlord requiring the questions he is challenging to be referred to arbitration under the 1986 Act. This is the only opportunity he

4 SI 1987/711.
5 Art 2(2), SI 1987/711.
6 Sch 3, Part II, para 10(c) Agricultural Holdings Act 1986.
7 Sch 3, Part III, para 10(b) ibid.
8 Arts 3(1) & (2), SI 1987/710.

has to challenge these three matters, and if he fails to do so he is precluded from raising them again at the notice to quit stage. The tenant's arbitration notice does not have to be in a prescribed form, but it must specify clearly those items in respect of which the tenant denies liability, those items he claims are unnecessary or unjustified, and also any method or material in respect of which he desires a substitution to be made.[9] If any of these matters are referred to arbitration, the tenant is not obliged to carry out the work which is the subject of the reference to arbitration until the arbitrator decides he is liable to do it. He must, however, carry out any work he is not referring to arbitration.

If the tenant chooses to refer any of the three matters above to arbitration, then he must also refer to arbitration at the same time any *other* question arising under the notice to work which he wishes to dispute,[10] eg he may want to allege that the time allowed for the completion of the work is unreasonable. He must do so by referring the matter to arbitration at the same time as questions (a), (b) or (c) above.

If the tenant is *not* requiring arbitration on any of the three matters above, he can either require arbitration at the notice to remedy stage or at the later notice to quit stage.[11] Moreover, even if he has referred the time allowed for the work to arbitration, he can still require arbitration on a subsequent notice to quit on the ground that something happened before the expiry of that time which rendered the time allowed to do the work unreasonably short.[12]

The arbitrator has wide powers to modify the notice so as to delete any items of work he considers unnecessary or unjustified. In doing so he must have regard to the overriding interests of good husbandry as respects the holding, and of sound management of the estate of which it forms part, or which it constitutes.[13] He may also, of course, decide that the tenant is under no obligation to do the work required, in which case the notice to do work will be of no effect. Where the tenant refers to arbitration the methods and materials to be used to carry out the work, the arbitrator can modify the notice to substitute different methods or materials, provided he is satisfied that those specified in the notice itself would involve undue difficulty or expense. The materials or methods substituted must, however, be as effective for the purpose as those originally specified in the notice.[14] The time within which work is to be done is extended until the termination of the arbitration.[15] The time stipulated in the notice is not extended, however, in respect of work which has not been referred to arbitration, and this must be completed by the tenant within the time allowed, on pain of notice to quit. If the tenant is referring his liability to do work to arbitration, he may wish to carry out any work which is the subject of that reference without waiting for the arbitrator's award. If he does so, and the arbitrator subsequently finds that he has carried out work which was not his liability, then the arbitrator can

9 Art 3(3) SI 1987/710.
10 Art 4(1) ibid.
11 Art 4(2) ibid.
12 Art 4(3) ibid.
13 Art 5(a) ibid.
14 Art 5(b) ibid.
15 Art 6(1) ibid.

determine the reasonable cost of the work that has been done and this will be recoverable from the landlord.[16]

Where the arbitrator finds that the tenant is liable to comply with a notice to do work, or part of it, he can further extend the time for doing that work by such period as he thinks fit.[17] Where an extension of time is allowed the arbitrator can, either on his own motion, or on an application made by the landlord not less than 14 days after the end of the arbitration, set a fixed date for the termination of the tenancy if the tenant fails to comply with the notice within the extended period.[18] That date cannot be earlier than the date on which the tenancy could have been terminated by notice to quit served on the expiration of the time *originally* specified in the notice to do work, or six months after the end of the extended period for compliance, whichever is the later.[19] If the landlord applies for the fixing of a termination date he must give notice of application to the tenant, who will then be entitled to be heard on the application. The question may, however, be determined as part of the arbitration proceedings on the arbitrator's own motion, and not by separate application. If the tenant then fails to do the work requested within the extended period, the landlord must serve his notice to quit within *one month* after the expiry of the extended time. If he does so, however, the notice to quit will be valid even though it does not expire on a term date of the tenancy and is of less than 12 months' duration, provided (of course) that it expires on the date for termination fixed by the arbitrator.[20]

(II) ARBITRATION ON NOTICE TO QUIT

If the tenant fails to comply with a notice to do work, the landlord can serve a Case D notice to quit. It is too late at this stage for the tenant to contest his liability to do the work, the necessity of any of the work required, or the methods or materials specified in the notice to do work. Neither can he challenge other matters previously raised on arbitration (other than the time allowed for compliance). He may wish to contest other issues, eg that he has done the work in question or that something has occurred which rendered the time originally allowed in the notice unreasonable. If he wishes to raise these or other matters he must serve a written notice within one month of service of the notice to quit, requiring them to be referred to arbitration under the 1986 Act.[1] The operation of the notice to quit is then suspended until the termination of the arbitration.[2] If the tenant is alleging that the time specified in the notice to do work, while originally reasonable, has become unreasonable by virtue of subsequent events, then the arbitrator has to extend the period allowed for the work to be done. His powers to do so are similar to those available at the notice to do work stage. He can extend the period allowed for the work to be completed by such period as he considers reasonable, having regard to the length of time which has elapsed since the original service of the notice to do work.[3] Where he does so, he has similar

16 Art 8 SI 1987/710.
17 Art 6(2) ibid.
18 Art 7(1) ibid.
19 Art 7(2) ibid.
20 Art 7(4) ibid.
 1 Art 9, SI 1987/710.
 2 Art 11(1) ibid.
 3 Art 14 ibid.

powers to those available at the earlier stage to fix a termination date of the tenancy in the event of non-compliance by the tenant within the extended period.[4] The landlord must then serve a second notice to quit within one month of the expiration of the extended term. The second notice to quit will be valid even though it is of less than 12 months' duration and expires on a date other than a term date of the tenancy.[5] The second notice cannot take effect, however, if the tenant serves a counter-notice within one month of service, unless the agricultural land tribunal has consented to its operation. On an application by the landlord for consent to the operation of his second notice to quit the tribunal *must* consent unless it appears to them that a fair and reasonable landlord would not insist on possession. In so deciding the tribunal must have regard to the extent to which the tenant has failed to comply with the notice to do work, the consequences of that failure and the circumstances surrounding it.[6]

Where the notice to quit has effect following an arbitration, or because a tribunal has consented to its operation, the tenant can apply to the arbitrator for a postponement of termination of the tenancy. If the notice to quit would come into operation within six months of the termination of the arbitration or the granting of tribunal consent, the tenant can *within* 14 days of the termination of arbitration or the giving of consent apply to the arbitrator, who has power to postpone the termination of the tenancy for a period not exceeding 12 months.[7] He must serve notice of application on the landlord, who has a right to be heard on the application.

If the tenant claims to have done the work in question he must show that he has complied with the notice in its entirety. Failure to comply with one of the requirements of a notice to do work, if the unfulfilled requirement is not *de minimis* and is in respect of a term of the tenancy which was consistent with the tenant's responsibility to farm in accordance with the rules of good husbandry, constitutes sufficient failure for the purposes of Case D.[8] Substantial compliance will not suffice. If the notice requires more than one breach of tenancy to be remedied then the period allowed for the work in the notice must be such as to allow time to remedy *all* the breaches specified. If the period allowed is insufficient to allow all the work specified to be done, then the notice to do work (and a subsequent notice to quit) would be invalid.[9] However, if the period specified is sufficient to remedy all such breaches, but it subsequently becomes impossible to remedy some of them due to changed circumstances, it seems the landlord *can* rely on those matters which have not been remedied to serve notice to quit. Thus in *Shepherd v Lomas*[10] a landlord served notice to do work specifying a reasonable period for compliance, but then failed to provide the materials needed to remedy one group of breaches until almost the end of the period, when it was clearly impossible for the work to be completed in time. Because the tenant had not remedied *any* of the breaches complained of, the landlord could rely on those in respect of which the tenant had to provide materials

4 See Art 15 SI 1987/710.
5 Art 15(4) ibid.
6 Art 15(6) ibid.
7 Art 13(1) ibid.
8 *Price v Romilly* [1960] 3 All ER 429.
9 See *Wykes v Davis* [1975] 1 All ER 399, CA especially at 404 per Buckley LCJ.
10 [1963] 2 All ER 902, CA.

himself to serve a valid notice to quit. Although the 'reasonableness', and hence the validity, of a notice to do work will depend largely upon the length of time allowed for the work required to remedy breaches of tenancy, nevertheless the personal circumstances of the tenant will also be relevant. The arbitrator, when deciding whether the time allowed is reasonable, must weigh the landlord's interest against factors relied on by the tenant for giving him a reasonable opportunity to fulfil his obligations.[11]

(III) TRIBUNAL CONSENT TO NOTICE TO QUIT

Section 28 of the 1986 Act places one final hurdle in the path of the landlord seeking possession. The tenant can, within one month of the giving of the notice to quit, serve a counter-notice requiring that section 28 shall apply, in which case the notice to quit is ineffective until the landlord obtains the tribunal's consent to its operation. The procedure is open to the tenant either instead of, or in addition to, demanding arbitration on the notice to quit.

The tenant's counter-notice must make it clear whether arbitration has also been demanded or not, on pain of invalidity for ambiguity. Arbitration prevails as a remedy, however. If a notice demanding arbitration is served within one month of notice to quit, the tenant's counter-notice is of no effect.

If a valid counter-notice is given the landlord must apply to the tribunal for consent to his notice to quit. On such an application the tribunal *must* consent unless it appears to them that, having regard:

(a)   to the extent to which the tenant has failed to comply with the notice to do work;

(b)   to the consequences of his failure to comply with it, and

(c)   to the circumstances surrounding the tenant's failure,

that a fair and reasonable landlord would not insist on possession (s 28(5)).

The identification of the issues which the tribunal should at this stage refer to (an amendment introduced by the Agricultural Holdings Act 1984, s 7) is clearly intended to restrict the tribunal's discretion by cutting out wider issues, such as hardship. Whether it completely does so may be questioned, however, as the criteria of 'circumstances surrounding any such failure' is quite wide. *Quaere*, therefore, whether this provision completely overrules the decision in *Clegg v Fraser*,[12] as was apparently the intention. The tribunal is clearly, however, entitled to look at issues of substantial compliance, and so the tenant who has (albeit belatedly) complied by the time of the hearing can procure a refusal of consent, and in so doing frustrate the landlord at the last stage of a lengthy procedure.

(b)   Form 3: notice to remedy not involving work

Any notice to remedy which does *not* involve the doing of any work of repair, maintenance or replacement by the tenant must be in Form 3, prescribed by the Agricultural Holdings (Forms of Notice to Pay Rent or to Remedy) Regulations 1987. The form used must, as with notices to do work, follow precisely that set out in the Schedule to the 1987 regulations if a

11 See *Sumnal v Statt* (1984) 271 EG 628, CA.
12 (1982) 264 EG 144.

valid notice to quit under Case D(b) is subsequently to be given. Notice to remedy in Form 3 is appropriate where, for instance, the tenant is failing to keep the premises adequately insured, or is allowing a sub-tenant in occupation to cause a public nuisance or commit other breaches of tenancy.

When notice to remedy is served the tenant cannot at that stage refer either his liability to comply, or any other question as to the validity of the notice, to arbitration. He can, however, claim arbitration on these issues later, if a notice to quit is subsequently served, on the ground that he has failed to comply with the notice to remedy. Where this happens he has one month following service of notice to quit in which to serve a notice requiring the validity of the notice to remedy, and his liability to comply with it, to arbitration. This is his only opportunity to challenge his liability to comply.

The period for compliance specified in the notice to remedy must be reasonable, but no minimum is prescribed. There are also no restrictions on the service of subsequent notices.[13]

During the arbitration the notice to quit is suspended.[14] It resumes effect if the arbitration upholds the notice to quit. In this case, however, if the notice would come into effect on or within six months after the termination of the arbitration, the tenant has 14 days after the end of the arbitration in which to apply for a postponement in its operation. The tribunal can postpone the termination of the tenancy for a period not exceeding 12 months.[15]

If the notice to remedy allowed a reasonable period for compliance, but that period has become unreasonable because of subsequent events, the arbitrator has power to extend the period by such amount as he considers reasonable.[16] He has power to specify a date for termination of the tenancy in the event of non-compliance by the tenant within the extended period.[17]

If the tenant fails to have the notice to quit struck down on arbitration, he cannot then go to the agricultural land tribunal. The landlord cannot be required to apply for tribunal consent to the operation of the notice to quit.[18]

5. Case E: irremediable breach of tenancy

Case E permits the landlord to serve notice to quit where there has been an irremediable breach by the tenant of a term or condition of the tenancy that was not inconsistent with the fulfilment by the tenant of his obligation to farm in accordance with the rules of good husbandry. The breach must also be one which causes material prejudice to the landlord's interest. The distinction between remediable and irremediable breaches of tenancy has already been discussed. Thus, for instance, Case E will apply where the tenant has assigned, sublet or parted with possession of the holding, without the landlord's consent, in breach of covenant.[19] It will also apply where the tenant is in breach of some other obligation of a non-recurrent nature, eg

13 *Cf* Form 2 (above).
14 Art 12, SI 1987/710.
15 Art 13 ibid.
16 Art 14 ibid.
17 Art 15 ibid.
18 *Cf* proceedings under Form 2, above.
19 See *Troop v Gibson* [1986] 1 EGLR 1, CA; *Lord Stradbroke v Mitchell* [1989] 2 EGLR 5, [1990] EGCS 109, CA.

failing to apply insurance moneys in reinstating the property within a reasonable period after damage by fire. The notice to quit must specify clearly that it is given under Case E, and must in particular make it clear that the breach complained of is irremediable, and not simply a remediable breach to which Case D will apply. If it fails to do so it will be void for ambiguity. For these purposes a conservation covenant is not to be regarded as inconsistent with the tenant's obligation to farm in accordance with the rules of good husbandry.[20]

A novel attempt to use Case E as a vehicle to contract out of security of tenure altogether, and to deny the tenant the right to refer an ordinary, unqualified notice to quit to a tribunal for consent, was defeated in *Johnson v Moreton*.[1] The landlord there inserted a clause in the lease whereby the tenant covenanted not to serve a counter-notice following notice to quit. If enforceable this covenant would have had the effect of denying the tenant the right to require the landlord to apply to the tribunal for consent to the operation of an unqualified notice to quit. When the landlord served notice to quit, the tenant nevertheless served a counter-notice, thus rendering the notice to quit ineffective without tribunal consent. The landlord then served a Case E notice to quit, claiming that the service of a counter-notice to his original notice to quit was an irremediable breach of tenancy, and materially prejudiced his interest. It was here held that the clause in the lease was void and unenforceable, being an attempt to contract out of the protective pro-visions of the Agricultural Holdings Acts.[2] Security of tenure is granted by the 1986 Act as a matter of public interest, and not private right, and contracting-out (in whatever form) is not permissable. It followed that the landlord could not rely on Case E, as there had been no breach of tenancy.

Special provision is made for tenancies of smallholdings let by a smallholdings authority or the Minister. By virtue of Sch 3, para 11(1), when considering whether the interest of the landlord has been 'materially prejudiced' by the breach complained of, regard must be had not simply to the narrow consideration of the effect of the breach on the holding itself, but also to its wider effect on the carrying out by the landlord of his arrangements for the letting and conduct of smallholdings. If a breach, such as unauthorised subletting, has the effect of frustrating the objects of a smallholding scheme, this may weigh as 'material prejudice' even if the landlord's reversionary interest has not been damaged in the narrower sense applicable in other cases.

Arbitration under Art 9 of the Arbitration on Notices Order 1987 is available following notice to quit, and is the only forum for questioning the reasons stated in the notice.

6.   Case F: insolvency of tenant

Notice to quit under Case F can be served where the tenant is insolvent. The protection given to agricultural landlords against the tenant's bankruptcy is extensive, and was further strengthened by amendments introduced in the

---

20 See Sch 3, Pt II, para 11(2) Agricultural Holdings Act 1986.
 1 [1980] AC 37.
 2 (1977) 35 P & CR 378 CA; affd on different grounds [1980] AC 37, HL. The relevant provision was, at that time, s 2(1) Agricultural Holdings (Notices to Quit) Act 1977.

Agricultural Holdings Act 1984. A tenant is insolvent for these purposes where either:

(a) if he is an individual, he has become bankrupt or has made a composition or arrangement with his creditors, or has had a receiving order made against him; or

(b) Where the tenant is a company, a winding-up order has been made against it, or a resolution for voluntary winding-up has been passed with respect to it. A resolution for a voluntary winding-up will not have this effect if it is passed solely for the purposes of a reconstruction, or for an amalgamation with another company.[3]

Where the tenant is insolvent, notice to quit does not have to be of 12 months' duration and short notice can be given.[4] Most leases will include a proviso for re-entry on bankruptcy, and so the landlord will have the option of proceeding instead by way of forfeiture proceedings under the general law. Under section 146(1) of the Law of Property Act 1925 the court has limited power to suspend forfeiture in bankruptcy cases. However, in the case of agricultural property even this limited power is excluded.[5]

Arbitration is not available to challenge a Case F notice to quit. The tenant will only be able to defend possession proceedings by alleging the notice to quit is bad in law, or that Case F does not apply at all (for instance because he is not bankrupt as alleged).

7. Case G: death of tenant

The security of tenure conferred by the 1986 Act is intended to accrue for the lifetime of the tenant, subject to the possibility of succession rights being available should Part IV of the 1986 Act apply.[6] Accordingly, Sch 3 Case G enables the landlord to serve notice to quit:

(a) following the death of a person who immediately before his death was the sole (or sole surviving) tenant under the contract of tenancy and

(b) not later than the end of a period of three months, beginning with the date on which notice in writing (a 'relevant notice') was served on him by the executor or administrator of the tenant's estate informing him of the tenant's death. If an application for succession is made, the landlord has three months from being given notice of application pursuant to s 40(5).[7]

'Relevant Notice'

For the purpose of time running against the landlord, the 'relevant notice' served by the deceased tenant's executors or personal representatives must be in terms which make it sufficiently clear to the ordinary landlord that the

3 See s 96(2) Agricultural Holdings Act 1986.
4 Section 25(2)(a) ibid.
5 See s 146(1)(a), Law of Property Act 1925.
6 See s 34 of the 1986 Act.
7 See Sch 3, Part III, para 12(b) ibid.

tenant is purporting to exercise his rights under the 1986 Act.[8] The fact that the landlord is aware of the tenant's death is irrelevant if no sufficient notice has been served, and time will not start running against him.[9] A cheque drawn by the executors in payment of rent, without more, is thus not a relevant notice for these purposes,[10] neither will a letter from solicitors stating that they do (or do not) act in connection with the estate of the late tenant.[11] The notice must be explicit, and clearly purport to put the landlord on notice of the tenants death for the purpose of Case G. It follows from para 12 of Sch 3 to the 1986 Act that if no executor has been appointed, or letters of administration obtained, no 'relevant notice' can be served.[12] Where notice is received from the tenant's executors or administrator, *and* a succession application ensues, the three-month period for notice to quit runs from the date of the *first* of those events to occur.[13]

The following points should be noted:

(i)   Joint tenancies

Until recast in its present form in 1976,[14] Case G enabled the landlord to give notice to quit on the death of the tenant with whom the contract of tenancy was made. The anomalous result was that notice to quit could be given on the original tenant's death even if he had (perhaps some considerable time previously) assigned the tenancy.[15] The reference in the remodelled Case G to 'the death of the sole (or sole surviving) tenant' removes this possibility. It does mean, however, that where the tenancy is vested in joint tenants, Case G can only be invoked on the death of the last surviving tenant. Moreover, if the joint tenancy includes a corporate tenant with perpetual succession, the right to invoke Case G cannot arise: such a tenant cannot 'die' in the required sense.[16] 'Quite clearly, landlords are well advised to avoid joint tenancies and, where the lease is oral or contains no non-assignment clause, to use the machinery provided by s 6 and Sch 1 to the 1986 Act to secure the insertion of a covenant against alienation.[17]

(ii)   It is specifically provided that the 'tenant' (the death of whom triggers Case G) does not include an executor, administrator, trustee in bankruptcy or other person deriving title from a tenant by operation of law. If the landlord fails to serve notice to quit within the 3 months allowed (see above), his position may be prejudiced in that the estate will vest in the tenant's

---

8 *Lees v Tatchell* [1990] 1 EGLR 10, 14 per Parker LJ.
9 The curious situation arose in *Lees v Tatchell* (above) that the landlord had attended the tenant's funeral, but was able to serve notice to quit because no sufficient notice of death was formally served.
10 *Lees v Tatchell* [1990] 1 EGLR 10.
11 *BSC Pension Fund Trustee Ltd v Downing* [1990] 1 EGLR 4.
12 *BSC Pension Fund v Downing* ibid.
13 Sch 3, para 12(b) (ii) Agricultural Holdings Act 1986.
14 By s 16 of the Agriculture (Miscellaneous Provisions) Act 1976.
15 See *Clarke v Hall* [1961] 2 QB 331.
16 There is evidence to suggest that the amendment to Case G effected in 1976 has led to more frequent assignment of farm leases, although it must be admitted that few modern leases fail to contain a prohibition on assignment and subletting (see Scammell and Densham's *Law of Agricultural Holdings* (7th Ed) at pp 192–3.)
17 See above Chapter 3 p 53 ff.

personal representatives, the subsequent death of whom will not trigger the applicability of Case G.[18]

(iii)   The notice to quit must be served *not later* than the expiry of three months of written notice of the tenant's death, or notice of a succession application. Notice to quit can, however, be validly given *prior* to receipt of written notice of death from the tenant's personal representatives.

(iv)   Where an application for succession to the tenancy is made under Part IV of the 1986 Act, the notice to quit has only qualified effect. By virtue of section 43 ibid it cannot have effect unless *either* no application to succeed to the tenancy is made within the time allowed, *or* none of the applicants is found to be eligible and suitable for succession, *or* the tribunal consents to the operation of the notice to quit under section 44. Where an applicant has been found 'eligible' and 'suitable' for succession, the latter provision gives the landlord a final opportunity to prevent a succession tenancy being awarded by applying for the tribunal's consent to the notice to quit. The tribunal can grant consent on one or more of the grounds specified in section 27, ie the notice is assessed in the same way as an unqualified notice given subject to the tribunal consent procedure. If the tribunal grant consent within three months prior to the original operative date of the notice to quit, or at any time thereafter, they can (on the tenant's application) specify that it take effect from a later date. The latter must be not later than the end of three months after the original operative date, or the date of granting consent, whichever last occurs.[19]

(v)   To be valid the notice to quit must state that it is given pursuant to Case G on the death of the sole (or sole surviving) tenant. It should be served on the tenant's personal representatives if they have obtained a grant and/or the person responsible for the control of management of the holding.[20] In the event of doubt, notice to quit should also be served on the President of the Family Division of the High Court.[1]

Case H: Ministry certificate

Case H enables the Minister of Agriculture, or Secretary of State for Wales (whichever is appropriate), to serve notice to quit in order to enable him to effect an amalgamation or reshaping of an agricultural unit. The Agriculture Act 1967 gives the Minister statutory power to acquire land for the purpose of reshaping or amalgamating holdings. Any tenancy of land so acquired should contain an acknowledgement that the tenancy is subject to Case H or s 29 of the 1967 Act. If it does so, then Case H enables the Minister to certify that the notice to quit is given for the purpose of enabling him to use, or dispose of, the land so as to effect an amalgamation or reshaping of an agricultural unit.[2] If a certificate is given the notice to quit will take effect

---

18 *Cf Costagliola v Bunting* [1958] 1 All ER 846.
19 See s 43(6) and (7) Agricultural Holdings Act 1986.
20 See s 93(3) ibid.
1 Notice addressed to the latter should be sent c/o the Treasury Solicitor, Queen Anne's Chambers, 28 Broadway, London SW1H 9JS: *Practice Direction* [1985] 1 All ER 832, Fam Div.
2 As to which see s 26(1) of the 1967 Act.

under Case H, arbitration not being available to challenge the notice in this instance.

C Servicemen tenants

The security of tenure provisions of the 1986 Act are modified in some respects by s 30 and Sch 5 *ibid* to confer additional protection on certain categories of serviceman tenant.

1. Qualifying servicemen

Protection extends to a serviceman who performs a period of 'relevant service',[3] other than a short period of training. This applies to most forms of service in the reserve and auxiliary services, though not to regular servicemen. A serviceman performing a period of 'relevant service', so defined, enjoys for present purposes a 'period of residence protection' comprising his period of service and the four months following its termination.[4] The special provisions of Sch 5 only apply, however, to an agricultural holding which comprises a dwelling-house occupied by the person responsible for the control of the farming of the holding[5] or any part of a larger agricultural holding, which part comprises or consists of such a dwelling-house.[6]

2. Control of notice to quit

Special rules apply where a serviceman tenant receives notice to quit during his period of residence protection.[7] By virtue of Sch 5, para 3, notwithstanding that notice to quit is given pursuant to Cases B to G, he can serve a counter notice requiring tribunal consent to its operation. When considering whether to grant consent, the tribunal must, if satisfied that any of Cases B to G are made out, consider whether, and to what extent, the existence of those circumstances is directly or indirectly attributable to the tenant's performing the service in question. They must also, in any case, consider to what extent the giving of consent to the notice to quit during the period of service residence protection would cause special hardship to the tenant. In doing so they must have regard to circumstances either directly or indirectly attributable to the serviceman's performing that period of service.[8] Similarly, protection applies where a tenant has received notice to quit, and subsequently enters into relevant service before the tribunal have decided whether or not to withhold consent to the operation of the notice to quit.[9]

---

3 As defined in s 64 of the Reserve and Auxiliary Forces (Protection of Civil Interests) Act 1951.
4 Sch 5, para 1 Agricultural Holdings Act 1986.
5 As to which see s 10 of the Rent Act 1977.
6 Sch 5, para 2(2) Agricultural Holdings Act 1986.
7 Sch 5, para 2(1) ibid.
8 Sch 5, para 3(2) ibid.
9 Sch 5, para 4 ibid.

Article 17(2) of the Arbitration on Notices Order[10] provides that the tribunal may, if the notice to quit was given pursuant to Case B, D or E and it is expedient to do so, require any of the reasons stated in the notice to be determined by arbitration before they consider whether to consent to the notice to quit. Article 17(3) modifies the operation of art 9 *ibid* so that a failure to demand arbitration on the notice to quit will not preclude the tenant from challenging the reasons stated in subsequent tribunal proceedings for consent.

D   Proviso for re-entry and forfeiture

It has been seen that the policy of the Agricultural Holdings Act 1986, unlike that of the business tenancy legislation, is not to prescribe a statutory mode of termination, but rather to leave a landlord free to pursue the normal modes of termination available at common law. It then provides security of tenure by subjecting the most commonly used method of termination – notice to quit – to extensive statutory restrictions. The natural corollary of this approach, however, is that the landlord's *other* remedies at common law remain unaffected. The landlord's remedies for breach of tenancy under the 1986 Act (above) therefore exist alongside the general law governing forfeiture for breach of covenant, and in no way exclude the application of the general law governing forfeiture pursuant to a proviso for re-entry in the lease itself. There is a question whether, as the courts generally strike down contractual terms which diminish the tenant's statutory protection,[11] the landlord must confine himself to the statutory cases for possession where these cover the breaches of covenant complained of, and not exercise a proviso for re-entry in the lease itself.[12] The validity of proceeding by way of forfeiture in such circumstances was, however, accepted *arguendo* in *Kent v Conniff*.[13] Furthermore, in *Parry v Million Pigs Ltd*[14] the requirements as to notice of re-entry in a forfeiture clause were examined in detail, no issue being made as to the availability of forfeiture as a remedy *per se*.

There can, therefore, be little doubt as to the availability of forfeiture under the general law as an alternative remedy alongside the statutory remedies provided for in Part II and Sch 3 of the 1986 Act.

1.   Proviso for re-entry

There is no implied proviso for re-entry. The lease must therefore include an express proviso permitting re-entry where (usually) the tenant is in breach of any of the covenants in the lease, or becomes bankrupt, or where the rent is unpaid for a fixed period. If the tenancy is oral, or is in writing but does *not*

10 SI 1987/710.
11 See *Johnson v Moreton* [1980] AC 37, HL; *Featherstone v Staples* [1986] 2 All ER 461.
12 This argument developed, for instance, in Yates & Hawkins, *Landlord & Tenant Law* (2nd Ed) at p 791.
13 [1953] 1 All ER 155, CA (the breaches of covenant at issue in this case would, it is suggested, equally have grounded action under what is now Case D to Sch. 3 of the 1986 Act, although the landlord there proceeded by way of forfeiture proceedings upon the proviso for re-entry in the lease itself).
14 [1980] 260 EG 281.

contain a proviso for re-entry, either party can refer the terms of the agreement to arbitration under Section 6 of the 1986 Act. A proviso for re-entry in the event of the tenant not performing his obligations under the tenancy is one of the matters specified in the First Schedule to the 1986 Act, and which the arbitrator must therefore include in his award. Sch 1 does not prescribe the form the proviso should take, and the special considerations applicable to agricultural leases should be considered in its terms.[15] The landlord's right to forfeit the lease under the general law is subject to the tenant's right to relief against forfeiture on payment of rent and costs, and on remedy of other breaches of covenant.

Forfeiture must be effected by either peaceful re-entry or proceedings for forfeiture.[16] The tenancy is terminated on judgment, which then relates back to terminate the tenancy from the date of issue of the writ.[17] The statutory restrictions on forfeiture vary according to whether forfeiture for non-payment of rent, or forfeiture for breach of other covenants, is in issue.

2.   Forfeiture for non-payment of rent

Unless the lease dispenses with the need to make formal demand, a formal demand for rent due must be made before proceedings can be commenced.[18] By virtue of Section 210 of the Common Law Procedure Act 1852 this is not necessary where six months' rent is in arrears and insufficient distress is to be found on the premises. Sections 16–18 of the Agricultural Holdings Act 1986[19] limit the goods on which distress can be levied by excluding agisted stock, and machinery and stock on hire from third parties. For Section 210 to apply there must, therefore, be insufficient distrainable goods to cover the rent owing, excluding those items protected by the 1986 Act.

County Court jurisdiction is limited to cases where the rateable value of the property concerned does not exceed £1,000.[20] Whether proceedings are pursued in the County Court or High Court the tenant will be entitled to relief if he pays into Court the rent owing and the landlord's expenses. Equity regards forfeiture as merely security for non-payment of rent.[1]

Where six months' rent is in arrears, and proceedings are in the High Court, sections 210–212 of the Common Law Procedure Act 1852 apply.[2]

---

15 Section 6 and Sch 1 para 8 of the 1986 Act. See Chapter 3 pp 62–3 ff for the requirement of notice of re-entry in agricultural leases.
16 Section 2 Protection from Eviction Act 1977 makes it unlawful to enforce forfeiture of a dwelling (such as a farm house) otherwise than by legal proceedings. Section 6 of the Criminal Law Act 1977 makes it a criminal offence to use or threaten violence in order to secure entry to premises against the wishes of someone present on those premises who is opposed to entry.
17 *Canas Property Co Ltd v KL Television Services* [1970] 2 QB 433, CA.
18 See *Doe d Dixon v Roe* (1849) 7 CB 134, *Acocks v Phillips* (1860) 5 H & N 183 for common law requirements.
19 See Chapter 5 p 98 ff above. Note also that unripe growing crops can be subject to distress – *Ex p Arnison* (1868) LR 3 Exch 56.
20 The County Court has jurisdiction where the rateable value of the property is £1,000 or less – CCA 1984, section 21 and AJA 1973 Sch 2.
 1 See for instance the statement of the doctrine in *Chandless v Nicholson* [1942] 2 KB 321, CA at 323 per Lord Greene MR.
 2 The 1852 Act does not apply at all if less than six months' rent is owing – *Standard Pattern Co Ltd v Ivey* [1962] Ch 432.

The tenant can stay the proceedings at any time up to trial by paying into court the rent owing and landlord's costs. If he is unable to pay the rent prior to judgment, he has six months after execution of the judgment in which to apply for relief, after which relief against forfeiture is barred. If less than six months' rent is owing, the tenant must fall back on the general equitable jurisdiction to grant relief.

In the County Court the tenant's right to relief is governed by Section 138 of the County Courts Act 1984. If the tenant pays rent and costs into court at least five days before the return day, he has an automatic right to relief. If the landlord makes out his case, the court must make an order for possession at the end of a period of at least four weeks, unless within that period the rent and costs are paid into court. The period for payment can be extended on the tenant's application.[3] If payment is not made within the stipulated period the tenant is 'barred from all relief'.[4] This is subject to the proviso that the tenant can apply for relief up to six months from the date on which the lessor recovers possession.[5]

3. Forfeiture for breach of other covenants

Section 146 of the Law of Property Act 1925 requires service of a formal written notice before forfeiture proceedings can commence. The notice must:[6]

(i) specify the breach complained of;
(ii) if the breach is capable of remedy, it must require the tenant to remedy the breach, and
(iii) it must require the tenant to make compensation in money for the breach.

If the tenant fails to remedy the breach within a reasonable time after service of the notice (where the breach is remediable) and fails to make reasonable compensation to the landlord's satisfaction, then the landlord can proceed to enforce the proviso for re-entry in forfeiture proceedings. All joint tenants must be served with a Section 146 notice.[7]

If the breach complained of is remediable an omission in the statutory notice to require it to be remedied will invalidate the notice. On the other hand, if the breach is irremediable the landlord need not leave a reasonable period after service of notice before issuing proceedings. The distinction between remediable and irremediable breaches is usually equated with that between breaches of a single obligation as opposed to a continuing one. Where a single obligation is involved a breach, once it occurs, cannot be undone. Where the obligation is a continuing one, however, past breaches can be remedied by resumption of observance of the obligation and the making of appropriate compensation. Reference to a 'continuing' breach

---

3 Section 138(3) CCA 1984.
4 Section 138(7) CCA 1984. Relief cannot be sought in the High Court. See *Di Palma v Victoria Square Property Co Ltd* [1986] Ch 150, CA.
5 Section 138(9A) CCA 1984, inserted by s 55 Administration of Justice Act 1985.
6 Section 146(1) Law of Property Act 1925.
7 *Blewett v Blewett* [1936] 2 All ER 188, CA.

simply means a breach of a continuing obligation and does not refer to the tenant's ability to remedy a single breach.[8]

Breach of a covenant against assignment, sub-letting or parting with possession is an irremediable breach, ie a breach once and for all and not a continuing breach.[9] Similarly, breach of a covenant to lay out insurance moneys in reinstating the property, being subject to an implied obligation to do so within a reasonable time, is a breach of a single obligation and irremediable.[10] A breach of covenant to keep premises insured, to reinstate after damage by fire, or to keep in good and tenantable repair, will be remediable and the landlord will have to allow a reasonable period for remedy before proceeding for possession. Where the breach is by a subtenant, such breach not having been known to, caused or permitted by an intermediate tenant (his immediate landlord), the breach by the intermediate tenant is not irremediable. The tenant's remedy is to take immediate steps to stop the breach as soon as it becomes known to him, and to initiate the commencement of an action for forfeiture of the sub lease within a reasonable period thereafter.[11] The landlord can avoid the problems caused by the distinction by phrasing his statutory notice in the alternative, specifying the breach complained of and requiring its remedy 'if it is capable of remedy'.[12] If he waits for a reasonable period before instituting proceedings his notice cannot then be challenged on the ground that the breach in issue is remediable, rather than irremediable.

Section 146(2) provides that at any time while the lessor 'is proceeding, by action or otherwise', to enforce a right of re-entry the tenant has the right to apply to the court for relief. The court can grant relief on such terms, if any, as to costs, expenses, damages, compensation, penalty or otherwise as it thinks fit. Section 146(4) extends the right to apply for relief to subtenants, and gives the Court power to 'make an order vesting, for the whole term of the lease or any less term, the property comprised in the lease or any part thereof in any person entitled as underlessee to any estate or interest in such property.' The court can grant relief to the subtenant on such terms as it thinks fit, although it cannot grant a term longer than that which the subtenant enjoyed under his original sublease.

The discretion of the court to grant relief is wide, and it is not possible to set down clear guidelines within which it will be exercised. Cozens-Hardy MR laid down the following general principles upon which the court will act in *Rose v Hyman*.[13] On appeal the House of Lords granted cautious approval to these principles, but stressed that rigid rules could not be laid down to guide the exercise of the court's discretion, and that they might therefore be departed from in appropriate cases:[14]

8 *Farimani v Gates* (1984) 271 EG 887, CA per Griffiths LJ.
9 *Scala House and District Property Co v Forbes* [1974] QB 575, CA, (reversing *Capital and Counties Property Co Ltd v Mills* (1966) 197 EG 775).
10 *Farimani v Gates* (supra).
11 *Glass v Kencakes Ltd* [1966] 1 QB 611.
12 This formula was approved by Paul J in *Glass v Kencakes* [1966] 1 QB 611 at 629.
13 [1911] 2 KB 234 especially at 234, CA. And see *Re Brompton Securities Ltd (No 2)* [1988] 3 All ER 677.
14 *Rose v Hyman* [1912] AC 623, HL Lord Loreburn thought that the principles enunciated by the Court of Appeal were 'doubtless useful maxims in general, and in general they reflect the point of view from which judges would regard an application for relief' ([1912] AC 623 at 631).

(a) the tenant must, as far as possible, remedy the breaches alleged and pay reasonable compensation for those which cannot be remedied.
(b) if the breach is of a negative character the tenant must undertake to observe the covenant in future, and
(c) if the act complained of is of such a nature that the court would have restrained it during the currency of the tenancy on the ground of waste, the tenant must undertake to make good the waste if it is possible to do so.
(d) if the breach is one for which damages might be recovered in an action on the covenant, the tenant must undertake not to repeat the wrongful act or to be guilty of a continuing breach.

The fact that the tenant has remedied the breach, or that it occurred without his knowledge or consent[15], are factors the court will take into account when weighing its discretion. Relief may not be granted, however, where the personal qualifications of the tenant are important for the preservation of the value or character of the property.[16] Agricultural property falls within this category, and Section 146(9) expressly excludes the protection of Section 146 where a landlord seeks to enforce a proviso for forfeiture on bankruptcy of the tenant in a lease of agricultural land.

The tenant cannot apply for relief under Section 146(2) once the landlord has re-entered,[17] or where he has obtained an order for possession, for in both cases the landlord is no longer 'proceeding by way of action or otherwise' within the meaning of the Section.[18]

The Leasehold Property (Repairs) Act 1938 imposes further restrictions on the landlord's right to enforce a proviso for re-entry for breach of repairing covenants. By virtue of s 51(1)(c) of the Landlord and Tenant Act 1954, the 1938 Act does not apply to agricultural holdings. It follows that the landlord of an agricultural holding who seeks forfeiture for breach of repairing obligations does not have to serve the additional notices required by the 1938 Act, or seek leave of the court to proceed.

It is not possible to exclude, by agreement or otherwise, the tenant's right to apply for relief against forfeiture. So, in *Richard Clarke & Co Ltd v Widnall*[19] a clause purporting to give the landlord a right to terminate the tenancy, on giving three months' notice, where the tenant was in breach of covenant was held to be in substance a proviso for re-entry. As such it was only enforceable if section 146 was complied with, and subject to the tenant's right to relief.

4. Waiver

One of the dangers for the landlord in forfeiture proceedings is that he may waive his right to forfeit by in some way acknowledging the continued existence of the tenancy. Demanding or accepting rent accruing due after

15 Eg *Glass v Kencakes Ltd* [1966] 1 QB 611.
16 See *Earl Bathurst v Fine* [1974] 1 WLR 905, CA (tenant of country mansion refused entry to UK by Home Office and consequently deemed unsuitable as a tenant – relief refused).
17 *Rogers v Rice* [1892] 2 Ch 170, CA.
18 *Pakwood Transport Ltd v 15 Beauchamp Place Ltd* (1978) 36 P & CR 112, CA per Orr LJ at 117.
19 [1976] 1 WLR 845, CA. And see *Plymouth Corpn v Harvey* [1971] 1 All ER 623.

proceedings have commenced will amount to a waiver, as will levying distress for rent falling due.[20] Waiver is not such a danger where the tenant's breach is of a continuing nature. The waiver of any breach up to a certain date by the landlord, where the breach is a continuing one, will not act as a waiver of future breaches. Moreover, it is unnecessary to serve a second Section 146 notice, following waiver, where the breach is a continuing one.[1] Where forfeiture is for breach of covenant to repair, entry by the landlord to do the necessary work followed by his distraining for his expenses will be a waiver. An agreement to allow a tenant more time to execute repairs does not act as a waiver, however, but merely as a suspension of the landlord's right to forfeit.[2]

5.   Forfeiture and the Agricultural Holdings Acts

The landlord's right to forfeit under the general law is a useful alternative remedy, and may be preferred in some situations to proceeding under Case D to Sch 3 of the 1986 Act. It has the advantage of avoiding the arbitration procedures available to the tenant under Case D. In rent cases it suffers from one major drawback, however, in that if the tenant pays the rent owing (with costs) into court before judgment, the court will invariably grant relief against forfeiture. Case D has the advantage that if the tenant fails to invoke the arbitration procedure, or does so unsuccessfully, the court has no jurisdiction to grant relief against forfeiture. In the case of forfeiture for breach of covenant to repair, the remedy by way of notice to do work or notice to remedy under Case D is hedged with so many procedural requirements that, in some cases, it may be preferable to pursue forfeiture proceedings based on a proviso for re-entry. It is also a useful alternative remedy if the landlord loses his right to proceed under the 1986 Act, eg by failure to comply with the strict time limits set out in the legislation.

Forfeiture pursuant to a proviso for re-entry will be a 'termination' of the tenancy entitling the parties to claim compensation for improvements and for dilapidations in the usual way.[3] Compensation for disturbance will probably not be payable however, as the tenancy will not have been terminated by notice to quit within the meaning of Section 60(1)(a) of the 1986 Act. The tenant will be able to claim for 'high farming' under Section 70, in which case he must serve notice of his intention to do so at least one month before the end of the tenancy.[4] The order for possession, when granted, terminates the tenancy on judgment and relates back to the date of service of the writ.[5] The proviso for re-entry should therefore provide for at least one month's notice of forfeiture proceedings to be given to the tenant, so that he can exercise his right to claim compensation under Sections 60(n) and 70. If it does not do so the clause may be void as an attempt to contract out of the compensation provisions of the 1986 Act.[6]

20 The reason being that one can only distrain for rent against a tenant.
 1 *Penton v Barnett* [1898] 1 QB 276, CA.
 2 *Doe d Rankin v Brinley* (1832) 4 B & Ad 84.
 3 Section 96(1) Agricultural Holdings Act 1986.
 4 Section 70(2) ibid.
 5 *Canas Property Co Ltd v KL Television Services* [1970] 2 QB 433, CA. And see *Parry v Million Pigs Ltd* (1980) 260 EG 281.
 6 *Re Disraeli's Agreement* [1939] Ch 382; *Coates v Diment* [1951] 1 All ER 890. And see Section 78 of the 1986 Act.

Chapter 8
Statutory succession to agricultural holdings

Part II of the Agriculture (Miscellaneous Provisions) Act 1976 effected a major extension in security of tenure for farm tenants by introducing provisions enabling a close relative of a deceased tenant to claim succession to his tenancy. The statutory succession scheme allows for two successions following the death of an agricultural tenant. The existence of two-generation succession rights has been criticised as a disincentive to landlords, and a factor contributing to the accelerating decline of the tenanted sector of agricultural land. The Agricultural Holdings Act 1984 consequently amended the statutory scheme in two ways:

1) Section 2 of the 1984 Act abolished succession rights for all new tenancies granted on or after 12th July 1984, with limited saving provisions. Abolition was agreed as part of the package deal between the NFU and CLA on which the 1984 Act was based, the *quid pro quo* being reform of the rent valuation provisions.[1]

2) The 1984 Act also enacted modifications to the scheme following suggestions by the Northfield Report in 1979.[2] The latter suggested there should be a maximum area of land to which a successor could succeed, and that stricter rules on 'eligibility' and 'suitability' for succession should be introduced, so as to encourage efficiency. Transfer to eligible successors prior to death should also be encouraged. Their suggestions on retirement were enacted by s 4 and Sch 2 to the 1984 Act.[3] The amended provisions governing succession are now consolidated in Part IV and Sch 6 to the Agricultural Holdings Act 1986.

The overall effect of the amendments made in 1984 is to create two classes of tenancy; those granted prior to 12th July 1984 to which full succession rights apply, and those granted on or after that date to which the scheme has no application. In the case of tenancies within the scheme the landlord's reversion is postponed (effectively) for three generations, with a consequent devaluation of the freehold interest. Not only has the non-retrospective nature of the changes made in 1984 caused added complexity, they have also arguably caused unfairness, in that a landlord's rights depend entirely upon the date at which a particular farm was let. The Law Commission has strongly criticised the anomalies created by the scheme in it's current reform,

---

1 As to which see Chapter 5 (above p 88 ff).
2 See the Report of the Committee of Inquiry into the Acquisition and Occupancy of Agricultural Land (1979) Cmnd 7599 paras 626–31.
3 See p 169 ff below.

and have again canvassed the possibility of abolition – as most of the tenancies accruing succession rights were already in existence when the scheme was introduced in 1976, tenants merely received 'an unexpected and uncovenanted benefit' upon its introduction, and that is all they would lose on abolition.[4] In any event, the number of tenancies to which the scheme applies will gradually diminish, as succession rights are exhausted, although the process could take a considerable length of time.

A   Scope of statutory succession scheme

Section 34(1) of the 1986 Act provides that succession rights shall not normally apply to any tenancy created on or after 12th July 1984. Tenancies granted after this date will therefore attract lifetime security of tenure only, and close relatives will have no right to apply to an Agricultural Land Tribunal for succession to the deceased tenant's tenancy.

Succession rights continue to apply in full to tenancies granted prior to 12th July 1984[5] and also in the following cases:[6]

(a)   Where a tenancy was granted (albeit after 12th July 1984) by an Agricultural Land Tribunal under the succession provisions. This permits the full two generation succession provided for in the 1986 Act to take place, as a tenancy granted pursuant to a tribunal order will still be subject to succession rights.

(b)   Where the tribunal has directed that a new tenancy be granted, but before it takes effect the landlord and successor make a fresh tenancy agreement. The tribunal direction will normally take effect twelve months after the end of the year of tenancy in which the deceased tenant died,[7] but by virtue of s 34(1)(b) any tenancy agreed between the landlord and successor in the intervening period, after the tribunal direction, will attract succession rights. This protects the successor against inadvertently signing away his succession rights.

(c)   The parties can provide that succession rights shall continue to apply, where the tenancy is concluded after 12th July 1984, provided there is a written contract of tenancy which 'indicates' (in whatever terms) that Part IV of the 1986 Act is to apply to it. One can therefore 'contract out' of the abolition of succession, a facility which is unlikely to be widely used in practice. It does, however, have limited usefulness. The ability to grant post-1984 tenancies with statutory succession rights is of utility, for instance, where a landlord wishes to rearrange holdings on an estate by agreement with tenants, as the latter may not agree to move to other (better) holdings if this meant losing succession rights. Re-organisation can, using the facility in s 34(1)(b)(iii), be effected without loss of succession rights by affected tenants.

4 See Law Comm No 145, 'Landlord and Tenant: Reform of the Law' (1987), paras 4.65 and 4.66.
5 Section 34(1)(a), Agricultural Holdings Act 1986.
6 See s 34(1)(b) ibid.
7 Section 46(1)(a) ibid.

(d) Part IV of the 1986 Act applies if the tenancy in question is granted in any other way to a tenant who immediately before 12th July 1984 was a tenant of the holding, or of a holding which comprised a substantial part of the holding concerned. This provision protects tenants who had succession rights under the 1976 Act from losing them by taking a new tenancy after the 1984 Act came into force.

B   Succession on death

1.   General

The succession scheme continues to apply to tenancies granted prior to 12th July 1984, and to those 'saved' by Section 34.[8] An application for succession can be made when the sole (or, in the case of joint tenancy, sole surviving) tenant dies and is survived by a close relative of his: section 35(2). The application must be made within 3 months of the tenant's death, beginning with the day after the date of death, and notice of application served on the landlord.[9] The applicant must demonstrate to the agricultural land tribunal that he is both 'eligible' and 'suitable' to succeed to the tenancy – he must, moreover, be eligible within the meaning of the Act both at the date of death and at the date of the proceedings.[10] 'Eligibility' and 'Suitability' are further discussed below. The statutory 3 month time limit for application is inflexible, and cannot be extended, *cf.* the period allowed for service of *notice* of application on the landlord can be extended at the tribunal's discretion.[11]

If an application for succession is made, any notice to quit given on the tenant's death is effectively suspended. By virtue of Section 43, a notice to quit given under Case G cannot have effect unless *either* no application is made within the allowed time, *or* none of the applications succeeds, *or* the tribunal consent to the operation of the notice to quit.[12]

2.   More than one application

(a)   General rule

Where more than one close relative applies for succession, section 39(3) requires the tribunal to determine the eligibility and suitability of each as if he were the only applicant. If only one application is made, and the applicant is found by the tribunal to be both eligible and suitable, then the tribunal must make a direction entitling him to a tenancy of the holding.[13] Where more than one application is made, however, and the respective applicants are found to be both 'eligible' and 'suitable' for succession, then

---

8 Section 35(1)(a) Agricultural Holdings Act 1986.
9 Section 39(1) ibid and Rule 5, SI 1984/1301.
10 See section 39(2) ibid.
11 *Kellett v Alexander* (1980) 257 EG 494 (Woolf J).
12 As to which, see section 44, (below p 166 ff).
13 Section 39(5) of the 1986 Act.

the tribunal must determine which of the applicants is the most suitable person to become tenant of the holding and make a direction in his favour accordingly.[14] The general rule, then, is that only one successor can take a tenancy by succession. Section 39(9) gives the tribunal power, however, to make an order entitling more than one applicant to take a joint tenancy of the holding, but *only* where the landlord consents. Clearly, where a joint tenancy is granted by way of succession, this will potentially extend the duration of the succession tenancy to the landlord's detriment. Whether there is one applicant, or multiple applications, the tribunal must in all cases give the landlord an opportunity to state his views as to the suitability of the applicant(s) before making a direction.[15] The landlord's views are not, however, binding on the tribunal (although they may be of persuasive force). The maximum number of applicants to whom a joint tenancy can be awarded, with the landlord's consent, is four.

(b)   Designation by will or codicil

Special rules apply where the deceased tenant has validly designated a person he wishes to succeed to the tenancy by will or codicil. Where more than one application for succession has been made, section 39(4) requires the tribunal to first make a determination as to the eligibility and suitability of the designated successor. If the latter is found to be 'eligible' and 'suitable', he will be awarded a direction entitling him to a tenancy of the holding. The tribunal can only go on to consider the eligibility and suitability of other applicants if the designated successor is not found to be an eligible or a suitable applicant for succession.[16]

For these purposes, a designation can be made either by will or codicil, but only if the latter is the subject of a grant of probate or administration. By virtue of Section 40, a designation will only be valid if either:

(i)   the will or codicil contains an effective specific bequest to the named successor of the deceased's tenancy of the holding; *or*

(ii)   in the absence of a specific bequest, it contains 'a statement specifically mentioning the holding or the deceased's tenancy of the holding, and exclusively designating that person (in whatever words, and whether by name or description) as the person whom the deceased wishes to succeed him as tenant of the holding'. If the will contains a statement designating different persons in different circumstances, this requirement is satisfied if, in the events which have happened, the statement exclusively designates a particular person to succeed to the tenancy.[17]

Once a tribunal direction in favour of a designated successor has been made, it is immaterial that the probate or administration of the deceased's will or codicil is subsequently revoked or varied.[18]

14   Section 39(6) ibid.
15   Section 39(7) ibid.
16   This is not very clearly expressed in s 39(4), as the provision does not deal with ruling out an ineligible 'designated' applicant other than by referring to a 'determination under sub-section (2)'.
17   See section 40(2) ibid.
18   Section 40(3) ibid.

3. Exclusion of insecure interests

The statutory succession scheme is an extension of the security of tenure provisions of the 1986 Act. Consequently, the Act prevents succession where the interest of the deceased was not such as to attract security of tenure. No application for succession can be made in the following circumstances:

(i) if the deceased's tenancy was a fixed term of which more than 27 months remained unexpired at his death;[19] *or*

(ii) if the deceased's interest was a fixed term of more than one but less than two years;[20] *or*

(iii) if the deceased received a notice to quit which had become binding and final prior to the date of death. This will be the case where tribunal consent has already been given, or no counter notice claiming security served, before the date of death. Similarly, no succession is possible if the tenant has received a notice to quit under Case C (Bad Husbandry) or Case F (Insolvency). If, prior to the tenant's death, the landlord served notice to quit under Cases B, D or E, then no succession is allowed if the arbitration procedures have been exhausted prior to the death, and the notice to quit upheld. This is also the case if the tenant failed to demand arbitration within the statutory time limits.[1]

(iv) No application for succession can be made if the holding consists of land held by a smallholdings authority (or the Ministry) for the purposes of smallholdings within the meaning of Part III of the Agriculture Act 1970.[2] This is expressly the case whether the tenancy was granted before or after the commencement of the 1970 Act.[3]

(v) No application can be made if the holding is vested in the trustees of a charitable trust for the settlement/employment in agriculture of ex-members of the armed forces.[4]

4. Two successions only

The statutory scheme allows for two transmissions of the tenancy. This basic principle is enshrined in somewhat complex terms in section 37.

(a) Succession on death

No application for succession can be made if, on each of the last two occasions when there died a sole surviving tenant of the holding:

(i) either a tenancy of the holding (or a related holding) was obtained by tribunal direction; *or*

(ii) a tenancy of the holding was granted by the landlord to a close relative

---

19 Section 36(2)(a) ibid.
20 Section 36(2)(b). Such tenancies do not enjoy statutory security (*Gladstone v Bower* [1960] 2 QB 384, CA).
1 See section 38(1), (2) and (3) ibid.
2 See section 38(4) ibid.
3 *Cf Saul v Norfolk County Council* [1984] QB 559, CA, reversed by statutory amendment in the 1984 Act.
4 Section 38(5), Agricultural Holdings Act 1986.

of the deceased who had become the sole remaining applicant for a direction. Note that a tribunal application must have been made if the tenancy is to count as one succession under the Act.[5] Also, the successor must be the *only*, or *sole* remaining, applicant for a direction. *Semble*, however, provided the applicant is a close relative of the deceased, the livelihood and commercial unit of occupancy tests (below p 157 ff) do not have to be made out for the tenancy to count under section 37.

(b)   Succession prior to death

(i)   To further encourage *agreed* successions, the 1984 Act introduced amendments facilitating the grant of new tenancies which can count as one succession under the scheme. Where, prior to the tenant's death, and as a result of an agreement between landlord and tenant, the holding was let to someone who is a close relative of the tenant, then that occasion counts as one succession under the statutory scheme.[6] An agreed transmission can now also be made by way of assignment of the existing tenancy to a close relative, or to joint tenants, *one* of whom is a close relative of the prior tenant.[7] These provisions only apply, however, to tenancies granted, or assignments made, after 12th September 1984.[8]

(ii)   A tenancy obtained following the *retirement* of the tenant, using the statutory provisions in the 1986 Act, counts as one succession for the purposes of the statutory scheme applying both on death and retirement.[9]

5.   Succession limited to close relatives

The policy underlying the succession provisions is to allow succession by only close relatives of the deceased tenant who have worked on the holding, and who have no other substantial agricultural concerns on which to rely. This is reflected in the eligibility rules which an applicant has to satisfy before he can be considered eligible for the grant of a tenancy under the Act (see below). In all cases, however, it is a fundamental prerequisite that the applicant be a 'close relative' of the deceased tenant.[10] Section 35(2) provides that the applicant must be either the wife or husband of the deceased tenant, his brother or sister, his child, or 'a child of the family', *viz*. 'any person who, in the case of any marriage to which the deceased was at any time a party, was treated by the deceased as a child of the family in relation to that marriage'. This definition is somewhat restrictive in scope.

5 Section 37(1) ibid.
6 Section 37(2) ibid. For the definition of 'close relative' for those purposes see below).
7 Sections 37(2)(b) and 37(5) ibid.
8 See section 37(8) ibid. Agreed retirement successions were possible prior to the 1984 Act, under s 18(6) Agriculture (Miscellaneous Provisions) Act 1976. The 1984 Act relaxed the provisions by providing (a) that it could be done by assignment; (b) it need not be to the whole of the holding and (c) it could be to joint tenants of whom only one was within the eligible degrees of kindred (Sch 1 para 2(7) of the 1984 Act). These amendments are now consolidated into s 37(2) of the 1986 Act.
9 Section 37(6) ibid.
10 Section 36(3) ibid.

There is no relaxation in favour of divorce, and succession rights will cease to apply on the grant of a decree absolute. More problematically, the restrictive definition of a 'child of the family' could lead to hardship in some cases. An unmarried tenant, for instance, could not pass on his tenancy to an adoptive child. *Semble*, neither could a grandparent to a grandchild whose parents have predeceased.

6. Eligibility for succession

To be an 'eligible person' the applicant must not only be a close relative of the deceased (above) but also satisfy two further eligibility conditions,[11] *viz*:

(i) in the seven years ending with the date of death, his only or principal source of livelihood throughout a continuous period of not less than five years, or two or more discontinuous periods together amounting to not less than five years, must have been derived from his agricultural work on the holding, or an agricultural unit of which the holding forms part (the 'livelihood condition'); *and*

(ii) he must not be the occupier of a commercial unit of agricultural land (the commercial unit 'occupancy' condition).

(a) The 'livelihood condition'

Where the applicant is the deceased's wife, it is specifically provided that the reference to agricultural work is to be read as a reference to agricultural work carried out by either the wife or the deceased (or both of them).[12] Prior to 1984, if a tenant wished his widow to succeed to the tenancy, he had to ensure she took a real part in running the farming enterprise if the livelihood condition were to be satisfied. A widow will now be automatically eligible to succeed, although it should be noted she will still have to establish her 'suitability' for succession. To do so, she will (as we shall see) have to prove she has sufficient experience and training in agriculture to enable her to farm the holding satisfactorily. *Semble*, it may still be advisable for her to be involved in managing the enterprise, if for different reasons.

Note, also that, the deeming provision in section 36(4) operates only in favour of a widow, and not in the case of a widower applicant.

For the purposes of calculating the five-year period required by section 36(4), any period during which an applicant was, during the seven years prior to the tenant's death, attending a full-time course at a university, college or other further education establishment, is to be treated as a period throughout which his only or principal source of livelihood was derived from his agricultural work on the holding. Not more than three years' attendance at an educational institution can be counted.[13]

The applicant's work must have been on the agricultural holding concerned or on an 'agricultural unit' of which the holding forms part. 'Agricultural unit' is defined by section 109(2) of the Agriculture Act 1947 in the following terms:

11 Section 36(3) ibid.
12 Section 36(4) ibid introduced by the Agricultural Holdings Act 1984, s 3(2).
13 Schedule 6, para 2 ibid.

'. . . the expression "agricultural unit" means land which is occupied as a unit for agricultural purposes, including –
(a) any dwelling-house or other building occupied by the same person for the purpose of farming the land, and
(b) any other land falling within the definition in this Act of the expression "agricultural land" which is in the occupation of the same person, being land as to which the Minister is satisfied that having regard to the character and situation thereof and other relevant circumstances it ought in the interests of full and efficient production to be farmed in conjunction with the agricultural unit, and directs accordingly.

Provided that the Minister shall not give a direction under this subsection as respects any land unless it is for the time being not in use for any purpose which appears to him to be substantial having regard to the use to which it may be put for agriculture.'

It follows from the wording of the section that, if different parcels of land are to be treated as one agricultural unit, they must be in single occupation.
The following points should also be noted:

'PRINCIPAL SOURCE OF LIVELIHOOD'

The Act directs attention to the applicant's source of 'livelihood', not simply his or her income. The test causes problems where the household expenditure of tenant and applicant are mixed, as will often be the case, eg where the deceased tenant and the applicant (a son for instance) lived together as one household. To correctly apply the livelihood condition, the tribunal must identify what proportion of the total expenditure on the livelihood of the household was attributable to the applicant, and what proportion was the tenant's. Only when his livelihood has been quantified in this way can the applicant's income be examined to see from which source his proportion of the relevant expenditure was funded. Clearly, the initial step of defining the applicant's 'livelihood' could itself involve difficult questions of fact.

'Principal source of livelihood' was defined in the following terms by Webster J in *Trinity College, Cambridge v Caines*.[14]

'The expression "source of livelihood" means what the applicant spends or consumes on her ordinary living expenses from time to time in money and/or kind and . . . it does not include money that she has available to spend but does not in fact spend for that purpose.'

It follows from the equation of 'livelihood' with 'ordinary living expenses' that, although some benefits in kind must be relevant, others must be ruled out; factors such as the provision of stock, animal feed and fuel must be ruled out, and relevant benefits in kind limited to household expenses. Undrawn profits from the farming enterprise, however, clearly do not count as part of the applicant's 'livelihood' in the required sense. The applicant's income spent on household expenses is the relevant criterion, and not his work on the holding *per se*.[15]

14 (1983) 272 EG 1287 at 1292.
15 And see (1987) Conv 387 (CR).

A 'PERIOD OF FIVE YEARS'

Within the seven years prior to the tenant's death, the applicant is entitled to choose which five-year period (or periods amounting to five years) he wishes to rely upon during which his livelihood was derived from work on the holding.[16] He may, therefore, be eligible even if for part of the seven-year period the enterprise was making losses, or even if he does not work on the holding itself for the two years prior to the tenant's death. Clearly, this allows considerable latitude to potential applicants to arrange their affairs so as to be sure of satisfying the statutory criteria.

'DERIVED FROM HIS WORK ON THE HOLDING'

The correct approach is to focus on the applicant's drawings from the farm accounts, and the proportion they bear to his total income. To be his 'principal' source of livelihood, such drawings must amount to not less than fifty per cent of his total expenditure on living expenses. *Semble*, the ultimate *source* of the monies drawn is irrelevant provided they are paid in return for agricultural work on the holding, or a unit of which the holding forms part. So, if the enterprise is making a loss, and monies drawn are derived from savings and capital put into the business by the (deceased) tenant, this is of no consequence as long as payments received by the applicant are clearly in return for his agricultural work on the holding.[17] Note also that the applicant's income must be derived from his work on the holding 'or an agricultural unit of which the holding forms part'.[18] This can prove important in many cases, eg where the tenant has other holdings and his son has worked on all of them.

(b)   The occupancy condition

A person is not eligible to succeed to a tenancy if he is the occupier of a 'commercial unit of agricultural land'.[19] The policy underlying this limb of the eligibility test is to ensure that only applicants who have no other viable agricultural concerns should be entitled to succession. The disqualification only applies, however, where the applicant 'occupies' a commercial unit, and not where he simply *manages* it on behalf of a third party.[20]

A 'commercial unit of agricultural land' is defined by Sch 6, para 3(1) of the 1986 Act as a unit of agricultural land which is capable, when farmed under competent management, of producing a net annual income of an amount not less than the aggregate of the average annual earnings of two full-time male agricultural workers aged twenty or over. The Minister pre-scribes, by Statutory Instrument, units of production for the purposes of calculating the productive capacity of a unit of agricultural land and the net income it is capable of generating.[1] MAFF also publishes regularly the average annual earnings of different classes of worker, including full-time males aged twenty or over. At the request of any person eligible to apply for

---

16 *Bailey v Sitwell* [1986] 2 EGLR 7.
17 See *Bailey v Sitwell*, ibid.
18 Section 36(3)(a) Agricultural Holdings Act 1986.
19 Section 36(3)(b) ibid.
20 *Trinity College Cambridge v Caines* (1983) 272 EG 1287.
 1 Schedule 6, paras 3(2) and 4. See currently SI 1990/1696 (operative from 12th Sept. 1990).

succession, or of the landlord, the Minister must carry out an investigation and issue a written statement of his views to the person making the request. The statement issued by the Minister is not conclusive and binding on the tribunal as to the commercial unit status (or otherwise) of the land in question, but is evidence of any facts stated in it as facts on which the Minister's view is based.[2]

Prior to amendments introduced in the 1984 Act the commercial unit disqualification caused considerable problems, and generated a not inconsiderable body of litigation.

(i)   Satisfaction of occupancy condition

In *Jackson v Hall*,[3] the House of Lords ruled that the applicant must satisfy the occupancy condition at the date of the tenant's death, at the date of application *and* at the date of the tribunal hearing. An applicant cannot render himself eligible by divesting himself of a 'commercial unit' between the tenant's death and the tribunal application. Similarly, the *acquisition* of an interest in a commercial unit during this interval will disqualify the applicant.

(ii)   Joint occupation of a commercial unit

In *Williamson v Thompson*,[4] the House of Lords ruled that a joint occupier of a commercial unit was also ineligible, even where joint occupiers had a commercial unit which was not sufficient to support them all. The 1984 Act therefore introduced amendments allowing for division of the potential income of a unit in appropriate cases.

Schedule 6, para 7 of the 1986 Act now enacts that where agricultural land is jointly occupied by an applicant for succession and one or more other persons either as:

(i)   beneficial joint tenants,
(ii)   tenants in common,
(iii)   joint tenants under a tenancy, *or*
(iv)   joint licensees

then while the survivor is still deemed to be occupying the whole of the land, the tribunal must assess his 'appropriate share' of the net income which the land is capable of producing. If his appropriate share of its income is less than the aggregate of the average annual earnings of two full-time agricultural workers, then he will not be treated as occupying a 'commercial unit' of agricultural land. The appropriate share of income attributable to the survivor is ascertained:

(i)   where he is a joint tenant, by dividing the net annual income which the land is capable of producing by the total number of joint tenants or licensees for the time being; *or*
(ii)   where he is a tenant in common, by dividing the net annual income in such a way as to attribute to him and the other tenants shares of

2 Schedule 6, para 5 ibid.
3 [1980] AC 854.
4 [1980] AC 854.

. the income proportionate to the extent for the time being of their undivided shares in the land.

(iii) Anti-avoidance provisions

The commercial unit test causes problems where a holding comprises land of mixed tenure, eg part may be freehold, and the remainder rented. If the tenant farms in partnership with close relatives, and the latter occupy as licensees or under a partnership tenancy, then if the freehold land so occupied is a commercial unit, succession to the tenancy of the rented land will be in jeopardy. Conversely, attempts to evade the occupancy condition have not been unknown, often by arranging for a commercial unit to be occupied under a bare licence, or for any interest in such land to be transferred by a potential applicant to a third party or company (the applicant often remaining in possession).

In order to clarify the operation of the condition, Schedule 6 to the 1986 Act now lays down in detail those interests which will trigger application of the condition (and those which are exempt), and contains complex provisions 'deeming' occupation by an applicant in certain cases in order to prevent evasion.

(iv) Excluded occupation

By virtue of Schedule 6, para 6, occupation in any of the following capacities is to be disregarded for the purposes of the occupancy condition:

   (i) occupation under a tenancy granted with Ministry consent under Section 2 of the Act, or under an exempt grazing or mowing agreement,
  (ii) occupation under a tenancy for more than one but less than two years (a '*Gladstone v Bower* tenancy'),
 (iii) occupation under any other tenancy not having effect as a contract of tenancy under the legislation,
  (iv) occupation under a tenancy for between two and five years, which does not continue as a yearly tenancy because the parties have obtained Ministry consent to the grant of the tenancy under Section 5 of the Act,
   (v) occupation as a licensee (see below),
  (vi) occupation as an executor, administrator, trustee in bankruptcy or person otherwise deriving title by operation of law.

These are all categories of agreement normally exempt from the operation of the 1986 Act, and therefore occupation of a commercial unit in any of these capacities will not disqualify the applicant from applying for succession to tenanted property elsewhere.

NB: OCCUPATION AS LICENSEE ONLY

When construing this exemption ((v) above), it should be remembered that section 2 of the 1986 Act, as intrepreted in *Harrison-Broadley v Smith*,[5] converts any contractual licence which confers exclusive possession into an annual tenancy with statutory security of tenure. Only a commercial unit

---

5 [1964] 1 All ER 867.

occupied under a gratuitous or unenforceable licence, or one of a non-exclusive nature, will escape the operation of the occupancy condition. Furthermore, it was held in *Brooks v Brown*,[6] per Forbes J., that occupation by an applicant as a partner in a family farming partnership was *not* occupation as a licensee 'only'. The exclusion is aimed at interests with no security in the land. Although a licensee, a partner's position is protected by the Partnership Act 1890, section 38 of which continues the partnership authority of the applicant after the tenant's death 'so far as may be necessary to wind up the affairs of the partnership, and to complete transactions begun but unfinished' at the time of the dissolution. *Sed Quaere*: there is an argument that the reference in the exclusion to occupation as a 'licensee only' was intended to distinguish between bare licenses and those converted by section 2 into annual tenancies with protection. Note also that the wording of section 18(2)(c) of the 1976 Act (occupation 'as a licensee only'), on which this decision was based, differs slightly from that of the 1986 Act ('occupies it only . . . (e) as a licensee'), although it is not thought this effects any change of substance to the exclusion.[7]

(v)   Deemed occupation

For the purposes of the commercial unit test, occupation by either the spouse of a survivor of the deceased, or by a body corporate controlled by a survivor of the deceased tenant, shall be treated as occupation by that survivor.[8] The exclusions of occupation listed above do not apply in the case of a licence or tenancy granted to a survivor of the deceased by his spouse or by a body corporate controlled by him.[9] The Act also tries to block evasion by a survivor granting an interest exempt from the operation of the legislation to a third party, where the latter does not gain security of tenure. Where land is held by a third party under one of the excluded classes of agreement or licence (above) and that interest was granted by the survivor or a 'connected person' himself entitled to occupy under an excluded class of tenancy or licence, then the survivor is deemed by Schedule 6 to be in occupation of the whole of the land.[10] A 'connected person' for these purposes means either the survivor's spouse or a corporate body controlled by the survivor. A company is to be treated as 'controlled' by a survivor if he and/or his spouse have power to secure that the affairs of the company are conducted in accordance with their wishes either:

(a)   by means of holding shares or possessing voting power in that or any other company (for instance a holding company), or

(b)   by virtue of provisions in the company's articles of association or any other document regulating the company's affairs.[11]

These complex provisions go some way to preventing abuse of the commercial unit test. They contain a number of loopholes, however, of which the following should be noted. Occupation is only attributed to a

---

6 (1985) (Unreported, Queens Bench Div., 1985 Co. No. 1552, 31 July 1985).
7 And see further (1986) Conv 320 (M Slatter) for a helpful discussion of the problems engendered by the interpretation adopted in *Brooks v Brown* ibid.
8 Schedule 6, para 9(1) Agricultural Holdings Act 1986.
9 Schedule 6, para 6(2) ibid.
10 Schedule 6, para 10 ibid.
11 Schedule 6, para 1(2) ibid.

survivor where an interest in a commercial unit is held by that survivor's spouse. Schedule 6 does not cover the case where an interest in a commercial unit is held by some other relative of the applicant, eg a brother/sister or child of the survivor. Avoidance of the test will still be possible if an interest in a commercial unit is transferred to such a relative prior to the tenant's death, with the survivor/applicant remaining in possession under an unprotected interest. Schedule 6 similarly does not cover the case of a family company controlled by brothers/sisters of the survivor, and not by his spouse. Likewise, if control of the company is maintained other than by a majority shareholding or by provisions in the articles, evasion may still be possible. Neither does the Schedule cover the case where control is maintained by a looser system of related shareholdings held (for instance) by trusted agents or brothers, sisters and other relatives (excepting the survivor's spouse).[12]

(c) Relaxation of livelihood condition

Where the applicant cannot fully satisfy the livelihood condition, section 41 enables him to make an application to the tribunal to be 'treated' as eligible. The application must be made within three months of the tenant's death, and at the same time and in the same form as the application to succeed to the tenancy.[13] If successful, his application for a tenancy under section 39 is to be treated as if made by an eligible person.[14]

For Section 41 to apply, a close relative must establish that:

(i) the occupancy condition is satisfied; *and*
(ii) the livelihood condition, though not fully satisfied, 'is satisfied to a material extent'; and
(iii) if satisfied as to (i) and (ii), the tribunal must determine whether it would be 'fair and reasonable' for the applicant to be able to *apply* for a succession direction. If they so determine, they must order that he be treated as eligible for the purposes of the Act.

'SATISFIED TO A MATERIAL EXTENT'

In *Littlewood v Rolfe*[15] it was held (thus resolving an earlier conflict in tribunal practice) that 'satisfied to a material extent' must be given a wide meaning, *viz*. 'material means substantial in terms of time and important in terms of value'.[16] Judge Edgar Fay QC here envisaged that in suitable cases, where the income from the holding formed a large part of the applicant's income, 50% satisfaction of the 'principal source of livelihood' test could be satisfaction to an extent that was material. It follows that an applicant can be 'treated' as eligible, in appropriate circumstances, with as little as two and a half years' work on the holding.[17]

---

12 *Semble*, also, Sch 6 has no application on the devise of a 'commercial unit' of land on discretionary trusts with a power of appointment, which latter is then exercised in favour of the deceased tenant's issue *after* a tribunal direction for succession has been obtained. For further discussion of points arising from the occupancy condition see *inter alia*, (1984) Conv 207 and (1985) Conv 111 (CR), and (1986) Conv 320 (M Slatter).
13 See SI 1984/1301, rule 3(2).
14 Section 41(4) Agricultural Holdings Act 1986.
15 [1981] 2 All ER 51.
16 [1981] 2 All ER 51, 58.
17 And see *Dagg v Lovett* (1980) 256 EG 491, CA.

The power to 'treat' applicants as eligible is of utility in two situations:

(i)   where the applicant has worked on the holding for a number of years but its *value* to him is not sufficient to make it his 'principal' source of income. The correct approach in such cases was discussed in *Wilson v Earl Spencer's Settlement Trustees*.[18] According to Hodgson J, the starting point must be the applicant's 'principal' source of livelihood. To be a *principal* source of livelihood, the holding must provide at least 50% of the applicant's income spent on household living expenses. The correct test, then, is to ask whether the applicant satisfied the 50% requirement 'to a material extent'. Adopting the wide definition of 'material' satisfaction sanctioned in *Littlewood v Rolfe (supra)*, the question in *value* cases is whether the income derived from the holding represents an important satisfaction of the 50% requirement of the applicant's living expenses. This involves a comparison of the applicant's total livelihood and his income from the holding. What constitutes an 'important' satisfaction of the test will be a question of fact for the tribunal, but clearly it could sanction applications for succession from applicants who have derived as little as 25% of their total livelihood from the holding concerned.

(ii)   Section 41 is also of use where the *length of time* the applicant has worked on the holding is less than the five years required by the livelihood condition. *Raine's Trustee v Raine*[19] exemplifies 'time' cases of this type, as here the applicant had only worked on the holding for three years in the seven prior to the tenant's death. Per Forbes J, the correct test in 'time' cases, applying the guidance in *Littlewood v Rolfe*, is whether the time spent working on the holding was a 'substantial' satisfaction of the five years required. Consequently, an applicant with as little as two and a half years work on the holding could qualify for eligibility on this basis. The five-year period required by section 36(3) is the starting point: the correct question is *not* whether the applicant has spent a substantial period of time working on the holding, but whether he has satisfied the requirement of eligibility (ie five years' work on the holding) to a 'substantial' degree. This is a question of fact for the tribunal.

(iii)   Section 41(6) also provides expressly that the section applies where the holding concerned is *too small* to provide the applicant with his principal source of livelihood. If the tenant had other farms or land, the applicant may also be assisted by the injunction to look at income derived from work on 'a unit of which the holding forms part'.[20]

APPLICATION: WHETHER 'FAIR AND REASONABLE' TO PROCEED

Once the tribunal is satisfied that section 41 applies, it can make a direction deeming the applicant eligible only 'if it appears to the tribunal that in all the circumstances, it would be fair and reasonable for the applicant to be able to apply . . . for a direction entitling him to a tenancy of the holding'.[1] This is in

18 [1985] 1 EGLR 3.
19 (1985) 275 EG 374.
20 Section 36(3), above pp 157–158.
 1 Section 36(3)(b) ibid.

the nature of a procedural bar. In *Raine's Trustee v Raine*, it was held that issues of hardship are irrelevant to whether the application should be allowed to proceed. If the landlord wishes to argue 'greater hardship', he should therefore serve notice to quit – in this event the question will arise, later in the proceedings, whether a 'fair and reasonable landlord' would demand possession, and questions of hardship will become relevant at this stage.

7. Succession to one commercial unit only

Succession is limited, on policy grounds, to one commercial unit of land from one landlord. Where an applicant obtains a tribunal direction entitling him to a tenancy of a particular holding, he is 'deemed' to be in occupation of that land for the purposes of the 'occupancy' condition.[2] If the land to which he has obtained succession is a commercial unit, he will be rendered ineligible to apply for succession to further holdings elsewhere.[3] If he succeeds as a joint tenant of the first holding, his 'appropriate share' of the income generated by the holding must be calculated for the purpose of deciding his eligibility to succeed to further tenancies.

8. 'Suitability' for succession

Once a candidate's eligibility for succession is established, he must prove to the tribunal's satisfaction that he is also a 'suitable' person to become tenant of the holding.[4] By virtue of section 39(8), the tribunal must have regard to 'all relevant matters' *including*: the extent of the applicant's training and practical experience in agriculture, the age, physical health and financial standing of the applicant and (finally) the view (if any) stated by the landlord on the suitability of the applicant. In *Dagg v Lovett*,[5] it was indicated that the scale of rent rise likely on the grant of a tenancy, and its impact on the profitability of the farm, could be a 'relevant factor' for consideration. Suitability is, ultimately, a question of fact for the tribunal.

9. Applications re more than one holding

It frequently occurs that the deceased held tenancies of more than one holding. Where multiple applications for succession to different holdings are made by one person, then the order in which they are dealt with by the tribunal can be decided by the applicant himself. Where, however, the applications are made by two or more persons, the order in which they are dealt with shall be decided by agreement between the applicants and in default of agreement by the tribunal chairman.[6] The chairman must have

---

2 Schedule 6, para 8 ibid.
3 And see s 42(2) and (3) as to order of determination of applications where there are multiple holdings. Below pp 165–166.
4 Section 39(2) ibid.
5 (1980) 256 EG 491, CA.
6 Section 42(2)(b) of the 1986 Act.

regard to the size of the holdings concerned, and direct that any application in respect of any holding which is larger than any other of those holdings shall be heard and determined by the tribunal before any application in respect of that other.[7] The applications must therefore be determined according to the size of the holdings concerned, starting with the largest in area and working down to the smallest.

10.   Landlord's notice to quit

The landlord may have served notice to quit (under Case G) following the tenant's death. In this event, as we have seen, the notice to quit is suspended if an application for succession is made, pending the outcome of the succession proceedings.[8] If at the end of the three-month period following death only one application has been made, then the landlord's application for consent must be made within four months after service on him of the first application for succession.[9] Where more than one application for succession has been made, the landlord's application for consent must be made either within four months of the service on him of the first application for succession, or within one month of the date on which the number of such applications is reduced to one, whichever is the later.[10] The secretary to the tribunal must inform the landlord of the start of the relevant period of four months, or one month where a reduction in the number of succession applications to one has occurred.[11] If the applicant for succession wishes to oppose the landlord's application for consent, as indeed he usually will, then he must file a Reply in the prescribed form within one month of the landlord's application being served on him.[12]

Where the applicant for succession has established he is both 'eligible' and 'suitable' for the grant of a tenancy, the tribunal must go on to consider the landlord's application for consent to the operation of his notice to quit *before* it makes a direction entitling the applicant to a tenancy. By virtue of section 44(2) of the 1986 Act the landlord must establish one of the five grounds for tribunal consent set out in section 27. The notice is treated, in other words, as a normal unqualified notice to quit. If the landlord is invoking the 'greater hardship' test and wishes to allege hardship to persons other than himself, he must give details in his application of those person(s) and the hardship on which he is relying.[13] Having established one of the five grounds in section 27 he must then also establish that a 'fair and reasonable landlord' would in the circumstances demand possession.

If the tribunal consent to the operation of the landlord's notice they must dismiss the application for succession. They have power to postpone the operation of the notice to quit if it is to take effect within three months of the tribunal's decision. On the tenant's application they may specify a new operative date, which may be not later than the end of three months beginning with either:

---

7 Section 42(3) ibid.
8 As to notice to quit on death see generally Chapter 7, p 141 ff above.
9 Rule 4(3), SI 1984/1301.
10 Rule 4(4) ibid.
11 Rule 4(5) ibid.
12 Rule 7 ibid.
13 SI 1984/1301, r 4(2).

(a)   the original operative date, or
(b)   the date on which the tribunal give their consent to the operation of the notice,

whichever is the later.[14]

11. Direction for succession tenancy: effects

If the applicant is found to be both eligible and suitable, and the tribunal refuse consent to the landlord's notice to quit (if any), then they must give a direction entitling the applicant to a tenancy of the holding.[15]

(a)   Commencement of succession tenancy

The tribunal direction entitles the applicant to a tenancy on the same terms as those on which it was let at the date of death.[16] The new tenancy is deemed to take effect either:

(a)   Where no notice to quit was given on the tenant's death, at the end of the twelve months immediately following the end of the year of tenancy in which the tenant died,
(b)   Where a Case G notice to quit was given, at the date on which that notice expired, or
(c)   If the deceased held under a fixed term tenancy with more than 27 months to run succession will be under the normal rules of inheritance. In other cases a Case G to notice to quit can be given, and the position will be as in (b).

Where the tribunal makes a direction for a new tenancy, but does so within the three months prior to the termination of the old tenancy, then it has limited power to extend the old tenancy on the tenant's application. The tribunal can specify a new termination date for the old tenancy falling within three months immediately following the original termination date. If the tribunal direction is itself made after the original termination date, then a new date can be substituted provided it is within three months of the direction.[17] The new tenancy is deemed to include a covenant against assignment.[18]

(b)   Succession to part of holding

If the applicant agrees, the tribunal can award a tenancy or joint tenancy of *part* only of the deceased's holding (Section 39(1)). In this event the tribunal must give their consent to the operation of the landlord's notice to quit (if one has been given) in relation to that part of the holding which is excluded from the tribunal direction under Section 39(10). The landlord does not, in this event, have to make out one of the grounds for consent.

14 See s 44(7) Agricultural Holdings Act 1986.
15 Section 39(5) ibid.
16 Sections 45(1) and 47 ibid. This is subject to the caveat that a covenant against assignment or subletting will be implied if there was none in the former tenancy: s 47(3).
17 See s 46(2) ibid.
18 Section 47(3) ibid.

(c)   Subtenancies: protective provisions ·

Subtenants enjoy no statutory security of tenure. A problem arises if the landlord introduces a supervening mesne tenancy after the grant of the deceased's interest. In this event the grant of a new tenancy by way of succession could turn the successor/tenant into a subtenant, his interest ante-dating that of the mesne lessee. The effect would be to destroy any security of tenure otherwise attaching to his interest.

To obviate this problem the 1984 Act introduced provisions (now contained in s 45(2) and (3) of the 1986 Act) whereby if the deceased's tenancy was not derived from the interest held by the immediate landlord of the successor at the relevant time, the succession tenancy is deemed to be granted by the person entitled to the immediate interest from which the deceased tenant's interest was originally derived (instead of by his immediate landlord, ie the mesne tenant). The supervening interest, in other words, is ignored, and the successor is deemed to be the tenant of the original landlord.

The deeming provision is triggered by the introduction of a 'supervening interest' subsequent to grant. This is widely defined in s 45(3) to mean 'any interest in the land comprised in the deceased's tenancy, being an interest created subsequently to that tenancy and *derived* (whether immediately or otherwise) *from the interest from which that tenancy was derived* and still subsisting at the relevant time' (italics added). There is a question whether the deeming provision would apply if a series of tenancies and subtenancies exists *ab initio*, and the landlord subsequently interposes a head lease between himself and his mesne tenant. *Semble* such an interest would not be an interest derived from that from which the deceased's tenant's interest was derived.

(d)   Death of applicant

The death of an applicant after securing a succession direction, but before it takes effect, is dealt with by the Agriculture (Miscellaneous Provisions) Act 1976 (Application of Provisions) Regulations 1977 (SI 1977/1215). If a person entitled to a joint tenancy dies, the direction takes effect as if made to the other applicant only.[19] In other cases, the succession scheme takes effect, with modifications as if the entitled successor were a deceased tenant.[20]

12.   Arbitration on terms of new tenancy

The terms of the new tenancy are the same as those of the original tenancy, except that the new tenancy is deemed to include a covenant against assignment and subletting even if the original lease contained no such clause. Section 48 provides for arbitration on the terms of the new tenancy. Either party can serve notice requiring arbitration as to either or both of two questions:

   (a)   what variation in the terms of the tenancy which has been awarded 'are justifiable having regard to the circumstances of the holding and the length of time since the holding was first let on those terms.' This is a question of fact for the arbitrator; *and*

19 Article 2(1), SI 1977/1215.
20 See SI 1977/1215, Schedule, para 2.

(b) the rent properly payable for the holding at the relevant time. Where question (a) is referred to arbitration, the arbitrator can include in his award compensation payable to the landlord on termination of the deceased's tenancy, and (similarly) compensation on such termination payable *by* the landlord.[1]

If the arbitrator varies the terms of the tenancy, he can make an adjustment of rent to reflect this, whether or not the rent properly payable (question (b)) has been referred to arbitration.[2]

Where the rent payable *is* referred to arbitration, the arbitrator must determine what rent might reasonably be obtained on letting by a prudent and willing landlord to a prudent and willing tenant, taking into account all relevant factors, including in every case the terms of the tenancy and all other factors referred to in Sch 2, para 1 of the 1986 Act. The rent must be determined, in other words, as on an ordinary review, and the landlord cannot obtain an uplift to market levels on commencement of the succession tenancy.[3]

Notice demanding arbitration must be served within the three months immediately following the tribunal direction or the 'relevant time', whichever is later. The 'relevant time' is (somewhat obscurely) defined to mean the end of the 12 months immediately following the end of the year of tenancy in which the deceased died, or where a Case G notice to quit was given the date on which it would expire. The three months will run from the end of that period, or from the tribunal direction if given subsequently.

C Succession on retirement

In order to encourage the transfer of tenancies prior to death, and to give effect to the majority recommendations of the Northfield Committee,[4] Schedule 2 to the 1984 Act introduced provisions enabling an existing farm tenant to 'retire' and nominate a qualifying successor to take over the holding. These provisions are now contained in ss 49–58 of the 1986 Act. The retirement scheme is an extension of the existing scheme applicable on death – the 'eligibility' and 'suitability' rules to be met by a potential successor, and the other detailed provisions, are therefore closely modelled on those applying on the tenant's death. Similarly, a retirement succession counts as one transfer for the purposes of the 'two-succession' rule limiting the duration of succession rights.[5] In particular, it must be appreciated that the right to apply for succession on retirement *only applies to tenancies to which succession rights on death already accrue* – either because the tenancy was granted prior to the coming into force of the Agricultural Holdings Act 1984, or because in the tenancy agreement (if granted subsequently) the parties have expressly provided for the succession scheme to continue to apply.[6]

The procedural rules governing retirement are complex, and must be carefully adhered to in order to claim the benefit of the new provisions.

1 Section 48(5) and (8) ibid.
2 Section 48(6) ibid.
3 See s 48(9) ibid. On the rent valuation provisions in Sch 2 see generally Ch 5, p 88 ff above.
4 Report of the Committee of Inquiry into the Acquisition and Occupancy of Agricultural Land (1979) Cmnd 7599, paras 633–636.
5 1986 Act, Sections 51 and 37.
6 As provided for in section 34(1)(b)(iii) of the 1986 Act.

1.   Retirement notice

The tenant of the holding (or in the case of a joint tenancy all the tenants) may give notice to the landlord indicating that he wishes a single 'eligible' person named in the retirement notice to succeed him as tenant of the holding from a specified date.[7] The date specified, at which succession is to take place, must be a date on which the tenancy could have been lawfully terminated by notice to quit given at the date of the retirement notice, *viz.* a contractual term date at least twelve months from the date of the notice.[8] That date must also be not less than one year, and not more than two years from the date of the notice. The definition of 'tenant' does not include an executor, administrator, trustee in bankruptcy or other person deriving title from a tenant by operation of law.[9] Thus, a person holding a tenancy in any of these capacities (for instance as the executor of a deceased tenant) will not be able to serve a retirement notice.

The right to use the retirement provisions can only be exercised once. If a retirement notice has been served by a retiring tenant, and an application for succession has been made to the Agricultural Land Tribunal by the nominated successor, then a further application for retirement succession cannot be made at a future date.[10] In particular, of course, if the tenant serves a retirement notice and his nominated successor is later adjudged to be unsuitable to become the tenant of the holding, a fresh retirement notice specifying an alternative successor will be ineffective. Similarly, the tenant will be unable to serve another retirement notice nominating the same successor at a later date when, perhaps, the latter's circumstances might have changed so as to render him 'suitable' to take the tenancy. Note, however, that if an application is withdrawn or abandoned it is to be treated as if it had never been made, with the result that a fresh retirement notice *can* be served.[11]

The right to apply for a new tenancy is excluded by s 51(3) *unless*:

(a)   On the date specified in the notice as the date from which the proposed succession is to take place the tenant will have attained the age of 65; where there is a joint tenancy all joint tenants must have achieved this age, or,

(b)   When he has not attained the age of 65, he is suffering from bodily or mental infirmity to an extent which is likely to prevent him permanently from conducting the farming of the holding so as to ensure compliance with the rules of good husbandry. In the case of joint tenants, all the tenants must meet the requirement as to ill-health. Agricultural Land Tribunals are free to decide for themselves how to evaluate ill health. It has, however, been restrictively interpreted to allow succession only where the tenant is too ill to manage, direct and control the farming enterprise. It is not sufficient that he is unable, through ill health, to do physical work on the holding. In other words, 'conducting' the farming of the holding means more

7   Agricultural Holdings Act 1986 Section 49(1)(b).
8   See s 25(1) ibid.
9   Section 49(2) and s 34(2) ibid.
10   Section 51(2) ibid.
11   Section 53(10) ibid.

than doing physical work and includes managing the farm enterprise.[12] If for any reason an application on grounds of ill health is dismissed, then a further application can only be made on the later death of the tenant.

By virtue of section 51(1), no succession pursuant to a retirement notice can take place where, on each of the last two occasions when the sole surviving tenant died, either

(a) a tenancy was granted to a successor under section 39 pursuant to a tribunal direction; *or*

(b) a tenancy was granted to a person who was the sole remaining applicant for a tribunal direction entitling him to succeed to the tenancy.[13]

When a nominated successor obtains a tenancy pursuant to an application following a retirement notice, then that succession (on retirement) is deemed to be one succession on death for the purposes of the scheme applying on death.[14] The overall result is that a retirement notice can only be served, and an application made, where there have not already been two successions – either on death or retirement.

2. Eligibility of nominated successor

The criteria for establishing the eligibility of the successor nominated in the retirement notice are modelled on the eligibility rules, laid down in sections 35 and 36, governing succession on death, and will only be summarised here. The one major difference is that there is no provision corresponding to section 41 enabling the 'nominated successor' to apply to be 'treated' as eligible. To be 'eligible' a successor must satisfy three criteria:

(a) He must be a 'close relative' of the retiring tenant. This is defined by s 49(3) in identical terms to the provisions applicable on death (above).

(b) He must satisfy the 'livelihood condition', and

(c) He must not be the occupier of a commercial unit of agricultural land, or if he is, he must occupy it as a licensee only (the occupancy condition).[15]

The nominated successor must be an 'eligible' person at the date of the giving of the retirement notice, and must continue to be eligible up to the determination of the application by the Tribunal. If, therefore, he occupies a commercial unit of agricultural land, other than as a licensee, this must be disposed of prior to the service of a retirement notice.

The livelihood and occupancy conditions are defined in identical terms to the provisions applicable on death by section 50.[16]

---

12 *Graves v Cropper* (1987) Northern Area ALT (unreported).
13 See section 37(1)(b) Agricultural Holdings Act 1986.
14 Section 37(6) ibid.
15 Section 50(2) ibid.
16 See above pp 157–163.

The anti-avoidance provisions in Sch 6 (discussed above) also apply as on death.[17]

3.   Application for tenancy

The nominated successor must, *within one month following service of the retirement notice*, apply to the Agricultural Land Tribunal for a direction entitling him to a tenancy of the holding. The application must be signed by both retiring tenant and nominated successor, and must be accompanied by a copy of the retirement notice.[18]

Suitability of nominated successor. If the Tribunal is satisfied that the nominated successor is 'eligible' for succession they must then determine whether he is in their opinion a 'suitable' person to become tenant of the holding.[19] When assessing the applicant's suitability they must have regard to:

(a)   the extent to which he has been trained in, or had practical experience of, agriculture,

(b)   his age, physical health and financial standing,

(c)   the views (if any) stated by the landlord as to his suitability.[20]

Before deciding the issue, the Tribunal must afford the landlord an opportunity to state his views as to the suitability of the applicant. The onus of proof is on the nominated successor, and the Tribunal has a wide discretion (within the above guidelines) to enter into a wide-ranging investigation of the successor's suitability. The successor will have to satisfy the Tribunal that he would be considered a suitable tenant by a reasonable and prudent landlord, ie he must be sufficiently competent to be able to realise the holding's potential. Tribunals accept modest standards of competence when operating the scheme for succession on death, and there is no reason to suppose a different standard will apply to succession applications on retirement.

If the nominated successor is both 'eligible' and 'suitable' he is *prima facie* entitled to succeed to the tenancy. The landlord has one further defence, however. By virtue of s 53(8) the tribunal *must* give a direction for succession to an eligible/suitable applicant, *unless*, on an application made by the landlord, it appears that greater hardship would be caused by giving the direction than by refusing the application.[1]

This will be a question of fact for the tribunal. If the application for succession is dismissed the retirement notice is treated as of no effect. As we have seen, the tenant will be precluded from serving a fresh notice specifying an alternative successor. It is therefore advisable to ensure, before serving a retirement notice, that the nominated successor is both eligible, and is likely to be adjudged a suitable person to succeed to the tenancy. If the application

---

17 Section 50(4) Agricultural Holdings Act 1986.
18 Sections 50(1) and 53(1)–(3) ibid.
19 Section 53(5) ibid.
20 Section 53(6) ibid.
1 The greater hardship rule was introduced to parallel the right on a 'death' application of a landlord to seek consent to this notice to quit. In a retirement application no notice to quit would normally be in prospect. See Sch 2 para 5(6) of the 1984 Act.

is withdrawn at some stage prior to its final determination, then it is treated as if it had never been made.[2] In the latter case, the retiring tenant will be able to serve a further retirement notice, as the bar on further retirement notices only applies where a notice has been followed by an application to the Tribunal by the nominated successor, and only continues while that application is outstanding or where it is dismissed.

4. Retirement notice and notices to quit

Where the landlord has served a notice to quit, the tenant may seek to evade his liabilities by serving a retirement notice and setting the retirement procedure in motion. To avoid this possibility, sections 51 and 52 set out complex procedural rules providing for the suspension of the operation of retirement notices in some circumstances where a notice to quit has been served. The rules depend on the point in time at which the notice to quit was served, and the ground on which it was based.

Where a retirement notice is served *after* the service of a valid notice to quit the holding the following rules are applied by s 51:

(a) If the tenancy is subject to a valid notice to quit served under section 26 of the 1986 Act, and either the month allowed to the tenant to serve a counter notice has expired, or the Tribunal has consented to the operation of the notice to quit, then the Tribunal has no jurisdiction to entertain an application for succession pursuant to the retirement notice.[3]

(b) The Tribunal has no jurisdiction to hear an application for succession if, at the date of service of the retirement notice, the tenancy was already subject to a notice to quit given before that date under Case C (certificate of bad husbandry) or Case F (insolvency of tenant) in Schedule 3 to the 1986 Act.[4] Such notices cannot be challenged by arbitration or the tribunal consent procedure.

(c) The Tribunal has no jurisdiction if, at the date of the retirement notice, the tenancy was subject to a notice to quit falling under Case B (land required for non-agricultural use), Case D (failure to pay rent or to remedy breach of tenancy) or Case E (irremediable breach of tenancy by tenant) *and either*:

    (i) the month allowed for reference to arbitration of the facts alleged in the notice to quit has elapsed; *or*

    (ii) the facts alleged in the notice to quit were referred to arbitration, and were upheld; *or*

    (iii) the Agricultural Land Tribunal consented to the operation of the notice to quit (where applicable).[5]

The notice to quit, in all these cases, will have become final *before* the retirement notice was given.

(d) Contrast the position where, at the date of service of the retirement

2 Section 53(10) Agricultural Holdings Act 1986.
3 Sections 38(1) and 51(1) ibid.
4 Sections 38(2) and 51(1) ibid.
5 See s 38(3) applied by s 51(1) ibid.

notice, the tenancy is subject to a valid notice to quit given under Cases B, D or E (as above), but the period during which a reference to arbitration can be made has not elapsed, *viz.* the notice to quit has not yet become final (*cf* (c) above). In this instance the operation of the retirement notice is *suspended until either*:

(i)   it is determined by arbitration that the notice to quit is invalid because the facts alleged in it are unsubstantiated; *or*

(ii) where the notice to quit was given on grounds of the tenant's failure to comply with a notice to do work, the Agricultural Land Tribunal has either withheld consent to the operation of the notice, or the period for application for consent has expired.[6]

Where either (i) or (ii) occurs, so as to 'revive' the retirement notice, the nominated successor has one month beginning with the date on which the arbitrator's award is served on him, *or* with the date of the Tribunal's decision to withhold consent *or* with the expiry of the period for making an application for consent (whichever applies), in which to make his application to the Tribunal for succession to the tenancy pursuant to the retirement notice.[7]

(e) One further point merits attention. It would appear from s 52(1)(a) and s 52(2)(b) that a notice to quit served by the landlord on or after the date of the retirement notice under Case C or D will *only* be effective if the certificate of bad husbandry was applied for, or the notice to pay rent or to remedy was given, *before* the retirement notice.

Where the tenancy becomes subject to a valid notice to quit given *on or after* the date of the retirement notice, but *before* the Tribunal have begun to hear an application by the nominated successor for the grant of a tenancy, different rules apply. If the notice to quit is given pursuant to Case B (land required for non agricultural use) or Case D (failure to pay rent or do work) then the retirement notice is *suspended* until either:

(a) it is determined by arbitration that the notice to quit is ineffective because of the invalidity of the reasons on which it is based; *or*

(b) in the case of alleged non-compliance with a notice to do work under Case D, where a counter notice has been served and the Tribunal subsequently withhold consent, or the time limit for the landlord to apply for consent expires.[8]

Where the retirement notice is 'revived' by the occurrence of either of these events the tenant has one month from the date of delivery of the arbitrator's award, the date of the Tribunal's refusal of consent or the expiry of the period to apply for consent (whichever applies), in which to apply for a direction entitling him to the grant of a tenancy.[9]

If the tenancy becomes subject to a notice to quit given (similarly) *on or after* the date of the giving of the retirement notice, but *before* the nominated successor has applied for a direction entitling him to a tenancy, then if the

6 See s 51(5) of the 1986 Act.
7 Section 51(6) ibid.
8 See s 52(2) and (3) ibid.
9 Section 52(4) ibid.

notice to quit is based on Case C (Certificate of Bad Husbandry) or Case F (insolvency of tenant) the retirement notice is of no effect and no proceedings can be taken upon it.[10] In these cases the notice to quit is final, unless challenged at common law, as the arbitration and tribunal consent requirements do not apply.

If an application by the nominated successor is invalidated by the operation of the above rules, it is treated as if it had never been made, with the result that if for any reason the tenant retains the tenancy (despite the notice to quit) he will be able to serve a fresh retirement notice at a future date.[11]

5. Landlord's notice to quit

Any notice to quit given to the tenant – either before or after the giving of a Retirement Notice – which does not fall within the above rules is deemed by s 54 to be of no effect during the one-month period for making application for succession, or during the course of succession proceedings if application is duly made. If the Tribunal direct that succession take place, then the notice to quit has no effect. This would apply, for instance, in the case of a notice to quit given under s 26(1), where the period allowed for referring the notice for tribunal consent had not expired at the date of the retirement notice.

6. Dismissal of application

Where the Tribunal disposes of the nominated successor's application other than by directing that a succession tenancy be granted, then the (unsuccessful) nominated successor is barred from applying for succession on the tenant's later death.[12] This will be the case even where a substantial period has elapsed between the Tribunal's refusal of succession and the tenant's later death, during which time the unsuccessful nominated successor may have become both an 'eligible' and 'suitable' candidate for succession.

7. Effect of direction entitling the nominated successor to a tenancy of the holding

A direction by the Tribunal entitling the nominated successor to a tenancy of the holding entitles him to a tenancy of the holding as from the retirement date specified in the retirement notice. The new tenancy is to be on the same terms as those on which the holding was let at the date of the giving of the retirement notice, and a tenancy on these terms is 'deemed' to be granted by the landlord to the nominated successor on the date specified in the notice as the date on which the proposed succession is to take place.[13]

The new tenancy is deemed to include a covenant not to assign, sub-let or

10 Section 52(1) ibid.
11 See s 52(5) ibid.
12 Section 57(4) ibid.
13 Section 55(1) and s 56(1) ibid.

part with possession of the whole or part of the holding without the landlord's consent in writing.[14]

The right to receive a tenancy pursuant to a Tribunal's direction is itself not assignable.[15] If the Tribunal's direction is given within three months prior to the retirement date the Tribunal can (on the tenant's application) specify as the date for commencement of the new tenancy any date within the period of three months following the retirement date. If the direction is itself made after the retirement date, the new tenancy can commence at any date during the period of three months immediately following the giving of the direction.[16]

8.   Sub-tenancies

The retirement provisions make identical provision to the rules applicable on death to protect the security of a subtenant whose landlord has created intervening leasehold interests subsequent to the grant of the original tenancy. Section 55(2) and (3) provide that the successor's tenancy, granted pursuant to the Tribunal order, is deemed to be granted by the person for the time being entitled to the interest from which the tenancy of the retiring tenant was originally derived, ie the freehold reversioner (in most cases) or a pre-existing head lessee. The 'supervening interest' of a mesne tenant inserted after the date of the original tenancy is disregarded.[17]

9.   Arbitration on the terms of the new tenancy

At any time between the giving of the Tribunal's direction and the end of three months from the date specified in the retirement notice as the date on which succession is to take place, either party may apply for arbitration as to the terms of the new tenancy.[18] The provisions as to arbitration set out in s 48 of the 1986 Act apply, in the same way as they do where succession takes place on the death of the tenant. Note that where retirement occurs, a demand for arbitration must normally be made within three months of the retirement date.

10.   Death of retiring tenant

If the retiring tenant dies after serving his retirement notice, but before the nominated successor's application has been 'finally disposed of' by the Tribunal, then the retirement notice is of no effect.[19] If proceedings have begun pursuant to the notice they must be discontinued and the issue of succession dealt with under ss 36 to 48 of the 1986 Act, *viz.* the nominated successor (or any other 'eligible' applicant) will have to make a fresh

14 Section 56(2) ibid.
15 Section 55(6) ibid.
16 See s 55(8) ibid.
17 And see p 168 above.
18 Sections 56(3) and 48 ibid.
19 Section 57(2) ibid.

application to the Tribunal for an order entitling him to succeed to the tenancy on death. Where proceedings on the retirement notice are well advanced, but an order not yet made, the result will be to lengthen substantially the Tribunal proceedings.

Where the retiring tenant dies *after* the Tribunal has made a direction entitling the nominated successor to succeed to the tenancy, but *before* the date on which succession is to take place, then the nominated successor succeeds to the tenancy under the retirement notice, and *not* ss 36–48 of the 1986 Act.[20] Provided the Tribunal has made a direction, therefore, a fresh application following the tenant's death will not need to be made.

As we have seen (above), where the tenant dies at any time after the Tribunal has disposed of an application by ruling the nominated successor to be 'ineligible' or 'unsuitable' for the grant of a tenancy, the nominated successor is barred from subsequently applying for succession under the 1986 Act.[1]

11.   Effect of direction on succession to other holdings

If the retiring tenant dies, and the nominated successor is for the time being entitled to a tenancy of the holding pursuant to a direction of the Tribunal, then he is 'deemed' (by s 58 of the 1986 Act) to be occupying that holding for the purposes of satisfying the occupancy condition[2] in relation to any other tenancies held by the deceased. Thus, if the holding to which he succeeds on retirement is a 'commercial unit' of agricultural land he will be ineligible to apply for a direction entitling him to succeed to any of the other tenancies held by the deceased tenant at his death.

12.   Interaction of retirement and death provisions

Where the nominated successor obtains a tenancy following a direction under s 53, then on his subsequent death the provisions providing for succession on death will apply in the usual way. If he dies leaving close relatives, they may apply for a further transmission of the tenancy (provided two successions have not already taken place). The grant of a new tenancy to the nominated successor on retirement counts as one transmission of the tenancy for the purposes of the succession scheme on death, and also for the purposes of future applications on retirement.[3]

13.   Voluntary succession on retirement

Section 37(2) of the 1986 Act provides that if a tenant retires, and the landlord grants a new tenancy to one of his close relatives who *would* (had the tenant died) have satisfied the 'eligibility' test in section 43(3), then the tenancy granted to that close relative is to be treated as one succession for

20 Section 57(3) ibid.
 1 Section 57(4) ibid.
 2 Section 36(3)(b) ibid. Above p 159 ff.
 3 See s 38, applied by s 51(1) of the 1986 Act, with modifications.

the purposes of the scheme of statutory succession. This is intended to encourage voluntary, agreed, retirements without the necessity and expense of a Tribunal application. No age limit is specified for retirement, and thus a tenant can retire at an earlier age than 65. From the landlord's point of view, a voluntary succession will not extend security of tenure from two generations to three. Following reforms introduced by the 1984 Act, agreed succession can be effected by assignment of the current tenancy, and can be to part only of the original holding. It will also count as one succession if the landlord grants a joint tenancy to persons one of whom would be eligible and suitable to succeed to the tenancy in the event of the tenant's death.

Chapter 9
Compensation on termination of tenancy

A   Introduction

At common law the tenant of an agricultural holding only enjoyed customary rights to compensation on termination of his tenancy, but compensation for improvements, such as the erection of buildings, was not generally payable. The statutory provisions providing for compensation now provide an important legislative framework of rights protecting the tenant's financial interest on termination of a tenancy. Customary rights to compensation play a much more restricted role than hitherto. Section 77 of the 1986 Act provides that the landlord or tenant of an agricultural holding shall not be entitled under custom to any compensation for any improvement or tenant right matter, unless the improvement concerned was began before 1st March 1948 and is of a kind specified in Schedule 7 (long term improvements) or Part I of Schedule 8 (short term improvements) to the 1986 Act.

B   Claims on termination – requirements

1.   Notice of intention to claim

By virtue of section 83(2) of the 1986 Act no claim, by either landlord or tenant, is enforceable unless before the expiry of two months from the termination of the tenancy, the claimant has served notice in writing on his landlord or tenant (whichever applies) of his intention to make a claim. The notice of intention to claim must clearly indicate the nature of the claim, although at this stage it will suffice to indicate the term of the tenancy, statutory provision or custom by virtue of which the claim is being made, without giving further particulars. Service in good time of notice under section 83 is an absolute requirement, non fulfilment of which bars the right of the party in default to receive compensation under the Act. There is no provision for extension of the time limit within which notice must be served. Moreover, the requirement of notice applies to any claim of whatever nature by tenant or landlord, whether it arises under the Act itself or under any custom or agreement, provided always that it arises on or out of the termination of the tenancy of the holding or part of it.[1]

All claims for compensation are assigned for determination by arbitration under the Act. The parties may, within the period of eight months from the termination of the tenancy, by agreement in writing, settle any claim for compensation.[2] Where, however, by the expiry of the eight month period from termination the parties' claims have not been settled by written agreement, then they must be determined by arbitration under the 1986 Act. When applying the two-month time limit from termination, for the purposes of section 83, the 'corresponding date' rule[3] will apply. Problems may arise where the tenancy is terminated by notice to quit, with the tenant holding over in possession as a tenant at will following termination. To prevent the working of an injustice by the notice of claim provisions, section 83(6) provides that where a tenant lawfully remains in occupation of part of a holding after the termination of a tenancy, references in section 83(2) to the service of notice within two months of termination shall, in the case of a claim relating to that part of the holding still occupied, be construed as a reference to termination of the tenant's occupation of the holding. Notice must therefore be served within two months following the termination of occupation of that part of the holding.

It has been held, albeit at first instance, that notice of intention to claim under section 83 can be validly served before the termination of the tenancy, ie that the requirement of service 'before the expiry of two months from the termination of the tenancy' does not *preclude* service prior to termination, which of necessity will also be service before a date two months after the date of termination of the tenancy (this being the requirement imposed by the Act).[4]

2.   Specific claims – additional requirements

In addition to notice of intention to claim[5], the making by landlord or tenant of specific claims allowed for under the 1986 Act involves further procedural formalities:

(a)   *Compensation for disturbance*. If the tenant wishes to make a claim for 'basic' compensation for disturbance of more than one year's rent[6] he must, not less than one month *before* the termination of the tenancy, give to the landlord notice in writing of his intention to make a claim under the relevant provisions.[7] Preliminary notice under section 60 must be served if the tenant's right to claim this

---

1 See s 83(1) Agricultural Holdings Act 1986.
2 Section 83(4) ibid.
3 See *Dodds v Walker* [1981] 2 All ER 609, HL and *E J Riley Investments Ltd v Eurostile Holdings Ltd* [1985] 2 EGLR 124, CA.
4 See *Lady Hallinan v Jones* (1984) 272 EG 1081 (CC), Langton Davies QC.
5 Under s 83 (above).
6 See s 60(3)(b) ibid.
7 Section 60(6) ibid.

additional sum is to be protected; this requirement is in addition to the requirements of section 83 as to service of notice of intention to claim *following* termination of the tenancy. There is a question whether service of a notice under section 60(6) also satisfies the requirements of section 83(2), *viz.* whether two notices need to be served, or whether one will suffice. Clearly, it may be prudent to serve two notices to avoid doubt.

(b) *Short-term improvements.* By virtue of section 68(1) a tenant shall not be entitled to compensation for an improvement specified in paragraph 1 of schedule 8 to the 1986 Act, unless not later than one month before the improvement was *begun* he gave notice in writing to the landlord of his intention to carry it out. This provision refers to mole drainage, and work carried out to secure its efficient functioning. Although the landlord's consent to the improvement is not necessary, it would be prudent to record the giving of notice *and* the date on which drainage works commenced to obviate any dispute as to claims for compensation on later termination of the tenancy.

(c) *Long-term improvements requiring consent.* By virtue of section 67(1) the tenant will not be entitled to compensation for 'a relevant improvement' specified in Schedule 7 (long-term improvements) unless the landlord has given his consent in writing to the carrying out of the improvement. The giving of consent is an absolute prerequisite to a claim for improvements under Schedule 7, Part 1. In the case of the most important improvements encountered in practice, however,[8] a tenant aggrieved by his landlord's refusal to grant consent can apply for the approval of an agricultural land tribunal to the execution of the works concerned. Although the Act does not require the giving of consent *prior* to the carrying out of the works in question, clearly it would be imprudent to carry out works without prior consent, as refusal to grant the latter will bar a claim for compensation. Consent, if given, must be in writing.

(d) *Claims for special system of farming.* If the tenant wishes to pursue a claim on termination to recompense him for the continuous adoption of a system of farming which has been more beneficial to the holding than that required by his contract, or than the system of farming normally practiced on comparable holdings,[9] then he must *not later than* one month before the termination of the tenancy give the landlord notice in writing of his intention to claim compensation in these terms.[10] Additionally, no claim can be made unless a record has been made of the condition of the holding and its fixed equipment, pursuant to section 22 of the 1986 Act.[11] No claim can be made for compensation in respect of a matter arising before the date on which the record was made.

---

8 For instance the erection of buildings.
9 See s 70(1) Agricultural Holdings Act 1986.
10 See s 70(2) ibid.
11 See Chapter 3 above.

(e)   *Landlord's claim for general deterioration of holding.* Section 72(4)
provides that the landlord cannot obtain compensation for general
deterioration of a holding unless, not later than one month before
the termination of the tenancy, he has given notice in writing to the
tenant of his intention to claim such compensation. In *Lady
Hallinan v Jones*[12] it was held that notice served in accordance with
this requirement, prior to termination, also satisfied the
requirements of section 83(2), *viz.* that a section 72 notice has all the
ingredients of a section 83 notice of claim and satisfies both
requirements. Consequently, one notice only need be served,
although prudence would dictate the service of separate notices for
the avoidance of doubt.

Milk quotas – special provisions. The tenant's right to compensation for milk
quota, on termination of his tenancy, is dealt with separately in Chapter 14.
It should be noted here, however, that schedule 1 paragraph 11 of the
Agriculture Act 1986 puts in place similar procedural requirements for the
making of a valid claim for quota compensation to those set out in section 83
of the Agricultural Holdings Act 1986 (above). Schedule 1, para 11(1)
provides that no claim for quota compensation is enforceable unless, before
the expiry of the period of two months from the termination of the tenancy in
question, the tenant serves notice in writing on his landlord of his intention
to make that claim. Disputes as to compensation for milk quota are assigned
to arbitration under the Agricultural Holdings Act 1986. As with other
claims on termination the parties can, within the period of eight months
from termination of the tenancy, settle the claim for quota compensation by
written agreement. If the claim has not been settled during that period it
must be determined by arbitration under the agricultural holdings
legislation.[13] The arbitration provisions of the Agricultural Holdings Act
apply to a quota arbitration on termination, with the one difference that the
arbitrator in a quota arbitration can fix the day for payment of the
compensation awarded to be not later than three months following the date
of the award – whereas in an ordinary arbitration the date fixed for payment
must be within *one* month of the date of that award.[14] As with ordinary claims
on termination, the two-month limit for service of notice of intention to claim
runs from the date on which the tenant's occupation of part of the holding
ceases, if he has remained in occupation following termination. This
provision protects the tenant holding over in possession.[15]

C   Tenant's claims on termination

1.   General

The statutory provisions governing compensation for improvements, tenant
right matters and compensation for disturbance all provide that

---

12 Above n 4.
13 Schedule 1, para 11(2), Agriculture Act 1986.
14 See Schedule 1, para 11(5), ibid.
15 See Schedule 1, para 11(4) ibid.

compensation is only payable on the termination of a tenancy, and on the tenant's quitting the holding.[16] In the context of compensation for disturbance it has been held that even if a landlord's notice to quit is bad, then provided it is accepted as good by the tenant, who quits the holding in reliance thereon, then compensation is payable.[17] This principle will apply, it is suggested, not only where notice to quit is bad for failure to comply with the contractual position between the parties, but also where a notice to quit is bad due to non-observance of some statutory provision (for instance the requirements as to minimum length of notice to quit).[18] If a notice to quit has been given, then the true meaning of the statutory provisions is that compensation will be payable where the tenant quits 'by reason of this document, good, bad, or indifferent, namely the notice to quit served by the landlord'.[19] Although the cases concern disturbance compensation, there seems no reason in principle why similar considerations should not also apply to compensation for improvements and tenant right matters.

Compensation is payable on 'termination' of the tenancy, which phrase is widely defined by section 96(1) to mean 'the cessor of the contract of tenancy by reason of effluxion of time or from any other cause'. Compensation will therefore be payable on termination of a fixed term by effluxion of time, and following termination by notice to quit, surrender, or forfeiture pursuant to a proviso for re-entry. Note, however, that compensation for disturbance is only payable where the tenant quits pursuant to a notice to quit given by the landlord.[20]

Compensation is payable by whoever is landlord at the time of termination of the tenancy. 'Landlord' is defined[1] to include any person for the time being entitled to receive the rents and profits of the land. Where the landlord has assigned the reversionary estate to a third party, then section 93(5) provides that unless or until the tenant has notice that the person who previously was entitled to receive the rents and profits of the holding (ie 'the original landlord') has ceased to be so entitled, together with notice of the name and address of the person who has become entitled to receive rents and profits (ie the new landlord), then any notice or document served on the original landlord is deemed for the purpose of the Act to have been served on or delivered to the landlord of the holding. Notice of claim served on termination of the tenancy upon the original landlord will, therefore, remain valid, unless the tenant has received prior notice of the name and address of his new landlord.

The identity of the landlord (and hence the person obliged to pay compensation on termination) may change between the giving of notice to quit and the subsequent termination of the tenancy. If notice to quit is given by the landlord, but takes effect after a sale by him of his reversionary estate, then the new reversionary owner will be the landlord receiving rents and profits for the purposes of paying compensation. By virtue of the ruling in *Lysaght v Edwards*[2], upon conclusion of a contract of sale the vendor

16 See sections 60(1), 64(1), 65(1) and 70(1) of the 1986 Act.
17 *Westlake v Page* [1926] 1 KB 299, CA.
18 See section 25 of the 1986 Act.
19 *Kestell v Langmaid* [1951] 1 KB 233 at 240, CA per Lord Evershed.
20 See s 60(1) Agricultural Holdings Act 1986.
 1 See s 96(1) ibid.
 2 (1876) 2 ChD 499.

becomes in equity a trustee of the reversionary estate for the purchaser, beneficial ownership in equity passing to the purchaser. Normally, however, the purchaser will only become entitled to receive rents and profits (and hence become the landlord for the purpose of the 1986 Act) from the date expressly fixed by the contract for completion of the purchase,[3] eg where the contract provides for apportionment of rent due as from the date of completion. If, however, the contract entitles the purchaser to receive rents and profits from the date of contract then he will at that date become the 'landlord' for the purposes of the compensation provisions of the legislation. Section 96(6) stipulates that the designation of landlord and tenant continues to apply to the parties until the conclusion of any proceedings taken under or pursuant to the Act in respect of compensation.

2.   Compensation for 'relevant' improvements

By virtue of s 64(1) the tenant is entitled on termination of his tenancy, on quitting the holding, to obtain from the landlord compensation for an improvement specified in Schedule 7 to the 1986 Act carried out on the holding by the tenant, being an improvement begun on or after 1st March 1948. Schedule 7 specifies two classes of long-term improvement begun on or after 1st March 1948, and for which compensation is payable. The measure of compensation payable is an amount equal to the increase, attributable to the improvement, in the value of the agricultural holding *as a holding*, having regard to the character and situation of the holding, and the average requirements of tenants reasonably skilled in husbandry.[4] This figure is usually arrived at by calculating the increase in letting value attributable to the improvement, and then multiplying by a number of years purchase to reflect the expected lifespan of the improvement concerned, thus arriving at a capital figure of compensation payable. The improvements for which compensation is payable are largely agricultural in nature. This could be of significance where diversification takes place, as improvements connected herewith may not qualify for compensation under Sch 7.

(a)   Long-term improvements requiring consent

Schedule 7, Part 1 lists a number of major improvements which require the consent of the landlord, *prior* to execution, if compensation is to be recoverable on the later termination of the tenancy. By virtue of section 67(1) the tenant is not entitled to compensation for a relevant improvement specified in Schedule 7 unless the landlord has given his consent in writing to the carrying out of the improvement. The consent can be given by the landlord unconditionally 'or upon such terms as to compensation or otherwise as may be agreed upon in writing between the landlord and the tenant'.[5] The parties can agree compensation, provided they do so in writing. There is a question whether they can agree that *no* compensation will be payable on termination. In the old case of *Mears v Callender*[6] it was held that

---

3 See *Dale v Hatfield Chase Corpn* [1922] 2 KB 282, CA; *Bradshaw v Bird* [1920] 3 KB 144, CA.
4 Section 66(1).
5 Section 67(2).
6 [1901] 2 Ch 388 (Cozens-Hardy J).

a stipulation that no compensation would ever be payable was void. This decision has, however, been consistently criticised and has not been followed in the Scottish courts.[7] In the absence of clear guidance the accepted view would appear to be that an agreement providing for no compensation to be payable would not infringe the terms of the Act.[8]

The long-term improvements for which the landlord's consent must be obtained in all cases, enumerated in Chapter 7, Part 1, are: the making or planting of osier beds, water meadows, watercress beds, planting of hops, planting of orchards or fruit bushes, the warping or weiring of land, making of gardens, and (finally) the provision of underground tanks on the holding.

(b)   Improvements requiring consent of landlord or tribunal

Part II of Schedule 7 specifies a number of improvements in respect of which, in the absence of the landlord's consent to their execution, a tenant can apply to an agricultural land tribunal for approval. Section 67(3) provides that, in the case of an improvement specified in Part 2, if the tenant is aggrieved by the refusal of his landlord to give consent, or is unwilling to agree to any terms subject to which the landlord is prepared to give that consent, he may apply to the tribunal for approval of the carrying out of the improvement. The tribunal has jurisdiction to approve the carrying out of the improvement, either unconditionally or upon such terms (whether as to reduction of compensation payable or other matters) as appear to them to be just. They may also withhold their approval if they feel this appropriate.[9] Where the tribunal give approval the landlord has the right, within one month of receiving notification of their decision, to serve notice in writing on both tribunal and tenant to the effect that he proposes to carry out the improvements himself.[10] If the tribunal grant approval for carrying out improvements then, if no notice is served by the landlord indicating his intention to carry out the works himself, or (if such a notice has been served) the tribunal later determines that the landlord has failed to carry out the improvements within a reasonable time, the tribunal's original approval has effect as if it were the consent of the landlord – with the result that compensation under Schedule 7 will be payable on later termination of the tenancy.[11] Any terms subject to which tribunal consent was given have effect as if they were contained in an agreement in writing between landlord and tenant.[12]

The improvements covered by Schedule 7, Part 2 are the most important likely to be encountered in practice. They include the following:

> (i)   The erection, alteration or enlargement of buildings, or making or improvement of permanent yards. *Semble* this would include buildings erected for a non-agricultural use connected with diversification of the farming enterprise.

7   See *Turnbull v Millar* 1942 SC 521 (and especially at 535 'the text books show that during the last forty years the opinion of Cozens-Hardy J has not been adopted by the settled practice of the profession and the agricultural community, and has remained the subject of discussion and controversy.')
8   See Muir-Watt, *Agricultural Holdings* (13th Edition) p 203, Scammell and Densham's *Law of Agricultural Holdings* (7th Edition) p 299, and see dicta in *Johnson v Moreton* [1980] AC 37 at p 58, HL, per Lord Hailsham LC.
9   Section 67(4) Agricultural Holdings Act 1986.
10   Section 67(5) ibid and SI 1978/259, rule 7(2).
11   See s 67(6) ibid.
12   Section 67(6) ibid.

(ii)   Carrying out works in compliance with an improvement notice under Part 7 of the Housing Act 1985 or Part 8 of the Housing Act 1974.
(iii)   Erection or construction of loading platforms, ramps, etc.
(iv)   Construction of silos.
(v)   Claiming of land.
(vi)   Marling of land.
(vii)   Making or improvement of roads and bridges.
(viii)   Making or improvement of water courses, culverts, ponds, wells or reservoirs or of works for the application of water power for agricultural or domestic purposes, etc.
(ix)   Making or removal of permanent fences.
(x)   Reclaiming waste land.
(xi)   Making or improving embankments and sluices.
(xii)   Erection of wire work for hop gardens.
(xiii)   Provision of permanent sheep dipping facilities.
(xiv)   Removal of bracken, gorse, tree roots, boulders or 'other obstructions to cultivation.'
(xv)   Land drainage.
(xvi)   The provision of electrical light and power.
(xvii)   Provision of facilities for storage and disposal of sewage or farm waste, eg slurry.
(xviii)   Repairs to fixed equipment.
(xix)   Grubbing up of orchards or fruit bushes.
(xx)   Planting trees (otherwise than as an orchard) and bushes (other than fruit bushes) eg planting trees that form screening.

3. Short-term improvements

By virtue of section 64(1) the tenant is also entitled to compensation on termination of his tenancy, on quitting the holding, for improvements specified in Part 1 of Schedule 8 to the Act, *viz.* short term improvements begun on or after the 1st March 1948. These are improvements which enure, for a period of limited duration, for the benefit of an incoming tenant by putting the land in good heart and condition. Compensation under Schedule 8, Part 1 can be claimed for: mole drainage and works carried out to secure its efficient functioning, protection of fruit trees against animals, clay burning, liming and chalking of the land, application of purchased manure and fertilizer and (finally) consumption on the holding of corn, cake or other feed stuff not produced on the holding, by horses, cattle, sheep, pigs or poultry. The landlord's consent to these improvements is not required as a precondition to a claim for compensation (*Cf* long-term improvements under Schedule 7 above). Section 66(2) provides that the amount of compensation for short-term improvements is the value of the improvement to an incoming tenant calculated in accordance with the prescribed regulations currently in force. The regulations currently in force are the Agriculture (Calculation of Value for Compensation) Regulations 1978 (as amended).[13] Part 1 to the Schedule of the 1978 Regulations sets out detailed rules for the

13 SI 1978/809 as amended successively by SI 1980/751, SI 1981/822 and SI 1983/1475.

calculation of compensation for Schedule 8 improvements. The value of most of these improvements reduces to nil after several years. So, for instance, the value of mole drainage reduces to nil after six years[14] and the value to the incoming tenant of purchased and organic manure applied to the land reduces to nil after three growing seasons.[15] Section 66(3) permits landlord and tenant to enter into an agreement in writing whereby, if any benefit is given or allowed to the tenant in consideration of his carrying out short-term improvements, that benefit can be taken into account in assessing compensation under the Act.

4.   Tenant right matters

Section 65(1) and Schedule 8, Part II provide for the entitlement of the tenant on termination of the tenancy, on quitting the holding, to obtain from his landlord compensation for 'tenant right' matters. The phrase 'tenant right' is used to describe those matters originally not recoverable under statute, but nevertheless customarily recoverable by an outgoing tenant. Where the tenant went into occupation of the holding on or after 1st March 1948 those tenant right matters for which compensation can be recovered are now set out in Schedule 8, Part 2 to the 1986 Act. If the tenant went into occupation prior to 1st March 1948 the tenant can elect, prior to termination of the tenancy and by notice in writing to the landlord, to claim compensation for tenant right under the statutory provisions. If he does not do so, however, his right to compensation will depend upon the custom of the country and the terms of the tenancy agreement, as formerly.[16] Where the tenancy terminates by reason of notice to quit, the landlord is entitled to put the tenant to his election by serving a written notice requiring him to elect whether section 65(1) is to govern claims for tenant right, or whether the claim is to be maintained under customary right or the tenancy agreement. The tenant is not entitled to elect for the statutory measure of compensation to apply after the expiry of one month from the giving of the landlord's notice of election, or (alternatively) one month from the termination of possession proceedings under the Act with the notice to quit having been upheld.[17] If no election is made in accordance with these provisions then the tenant's claim under custom is barred by virtue of section 77(1) of the 1986 Act.

The matters listed in Schedule 8, part 2 for which compensation can be recovered include the value of growing crops, or that of harvested crops and produce grown in the last year of the tenancy and which the tenant has no right to sell or remove.[18] The tenant can also recover the reasonable cost of

14 Schedule 1, para 1, SI 1978/809.
15 Schedule 1, para 6 and tables 2 to 5.
16 Schedule 12, para 6 of the 1986 Act.
17 See Schedule 12, para 6(2).
18 Schedule 8, para 7.

his acts of husbandry – for instance sowing seeds, cultivations, fallows and any other acts of husbandry performed on the holding at his expense.[19] Compensation is also recoverable in respect of pasture laid down with clover, grass, lucerne, sainfoin or other seeds at the tenant's expense, otherwise than in compliance with an obligation imposed upon him by an agreement in writing to lay it down to replace temporary pasture comprised in the holding.[20] A claim can also be made in appropriate cases for the value attributable to acclimatisation, hefting or settlement of hill sheep on hill land.[1] This refers to the value attributable to a flock due to it having been reared and managed on a particular hill or mountain and having thereby developed an instinct not to stray from the particular grazing concerned (which may well be unfenced). Likewise, an outgoing tenant can claim compensation for the residual fertility value of the sod of what are referred to as excess 'qualifying leys' on the holding.[2]

By virtue of section 66(2) the amount of compensation for tenant right matters is the value of the improvement to an incoming tenant, calculated in accordance with the prescribed regulations currently in force. Those currently in force are the Agriculture (Calculation of Value for Compensation) Regulations 1978[3], Part 2 of the Schedule to which contains detailed rules for assessing the value of tenant right matters to an incoming tenant. The value of growing crops left on the holding will be the reasonable cost of seed sold and of cultivations, fallows, and acts of husbandry performed taking into account current costs of labour, hire of equipment, etc.[4] By virtue of section 66(4) of the 1986 Act the parties are free to substitute for the measure of compensation specified in the regulations such measure of compensation, to be calculated according to such method, as may be specified in the written contract of tenancy.

The tenant is *not* entitled to compensation under the Act for tenant right in respect of crops or produce grown, seeds sown, cultivations, fallows or acts of husbandry performed or pasture laid down, if this is in contravention of the terms of the tenancy agreement, which latter must be in writing.[5] Notwithstanding contravention of the terms of the tenancy, however, compensation will be recoverable for tenant right matters if the term of the contract is shown to be inconsistent with the fulfilment by the tenant of his responsibilities to farm the holding in accordance with the rules of good husbandry.[6] The latter therefore override the terms of the tenancy agreement.

5.   Improvements begun before 1st March 1948

By virtue of section 64(4) the provisions of Schedule 9, Part 1 govern the rights of a tenant of an agricultural holding to compensation for those

---

19 Schedule 8, para 8.
20 Schedule 8, para 9.
 1 See Schedule 8, para 10.
 2 Schedule 8, para 11.
 3 SI 1978/809 as amended (above).
 4 Schedule, Part 2, paras 8 and 9.
 5 Section 65(2).
 6 As to which see section 11 of the Agriculture Act 1947 and see Chapter 3 p 56 ff.

improvements[7] carried out on the holding (if any) which were begun before 1st March 1948.[8] These are not commonly encountered in practice, and will therefore not be treated *in extenso* here. Certain salient differences between the codes of compensation applicable to pre-1st March 1948 improvements, and those executed post that date, are of importance, however, and merit attention.

'Old' improvements for which compensation is payable broadly encompass those covered by parts 1 and 2 of schedule 7 ('new' long-term improvements), eg the erection or alteration of buildings, making or removal of permanent fences, drainage work, etc. The amount of compensation for 'old' improvements is calculated on the same basis as for new improvements, *viz*. the amount payable is an amount equal to the increase, attributable to the improvement, in the value of the holding as a holding, having regard to the character and situation of the holding and the average requirements of tenants reasonably skilled in husbandry.[9] The tenant is not entitled to compensation under Schedule 9, however, for an improvement which he was required to carry out by the terms of his tenancy and which was made before 1st January 1921.[10] The most important differences between the code governing old and new improvements are twofold:

(a) The tenant can contract out of his right to compensation for 'old' improvements, or alternatively can claim compensation under custom in lieu of statutory compensation.[11] Contracting out of compensation rights is not allowed in the case of 'new' improvements, and (as already noted) customary compensation has been abolished for new improvements by the provision now contained in section 77(1) of the 1986 Act; *and*

(b) In order to claim compensation for any old improvement (other than drainage) the landlord must have given his consent in writing to the execution of the improvement concerned *prior to* that improvement being carried out.[12] In the case of drainage improvements, compensation is not payable unless, not more than three nor less than two months before beginning to execute the drainage works concerned, notice in writing under section 3 of the Agricultural Holdings Act 1923 signifying the tenant's intention to execute the improvement concerned was served on the landlord, and the parties either agreed the terms on which the work was to be executed or the landlord failed to exercise his statutory right to execute the improvements himself within a reasonable time.[13] In the case of 'new' improvements begun on or after 1st March 1948

---

7 These are specified in Part 2 of Sch 9 ibid.
8 These are commonly termed 'old improvements' – see Schedule 9, para 1(2).
9 Schedule 9, para 2.
10 See Schedule 9, para 1(3).
11 Schedule 9, para 1(4).
12 Schedule 9, para 3(1).
13 Schedule 9, para 4(1) ibid.

there is no requirement that the landlord's consent be obtained before the improvement in question is carried out – albeit prudence would dictate that consent be obtained prior to the incurring of substantial expenditure. Similarly the code for old improvements provides no procedure whereby the tenant can obtain the consent of an agricultural land tribunal if the landlord withholds consent.

6.   Compensation for adoption of special system of farming

Section 70 of the 1986 Act entitles the tenant to claim compensation, additional to that attributable to individual improvements, if he can show that by the continuous adoption of a system of farming more beneficial to the holding than either:

(a)   The system of farming required by his contract of tenancy or
(b)   In the absence of a contractual requirement, the system of farming normally practiced on comparable agricultural holdings,

the value of the holding *as a holding* has been increased during the tenancy. When ascertaining the relevant increase in letting value regard must be had to the character and situation of the holding and the average requirements of tenants reasonably skilled in husbandry.[14]

When assessing the value of the holding for these purposes allowance has to be made for any compensation agreed, or awarded to the tenant, for long or short term improvements or tenant right matters where the latter have caused or contributed to the additional benefit to the holding. In practice it will be difficult to establish an additional benefit to the holding *as a holding* in addition to an increase in value attributable to specific improvements. Furthermore section 70(2) imposes additional conditions on a claim for 'high farming' under this provision, namely, that:

(a)   As already noted, the tenant must not later than one month before the termination of the tenancy have given to the landlord notice in writing of his intention to claim compensation under section 70, and also
(b)   A record of the condition of the holding must have been made under section 22, recording the condition of the fixed equipment on the holding and the general condition of the holding itself. Compensation cannot be recovered in respect of any matter arising before the date of the making of the record.[15]

---

14 See s 70(1) ibid.
15 See s 70(3) ibid.

7. Compensation for disturbance

The tenant's right to compensation for disturbance is of considerable importance. It is now dealt with in ss 60–63 of the 1986 Act and is payable in addition to any compensation to which the tenant may otherwise be entitled under the 1986 Act.[16]

(a) Qualifying conditions

By virtue of s 60(1), disturbance compensation is only payable where the tenancy terminates by reason of a notice to quit given by the landlord, or following a counter-notice by the tenant enlarging a landlord's notice to quit part of the holding.[17] Furthermore, the tenant must 'quit the holding in consequence of the notice or counter-notice' – and not, for instance, following a surrender or forfeiture under the general law.[18] In the case of a fixed term of two years or more, granted on or after 12th September 1984, which terminates following the tenant's death, section 4(3) deems termination to be by landlord's notice to quit, thus preserving the right to compensation for disturbance.

'*In consequence of the notice*'. Whether the tenant has quit in consequence of a notice to quit (or counter notice enlarging the landlord's notice to quit part) is to be decided not by whether there is an interval of time between the expiration of the notice and the tenant's departure, but rather whether there was any break in the causation or sequence between the giving of notice and the tenant's quitting the holding.[19] So, if the tenant remains in possession pending the outcome of tribunal or arbitration proceedings to establish the validity of a notice to quit, and then quits later when the notice is upheld, he will have quit 'in consequence of' the notice and disturbance compensation will be payable.[20] If the landlord's notice to quit is bad in law (for instance for ambiguity or uncertainty) then provided the tenant accepts the notice as good and quits compensation will be payable.[1] The same principle has been applied where a notice to quit is bad for failure to meet statutory requirements.[2] Although the question is not free of doubt, it is thought that a notice to quit which fails to give the statutory minimum notice of 12 months, and is therefore rendered 'invalid' by s 25(1) of the 1986 Act, will engage liability for disturbance compensation if the tenant subsequently quits. Section 25(1) renders the notice to quit 'invalid', ie of no effect to terminate the tenancy, and not a nullity *per se*. If the tenant acts on it to his detriment by quitting the principle in *Westlake v Page*[3] dictates that compensation should

---

16 Section 60(7) Agricultural Holdings Act 1986.
17 As to which see s 32 ibid.
18 It follows that, if compensation is agreed between the parties, any document recording the agreed terms should scrupulously avoid any implication that it records a surrender of the tenancy. If it fails to do so, payments received thereunder may not be regarded as disturbance compensation at all, with significant tax consequences – disturbance compensation is not chargeable to Capital Gains Tax. See *Davis v Powell* [1977] 1 All ER 471. Any other payment received on disposal of the lease (eg by surrender) may well be.
19 *Preston v Norfolk County Council* [1944] KB 775.
20 See *Gulliver v Catt* [1952] 2 QB 308, CA.
 1 *Westlake v Page* [1926] 1 KB 299, CA.
 2 *Kestell v Langmaid* [1950] 1 KB 233, CA (contravention of Defence (General) Regs 1939 rendering notice to quit thereby 'null and void'. Compensation for disturbance payable).
 3 See above n. 1.

be payable. It would indeed be strange were the landlord's culpability in serving an invalid notice to have the effect of depriving the tenant of his statutory right to compensation for disturbance.[4] The true meaning of s 60(1) is that compensation is payable where the tenant quits 'by reason of this document, good, bad or indifferent, namely the notice to quit served by the landlord'.[5]

The claim for disturbance compensation has two elements; the 1986 Act distinguishes between 'basic compensation' and 'additional' compensation.[6]

(b) 'Basic' compensation for disturbance

By virtue of s 60(3) the tenants claim for 'basic' compensation entitles him to:

(i) an amount equal to one year's rent of the holding, at the rate at which rent was payable immediately before the termination of the tenancy; *or*

(ii) a greater amount, reflecting the tenants actual loss or two years' rent of the holding, whichever is less. One year's rent is payable as of right, without proof of loss. If the tenant wishes to claim compensation for loss exceeding this amount, subject to the maximum of two years' rent, the requirements of s 60(6) must be complied with. These are:

(a) Not less than one month before the termination of the tenancy the tenant must give the landlord notice of his intention to make the claim (see p 180 above). It has been held that notice of claim can be validly served by one out of joint tenants.[7] Prudence dictates, however, that all joint tenants join in serving the appropriate notice.

(b) The tenant must, before their sale, give the landlord a reasonable opportunity of making a valuation of any goods, stock, implements, fixtures or produce in respect of which compensation for disturbance is being claimed.[8]

MEASURE OF BASIC COMPENSATION

Where more than one year's rent is claimed, the measure of compensation is prima facie 'the amount of the tenants actual loss'.[9] This is defined more closely by s 60(5) to mean 'the amount of the loss or expense directly attributable to the quitting of the holding which is *unavoidably* incurred by the tenant upon or in connection with the sale or removal of his household goods, implements of husbandry, fixtures, farm produce or farm stock on or used in connection with the holding, and includes any expenses reasonably incurred by him in the preparation of his claim for basic compensation.'

---

4 See the doubts expressed in *Kestell v Langmaid* [1950] 1 KB 233, 239, CA, per Evershed MR. *Cf* however *Thomas v National Farmers Union Mutual Insurance Society Ltd* [1961] 1 WLR 386.

5 *Kestell v Langmaid* [1950] 1 KB 233, 240, CA.

6 See s 60(2).

7 *Howson v Buxton* [1928] All ER Rep 434, CA. And see *Lloyd v Sadler* [1978] QB 774, CA; *Featherstone v Staples* [1986] 2 All ER 461, CA; *Combey v Gumbrill* [1990] 27 EG 85 and, further, p 113 ff above.

8 Whether such opportunity has been given is a question of fact for the arbitrator: *Dale v Hatfield Chase Corpn* [1922] 2 KB 282, CA.

9 Section 60(3)(b) Agricultural Holdings Act 1986.

Costs of an arbitration to determine liability for compensation are not, however, recoverable as basic compensation. Losses incurred on the forced sale of stock and implements will be recoverable. Valuers fees incurred in preparing a claim for compensation are also recoverable, provided they are reasonably incurred by the tenant in the preparation of his claim – even if a claim for compensation is not subsequently made.[10] Whether a loss is too remote to be properly 'directly attributable' to the tenant's quitting the holding is a question of fact. Valuer's fees for the valuation of stock *prior* to the sale is not, for instance, an unavoidable expense of the sale and is prima facie not recoverable.[11]

EXCLUSION OF BASIC COMPENSATION

By virtue of s 61(1) neither basic nor 'additional' compensation are payable where the tenant's right to serve a counter-notice under s 26(1) is excluded by Cases C, D, E, F or G. This refers to the situation where the landlord's notice to quit is expressly given pursuant to one of specified Cases for possession in Sch 3 to the 1986 Act (for instance for failure to pay rent, irremediable breach of the tenancy or following the tenant's death), thus excluding the tenant's right to serve a counter notice and subject the notice to the requirement of tribunal consent. Basic compensation *will* be payable if the landlord's notice to quit is a plain notice, or if it is served pursuant to Cases A, B or H in Sch 3 to the 1986 Act. Further restrictions apply to the availability of 'additional' compensation for disturbance.[12] *Semble* the right to claim both basic and additional compensation will be excluded where the tenancy is terminated not by notice to quit, but by forfeiture in reliance on a priviso for re-entry in the lease – in this event the requirements of s 60(1) will not have been satisfied.[13] This will not, it is thought, work an injustice. Compensation is excluded by s 61 where notice to quit is given for non-payment of rent or other breaches of covenant. There would appear to be no valid reason why either basic or additional compensation should be available in the event of the landlord choosing to proceed, instead, by way of forfeiture for breach of covenant under the general law. Note also that neither basic nor additional compensation can be claimed under the 1986 Act on a surrender of the tenant's interest, a factor of considerable significance when negotiating the terms on which surrender is to take place.

(c)   'Additional' compensation for disturbance

By virtue of s 60(2)(b) and (4) the tenant may be entitled to an amount of *additional* compensation equal to four year's rent of the holding, at the rate at which rent was payable immediately prior to termination of the tenancy, provided certain requirements are met. Additional compensation is not payable if the landlord's notice to quit was given pursuant to any of the cases for possession in Schedule 3 to the 1986 Act, *other than* Case B ie where land is required for a non-agricultural use for which planning permission has been obtained, or for which it is not required by virtue of Crown immunity or exemption in non-planning legislation. Additional compensation is also not

10 *Dunstan v Benney* [1938] 2 KB 1, CA.
11 *Re Evans and Glamorgan County Council's Arbitration* (1912) 76 JP 468.
12 See below pp 193 and 194 ff.
13 To the same effect see *Muir Watt*, Agricultural Holdings (13th ed) p 444.

available if the notice to quit, rather than specifying one of the cases for possession, is a plain notice but states that the carrying out of the purpose for which the landlord proposes to terminate the tenancy is desirable on any of the grounds set out in paragraphs (a) to (c) of section 27(3), or that the landlord will suffer hardship unless the notice has effect. Where a plain notice to quit is given it follows that additional compensation for disturbance is only available if the notice purports to terminate the tenancy for the purpose of a non-agricultural use *not* falling within Case B (ie one which does not require planning permission by virtue of some provision in the Planning legislation itself) or that the carrying out of the landlord's purposes is desirable for the purposes of the enactments relating to allotments. Note however that, if it is to exclude compensation for disturbance, s 61(3) requires the notice to quit to contain a statement to the effect that the carrying out of the purpose for which the landlord proposes to terminate the tenancy is desirable on one of the enumerated grounds in section 27(3). It follows that a notice to quit which fails to specify the grounds on which tribunal consent under section 27 will be sought could lead to a claim for additional (as well as basic) compensation for disturbance. Additional compensation is, in any event, only excluded if an application for consent to the operation of the notice is made to an agricultural land tribunal, and the tribunal grant consent on the grounds in section 27(3) enumerated above.[14] If the tribunal's reasons for giving consent include a statement, however, that they are *also* satisfied that the land is required for a non-agricultural use for which planning permission is not required[15] additional compensation is payable.[16] By virtue of section 61(5) additional compensation is similarly available if the landlord's notice specifies sound management[17] as a ground for consent, and the tribunal, although satisfied as to that ground, would also have been satisfied (had it been pleaded) as to the non-agricultural use ground.[18] The tribunal must include a statement to that effect in the reasons for their decision if additional compensation is to be payable. The complex provisions now found in section 61 are intended to provide additional compensation where the tenant is displaced to enable the land to be used for development, forestry or other non-agricultural purposes. The additional sum of disturbance compensation of four years' rent is payable without proof of loss (*cf* the basic compensation payable under section 60(3)). The complex entitlement rules reflect this general policy, albeit imperfectly.

(d)   Consequential provisions

(i)   *Sub-tenancies.* Where a sub-tenancy of an agricultural holding terminates by operation of law[19] section 63(1) preserves the sub-tenant's right to claim compensation for disturbance – notwithstanding the technical objection that he has not quit

---

14 Section 61(3)(b).
15 Ie section 27(3)(f).
16 Section 61(4).
17 Ie section 27(3)(b).
18 Ie section 27(3)(f) above.
19 For instance where a landlord serves notice to quit on his tenant, and the latter then fails to himself serve notice to quit on any sub-tenant.

pursuant to a notice to quit as required by section 60. Similarly, section 63(2) preserves the mesne tenant's right to compensation as against his immediate landlord notwithstanding the technical objection that he (not being in occupation of the holding) does not quit the holding in the required sense.

(ii) *Notice to quit part.* The tenant's right to claim compensation for disturbance is limited, in some instances, where the landlord serves notice to quit part of the holding and the tenant elects to treat it as a notice to quit the whole holding. If the part subject to notice to quit, taken with any other part of the holding affected by a previous notice to quit, is less than one fourth part of the original holding, *and* the holding as diminished would be reasonably capable of being farmed as a separate holding, then compensation is only payable in respect of that part of the holding to which the notice to quit itself relates.[20]

(iii) *Agreed compensation.* The parties cannot contract out of the tenant's right to claim compensation for disturbance on the statutory basis.[21] They are free, however, to agree that additional compensation exceeding the statutory quantum shall be payable, whether in the contract of tenancy itself or a supplementary agreement. The courts will construe a term giving additional relief in very general and wide terms, and going beyond the statutory provisions, as intended to give a greater measure of relief, for instance where a clause in a tenancy agreement gave the tenant the right to claim compensation for 'any loss or damage he may sustain through . . . disturbance'.[1]

8.   Improvements, disturbance and tenant right: special provisions

(a)   Early resumption clauses

Section 62 applies special rules where the lease contains an early resumption clause enabling the landlord to repossess the holding for some specified use other than agriculture, on giving less than the statutory minimum notice to quit.[2] Where the tenant quits in these circumstances the landlord is liable to pay an additional sum in compensation, equal to the value of the *additional benefit* (if any) which would have accrued to the tenant had the tenancy been terminated (as would otherwise be the case) by 12 months' notice ending on a term date.[3] The tenant's position, for compensation purposes, is to be treated as the same as if he had been given the normal statutory notice to quit, of at least 12 months' duration.

---

20 Section 63(3).
21 See s 78 discussed below.
 1 See *Dean v Secretary of State for War* [1951] 1 All ER 344, CA. Here the tenant was subsequently able to claim loss of profits.
 2 See s 25(2)(b) and Chapter 3 p 62 ff above.
 3 Section 62(2).

(b)   Improvements: deemed consent of landlord

(I)   SUB-TENANCIES – SPECIAL CASES

By virtue of s 68(2), where a sub-tenant obtains a tribunal direction requiring his immediate landlord to provide fixed equipment, the requirement of consent to improvements[4] does not apply in the case of any claim for compensation for improvements by the immediate landlord in respect of that work. This protects the position of the immediate landlord and enables him to claim compensation, in turn, from the superior landlord of the holding. If the sub-tenant himself carries out the improvements, the immediate landlord having failed to comply with a tribunal direction, the latter's position is similarly protected by a provision deeming the work to have been carried out by the immediate landlord for the purposes of his claiming compensation under the 1986 Act.[5]

(II)   HILL FARMING IMPROVEMENTS

By virtue of s 68(3) the landlord's consent to the implementation of a hill farming land improvement scheme, pursuant to the Hill Farming Act 1946,[6] shall be taken as consent to the carrying out of improvements executed thereunder by the tenant, for the purposes of claiming compensation for improvements under the 1986 Act.[7] Agreement as to compensation is likewise enforceable in the same manner as if made in compliance with s 67(2).[8] Improvement grants paid under the 1946 Act are to be taken into account, when calculating compensation on quitting, as if it had been a benefit allowed to the tenant in consideration of executing the improvements.[9]

(III)   HOUSING ACT IMPROVEMENTS

The requirements of the landlord's prior consent to improvements are dispensed with if the work concerned is carried out in compliance with an improvement notice or undertaking given under Part VII of the Housing Act 1985 or Part VIII of the Housing Act 1974. Compensation on quitting can be claimed for such improvements notwithstanding the absence of prior landlord's consent.[10] Financial contributions by third parties towards the cost of the improvements must be taken into account when assessing compensation.

---

4 Above p 184 ff.
5 See s 68(2)(b).
6 See s 1 Hill Farming Act 1946.
7 The consent to the scheme counts as consent for the purposes of s 67(1) and (2) of the 1986 Act, as to which see p 184 ff.
8 Section 68(3)(b).
9 Section 68(4).
10 Section 68(5).

(c) Successive tenancies

Section 69 of the 1986 Act makes special provision for the position arising where a tenant remains in occupation of a holding under successive tenancies, eg following surrender and re-grant. Compensation for relevant improvements can be claimed by the tenant, notwithstanding that these improvements were made during an earlier tenancy other than the one at the termination of which he quits the holding.[11] This saving provision only applies where the identity of the tenant remains the same, and not, eg in the cases of succession tenancies awarded under Part IV of the 1986 Act, or of re-grant to a farming company (even if controlled by the former tenant). Special provision is also made for improvements for which an incoming tenant has paid compensation on entry – either (with the landlord's written consent) to the outgoing tenant or to the landlord himself. The incoming tenant can, on later quitting the holding, claim such compensation for the improvements as the outgoing tenant would have claimed had he remained as tenant.[12]

(d) Notice to quit part of holding

By virtue of s 74 of the 1986 Act, where the landlord resumes possession of part of a holding in any of the three ways indicated below, the tenant can claim compensation under the Act as if it were a *separate holding* which he had quitted in consequence of notice to quit. This concession applies:

(i) Where notice to quit part is given pursuant to s 31, ie for one of the specified purposes enumerated therein, such as the erection of farm workers' cottages[13] *or*

(ii) Where possession of part is resumed pursuant to a partial recovery clause in the lease itself.[14] If any relief or benefit has been allowed to the tenant in consideration of the taking of such a clause, it must be taken into account by an arbitrator when calculating compensation – but only, it should be noted, where the relief/benefit is recorded in the contract of tenancy itself.[15] *or*

(iii) Where the owner of a severed portion of the reversionary estate serves notice to quit part in reliance on the right in that behalf conferred by Law of Property Act 1925, s 140. Special rules apply for the purposes of *compensation for disturbance* where the tenant exercises his statutory right to enlarge the notice into notice to quit the whole building. These have already been considered.[16]

11 Section 69(1).
12 See s 69(2).
13 Section 74(1).
14 Section 74(2), as to which see Chapter 3 p 62 ff above. Note *Coates v Diment* [1951] 1 All ER 890; *Re Disraeli's Agreement* [1939] Ch 382; *Parry v Milion Pigs Ltd* (1980) 260 EG 281 on the requirement of sufficient notice of repossession if such a clause is to be valid.
15 See s 74(2)(b).
16 Above p 195 ff.

(e)   Severance of reversionary estate

By virtue of s 75(1) of the 1986 Act, where the reversionary estate has been severed, and is for the time being vested in more than one person in several parts, the tenant of the entirety is entitled to require that the compensation payable under the Act be determined as if the reversion were not severed. He is, by this provision, *enabled* to do so eg if it is to his financial advantage to have compensation calculated as to the whole holding rather than the severed parts. He cannot, however, be compelled to have compensation so calculated. Where the tenant elects to have compensation calculated as if no severance has occurred, the arbitrator is directed[17] to apportion the amount awarded between the several owners of the reversionary estate (more precisely, between 'the persons who for the purposes of this Act together constitute the landlord of the holding', ie the persons entitled to receive rent and profits).[18] No guidance is given in the 1986 Act as to the basis of apportionment to be used by an arbitrator engaged in this exercise.

(f)   Permanent pasture

The tenant who has been allowed, pursuant to an arbitrator's award, to reduce the area of permanent pasture on his holding[19] cannot subsequently claim compensation for restoring the pasture area ploughed up in accordance with the arbitrator's directions.[20] Similarly, when assessing compensation the value per hectare of the tenant's pasture must not be taken to exceed the average value per hectare of the whole of the tenant's pasture comprised in the holding on termination of the tenancy. This prevents the tenant selecting the superior pasture on the holding for the purposes of a compensation claim, and disclaiming inferior pasture land, where some of the holding has been ploughed and reseeded pursuant to a s 14 arbitration award.[1] Similar considerations prevent a tenant claiming compensation for work carried out to restore the condition of the holding after he has exercised his statutory rights to disposal of produce and freedom of cropping.[2] Contracting out of these special provisions is not allowed.[3]

9.   No contracting out

Section 78(1) of the 1986 Act provides that, save as expressly allowed in the Act itself, in any case for which compensation is provided by the statutory provisions, a tenant (or landlord) will be entitled to compensation in accordance with those provisions 'and not otherwise, and shall be so entitled notwithstanding any agreement to the contrary'. This provision does not prevent the parties agreeing that compensation additional to that provided

---

17 See s 75(2).
18 Sections 75(2), 96(1).
19 As to which see s 14 of the 1986 Act and Chapter 3 p 58 ff above.
20 Section 76(1).
 1 See s 76(1)(b).
 2 Section 76(2). For these rights and the duty of reinstatement see s 15, and further Chapter 3 p 58 ff above.
 3 See s 76(1); 'notwithstanding anything in this Act or any custom or agreement . . .'

for in the Act should be payable, but to be enforceable such additional matters must be contained in a written agreement.[4] Section 78(1) will void any agreement purporting to exclude or reduce a statutory claim for compensation[5], as also any clause in the tenancy purporting to give the landlord a right to repossess without sufficient time being left to the tenant to enable service of notices to claim additional compensation for disturbance or for 'high' farming, eg a short notice clause[6] or a proviso for re-entry[7] providing for less than one month's notice of re-entry.

D Landlord's claims for dilapidations

On termination of the tenancy the landlord may have a claim for compensation for disrepair and dilapidations. The 1986 Act itself provides for these heads of claim on termination. Additionally, the landlord could pursue an action for breach of repairing covenant during the currency of the tenancy, prior to termination.[8] The claims available on termination are the following.

1. Statutory claim for dilapidations

On the tenant's quitting the holding on termination of the tenancy, section 71(1) of the 1986 Act gives the landlord the right to claim compensation in respect of any dilapidation or deterioration of, or damage to, any part of the holding, or anything in or on the holding. The amount of compensation recoverable is the cost, if any, of making good the dilapidation, deterioration or damage.[9]

For compensation to be recoverable under either section 71(1), or on the section 71(3) claim for contractual damages,[10] the deterioration or damage complained of must be the result of non-fulfilment by the tenant of his responsibility to farm in accordance with the rules of good husbandry. The rules of good husbandry laid down in section 11 of the Agriculture Act 1947 apply for this purpose.[11] These make it clear that in addition to the carrying out of a suitable mode of farming on the holding, fixed equipment provided on the holding must be maintained. They do not specify, however, on whom this obligation falls. Where the contract of tenancy is silent, the model clauses in the Agriculture (Maintenance, Repair and Insurance of Fixed Equipment) Regulations 1973 place the liability to maintain on the tenant.[12]

---

4 Section 78(3) ibid and see *Dean v Secretary of State for War* [1950] 1 All ER 344, CA.
5 Eg *Mears v Callender* [1901] 2 Ch 388.
6 *Coates v Diment* [1951] 1 All ER 890; *Re Disraeli's Agreement* [1939] Ch 382.
7 *Parry v Million Pigs Ltd* (1980) 260 EG 281.
8 See *Kent v Conniff* [1953] 1 QB 361, CA.
9 See s 71(2).
10 Discussed below p 201 ff.
11 See s 96(3) of the 1986 Act. On the rules themselves see Chapter 3 p 56 ff above.
12 For principles of incorporation see s 7 and *Burden v Hannaford* [1956] 198 142, CA.

But in so far as the contract places an obligation to maintain fixed equipment on the landlord the model clauses are disapplied. When assessing the tenant's responsibility to farm in accordance with the rules of good husbandry, the arbitrator must therefore take into account any specific obligations which the contract places on the landlord.[13] It should also be appreciated that the tenant may be in breach of the statutory standards of husbandry as a consequence of diversifying into non-agricultural activities eg with grant and under the Farm Diversification Scheme. Section 71 is premised on the tenant's underlying duty to maintain efficient agricultural production, and contains no concession providing for the possibility of set aside of land or diversification.

The landlord's claim for damage to parts of the holding under section 71(1) should be clearly distinguished from his claim for general deterioration under section 72, discussed below. The claim for dilapidations under section 71(1) relates to *specific* breaches of the rules of good husbandry which have caused damage or deterioration to the holding, eg a failure by the tenant to fence adequately or maintain buildings. The reference to 'deterioration' in section 71(1) also brings within that claim, however, claims for damage requiring longer term remedy. The claim under section 72, in contrast, lies where the landlord can prove 'a general depreciation of his farm as a whole'[15] over and above the cost of making good specific breaches covered by section 71(1). Thus in *Evans v Jones*[16] it was held that where a tenant has failed to farm in accordance with the rules of good husbandry in respect of specific fields, by not adequately fertilising them, the landlord can claim the cost of bringing those fields back into a proper state of health under section 71(1), and additionally claim under section 72 for any general depreciation in the value of the farm over and above this. Any amounts recovered under section 71 must be brought into account when assessing damages for general depreciation, so that the landlord cannot recover compensation twice over.[17] The distinction between the two claims may be important in some cases, for in order to make a claim under section 72 the landlord has to serve notice of intention to claim at least one month prior to termination of the tenancy.

The measure of compensation payable on a claim under section 71(1) is fixed by section 71(2) as 'the cost, as at the date of the tenant's quitting the holding, of making good the dilapidation, deterioration or damage.' The claim under s 71(1) is subject to the *caveat*, however, that the amount of compensation recoverable 'shall in no case exceed the amount (if any) by which the value of the landlord's reversion in the holding is diminished owing to the dilapidation, deterioration or damage in question.'[18] The measure of damages under section 71(1) is therefore the actual cost of

13 *Barrow Green Estate Co v Walker's Executors* [1954] 1 All ER 204, CA.
14 SI 1973/1473.
15 See *Evans v Jones* [1955] 2 All ER 118, 121, CA for judicial consideration of the relationship between the two claims.
16 [1955] 2 All ER 118, CA.
17 Section 72(2).
18 Section 71(5).

making good the deterioration or damage concerned, subject to a ceiling of the injury to the value of the landlord's reversion. If the latter is less than the cost of making good, then only the lesser amount will be recoverable.

2.   Claim under contract of tenancy

The landlord has the option either to pursue a claim for the cost of making good any damage and deterioration under section 71(1), or by virtue of section 71(3) of pursuing an alternative claim under the terms of the contract of tenancy. For the contractual claim to be available, the contract of tenancy must be in writing. Compensation under section 71(3) is only recoverable on the tenant's quitting on termination of the tenancy, and compensation cannot be claimed in respect of any one holding under both sections 71(1) and 71(3).[19] The landlord must elect either to pursue a claim under section 71(1), or section 71(3), and cannot claim in respect of some items of damage under one head, and as to other items under the other. The alternative contractual claim under section 71(3) covers the possibility of the contract of tenancy putting on the tenant a liability to repair greater than that imposed by Statute[20] or the rules of good husbandry.

Although section 71(4)(b) provides that compensation cannot be claimed in respect of any one holding both under section 71(1) (above) and under the contract, this does not prohibit the landlord's statement of claim being made in the alternative. The true construction of the section is that no one is to have an *enforceable* and effective claim to compensation under both provisions. In putting forward his claim on both grounds, the landlord is not thereby disqualified from receiving compensation on either ground.[1] He can validly frame his notice of claim in the alternative, but must elect which claim he wishes to pursue by the date of the subsequent arbitration. Note, however, that problems may arise where the landlord's statement of claim intermixes, in respect of different items comprised in the same holding, claims under section 71(1) *and* claims under the contract. It may well be that he will not be able to produce a good claim out of a notice so framed, ie a claim only under the tenancy agreement, or alternatively only under section 71(1).[2] The claim must be pursued exclusively under either the contract or section 71(1), and the landlord's statement of case must be framed accordingly.

Where a contractual claim is made under section 71(3) the measure of damages is prima facie the injury to the landlord's reversion occasioned by the breaches complained of.

3.   Measure of compensation for dilapidations

Where claims are made on termination of the tenancy under section 71, the measure of damages will be:

19 See s 71(4).
20 *Viz* s 7 and SI 1973/1473 (the 'model clauses').
 1 *Boyd v Wilton* [1957] 2 QB 277, CA.
 2 See the comments in *Boyd v Wilson* at 287 per Jenkins J.

(i)   on a claim under section 71(1), the cost of making good dilapidations, deterioration and damage to the holding. No costs can be recovered, however, in so far as they exceed in amount any reductions in the value of the landlord's reversion caused by the dilapidations complained of.[3]

(ii) on a contractual claim under Section 71(3), the diminution in value of the landlord's reversion *prima facie* provides the measure of damages itself.[4]

Quantifying the loss in value of the landlord's reversion will therefore be important in assessing claims under both heads, though for differing reasons. This is, in itself, often a matter of no small difficulty.[5]

Where compensation is claimed on termination, what must be considered is the diminution in the value of the reversion at the end of the lease, by which is meant the diminution in the landlord's *then* interest in the property. Some useful guidelines for assessing this depreciation were suggested in *Smiley v Townshend*,[6] viz:

(i)   The basic test of the measure of damages is the difference in the value of the reversion at the end of the lease between the property in its then state of disrepair and in the state it would have been in if the repairing covenants had been fulfilled.[7] In other words, the question is how much was the market value of the landlord's interest diminished at the end of the lease by reason of the disrepair?

(ii) Although the landlord's reversion means his *then* interest in the property (ie his interest at termination) it does not follow that future probabilities are to be totally disregarded. So, for instance, if buildings on the holding are to be pulled down after the end of the lease, so that repairs would have been useless, this will reduce the landlord's compensation accordingly. The occurrence of some event after termination can only be taken into account, however, in so far as it provides strong evidence of what the landlord intended at the date of termination of the lease.[8]

(iii) Where repairs have been, or are going to be, done by the landlord himself, the cost of executing those repairs will provide a good guide to the damage to the reversion.[9] The measure of damages in this case will be the sum it will take to put the property into the state of repair in which the tenant ought to have left it according to his

---

3 Section 71(5) of the 1986 Act.
4 See also s 71(5) *ibid* which also applies to the contractual claim.
5 Similar considerations apply under s 18 Landlord and Tenant Act 1927, which limits damages claims under the general law in similar terms.
6 [1950] 2 KB 311, CA.
7 See *Hanson v Newman* [1934] Ch 298, CA.
8 *Family Management v Gray* (1979) 253 EG 369, CA.
9 See *Jones v Herxheimer* [1950] 2 KB 106, CA.

covenant or statutory duty.[10] Where the landlord has relet on a full repairing lease to a third party before the end of the lease, the sitting tenant is not thereby released from his obligation to repair, and will be liable for such sum as the landlord proves to be a reasonable and proper amount for putting the property into the state of repair in which it should have been left.[11] Where the landlord does not intend to carry out the repairs himself, the proper basis for valuation of the reversion will be the rent which the property would be likely to produce immediately following the termination of the lease.[12] Where the property is relet, the injury to the reversion will be quantifiable by reference to the diminution in the rent obtained by the landlord on reletting, or the allowance he will have to make to an incoming tenant for the state of disrepair of the holding.[13]

4. Claim for general deterioration

Where, on the tenant's quitting the holding, the landlord shows that the value of the holding generally has been reduced either by reason of dilapidations or failure to repair, or otherwise by non-fulfilment by the tenant of his responsibilities to farm in accordance with the rules of good husbandry, the landlord can claim additional compensation under section 72 equal to the loss in the value of the holding *as a holding*.

Compensation for loss of value under section 72 is recoverable in addition to compensation under sections 71(1) or 71(3). The aim is to compensate the landlord for any general depreciation in the value of the farm as a whole, over and above the cost of repairs and loss of rental value recoverable under section 71. Any compensation recovered under section 71 must, however, be brought into account so as to avoid a double relief.[14] The measure of damages recoverable under section 72 is an amount equal to the decrease, attributable to the matters in question, in the value of the holding as a holding, having regard to the character and situation of the holding and the average requirements of tenants reasonably skilled in husbandry.[15] Such decrease must be attributable to the tenant's breach of covenant or failure to farm in accordance with the rules of good husbandry. Calculating a *general* decrease in value of this nature poses obvious problems, and it will be of assistance if a record of the condition of the holding has been made at some time during the tenancy. The decrease in the value of the holding will *prima facie* be the difference between the value of the holding in the condition in which the tenant left it, and its value had the buildings, fixtures and fittings been left in good repair, and the land clean and in good heart.[16]

It is a condition precedent to recovering compensation under section 72,

10 *Ebbelto v Conquest* [1895] 2 Ch 377, 384, CA.
11 *Joyner v Weeks* [1891] 2 QB 31, 43, CA.
12 *Family Management v Gray* (1979) 253 EG 369, CA.
13 *Williams v Lewis* [1915] 3 KB 493.
14 See s 72(2).
15 Section 72(3).
16 On the relationship of the claim under s 72 to that under s 71 see generally *Evans v Jones* [1955] 2 QB 58, CA.

that the landlord must, not later than one month before the termination of the tenancy, give notice to the tenant of his intention to claim compensation for general deterioration under the section.[17] The additional procedural requirements following termination apply to claims under section 72 as well as section 71, so that a notice of claim under section 83 will also have to be served within two months following termination of the tenancy.[18]

5.   Contracting out

By virtue of s 78(1) of the 1986 Act[19] save as expressly provided in the Act itself, in any case in which the provisions of the 1986 Act provide for compensation, a tenant or landlord shall be entitled to compensation in accordance with the statutory provisions 'and not otherwise', and shall be so entitled notwithstanding any agreement to the contrary. The application of this provision to prevent contracting out of the tenant's rights to compensation on quitting has already been considered.[20] Two facets of the statutory provision against 'contracting out' merit attention in its application to the landlord's claim for dilapidations.

(a)   Contracting out simpliciter

As a result of s 78(1), in any case for which the Act provides compensation, then save as expressly provided in the Act itself, the landlord will be entitled to compensation in accordance with the Act, and will be so entitled notwithstanding any agreement to the contrary. Section 71(1) itself, however, provides one instance where the Act expressly permits a form of contracting out. If there is a written tenancy varying the tenant's normal liability for repairs the landlord can pursue his contractual claim under Section 71(3) instead of the statutory claim under section 71(1).

(b)   Claim for damages during currency of lease

Notwithstanding s 78(1) the landlord can sue for damages for breach of a covenant to repair *during* the currency of the tenancy. Section 78(1) of the 1986 Act provides that 'in any case for which' the Act provides compensation, the landlord and tenant shall be entitled to compensation in accordance with those provisions 'and not otherwise', and notwithstanding any agreement to the contrary. In *Kent v Conniff*,[1] it was held that as Sections 71 and 72[2] only provide compensation on *termination* of the tenancy, the landlord is not barred by section 78 from claiming damages for breach of covenant *during* the tenancy. The latter is not a situation provided for in the 1986 Act at all, and the landlord's contractual claim for damages is therefore preserved. The measure of damages will be the amount by which the value of the landlord's reversion has diminished as a result of the breaches complained of. Note, however, that section 78(1) *does* deprive the

17 Section 72(4).
18 See above, p 179 ff.
19 See above p 198 ff.
20 See p 198 above.
 1 [1953] 1 QB 361.
 2 Or in that case, the corresponding provisions in the 1948 Act.

landlord of the right to claim compensation during the tenancy in one case. Section 15(5) of the 1986 Act provides that if the tenant exercises his rights to freedom of cropping, and to dispose of the produce of the holding, in such a way as to injure or deteriorate the holding, then the landlord has the remedies laid down in section 15 itself 'but no others'. The remedies prescribed by section 15(5) are an injunction to restrain the exercise of the tenant's rights in this way, and a statutory claim for damages on the tenant's quitting the holding. It was held in *Kent v Conniff* that in cases within section 15 the right to damages was preserved, but postponed to the end of the tenancy, and that an action for damages under this head could not therefore be brought during the tenancy.

Note that, where breach of a covenant to repair is complained of during the currency of the lease, s 18 of the Landlord and Tenant Act 1927 provides that damages shall in no case exceed the amount (if any) by which the landlords reversion in the property is diminished by reason of the breach complained of.[3] It should also be noted that, where the 'model clauses' are incorporated into the tenancy, the Agriculture (Maintenance, Repair and Insurance of Fixed Equipment) Regs 1973[4] provide an alternative remedy for disrepair.[5]

6. Series of tenancies

Section 73 deals with the case where the tenant has remained in occupation of the holding during two or more tenancies.[6] It may happen that the parties enter into a new tenancy agreement, perhaps with modified terms, without disrupting the continuing landlord/tenant relationship. Where this happens, section 73 provides that the landlord's right to claim compensation is preserved where the dilapidation occurred during an earlier tenancy of the holding. Note, however, that section 73 only operates to preserve the landlord's claims where the second and successive tenancies are granted to the same 'tenant' and relate to the same 'holding'. The section will not apply where the parties to the tenancy have altered – for instance if an additional tenant has been brought in – or if the boundaries of the holding have been altered in a way which is other than *de minimis*. Where this occurs the landlord will have to exercise his rights to compensation on termination of the original tenancy.

7. Compensation as to part of holding

It may be that the landlord resumes possession of part only of the holding, either pursuant to a clause allowing repossession of part in the tenancy

---

3 For the applicable principles in quantifying damages on this basis see above p 202 ff. The same ceiling on liability applies to claims on termination of tenancy by virtue of s 71(5) of the 1986 Act.
4 SI 1973/1473.
5 See SI 1973/1473, Art 4, above Chapter 4 p 75 ff.
6 *Cf* its counterpart s 69, discussed above, which protects the tenant's claims.

agreement itself, or by virtue of the provisions of section 31 of the 1986 Act. Where he does so, section 74 of the 1986 Act safeguards the landlord's right to compensation by providing that, for the purposes of any claim for compensation, the part of the holding repossessed is treated as if it were a separate holding which the tenant had quitted in consequence of a notice to quit. Compensation can be claimed in respect of dilapidations to that part of the holding as if it were a separate holding. Where possession is resumed pursuant to a term of the contract of tenancy, then when assessing the compensation payable the arbitrator must take into consideration any benefit or relief allowed to the tenant under the tenancy agreement.

Further, s 74(3) provides that where a person entitled to a severed part of the reversionary estate resumes possession of part of the holding by virtue of a notice to quit,[7] then compensation can be claimed as if the part repossessed were a separate holding of which the reversioner is landlord.[8]

E   Special provision for limited and special owners

The 1986 Act contains a number of miscellaneous provisions dealing with the powers of limited owners, and making special provision for certain classes of landlord, eg the Crown and ecclesiastical landowners, and landlords holding as tenants for life under a strict settlement.

1.   Power of limited owners to give consent

Section 88 of the 1986 Act provides that the landlord of an agricultural holding can, whatever his estate or interest therein, give any consent, make any agreement and do any other act required by the 1986 Act which he might give, make or have done had he been the owner in fee simple. If his interest is an interest in leasehold, he can give any consents, make agreements and do any other act required by the Act, as if he were absolutely entitled to that leasehold.

2.   Settlements: application of capital moneys for improvements

Section 89 provides that where, under powers conferred by the Settled Land Act 1925 or the Law of Property Act 1925, capital money is applied in or about the execution of any improvement specified in Schedule 7 to the 1986 Act, no provision shall be made for requiring the money so spent to be replaced out of income. Improvements under Schedule 7 of the 1986 Act are deemed to be improvements authorised by Part I of the Third Schedule to the Settled Land Act 1925.[9] Similar provisions apply where capital moneys are applied in paying for an improvement pursuant to powers conferred by the Universities and Colleges Estates Act 1925.[10] In the latter case capital

---

7 As to which see s 140 Law of Property Act 1925.
8 This amendment was introduced by the Agricultural Holdings Act 1984, Sch 3, para 14, and is now consolidated in s 74(3) of the 1986 Act.
9 Section 89(1) Agricultural Holdings Act 1986.
10 Section 89(2) ibid.

need not be replaced out of income unless the College or University concerned itself decides otherwise,[11] or the Minister requires it to make provision for replacement out of income using his statutory powers.[12]

The practical significance of these provisions is that they allow the tenant for life of settled land to shift the burden of paying for improvements from income to capital, and in some circumstances to demand reimbursement out of capital where he has incurred expenditure in effecting improvements. The interaction of the relevant provisions of the Agricultural Holdings Act 1986 with the Settled Land Act 1925 has, however, given rise to a number of uncertainties.[13] The following points should be noted:

(i) Section 89 does not confer power to *apply* capital for improvements – it simply provides that capital lawfully expended on improvements need not be replaced out of income. Section 73(1)(iv) of the Settled Land Act 1925 permits the application of capital in payment of 'any money expended and costs incurred by a landlord' under the 1986 Act 'in or about the execution of any improvement comprised in the Schedule 7 to the said Agricultural Holdings Act'.[14] It would appear to follow that capital cannot be applied to reimburse a tenant for life for compensation for improvements paid to a tenant on quitting.[15] It is clear, however, that the section *will* apply to legitimate payments out of capital where the landlord/life tenant carries out improvements himself.

(ii) If the landlord wishes to enforce payment for improvements out of capital, he can only do so in an indirect manner. If he pays compensation to the tenant, he can obtain a charging order from the Minister charging the holding with repayment.[16] Section 73(1)(ii) of the Settled Land Act authorises payments out of capital to redeem any charge created on an agricultural holding in respect of an improvement. The landlord can therefore arrange for the charge to be redeemed out of capital.[17]

(iii) There is no power to pay compensation for disturbance out of capital. Neither can the landlord do so indirectly, as Section 73(1)(ii) only authorises the redemption out of capital of charges created in respect of improvements.

---

11 Under s 2 Universities and College Estates Act 1964.

12 Ie under s 26(5) University and College Estates Act 1925.

13 The forerunner of s 89 of the 1986 Act was referred to by Vaisey J in Re Northumberland [1950] 2 All ER 1181 at 1185 as '. . . a very inappropriate and inconvenient use of what may be called "referential legislation".' For an interesting article on the interaction of the 1948 and 1925 Acts see (1951) 15 Conv. (NS) 415 (E H Scammell). And see Muir Watt *Agricultural Holdings* (13th ed) pp 321–5 for a detailed critique of the interaction of the relevant provisions.

14 Section 73(1)(iv), Settled Land Act 1925, as amended Agricultural Holdings Act 1986, ss 99, 100, Sch 13 para 3, Sch 14, para 11.

15 Payments made 'in or about the execution' of an improvement cannot cover compensation for improvements executed by someone else. And see *Re Duke of Wellington's Estates* [1971] 2 All ER 1140.

16 Section 86 of the 1986 Act.

17 See *Re Duke of Wellington's Estates* [1971] 2 All ER 1140 at 1143 per Plowman J.

(iv) *Provision and Repair of Fixed Equipment.* It has been held, notwithstanding difficulties of interpretation, that the cost of repairs to
fixed equipment on an agricultural holding forming part of a settled
estate, *can* be paid out of capital, whether or not the landlord is
liable to carry out those repairs and whether or not the life tenant is
a landlord at all within the meaning of the 1986 Act.[18]

There is no general right, however, to reimbursement out of
capital for expenditure incurred in *providing* fixed equipment on a
holding. The provision of most major items of fixed equipment is
classified by Schedule 7 of the 1948 Act as an improvement,
however. Thus the cost of providing and erecting buildings,[19] silos,[20]
roads, bridges[1] and other major items of fixed equipment will be
recoverable out of capital.

---

19 *See re Duke of Northumberland* [1950] 2 All ER 1181; *Re Lord Brougham and Vaux's
Settled Estates* [1953] 2 All ER 655. The interpretive difficulties arise from s 73(1)(iv) of the
Settled Land Act and Sch 7 para 26 of the Agricultural Holdings Act 1986, when read
together, as to which see *Re Sutherland Settlement Trust* [1953] 2 All ER 27; *Re Boston's Will
Trusts [1956]* 1 All ER 593; *Re Pelly's Will Trusts* [1956] 2 All ER 326.
20 Sch 7, para 9 of the 1986 Act.
 1 Sch 7, para 12 ibid.
 2 Sch 7, para 15 ibid.

Chapter 10
Taxation of agricultural land

A   Introduction

Farming is a capital-intensive activity generating a low yield in relation to the capital asset employed; this applies whether the land is owned by the working farmer or by a landlord, as rents of agricultural property rarely exceed 3% of the capital value of the asset. Such a capital-intensive industry is particularly vulnerable to capital taxation. If funds are borrowed to pay the tax, the interest on the loan, even at modest rates, may be difficult to service out of income. The alternative method of funding the tax liability, by selling part of the capital asset, may not only reduce the viability of the remainder of the farm, but may also trigger off a charge to capital gains tax so compounding the problem.

If a farm is worked and kept within the family, the impact of capital gains tax may be greatly relieved by the availability of the hold-over and roll-over provisions, so that the tax may be indefinitely postponed or even eliminated (as on retirement or on a death) provided the landowner continues in business until that time.

The impact of inheritance tax, whilst not potentially eliminated to the extent of capital gains tax, has been progressively mitigated since its original introduction as capital transfer tax. The relief available to landlords and agricultural property was increased to 30% by the Finance Act 1984 and inheritance tax at a flat rate of 40% applies in respect of dispositions made after 14th March 1987. The concept of the potentially exempt transfer introduced in the Finance Act 1986 gives an added incentive to making lifetime gifts where the donor is likely to survive the gift by seven years, provided he can overcome the hurdle of the reservation of benefit provisions. To take advantage of the reliefs available requires advance planning by the taxpayer as the opportunities for death-bed planning are restricted.[1]

In a single chapter on taxation in a book relating to agricultural law in general it is not possible, nor indeed intended, to set out the detailed taxation provisions. This chapter will confine itself to considering the two taxes currently affecting agricultural property, capital gains tax and inheritance tax. A working knowledge of the two taxes is presumed, for the detailed provisions of which reference should be made to the standard works currently available. The objective of this chapter is to highlight aspects of

---

1 Although some possibilities are considered later at p 228.

these two capital taxes, particularly those relevent to mitigating tax for the farmer and the farm owner.

B   Inheritance tax

Following the introduction of the concept of the potentially exempt transfer in respect of gifts made on or after 18th March 1986,[2] a donor may be particularly anxious to make a gift at an early stage so that if he survives the gift by seven years it will be exempt, subject to the donor reserving no benefit in the gift.

Nevertheless, the donor should consider delaying making any gift until such time as he qualifies for agricultural property relief so that if he should die within seven years of the gift the relief will be available.

Consideration must therefore be given to the requirements for establishing the right to agricultural property relief, the two rates of relief available and their inter-relationship in different circumstances to maximise the relief.

To *qualify* for agricultural property relief, the transferor must establish one of two requirements.[3] *Either*:

(a)   He must have occupied the property for the purpose of agriculture throughout the period of two years ending with the date of the transfer. The only requirement here is occupation for the purpose of agriculture for the two years ending with the date of transfer, which is regardless of any period of ownership. Accordingly, a farmer who has been in possession for over two years and who then purchases the freehold reversion can immediately make a transfer of the property and qualify for relief; *or*

(b)   He must have owned the property throughout the period of seven years ending with the date of the transfer and it has been occupied by himself or another throughout for agricultural purposes. This would cover, for example, a landlord who has not taken possession.

The *relief* given is to reduce the chargeable value of the agricultural value of the property by 50% if the transferor has vacant possession of the property or the right to obtain it within twelve months of the transfer; otherwise, the reduction is 30% in all other cases.[4]

While the broad objective of these provisions is to give working farmers relief at 50% and landlords relief at 30%, there are occasions when a landlord may qualify for 50% relief and the owner-occupier for only 30% relief.

If the taxpayer has owned the property for seven years without having been in possession for two years, but his interest at the date of the transfer carries the right to immediate possession, he may still qualify for 50% relief. This could arise if the landowner takes the land in hand shortly before the transfer or serves an effective notice to quit before the transfer, which notice

2 IHTA 1984, s 3A.
3 Ibid, s 117.
4 Ibid, s 116.

is to expire in less than twelve months from the date of the transfer. On the other hand, where the landlord has served a notice to quit expiring in more than twelve months and to which the tenant has failed to serve a counter-notice, if a chargeable transfer is made when more than 12 months have to run to the expiry of the notice, only 30% relief will be available. Similarly, only 30% relief is available where the transfer is made during the first part of a *Gladstone v Bower*[5] tenancy of more than 12 months and less than two years, when more than 12 months still have to elapse. The same principle also applies during the first part of a tenancy for longer than twelve months granted with the consent of the Ministry of Agriculture.[6] It is therefore particularly important in these situations that the transfer should not be made until the maximum rate of relief can be utilised.

Conversely it is possible for the vacant possession value to apply to tenanted property whereby only 30% relief is available on that higher value. This will arise where the associated operations rule applies when the taxpayer has granted a tenancy for full consideration in money or money's worth but has made a disposal of the reversion within three years, or has granted a tenancy after 26th March 1974 for less than full consideration and made a disposal of the reversion at any time thereafter.[7] The existence of the tenancy is ignored for the purpose of valuation under the associated operations rule but, as the property is *actually* subject to a tenancy, relief at only 30% is available. A similar problem may arise when the related property rules operate,[8] where a taxpayer grants a tenancy to his spouse, or in certain circumstances to a charity, and then disposes of the freehold reversion. For the purpose of valuation the value of the freehold reversion and the tenancy are added together so providing a vacant possession value, but as the property is *actually* subject to a tenancy, relief at only 30% is available.

The reversionary lease

While the legislation provides for a continuous period of two years' occupation by the transferor for the purpose of agriculture to qualify for relief and requires that the transferor's interest in the property immediately before the transfer carries the right to vacant possession or early possession, there is no requirement of any minimum period during which the transferor continues to have vacant possession after he has made a transfer of value. Accordingly, there is no reason why a reversionary lease cannot be granted before the land is gifted with vacant possession but subject to the lease. When the transferor makes the gift he will still have vacant possession and so attract 50% relief but, as the lease has been granted before the gift, the value of the freehold land would be reduced from vacant possession value to near tenanted value. To avoid the scheme falling foul of the associated operations provisions, more than three years should elapse between the granting of the

5 [1960] 2 QB 384, CA.
6 Under ss 2 or 5 of the 1986 Act.
7 IHTA 1984, s 268.
8 Under ibid s 161.

lease and the transfer of the freehold reversion.[9] The procedure would be to grant a lease at a rack rent to commence in, say, three and a half years' time and then shortly after the expiry of three years from the date of the granting of that lease make a gift of the freehold reversion at a time the transferor has vacant possession, so attracting the 50% relief but subject to the lease commencing less than six months hence and therefore at only tenanted value. The subsection[10] does refer to the 'granting' of a lease and therefore it is advisable in view of the possible strict interpretation of these provisions that a formal deed should be entered into rather than relying on a mere agreement for a lease. The granting of such a tenancy of agricultural property in the UK for use for agricultural purposes, even though it may reduce the value of the freehold reversion, is not to be treated as a transfer of value by the grantor if he makes it for full consideration for money or money's worth.[11]

Adopting the same principle a further possibility is for the partner who owns freehold land which is being farmed by a farming partnership to consider the granting of an option to his partners to take a lease of the land should he cease to be a partner for any reason. If the freeholder should then die while the partnership was still in existence, the value of the freehold would be considerably diminished because of the probability that the option to take the tenancy would be exercised, but at the point in time the freehold owner dies, assuming that no tenancy has been granted to the partnership at that time, the freeholder carries the right to vacant possession and so qualifies for the 50% relief. It is, of course, essential that the agreement should only contain an option to grant a *lease* and not a binding agreement to *sell*, as otherwise in the latter event all relief may be lost.[12]

Preservation of the 'working farmer' relief

When capital transfer tax was first introduced relief was given to agricultural property on the basis of the concept of the 'working farmer'. This test was introduced to avoid the abuse of death-bed purchases of agricultural property which used to be available under the old estate duty provisions. The qualifications for the relief were contained in Schedule 8 of the Finance Act 1975 whereby if a person's principal source of earned income was from farming, he would qualify for 50% relief on agricultural property of which he had possession (subject to certain limitations as to value and area). This was intended to provide relief for the genuine farmer owning and occupying his own property. However, by taking advantage of the fact that the value of

---

9 Ibid, s 268(2). It is the date of the *granting* of the lease which is the relevant date under the sub-section, not the date on which the lease takes effect in possession.

10 Ibid, s 268(2).

11 Ibid, s 16(1). If the transferor is not prepared to wait the three years between granting of the reversionary lease and the gift of the freehold as required under IHTA, s 26(2), it may be possible to avoid this requirement by granting a tenancy to one person, say his son, and the freehold reversion to another person, say the tenant of a settlement for the benefit of another person. This should be construed as two different dispositions and not as one disposition by associated operations. The author must say he has not yet tested this device with the Revenue and unless time is critical would prefer to comply with s 26(2).

12 Under ibid, s 124.

property protected under the Agricultural Holdings Legislation is substantially lower than its vacant possession value, a 'double discount' could effectively be achieved by claiming 50% relief on the tenanted value of agricultural property of which the transferor was in possession as a member of the partnership which held the tenancy. This was achieved if there was already a tenancy of the property created before 27th March 1974 or a tenancy granted on or after that date at a full commercial rent which had run for three years before the making of a transfer of the freehold reversion, so avoiding the associated operations provisions.[13] Thereby the chargeable value of agricultural property was effectively reduced to approaching one-quarter of its full vacant possession value. There was some debate as to whether the granting of the tenancy by the transferor to the partnership of which he was a member could itself be regarded as a transfer of value, as it effectively reduced the value of the transferor's estate. This potential problem was resolved by the Finance Act 1981 which provided that there was no transfer of value by the granting of a tenancy in those circumstances.[14] However, the same Act also prevented the use of this device after 9th March 1981, but under the transitional provisions of that Act preserved it in respect of circumstances where there was a subsisting tenancy before 10th March 1981.

Where relief is available under these transitional provisions, extreme care should be taken to ensure that the benefit is not lost. The relief under the transitional provisions provides that this double relief is available if *all* the following conditions are satisfied:[15]

(a) The conditions for working farmer relief were satisfied on 9th March 1981, which broadly required that the taxpayer should be a full-time working farmer (which is automatically evidenced if 75% of his *earned* income was derived from farming) or a person undergoing full-time education *and* the transferor is in occupation (as a tenant farmer or through the control of a company) of the agricultural property now transferred for the purpose of agriculture and must have so occupied it for at least two years immediately preceding the transfer.

(b) At no time between 10th March 1981 and the date of the relevant transfer was there a right to vacant possession; and

(c) Such a right has not been eliminated by any act or deliberate omission by the transferor during that period.

From this it will be appreciated that the valuable relief given under these provisions will be lost if the taxpayer ceases to be a full-time working farmer such as, for example, should he retire before making the transfer, should he cease to be in occupation of the agricultural property and if at any time after 9th March 1981 a right to vacant possession of the property arises. There is a danger that the latter requirement could be inadvertently breached if the tenancy comes to an end, such as on the death or retirement of a partner, so that the tenancy and the freehold become vested in the same person or

13 Under ibid, s 268.
14 Ibid, s 16 formerly FA 1981, s 97(1).
15 Now retained in ibid, s 116.

persons. Once a right to vacant possession has arisen, then any subsequently created tenancy cannot benefit under the transitional provisions.

A right to vacant possession may come about by an act of the parties. A father may own the farm, which is tenanted by himself and his son as partners under a tenancy agreement created before 10th March 1974, or after that date at a full market rental. The father may be somewhat reluctant to transfer the whole farm into his son's sole name and may instead decide to transfer a half share of the farm into the name of his son so that the property then becomes vested in the names of his son and himself. This will terminate the tenancy as the freehold reversion and the lease are vested in the same persons.[16] The transitional relief will be lost on the father's death when he gives his retained half-share to his son by will. If the father dies within seven years of the lifetime gift, a substantially higher tax liability will be incurred than if he had delayed making any gift of the farm until his death.

If there is a danger that the right to vacant possession may arise, it is suggested that the taxpayer should consider an assignment of the lease to more than one tenant to avoid this. However, when doing so, one must bear in mind the requirements that such a right to vacant possession must not have been eliminated by any act or deliberate omission by the transferor after 9th March 1981. Therefore on any assignment the terms of the lease should be strictly complied with as otherwise there is a possibility that the landlord/transferor may have had grounds for forfeiting the lease and as such omitted to act to obtain vacant possession when he had a right to do so.[17]

Where relief is claimed under these transitional provisions at 50% on the tenanted value and the transferor is a member of the tenant partnership, the Revenue claim that the tenancy has a value which falls to be included as a partnership asset in ascertaining the transferor's interest in the partnership. It is arguable that where the tenancy is non-assignable the tenancy has little value. In practice it may be difficult to contend that such a non-assignable agricultural tenancy has no value, particularly following the decision of *Baird's Executors v IRC*.[17a] If a landlord is negotiating the surrender of such a lease by the tenant or conversely the tenant is negotiating the purchase of the freehold reversion from the landlord, it would be difficult to argue that the lease has no value. In these circumstances the Revenue contend that the value of the lease is a figure representing approximately half the difference between the vacant possession and sitting tenant values of the property. This value is then added to the partnership assets and the transferor's share attributed to him.

The contention by the Revenue can be mitigated in two ways. First, when arriving at the value of the transferor's share in the tenancy, it should be discounted between 10% and 15% as being jointly owned property. Secondly, the value of the transferor's share in the tenancy so attributed to the partnership will qualify for business property relief as a partnership asset.[18]

---

16 *Rye v Rye* [1962] AC 496, HL.
17 IHTA 1984, s 3(3).
17a 1991 SLT (Lands Tr) 9, [1991] 09 EG 129, 10 EG 153. For comment see Capital Taxes News and Reports Vol 9 p 122 & Vol 10 p 211.
18 Being relevant business property if in business for at least two years under ibid ss 105, 106.

Letting to reduce value

As the transitional provisions are not available in respect of tenancies created after 9th March 1981, a taxpayer has to consider whether it is worthwhile creating a tenancy of agricultural property at a full market rental to reduce its value and then after three years, to avoid the associated operations provisions, making a gift of the freehold reversion. Unless one is prepared to use the reversionary lease device outlined above, such an operation may have been justified when the rate of relief on tenanted property was 20%, but now that that relief has been increased to 30% it is less likely to be advantageous to let the farm to a family partnership. Whether such an exercise is justified will depend, of course, on the reduction of the value of the property by virtue of the fact that it is tenanted; the 'break-even' point at which it may be considered is when the tenanted value is less than 70.50% of the vacant possession value. The inter-relation of the reliefs and values is shown below.

Vacant possession value	Tenanted value as % of column 1	Actual value	Relief at 30%	Relieved IHT values	
				Tenanted	Vacant possession
1,000,000	80	800,000	240,000	560,000	500,000
1,000,000	71½	715,000	214,500	500,500	500,000
1,000,000	70	700,000	210,000	490,000	500,000
1,000,000	65	650,000	196,000	455,000	500,000
1,000,000	60	600,000	180,000	420,000	500,000
1,000,000	50	500,000	150,000	350,000	500,000

The disadvantage of such an exercise is that if the transferor should make the gift or die within three years, then the granting of the tenancy and the subsequent transfer of the freehold reversion will be an associated operation;[19] consequently the property will be valued on a vacant possession basis with relief only being given at 30%. A further obvious disadvantage is that having to wait three years before making a gift of the freehold reversion may prove critical for surviving the seven year period necessary to qualify as an exempt transfer.

Maximising the relief

Having established the right to the relief, it is equally important that full advantage is taken of the relief given. It is obvious that if a relieved asset is given to an exempt transferee the whole benefit of the relief which may only be utilised by a chargeable transferee, is wasted. Accordingly, if an estate contains agricultural property, subject to the proviso in the next paragraph,

19 Ibid, s 268.

the relieved property should not be given to a spouse or charity when the benefit of the relief is lost on an exempt transferee. For example, if a deceased having an estate of £560,000, including £280,000 farm property which qualifies for 50% relief, makes a gift of the farm to his wife and the residue to the son, the tax on the residue of £280,000 will be £56,000. On the other hand, if he gives the farm to the son and the residue to the widow the tax on the gift of the farm to the son would be based on half of £280,000, which would fall within the nil-rate tax band.[20]

While generally agricultural property should not be given to a spouse to avoid the relief being wasted, an exception to this rule is where the deceased has not fully qualified for the relief at the date of his death. If the surviving spouse becomes entitled to the agricultural property on death, the period of occupation and ownership by the deceased spouse can be added to that of the surviving spouse.[1] This may arise, for example, where the deceased spouse before the date at his death has been in occupation of the agricultural property for a period less than two years or has been a landlord of agricultural property for less than seven years. In these circumstances the property should be given by will to the surviving spouse who then completes the period of occupation or ownership before making the intended gift. If the testator has provided in his will for the property to pass elsewhere, such as to his son, then a deed of variation should be effected to achieve this result. It is important to appreciate that the transferee spouse under a *lifetime* gift cannot utilise the period of occupation or ownership of the transferor: this provision only applies where the spouse receives the agricultural property on death.

Charged debts

A charged debt is deducted from the value of the asset on which it is charged and it is the net value which attracts valuation relief.[2] Consequently if the charge on qualifying agricultural property is removed in advance of making a transfer relief will be obtained on the whole value of the property rather than the net value after deduction of the charged debt. Consider a farmer who has a farm valued at one million pounds which qualifies for 50% relief and also has other assets not qualifying for relief (ie life policies, development land, etc) amounting to £500,000. If there is a mortgage on the farm of £500,000 the tax will be shown as in column (a) below. If the debt is rearranged so as to be secured on the unqualifying assets the tax will be as shown in column (b) below.

Furthermore, not only is £100,000 saved in tax by rearranging the debt, but the whole of the tax on that smaller sum qualifies for payment by ten interest-free instalments[3] whereas only one third of the larger tax liability qualifies for that relief.

It will therefore be realised that if the charge on the asset can be removed in advance of making a transfer, relief will be obtained on the whole value of the asset rather than the net value after deduction of the charged debt. It is

20 1991/92.
 1 Ibid, s 120(1), (2).
 2 Ibid, s 162(4).
 3 Under ibid, s 234(1).

	(a) £	(b) £
Value of farm	1,000,000	1,000,000
Less mortgage	500,000	–
Net	500,000	1,000,000
Relief at 50%	250,000	500,000
Net value	250,000	500,000
Add unrelieved assets	500,000	500,000
	750,000	1,000,000
Deduct unsecured debt	–	500,000
Chargeable estate	750,000	500,000
Tax on estate	244,000	144,000

appreciated that it is not always easy to persuade a bank manager who has a charge on a farm to release it and secure it on other assets, but a temporary arrangement could be made for this purpose shortly before making a lifetime transfer or in a death-bed situation. For example, the intended transferee of a lifetime gift or devisee under the will could guarantee the overdraft to enable the charge to be removed before the transfer.

Utilisation of the nil-rate tax band

Where a testator leaves a surviving spouse, from the inheritance tax point of view it is generally advisable for the nil-rate tax band, currently £140,000 (1991/92), to be left to beneficiaries other than the spouse. In the case of agricultural property qualifying for 50% relief this effectively amounts to £280,000. There is a considerable virtue in transferring assets above that sum to the other spouse, either absolutely or for life, so as to postpone the payment of the tax until the second death or indeed enable the surviving spouse to make lifetime transfers and hope to survive seven years. Many wills made prior to the Finance Act 1987, when a flat rate of 40% of tax was introduced, were made with a view to equalising estates to utilise in both estates the lower bands of tax that then applied. Such wills may now no longer be tax efficient. Nevertheless, if not remedied by the testator in his lifetime, they may be still effectively redrawn by agreement between the beneficiaries by means of a deed of variation made within two years of the date of death.[4]

4 Under ibid, s 142. See infra at p 229.

Gifts with reservation

The gift with reservation provisions reintroduced by the Finance Act 1986 are intended to prevent a donor escaping tax by simply surviving the gift by seven years but nevertheless continuing to derive a benefit from the gifted property.

These provisions can apply particularly harshly where a person's whole wealth is tied up in a business or property, such as a farm, as a relatively small reservation of benefit may invoke the application of these provisions to the whole of the property transferred.

In the context of farming, there are two particular practical considerations arising out of these provisions. A farmer may be anxious to make a gift of the farm to his son, but nevertheless to continue to live in the farmhouse; he may also wish to continue to participate in, and so derive a benefit from, the farming business. Both these objectives can be achieved, but extreme care must be taken in achieving these objectives.

A distinction must be made between retaining an interest in an asset before gifting it and reserving a benefit out of a gifted asset after it has been gifted. The distinction may be fine, but is absolutely critical in the context of the gift with reservation provisions.

If a father wishing to retire, gifts the entire farm, including his farmhouse, to his son but continues to live in the farmhouse, he will be reserving a benefit in the gifted property thereby invoking the gift with reservation provisions. Conversely, if the father gifts the farm, excluding the farmhouse, but continues to live in the farmhouse, he is not reserving a benefit out of the gifted property, ie the farm excluding the farmhouse, as he has physically excluded the farmhouse from the subject matter of the gift.

Alternatively, the asset from which the donor wishes to benefit can be legally, rather than physically, excluded from the subject matter of the gift prior to the making of the gift. This may arise where a donor of a farm wishes to continue in the farming business after having made a gift of the farm to, say his son. If there is an existing tenancy in favour of the business carried on by the father and the son prior to the making of the gift of the farm, the subject matter of the gift will not be the entire interest in the land but the father's interest in the property subject to the rights of the partnership: the father will not be deemed to be reserving a benefit out of the gifted property as the subject matter of the gift is the farm excluding the pre-existing rights of the partnership.[5] Conversely, if the father gifts the property to his son and *subsequently* a tenancy is created in favour of the partnership of which the donor is a member, the donor will be deemed to be reserving a benefit in the gifted property[6] unless the tenancy back is for full consideration in money or money's worth.[7] If the tenancy back to the donor is even slightly less than a market rental, or is otherwise not on a commercial basis, the property will be subject to a reservation to the donor. Indeed, even if the rent is initially at a full market rental, but is not reviewed on a commercial basis throughout the period of seven years before the date at death, the property may subsequently become subject to a reservation.[8] In the case of agricultural tenancies this

5 *Munro v Stamp Duties Comr* [1934] AC 61, PC.
6 *Chick v Stamp Duties Comr* [1958] AC 435, PC.
7 FA 1986, Sch 20, para 6(1)(a).
8 Ibid, s 102(1).

effectively means that the rental should be reviewed every three years on a commercial basis as otherwise the full rigour of the gift with reservation provisions will apply: even if the granting of the tenancy is not initially a reservation of benefit, it may subsequently become one if the rent falls below a commercial level.

In relation to gifts of land or chattels, actual occupation of the land, or actual enjoyment of an incomparable right over the land or actual possession of the latter by law, shall be disregarded if it is for full consideration in money or money's worth.[9] Quite apart from payment of rent, in determining whether a full consideration has been given to satisfy this relaxation, the Revenue will take into account all the circumstances surrounding the arrangement including the share of the profits and losses, the donor's and the donee's interests in the land and their respective commitment and expertise.

The Inland Revenue's approach to gifts involving family businesses or farms is as follows:[10]

'A gift involving a family business or farm will not necessarily amount to a gift with reservation merely because the donor remains in the business, perhaps as a director or partner. For example, where the gift is of shares of a company, the continuation of reasonable commercial arrangements in the form of remuneration for the donor's ongoing services to the company entered into before the gift will not of itself amount to a reservation provided the remuneration is in no way linked to or beneficially affected by the gift. Similar considerations will apply in the case where the gift is into trust which empowered a trustee, who may be the donor, to retain director's fees, etc for his own benefit.

The "*Munro*" principle[11] will also be relevant in determining the tax treatment of gifts affecting family farms where the donor and the donee continue to farm the land in pursuance of an arrangement entered into prior to and independently of the gift. In cases where this principle does not apply, the test of "full consideration" for the purposes of para 6(1)(a)[12] will need to be satisfied with regard to the donor's occupation of the land. In applying that test we shall take account of all the circumstances surrounding the arrangements including the sharing of profits and losses, the donor's and the donee's interests in the land, and their respective commitment and expertise.'

This statement of practice therefore reiterates the *Munro* principle that gifts of assets which are subject to pre-existing arrangements are not to be treated as gifts with reservation where those pre-existing arrangements continue to be enjoyed by the donor.

C Capital gains tax considerations

Following the introduction of capital transfer tax by the Finance Act 1975, there remained in many cases a positive deterrent against making lifetime gifts because of the potential charge to capital gains tax. A lifetime gift constituted a disposal and as such triggered a charge to capital gains tax. At

---

9 Ibid, Sch 20, para 6(1)(a).
10 Extract of a letter of 18th May 1987 from the Inland Revenue to the Law Society.
11 *Munro v Stamp Duties Comr*, supra.
12 FA 1986, Sch 20, para 6(1)(a).

that time capital gains tax had been in existence for over ten years and as no indexation allowance was available during a period of substantial inflation, there was a potentially large capital gains tax liability built into any lifetime gift to the next generation.

However, following the Finance Act 1980, which made hold-over relief generally available, the climate for making lifetime gifts has progressively improved. With the introduction of the concept of the potentially exempt transfer by the Finance Act 1986, the final incentive was given to lifetime gifts as capital gains tax could be held over, stamp duty on gifts had been abolished and no inheritance tax was payable provided the donor survived the gift by seven years and reserved no benefit in it. Accordingly, through the combined effects of roll-over relief and hold-over relief, capital gains tax had been virtually reduced to a voluntary tax. For the working farmer this still applies, even following the general loss of hold-over relief on gifts made after 13th March 1989.

Roll-over relief

The roll-over relief provisions are still principally contained in CGTA 1979,[13] although many of the provisions concerning the relief are Revenue concessions. The purpose of the relief is to remove the disincentive to the businessman, including of course the farmer, from selling business assets and purchasing replacement assets with the proceeds of sale. The relief is available when certain categories of capital assets are disposed of and the proceeds of sale reinvested in new capital assets. The capital gain which would otherwise have been chargeable on the sale is deducted from the acquisition value of the new asset. Consequently the tax is only deferred, but may ultimately be reduced or eliminated by business retirement relief[14] or on death.

The relief is available provided the disposal is of a qualifying asset used in the business during the time of ownership. To qualify as an asset it must comprise land and buildings, fixed plant and machinery which does not form part of a building, ships, aircraft, hovercraft and goodwill.[15] This has been extended to milk and potato quotas.[16] Provided the original assets and replacement assets fall within the relevant classes, businesses need not be of the same type; for example, the sale of the farm may be rolled-over into the purchase of a public house or an aircraft for business use! Secondly, to obtain the full relief, the taxpayer must have used the asset in his business during the whole time that he owned it,[17] otherwise only partial roll-over is allowed.[18] For example, if a farmer purchases a farm in 1982, farms it until 1986 when he lets it before ultimately disposing of it in 1990, the roll-over relief will only be available on half the gain. It should be noted that building land must be occupied as well as used for the purpose of the taxpayer's business to qualify for the relief.[19]

---

13 Sections 115–126.
14 See p 221.
15 CGTA 1979, s 118.
16 FA 1988, s 112.
17 CGTA 1979, s 115(1).
18 Ibid, s 115(6).
19 Ibid, s 118, Class 1, Head A.

Provided the new asset is acquired within one year before or three years after the disposal of the original asset, there is no loss of roll-over relief.[20]

Where the whole of the proceeds of sale are not reinvested in acquiring the new asset, there will be a chargeable gain equivalent to the amount not reinvested and only the balance may be rolled-over. This effectively means that if the purchase price of the new asset does not exceed the acquisition cost of the original asset, the whole gain is chargeable.[1]

Hold-over relief

Where hold-over relief is available, it enables the assessment and payment of capital gains tax to be postponed by an election made by the donor and donee to hold over the gain. The effect of such an election is that the donee is deemed to have acquired the asset at the donor's original cost and at that time, so effectively holding over the gain until such time as the donee in turn disposes of the asset, when payment of tax may be reduced or eliminated by business retirement relief if the donee so qualifies, or eliminated if the asset passes into the estate of the donee on his death.

While the availability of hold-over relief has been severely curtailed by the Finance Act 1989 in respect of gifts made after 13th March 1989, it is still available in respect of gifts of business assets,[2] and also gifts which would attract an immediate charge to inheritance tax, gifts to political parties and certain other gifts for public benefit.[3]

Qualifying business assets include an asset used for the purpose of a trade, profession or vocation carried on by the transferor or his family and also includes agricultural property which qualifies for agricultural property relief for inheritance tax purposes,[4] which may therefore include a gift of a tenanted farm. It is therefore particularly important to ensure before making a lifetime gift of agricultural property that it qualifies for relief for inheritance tax purposes under the provisions already considered[5] to ensure that it also qualifies for hold-over relief for capital gains tax purposes.[6]

It should be noted that any inheritance tax paid on a gift relieved under these provisions, such as if the donee has to pay tax by reason of the death of the donor within seven years of the gift, may be deducted from the donee's gain when he disposes of the asset.

Business retirement relief

Where a farmer has attained the age of fifty-five and disposes of the whole or part of a business which he has owned for the last ten years, he is exempt from capital gains tax on the first £150,000 of any gain and on the next £450,000 of the gain 50% relief is given[7]. Accordingly, if the disposal of the

---

20 Ibid, s 115(3).
 1 Ibid, s 116.
 2 Ibid, ss 126, 126A and 126B.
 3 Ibid, s 147A(2).
 4 Ibid, s 126(1A).
 5 *Supra*, p 210.
 6 CGTA 1979, s 126(9).
 7 1991/92. Previously the limits were £125,000 and £375,000 respectively.

business realises a gain of £600,000, the first £150,000 is exempt from tax as is one-half of the next £450,000.

Three conditions must be satisfied before the relief is available: a personal qualification, an ownership qualification and a material disposal of business assets.

First, the individual must have attained the age of fifty-five years at the date of the disposal or have retired before that age on the grounds of ill health.[8] Subject to the comments below relating to disposal of the assets of the business, generally a taxpayer does not have to actually retire from the business to qualify for the relief. To satisfy the grounds of ill health requirement, the Board must be satisfied on this point and consequently their decision is not subject to appeal.

Secondly, to utilise the full relief the business asset must have been owned for ten years prior to the date of disposal. However, provided the asset has been owned for at least one year, the relief will be proportionately reduced according to the time the asset has been owned, calculated precisely in months and days.[9]

Thirdly, the transferor must make a material disposal of business assets. This definition includes a disposal of the whole or part of the business[10] and also extends to a disposal of assets which, at the time when the business ceased to be carried on, were in use for the purposes of that business.[11] The conditions for the relief must be satisfied at the date when the business ceased (that is the requirements of age, ill-health and ownership of the business for a minimum of one year),[12] but the disposal of the asset itself may occur within a period of one year thereafter[13] or such longer period as the Revenue by notice in writing may allow.[14]

It is important to realise that relief is not available for the disposal of assets of the business as opposed to the business itself, unless the taxpayer ceases business.[15] Where the business continues, it will be necessary to determine whether the disposal is of part of the business itself which qualifies, or merely of assets used in the business, which do not qualify.[16] This is particularly relevant in the case of a farm where part only of the property is sold but the farmer nevertheless continues to farm the balance of the land.[17] Accordingly, if a farmer owns 200 acres of land and sells off 10 acres at a substantial gain for development, the gain realised on the development land will not qualify for the relief as he has sold an asset of the business rather than part of the business itself which continued after the disposal. Conversely, if the farmer had sold the entirety of the business, including the

---

8 FA 1985, s 69(1). Prior to 1991/92 the age was sixty years.
9 Ibid, Sch 20, para 13(1). From 6th April 1988 the proportional reduction is applied separately to the full and 50% relief.
10 Ibid, s 69(2)(a).
11 Ibid, s 69(2)(b).
12 Ibid, s 69(4)(a), (b).
13 Ibid, s 69(4)(c) 'the permitted period' is defined in Sch 20 para 1(2).
14 Ibid, Sch 20, para 1(2).
15 Ibid, s 69(2)(b).
16 *McGregor v Adcock* [1977] 3 All ER 65 where a farmer who had sold 4.8 acres of his 35 acre farm was held to have disposed of an asset, not part of the business.
17 CGTA 1979, s 49(1).

farm with the development land, then it would have qualified for relief. Alternatively, he could have simply ceased business.

Inter-relation of reliefs

While the capital gains tax can be regarded largely as a voluntary tax in the circumstances envisaged above, one cannot ignore its existence altogether. If assets in respect of which there is an unrealised gain are retained until death, there is a capital gains tax uplift so that the gain will be completely eliminated. The beneficiaries of those assets will acquire them at their market value at the date of death thus establishing an uplifted base value. Because of this uplift in value at the date of death for capital gains tax purposes, in the case of relatively small estates it may actually be an advantage to retain assets until death, rather than make a lifetime disposition with the donee holding over the gain. This is particularly so in the case of property on which the value of the asset is reduced for inheritance tax purposes. Where the value of an asset has been determined for inheritance tax purposes, the same value is taken for capital gains tax purposes.[18] That value, however, is not reduced by any agricultural or business property relief: consequently for capital gains tax purposes the base value established at the death will be the full unrelieved value of the assets. The maximum rate of capital gains tax is 40% and if an estate contains virtually all agricultural or business property on which the 50% relief is available, it may be worth considering passing the property through the estate to obtain a capital gains tax uplift and paying some inheritance tax. This is particularly so bearing in mind that the flat rate of inheritance tax has now been reduced to 40% and with the application of 50% agricultural property relief, the rate of tax is effectively 20%. It is therefore possible to envisage circumstances where a lifetime gift may save inheritance tax but result in capital gains tax of 40% on a subsequent disposal by the donee, such as if there is a very low held-over base value and the donee makes a disposal of the gifted property without himself being able to hold it over. All the circumstances will have to be considered when balancing the capital gains tax uplift on a death against the inheritance tax chargeable. One should particularly consider whether the donee is likely to dispose of the gifted asset.

If the gift on death is to a spouse, the best of both taxes may be achieved with a capital gains tax uplift but attracting no inheritance tax.[19]

Conversely, there are circumstances in which one may suffer the worst effects of both taxes. If a transferor makes a lifetime disposition with an election for hold-over relief and then dies within seven years, the donor's cumulative total will be utilised against the nil-rate tax band in his estate, even if no inheritance tax is payable on the lifetime gift as falling within the inheritance tax threshold, yet without the advantage of a capital gains tax uplift which would have applied on death. So, where the life expectancy of the donor is limited, it is generally better to gift the property by will rather than by a lifetime gift.

Where there is a sale at an undervalue only the gift element of the disposal may be held over but, to the extent the donee pays any of the price, the relief

18 Ibid, s 153.
19 Considered later at p 228 as part of death-bed planning.

is lost. The effect of this is to make gifts (rather than sales) desirable when rearranging ownership of assets. Problems may arise from the possible inter-relation of hold-over relief and other reliefs. If the donor is eligible for retirement relief, this operates by way of reducing the gross gain[20] so that only the balance after deducting retirement relief is a chargeable gain. Accordingly, the retirement relief will first reduce the gain and only then any remaining chargeable gain may be held over. This may be thought to be desirable as outright exemption is given rather than a mere postponement of tax. On the other hand, the transferor may wish to utilise the retirement exemption towards the disposal which realises cash and which consequently cannot be held over. The solution in this situation is to make the disposals in the correct sequence, first making a cash disposal utilising the retirement relief and then making the gift on which the tax may be held over. If the order is reversed by first making the gift, the gain is utilised first towards the retirement relief and only after the retirement relief is exhausted is the balance held over; if the donor then makes a cash disposal he will pay capital gains tax on it.

If hold-over relief is claimed, any inheritance tax which became chargeable on the gift by reason of the death of the donor within seven years of the gift or the donor having reserved a benefit in the gift, is calculated without taking into account possible capital gains tax liability. Accordingly, if the donee sells the property and becomes liable to pay capital gains tax on the donor's held-over gain as well as his own, the combined taxes on the two transactions (the gift and sale) will effectively be on the whole gain since the original acquisition by the donor. This may be greater than the charge to tax if capital gains tax had been paid at the time of the original gift by the donee and hence enabling it to be deducted from the value transferred for inheritance purposes.[1]

D   General considerations

Whilst a charge to capital gains tax can be virtually eliminated by hold-over and roll-over reliefs, the charge to inheritance tax may be such as to force a family farm out of business. The value of a quite modest farm on current values can be in the region of £1,000,000 including farming stock and agricultural implements. If the owner holds virtually no other assets then, even allowing for 50% agricultural property and business property reliefs, the gift of such an estate to a non-exempt person, such as a son, will on death attract inheritance tax of £144,000.[2] This could be crippling for the successor's farming activities, even if repaid by ten interest-free instalments and borrowing for the instalments as they arise. If a sale of part of the property is effected to raise the capital, this may reduce the viability of the farm and may in turn trigger off a charge to capital gains tax, although there is less likelihood of this following a death in view of the capital gains tax uplift on a death.

20 FA 1985, Sch 20, para 6.
 1 IHTA 1984, s 165(2).
 2 1991/92 rate.

Gifts

To mitigate potential tax liability the taxpayer should consider making gifts at a fairly early stage so as to take advantage of the substantial concessions given in the reforms over the last few years. Gifts should be considered whilst these concessions are still available as they may be changed by a future Parliament. At this stage it may be helpful to consider the advantages and disadvantages of making lifetime gifts.

(I)   Advantages of lifetime gifts

The merits of making lifetime gifts are fairly obvious. Assuming the gift is a potentially exempt transfer, there will be no immediate change to inheritance tax and time will start to run towards the seven years required to ensure that the gift will be exempt from inheritance tax and also drop out of the cumulative total on death.

Further, the value of the gift is established at the date of the gift; in times of inflation this is an important factor, but of course at other times it may be regarded as a neutral or negative factor.

If tax is payable by reason of the death of the donor within seven years of the gift, tapered relief on any inheritance tax payable will be available after three years. However, unless the gift is sufficiently substantial to attract tax (which in the case of an agricultural property means it must exceed £280,000 (or £292,000 if two years' annual exemption can also be utilised),[3] unless the donor survives the seven years there is little merit in the gift apart from establishing its value at that time rather than at the date of death as the gift will be cumulated with his estate anyway. In this connection it is important for the donor to appreciate that the making of a lifetime gift which has not dropped out of the cumulative total on death may partly or wholly exhaust the nil-rate tax band and thereby substantially increase the tax payable by the beneficiaries of his estate.

(II)   The disadvantages of lifetime gifts

There are a number of disadvantages of making lifetime gifts, some obvious, others less so. These disadvantages may be summarised as follows:

(i)   A gift is irrevocable and the donor may be hesitant to transfer substantial assets to the next generation. However, this objection can be overcome by the use of a trust set up in the transferor's lifetime, but retaining the power to elect the ultimate beneficiaries by a power of appointment. This may be achieved by an accumulation and maintenance trust,[4] which qualifies as a potentially exempt transfer, or an under a wider discretionary trust which does not so qualify but will not attract any inheritance tax on its creation provided it is kept within the nil-rate tax band.

(ii)   If inheritance tax becomes payable on a lifetime chargeable transfer (such as gifts into discretionary trusts or gifts by or to a company), effectively the tax has to be paid in advance.

(iii)   As already considered above, there is a danger of the donor's

3 1991/92.
4 Under IHTA 1984, s 71.

death within seven years of the date of gift; the nil-rate tax band otherwise available to the estate on death will be partially or wholly utilised by the gift and to the extent the threshold is exceeded tax thereon will be payable by the donee. The donor should bear the latter fact in mind; if he wishes the donee to receive the asset free of tax he must specifically provide in his will for the payment of that tax out of his estate: the usual rule that in the absence of contrary provision the tax on an estate is borne out of the residue does not apply to a tax on lifetime gifts. Conversely, the donor should be aware that the inclusion of the gift in the cumulative total on death may substantially increase the tax burden on his estate.

(iv)   If an election is made to hold over the capital gain, there is no uplift in the base value of the asset on the subsequent death of the donor. If the donor dies within seven years of the gift, the donee will suffer the worst aspect of both taxes.[5]

(v)   If the donee himself makes a gift or sells the agricultural property within the seven years before the donor's death, the agricultural property relief will be lost.[6]

(vi)   If the gift is to the donor's spouse, for example to provide that spouse with sufficient assets in his or her estate to utilise the nil-rate tax band on his or her death, if that donee spouse dies before he or she has qualified for agricultural property relief or business property relief, the periods of ownership or occupation by the donor spouse cannot be added to that of the donee spouse. On the other hand, if the gift had been made by will, the donee could have utilised the testator's periods of ownership or occupation.[7]

(vii) There is always the possibility of the donee predeceasing the donor.

(viii) The donee's property will become available for consideration in any matrimonial settlement on a divorce of the donee or indeed on a donee's bankruptcy.

Once a decision has been made to make a gift, then it is generally advisable to proceed with the gift as soon as possible so that time will start running towards the seven years after which the gift will drop out of account. However, because of the possibility of the donor dying within seven years of the gift, it should not generally be made until such time as the donor qualifies for the business and agricultural property reliefs.

Finally, before making a gift it is important to check that no gifts have been made by the donor within the seven years preceding the gift which would be 'locked-in' to his cumulative total. Where a potentially exempt transfer is made within seven years after an earlier chargeable transfer and the potentially exempt transfer itself becomes chargeable by virtue of the donor's death within seven years thereafter, tax on that potentially exempt transfer is calculated by including the earlier transfer in the donor's

---

5 See *supra* p 223.
6 IHTA 1984, s 124A.
7 Ibid, s 120(1), (2) and considered *supra* at p 223.

cumulative total. This effectively extends the cumulation period by a further seven years by 'locking-in' the earlier chargeable transfer. While no additional tax becomes payable on the earlier chargeable transfer as the cumulative total increased the available nil-rate tax band will be reduced on the later gift and on the estate.

Sale and loan-back

Following the introduction of capital transfer tax, at a time of high inflation sales with loan-backs of the whole consideration were sometimes advocated. Such arrangements cannot generally be advised in relation to assets which attract agricultural property or business property relief. First, a sale may attract a charge to capital gains tax; while this may be covered by retirement relief that relief may be required for other disposals. Secondly, the fact that the vendor/transferor has effected a sale will result in the creation of an asset in his estate, viz the outstanding loan, on which no relief is available. Consequently the relief will be wholly lost following the sale.[8]

Farming partnerships

The establishment of a farming partnership may itself be a useful method of mitigating inheritance tax. On the formation of a partnership all partners would normally be expected to contribute towards the capital, but in the case of a family partnership the only capital contribution is often by the existing sole trader. This frequently arises where a father takes his son into partnership when he and his son continue farming the property. The father's capital account is credited with the assets of the existing business, although to utilise his annual exemption the father may credit the account of his son with the previous and current years' annual inheritance tax exemptions. However, if substantially more assets are transferred into the son's name, such as crediting his capital account with the assets of the business, the question may then arise as to whether there has been any transfer of value by the father to the son on the formation of the partnership. A transfer of value is the *net* loss to the estate of the transferor. If the partnership agreement provides that in consideration of the father crediting capital to the son's account on the basis that the father need only give such time and attention to the business as he considers fit whereas the son commits himself to giving his full time and attention to the business, if the father still remains entitled to receive a substantial proportion of the profits of the business he effectively commutes his capital into future income, so reducing or eliminating the net loss to his estate. While in the case of a substantial business there may be some difficulty in ensuring that the consideration given by the son devoting his whole time to the business equals the value of the contribution of the capital by the father, it will at least partially reduce the value of the gift. Furthermore, the son may undertake a liability, such as to provide an annuity for his father and/or widow out of the partnership. Cases involving

8 Ibid, s 124.

estate duty have shown that a covenant by a son to devote his energy whole time to partnership business can provide such an adequate consideration.[9]

When drafting partnership agreements, careful consideration should be given to the provisions that are to operate on the death of a partner; care should be taken that such clauses cannot be construed as contracts for sale although not to operate until a partner dies. This may arise whereby in the partnership agreement the partners effectively enter into a buy/sell agreement under which in the event of the death of one of the partners before retirement his personal representatives are obliged to sell the deceased partner's share to the surviving partners, who are in turn obliged to buy. As this is a binding contract, not merely an option to buy, the business relief which might otherwise be available on the deceased partner's share may be totally lost.[10] The same would apply if the partnership agreement contains a binding obligation to sell the deceased partner's share in the property; the relief normally available on agricultural property may otherwise be lost.[11] Such clauses should therefore ideally be drafted as only options to buy.[12]

Death-bed planning

While the scope for death-bed planning is limited, there are a number of situations where if it is known or anticipated that the life expectancy of the intending donor is limited, there are steps which may be taken to mitigate both inheritance tax and capital gains tax:

    (i)   Agricultural property relief will not be available if at the date of his death the donor has not at that time satisfied the two years' occupation or seven years' ownership qualifying periods necessary to obtain agricultural property relief. In this event the intending donor should not make a lifetime gift at all but should instead make a gift of the property in his will to his spouse, who may then utilise any period of occupation or ownership of the deceased with her own, so that when she qualifies for the relief she can herself then make the intended gift.[13]

    (ii)   Ensure that the nil-rate tax band will be utilised on the first death.[14]

    (iii) If there is a charge on the agricultural property, arrange for this to be transferred to other assets which do not qualify as outlined above.[15]

    (iv) If the likely surviving spouse has assets of his own which are pregnant with gain, he should consider giving these by lifetime gift to the terminally ill spouse who then gifts them back by will to the surviving spouse. In this way no inheritance tax will be payable on

---

9 *AG v Baden* [1912] 1 KB 539.
10 Under IHTA 1984, s 113.
11 Under ibid, s 124.
12 See Revenue Statement of Practice SP 12/80.
13 IHTA 1984, s 120(1), (2), see supra p 215. The same principle applies to business property relief under *ibid*, s 108.
14 Ibid s 108, see supra p 217.
15 See *supra* p 216.

either the lifetime gift or the gift under the will, but there will be a capital gains tax uplift on the gift by will to the surviving spouse.

Post-death planning

A will may be varied or the intestacy provisions changed or disclaimed and treated for inheritance tax and/or capital gains tax purposes as having been effected by the deceased provided the variation or disclaimer is made within two years of the date of death and notice given to the Revenue within six months thereof.[16] With the agreement of the beneficiaries entitled to the estate under the will or intestacy, it is therefore possible to redistribute the deceased's estate to mitigate tax with the benefit of hindsight!

While the beneficiaries under a will or intestacy may vary the distribution of an estate, this does require their agreement. which may not be forthcoming, and their capacity to do so, which may not be possible in the case of beneficiaries who are minors without an application to the Court. Accordingly, a testator may wish to incorporate a provision whereby a specific asset, a legacy or the residue of the estate is given to the executors or nominated trustees on discretionary trusts with the widest possible powers of appointment amongst a class comprising all the persons whom the testator may possibly wish to benefit. Such appointments, when exercised, are then effectively deemed to have been made by the testator for the purposes of inheritance tax, but not for capital gains tax.[17] These are separately considered below.

Variations and disclaimers

While the use of variations and disclaimers may be used for all estates, in relation to the farmer and farm owner, there are a number of specific situations where they may prove particularly helpful:

(a) Over or under utilisation of the nil-rate tax band. While this is applicable to all estates, it should be remembered that in the case of assets carrying agricultural or business property relief with 50% relief the tax threshold is effectively £280,000.[18]

(b) The reliefs available for agricultural and business property may only be utilised if the gift is to a chargeable transferee. Accordingly if, for example, an asset that qualifies for relief is given to a spouse, by a deed of variation it may be redirected to another beneficiary who can utilise the relief.

(c) Where the deceased at the date of his death does not qualify for agricultural property or business property relief and the asset has been given to a chargeable transferee, a deed of variation may redirect that property to the deceased's spouse who can utilise the deceased's period of occupation or ownership and add to his own before ultimately making the intended gift.[19]

16 IHTA 1984, s 142 and CGTA 1979, s 49(6)–(10) respectively.
17 IHTA 1984, s 144.
18 1991/92.
19 IHTA 1984, s 120(1), 2 and s 108 respectively, considered *supra* at p 216.

Two-year discretionary trusts

Provided a testator is secure in the knowledge that his executors will carry out his wishes on his death, he can leave his estate or particular assets of his estate to his executors on discretionary trusts. If an appointment is made within two years of the testator's death, for inheritance tax (but not capital gains tax) purposes the distribution in accordance with the power of appointment is effectively treated as if it had been written back into the deceased's will as at the date of death.[20] The application of this provision is automatic and no election is required.

These provisions apply regardless of whether the discretionary trust is set up as a two-year discretionary trust or is a full eighty-year discretionary trust, provided the appointment is made out of the trust within two years of the date of death. For flexibility it may therefore be better to form the trust as an eighty-year trust, particularly as no hold-over relief is available for capital gains tax purposes if the distribution is made within two years of death. The executors are therefore given an ability to distribute the estate within two years of date of death or later to maximise the tax advantages and also take into account any changed circumstances of the beneficiaries during that time.

Quite apart from the tax advantage of such a discretionary trust, this can be an exceedingly useful device where a testator owns a home farm, which he wishes to give to his son, and also holds an agricultural tenancy, which he also wishes to be transmitted to his son on his death. If by his will he leaves his home farm to his son, the son may be precluded from taking a transmission of the tenancy on the grounds that he occupies another viable unit.[1] However, if instead of making the gift to his son in his will the testator leaves his farm on discretionary trusts with a wide class of potential beneficiaries, including the son, the son would not be entitled as of right to the home farm. Accordingly, the son could then make an application for a transmission of the tenancy to himself and after this has been achieved the executors would be able to appoint the home farm to the son.

The Agricultural Holdings Act

Finally, one must consider whether there are any tax implications where a tenant joins with his nominee in making an application to the agricultural land tribunal for a direction by the tribunal that a new tenancy be granted to the nominated successor. The circumstances in which such a Retirement Notice can be served are detailed in Chapter 8 to which reference should be made for general discussion of succession on retirement. If such an application is successful, the direction by the tribunal entitling the nominated successor to a tenancy of the holding entitles him to a tenancy of the holding as from the date specified in the Retirement Notice. The new tenancy is to be on the same terms as those on which the holding was let at the date of the giving of the Retirement Notice, and a tenancy on these terms is 'deemed' to be granted by the landlord to the nominated successor on the date specified in the Notice as the date on which the proposed succession is to take place.[2] There is therefore

---

20 Ibid, s 144.
  1 Under the 1986 Act, Part IV s 34 ff. See supra p 153 ff.
  2 Ibid, ss 55(1), 56(1) and supra p 175 ff.

not an assignment of the existing tenancy, but effectively an extinction of the existing tenancy and the granting of a new tenancy.

What are the capital gains tax implications of a successful application? Looking at it from the viewpoint of the existing tenant, prior to the tribunal granting its consent he has an asset, namely his tenancy. One must then consider whether this asset has a value which, following the decision of *Baird's Executors v IRC*,[3] it now undoubtedly has. The value of the tenancy will depend on all the circumstances, including the terms of the tenancy. If it is an oral tenancy which has not yet been reduced to writing, it may be freely assignable as no covenant against assignment will be implied. However, this is not likely to arise in practice very often in view of the fact that either the landlord or the tenant can make an application to reduce the tenancy agreement to writing, and that an absolute covenant against assignment is now incorporated in any written agreement.[4] Also, unless the tenant has already assigned an oral tenancy before a reference to arbitration to reduce the terms of the tenancy to writing has been made, he will be precluded from assigning pending the arbitration.[5] Even if there is an absolute covenant against assignment, however, can one attribute a value to the tenancy? In these circumstances the value of the tenancy must be the surrender value to a special purchaser, the landlord; the particular circumstances under which there is an application to the tribunal are such that it is highly likely that the landlord would be a landlord willing to acquire the tenancy. When negotiating the surrender of a tenancy one often looks at a figure some way between the difference of the tenanted value and the vacant possession value of the property. Likewise, when one is considering the purchase by the tenant of the freehold reversion, a sale price is generally negotiated at a figure some way between the tenanted value and the vacant possession value. In these circumstances it may be said that the tenancy has a value, which may be quite substantial. When the tribunal gives its direction the existing tenancy held by the retiring tenant is extinguished and a new tenancy in favour of the nominated successor is deemed to be granted. The extinction of an asset constitutes a disposal of that asset, whether or not any capital sum (by way of compensation or otherwise) is received in respect of the extinction of the asset.[6] Furthermore, even if a tenancy is not assignable, it can be an asset for capital gains tax purposes[7] even though the law does not necessarily attribute a value to it as an asset. If it can be said that the transaction, by virtue of which the asset (the tenancy) came to be extinguished, is by way of a bargain made at arm's length, then that would normally be the end of the matter as there is no mechanism for substituting a value. However, the retiring tenant and the nominated successor will of necessity always be connected persons in establishing the successor's eligibility. Consequently the parties will be treated as parties to a transaction otherwise than by way of a bargain at arm's length and a deemed market value for the disposal will be substituted.[8] In

---

3 1991 SLT (Lands Tr) 9, [1991] 09 EG 129, 10 EG 153. For comment see *Capital Taxes News and Reports* Vol 9 p 122 & Vol 10 p 211.
4 Ibid, Sch 1, para 9.
5 Ibid, s 6, discussed further supra Chapter 3 p 53 ff.
6 CGTA 1979, s 22(1).
7 *O'Brien v Benson's Hosiery (Holdings) Ltd* [1980] AC 562, HL.
8 CGTA 1979, s 29A.

considering the value to be attributed to the surrender of the old tenancy, the value deemed to be received is the market value of the new tenancy in the hands of the nominated successor; that same value will then be the acquisition cost to the new tenant. This is the current view of the Revenue.[9] As the retiring tenant cannot normally make an application until he has attained sixty-five,[10] in the majority of cases the retiring tenant will be able to claim retirement relief. To the extent that retirement relief may not be available or insufficient to wholly cover the gain, business hold-over relief may still be available.[11]

There is, of course, no problem of capital gains tax arising when the succession is on a death where there is a capital gains tax free uplift.[12]

As far as inheritance tax is concerned one must consider whether there has been a transfer of value, *viz* a disposition by the retiring tenant as a result of which the value of his estate immediately after that disposition is less than it would have been but for the disposition.[13] If it is accepted that the tenancy is an asset which has a value, the estate of the retiring tenant after the tribunal's direction will have been reduced by the value of the tenancy as a result of the joint application by the retiring tenant and the nominated successor. Although there is no transfer of the tenancy to the nominated successor, but rather a deemed granting of a new tenancy to the successor, the absence of a transferee should not preclude the possibility of a charge to inheritance tax. The word to be construed under IHTA 1984 section 3(1) is 'disposition', not transfer, and there appears to be no reason why the extinction of an asset should not be regarded as a disposition. There must therefore be a serious risk that a successful application for succession would amount to a chargeable transfer by the retiring tenant (unless, of course, the nominated successor was his spouse), particularly as the parties will of necessity always be connected persons in establishing the successor's eligibility. Although such a transfer of value will normally constitute a potentially exempt transfer, in view of the age of the retiring tenant it is quite possible that he will not survive the outcome of a successful application by seven years. A possible, but doubtful defence is provided by IHTA 1984, s 10, which provides that a disposition is *not* to be treated as a transfer of value if it can be shown that it was not intended, and was not made in a transaction intended, to confer any gratuitous benefit on any person and that it was a transaction which might be expected to be made in dealings at arm's length between persons not connected with each other. If a chargeable transfer does arise in these circumstances, it will at least normally qualify for business property relief.[14]

This problem does not arise on death, as in that situation the new tenant becomes entitled by virtue of his *own* application to the tribunal. In the case of a lifetime application on the other hand there is a *joint* application on the part of the retiring tenant and the nominated successor, as a result of which the retiring tenant gives up an asset of value.

9 Per letter to author of 28 February 1991.
10 He may only serve a retirement notice prior to the age of 65 if suffering from a mental or physical disability which is likely to be permanent.
11 Under CGTA 1979, ss 126, 126A and 126B, see supra p 220.
12 Ibid, s 49(1).
13 IHTA 1984, s 3.
14 Under IHTA 1984, s 105.

Chapter 11
Tied agricultural accommodation

A Introduction

Agricultural workers in tied accommodation are commonly either service occupiers, or pay rent lower than the threshold to attract Rent Act protection.[1] The Rent (Agriculture) Act 1976 introduced statutory protection and rent control, modelled on the Rent Acts, guaranteeing security of tenure after an occupier's employment ceases, subject to the landlord's right to relet to another agricultural employee if alternative accommodation is available for the protected occupier. The regime under the 1976 Act was replaced by the Housing Act 1988 for new lettings on or after 15th January 1989. All occupancies granted *after* that date will be 'assured' agricultural occupancies governed by the 1988 Act. In broad terms, the 'assured' occupier will enjoy similar security of tenure to that available under the 1976 Act, but restriction of rents on 'fair rent' principles no longer applies. The landlord is free to demand a market rent, with increases being subject to review by the rent assessment committee.[2]

Although modelled on the Rent Acts, the Rent (Agriculture) Act 1976 employed its own specialist terminology to define occupancies to which protection extends. The occupier must have been granted a 'relevant tenancy or licence' of property in 'qualifying ownership', and the occupier must himself be a 'qualifying worker' within the meaning of Schedules 2 and 3 to the 1976 Act.[3] Some of these qualifying conditions, set out in Schedules 2 and 3 of the 1976 Act, are also employed by the Housing Act 1988 to define 'assured agricultural occupancies' granted after its commencement. The 1976 Act continues to apply to most occupancies created prior to the commencement of the 1988 Act. The protection afforded by the 1976 Act is, moreover, retrospective and applies to occupancies granted prior to its commencement, as if it had 'at all material times' been in force.[4] The existence of separate regimes for occupancies created prior to 15th January 1989, and those created on or after that date, is a source of considerable complexity. 'Protected' agricultural occupancies within the 1976 Act are discussed in Section B below. 'Assured' agricultural occupancies governed by the Housing Act 1988 are discussed in Section D, the two being linked by discussion (in Section C) of the transitional provisions to be found in the 1988 Act.

1 Rent Act 1977, s 5(1).
2 Sections 13 and 14 Housing Act 1988.
3 See s 2 Rent (Agriculture) Act 1976.
4 *Skinner v Cooper* [1979] 2 All ER 836, CA.

B Protected agricultural occupancies

1. Qualifying for protection

The Rent (Agriculture) Act 1976 employs complex terminology to define occupancies to which protection extends. The occupier must have been granted a 'relevant licence or tenancy' of property in 'qualifying ownership', and the occupier must usually be a 'qualifying worker'. If these conditions are met the employee becomes a 'protected occupier in his own right'. On termination of his contractual tenancy or licence he will be a 'statutory tenant in his own right'. The code of protection for 'protected' agricultural occupiers, contained in the Rent (Agriculture) Act 1976, continues to apply where the tenancy or licence was granted *prior* to commencement of the Housing Act 1988 on 15th January 1989.

(a) Protected occupiers in their own right

By virtue of section 2(1) of the 1976 Act, an employee will be a 'protected occupier in his own right' if three conditions are satisfied:

  (i)   he has a 'relevant licence or tenancy'
  (ii) the dwelling is in 'qualifying ownership', or has been at any time during the subsistence of the tenancy or licence'[5] and
  (iii) the occupier is a 'qualifying worker', or he *has been* a qualifying worker *at any time* during the subsistence of the licence or tenancy.[6] Once the occupier has become a 'qualifying worker' his protected status will be unaffected by his ceasing to be employed in agriculture, or employed by his landlord. Once satisfied, the qualifying worker condition cannot be disapplied.[7]

An occupier will qualify for protection if he satisfies (i) and (ii) but has been incapable of whole time work in agriculture as a consequence of a qualifying injury or disease.[8] Similarly, he will remain a protected occupier in his own right where there has been (i) a surrender and re-grant in circumstances where he was, prior to re-grant, a protected occupier; and (ii) where the licence or tenancy was granted in consideration of his giving up possession of another dwelling house of which he was a protected occupier.[9]

(b) Relevant tenancy or licence

The 1976 Act applies whenever a qualifying worker (see below) has exclusive occupation of a dwelling house as a separate dwelling. Occupation can be under either a licence or tenancy, though if the employee has a licence, it is a prerequisite of protection that he have exclusive occupation of the property as a dwelling.[10] If the occupier has a tenancy, the qualifying

---

5 Whether or not it was at that time a 'relevant' licence or tenancy: s 2(1) ibid.
6 Section 2(1)(b) *ibid.*
7 *Cf* the agricultural worker condition for 'Assured' occupancy protection under the Housing Act 1988, which clearly *can* cease to be fulfilled. See p 249 ff below.
8 Section 2(2) and (4) Rent (Agriculture) Act 1976.
9 Section 2(3) and (4) ibid.
10 Schedule 2, para 1 ibid.

conditions of the Rent Act 1977 are modified. A 'relevant tenancy' is one under which a dwelling house is let as a separate dwelling.[11] It will qualify for protection under the 1976 Act, however, even if the rent is less than the threshold for full Rent Act protection,[12] and if the dwelling is comprised in an agricultural holding.[13] A tenancy will be outside the 1976 Act if it is a bona fide term that the landlord provides the tenant with board or attendance, but meals provided by the landlord in the course of the occupier's employment do not constitute 'board' for his purpose.[14] Apart from these modifications the qualifying conditions for full protection under the Rent Act 1977 must be satisfied, and apply whether the occupier's interest is a licence or tenancy. A 'protected' occupany cannot arise, for instance, if the landlord's interest belongs to the Crown or a local authority, or the landlord is a resident landlord within the meaning of the 1977 Act.[15]

(c) Qualifying ownership

A dwelling is in 'qualifying ownership' for the purposes of the 1976 Act at any time if, at that time, the occupier is employed in agriculture and the occupier's employer is *either* the owner of the dwelling house *or* has made arrangements with the owner for it to be used as housing accommodation for persons employed by him in agriculture.[16]

(d) Qualifying worker

For protection to accrue, the occupier must have been a 'qualifying worker' at some time during the subsistence of the tenancy or licence – not necessarily, note, at the date on which protection is claimed.[17] By virtue of Sch 3, para 1 a person is a qualifying worker if, *at any time*, he has worked whole time in agriculture, or has worked in agriculture as a permit worker, for not less than 91 out of the last 104 weeks. For the purpose of calculating the number of weeks worked in agriculture, a week will 'count' if the number of hours for which he works for his employer is not less than 35 hours.[18] Certain weeks will count towards the occupier's entitlement even if he does not work during them. These are:

(i) any week during which, by agreement with his employer, he works less than the standard number of hours (ie 35 hours).[19]

(ii) any week during which he is absent from work in agriculture by reason of taking a holiday to which he is entitled.

(iii) any week in which he is absent from work in agriculture with the consent of his employer.

11 *Cf* s 2 Rent Act 1977; s 1(1) Housing Act 1988. This formula has been used in successive Rent Acts, and has generated a not inconsiderable body of case law, as to which see *Megarry, The Rent Acts* (11th ed 1989) Ch 5 p 87 ff.
12 Ie less than two-thirds the rateable value of the dwelling on the relevant date, as otherwise required by Rent Act 1977, s 5, where the tenancy was granted prior to 1 April 1990.
13 Schedule 2, para 3 Rent (Agriculture) Act 1976.
14 Schedule 2, para 3(3) and (4) ibid.
15 See s 17, 13 and 14 Rent Act 1977.
16 Schedule 3, para 3 Rent (Agriculture) Act 1976.
17 Section 2(1) ibid.
18 Schedule 3, paras 4(2) and 12 ibid.
19 Schedule 3, para 4(3) ibid.

(iv)   any week during which he is absent in consequence of an injury or disease (whether a 'qualifying' injury or disease or not).[20]

Where an occupier is suffering from a 'qualifying' injury or disease, any week of absence will count as a week of whole time work in agriculture, whether or not that person is employed in agriculture as a whole time worker or not.[1]

Note that the qualifying employment need not be with the same employer – if an agricultural worker *at any time* works for 91 out of the previous 104 weeks full time in agriculture, he achieves the *status* of 'qualifying worker'. If he is offered accommodation thereafter on terms which constitute a 'relevant licence or tenancy', and the premises are in 'qualifying ownership', the protection of the 1976 Act will apply *ab initio*. It is therefore important for an employer offering accommodation to agricultural employees to ascertain the precise nature of their previous employment status at the outset. It is also important to note that, once a protected agricultural occupancy has arisen, it will continue to be protected notwithstanding that the occupier later ceases to be employed full time in agriculture – indeed, he may cease to be employed at all. Once the agricultural worker condition has been satisfied it gives the occupier an ongoing *status* which confers protection. Likewise, as soon as the occupier becomes a 'protected agricultural occupier' this status attaches to the property irrespective of his future employment record, provided he continues to occupy the dwelling as his residence. Although, in most cases to which the 1976 Act applies in practice, the occupier will have completed 91 weeks' work with the same employer, by whom the accommodation has also been provided, potentially the scope of the Act is considerably wider.

Special provision is made for two categories of employee:

(I)   PERMIT WORKERS

An employee is entitled to count towards his entitlement any week during which he has worked in agriculture as a 'permit worker'.[2] Where an employee is suffering from a physical or mental incapacity which prevents him earning the minimum rate of pay prescribed by an Agricultural Wages Order, the Agricultural Wages Board may grant him a permit, exempting his employment from the statutory restrictions otherwise applicable under the terms of the Agricultural Wages Act 1948.[3] Any week worked as a permit worker can be counted irrespective of whether 35 hours are worked or not. In this way, therefore, the Act ensures its benefits are extended to incapacitated employees who are unable to comply with the more stringent qualifying conditions applicable to others. As with other employees, weeks during which absence is due to holiday leave, agreed absence or injury, may be counted towards the 91 week qualifying period.

(II)   EMPLOYEES SUFFERING 'QUALIFYING DISEASE OR INJURY'

An employee can count towards his entitlement any week in which he is incapable of work by reason of any qualifying injury or disease[4] *viz* an injury caused by an accident arising out of and in the course of his agricultural

---

20 For exceptions (ii)–(iv) see Sch 3, para 4(4) ibid.
1 Schedule 3, para 4(5) ibid.
2 Schedule 3, para 1 and Sch 3, para 5 ibid.
3 See s 5 Agricultural Wages Act 1948.
4 Schedule 3, para 4(5) Rent (Agriculture) Act 1976.

employment, or an injury prescribed in relation to agricultural workers under the Social Security legislation.[5] Furthermore, where an occupier suffers a qualifying injury or disease during the course of his employment, rendering him incapable of whole time work in agriculture, he will be a protected occupier irrespective of whether he has 91 weeks' work in agriculture or not.[6] Workers suffering injuries in the course of their employment therefore enjoy the residential security conferred by the 1976 Act irrespective of the length of their employment. The 1976 Act will apply if an injury is sustained during the early part of an occupiers agricultural career. Moreover, while he is unable to work, as a consequence, weeks will count towards his statutory entitlement so that after 91 weeks he will achieve the status of 'protected occupier'. This will ensure continual protection under the 1976 Act if, on his return to health, he subsequently ceases to be employed in agriculture or is employed by a different employer who offers him tied accommodation. Anomalously, however, if one returns to health during the initial 91 week qualifying period, statutory protection will cease to apply until the qualifying period has elapsed. The concession of automatic protection only applies 'if and so long as' the occupier is incapable of whole time work in agriculture, or work as a permit worker, in consequence of a qualifying injury or disease.[7]

(e) Employment in 'agriculture'

An occupier must be employed in agriculture pursuant to a contract of employment *viz* a contract of employment, or apprenticeship, whether express or implied, written or oral.[8] The protection of the 1976 Act does not extend, therefore, to self-employed agricultural contractors. The occupier must also be employed, for the requisite period of time (above), in 'agriculture' as statutorily defined.

'Agriculture' is defined by the 1976 Act in terms which differ in material respects from the definition contained in the Agricultural Holdings Act 1986,[9] and which are somewhat wider.

By virtue of Section 1 of the 1976 Act 'agriculture' includes dairy-farming and livestock keeping and breeding, the production of any consumable produce grown for sale or consumption (or use in another trade or business), the use of land as grazing, meadow or pasture land, as orchards or osier land, the use of land for market gardens or nurseries,[10] and also forestry. This definition, it should be noted, is inclusive but not exhaustive. Decisions on the analogous provisions of the Agricultural Holdings Act 1986, the General Rate Act 1967, Rating Act 1971 and the Town and Country Planning Acts are thus of assistance, if not strictly authority.[11] The definition was apparently not intended to encompass every rural activity, but was intended to include all operations involved in farming land for commercial purposes.[12] Arable

---

5 Schedule 3, para 2(1) ibid.
6 Section 2(2) ibid.
7 Section 2(2) ibid.
8 Schedule 3, para 11 ibid.
9 Section 1 Agricultural Holdings Act 1986. See generally chapter 2.
10 As to which see *Short v Greeves* [1988] 1 EGLR 1, CA; (1988) NLJ 329 (Wilkinson); (1988) Comm 430 (Rodgers) and (1988) 14 EG 51 Muir Watt.
11 See s 1 Agricultural Holdings Act 1986, s 26(3) General Rate Act 1967, s 336(1) Town and Country Planning Act 1990.
12 *Lord Glendyne v Rapley* [1978] 1 WLR 601, CA.

farming is therefore included, though not specified, but not (apparently) growing crops and weeds for testing commercial weed killers.[13] Grazing is *per se* an agricultural activity, even though the animals concerned may not be 'livestock' within the statutory definition of the latter, eg racehorses.[14]

'Livestock' includes, by virtue of section 1(2) *ibid*, any animal which is kept for the production of food, wool, skins or fur, or for the purposes of its use in the carrying on of any agricultural activity. For the purpose of this definition 'animal' includes birds, but not fish, thus seemingly excluding fish farming from the scope of 'agriculture' in this context.[15] By contrast, mink farming would clearly be within the statutory definition. Pheasants and other game reared primarily for sport are not livestock, and gamekeepers employed for this purpose are not protected by either the 1976 or 1988 Acts.[16] 'Animals reared for sport or entertainment or for their decorative qualities cannot . . . be regarded as being reared in the course of the activity of farming'.[17] Racehorses are thus not livestock within the definition.[18]

Note that an employee employed in general farm work, such as a farm mechanic, will be employed in 'agricultural' work even though his contractual duties may not, taken alone, be agricultural by definition. The definition in section 1 of the 1976 Act is directed towards including *all* operations, including repair and maintenance of farm machinery, which are involved in farming land for commercial purposes.[19] Further, protection will not automatically be lost if the occupier ceases to be employed in agriculture and commences a non-agricultural user of the premises, eg by using the dwelling to run a jobbing builders premises.[20] Such user may, however, constitute a breach of the terms of the statutory tenancy.

(f)   Statutory tenants in their own right

Where an occupier satisfies the agricultural worker condition and becomes a 'protected occupier in his own right' then, on termination of the protected occupancy, he becomes a 'statutory tenant in his own right'.[1] The statutory tenancy subsists only if and so long as the occupier occupies the dwellinghouse as his residence.[2] It confers merely a personal right of occupation, not a tenancy vesting in possession, and will therefore terminate on the tenant's later death without successors, or on his vacating the dwelling without sufficient *animus revertendi*. In this respect the 1976 Act differs from

---

13 *McClinton v McFall* (1974) 232 EG 707, CA. *Cf Dow Agrochemicals Ltd v EA Lane (North Lynn) Ltd* (1965) 192 EG 737, CCA.

14 See *Hemens v Whitsbury Farm and Stud Ltd* [1987] 1 All ER 430, 436, CA; affd [1988] 1 All ER 72, HL; and see *Belmont Farm Ltd v Minister of Housing and Local Government* (1962) 13 P & CR 417; *Bracey v Read* [1963] Ch 88; *University of Reading v Johnson-Houghton* [1985] 2 EGLR 113; (1986) Conv. 275 (Rodgers).

15 *Cf Jones v Bateman* (1974) 232 EG 1392, CA; *Wallace v Perth and Kinross Assessor* 1975 SLT 118; *Gunter v Newtown Oyster Fishery Ld* (1977) 244 EG 140; *Cresswell v British Oxygen Co Ltd* [1980] 3 All ER 443, CA and other rating decisions.

16 See *Lord Glendyne v Rapley* [1978] 1 WLR 601, CA; *Earl of Normanton v Giles* (1978) 248 EG 869, CA, also *Reeve v Atterby* [1978] CLY 73.

17 *Forth Stud Ltd v East Lothian Assessor* [1969] RA 35, 46 per Lord Avondale.

18 *Hemens v Whitsbury Farm and Stud Ltd* (above).

19 *McPhail v Greensmith* (6th August 1987, unreported) Lexis transcript; *Lord Glendyne v Rapley* (above).

20 See *Durman v Bell* [1988] 2 EGLR 117, CA.

1 Sections 2(4) and 4(1) Rent (Agriculture) Act 1976.

2 Section 4(1) ibid.

the code for 'assured' agricultural occupancies under the Housing Act 1988, which latter confers a tenancy vesting in possession on those employees occupying tied accommodation to which it applies.[3] The statutory tenancy arises automatically when the protected occupancy is terminated, whether by notice to quit, by a notice of rent increase,[4] 'or otherwise',[5] eg by the tenant accepting a registered 'fair' rent fixed by the Rent Officer.[6] A single succession to the statutory tenancy is provided for by the 1976 Act.[7]

2. The statutory tenancy

(a) Control of rent

Following termination of his employment, the landlord may wish to charge a protected occupier an economic rent for the accommodation provided. The parties can at any time agree a rent payable under the statutory tenancy. By virtue of section 11(3) of the 1976 Act, however, a rent 'ceiling' is applied, in that the agreed rent cannot exceed either the registered fair rent for the dwelling or (if no rent is registered) the weekly or other periodic equivalent of a rent fixed at one and a half times the rateable value of the dwelling.[8] The 'fair rent' provisions of Part IV Rent Act 1977 are applied to tied cottages by section 13 of the 1976 Act, enabling either party to apply for the registration of a 'fair rent' for the dwelling, quantified in accordance with the 1977 Act[9].

If no rent has been registered, and the agreed rent is less than the periodic equivalent of one and a half times the rateable value of the dwelling, the rent can be increased to this level by a notice of increase under section 12(2). Where a fair rent *has* been registered, the agreed rent can be raised to the level of the registered rent by a notice of increase under section 14(2).[10] An agreed rent is irrecoverable from the tenant insofar as it exceeds the rent ceiling imposed by the 1976 Act.[11] *Cf* 'Assured' agricultural occupancies granted after commencement of the Housing Act 1988 enjoy no rent control on fair rent principles.

(b) Other terms of the statutory tenancy

The statutory tenancy arises immediately upon termination of the occupier's contractual licence or tenancy. The terms of the statutory tenancy are set out in section 10 and Sch 5 to the 1976 Act.

Rent. No rent is payable under a statutory tenancy until there is an agreed rent or notice of increase under sections 12 or 14 (above).[12] Rent under a

---

3 See below pp 251 ff.
4 Ie pursuant to s 16(3), see below.
5 Section 4(1) ibid.
6 *Durman v Bell* [1988] 2 EGLR 117, CA. Here the protected tenancy ceased, and statutory tenancy commenced, by operation of law upon the parties impliedly agreeing to a statutory tenancy.
7 See below pp 243 ff and ss 3 and 4 Rent (Agriculture) Act 1976.
8 Section 12(7) and (9) ibid.
9 See s 70 Rent Act 1977.
10 See s 15 Rent (Agriculture) Act 1976.
11 See s 11(3) and (8) ibid.
12 Section 10(2) ibid.

statutory tenancy is payable weekly in arrears, subject to agreement to the contrary.[13] A covenant to pay rent in accordance with the provisions of the 1976 Act is implied.[14]

With regard to other obligations, the general principle is that, as long as the statutory tenant retains possession, all the terms of the original contract remain enforceable by the parties *inter se*.[15] Subject to this, Sch 5 makes special provision for the following.

Licences. Where the original contract was a licence, the statutory tenancy is a weekly tenancy, and includes all terms which would have been implied if it had been a contract of tenancy, eg the landlord's covenant for quiet enjoyment.[16]

Non-contractual arrangements. The landlord must continue to supply any facilities or services which he previously supplied, but not under the contract, provided these are reasonably necessary for any person occupying the dwellinghouse as a statutory tenant.[17] An example would be the supply of electricity or water supplies by the landlord from his own installations.

Repairing obligations. Section 11 of the Landlord and Tenant Act 1985 applies.[18] This implies a covenant on the part of the landlord to keep the structure and exterior of the property in repair, as well as installations for the supply of water, gas and electicity.

Non assignment and user. It is a condition of the statutory tenancy that the tenant will not use the dwellinghouse, or any part of it, for purposes other than those of a private dwellinghouse.[19] This obligation will be breached by significant business use of the premises, but such breach can be waived by the landlord and made good, in which event the court may refuse as a matter of discretion to order possession.[20] The tenant cannot assign, sublet or part with possession of the dwellinghouse or any part of it.[1]

Access. The tenant must allow reasonable access for the execution of repairs. Likewise the landlord must afford such right of access to the premises as is reasonable in all the circumstances eg over adjoining land not subject to the statutory tenancy.[2]

Notice to quit. The tenant must give at least four weeks' notice to quit, if the original tenancy or licence failed to make provision in this regard.[3]

Schedule 5, para 12 entitles the parties to vary the terms of the statutory tenancy, provided they do so by agreement in writing. Certain basic terms cannot, however, be varied in this way, eg the application of Landlord and Tenant Act 1985, s 11, or a substantial addition to the land and premises

13 Section 10(3) ibid. If rent was paid under the protected tenancy on a different basis, that will prevail.
14 Section 10(5) ibid.
15 Schedule 5, para 2 ibid.
16 Schedule 5, paras 3 and 4 ibid.
17 Schedule 5, para 5 ibid.
18 Schedule 5, para 6(1) and (2) ibid.
19 Schedule 5, para 7(i) ibid.
20 See *Durman v Bell* [1988] 2 EGLR 117, CA.
 1 Schedule 5, para 7(2) Rent (Agriculture) Act 1976.
 2 Schedule 5, paras 8 and 9 ibid.
 3 Schedule 5, para 10 ibid.

which the tenant is entitled to occupy, or variation of the circumstances in which the tenant can give notice to quit.[4]

3. Security of tenure

The security of tenure provisions are modelled closely on those of the Rent Act 1977. By virtue of section 6(1) a court cannot make an order for possession of a dwelling house subject to a protected or statutory occupancy unless one of the Cases in Schedule 4 is made out. The cases are similar to those in the Rent Act 1977, and like the latter are divided into mandatory and discretionary cases for possession. In the case of a discretionary ground, the court cannot make an order for possession unless it considers it reasonable to do so.[5] Moreover, where one of the discretionary grounds is relied on the court has power to stay or suspend execution of an order for possession, or to postpone the date of possession for such period(s) as it thinks fit.[6] The court also has discretionary power to adjourn the proceedings.[7]

The discretionary grounds for possession are contained in Schedule 4, Part I of the 1976 Act. A major policy consideration underlying the legislation is that security of tenure should not interfere with the efficient organisation of agriculture by tying up agricultural accommodation indefinitely, thus preventing its use for housing new employees. Cases I and II to Schedule 4 therefore permit repossession where suitable alternative accommodation is provided either by the landlord or the housing authority. Although this ground is discretionary, it is reinforced in the agricultural context by section 27 of the 1976 Act, which enables an agricultural landlord to apply to the housing authority on the ground that it ought 'in the interests of efficient agriculture' to provide suitable alternative accommodation for a protected occupier. Section 29 establishes agricultural dwelling house advisory committees to advise housing authorities on the merits of applications and the interests of efficient agriculture. Agricultural landlords therefore enjoy powers of compulsion, lacking under the Rent Act 1977, to compel housing authorities to consider providing alternative accommodation.[8] The 'suitability' of alternative accommodation is to be judged by criteria similar to those applicable under the Rent Act 1977. Where the landlord offers alternative accommodation it must be 'suitable' by reference to the tenant's needs as to the character and extent of the property, and equivalence of terms and security of tenure with the existing property.[9] If alternative accommodation is offered by the housing authority, Case II will be satisfied if either:

  (i) an offer of suitable accommodation is made, giving the tenant not less than 14 days in which to accept it; *or*
 (ii) the housing authority notify the tenant that they have received,

---

4 Schedule 5, para 12(3) and (4) ibid.
5 Section 7(2) ibid.
6 Section 7(3) ibid.
7 Section 7(2A) ibid. And see s 7(4) for the court's power to order a suspension or postponement subject to such conditions as to payment of arrears of rent etc as it thinks fit.
8 See further p 255 ff. below.
9 See Sch 4, Case I, paras 2, 3 and 4 ibid.

from a third party, an offer of alternative accommodation, and the tenant has accepted within the time allowed: *or*

(iii)   the landlord shows that the tenant did not accept the offer, and in so doing acted unreasonably in refusing the housing authority's offer of alternative accommodation.

The other discretionary grounds mirror those available under the Rent Act 1977. Possession can be obtained if rent lawfully due is unpaid or other obligations of the tenant have been breached,[10] if the tenant or his lodger or subtenant has been guilty of conduct which is a nuisance or annoyance to adjoining occupiers,[11] or if the condition of the dwelling house or furniture provided by the landlord has deteriorated owing to the neglect or default of the tenant.[12] A further discretionary ground applies where the tenant has, without the consent of the landlord, assigned, sublet or parted with possession of the dwelling house or any part of it,[13] and where the premises have been sublet (with or without consent) at a rent exceeding the maximum recoverable under the 1976 Act or Rent Act 1977.[14] Where the tenant has given notice to quit, and the landlord has contracted to sell or let the dwelling house, or taken other steps as a result of which he would be seriously prejudiced by being unable to obtain possession, the landlord has a discretionary ground for possession.[15] This ground does not apply, however, where the tenancy has been terminated not by notice to quit, but by the tenant giving notice to terminate his employment. A further discretionary ground applies where the dwelling is reasonably required by the landlord as a residence for himself, his son or daughter, parents or grandparents, provided he did not become landlord by purchasing the reversion in the dwelling house after 12th April 1976.[16] This ground is subject to a further requirement, *viz* that the court must be satisfied that no greater hardship would be caused by granting possession than by refusing it.[17]

The mandatory grounds for possession are contained in Schedule 4, Part II of the 1976 Act. Where a mandatory ground is made out by the landlord, the court does not have an overriding discretion to refuse to make a possession order.[18] The mandatory grounds provide for the following cases:

(a)   Where the person granting the tenancy was an owner occupier and the court is satisfied that the dwelling house is required as a residence for the original occupier or a member of his family who resided with him when he last occupied the dwelling as a residence.[19] Notice must have been given at the commencement of the tenancy that possession might be recovered under this ground.

(b)   Where the person granting the original tenancy had acquired the dwelling with a view to occupying it as a residence upon retirement, and he now requires it as a retirement home, or (if he has died) it is

10 Schedule 4, Case III ibid.
11 Schedule 4, Case IV ibid.
12 Schedule 4, Cases V and VI ibid.
13 Schedule 4, Case VIII ibid.
14 Schedule 4, Case X ibid.
15 Schedule 4, Case VII ibid.
16 Schedule 4, Case IX ibid.
17 Schedule 4, Case IX, para 2 ibid. Cf Sch 15, Case 9 Rent Act 1977.
18 Section 6(6) Rent (Agriculture) Act 1976.
19 Schedule 4, Case XI ibid.

so required by a member of his family who was residing with him at the date of his death.[20] Notice must have been given on commencement of the tenancy if this ground is to be available.

(c) Where the dwelling house is overcrowded in circumstances rendering the occupier guilty of an offence under the housing legislation.[1]

4. Sub-tenants

Sub-tenants are protected by section 9 of the 1976 Act. Broadly, where a statutory tenancy is terminated, any sub-tenant who has been lawfully sublet the dwelling house or any part of it is protected and becomes a direct tenant of the landlord on the same terms as the statutory tenant – provided, always, that he himself qualifies as a protected occupier or statutory tenant under the 1976 Act.[2]

5. Succession rights

Section 4 of the 1976 Act provides for one succession to a protected occupancy. The succession provisions have been amended, however, where the protected occupier dies after the commencement of the Housing Act 1988. Succession rights accrue in either of two situations:

(i) if the original occupier died leaving a spouse who was residing with him at his death, then if the latter is not a protected occupier in his own right, he becomes the statutory tenant if and so long as he occupies the dwelling as his residence. Part II of Schedule 4 to the 1988 Act amends the 1976 Act[3] to provide that a cohabitee will be so treated if he or she 'was living with the original occupier as his or her wife or husband'. This mirrors the similar changes made to the succession scheme for protected and statutory Rent Act tenancies by the 1988 Act, and removes the uncertainty surrounding the position of common-law spouses and cohabitees.[4] If there is more than one person who fulfils this requirement, then in default of agreement it is for the county court to decide who shall be statutory tenant.[5]

(ii) if the occupier had no spouse living with him in the dwelling at his death, then an *assured* tenancy by succession is conferred on any member of his family who was residing with him in the dwelling house at the time of, and for the two years immediately preceding, his death. The requirement of residence in the dwelling house itself, rather than simply with the deceased occupier, was added by paragraph 10 of Schedule 4 to the 1988 Act. The latter also extended the qualifying period of residence from six months to two years. If

20 Schedule 4, Case XII ibid.
1 Schedule 4, Case XIII ibid.
2 Section 9(2) ibid.
3 Section 4(5) ibid.
4 As to which see *inter alia, Dyson Holdings Ltd v Fox* [1976] QB 503, *Helloy v Rafferty* [1978] 3 All ER 1016, *Chios Property Investments Co Ltd v Lopez* [1988] 05 EG 57.
5 Section 4 (5B) inserted by Housing Act 1988, Sch 4, para 12.

more than one family member fulfils this requirement, the assured tenant shall be, in default of agreement, such one as the court directs.

It should be noted that the Housing Act 1988 provides that in the case of deaths occurring after its commencement, family members other than spouses shall occupy by virtue of an assured tenancy by succession,[6] cf the statutory tenancy by succession enjoyed by widows or widowers, and previously enjoyed by other family members. The effect, broadly, is to confer greater security of tenure on the former than the latter from the date of the Act's commencement. There will also be no control of rents on fair rent principles where a family member succeeds to an assured tenancy by succession. Existing statutory tenancies by succession remain unaffected, however.

C   Transitional provisions

A licence or tenancy granted after the commencement of the Housing Act 1988 will normally be an 'assured' agricultural occupancy (below). Protected occupancy status under the 1976 Act is preserved for licences and tenancies granted after this date by the 1988 Act[7] in three situations only, *viz*:

(i)   if they are entered into pursuant to a contract entered into prior to the commencement of the 1988 Act. *Semble*, this would include occupancies granted as a term of a contract of employment entered into prior to the 1988 Act's commencement; *or*

(ii)   if the tenancy or licence is granted to a person who immediately before its grant was the protected or statutory occupier of tied accommodation. The occupier's protected status is therefore continued in the event of surrender and re-grant, provided the re-grant is by the person who was landlord or licensor (or one out of joint landlords/licensors) under the previous protected occupancy or statutory tenancy; *or*

(iii) prior to the grant of the tenancy, an order for possession was granted under Case I to Schedule 4 of the 1976 Act (ie suitable alternative accommodation) and the premises occupied are suitable alternative accommodation provided by the landlord, the tenancy of which the court directed should be a protected tenancy.[8]

It will be appreciated that the transitional provisions define those tenancies and licences which *can* remain protected under the 1976 Act, without stating clearly those which will fall to be protected instead by the 1988 Act. Under both Acts[9] protection only accrues once the agricultural worker condition has been satisfied *viz* when the occupier is a qualifying worker who has worked whole time in agriculture (or has thus worked as a permit worker) for 91 out of the last 104 weeks.[10] A problem may arise where an agricultural worker was granted a tenancy or licence prior to 15th January

6 Ibid Sch 4, para 11(b).
7 See s 34(1) and (4) Housing Act 1988.
8 Section 34 1(c)(i) *ibid*.
9 Sections 2(1) Rent (Agriculture) Act 1976; s 24(1) Housing Act 1988.
10 Schedule 3, para 1 Rent (Agriculture) Act 1976; Sch 3, para 2 Housing Act 1988.

1989 (the commencement date of the 1988 Act) but satisfied the agricultural worker condition *after* that date, eg he may have entered into a tenancy or licence 90 weeks before 15th January 1989. At the commencement of the 1988 Act regime he was not a qualifying worker; but he will become protected *after* commencement of the 1988 Act, having then completed 91 weeks' employment in agriculture.[11] Does the employee have in these circumstances a 'protected' or an 'assured' agricultural occupancy, *viz* does the 1976 Act apply, or the assured tenancy code of the 1988 Act? The better view, it is suggested, is that the Rent (Agriculture) Act 1976 will continue to apply in such circumstances, albeit that its protection may have accrued after the commencement of the 1988 Act. The occupancy will have been granted pursuant to a contract made before the commencement of the 1988 Act, and so will be covered by the saving provisions in Section 34 *ibid*.[12] Although there is no provision which expressly *excludes* protection under the 1988 Act, an assured agricultural occupancy cannot arise in these circumstances. For protection under the 1988 Act there must be an assured tenancy, or an interest which *would* be such if certain factors (eg a low rent) were discarded. But Schedule 1, para 1 of the 1988 Act specifies that a tenancy entered into before, or pursuant to a contract made before, 15th January 1989 *cannot* be an assured tenancy. Reading the assured agricultural occupancy provisions with Sch. 1 to the 1988 Act,[13] then, it is clear that an occupancy granted prior to 15th January 1989, but which becomes protected only after that date, will confer on the occupier the more extensive protection of the Rent (Agriculture) Act 1976, and not that of the 1988 Act.

D   Assured agricultural occupancies

The Housing Act 1988 introduced a new regime – 'assured' agricultural occupancies – applicable to licences and tenancies granted after the commencement of Part I of that Act. The broad features of the new regime are a reduced degree of security of tenure for agricultural occupiers, and the absence of rent control once the occupier's employment has ceased, other than the limited control on rents afforded to assured tenants by sections 13 and 14 of the 1988 Act.

1.   Qualifying for protection

A tenancy or licence will be an 'assured agricultural occupancy' if two conditions are satisfied.[14] For these purposes, any assured agricultural occupancy which is not an assured tenancy, ie a licence, shall be treated as if it were an assured tenancy and the provisions of Part I of the Act will apply accordingly.[15]

The two qualifying conditions are:

11 In the example given, protection will accrue one week after 15th January 1989.
12 See s 34(4)(a) of the 1988 Act.
13 Ie s 24(2) and Sch 1, para 1 ibid.
14 Section 24 Housing Act 1988.
15 Section 24(3) ibid.

    (a)   that the licence or tenancy –
        (i)   is an assured tenancy other than an assured shorthold tenancy. The protection will not apply, therefore, where the landlord grants an assured shorthold tenancy of agricultural accommodation.[16] The limited rent control provided for shortholds, based on comparability of rents, may be problematical given the probable lack of comparable shorthold lettings 'in the locality', suggesting (perhaps) a fruitful avenue of avoidance for agricultural landlords[17]; *or*
        (ii)   the tenancy is not an assured tenancy by virtue only of the fact that it is granted at a low rent (ie if granted after 1 April 1990 less than £1000 pa Greater London or £250 pa, (elsewhere)); *or* the dwelling is comprised in an agricultural holding and is occupied by the person responsible for the farming of the holding;[18] *or*
        (iii)   the occupancy is conferred by a licence under which a person has exclusive possession of a dwelling house and which, if it conferred a sufficient interest in land, would be a tenancy falling within (i) or (ii) above. Notwithstanding the House of Lords' ruling in *Street v Mountford*[19] many such occupancies will remain licences, given the grant of exclusive possession, owing to the service occupancy element present; *and*
    (b)   the 'agricultural worker condition', as defined by Schedule 3 to the 1988 Act, must be satisfied for the time being with respect to the dwelling house subject to the licence or tenancy.[20] This condition, which is discussed further below, requires that the worker have worked in agriculture for 91 out of the last 104 weeks before protection under the Act applies.

The assured agricultural occupancy under the 1988 Act is merely a variant of the Assured Tenancy, which latter is the regime applicable to all private sector lettings after 15th January 1989. This is reflected in the qualifying conditions (above) – the tenancy or licence must either *be* an assured tenancy, or be such that it *would* be one if the dwelling were let at a low rent etc. There is no control of rents on fair rent principles, however, and the landlord is free to charge a market rent on commencement of the agreement if he wishes. Previously the amount recoverable by agreement was limited by the 1976 Act.[1] If a market rent is now charged, the occupier retains his assured agricultural occupancy under the 1988 Act. This is unlikely to arise in practice, as most farmers make no charge for tied accommodation. Nevertheless, the legal implications of exacting a rent in such circumstances should be appreciated:

    (i)   If a tenancy is granted to an employee who has not been employed in agriculture for 91 out of the last 104 weeks, then if he is charged a

---

16 See ibid Part I, Chapter II, ss 20–23.
17 Ibid s 22(3).
18 Ibid Sch 1, paras 3, 3A and 7 (amended SI 1990/434).
19 [1985] 2 All ER 289, HL.
20 Section 24(1)(b) Housing Act 1988.
 1 By virtue of s 11 Rent (Agriculture) Act 1976 any agreed rent is irrecoverable insofar as it exceeds either the registered rent or (if more) one and a half times the rateable value of the dwelling. See pp 239 ff.

rent of less than the applicable rent limit[1a] he will enjoy no protection under the 1988 Act. He will, however, *become* an assured agricultural occupant as soon as he has 91 weeks' qualifying employment (see below).[2] The same result ensued under the Rent (Agriculture) Act 1976, leading to the creation of a protected agricultural occupancy once 91 weeks' qualifying employment has elapsed.

(ii)   If tied accommodation is let to an agricultural worker for a rent of *more* than the applicable rent limit then, the full protection of the Assured Tenancy Code under Part I of the 1988 Act will apply – unless one of the relevant exclusions in Schedule 1 applies, so as to prevent an assured tenancy arising.[3] The same employee would, under the old regime, have enjoyed protection under the Rent Act 1977.

(iii)   Once an employee granted an assured tenancy has completed 91 weeks qualifying employment, his interest will cease to be an assured tenancy *simpliciter* and will *become* an assured agricultural occupancy.[4] Although fully protected in the intervening period, the employee will at this point find himself in exactly the same position as an agricultural employee who has paid rent or a licence fee *ab initio* of *less* than the applicable rent limit (see fn 1a). He therefore receives no return for having paid a full rent from the outset. The position under the 1988 Act might be compared with that obtaining under the Rent (Agriculture) Act 1976. Under the old regime an employee paying a full rent would have been fully protected by the Rent Act 1977, and would have remained so even after the qualifying period of employment had elapsed – a protected occupancy under the 1976 Act only arose where the rent paid was less than ⅔ the rateable value of the dwelling.[5] Although the tenancy would in such circumstances be a regulated tenancy under the 1977 Act, however, the local authority rehousing provisions[6] remained available to the landlord/farmer by virtue of section 27(2) of the 1976 Act. This approach, it is suggested, has more to commend it than that adopted by the 1988 Act.

(iv)   Although a landlord/farmer is in theory free to charge a full rent when letting to an employee, it must be appreciated that the Agricultural Wages Orders limit the amount which may be deducted from an employee's wages by way of rent.[6a] This means that it is unlikely in practice that an employee will be paying a rent sufficiently large to lead to the creation of an assured tenancy *simpliciter* – although an assured agricultural occupancy will in such cases arise once the period of qualifying employment has been completed.

1a Ie less than ⅔ rateable value; *or* less than £1000 pa (London) or £250 (elsewhere) if the tenancy is granted on or after 1 April 1990.

2 The tenancy will then be within s 24(2)(b) of the 1988 Act *viz* it is a tenancy which is not assured solely because Sch 1, para 3 (tenancy at a low rent) is not satisfied. Section 24(1)(b) (agricultural worker condition) will also now be satisfied.

3 See Sch 1, para 6 (letting of land exceeding two acres with dwellinghouse) and 7 (letting of dwellinghouse occupied by person controlling farming of agricultural holding).

4 This conclusion follows inevitably from the interaction of s 24(2)(a) and s 24(1).

5 Schedule 2, para 2 Rent (Agriculture) Act 1976.

6 See below p 255 ff.

6a See the Agricultural Wages Order 1990 (1990 AWB No 1).

2.   The agricultural worker condition

This definition has two functions:

(a)   it limits the scope of protection by defining those agricultural employees on whom an assured agricultural occupancy is conferred; and

(b)   it triggers the distinctive security of tenure provisions applicable to agricultural occupancies, as opposed to other forms of assured tenancy.

If at any time the agricultural worker condition ceases to be fulfilled, the tenancy will cease to be an assured agricultural occupancy.[7] It then becomes a normal assured tenancy, and the special security of tenure provisions requisite to agricultural occupation cease to apply – in particular Ground 16 becomes available giving the landlord a discretionary ground for possession upon cessation of the occupier's employment (as to which see below).

(a)   'Agricultural worker' – the statutory definition

By virtue of paragraph 2 of Schedule 3 to the 1988 Act, two requirements must be met before the condition is satisfied, *viz*:

(i)   *The landlord condition.* The dwelling house must be, or have been, in 'qualifying ownership' at any time during the subsistence of the tenancy or licence. 'Qualifying ownership' is defined by reference to Schedule 3 to the 1976 Act, paragraph 3 of which requires that the occupier must be employed in agriculture and his employer be either the owner of the dwelling house or someone who has made arrangements with the owner for it to be used to house agricultural workers; and

(ii)   *The occupier condition.* The occupier (or one out of joint occupants) must be a 'qualifying worker', or *have been* a qualifying worker at any time during the subsistence of the licence or tenancy. Alternatively, the occupier must be incapable of whole time work in agriculture, or of permit work, by reason of a qualifying injury or disease suffered in the course of his agricultural employment with the landlord (see paragraph 2 of Schedule 2 to the 1976 Act).

'*Qualifying Worker*'. An occupier is a qualifying worker for these purposes if, at the relevant time, he has worked whole time in agriculture, or has worked in agriculture as a permit worker, for not less than 91 out of the past 104 weeks.[8]

(iii)   *Extension to qualifying spouses and members of occupier's family.* Where a qualifying worker has died, the agricultural worker condition is deemed to be satisfied if the occupier is either the 'qualifying widow or widower' of the previous occupier, or is a 'qualifying member of that previous occupier's family'.[9] A widow or widower qualifies under this provision if he or she was residing with the previous occupier in the dwelling house immediately

---

7 Section 24(1)(a) Housing Act 1988 – 'the agricultural worker condition is *for the time being* fulfilled etc' (emphasis added).
8 Schedule 3, para 1 Rent (Agriculture) Act 1976.
9 Schedule 3, para 3(1) Housing Act 1988.

before his or her death.[10] In the case of other members of his family, they qualify only if there was at the occupier's death no qualifying widow or widower, and the member of the family concerned was residing in the dwelling house with the occupier at the time of, and for two years before, his or her death.[11] If there is more than one member of the occupier's family who qualifies, then in default of agreement, that member of the deceased's family who the county court so decides, shall be the qualifying occupier for the purposes of the Act.[12] For these purposes, someone living with the deceased occupier 'as' his or her husband or wife is deemed to be his or her spouse.

One succession to an assured agricultural occupancy is, therefore, possible, subject to the same conditions as apply to succession to protected occupancies under the 1976 Act (as amended) where the occupier dies after the commencement of the 1988 Act.[13] The spouse succeeding to an assured occupancy granted after commencement will only have an assured tenancy, however, whereas a protected or statutory tenancy by succession is available if the occupancy was originally granted pre-commencement.

(iv) *Substitutionary licences/tenancies.* The agricultural worker condition is satisfied, and the occupier protected, if the tenancy or licence which he currently enjoys was granted in consideration of his giving up possession of another dwelling house in respect of which, at the time of surrender, the condition was satisfied.[14] In other words, the occupier who vacates voluntarily to enable his employer to relet to (for example) a replacement employee, does not thereby lose his assured occupancy status. Similarly, the latter is preserved where there is a surrender and re-grant of a licence or tenancy in relation to the same dwelling, thus protecting the occupier's status, even though the agricultural worker condition is not satisfied at the time of the re-grant.[15]

(b) Cessation of agricultural worker condition

It will be noted that the assured agricultural occupancy will only continue if the agricultural worker condition is *for the time being* fulfilled with respect to the dwelling house.[16] It is envisaged, clearly, that the condition can *cease* to be satisfied, in which event the distinctive protection of the assured agricultural occupancy provisions will cease to apply. In that event, also, the landlord would cease to have the benefit of the local authority's obligation to consider rehousing agricultural employees.[17] In this respect the assured agricultural occupancy provisions differ from the parallel provisions of the Rent (Agriculture) Act 1976, which make no provision for the cessation of 'protected' agricultural occupancy status if the occupier ceases to be a qualifying worker.[18]

Interpretation of the provisions providing for cessation of the agricultural

10 Ibid para 3(2).
11 Ibid para 3(3).
12 Ibid paras 3 and 4.
13 See pp 242 ff above.
14 Schedule 3, para 4 Housing Act 1988.
15 Ibid para 5.
16 Section 24(1)(b) Housing Act 1988 (italics added). And see s 25(1)(a) ibid.
17 Section 27 Rent (Agriculture) Act 1976, discussed below pp 255 ff.
18 See s 2(1)(a) and (b) ibid.

worker condition is not without difficulty. It might be thought that the condition ceases to be satisfied upon an employee retiring, or ceasing to be employed in agriculture for upwards of 13 weeks, or on moving to part time work. This is not, however, the case. By virtue of Schedule 3, para 2(b) of the 1988 Act, the agricultural worker condition is satisfied if the occupier has been a qualifying worker *at any time* during the subsistence of the tenancy or licence. Once the occupier has satisfied the condition by completing 91 weeks' work in agriculture out of the last 104 he will remain protected – even if he retires, moves to part time work or is dismissed. Once the condition is satisfied, the assured agricultural occupancy effectively acts *in rem*, and binds the dwelling irrespective of the personal employment status, thereafter, of the occupier.[19] In this respect the 1988 Act follows the same policy as that of the Rent (Agriculture) Act 1976.

The agricultural worker condition will only cease to be satisfied, as envisaged by the 1988 Act, in very limited circumstances. These arise from the distinctive nature of the assured occupancy as a variant of the Assured Tenancy *simpliciter*. By virtue of section 5 of the 1988 Act a periodic assured tenancy cannot be brought to an end without a court order and, furthermore, on termination of a fixed term assured tenancy a statutory periodic tenancy arises. By virtue of section 5(3)(a) the latter takes effect in possession, immediately on the coming to an end of the fixed term tenancy. It is not merely a right *in personam*, as is the statutory tenancy under the Rent Act 1977 or Rent (Agriculture) Act 1976. Being an interest in possession the statutory tenancy can be assigned or devised by will, and can pass on intestacy. The 1988 Act implies an absolute covenant against assignment in all periodic lettings of residential accommodation, but not where a fixed term assured tenancy is granted. It follows that the agricultural worker condition could *cease* to be satisfied if a fixed term tenancy of tied agricultural accommodation were assigned to a non-qualifying worker, or any other person not satisfying the requirement of 91 weeks' work in agriculture. Similarly, it could cease to be satisfied if, on the tenant's death, the tenancy vested in a third party (other than a spouse with succession rights) and the latter was a non-qualifying person. Where a periodic assured tenancy devolves under the will or intestacy of the former tenant, the 1988 Act gives the landlord a mandatory ground for possession, providing proceedings are begun not less than 12 months after the tenant's death.[20] Cessation of the agricultural worker condition will be of most importance, then, where a fixed term tenancy has been granted to an agricultural employee and is subsequently assigned, devised by will, or passed on insolvency, to a non-qualifying occupant. It might be noted that a similar result was achieved by the 1976 Act, but by different means. Section 4 of the 1976 Act conferred on the occupier a statutory tenancy, following termination of his licence or tenancy, but this was a personal right which only continued 'if and so long as he [the occupier] occupies the dwellinghouse as his residence'. On his ceasing to do so, the statutory tenancy ceases automatically. The inclusion of provisions in the 1988 Act for cesser of the assured agricultural occupancy is a necessary consequence of the nature of the assured tenancy as an interest *in rem*.

19 Section 5(2) Housing Act 1988.
20 See Sch 2, Ground 7 ibid.

(c)   Cesser of agricultural worker condition – effects

As we have seen, an assured agricultural occupancy can be either (a) an assured tenancy; (b) a tenancy which would be assured if not let (for instance) at a low rent or (c) a licence giving exclusive possession. By virtue of s 24(3) assured agricultural occupancies which are *not* assured tenancies, (ie b) and (c) above) are to be treated as assured tenancies. It follows that if a tenancy at a low rent, or a licence, ceases to be an assured agricultural occupancy, for instance due to cesser of the agricultural worker condition, the deeming provision in s 24(3) will cease to apply. Where an agricultural employee has a tenancy at a low rent or a licence, therefore, cesser of the agricultural worker condition will entitle the landlord to repossess following notice to quit, unhampered by the restrictions on possession in the 1988 Act. If the tenancy was an assured tenancy, the rent payable being above the rateable value or rent thresholds, the 1988 Act will continue to apply. In this event, however, Ground 16 in Sch 2 will become available to the landlord (in addition to the other Grounds for Possession) and will give a discretionary ground for possession on the basis that the dwelling house was let in consequence of the tenant's employment, which latter has now ceased. If a fixed term occupancy has been assigned in breach of a covenant against assignment or underletting, the landlord will also be able to invoke Ground 12 (breach of obligation other than as to rent).

3.   Security of tenure and Rent Control

As we have seen, the assured agricultural occupancy is a variant of the assured tenancy provided for in Part I of the Housing Act 1988. The general provisions applicable to assured tenancies apply, also, to assured agricultural occupancies. Protection is assured for agricultural occupants by conferring on the occupier a statutory periodic tenancy, but varying its terms and the grounds for possession to confer special protection.

(a)   Statutory periodic tenancy

On termination of the original licence[1] or tenancy, a 'statutory periodic tenancy' arises.[2] By virtue of section 5(3) of the 1988 Act this takes effect in possession immediately on the coming to an end of the former tenancy, and subject to the same terms as those of the former tenancy. If the occupancy was pursuant to a periodic tenancy, rather than a fixed term, the tenancy cannot be brought to an end by the landlord except by obtaining a court order.[3]

Prima facie, if the former tenancy was a fixed term the periods of tenancy will be the same as those for which rent was last payable.[4] Clearly, however, no rent will have been payable under many agricultural occupancies. The

---

1 A licence which constitutes an assured agricultural occupancy is deemed to be an assured tenancy for the purposes of Part 1 of the 1988 Act.
2 Section 5(2) Housing Act 1988. The statutory periodic tenancy will not arise if the tenancy was ended by a court order or a surrender.
3 Section 5(1) ibid.
4 *Section* 5(3)(d) ibid.

1988 Act[5] therefore provides that, in this event, the periods of tenancy shall be monthly, beginning on the day following the expiry or termination of the licence or tenancy. It is an implied term of every *periodic* assured tenancy that, except with the landlords consent, the tenant will not assign the tenancy, or sublet, or part with possession of, the whole or part of the dwelling.[6] This will be implied in all statutory periodic tenancies, but will not be implied into a fixed term, or where a premium is paid on grant. It is not an incident of the implied covenant that the landlord have to establish the reasonableness of any refusal of consent to assign etc.[7] There is also an implied term in every assured tenancy that the tenant shall afford access to the landlord, and all reasonable facilities, for executing repairs.[8]

(b)   Control of rent

One of the characteristics of 'assured' occupancies, when compared to 'protected' occupancies under the 1976 Act, is the absence of rent control on fair rent principles. The 1988 Act places no restriction on the rent which may be agreed between the parties at the outset. Section 13 provides, however, a procedure by which proposed rent *increases* can be controlled once a statutory periodic tenancy has arisen, or where a periodic tenancy itself has no rent review clause. The rent control provisions have no application in the case of a fixed term.

To obtain an increase in rent, the landlord must serve a notice of increase, to take effect at the beginning of a new period of tenancy.[9] The latter must be a date not earlier than the first anniversary of the commencement of the tenancy, except where a statutory periodic tenancy has arisen on determination of a fixed term.[10] There is also a requirement that notice of increase be of at least the 'minimum period' prescribed by the Act – six months in the case of a yearly tenancy, one month in the case of a tenancy of less than a month, and the period of tenancy in any other case.[11] The proposed date for rent increase must also be not less than twelve months from the date on which the last increase of rent took effect.[12] The tenant can refer a proposed rent increase to the Rent Assessment Committee for adjudication at any time before it comes into effect.[13] In default of reference, the rent proposed takes effect on the date proposed in the landlord's notice of increase.[14] On a reference under section 13, the Rent Assessment Committee are to fix the rent as that 'at which . . . [they] consider the dwellinghouse concerned might reasonably be expected to be let in the open market by a willing landlord under an assured tenancy.'[15] In doing so they

5 Section 25(1) ibid.
6 Section 15(1)(3) ibid.
7 Section 15(2) ibid, ie s 19 Landlord and Tenant Act 1927 does not apply.
8 Section 16 ibid.
9 Section 13(2) Housing Act 1988. The notice must be in prescribed form, for which see the Assured Tenancies and Agricultural Occupancies (Forms) Regulations 1988, SI 1988, SI 1988/2203.
10 Section 13(2)(b) ibid.
11 Section 13(3) ibid.
12 Section 13(1)(c) ibid.
13 Notice in prescribed form, referring the matter to the Rent Assessment Committee, must be served on the landlord: s 13(4) *ibid* For the prescribed form see SI 1988/2203 (above n. 9).
14 Section 13(4) ibid.
15 Section 14(1) ibid.

must assume the tenancy is an assured periodic tenancy having the same periods as those of the tenancy under consideration, subject to the same terms as the latter, and in relation to which the same notices have been served for the purposes of the mandatory grounds for possession (as to which see below). The committee must make several statutory 'disregards', discounting, *inter alia*, any value attributable to there being a sitting tenant, qualifying tenant's improvements,[16] and any tenants dilapidations.[17]

It should be appreciated that the rent control procedure only applies where the landlord seeks an increase – it is not open to the tenant to seek a *reduction* in rent, unless the landlord has served a notice of increase. In many cases, an assured agricultural occupant will have paid no rent during his period of employment. The 1988 Act enables the landlord to increase the rent to a free market level by notice of increase. There are, moreover, no provisions for the phasing of rent increases analogous to those previously available under the Rent (Agriculture) Act 1976. The only saving provision is section 14(7), which enables the committee to delay implementation of a rent increase, following adjudication, where it would cause 'undue hardship' if it came into effect on the date proposed in the landlord's notice of increase.

(c) Grounds for possession

By virtue of section 7(1), the court cannot grant an order for possession of a dwelling house let on an assured tenancy unless one or more of the grounds set out in Schedule 2 are satisfied. As with the 1976 Act grounds, the grounds in Schedule 2 to the 1988 Act are divided into mandatory and discretionary grounds for possession. In cases involving the discretionary grounds the court may make a possession order only if it considers it reasonable to do so.[18] Further, it has power to suspend proceedings, or stay execution of a possession order, on terms as to payment of rent, and may impose such other conditions as it thinks fit.[19] Where the mandatory grounds are at issue, the courts suspensory powers do not apply,[20] and if satisfied that one of the grounds is made out the court *must* make an order for possession.[1] The grounds for possession are themselves more generous than those available under the 1976 Act.[2]

(I) MANDATORY GROUNDS

These are contained in Schedule 2, Part I. As with the Rent Act grounds, the availability of Grounds 1 to 5 in Schedule 2 depends upon notice having been served prior to commencement of the tenancy informing the tenant that the relevant ground may be relied on. Schedule 2 provides a mandatory owner/occupier ground[3] of wider scope than its Rent Act counterpart, in that a

16 For qualifying improvements see s 14(3) ibid.
17 Section 14(2) ibid.
18 See s 7(4) ibid.
19 Section 9 ibid.
20 Section 9(6) ibid.
 1 Section 7(3) ibid. There are additional restrictions on the making of possession orders during a fixed term assured tenancy (see s 7(6)), but these are unlikely to be applicable to many assured agricultural occupancies, which are commonly periodic in nature.
 2 The grounds are summarised here, and not treated *in extenso*. See further Megarry, *The Rent Acts* (11th ed) vol 3 chapters 13 and 14; Martin, *Residential Security* (1989) p 205 ff; Rodgers, *Housing – the New Law* (1989) p 26 ff.
 3 Sch 2, Part I, Ground I ibid.

requirement for the dwelling as a residence need not be proved. This ground is also available to a non owner/occupier, in which event there is a requirement that he prove he requires the dwelling as his or his spouse's 'principal' home. Further mandatory grounds make provision for the following:

- repossession of holiday and student accommodation, and premises let to ministers of religion.
- repossession for the purpose of demolition and/or reconstruction of the dwelling or any building of which it forms part.
- where the assured tenancy has devolved on the death of the tenant either under his will or intestacy. Note that in this context the tenancy may cease to be an assured agricultural occupancy altogether, upon the 'agricultural worker condition' ceasing to be fulfilled. This ground will be available if the deceased tenant held pursuant to a fixed term or periodic assured tenancy, rather than a licence *treated* as a tenancy by virtue of the agricultural occupancy conditions.[4]
- where three weeks' rent is in arrears both at the date of notice of proceedings and hearing.

(II)   DISCRETIONARY GROUNDS

These are contained in Schedule 2, Part II, and make provision for the following grounds for possession:

- where suitable alternative accommodation is available for the tenant, or will be available for him when the possession order takes effect (Ground 9). Suitability is defined in terms similar to the existing criteria under the Rent Acts, *viz* by reference to the tenant's needs as to the character and extent of the property, and equivalence of terms and security of tenure with the existing tenancy.[5] This ground is particularly important, given the power enjoyed by agricultural landlords to compel the local housing authority to give consideration to rehousing former agricultural employees (see below).
- where there are rent arrears, persistent delay in paying rent or breach of other terms of the tenancy.
- where there is deterioration of the dwellinghouse, or furniture provided by the landlord, as a consequence of the tenant's neglect or default, and where the tenant's conduct has caused nuisance and/or annoyance to adjoining occupiers.
- where the dwelling was let to the tenant in consequence of his employment by the landlord seeking possession (or a previous landlord), and that employment has now ceased (Ground 16). By virtue of s 25(3) this ground does not apply while the tenancy qualifies as an 'assured agricultural occupancy'. The aims of the Act being to prevent arbitrary eviction of agricultural workers upon termination of employment, this exception is of the first importance. Many landlords may wish to seek possession upon termination of the occupier's employment, and the availability of Ground 16 would remove such

4 In this case the 1988 Act will cease to apply at all. If the tenancy was assured, it will revert to being an assured tenancy *simpliciter* without the distinctive protection afforded to agricultural occupancies.
5 See Sch 2, Part III Housing Act 1988.

security of tenure as the occupier otherwise enjoys. Notice given to terminate employment, if given by the tenant, does not constitute notice to quit and his security is not thereby prejudiced.[6] An *actual* notice to quit will, however, terminate the occupancy. If the tenancy ceases to be an assured agricultural occupancy, eg upon the agricultural worker condition ceasing to be fulfilled, Ground 16 will become available.

E Rehousing former agricultural workers

It would clearly be contrary to the needs of efficient agricultural production if property needed to house essential workers were rendered indefinitely unavailable to an agricultural employer, and the protection of former employees extended indefinitely. Of the grounds for possession, the availability of suitable alternative accommodation will be of particular importance to agricultural employers, enabling the relocation of former employees in alternative accommodation and the freeing of formerly tied accommodation for letting to essential workers. The suitability of alternative accommodation is assessed for assured agricultural occupancies in the same manner as with other assured tenancies, *viz* in accordance with Part III of Schedule 2 to the 1988 Act. The availability of alternative accommodation also furnishes one of the principal grounds for possession under the 1976 Act.[7] The security of the 'assured' agricultural occupier under the 1988 Act is, in this respect, broadly similar, as this ground for possession remains discretionary.

The agricultural occupancy provisions differ markedly from the regime applicable to other residential lettings, in that they enable an estate owner who is himself unable to provide accommodation to make application to the housing authorities, and to compel the latter to consider making accommodation available. This is, apparently, another facet of the underlying legislative policy of promoting the efficient organisation of agriculture.[8]

Section 27 of the 1976 Act enables a landlord to apply to the relevant housing authority on the ground that vacant possession is or will be needed of a dwelling house which is subject to either a protected or assured occupancy, in order to house a person who is, or is to be, employed by the landlord in agriculture. The latter must establish that he is himself unable to provide, by any reasonable means, suitable alternative accommodation himself, and that it's provision by the authority would be 'in the interests of efficient agriculture' (the key concept). In assessing the merits of the application, and in particular the requirements of 'efficient agriculture', the authority can obtain advice from the Agricultural Dwellinghouse Advisory Committee for the area concerned. The latter are constituted under section 29 of the 1976 Act specifically for this purpose, and are established in the area of each agricultural wages committee. The committee must tender its advice in writing making copies available to both landlord and tenant.[9] Although its

---

6 Section 25(4) ibid.
7 Rent (Agriculture) Act 1976, Sch 4 Cases I and II, above pp 241 ff.
8 See *R v Agricultural Dwelling-House Advisory Committee for Bedfordshire, Cambridgeshire and Northamptonshire, ex p Brough* (1986) 282 EG 1542, 1545 per Hodgson J.
9 Section 28(4) Rent (Agriculture) Act 1976.

ruling is advisory only, and not binding on the authority, it can be quashed by certiorari if insufficient or inadequate reasons are given. The committee's rulings are influential and invariably followed by housing authorities, and can therefore lead directly to a later decision adverse to the parties' rights. For this reason they can be subjected to judicial review.[10] If the housing authority is satisfied that the landlord's case is made out, it has a statutory duty to use its 'best endeavours' to provide suitable alternative accommodation.[11] When assessing the priority of the landlord's claim on its resources, the authority must give account to the urgency of the case, the competing claims on the accommodation which they can provide and the resources at their disposal. They must, moreover, treat an ex-employee as an applicant in a special category, and not simply by reference to a 'priority needs category' established under the Housing Act 1985.[12]

The rehousing provisions of the 1976 Act are applied to assured agricultural occupancies by Section 26 of the 1988 Act. Coupled with the wider grounds for possession applicable to Assured Tenancies, this will further enhance the landlord's ability to repossess dwellings for reletting to agricultural employees, where the occupancy was granted on or after 15th January 1989, and commensurately reduce the protection afforded to former employees.

10 See *R v Agricultural Dwelling-House Advisory Committee for Bedfordshire, Cambridgeshire and Northamptonshire, ex p Brough* (1986) 282 EG 1542.
11 Section 28(7) Rent (Agriculture) Act 1976.
12 See generally *R v East Hertfordshire District Council, ex p Dallhold Resources Management (UK) Pty Ltd* (1989) 22 HLR 77 (Pill J).

Chapter 12

Public control of land use I: planning and conservation

Agriculture is largely outside the control of the Town and Country Planning legislation. Many agricultural usages are exempt from the requirement of planning permission, while the Town and Country Planning (General Development) Order 1988[1] grants automatic permission for certain categories of building and engineering operation on agricultural land.[2] Development rights are subjected by the 1988 Order to conditions aimed at controlling the potentially harmful effects of intensive agricultural development eg near dwellings and roads. Additionally, major projects which may have a significant effect on the environment, and which require planning permission, will in future be subjected to an environmental assessment before permission can be granted.[3] While planning control is important in regulating development in the countryside, the main thrust of legislation concerned with conservation *per se* has been to encourage the voluntary participation of farmers and landowners in conservation measures eg by the conclusion of management agreements. The use of planning control to reinforce the voluntary principle is reserved principally for sites of particular importance, such as National Parks.[4]

A   Agricultural user and development rights

1.   Introduction

In principle, planning permission is required before any 'development' of land or buildings can take place. 'Development' requiring permission includes 'the carrying out of building, engineering, mining or other operations in, on, over or under land, or the making of any material change in the use of any buildings or other land.[5] The approach of the Town and Country Planning legislation to agricultural development is two-fold. Firstly, planning permission is automatically granted (subject to conditions) for three classes of development, which would otherwise require planning

1 SI 1988/1813.
2 *Ibid* Sch 2, Part 6, Class A, discussed further below p 261 ff.
3 Under the Town and Country Planning (Assessment of Environmental Effects) Regs 1988, SI 1988/1199. See below p 269 ff.
4 Eg in relation to Article 1(5) Land and Article 1(6) Land in National Parks etc, pursuant to the Town and Country Planning General Development Order 1988, SI 1988/1813.
5 Sections 55(1) and 57 Town and Country Planning Act 1990.

permission, by art 3 and sch 2 to the General Development Order 1988.[6] Secondly, Section 55(2)(e) of the Town and Country Planning Act 1990 exempts from the definition of 'development'[7] the *use* of land and existing buildings for agricultural purposes, and any change of use to agricultural user.

When preparing Local Plans and Structure Plans, or amendments thereto, local authorities are subject to publicity and consultation requirements.[8] They are, further, encouraged to consult MAFF when preparing development plans.[9] Where MAFF have objected to development plans they can, by virtue of Section 43(6) of the 1990 Act, require the local authority to send to the Secretary of State details of their objections, and the authority's reasons for modifying the proposed plans accordingly. Where MAFF have objected to the making or amendment of development plans, the local authority are barred from adopting them unless authorised to do so by the Secretary of State.[10]

2. Planning permission: agricultural user exemption

By virtue of Section 55(2)(e) of the 1990 Act 'the use of any land for the purposes of agriculture or forestry . . . and the use for any of those purposes of any building occupied together with land so used' does not constitute development, and does not require planning permission. A change of use of land or buildings from a non agricultural use to an agricultural user does not, therefore, require planning permission.[11] Similarly, s 55(2)(e) has the effect of exempting from planning control a change in the *use* of land/buildings from one agricultural use to another. If it is proposed to erect new buildings etc, however, or to modify or extend existing buildings, planning permission will be required – either expressly or under the terms of the General Development Order (below). Planning permission will be required if a change of use involves 'building, engineering, mining or other operations' in, on or over the land.[12] Note, however, that merely placing an existing structure on agricultural land will not constitute a building operation requiring permission. If its intended user is agricultural, there will be no material change of use and planning permission will not be needed.[13] So, for instance, the placing of a residential caravan on agricultural land, for the purpose of providing a weatherproof store and mixing place for cattle food, will not constitute 'development' and will not require planning permission.[14] The placing of an object or structure on farmland will only be outside planning control, however, if its siting and intended user is ancillary to the agricultural use of the relevant planning unit, which latter may encompass several parcels of land and not simply the site on which the structure is placed.[15] Where there

6 SI 1988/1813 Sch 2, Part 6.
7 See s 55(1) Town and Country Planning Act 1990.
8 Sections 33 and 39 *ibid.*
9 See DoE Circular 16/87 Annex A and DoE Circular 22/84 Annex C.
10 Section 43(6)(b) Town and Country Planning Act 1990. The Ministry make sparing use of this power.
11 *McKellan v Minister of Housing and Local Government* (1966) 198 EG 683.
12 Section 55(1) Town and Country Planning Act 1990.
13 *Restormel Borough Council v Secretary of State for the Environment* [1982] JPL 785.
14 *Wealden District Council v Secretary of State for the Environment* (1988) 56 P & CR 286, CA.
15 *G Percy Trentham v Gloucestershire County Council* [1961] 1 WLR 506, CA.

is a change of user from one agricultural use to another, the question whether it is a 'material' change of use is irrelevant – planning permission is not required, irrespective of the aesthetic merits of the changed agricultural use.[16]

(a) Material change of use

If no building or other operations are involved, planning permission will not be required unless there is a 'material change of use' of existing land or buildings etc. The change must, moreover, be from an agricultural to a non-agricultural user. A material change of use can occur when the ancillary uses to which land or buildings are put cease to be agricultural, or cease to be 'ancillary' to the primary agricultural user. For the purpose of deciding whether a change of use which is 'material' has occurred, regard must be had to the existing user of the planning unit *viz* the whole of the area which was used for a particular purpose or activities ancillary thereto. So, for instance, the creation on a holding of a 'lairage', for the transport and storage of livestock from other farms, will be a development requiring planning permission.[17] Cf. the conversion of buildings for such use for the purpose of exporting stock from the subject holding alone would probably *not* amount to a material change of use. Similarly, selling farm produce grown other than on the subject holding may constitute a material change of use requiring planning permission, as it is not an activity ancillary to the conduct of agriculture on the subject holding itself.[18] The sale of farm produce *per se* is a retail use, and not agricultural, and can only be exempted from planning control if truly incidental to the conduct of agriculture on the relevant planning unit. An ancillary agricultural use can also lose its protection if the primary user of the holding ceases to be agricultural. This is a question of fact and degree.[19]

(b) 'Land' defined

Land is defined by s 336(1) to mean 'any corporeal heriditament, including a building'. Taken with s 55(2)(e), it follows that planning permission is not required to put any existing building to agricultural use, whatever its design, appearance or present use.[20] Note, also, that s 55(2)(e) itself permits the use for agriculture not only of land, but of 'any building occupied with land so used'. It is not unlikely that this provision was intended to cover cases where there is an agricultural unit with a building which is not actually within the unit, but is occupied with the land so used eg a nearby farm cottage.[1]

---

16 See *Crowborough Parish Council v Secretary of State for the Environment* [1981] JPL 281.
17 *Warnock v Secretary of State for the Environment* [1980] JPL 590.
18 *Williams v Minister of Housing and Local Government* (1967) 18 P & CR 514.
19 *Cf. Pitman v Secretary of State for the Environment* [1988] JPL 391; *Birmingham Corpn v Minister of Housing and Local Government* [1964] 1 QB 178; *James v Minister of Housing and Local Government* [1966] 3 All ER 964.
20 See *North Warwickshire Borough Council v Secretary of State for the Environment* (1980) 50 P & CR 47.
1 See arguendo *North Warwickshire Borough Council v Secretary of State for the Environment ibid.*

(c)   'Agriculture' defined

By virtue of s 336(1), 'agriculture' is defined to include horticulture, fruit growing, seed growing, dairy farming, the breeding and keeping of livestock (including any creature kept for the production of food, wool, skins, or fur, or for the purpose of its use in farming the land), the use of land as grazing land, meadow land, osier land, market gardens and nursery grounds, and the use of land for woodlands where that use is ancillary to the farming of land for other agricultural purposes. Only use which is agricultural, within the extended meaning given by s 336(1), will be exempt from planning control. The definition is similar, but not identical, to the parallel provisions in the Agricultural Holdings Act 1986[2] and Rent (Agriculture) Act 1976[3] eg 'livestock' within s 336(1) would clearly include fish, thus exempting the mere *use* of land or buildings for fish farming. Fish are, however, not 'livestock' within the meaning of the Rent (Agriculture) Act 1976, and a worker employed in fish farming may not, therefore, enjoy the protection of the tied cottage legislation. Although decisions on the parallel definitions in the 1976 and 1986 Acts are not of authority, they may be of assistance.[4] The definition in s 336(1) is inclusive in nature, and not exhaustive – some common agricultural practices, such as arable farming, are not expressly included. Although the definition will extend to cognate agricultural activities, however, the constituent parts of the definition cannot be expanded by reference to their ordinary and natural meaning, irrespective of the agricultural context. So, for instance, the term 'livestock' is limited to animals normally kept for the production of food etc, and will not include the keeping of cats, dogs or even racehorses.[5] Guidance on the construction of inclusive definitions of this type was given in *Hemens v Whitsbury Farm and Stud Ltd*.[6] The following features of the definition should also be noted:

Breeding and keeping of livestock. 'Livestock' is defined as including any 'creature' kept for the production of food etc, and would include fish.[7] *Semble*, however, it would not encompass the raising of fish for ornamental purposes or restocking. It has also been held, for the purposes of the tied cottage legislation,[8] that pheasants and other game birds raised for sporting purposes are not 'livestock'.[9] Racehorses, similarly, cannot be regarded as livestock,[10] although foxes kept for the production of skins and fur may be.[11]

Grazing land. The use of land as grazing land is, in itself, an 'agricultural' user within the meaning of s 336(1), even if the animals grazed are not livestock. It will not suffice to turn animals onto the land for the occasional 'snack' of grass;

2 See Sch 1 Agricultural Holdings Act 1986 and Ch 2 p 17 above.
3 See s 1 Rent (Agriculture) Act 1976, and further Ch 11 above.
4 For more detailed discussion see Ch 2 p 17 and Ch 11 p 237 above.
5 *Hermens v Whitsbury Farm and Stud Ltd* [1988] 1 All ER 72, HL.
6 *Ibid* at 77 h–j and 78 a–c per Lord Keith.
7 See *Jones v Bateman* (1974) 232 EG 1392, CA; *Wallace v Perth and Kinross Assessor* 1975 SLT 118 and *Cresswell v British Oxygen Co Ltd* [1980] 3 All ER 443, CA. And see generally Howarth [1987] JPEL 484.
8 As to which see Ch 11 above.
9 *Lord Glendyne v Rapley* [1978] 1 WLR 601, CA; *Earl of Normanton v Giles* (1978) 248 EG 869; *Forth Stud v East Lothian Assessor* [1969] RA 35, 46.
10 *Hemens v Whitsbury Farm and Stud Ltd* [1988] 1 All ER 72, HL.
11 *North Warwickshire Borough Council v Secretary of State for the Environment* (1983) 50 P & CR 47.

they must be turned onto the land with a view to feeding them from the land.[12] Land, for planning purposes, includes buildings, and buildings used solely for purposes ancillary to grazing will be within the definition of agriculture.[13] Land and buildings used solely for the purpose of keeping animals (such as racehorses), and not for grazing, are not used thereby for agriculture.[14]

Recreational use. For the agricultural user exemption to apply it is not necessary that agricultural user be for the purposes of a trade or business cf. under the Agricultural Holdings Act 1986 use for the purpose of a trade or business is a prerequisite for protection.[15] Recreational use of an agricultural nature will suffice. So, for instance, grazing ponies kept for recreational purposes will not require planning permission – the mere keeping of racehorses or ponies will, however. Cf. for development rights under the General Development Order 1988 to apply, however, the user must be in connection with a trade or business.[16]

3. Permitted agricultural development rights

The agricultural user exemption in s 55(2)(e) of the 1990 Act (above) permits only of the *use* of land and/or existing buildings for agricultural purposes without planning permission. This is supplemented by s 59 *ibid* and the Town and Country Planning General Development Order 1988,[17] which grants planning permission for a wide range of operations involving development on agricultural land. Schedule 2 Part 6 of the General Development Order grants planning permission for, *inter alia*, the erection and modification of buildings, excavation and engineering operations. These permitted development rights are, however, subjected to numerous exceptions and conditions on their exercise. These are considered below.

Permitted development rights under Sch 2, Part 6 can be limited in two situations. By virtue of article 4 of the General Development Order, the Secretary of State or planning authority can give a direction that permitted development rights shall not apply, either within a particular area or in relation to a particular development. Further, in the case of land designated by Art 1(5) or 1(6) *ibid* development rights under Part 6 are expressly limited. So, in the case of Art 1(6) land, notice of intended building operations has to be given to the local planning authority, who can (if they so wish) impose conditions on the siting, design or appearance of any building erected. This additional control applies principally to development in National Parks, and certain specified areas adjacent thereto.[18] Cf. Agricultural user rights under s 55(2)(e) cannot be restricted by an article 4 order, neither are they affected in any way if land is within a National Park or other designated site. A distinction must be drawn, therefore, between the use of existing buildings and land for agricultural purposes (s 55(2)(e)) and

12 See *Sykes v Secretary of State for the Environment* [1981] 1 WLR 1092.
13 *McClinton v McFall* (1974) 232 EG 707, CA.
14 *Belmont Farm Ltd v Minister of Housing and Local Government* (1962) 13 P & CR 417.
15 See Ch 2, p 24 above.
16 See p 262 below.
17 SI 1988/1813.
18 Adjacent areas subjected to special control are specified in some detail in Sch 1 Part II *ibid*.

the erection of buildings or other installations (to which Sch 2, Part 6 applies).

The development rights conferred by Sched 2 Part 6 of the 1988 Order are divided into three classes:

Class A: the erection, extension and alteration of buildings, and any excavation and/or engineering operations.

Class B: winning or working of minerals for agricultural purposes.

Class C: construction of fishponds, and other operations, for the purpose of fish farming.

(a)   Building, excavation and engineering operations – class A

Class A grants permission for the carrying out on agricultural land comprised in an agricultural unit of works for the erection, extension or alteration of a building, or any excavation or engineering operations, reasonably necessary for the purposes of agriculture within that unit. Where Class A applies, development rights are subject to various conditions and limitations, considered below.

For Class A rights to apply, proposed operations must be carried out on 'agricultural land' comprised in an 'agricultural unit', and must furthermore be 'reasonably necessary' for the purposes of agriculture within that unit. Part 6 rights must be assessed by reference to the agricultural unit within which land is situate. This is not to be confused with the 'planning unit', which latter is of importance in deciding whether a material change of use requiring planning permission has occurred. Before the conditions applicable to the exercise of Class A rights are considered, the definition of the concepts delimiting the scope of Class A must be examined.

Agricultural Land
This is defined by Schedule 2 Part 6 Class D to mean 'land which, before development permitted by this Part is carried out, is land in use for agriculture and which is so used for the purposes of a trade or business, and excludes any dwellinghouse or garden'. The definition of agriculture for planning purposes has already been considered.[19] Note that development rights under Part 6 do not apply, however, if the agricultural user is recreational eg if buildings are to be erected for stabling ponies kept for recreational purposes. 'Trade or business' is not defined. *Semble*, however, it has a wide meaning and connotes any occupation by which one earns a living, as opposed to an activity for pleasure and social enjoyment.[20] A 'business' will, furthermore, encompass any 'serious occupation, not necessarly confined to commercial or profit-making undertakings'.[1] The express exclusion from the definition of agricultural land of any dwellinghouse and garden was added by the 1988 Order. Part 6 rights do not apply, therefore, to allow development in the garden of a farm cottage or farmhouse.[2]

19 See p 260 ff above.
20 *Customs and Excise Comrs v Fisher* [1981] 2 All ER 147; *South Oxfordshire District Council v East* [1987] 56 P & CR 112.
 1 *Town Investments Ltd v Department of the Environment* [1978] AC 359, HL.
 2 See *Tyack v Secretary of State* [1989] 1 WLR 1392, HL, decided under the Town and Country Planning General Development Order 1977.

'Agricultural Unit'

For development rights to apply under Class A, works or operations must be carried out on agricultural land comprised in an 'agricultural unit', and they must be 'reasonably necessary' for the purposes of agriculture *within that unit*. An agricultural unit is defined by Class A.3(2) to mean agricultural land which is occupied as a unit for the purposes of agriculture. This includes any building or dwelling on the land which is occupied for the purpose of farming that land by the person occupying the unit, and also includes any dwelling on the land occupied by a farm worker. It should be appreciated that an 'agricultural unit', thus described, can include separate parcels of land. Development rights are intended, however, to apply only to operations on land comprised in a working farm. Thus development is not permitted under Class A where land is included in a larger unit which is not agricultural in use.

'Reasonably necessary'

For Class A to apply, works or operations must be reasonably necessary for the purpose of agriculture within the agricultural unit concerned. In this respect the 1988 Order is considerably wider in application than its predecessors,[3] which required that development be 'requisite' for the purposes of agriculture. The latter requirement had been given a wide interpretation by the courts, who insisted only that some agricultural use should already exist on the land.[4] It was not required however, that a development be ancillary to a particular agricultural use, already carried out on the land. The requirements of the 1988 Order – that work be 'reasonably necessary' for the purposes of agriculture within the agricultural unit – re-emphasise the broad nature of the test to be adopted. Whether work is 'reasonably necessary' is to be ascertained by looking at the agricultural unit as a whole, which may constitute scattered parcels of land, and not the site on which the development is proposed to be carried out.

Minimum area of land

By virtue of Class A.1(a) development is not permitted if it would be carried out on agricultural land less than 0.4 hectares in area. For these purposes the 0.4 hectares limit is to be calculated without taking into account separate parcels of land.[5] It follows that the question whether development is on land exceeding 0.4 hectres is to be decided by looking at the individual parcel of land on which it is to take place, and not the agricultural unit as a whole. If the site itself exceeds 0.4 hectares, the question whether development is reasonably necessary for the purposes of agriculture etc is *then* decided by looking at the user of the agricultural unit as a whole, taking its several parts together. It follows that silage facilities, livestock housing, or other agricultural facilities, could be erected on one parcel of land, of the minimum 0.4 hectares in extent, although those facilities will benefit agricultural activities carried on elsewhere on other parcels of land included in the holding. Disallowance of the aggregation of individual parcels of land, for the purpose of calculating the 0.4 hectare minimum area for development, was introduced for the first time in the 1988, and confirms

3 See Town and Country Planning General Development Order 1977, Sch 1 Parts VI and VII.
4 See *Jones v Metropolitan Borough of Stockport* [1983] 50 P & CR 299, CA; *Fayrewood Fish Farms v Secretary of State for the Environment* [1984] JPL 267.
5 SI 1988/1813 Sch 2 Part 6 Class A 3(1)(a).

the decision of the House of Lords in *Tyack v Secretary of State for the Environment*.[6] As has already been noted, a dwellinghouse is not 'agricultural land', and it follows that it cannot be included when calculating the minimum size of the parcel of land to be developed.[7] In this respect, also, the 1988 Order confirms the ruling in *Tyack*, where it was held that a house and curtilege, on neighouring but physically separate land farmed by the occupier, were not part of a single agricultural unit, and that neither could the house and curtilege be considered agricultural land for the purposes of the General Development Order. It should be noted that although separate parcels of land will be taken together as forming the 'agricultural unit' for the purposes of Part 6, each parcel of land *may be* a 'planning unit' for the purposes of assessing whether there has been a 'material change of use'· requiring planning permission. So, in *Fuller v Secretary of State*[8] there was a material change of use where a grain silo was used for storing grain produced on other parts of the holding separate and distinct from the land on which the silo was situated. Although the farm as a whole was one agricultural unit, the separate parcels of land were constituted separate planning units.

(i)   *Permitted development under Class A*
Class A rights apply to development which consists of *either* works for the erection, extension or alteration of a building *and/or* excavation or engineering operations. By virtue of section 336(1) of the 1990 Act a building 'includes any structure or erection, and any part of the building, but not plant or machinery comprised in a building'. The 1988 Order further provides[9] that a 'building' does not include anything resulting from engineering operations. The erection of gates, fences and walls is not, therefore, regulated by Part 6, although it is separately regulated by Part 2 of the General Development Order. It follows, also, that unless covered by the separate permission for engineering operations (below) the installation or modification of fixed equipment is not covered by Class A.

Although Class A authorises excavation or engineering operations for agricultural purposes, it does not authorise the mining of minerals *per se*, even if they are to be used for agriculture on the holding, and not moved off it. Mining operations are separately dealt with by Class B (discussed below). Further, Class A.2(b) provides that if the development involves either the extraction of minerals from the land (or any disused railway embankment on the land) *or* the removal of any mineral from any mineral working deposits on the land, then the minerals shall not be moved off the land unless planning permission for the winning and working of the minerals concerned has been granted. Class A rights would, however, clearly encompass levelling and infilling to improve the agricultural quality of the land.

(ii)   *Buildings: Additional limitations*
The permission granted by Class A for development involving the erection, extension or alteration of buildings etc, is subjected to a number of additional limitations. These additional restrictions do not apply to excavation or engineering operations (above). In order to prevent the erection of buildings not designed for agricultural use Class A.1 expressly

---

6 [1989] 1 WLR 1392; affirming Court of Appeal (1988) 57 P & CR 140.
7 SI 1988/1813, Sch 2, Part 6, class D.
8 *Fuller v Secretary of State for the Environment* [1987] 56 P & CR 84. See above p 259.
9 SI 1988/1813 Sch 2, Part 6, Class A.3(2).

forbids development which would consist of or include the erection, extension or alteration of a dwelling. Further, whether a building or structure is 'designed' for the purposes of agriculture is to be decided by its physical appearance and layout.[10] It has been held, therefore, that an aircraft hanger is not a building 'designed' for the purposes of agriculture.[11]

Class A also imposes limitations on the size or ground area of permitted building operations. Development is not permitted if the ground area to be covered would exceed 465 square metres. This limitation applies to two types of development. Firstly, any works or structure (other than a fence) for the purposes of accommodating livestock, or any plant or machinery arising from engineering operations, must not exceed 465 square metres in ground area. Secondly, the limit applies to any building erected, or any building altered or extended, by virtue of Class A. The relevant ground area, for the purpose of assessing whether it complies with the 465 square metre rule, is

(1) the ground area which would be covered by the proposed development, *plus*

(2) the ground area of any building (other than a dwelling), or any structure, works, plant or machinery within the same unit which is being provided, or has been provided within the preceding two years, and any part of which would be within 90 metres of the proposed development.[12]

If the development, taking the aggregate of its ground area together with that of structures or buildings provided within the last two years within a radius of 90 metres, would exceed 465 square metres in area then planning permission will be required. Note, however, that aggregation only applies where, (1) buildings are within ninety metres of the proposed development, and, (2), to buildings which have been erected in the previous two years. The intent is to prevent extensive development of small areas of land. If a building is to be placed within ninety metres of one previously built within the last two years, planning permission will be required unless a two-year period is allowed to expire. This facilitates the staging of development without planning permission, provided the terms of Class A are satisfied. Further, it should be appreciated that there is no control of buildings on an area of less than 465 square metres, provided they are spaced so that none impinges within a radius of 90 metres around any other. If this happens the ground area of the buildings must be aggregated (for the purposes of Class A) and if the aggregated area exceeds 465 square metres either planning permission will be required, or there must be a delay in development until the two-year period has elapsed.

Development is not permitted in close proximity to aerodromes. Class A.1(e) and (f) specify that if any part of the proposed development is within three kilometres of the perimeter of an aerodrome, then it is not permitted if the height of any part of the building, structure or works concerned would exceed three metres. Where a development is to take place *outside* the three kilometre radius of an aerodrome, development control is relaxed, in that development is not permitted if any part of the building or structural works would exceed twelve metres in height. Similarly, development within close proximity to metalled roads is subjected to limitations. If any part of a

---

10 See *Harding v Secretary of State for the Environment* [1984] JPL 503.
11 *Belmont Farm v Minister of Housing and Local Government* (1962) 13 P & CR 417.
12 SI 1988/1813 Sch 2, Part 6, Class A.3.(1)(b).

proposed development is within twenty-five metres of the metalled portion of a trunk or classified road, the development as a whole will not be authorised by Class A – and not just that portion which is within the twenty-five metre radius.[13] Where access is sought to a permitted development within Class 6, works providing access are allowed by Part 2 Class B, but only if the road to which access is sought is unclassified. Further, Article 35 of the 1988 Order provides that if access is sought to a classified or trunk road, then Class 6 rights do not include the building or material widening of an existing access road. The restrictions contained in Class A do not apply to unclassified roads.

Engineering operations connected with fish farming are expressly excluded from Class A development rights, being dealt with separately in Class C (below).[14]

(iii)   *Siting of livestock units, slurry and sludge storage facilities*
By virtue of Class A(1)(J), development is not permitted if it would consist of, or include, the erection or construction of, or the carrying out of any works to, a building, structure or excavation, used or to be used, for the accommodation of livestock, or for the storage of slurry or sewage sludge, if the building/structure etc is, or would be, within 400 metres of the curtilege of any 'protected' building. This restriction is intended to minimise the nuisance to residential occupiers caused by the insensitive siting of slurry and sludge facilities etc. Protected buildings, proximity to which is prohibited, are defined to include any permanent building which is normally occupied by people, or would be so occupied if used for the purposes for which it is apt.[15] Any building within the agricultural unit itself is not, however, a protected building for these purposes, neither is an agricultural building on an adjacent unit.

(iv)   *Development rights: conditions on exercise*
Where development rights under Class A accrue, their exercise may, in certain circumstances, be subject to conditions. These are specified in Class A.2(1).

In order to prevent evasion of development control as to the siting etc of livestock units, slurry and sludge facilities (above), condition A.2(1)(a) provides that where a permitted development is carried out within 400 metres of the curtilege of a protected building, any building or structure etc which is erected or made cannot be *used* for the accommodation of livestock, or the storage of slurry or sewage sludge, within five years of the development.[16] Note, however, that although the erection of such facilities within a 400 metre radius of protected buildings is controlled, section 55(2)(a) of the 1990 Act permits the carrying out of maintenance, alterations or improvements to an existing building, provided always that the external appearance of the latter is not materially affected. The condition limiting user for slurry or sludge storage etc for five years operates to prevent the erection of agricultural buildings under the permission granted by Class A (above), and their subsequent conversion to use for livestock housing, or

---

.13 See *Fayrewood Fish Farms v Secretary of State for the Environment* (1984) JPL 267.
14 SI 1988/1813 Sch 2, Part 6, Class A.1(R).
15 *Ibid* Class A.3(2).
16 Art 1(2) *ibid*. defines slurry to mean animal faeces and urine, irrespective of whether water is added to facilitate handling.

slurry/sludge facilities, thus avoiding planning control on the siting of facilities of this kind.

Where minerals are extracted in the course of agricultural operations authorised by the General Development Order, Class A.2(1)(b) provides that they cannot be moved off the land without express planning permission. The mining of minerals is separately dealt with by Class B (below). This condition would apply, for instance, to shale and gravel removed incidentally to the levelling and improvement of land for agricultural purposes. Note, additionally, that there is no restriction on the *importation* of building materials or other material (eg soil) which does not constitute waste. Where it is proposed to import *waste* material onto an agricultural unit, however, the type of material which may be brought onto the land without planning permission is controlled. The only waste material which may be imported is that intended for use in building works, or for the creation of a hard surface.[17] In both cases, moreover, the material must be incorporated into the building or surface forthwith. Waste is not statutorily defined, but clearly includes material which is surplus to the requirements of the supplier and of no intrinsic use to him eg the by-products of building works. This condition on permitted development is intended to prevent unauthorised waste disposal on agricultural land, under the guise of permitted agricultural operations within Part 6.[18]

(v)   *Buildings in National Parks etc: Special Control*
Additional restrictions apply to development rights in 'Article 1(6) Land' ie land in National Parks and other protected areas specified in Schedule 1 Part 2 of the General Development Order. In such areas Part 6 development rights are qualified by the requirement that the developer give written notice to the local Planning Authority of any proposed development which consists of the erection, extension or alteration of a building, or the formation or alteration of a private way. Following notification, the local Planning Authority have twenty-eight days in which, if they so wish, to give the developer notice in writing that the development must not be done without their prior approval as to the siting, design and external appearance of the building. The local Planning Authority can also subject the siting and means of construction of a private way to their approval.[18] If the Authority have given notice, then the development must be carried out in accordance with details as to siting, external appearance etc approved by the Authority, unless the latter have agreed otherwise in writing.[19] Where the Authority fails to serve notice exercising their right of control, the development must in any event proceed in accordance with the description and indication of siting initially given by the developer.[20] In any event, the development must be carried out within five years of either the initial submission of written details (above) or the date of approval by the local Planning Authority, whichever applies.

17 *Ibid* Class A.2.1.(c).
18 See *Northern District Council v Secretary of State for the Environment* [1981] JPL 114; *Bilboe v Secretary of State for the Environment* (1980) 39 P & CR 495, CA.
19 SI 1988/1813, Sch 2, Part 6, Class A.2(2) as amended, SI 1989/603.
20 *Ibid* Class A.2(2)(c).

(b) Winning and working of minerals: Class B

Class B grants permission for the winning and working, on land held or occupied with land used for the purposes of agriculture, 'of any minerals reasonably necessary for agricultural purposes within the agricultural unit of which the land forms part'. For this purpose agriculture is deemed to include fertilising land used for the purposes of agriculture, and the maintenance, improvement and alteration of any buildings, structures or works occupied or used for such purposes on land so used.[1] This permitted development right applies where minerals are mined, as opposed to extracted in the course of agricultural operations authorised by Class A (above). Class B rights are subject to the condition that no mineral extracted can be removed outside the land from which it was extracted, except to land held or occupied with that land, and which is also used for the purpose of agriculture.[2] It is permissible, therefore, to extract minerals on one part of an agricultural unit for use on a separate part of the same unit, without planning permission.[3] Development rights under Class B are subjected to the additional condition that development is not permitted if any excavation connected therewith would be made within twenty-five metres of the metalled portion of a trunk or classified road. This restriction does not, however, limit development adjacent to unclassified roads.

(c) Fish and shellfish farming: Class C

Class C permits the carrying out on agricultural land used for the purposes of any registered business of fish farming, or of shellfish farming, of operations for the construction of fish ponds, or other engineering operations for the purposes of that business. Operations connected with fish farming are expressly exempted from Class A rights (above), a special regime being applied by Class C, with intent to prevent farmers exploiting permitted development rights by engaging in extractive mineral operations under the guise of constructing installations necessary for fish farming. For this reason the permission granted by Class C is more limited than that more generally available under Class A (above) eg Class C rights are limited to operations for the construction of fish ponds or related engineering operations.

'Construction of fish ponds'. This is defined to include the excavation of land and the winning or working of land for that purpose (and that purpose only).[4] A 'fish pond' is defined to include any pond, tank, reservoir, stew or other structure used for the keeping of live fish, or for the cultivation and propagation of shellfish. It should be appreciated, also, that development rights are restricted by Class C to *registered* fish farm businesses only.

Class C.2. imposes further restrictions on development rights applicable to fish farming. Firstly, the site within which the operations would be carried out must not exceed two hectares. Note that it is the area of the *site*, and not the actual area to be excavated, which must not exceed two hectares. It is further provided that no part of the operation must be carried out within

---

1 *Ibid* Class B.3.
2 *Ibid* Class B.2.
3 See the definition of agricultural unit, *ibid* Class A.3(2); this could clearly include scattered parcels of land.
4 Class C. 2.

twenty-five metres of the metalled portion of a trunk or classified road. As with the parallel restriction on Class A development rights (above), if any *part* of the operation infringes the twenty-five metre limit, the whole operation will be unauthorised. Further, if the operation involves the winning or working of minerals, it is not authorised if any excavation were to exceed 2.5 metres in depth, or if the area of the excavation (taken with any other excavations during the prior two years) would exceed 0.2 hectares. The intent is to limit the area of permitted excavation to that reasonable for the construction of fish tanks, ponds etc, thus reducing the likelihood of the extraction of minerals taking place under the guise of permitted agricultural development under Class C.

4. Environmental assessment of planning applications

European Council directive 85/337/EEC (the Environmental Assessment Directive) requires member states to ensure, before consent to certain types of development is given, that projects likely to have a 'significant effect' on the environment by virtue of their nature, size or location are made subject to an assessment of their environmental effects. The EEC provisions do, however, envisage that environmental assessment can be integrated into existing procedures adopted by member states for giving consent to projects or development.[5] Development requiring environmental assessment is divided by the Directive into two categories: that which requires environmental assessment in every case (listed in Annex 1 thereto) and that which requires environmental assessment when member states consider that its characteristics so require (listed in Annex 2). Where the requirement of environmental assessment applies, a developer must provide information about the effects of the proposed operation, both directly and indirectly, on matters specified in article 3 to the Directive *viz* human beings, flora and fauna, soil, water, air, climate and landscape, material assets and the material heritage.[6] By virtue of Annex 2, para 1 of the Directive, certain agricultural operations fall within the category which member states *can* make subject to environmental assessment if they consider their characteristics so require. The Directive places the following agricultural operations within this category:

Projects for the restructuring of rural land holdings
Projects for the use of uncultivated land or semi natural areas for intensive agricultural purposes
Water management projects for agriculture
Initial afforestation where this may lead to adverse ecological changes
Poultry rearing installations
Pig rearing installations
Salmon breeding, and
Reclamation of land from the sea

The Environmental Assessment Directive has been implemented in domestic law using existing planning consent procedures[7], and procedures on

5 See Art. 2 Council Directive 85/337/EEC.
6 The information to be supplied is specified in more detail in Annex 3 to the Directive.
7 By the Town and Country Planning (Assessment of Environmental Effects) Regs. 1988, SI 1988/1199.

application for capital grants. By virtue of section 17(1) of the Agriculture Act 1986 the Minister, when discharging any functions connected with agriculture in relation to any land, must have regard to, and endeavour to achieve, a reasonable balance between the promotion and maintenance of a stable and efficient agriculture industry, the economic and social interests of rural areas, the conservation and enhancement of the natural beauty and amenity of the countryside, and the promotion of its enjoyment by the public. It follows that the environmental impact of proposed works will be relevant to the resolution of applications for grant aid eg under section 29 Agriculture Act 1970 or the Farmland and Rural Development Act 1988. Environmental assessment does not apply, however, where detrimental operations are carried out without applying for capital grant aid. If such operations do not require planning permission, moreover, the possibility of assessment does not arise. This is arguably a deficiency in the implementation of the Environmental Assessment Directive in domestic law.

(a)   Environmental assessment in planning law

The Town & Country Planning (Assessment of Environmental Effects) Regulations 1988 complement the Agriculture Act 1986 (above) by requiring environmental assessment of certain planning applications. The 1988 Regulations require a planning authority, when considering applications for planning permission, to have regard in some cases to an environmental statement as to the likely effects of the proposed development. Those requiring environmental assessment in every case are specified in Schedule 1 to the Regulations. Those listed in Schedule 2 require environmental assessment if they are likely to have 'significant effects' on the environment by virtue of their nature, size or location.[8] Schedule 2, para 1 specifies a number of agricultural operations which are potentially subject to environmental assessment, depending on their likely effect on the environment. These include:

> Water management for agriculture,
> Poultry rearing,
> Pig rearing,
> Salmon hatcheries,
> Installations for rearing salmon,
> Reclamation of land from the sea.

Proposed developments within these categories will be subjected to environmental assessment if they are likely to have 'significant' effects on the environment. Identifying projects likely to have this effect, and therefore requiring assessment, is provided for in the following manner:

(i)   By virtue of Regulation 2(2) the Secretary of State can give a conclusive direction as to whether a development would or would not have significant effects on the environment.

(ii)   Regulation 4(4) further provides that a project is to be taken as likely to have a significant effect on the environment, and thus to require environmental assessment, if the applicant for planning permission and the local Planning Authority agree that it is likely to

---

8 *Ibid* reg. 2(1).

have this effect, if the applicant submits an environmental statement expressed to be for the purposes of the Regulations, or (thirdly) if the Secretary of State directs that the consideration of environmental information is necessary.

(iii) In other cases, whether the Regulations will apply depends upon the facts of the case and the likely environmental effect of the proposed operations ie whether they are likely to have significant effects on the environment or not.

Regulation 4(2) prevents the Authority from granting planning permission, where a proposed operation will have significant effect on the environment, unless they have first taken environmental information supplied in accordance with the Regulations into account.

The Regulations enable potential applicants to request the local Planning Authority to state in writing whether, in their opinion, the proposed development is within schedule 2,[9] and whether an environmental statement would have to be considered before planning permission could be granted. The Authority have three weeks in which to reply, and if of the opinion that an environmental assessment *is* required, they must state the reasons for their conclusion.[10] If the Authority decide that an environmental statement is required, or fail to respond, the applicant can apply to the Secretary of State for a direction.[11] Further, it should be noted that the Town & Country Planning General Development Order 1988 now gives the Secretary of State power to give directions exempting a proposed development, or class of development, from the environmental assessment requirements, and stating whether it is or is not one in respect of which the Regulations require the consideration of an environmental statement.[12] These powers enable the Secretary of State to decide conclusively whether or not a particular project requires environmental assessment, and will normally be applied where a developer applies for a direction under the terms of the Environmental Assessment Regulations.[13]

(b) Projects subject to assessment

Ministerial guidance indicates that in the Secretary of State's view, environmental assessment will normally be needed for Schedule 2 projects in three types of case only:

(i) For major projects of more than local importance,
(ii) Occasionally, for projects on a smaller scale which are proposed for sensitive or vulnerable locations, and
(iii) In a small number of cases, for projects of unusually complex and potentially adverse environmental effect, where expert and detailed analysis of those effects would be desirable, and relevant

---

9 *Ibid* reg 5(1).
10 *Ibid* reg 5(4).
11 *Ibid* reg 5(6).
12 SI 1988/1813, Art 14. And see SI 1988/1199, reg 3, extending the Secretary of State's power to give directions in a General Development Order.
13 Ie under regs 5 or 6, SI 1988/1199.

to the issue of principle as to whether or not the development should be permitted.[14]

Department of the Environment Circular 15/1988 gives indicative criteria and thresholds, for the purpose of guiding local Planning Authorities when identifying Schedule 2 projects which will require environmental assessment.[15] Agricultural operations which are specified, and which may therefore require environmental assessment, include the following:

(a)   *New pig rearing installations*

These will not generally require assessment, but those designed to house more than 400 sows or five thousand fattening pigs may require environmental assessment.

(b)   *Poultry rearing installations*

Those designed to house more than a hundred thousand broilers or fifty thousand layers, turkeys or other poultry may require environmental assessment.

(c)   *Salmon farming*

Salmon hatcheries and installations for rearing salmon are both Schedule 2 matters potentially requiring environmental assessment. Whether they require assessment will depend on the environmental effect of each proposed development. Ministry guidance, however, indicates that small projects designed to produce less than one hundred tons of fish a year would not normally require environmental assessment. Note that different criteria apply to salmon farming in coastal waters.

(d)   *Drainage works*

Drainage and flood defence works may require assessment if it emerges from consultation with drainage and conservation bodies that the project in question is likely to have a significant environmental effect. Ministry guidance indicates that the Secretary of State will decide on the need for assessment after taking into account the views of the relevant agriculture Minister, the latter having statutory responsiblities under the Drainage Act 1976.

The above are guidelines only. It should be appreciated that whether environmental assessment will be required, in an individual case, will depend upon whether the planned development will have significant environmental effects. Those aspects of the environment which might be significantly affected by a project include 'human beings, flora and fauna, soil, water, air, climate, the landscape, the interaction of any of these material assets and the cultural heritage'.[16] Consideration may also be given to the use of natural resources, the emission of pollutants, the creation of nuisances, and the elimination of waste.[17]

---

14 DoE Circular 15/1988 para 20. And see paras 22–9 *ibid* for detailed consideration of these heads.
15 See *ibid* Appendix A.
16 SI 1985/1199 Sch 3, para 2.
17 *Ibid* Sch 3, para 3.

(d)   The environmental statement

Where an agricultural project has been determined as requiring environmental assessment, an environmental statement will have to be submitted with the application for planning permission. Although no form is prescribed, it must contain the information specified in Schedule 3 para 2 of the Regulations. The latter require the local Planning Authority to inform relevant public bodies that environmental assessment of a project has been determined as necessary.[18] Those bodies are under an obligation to make available to the developer any information in their possession which is relevant to the preparation of an environmental statement.[19] The public bodies specified, and which are subjected to the duty of consultation, include the Nature Conservancy Councils and Countryside Commissions, the principal Council of the area concerned, and those bodies which would be statutory consultees under article 15 of the General Development Order for any planning application for the proposed development.[20] The Planning Authority is under a duty to consult with the statutory consultees, and the developer must supply one copy of the environmental statement for each free of charge when applying for planning permission.

The Local Authority must forward a copy of the environmental statement to the Secretary of State and Department of the Environment Regional Office (or Welsh Office if appropriate). In all other respects, however, they must treat the planning application in the same way as any other. The environmental statement, in addition to the application itself, must be placed on Part 1 of the Planning Register together with any direction or opinion given during the pre-application procedures (above). The Planning Authority have sixteen weeks from the receipt of the environmental statement to determine the application.[1] The publicity requirements of the Town and Country Planning Act 1990 apply to the application, requiring public notices to be posted on site and in the local press.[2] The relevant notices must specify that a copy of the environmental statement is available for inspection by the public, and give an address at which it may be inspected.[3]

When considering the application, the Planning Authority are required to have regard to all the environmental information contained in the statement, and to any observations made by the public bodies consulted on the application, in addition to any representations made by the public and other material considerations. Where insufficient information is supplied the Planning Authority have power[4] to require an applicant to supply additional information. Upon determination of the application the Planning Authority must notify the Secretary of State, in addition to notifying the applicant and to placing a copy of the decision on the Planning Register. The special nature of the application, and the requirement of environmental assessment, do not affect the applicant's rights of appeal.

18 *Ibid* reg 8.
19 *Ibid* reg 22.
20 *Ibid* reg 8. Public bodies can make a reasonable charge for providing information.
 1 *Ibid* reg 16(2). Cf the normal time limit is 8 weeks, pursuant to SI 1988/1813, art 7.
 2 Section 25 Town and Country Planning Act 1990.
 3 SI 1988/1199 reg 12.
 4 See *ibid* reg 21(1).

B   Agriculture, conservation and land use

1. Conservation legislation

The volume of conservation legislation affecting agricultural land use has increased considerably in recent years. While some conservation measures originate in European community requirements (eg the set aside scheme), other measures have domestic origins. The policy consistently pursued by the domestic legislation, in its application to agriculture, has been to encourage the voluntary participation of farmers and land owners in conservation measures.

Conservation protection, and the associated control of agricultural practices, is provided for in a variety of legislative measures, which latter fall into several categories. Of primary importance is legislation providing for the designation of environmentally important sites, and their protection by the conclusion of voluntary or mandatory management agreements controlling the future management and cultivation on conservation grounds.[4a] Land considered of environmental importance by the relevant Nature Conservancy Council can, for instance, be designated a site of special scientific interest under the Wildlife and Countryside Act 1981. The broad effect of designation is to restrict certain proscribed agricultural operations pending the conclusion of a management agreement with the owner or occupier. Management agreements can also be secured in relation to Nature Reserves under the National Parks and Access to the Countryside Act 1949, and in relation to environmentally sensitive areas under the Agriculture Act 1986. The use of management agreements has become widespread, and underpins the voluntary principle in its application to conservation and protection of the countryside. The use of management agreements is supplemented, in limited circumstances, by the use of planning control to enforce compulsory restrictions on agricultural activity. The use of planning measures is restricted primarily to the protection of areas of national significance eg in relation to land designated as National Parks under the 1949 Act. Environmental assessment of the effects of agricultural operations, provided they require planning permission,[5] has already been considered.[6] The use of designation powers, management agreements and planning control, has now been supplemented by measures introducing agricultural grants to encourage the adoption of conservation measures. Financial subsidies have, for instance, been introduced to encourage farmers to take land out of production altogether under the set aside scheme[7] and to encourage farmers to introduce fixed equipment and improvements specifically intended to prevent pollution and to conserve the environment.[8] As we have seen applications for capital grant are now, by virtue of section 17(1) of the Agriculture Act 1986, subjected to assessment on environmental as well as agricultural grounds.

4a For designation of Nitrate Sensitive Areas under the Water Act 1989, and management agreements thereunder see Appendix 4.
5 As to which see p 261 above.
6 See p 269 ff above.
7 Implemented by the Set Aside Regulations 1988, SI 1988/1352, (below Ch 13).
8 See eg Farm and Conservation Grant Scheme 1989 SI 1989/128.

2. Nature Conservancy Councils – role

The central role in providing a comprehensive framework of control is played by the Nature Conservancy Council (NCC). By virtue of Part 7 of the Environmental Protection Act 1990 the Nature Conservancy Council has now been divided into three separate bodies: the Nature Conservancy Council for England, the Nature Conservancy Council for Scotland and the Countryside Council for Wales. Designation powers formerly enjoyed by the Nature Conservancy Council under various conservation measures (discussed below) will in future be exercisable in relation to England, Scotland and Wales respectively by the successor bodies to the NCC constituted by the 1990 Act.

The NCCs have the duty of advising on the implementation of conservation policies in the UK, and have a specific role by statute in several areas. They are responsible for designating sites of special scientific interest under the Wildlife and Countryside Act 1981, for the establishment and management of National Nature Reserves under the National Parks and Access to the Countryside Act 1949 and for giving support for education on conservation. The NCCs also have power under the 1981 Act[9] to make financial grants and loans for the purpose of fostering the understanding of nature conservation, and *inter alia* to cover expenditure by an individual in doing anything conducive to nature conservation. The Councils also give a wide range of advice to public bodies on conservation issues, as to private individuals.[10]

The Environmental Protection Act 1990 makes detailed provision for the reallocation of many of the nature conservation functions of the NCC to the new Councils constituted by Part 7 thereof. Section 132 of the 1990 Act transfers to the new Councils the following conservation functions, previously exercised by the NCC on a national basis. In exercising these functions the new Councils are directed to 'take appropriate account of actual or possible ecological changes'.[11] The Secretary of State has power to give the Council directions of a 'general or specific character with regard to the discharge of any of their nature conservation functions'. This power, however, does not apply to their powers to designate areas for special protection eg as sites of special scientific interest.[12] The nature conservation functions transferred by the 1990 Act to the new Councils are:

(i) Such functions previously discharged by the Nature Conservancy Council as are specificed in Schedule 9 to the 1990 Act. These include, inter alia, the Council's former functions in designating sites of special scientific interest and nature reserves, together with ancillary functions eg in relation to management agreements.

(ii) The provision of advice for the Secretary of State or other Ministers on the development and implementation of nature conservation policy.

(iii) The provision of advice and dissimination of knowledge to any other person about nature conservation in their area, or about grants and loans to support conservation projects.

9 Section 38 Wildlife and Countryside Act 1981.
10 For guidance on conservation policy generally see DoE Circular 27/1987.
11 Section 131(2) Environmental Protection Act 1990. These powers will become exercisable upon the relevant provisions of the 1990 Act being brought into force by order.
12 Section 131(4) *ibid.*

(iv)   The commissioning or support of research relevant to the exercise of the Council's conservation functions.

The 1990 Act also allocates additional 'special' functions to the new Councils, which latter can only be exercised by a Joint Committee made up of the chairman and one other member of each of the Councils, plus non-voting members appointed by the Secretary of State.[13] These functions include the provision of advice to Government on the implementation of nature conservation policy in Great Britain or elsewhere, the provision of advice etc and dissemination of knowledge about conservation in Great Britain or elsewhere, the establishment of common standards for monitoring nature conservation, and the conducting of research relevant to conservation matters of a national character. It should also be appreciated that in relation to Wales (only), in addition to functions previously exercised by the NCC on a national basis, the Countryside Council for Wales has assumed functions previously exercised by the Countryside Commission. The most important of these are the Countryside Council's functions in designating and managing National Parks and areas of outstanding national beauty.[14] In contrast, the functions of the Countryside Council in England and Scotland have not been transferred to the new Nature Conservancy Councils for England and Scotland respectively.

In the following account of the designation and protection of special areas (below), for ease of reference the designating body is referred to as 'the relevant Council'. Where land is geographically situated in England this will be the NCC for England, where land is situated in Scotland this will be the Nature Conservancy Council for Scotland, and where land is geographically situate in Wales the relevant body will be the Countryside Council for Wales.

3.   Designation of special areas for protection

(a)   Sites of special scientific interest

By virtue of section 28 of the Wildlife and Countryside Act 1981[15] the relevant Council has wide powers to designate areas as 'sites of special scientific interest' (SSSIs) and to notify them to the relevant local Planning Authority. Section 28(1) *ibid* provides that where the Council are of the opinion that an area of land is 'of special interest by reason of any of its flora, fauna or geological/physiological features' they must notify that fact to the Planning Authority, the owner and occupier of the land concerned and to the Secretary of State. A notification made under section 28 must specify the features by reason of which the land is considered of special interest and, moreover, must specify any operations which the Council believes would be likely to damage the flora, fauna or

---

13   Section s 133 *ibid*.
14   Section 130(1) and Sch 8 *ibid*.
15   These powers were formerly contained in s 23 National Parks and Access to the Countryside Act 1949.

other features of the site.[16] Agricultural operations, such as ploughing, reseeding, or drainage work etc will commonly be operations specified as likely to damage designated SSSIs. The notification must specify a period of not less than three months within which representations and objections can be made.[17]

By virtue of section 28(4A), following notification the relevant Council have nine months, beginning on the date it was served on the Secretary of State, in which to either give notice to persons affected withdrawing or confirming the notification. A notification will cease to have effect upon notice of withdrawal being given, or on expiry of the nine month period if no notice of withdrawal or confirmation is given within that time.[18] The relevant Council have power, when confirming a notification, to do so with or with modifications. This power cannot be exercised so as to add to the prohibited operations specified in the notification, or to extend the area to which it applies.[19] If the relevant Council confirm the designation with modifications, it takes effect from the date of service of the Councils notice of confirmation, and has effect in its modified form to so much of the land originally notified which remains subject to it.[20]

Following designation of a site as an SSSI, the owner or occupier of land within the site must not carry out (or cause or permit to be carried out) while the notification remains in force, any operation which is prescribed in the notification.[1] Operations can only be carried out if *both* of the following conditions are satisfied:

(i) The owner or occupier must give the Council written notice of his proposal to carry out the operation, including a specification of its nature and the land on which it is proposed to carry it out; and

(ii) One of three conditions contained in section 28(6) is satisfied. The latter provision specifies that the operation must either be carried out with the relevant Council's written consent, or be in accordance with a management agreement,[2] or that a period of four months must have expired from the giving of notice to the Council of the operation proposed. The relevant Council then have four months in which to respond to a notice proposing the carrying out of proscribed operations. If written agreement is reached between the relevant Council and the owner/occupier that the four months' condition is not to apply, then the operations proposed will only be lawful if carried out with the written consent of the Council or pursuant to a management agreement.[3] The land owner or occupier may subsequently terminate the agreement, in which event the carrying out of the operations is further prohibited for one month or such longer period as the owner or occupier himself specifies.[4]

16 Section 28(4) Wildlife and Countryside Act 1981.
17 The NCC have a duty to consider the objections within the time allowed: s 28(2) *ibid*, added by s 2 Wildlife & Countryside (Amendment) Act 1985.
18 Section 28(4A) ibid, added by Wildlife & Countryside (Amendment) Act 1985, s 2.
19 Section 28(4B) Wildlife and Countryside Act 1981.
20 Section 28(4C) *ibid*.
1 Section 28(5) *ibid*.
2 Entered into under s 16 National Parks and Access to the Countryside Act 1949 or s 15 Countryside Act 1968.
3 Section 28(6A) Wildlife and Countryside Act 1981.
4 Section 28(6B) *ibid*.

The four month period, during which notified operations cannot be carried out, enables the relevant Council to enter into negotiations for the conclusion of a management agreement protecting the site. Once this period, as extended, has expired without agreement, however, the proposed agricultural operations may be carried out. If a management agreement cannot be concluded, they can only be prohibited if the Secretary of State (after consultation with the relevant Council) has made a Nature Conservation Order. These are discussed below. The effect of the making of a Nature Conservation Order will be to further extend the period of negotiation, during which the carrying out of agricultural operations contrary to the SSSI designation is prohibited.

Notification of land as an SSSI can be registered by the relevant Councils as a local Land Charge.[5]

Although an owner or occupier of agricultural land is not obliged to give the relevant Council notice of an operation for which planning permission has been granted, the local Planning Authority is required to notify the Council of an application for planning permission for development within an SSSI.[6] The Nature Conservancy Council's views will be taken into account on the merits of the planning application. If permission is granted, the existence of planning consent is deemed to constitute a 'reasonable excuse' relieving the owner or occupier of liability for carrying out a prohibited operation.[7] Local Planning Authorities are also encouraged[8] to assist the relevant Nature Conservancy Councils by notifying them of potentially damaging operations which come to their attention, whether or not they need planning permission.

It is a criminal offence for any person, without reasonable excuse, to contravene the prohibition of operations contained in the notification. On summary conviction, this offence carries a fine not exceeding £1,000.[9] A prescribed operation will be carried out with 'reasonable excuse' if, *either* the operation was authorised by a grant of planning permission on an application under Part III of the Town and Country Planning Act 1990,[10] or the operation was an 'emergency operation', details of which were notified to the relevant Council as soon as practicable after commencement of the operation.[11]

(b) Nature conservation orders

Section 29 of the Wildlife and Countryside Act 1981 enables the Secretary of State, after consultation with the relevant Council, to make a Nature Conservation Order. As we have seen, the relevant Council may request an Order where notified operations are likely to have a damaging effect on an SSSI. In this instance the effect of a Nature Conservation Order will be to lengthen the consultation period during which a notified agricultural operation cannot be carried out. The period of notice required before an

---

5 Section 28(11) *ibid.*
6 SI 1988/1813 para 18(1)(t).
7 Section 28(8) Wildlife and Countryside Act 1981.
8 See DoE Circular 27/1981 ('Nature Conservation').
9 Section 28(7) *ibid.*
10 Note that planning permission must be granted under Part III Town and Country Planning Act 1990 – deemed permission under the General Development Order 1988 will not suffice.
11 Section 28(8) Wildlife and Countryside Act 1981.

operation is carried out is extended to twelve months if the relevant Council have offered a management agreement.

A Nature Conservation Order can only be made if the Secretary of State considers it expedient to do so in order to secure the survival in Great Britain of any kind of animal or plant, or compliance with international obligations. He may also designate a site if he considers it expedient for the purpose of conserving its flora or fauna, or geological or physiological features. In both cases, however, the Secretary of State must also consider the site to be of special interest and, where preservation of fauna, flora etc is at issue, to be of national importance by reason of any of its flora, fauna, or geological or physiological features. The Secretary of State has a duty to consult with the relevant Council before making an Order. Schedule 11 to the Wildlife and Countryside Act 1981 prescribes a detailed procedure to be followed by the Secretary of State, and makes provision for publicity and consultation in the making and confirming of Nature Conservancy Orders. Although an Order will come into operation on being made, the Secretary of State has a duty to subsequently consider and (if appropriate) confirm the Order. If he fails to confirm an Order, it will cease to have effect nine months after being made.[12] Appeal against the making or confirmation of a Nature Conservation Order lies to the High Court, within six weeks of notice of designation (or confirmation of designation, if appropriate) on the grounds that the order is not within the powers conferred by section 29 (above) or that the consultation and publicity requirements of Schedule 11 have not been complied with.[13]

The designation of land by a Nature Conservation Order places further restrictions on agricultural operations, additional to those flowing from the designation of a site as of special scientific interest. By virtue of section 29(3), where an Order has been made no person can carry out any operation specified in the Order which is, in the opinion of the Secretary of State, likely to destroy or damage the flora, fauna, or geological/physiological features of the site. The prohibition on agricultural operations is wider than that applicable to SSSIs, in that a prohibition contained in a Nature Conservation Order extends to prohibit action by third parties, and not solely the owners/ occupiers of the site itself. It is an offence for any person, without reasonable excuse, to contravene the prohibitions in a Nature Conservation Order.[14] As with operations in a designated SSSI it is a defence (ie a reasonable excuse) for operations to be carried out pursuant to a grant of planning permission, or where they constitute 'emergency operations' details of which were notified to the relevant Council as soon as practicable after commencement of the operation.[15]

An owner or occupier can give notice to the relevant Council that he intends to carry out a proscribed operation. By virtue of section 29(4) and (5)[15a] agricultural operations can, when notified to the relevant Council, only be carried out if *either*:

---

12 Schedule 11, para 1(2) *ibid*.
13 Schedule 11, para 7 ibid.
14 Offences under s 29(3) *ibid* are punishable on indictment by a fine and on summary conviction by a fine not exceeding the statutory minimum.
15 Section 29(9) *ibid*.
15a As amended, Environmental Protection Act 1990, Sch 9, para 11(9).

(i)   They are carried out with the relevant Council's consent, or
(ii) If carried out in accordance with a management agreement or
(iii) Three months has elapsed since notice of the proposed operations
      was given to the relevant Council. If the relevant Nature
      Conservancy Council offer to enter into an agreement to acquire
      the land (or the occupiers interest in it) before the end of the three
      month period allowed, or offer a management agreement, the
      period of notice during which operations are proscribed is
      statutorily extended by up to a further nine months. If a
      management agreement is concluded before the expiration of
      twelve months from the giving of notice of the intended operations,
      the period of proscription ends with the conclusion of the
      agreement. Similarly, where the relevant Council propose to
      acquire the owner's or occupier's interest in the land, the period of
      proscription is extended to twelve months from the giving of the
      notice of intended operations.

If the relevant Council make an offer of a management agreement, or
acquisition, which is rejected, the period of proscription is extended to three
months from the rejection or withdrawal of the agreement.[16] This gives the
relevant Council, as a last resort, an opportunity to consider using
compulsory purchase powers to acquire the site. If compulsory purchase is
sought, agricultural operations are proscribed for a further period expiring
on the day on which the Secretary of State withdraws the compulsory
purchase Order or decides not to confirm it.[17] A person convicted of an
offence under section 29 may be ordered by the Court to carry out, within a
specified period, 'such operations for the purpose of restoring the land to its
former condition as may be so specified'.[18] The power to make a restoration
order is unique to the regime applicable to Nature Conservation Orders,
and is not available to the Court where a damaged site is an SSSI *simpliciter*.
Once made, a restoration order can be varied or revoked at any time
before it has been fully complied with, if it appears to the Court that a change
of circumstances has made it impracticable or unnecessary.[19] A person who
fails to comply with a restoration order within the time allowed will be liable
in the first instance on summary conviction to a fine not exceeding £1,000. In
the case of further convictions the Court can impose a further fine of up to
£100 for each day during which the offence continues, so as to compel
compliance. By virtue of Section 31(6) the NCC have power, as a last resort,
to enter and carry out operations which have not been carried out pursuant
to a restoration order. In this event expenses reasonably incurred in doing
so are recoverable from the defendant.

Because of the limiting effect of a designation, the 1981 Act makes provision
for compensation where land has been included in an Order under section
29. By virtue of section 30(2) the relevant Council must pay compensation to
any person having an interest in an agricultural unit comprising land
included in a Nature Conservation Order if, as a result of its designation

16 Section 29(6) *ibid*.
17 Section 29(7) *ibid*.
18 Section 31 *ibid*.
19 Section 31(4) *ibid*.

under section 29, the value of his interest in the land is less than it would have been otherwise. Compensation is valued as the difference between the unincumbered value of the claimants interest, and its value with a Nature Conservation Order in place restricting the carrying out of specified agricultural operations.[20] The relevant Council must also pay compensation to an owner or occupier of land who notifies it of his intention to carry out agricultural operations restricted by a Nature Conservation Order.[1] Compensation is payable if the period of proscription, during which operations cannot be carried out, is extended following the relevant Council having offered a management agreement or purchase of the claimant's interest in the land. In this event the claimant can claim compensation if he has reasonably incurred expenditure which has been rendered abortive by the statutory extension of the prohibition of operations, following an offer of purchase or a management agreement. The Council must also pay compensation for any loss or damage suffered by reason of the owner or occupier having to wait to carry out the operations concerned due to the extension of the period of proscription.[2]

(c) Environmentally sensitive areas

By virtue of section 18 of the Agriculture Act 1986, the Minister[3] has power to designate an area of land an 'Environmentally Sensitive Area'. Designation is by statutory instrument, subject to the negative resolution procedure of either House of Parliament.[4] The Minister's power of designation is exercisable if he considers that the adoption of a particular agricultural method is likely to facilitate the conservation and enhancement of the natural beauty of an area, or conservation of the flora, fauna, geological/physiological features of an area, or the protection of buildings or other objects of archeological, architectural or historical interest in an area, *and* (in all cases) that conservation of those features is particularly desirable. Prior to designation, the Minister must consult the Countryside Commission and the relevant Nature Conservancy Council, and must obtain the consent of the Treasury.[5] The Environmentally Sensitive Area scheme implements in domestic law the requirements of title V of Council Regulation (EEC) No 797/85 on improving the efficiency of agricultural structures.

Where land has been designated to an Environmentally Sensitive Area the Minister is empowered by section 18(3) to enter into management agreements wherever it appears to him that any of the conservation purposes (above) set out in the 1986 Act are likely to be facilitated in a designated area by him doing so. The terms of proposed management agreements are prescribed in detail in designation orders made under the 1986 Act, and in most cases include detailed proscriptions as to farming methods, stocking levels, preservation of vernacular buildings etc, and restrictions on the application of fertilisers and herbicides/pesticides. The Environmentally

20 Section 10 Land Compensation Act 1973 and s 5 Land Compensation Act 1961 apply to assess compensation claims. And see Wildlife and Countryside Act 1981, s 30(4) and (5).
1 Section 29(3) *ibid.*
2 Section 30(3) *ibid.*
3 Ie Minister of Agriculture or (in Wales) the Secretary of State for Wales.
4 Section 18(2) Agriculture Act 1986.
5 Section 18(2) *ibid.*

Sensitive Area provisions are firmly based on the voluntary principle, in that the 1986 Act makes no provision for the compulling of land owners or occupiers to enter into management agreements in appropriate cases cf. the residual power of compulsion exercisable by Nature Conservation Orders where a site has been designated an SSSI (above). The Minister is empowered to conclude management agreements with any person having a sufficient interest in land.[6] He cannot, however, enter into a management agreement unless the other party has certified that he is either the owner of the land, or that he has notified the owner of his intention to enter into an agreement. Where the occupier is a tenant, therefore, the 1986 Act obliges him to give notice of his intention to enter into a management agreement to his landlord. The 1986 Act does not, however, require a tenant to obtain his landlord's consent prior to him entering the Environmentally Sensitive Area scheme. Observance of the terms of a management agreement may, however, involve questions of potential breach of tenancy, and receipt of grant moneys may have implications for future rent reviews. These issues are discussed below.[7] The Minister is empowered to offer grant aid, pursuant to a management agreement, to landowners and occupiers of agricultural land participating in the Environmentally Sensitive Area scheme. Rates of payment per hectare are prescribed in the designating statutory instruments. Designations under the 1986 Act have been made in relation to fourteen areas, encompassing extensive tracts of agricultural land.[8]

(d) National Parks

By virtue of section 5 of the National Parks and Access to the Countryside Act 1949 the Countryside Commission[9] has power to designate as a National Park those 'extensive tracts' of countryside which, by reason of their natural beauty and the opportunities they offer for open-air recreation, necessitate measures being taken to preserve and enhance their natural beauty. Designation orders must be confirmed by the Minister before taking effect. Section 6, further, requires the Commission to make recommendations to the Minister and Local Authorities as to the enhancement and preservation of the areas natural beauty, and they have a duty both to assist Local Planning Authorities in formulating proposals as to the exercise of their planning powers to further the objects of the designation, and to give advice as to administration of the area as a National Park.[10] Before making a designation the Commission must consult every joint Planning Board, District Council and Borough Council whose area includes land to be designated a National Park.[11] Detailed provisions as to the making, confirmation and variation of designation orders are set out in Schedule 1 to

---

6 Section 18(3) *ibid*.

7 See p 288 ff below.

8 The areas designated are: South Downs (SI 1986/2289), West Fenwick (SI 1986/2252), Somerset Levels (SI 1986/2252), Pennine Dales (SI 1986/2253), Broads (SI 1986/2254), Cambrian Mountains (SI 1986/2257 and 1987/2026), Lleyn Peninsula (SI 1987/2027), Breckland (SI 1987/2029), North Peak (SI 1987/2030), Shropshire Borders (SI 1987/2031), South Downs (Extension) (SI 1987/2032), Suffolk River Valleys (SI 1987/2033), Test Valley (SI 1987/2034).

9 In Wales the Countryside Council for Wales: Environmental Protection Act 1990, s 130(1) and Sch 8.

10 See especially, s 6(4) National Parks and Access to the Countryside Act 1949.

11 Section 7 *ibid*.

the 1949 Act. These provide, inter alia, for publication in the Gazette, two national newspapers and one local newspaper, and the holding of Public Inquiries to consider objections.

Following designation, special planning control applies to the erection, extension and alteration of buildings, or the formation or alteration of private rights of way, in a National Park. These have already been considered.[12] Additionally, section 11 of the 1949 Act confers upon a Local Planning Authority whose area consists of or includes a National Park, power to take all action which appears expedient to attain the objectives for which the Park was established. Section 44 of the Wildlife and Countryside Act 1981, further, confers specific power on a County Planning Authority to give financial assistance by way of grant or loan in order to fund expenditure which is conducive to the enhancement of the natural beauty of a National Park and its enjoyment by the public. Conditions can be imposed on financial aid, including terms making provision for repayment in certain circumstances. Section 42 of the 1981 Act confers on the Minister power to impose additional restrictions on the carrying out of agricultural operations on land which comprises moor and/or heath within a designated National Park. This power is exercisable by Order. In this event it will become a criminal offence to plough, or otherwise convert into agricultural land, any land which is moor and heath and which has not been agricultural land within the preceding twenty years.[13] It is also an offence under the 1981 Act to carry out, on such land, other agricultural operations which appear to the Minister likely to affect the character or appearance of the land, and which are for that reason specified in an Order made under section 42. An owner or occupier of agricultural land can give notice of a proposed operation to the County Planning Authority, but can only carry it out without committing a criminal offence if the latter have:

(a)   Given their consent, or
(b)   Failed to respond within three months of receiving notice by either giving or refusing consent, or
(c)   Where they have refused consent, where twelve months have elapsed from the giving of the notice.[14] The Authority, consequently, have twelve months in which to offer a management agreement using their general power to do so under section 39 of the Wildlife and Countryside Act 1981 (below).

Notices of proposed operations on moor and heath must also be sent to the relevant Nature Conservancy Council and the Countryside Commission by the relevant Planning Authority.

(e)   Areas of outstanding natural beauty

Section 87 of the National Parks and Access to the Countryside Act 1949 confers power on the Countryside Commission to designate an area an 'area of outstanding natural beauty'. Designation orders must be confirmed by the Minister before coming into effect, and must be preceded by consultation with the Local Authorities and publication of the Commission's

12 See p 267 above.
13 Section 42(2) Wildlife and Countryside Act 1981.
14 See s 42(3) and (4) *ibid*.

proposals in the Gazette and at least one local newspaper. Conservation policy in designated areas of outstanding natural beauty is exercised by Local Authorities, who enjoy the same powers to make financial grants etc as are exercisable in relation to a National Park under section 11 of the 1949 Act (above). Section 90 *ibid* gives the Local Planning Authority power to make bylaws to protect land in an area of outstanding natural beauty. Further, by virtue of section 88 the Countryside Commission must be consulted on development plans in an area of outstanding natural beauty and have power to give advice on development proposals.[15] Land within an area of outstanding natural beauty is, further, 'article 1(5) land' within the meaning of the General Development Order 1988, with the consequence that the range of permitted domestic or industrial development rights is restricted. The restrictions on agricultural operations applicable to agricultural land within a National Park (discussed above) do not apply, however, to an area of outstanding natural beauty.

(f)   Nature Reserves

By virtue of sections 15 to 17 of the 1949 Act, Nature Reserves are designated by the relevant Nature Conservancy Council.[16] Section 16 of the 1949 Act empowers the relevant Council to enter into management agreements with the owner, lessee or occupier of land which they consider should be managed as a Nature Reserve in the national interest. Management agreements under the 1949 Act can impose restrictions on the exercise of the owner or occupier's rights over the land, and provide for its management in such manner as seems appropriate to achieve the satisfactory maintenance of the land as a Nature Reserve. Management agreements can also bind the Council to defray the costs of managing the land and make provision for payment of compensation to an owner or occupier in respect of agreed restrictions on agricultural operations on the land.

Although the use of management agreements is the chief method of protecting areas designated as Nature Reserves, if an agreement cannot be reached section 17 confers on the relevant Council powers of compulsory acquisition.

The use of management agreements to protect Nature Reserves is supplemented by section 20 of the 1949 Act. This confers on the relevant Council the power to make bylaws for the protection of Nature Reserves. Bylaws made under section 20 may, inter alia, prohibit or restrict entry to, or movement within, a Nature Reserve of both people, animals, and vehicles, and restrict the killing of animals or destruction of vegetation.[17] Bylaws made under the Act cannot, however, interfere with the exercise by any person of a right vested in him as an owner, lessee or occupier of land within a Nature Reserve, neither can they interfere with the exercise of public rights of way.

If land is being managed as a Nature Reserve, whether by the relevant Nature Conservancy Council or pursuant to a management agreement, section 35 of the Wildlife and Countryside Act 1981 enables the relevant

15 See s 88 and 89 National Parks and Access to the Countryside Act 1949.
16 In Wales the Countryside Council for Wales: see p 274–5 above.
17 See section 20(2) National Parks and Access to the Countryside Act 1949.

Council to declare the land a National Nature Reserve. Following designation, the relevant Council can make bylaws for the management of a National Nature Reserve by an approved Body subject to the same limitations as apply to Nature Reserve *simpliciter*.[18]

(g)   Limestone Pavement Orders

Limestone pavements are protected under the terms of the Wildlife and Countryside Act 1981. These are areas of limestone wholly or partly exposed on the surface of the ground and which have been fissured by natural erosion.[19] They are a natural feature of certain parts of the country only, and are by their nature vulnerable to damage from unsympathetic agricultural operations. Accordingly, section 34 of the 1981 Act confers special protection on areas on which limestone pavements are present. Where the relevant Nature Conservancy Council or the Countryside Commission are of the opinion that a limestone pavement is of special interest by reason of its flora, fauna or geological/physiological features, they must notify the Planning Authority in whose area the land is situate.[20] If the Planning Authority (or the Secretary of State) believes the character or appearance of the land would be likely to be adversely affected by the removal or disturbance of limestone, they have power to make a Limestone Pavement Order protecting the site. By virtue of section 34(2) a Limestone Pavement Order prohibits the removal or disturbance of limestone on or in the land designated. An Order under section 34 has the effect of absolutely prohibiting agricultural operations likely to damage, or involving the removal of, limestone. The only circumstances in which agricultural operations can be carried out is where they are sanctioned by planning permission obtained on application under Part III of the Town and Country Planning Act 1990.[1] Contravention of a Limestone Pavement Order is a criminal offence punishable on summary conviction by a fine not exceeding the statutory maximum, and on indictment by a fine.[2] The publication and notice provisions of schedule 11 of the 1981 Act, applicable to the making of Nature Conservation Orders, apply also to the making and revoking of Limestone Pavement Orders.

4.   Management agreements

The relevant Nature Conservancy Councils, and in some instances Local Authorities, have power to conclude Management Agreements in a variety of situations.

(a)   Availablity of management agreements

Management Agreements are available in the following circumstances:

---

18 Section 35(3) and (4) Wildlife and Countryside Act 1981.
19 See the definition in s 34(6) *ibid.*
20 Section 34(1) *ibid.*
 1 Section 34(5).
 2 Section 34(4).

(i)   *Nature reserves*
      Where the relevant Nature Conservancy Council[3] consider it would
      be in the national interest that land should be managed as a Nature
      Reserve, they have power under section 16 of the National Parks and
      Access to the Countryside Act 1949 to conclude management
      agreements with every owner, lessee or occupier of agricultural land.
      Under the 1949 Act management agreements are intended to limit
      the exercise of legal rights over the land, whether of user or otherwise,
      and the agreement can, therefore, impose such conditions as seem
      expedient on the exercise of rights over the land by the land owner or
      other occupier. By virtue of section 16(3) conditions which may be
      included in a management agreement include provision for the
      management of the land in such manner, and the doing of such work
      etc as seemed expedient for the purposes of the agreement, and it can
      provide for the cost of performing the agreement to be defrayed by
      the relevant Council or the owner or occupier, or partly by each party.
      Similarly, the agreement may make other provision as to the making
      of payments by the relevant Council, and the payment of compensation
      for the effect of restrictions, as may be specified in the agreement. The
      management agreement provisions are supplemented by sections 17
      and 18 of the 1949 Act, which give the relevant Council powers of
      compulsory purchase exercisable where they cannot conclude a satis-
      factory agreement, or where a party is in breach of the terms of a
      management agreement previously entered into.

(ii) *Sites of special scientific interest*
      By virtue of section 15 of the Countryside Act 1968, the relevant
      Council has power to enter into management agreements where land
      is included in a notified site of special scientific interest. A
      management agreement will commonly be offered where the owner
      or occupier has notified the Council of his intention to carry out
      proscribed operations within an SSSI, contrary to the order
      designating the site. Once a designation order has been made
      however, an owner or occupier is entitled to seek a management
      agreement with the relevant Council at any time.

(iii) *Refusal of capital grant*
      Where the owner or occupier of agricultural land has made an
      application for capital grant (eg for improvements) pursuant to
      section 29 of the Agriculture Act 1970, but the application is refused
      on conversation grounds after objections by the relevant Council or
      Local Authority, the owner or occupier can in some circumstances
      compel the objecting bodies to offer a management agreement.[4]
      When considering an application for capital grant for agricultural
      operations on land within a notified SSSI, the Minister has a duty to
      exercise his function so as to further the conservation of flora, fauna,

---

3 Ie Nature Conservancy Council for England, Nature Conservancy Council for Scotland,
  Countryside Council for Wales: Environmental Protection Act 1990, Sch 4.
4 See 32(2) Wildlife and Countryside Act 1981.

geological and physiological features of the designated site.[5] If the relevant Council object to the making of a grant, the Minister cannot make financial aid available without considering the terms of the relevant Council's objection. Similarly, where land is within a designated National Park, the relevant Planning Authority has power to object to the making of a capital grant for improvements, in which event the Minister will have to consider objections before making a decision.[6] If the application is refused as a consequence of such objections, the relevant Council (or Authority if appropriate) must, within three months of receiving notice of refusal, offer to enter into a management agreement with the applicant. The management agreement offered must make provision for restrictions on the activities in respect of which grant has, on conservation grounds, been refused and for making payments to the applicant(s) in consideration thereof.[7]

(iv) *Environmentally sensitive areas*

Where land is within a designated Environmentally Sensitive Area, section 18(3) of the Agriculture Act 1986 gives the Minister power to enter into management agreements with 'any person having an interest in agricultural land' wholly or partly within the designated area. The terms of each management agreement will be specified in the statutory instrument designating the area as an Environmentally Sensitive Area, and the management agreement offered must include the detailed restrictions provided for in the designation order. By virtue of section 18(4) the latter may specify those requirements as to agricultural practices, methods and operations, and the installation or use of equipment, which must be included in management agreements. It may also specify the minimum period for which agreements are to impose restrictions on farming methods, or a fixed period for which agreements are to run eg five years. Provision can also be made by the designating Instrument for the rates of payment to be made under management agreements in the area covered, and for repayment on breach of the requirements imposed by such agreements. The Minister must arrange for reviews to be carried out as to the effect, on each designated area as a whole, of the performance of management agreements under the Act.[8]

(v) *Management agreements: general powers*

The Wildlife and Countryside Act 1981 confers a general power upon County and Local Planning Authorities to enter into management agreements for the purpose of conserving and enhancing the natural beauty or amenity of land which is in the countryside and within their

5 Section 32(1) *ibid*.
6 See s 39(5) and s 41 *ibid*.
7 Section 32(2) and 41(4) *ibid*.
8 See s 18(8) Agriculture Act 1986. Management agreements under s 18 will commonly include restrictions on stocking levels, and contain restrictions on the application of herbicides and pesticides. They commonly also provide for the maintenance of vernacular buildings and other traditional landscape features (hedges etc). And see p 281 ff above.

area, or for promoting its enjoyment by the public.[9] This power enables the Authority to conclude an agreement with 'any person having an interest in the land' concerned (eg a tenant as well as a freehold owner), and is exercisable irrespective of whether the land is within a designated site of special scientific interest or any other area given protection by statutory designation. Local Authorities have a general duty under the Countryside Act 1968[10] to have regard in the exercise of their functions to the desirability of conserving the natural beauty and amenity of the countryside. The use of management agreements is one facility available to further this objective, and is actively encouraged by central government.[11] A management agreement concluded under these powers can impose restrictions on the methods used to cultivate the land, on its use for agricultural purposes, or the exercise of rights over the land. It may also impose obligations on the owner or other occupier to carry out works or agricultural/forestry operations. Additionally, a management agreement can confer on the Authority power to carry out works necessary to the performance of its functions under the National Parks and Access to the Countryside Act 1949 and the Countryside Act 1968. It may also contain such incidental and consequential provisions as appear necessary or expedient for the purposes of a management agreement eg making provision for payments to the owner or occupier.[12]

(b)   Landlord and tenant: some problems

The relevant statutory provisions all enable the relevant Council, Minister or Local Authority (whichever is applicable) to enter into management agreements with 'any person having an interest in the land' to which the agreement relates.[13] It follows, therefore, that an agreement can be concluded not only with a freehold owner of agricultural land, but also with a tenant or other person having a legal interest sufficient to enable him to gurantee performance of the terms of a management agreement. A share farmer, however, would normally not have a sufficient interest to guarantee performance of the terms of a management agreement, and will in any event not have an interest in the land.[14] The statutory provisions variously make provision for management agreements being concluded with the holder of an interest in the land less than freehold. The provisions in relation to tenants are not, however, uniform in their application.

---

9 Section 39 Wildlife and Countryside Act 1981.
10 Section 11 Countryside Act 1968.
11 See DoE Circular 27/87 paras 39(k) and 40.
12 See s 39(2) Wildlife and Countryside Act 1981.
13 See s 18(3) Agriculture Act 1986 (Environmentally Sensitive Areas), s 15 Countryside Act 1968 (Sites of Special Scientific Interest), s 39 Wildlife and Countryside Act 1981 (general powers).
14 In most cases a share farmer will not have exclusive possession and will, therefore, have no leasehold interest. See Ch 2 p 39 ff above.

Sites of special scientific interest
If a management agreement is concluded in respect of land within a site of special scientific interest, the Wildlife and Countryside Act 1981 imposes no obligation on the tenant to notify the owner. Similarly, where an agreement has been concluded with the local Planning Authority under the terms of the 1981 Act, the latter imposes no obligation on a tenant to inform his landlord of his intention to enter into an agreement. In practice, however, the concurrence of the owner will be necessary to secure the long term performance of a management agreement. The provisions of an agreement will be binding on the successors in title of the party with whom the agreement was made.[15] It would, for instance, bind assignees of a lease, but not a landlord resuming possession on termination or forfeiture of a tenancy. In any event, performance of the proscriptions in a management agreement may involve a tenant in breaches of his tenancy agreement, thus entitling a landlord to serve notice to quit (below). Ministerial guidance therefore indicates, where an agreement is offered in respect of a designated SSSI or following refusal of capital grant, that the relevant Council should require a tenant to give a written assurance that his landlord has been informed of the land to be included within the proposed agreement, of the proposed agricultural operations which have led to the offer of an agreement under the terms of the Wildlife and Countryside Act 1981, and that the offer of an agreement is likely to be accepted by the tenant.[16] Ministerial guidance also indicates that the relevant Council should, in any event, seek to secure the *long term* protection of a designated site by including the landlord's interest in the principal agreement, or (alternatively) by concluding a complementary agreement with the latter. A landlord entering into a complementary agreement will normally be entitled to a nominal payment only, to secure his agreement, as his rights are otherwise secured by the Agricultural Holding Act 1986.[17] The policy of the Nature Conservancy Council in such circumstances, has been to include the landlord's interest in the principal management agreement, and to include therein an undertaking by him not to serve on the tenant, notice to remedy breaches of tenancy contrary to the intentions of the management agreement.[18]

Environmentally sensitive areas
Section 18(6) of the Agriculture Act 1986 stipulates that the Minister cannot enter into a management agreement under the Environmentally Sensitive Area scheme unless a tenant has certified that he has notified the owner in writing of his intention to make an agreement. As with agreements made in relation to an SSSI (above), a management agreement will be binding on a successor in title or person deriving title under or through the offeree, and be enforceable accordingly.[19] It follows that an agreement will not bind all future occupiers eg the owner, if land is taken in hand, or future tenants other than assignees of the leasehold estate. Additionally, it may be necessary to include the landlord's interest within a management agreement

15 Section 39(3) Wildlife and Countryside Act 1981.
16 DoE Circular 4/1983, para 7.
17 See generally DoE Circular 4/1983 para 8.
18 'Sites of Special Scientific Interest' (Nature Conservancy Council 1988) p 13, DoE Circular 4/1983 para 8.
19 Section 18(7) Agriculture Act 1986.

to secure the long term performance of the latter, as the tenants obligations thereunder may involve breaches of tenancy (below).

Nature reserves
It is expressly provided, by virtue of section 16 of the National Parks and Access to the Countryside Act 1949, that a lessee may be a party to a management agreement entered into thereunder. Similar considerations as to the long term performance of the agreement, however, apply.

(i)   Leasehold obligations

The rules of good husbandry, set out in section 11 to the Agriculture Act 1947, lay down statutory standards of good husbandry. Although not enforceable directly, the rules can be enforced *indirectly* in possession proceedings where a tenant is failing to observe the standards therein laid down. This can be done, eg by proceeding pursuant to case C in Schedule 3 to the Agricultural Holdings Act 1986 where a certificate of bad husbandry has been issued, or in proceedings under case D where the tenancy agreement (as is common) makes observance of the rules a term of the tenancy.[20] The rules are intended to ensure the adoption of efficient farming methods by a tenant, untempered by considerations of conservation, and their observance could in some situations be in contradiction to conservation objectives contained in a management agreement. The Agriculture Act 1947 imposes obligations, for instance, requiring a tenant to maintain permanent pasture in a state of good cultivation and fertility and properly mown and/or grazed, and to crop arable land in a way which maintains the latter in a clean and good state of cultivation and fertility. The rules also require livestock farms to be properly stocked and an efficient standard of management maintained. A tenant must also, *inter alia*, take steps to keep crops and livestock free from disease and infestation by pests and insects, and carry out 'necessary' work of maintenance to fixed equipment and buildings where the obligation to do so falls on him.[1] A management agreement will, in many cases, oblige a tenant to reduce stocking levels and refrain from using specified herbicides or pesticides. In this event observance of the terms of the agreement may well involve technical breaches of the tenant's contract of tenancy. Additionally, observance of prescriptions commonly included in management agreements may also involve a tenant in breach of the model clauses implied into tenancies by section 7 of the Agricultural Holdings Act 1986.[2]

(ii)   Conservation covenants

By virtue of schedule 3 paragraphs 9(2), 10(1)(d) and 11(2) of the Agricultural Holdings Act 1986, a tenant will be protected in possession proceedings brought under (respectively) cases C, D or E if the tenancy includes a suitably phrased conservation covenant. Schedule 3 paragraph 9(2) provides that when deciding whether to issue a certificate of bad husbandry, an agricultural land tribunal must disregard any practice

---

20 See Ch 7 p 133 ff above.
  1 See s 11 Agriculture Act 1947, discussed further p 55 ff above.
  2 Ie the Agriculture (Maintenance, Repair and Insurance of Fixed Equipment) Regs 1973, SI 1973/1473 eg a tenant may not be able to *replace* fixed equipment (such as fences) as required by the model clauses, if a management agreement prevents this.

adopted by the tenant in pursuance of a provision in the contract of tenancy (or in any other agreement in writing with the landlord) which indicates that its object is the furtherance of the conservation of flora and fauna, the protection of buildings or other objects of archeological, architectural or historical interest, the conservation and enhancement of the natural beauty of the countryside, or the promotion of its enjoyment by the public. It is further provided that for the purposes of cases D and E a conservation covenant[3] in this form is to be regarded as a term of the tenancy which *is not* inconsistent with the tenant's duty to farm in accordance with the rules of good husbandry. Clearly, where management agreements are negotiated with a tenant, the long term protection of the site concerned can best be preserved by including a conservation covenant in the tenancy agreement, or other written agreement with the landlord, in return for an appropriate payment – this will remove the possibility of possession proceedings arising, under the Agricultural Holdings Act, from performance of the obligations in a management agreement.

(c)   Payments under management agreements

Ministerial circular No 4/83 ('Wildlife and Countryside Act 1981 – Financial Guidelines for Management Agreements') gives guidance as to payments to be made by the offeror of a management agreement. By virtue of section 50(1) of the Wildlife and Countryside Act 1981 this guidance has statutory effect in relation to management agreements entered into in three situations:

(i)   In a site of special scientific interest, where the relevant Council has been notified of an agricultural operation and offers a management agreement to prevent damage to the site;

(ii)   In a site of special scientific interest, national park or other designated area, where farm capital grant has been refused because of an objection on conservation grounds, and

(iii)   Where the relevant Council has undertaken to voluntarily apply the guidelines by virtue of section 32(2) of the 1981 Act whenever other types of capital grant have been refused eg EEC Development grants.[4]

Payments under management agreements offered in Environmentally Sensitive and Nitrate Sensitive Areas are proscribed by the designation Orders relative thereto, on a flat rate basis per hectare, and vary from one designated area to another.

While negotiations for a long term management agreement are proceeding, the parties are recommended to conclude a short term agreement, within three months of notification, such agreement to be for a fixed period of (normally) between six and twelve months. Payments under a short term agreement will normally be nominal.[5] Where a long term agreement is concluded, payments thereunder can either be by way of lump sum or

---

3   Sch 3, paras 10(1)(d) (Case D – remediable breach of tenancy), Sch 3, para 11(2) (Case E – irremediable breach of tenancy).
4   See DoE Circular 4/83 para 4. Also s 20 Agriculture Act 1986, bringing EEC Development Grants within the scope of the Wildlife and Countryside Act 1981, s 32(2).
5   Circular 4/1983, para 12.

annual payments. Owners and owners/ occupiers can choose either lump sum or annual payments. Where the offeree is a tenant, however, only annual payments are available.

Lump sum payments
Ministerial guidance indicates that payment will be made at the commencement of the agreement in return for a management agreement extending over a period of *twenty years*. The amount paid should be equal to the difference between the restricted and unrestricted value of the owner or owner/occupier's interest in the land, calculated using the rules of assessment set out in section 5 of the Land Compensation Act 1961.[6]

Annual payments
The management agreement should provide for payment of annual sums over a twenty-year period, or such other period as is agreed, such payments to reflect the net profits foregone by the occupier by reason of the existence of the restrictions on agricultural operations contained in the agreement. Where the offeree is a tenant annual payments will only continue while he is in occupation. In the case of landlords the annual payment will be nominal.[7] Where well defined categories of land and/or agricultural operation are involved, the offeror (for instance the relevant Council) may determine and periodically revise standard rates of payment per hectare.

The following provisions should be noted:

(i)   *Deemed eligibility for capital grant*
For the purposes of calculating payments under a management agreement it is to be assumed that farm capital grant would have been payable to carry out the agricultural operation which the offeree was proposing to carry out, and which the agreement will oblige him to refrain from executing.[8] Deemed eligibility does not apply, however, if the operation is ineligible for grant, the applicant's business is non-agricultural, or the operation in question had begun before the Minister determined the application for grant. In these circumstances, if a management agreement is offered voluntarily it is to be assumed that farm capital grant would not have been payable. Similarly, payments should be calculated without allowance of grant if the offeree refuses to consent to details of his investment limit for capital grant being divulged to the relevant Council.[9]

(ii)   *Arbitration*
By virtue of section 50(3) of the 1981 Act, if the offeree disputes the terms of the proposed management agreement he can, within one month of receiving a formal offer, require determination of the amount payable by way of arbitration. Where the offer of an agreement was mandatory, and the arbitrator awards a higher payment than that offered, the offeror must amend his offer accordingly. Where the management agreement was offered voluntarily, however, the offeror can either withdraw its offer altogether or offer the higher sum determined by the arbitrator.[10] The formal offer of a management agreement must, moreover, contain a

6 Para 14 *ibid*.
7 Paras 16–18 *ibid*.
8 Para 23 *ibid*.
9 Paras 24–6 *ibid*.
10 Paras 35 and 36 *ibid*.

statement informing the offeree of his right to refer the amount payable under the agreement to arbitration.[11]

(iii) *Commencement of payments*

Payments should commence on completion of the agreement, and interest should be paid in respect of the intervening period between the effective date of the agreement and completion. The effective date of the agreement should be the date it is signed, or three months after receipt by the offeror of notice of the proposed operation leading to the offer of a management agreement, (whichever is the earlier). Where a lump sum payment is made the valuation of the owner's interest should be made at the effective date of the agreement. Where, on the other hand, the offeree has chosen to receive annual payments, the first payment should be back dated to the effective date and interest paid on completion.[12] The offeror, moreover, should offer to pay the reasonable costs of the offeree in concluding the management agreement, including his costs in retaining professional advisers. The agreement should also provide for the payment of costs in preparing to execute an agricultural operation notified to the offeror, provided those costs were incurred within the twelve month period prior to notification.[13]

(iv) *Miscellaneous*

The management agreement should contain provision whereby, if the offeree breaches the terms of the agreement by his deliberate action, the offeror authority will be entitled to rescind and claim a proportion of the moneys already paid under the agreement. If the agreement provided for a lump sum payment on commencement, it should provide for the offeree to recoup a proportional part of the sum paid ie a sum which would represent the value of the notional management agreement offered for the remainder of the unexpired term.[14] If the agreement becomes impossible to fulfil it should be terminable. Whether this results from the act of third party or by natural or accidental causes, the offeror should have the right to recoup a proportion of any lump sum payment made, on the same basis as if the offeree were in breach of the agreement (above), or to discontinue annual payments where this mode of payment has been selected.[15] Where renewal of a management agreement is sought, the offeror should initiate negotiations for possible renewal at least two years before the agreement is due to expire. Moreover, in all cases it should, at least one year before expiry, inform the offeree whether it wishes in principle to renew the agreement.[16]

11 Para 32 *ibid.*
12 Paras 38 and 39 *ibid.*
13 Paras 29 and 30 *ibid.* There is a duty on the offeree to minimise this loss.
14 Para 43 *ibid.*
15 Para 44 *ibid.*
16 Para 46 *ibid.*

Chapter 13
Public control of land use II: set aside and diversification

A   Set aside of agricultural land

Implementing European Community obligations'[1] the Set Aside Regulations 1988[2] introduced provisions designed to encourage the set aside of agricultural land previously used for production of specific arable crops. The European regulations require member states to establish schemes of aid to encourage the removal of arable land from agricultural production. Under the European provisions, national set aside schemes must provide for land withdrawn from production to represent at least 20% of the arable land on a holding during the reference period, and for that land to be set aside for a period of five years. The environmental features of the set aside scheme were enhanced by amendments introduced in the Set Aside (Amendment) Regulations 1990[3], which latter introduced a limited 'grazed fallow' option for set aside land, and placed additional restrictions on the use of land set aside from production, with a view to preserving its environmental features.

1.   Eligibility for set aside

The set aside scheme operates on voluntary principles, participation being available to all producers who qualify as 'eligible persons' within the meaning of the Set Aside Regulations 1988 ie any person 'who on the date of the submission of his application occupies a holding comprising arable land as an owner or tenant and who at the commencement of the set aside period will have so occupied that holding for a period of at least twelve months'.[4] The classes of tenant entitled to participate is restricted to those that occupy in one of the following ways:[5]

(a)   Under an agreement for a letting from year to year; or
(b)   Under an agreement which has effect as such by virtue of section 2 of the Agricultural Holdings Act 1986;[6] or

1 See Council Reg (EEC) No 1094/1988 and Comm. Reg (EEC) 1272/1988.
2 SI 1988/1352.
3 SI 1990/1716.
4 SI 1988/1352 reg 2(1).
5 *Ibid* reg 2(1) definition of 'tenant'.
6 Ie a licence giving ex poss: See *Harrison-Broadley v Smith* [1964] 1 All ER 867, CA; *Bahamas International Trust Co Ltd v Threadgold* [1974] 3 All ER 881, HL, above Ch 2 p 25 ff.

(c)   Under a fixed term of years of which at least five years remain unexpired at the commencement of the set aside period. This additional qualification is imposed to ensure that the tenant's interest will, in any event, be of sufficient duration to ensure compliance with set aside obligations during the whole of the set aside period, which latter would normally be of five years' duration (see below).

The requirement that an applicant, to be eligible, must 'occupy' a holding for twelve months prior to application means that a share farmer will not normally qualify. Share farming arrangements for arable crops normally provide for ownership of crops to vest in the owner until severance and sale, thus reserving occupation of the land to the owner, and precluding exclusive possession arising in a share farmer. *Cf* The freehold owner will, in this instance, retain exclusive possession of the land and may be entitled to enter the set aside scheme. Before doing so, however, the terms of the share farming contract will have to be considered carefully to ensure that entry to the scheme does not give rise to actionable breaches of contract.

Arable land

The set aside scheme only applies to land which was 'arable land' during the reference period ie during the period commencing on the 1st July 1987 and ending on 30th June 1988. The land to be set aside must also be arable land or temporary grass land at the time undertakings under the set aside scheme are given.[7] 'Arable land' means land used for rotational fallow or for the production of specified arable crops *viz* common wheat, durum wheat, rye, barley, oats, grain maize, buck wheat, millet, canary seed, triticale, fresh vegetables, peas and beans harvested in dried form, sugarbeet, hops, and, *inter alia*, oilseed rape, forage foots, lucerne, sainfoin, clover, lupins, vetches, fodder kale, fodder rape, maize and certain other kinds of seeds.[8]

2. Set aside obligations

In order to participate in set aside, an applicant must undertake for a period of five years (referred to as 'the set aside period') to set aside and withdraw from production an area of arable land equal to at least 20% of the arable land on the holding in the reference period.[9] Further, the area set aside cannot exceed the total area used for arable production during the reference period. The Set Aside Regulations 1988[10] make provision for land withdrawn from production to be put to one or more of several optional uses. Land can, at the applicant's option, be used as permanent or rotational fallow, grazed fallow (subject to conditions), converted to woodland, or used for non-agricultural purposes, during the five-year set aside period. Following amendments introduced in 1990[11] land which has been set aside for non-agricultural purposes or woodland can now also be put to a

7 SI 1988/1352 reg 3(1)(a), amended by SI 1989/1042.
8 SI 1988/1352 Sch 1, amended SI 1989/1042 reg 8.
9 Ie in the period 1st July 1987 to 30th June 1988.
10 SI 1988/1352 reg 3(1)(a) and (b), as amended by SI 1990/1716.
11 SI 1990/1716.

combined use with either grazed fallow or permanent/rotational fallow (but not both). It is not permissible to set land aside, and then increase the amount of land used for arable to make good any shortfall. To this end, the regulations require the applicant to undertake to ensure that the total arable land on his holding does not exceed the relevant arable land during the reference period, minus the area set aside. Additional land may be set aside during the first three years of the set aside period.[12] Note, however, that if land has already been set aside for permanent or rotational fallow, the additional area set aside cannot be used for grazed fallow. Similarly, where the grazed fallow option has been used, any additional land set aside cannot be used for permanent or rotational fallow.[13]

It may be that a holding is enlarged by the acquisition of arable land or permanent pasture *during* the set aside period. In this event some or all of the additional land can be set aside, provided the land in question was arable land during the reference period, and the application for set aside is made within four years from the date of acceptance of the original application.[14]

Whatever the area of land set aside, it must include a minimum of one whole field amounting to at least one hectare, or an area consisting of adjacent whole fields amounting to at least one hectare. If a strip of land, the area set aside must be at least fifteen metres wide.[15] The obligations imposed in relation to set aside land depend upon whether the applicant undertakes to use the land for fallow, grazed fallow, woodland or non-agricultural use.

(a) Fallow option

Schedule 2 to the Set Aside Regulations 1988 applies requirements aimed at ensuring the maintenance of adequate plant cover, and the enhancement of the environment, where land is set aside for permanent or rotational fallow.[16] Following amendments introduced in 1990,[17] applicants are now required to agree to cut plant cover at least twice a year and to maintain unimproved grass, moorland and heath, vernacular buildings (ie those traditionally found in the locality) and stone walls on their holdings. If land is to be used for rotational fallow, moreover, the Minister must be notified every year (before the 1st October) of the location and area of land to be set aside during the following twelve months.[18]

The set aside regulations require that plant cover be established immediately after the commencement of the set aside period, or as soon as the previous crop has been harvested.[19] Plant cover, once established, must be maintained throughout the set aside period, and its destruction is only permitted for the preparation of a crop, control of weeds or establishment of an alternative plant cover.[20] Where the applicant's undertakings have been given on or after 1st October 1990 plant cover must be cut twice each year,

---

12 Reg 3(1)(c) SI 1988/1352.
13 Reg 3(2)(b), amended SI 1990/1716.
14 Reg 3(4) *ibid.*
15 Reg 4 *ibid.*
16 Reg 7 and Sch 2 *ibid.*
17 Ie by SI 1990/1716.
18 Reg 7(3) *ibid.*
19 Sch 2, para 1 *ibid.* Plant cover can be naturally occurring vegetation.
20 Sch 2, para 3 *ibid.*

although cuttings cannot be sold or used for feeding livestock.[1] Where undertakings were given before the 1st October 1990 the applicant must cut the plant cover at least once every year, but can elect to observe the new requirements and cut the plant cover at least twice a year (in consideration of which enhanced grant payments will be available – see below).[2] Inorganic fertilizers containing nitrogen cannot be used at any time between the end of the previous harvest and the establishment of a subsequent crop. Furthermore, inorganic fertilizers not containing nitrogen cannot be used before the 1st August in the year in which a crop is to be established.[3] The dumping of organic or inorganic material is prohibited, and organic fertilizers cannot be applied at any time between the end of the previous harvest and the establishment of subsequent crops. The application of slurry or manure, however, can be authorised to prevent soil erosion.[4] The use of herbicides and/or pesticides is generally prohibited, with the *caveat* that the Ministry can sanction the use of specified herbicides if they are of a type normally absorbed primarily through the leaves and stem and have little persistence in water or soil.[5] Existing environmental features – hedges, rows of trees, lakes, ponds, watercourses etc – must be maintained if they are on, or on land adjacent to, the land set aside.[6] Where set aside undertakings are given on or after 1st October 1990 the applicant will also have to undertake to maintain unimproved grassland, moor and heath, vernacular buildings and stone walls. Participants who entered the scheme prior to the 1st October 1990 can elect to observe these additional obligations in return for enhanced payments (below).[7] The installation of new drainage systems or the modification of existing systems is prohibited.[8]

Amendments introduced to the scheme in 1990[9] now enable applicants who set land aside for *rotational* fallow to offset reductions in the area set aside in one year with increases in a previous year. The amount of land set aside cannot be increased or reduced by more than 10%, neither can it be reduced below 20% of the relevant arable land on the holding in the reference period. Moreover, an applicant may only reduce land already set aside for rotational fallow if he has in a previous year increased the area of land which he undertook to set aside for rotational fallow by at least that same amount. These amendments implement European Community requirements.[10]

(b) Grazed fallow option

A limited grazed fallow option was introduced with effect from 1st October 1990.[11] Under this option an applicant who had livestock in the reference

---

1 Sch 2, para 4(a) *ibid.*
2 Sch 2, para 4(b) and reg 7(2) *ibid.*
3 Sch 2, paras 6 and 7 *ibid.*
4 See s 2, paras 8 and 9 *ibid.*
5 Sch 2, paras 10–12 *ibid.*
6 Sch 2, para 13 *ibid.*
7 Sch 2, para 13 *ibid.* (Amended SI 1990/1716).
8 Sch 2, para 14 *ibid.*
9 SI 1990/1716 reg 8, in the new reg 7(4) *ibid.*
10 Ie Comm Regs (EEC) No 1272/88 and 3981/89.
11 By SI 1990/1716, pursuant to Council Reg (EEC) 1094/88 and Comm Reg (EEC) 1272/88.

period (ie 1st July 1987 to 30th June 1988) can opt to graze on his holding no more than the equivalent of the maximum number of 'livestock units' on the land during the reference period.[12] Livestock units are defined in accordance with Schedule 4 to the Set Aside Regulations (as amended). A bull, cow or other bovine animal over two years, or equine animal over six months, counts for this purpose as one livestock unit; a bovine animal between six months to two years as 0.60 livestock units; a sheep as 0.15 livestock unit and a goat or deer as 0.15 livestock unit.[13] If no livestock were kept during the reference period the applicant can only use fallow land as grazed fallow for deer and goats up to one livestock unit per forage hectare.[14] Where the grazed fallow option is used, applicants have to comply with certain requirements additional to those applicable to permanent and rotational fallow (above). These are contained in Schedule 3 to the Set Aside Regulations 1988.[15] The additional requirements require that the area to be grazed must be sown with grass and maintained as grass land throughout the set aside period. Clover cannot be sown, with the exception of white clover whose seed content by weight is no more than 5% or 1.5 kilograms per hectare (whichever is less), and irrigation is prohibited. Moreover, for the limited period of twelve months (only) from the date of sowing grass cover, fertilizer can be applied. After that date, however, no organic or inorganic fertilizer can be applied other than manure produced by livestock grazing the land. Pesticides and herbicides cannot be applied other than during the initial twelve months following sowing. Grass cover cannot be cut more than once a year and cuttings cannot be sold. Cuttings can, however, be used to feed livestock *cf* rotational/permanent fallow where grass cuttings can neither be sold nor fed to livestock. Environmental features on or adjacent to the area set aside must be maintained including all existing hedgerows and trees, lakes, and unimproved grassland, moorland and heath, and all vernacular buildings and stone walls. The installation of new drainage systems is prohibited, as is the substantial modification of existing systems.

(c)   Woodland option

Where a beneficiary has undertaken to use set aside land for woodland, he must maintain the land as permanent or rotational fallow and have observed the requirements relating thereto (above) until planting commences.[16] Where set aside undertakings are given on or after 1st October 1990, moreover, the land can only be used as permanent fallow until planting commences.[17] If the applicant has applied for a grant under the woodland grant scheme or the farm woodland scheme, he must not start planting on set aside land until the application has been approved.[18]

---

12 Reg 7A(1) *ibid.*
13 Reg 7A(5) and Sch 4 *ibid*, introduced by SI 1990/1716.
14 Reg 7A (2) *ibid.*
15 Inserted by reg 20 and Sch 2 SI 1990/1716.
16 Reg 8(1) *ibid.*
17 *Ibid* as amended SI 1990/1716 reg 10.
18 Reg 8(2) *ibid.*

(d) Non-agricultural user option

Where the non-agricultural user option is pursued, land must be administered as permanent or rotational fallow in accordance with Schedule 2 (above) until non-agricultural user commences.[19] Where set aside undertakings are given on or after 1st October 1990, moreover, land can only be used for permanent fallow pending commencement of a proposed non-agricultural use.[20] Land can be set aside to any non-agricultural use, with the exception of the extraction of minerals or the erection of buildings or other permanent structures with a view to carrying on an industrial process, the wholesale or retail sale of goods, residential use, office accommodation or the use of buildings as storage or a distribution centre.[1] Buildings may be erected if they are to be used for the purposes of a business approved in the schedule to the Farm Business Specification Order 1987.[2]

3. Set aside grant payments

Applications for grant aid under the set aside scheme must include a map of the holding showing its boundaries and internal field boundaries, the area it is proposed to set aside and the area on which it is proposed to continue arable cropping.[3] The Minister cannot accept an application to set aside land within a site of special scientific interest, a national park or the Broads unless satisfied that the applicant has notified the relevant Nature Conservancy Council, National Park Authority or Broads Authority (whichever is appropriate) of his intended application. Where it is proposed to set aside land pursuant to the woodland option (above), and the area to be set aside is more than 0.25 hectares, the application must be refused unless the applicant has applied to the Forestry Commission for grant aid under the Woodland Grant Scheme, or to the Minister under the Farm Woodland Scheme 1988.[4] An application can also be refused on the grounds that it would frustrate the purposes of assistance previously given out of Government or EEC funds or would duplicate assistance previously given.[5]

The amount of aid payable during each of the five years of set aside is prescribed in Schedule 1 to the Set Aside Regulations 1988, and varies according to the use to which set aside land is to be put.[6] The annual payment per hectare of set aside land makes differential provision for payments in less favoured areas, and other areas, and prescribes enhanced payments for applications made up to 1st October 1990 where the additional requirements prescribed by the Set Aside (Amendment) Regulations 1990 apply.

Where land is set aside under the Farm Woodland Scheme the applicant will receive the rate of payment for permanent fallow in respect of any year prior to that in which planting commences. In the year in which planting

---

19 Reg 9(1) *ibid.*
20 Reg 9(1) as amended SI 1990/1716 reg 11.
1 Reg 9(2) *ibid.*
2 SI 1987/1948. For planning permission requirements see p 304 ff.
3 See generally reg 5 *ibid.*
4 Reg 6(3) and (4) *ibid.*
5 Regs 6(5) and (6) *ibid.*
6 Reg 13 and Sch 1 *ibid.*

commences, and any subsequent year, he will receive the rate provided for in the scheme.[7] Where the Woodland Grant Scheme option is used, on the other hand, the applicant will receive planting grants from the Forestry Commission at the appropriate rate per hectare planted, in addition to the woodland set aside payments prescribed by the Set Aside regulations. Where the non-agricultural use option is pursued, the grant for permanent fallow is payable for any year prior to that in which conversion to a non-agricultural use takes place. The Minister is empowered, furthermore, to deduct from set aside payments any aid paid to a beneficiary under the Environmentally Sensitive Area scheme.[8]

The Regulations empower the Minister to withhold or recover grant aid in specified situations.[9] Grant aid can be recovered, for instance, where the applicant fails to comply with any of the set aside obligations (above) or where he has failed without reasonable excuse to notify the Minister of the proposed change of use, of withdrawal from set aside, or of land to be left fallow in rotation. Grant aid can also be withheld or recovered where the applicant fails to allow entry and inspection by an authorised officer, and where he has planted woodland under the Woodland Grant Scheme if it appears to the Minister that the applicant has not complied with its' requirements. Provision is also made for grant aid to be withheld if the applicant makes false statements or furnishes false or misleading information in order to obtain payment of set aside grant aid.

4.   Withdrawal from set aside

A participant can withdraw from the scheme, and from his undertakings thereunder, if he gives notice to do so within the first three years of the set aside period. Termination of set aside cannot take effect before the expiry of the first three years of the set aside period.[10] An applicant can now also withdraw *part* of land set aside, provided he does not thereby reduce the area set aside below 20% of the relevant arable land on the holding in the reference period.[11] Where an applicant withdraws land from the set aside scheme, the Minister cannot accept an application for aid in respect of the withdrawn land within two years of termination.[12]

5.   Change of use

The Set Aside regulations make provision[13] for an applicant to change the use of set aside land (other than woodland) from the use to which he has undertaken to put it to one or more of the other set aside options provided for, if he does so within the first three years of the set aside period.

7 Reg 15(2) *ibid.*
8 Reg 13(5) *ibid.*
9 Reg 16 *ibid.*
10 Reg 10(1) *ibid.*
11 *Ibid* amended by SI 1990/1716 reg 12.
12 Reg 10(4) *ibid.*
13 See reg 11 *ibid.*

User can now also be changed to a combination of permanent fallow, woodland and/or non-agricultural use.[14] The change must be notified to the Minister, in default of which aid can be withdrawn and/or withheld. For the purpose of calculating grant payments, the change of use is deemed to take effect on the 1st October following the approval of the change by the Minister.[15] A change of use to set aside woodland or non-agricultural use cannot be approved, if the beneficiary is a tenant, unless he has the written consent of his landlord for the proposed change of use.[16]

6. Landlord and tenant

The impact of entry into set aside undertakings on the private law obligations of tenant farmers are not dealt with by the Set Aside Regulations 1988. The interaction of set aside obligations with those arising under a contract of tenancy and/or the Agricultural Holdings Act 1986 may give rise to difficulties.

(a) Permanent, rotational and grazed fallow options

The Minister cannot accept an application for set aside on the permanent, rotational or grazed fallow options unless satisfied that a tenant has given his landlord written notice of his intention to make the application.[17] The landlord's consent is not, however, a condition precedent to the set aside of land under one or more of these options. It by no means follows, however, that set aside has no impact on the tenant's obligations under his contract of tenancy. So, for instance, entering into set aside may put the tenant in breach of the rules of good husbandry contained in section 11 of the Agriculture Act 1947, and give rise to similar problems to those already considered in relation to management agreements under eg the Environmentally Sensitive Area scheme[18]. The rules of good husbandry provide, for instance, that a tenant must maintain a reasonable standard of efficient production as respects both the kind, quantity and quality of produce, and must maintain the agricultural unit in a condition to enable such a standard to be maintained in the future.[19] Section 11(2) of the 1947 Act specifies certain objectives to which regard is to be had in determining whether the rules have been satisfied. These make no allowance for conservation management, a concept which has become more prevalent since 1947. In particular, permanent pasture must be properly mown or grazed, and must be maintained in a good state of cultivation and fertility and in good condition. Arable land must be cropped in a manner which 'is such as to maintain the land clean and in a good state of cultivation and fertility and in good condition'. Necessary work of maintenance and repair must, furthermore, be carried out. Breach of the rules can be enforced by

14 Reg 13(1) amended SI 1990/1716 reg 13.
15 Reg 11(3) *ibid.*
16 Reg 11(5) *ibid.*
17 Reg 6(2) *ibid.*
18 See Ch 12, p 288 ff.
19 Section 11(1) Agriculture Act 1947. See above Ch 3 p 90 ff.

proceedings pursuant to case C of Schedule 3 to the Agricultural Holdings Act 1986 for the issue of a certificate of bad husbandry. Furthermore, if the tenancy agreement incorporates the rules as a term of the tenancy, breach of the statutory standards of husbandry could lead to service of a notice to remedy breaches of tenancy, and notice to quit under case D to Schedule 3 ibid. There may be a question whether set aside of land under the rotational fallow option constitutes a clear breach of the rules of good husbandry. Set aside pursuant to the permanent fallow option would appear, however, to be in conflict with the statutory standards of efficient production laid down in section 11 of the 1947 Act.

The 1986 Act[20] makes provision for the adoption of a practice whose object is *inter alia* the conservation of flora or fauna, the conservation or enhancement of the natural beauty or amenity of the countryside, or the promotion of its enjoyment by the public, where this is reflected in a covenant in the tenancy agreement or other written agreement with the landlord. It follows that a tenant considering entry into set aside under the permanent fallow option (and possibly one entering under the rotational fallow option) should obtain a variation of the tenancy to permit entry, or otherwise obtain the landlord's consent to his doing so prior to entry. Failure to do so could, depending on the terms of the particular contract of tenancy, put the tenant in the position of having conflicting contractual obligations to his landlord under his tenancy, and to the Ministry under the set aside regulations. There may, in any event, be a question whether the set aside of land under the 1988 Regulations constitutes a practice whose primary objective is 'the conservation of flora and fauna, the conservation or enhancement of the natural beauty or amenity of the countryside etc' as envisaged by the relevant provisions of the Agricultural Holdings Act 1986. The primary objective of the relevant EEC Regulations is to take land out of agricultural production, and to eliminate structural surpluses in the arable sector. Article 1(a)(3) of Council Regulation (EEC) 1094/1988 permits member states to introduce measures to ensure that land withdrawn from production is maintained with a view to protecting environmental and natural resources. The Set Aside Regulations 1988 make provision for the maintenance of environmental features of set aside and adjacent land, but this is not the only (or arguably the primary) objective of the set aside scheme. There must, therefore, be a question whether a conservation covenant, as envisaged by the Agricultural Holdings Act 1986, would protect the tenant entering into set aside under the permanent fallow option. It may therefore be necessary to secure a covenant, or variation of tenancy, explicitly covering the set aside of land pursuant to the fallow options.

(b)   Non-agricultural use and woodland options

No application to set aside land for woodland or non-agricultural purposes can be accepted unless the Minister is satisfied that the applicant has obtained the written consent of his landlord to the application.[1] No doubt because of the change this form of set aside would have on the long term nature of the land, the landlord has a right to prevent set aside by the tenant

---

20 Sch 3, paras 9(2), 10(1)(d) Agricultural Holdings Act 1986. Discussed above p 289.
1 Reg 6(1) Set Aside Regs 1988 SI 1988/1352.

in this manner without his prior consent. Even where consent has been obtained, however, there may be further legal consequences following entry into set aside pursuant to the non-agricultural use or woodland options.

Where land is converted to non-agricultural use the tenancy may in some circumstances cease to be that of an agricultural holding at all, with serious consequences for the tenant's security of tenure. If a substantial part of the tenant's holding is set aside for non-agricultural use a question may arise whether the substantial user of the land remains agricultural.[2] No severance of the holding into agricultural and non-agricultural land is possible for the purpose of ascertaining its status as an agricultural holding or otherwise.[3] For a holding to lose its status as an agricultural holding, agricultural activity must have been wholly or substantially abandoned by the tenant, which question involves a consideration of all the circumstances and not solely the physical use of the land itself, eg the turnover of the farming business will be relevant, as will the sources (agricultural or non-agricultural) of that turnover, the terms of the tenancy and the proportion of the holding set aside. The rules appertaining to cesser of agricultural use, in the context of the protection of the Agricultural Holdings Act 1986, will therefore have to be carefully considered.[4] Clearly, however, the contribution made by grant aid payments under the scheme, as a proportion of the applicant's gross turnover, could be relevant.[5] Further, if the non-agricultural user in question is of a commercial character the tenancy may come within the scope of the Landlord and Tenant Act 1954. Although abandonment of agricultural user does not of itself bring a tenancy within any of the alternative codes of tenancy protection, the requirement of the landlord's written consent before set aside under this option *may* constitute a variation of the contract of tenancy bringing it within the 1954 Act, if the requirements of the latter are otherwise satisfied.[6] The security of tenure afforded to the tenant under the 1954 Act is, in any event, less extensive than that under the Agricultural Holdings Act 1986 eg the landlord will have the right to resist leasehold renewals under the 1954 Act if he wishes to redevelop the property or to repossess for his own use.[7]

(c) Agricultural rents

Grant payments under the set aside scheme will, it is suggested, constitute a 'relevant factor' influencing the rent properly payable for an agricultural holding within the meaning of Schedule 2, paragraph 1 of the Agricultural Holdings Act 1986. An arbitrator determining the rent payable must have regard *inter alia* to the productive and related earning capacities of the holding.[8] 'Related earning capacity' is defined by reference to income generated by agricultural production on the holding[9] and would not, it appears, include grant payments received for cessation of production. There

---

2 As required by section 1(1) Agricultural Holdings Act 1986.
3 See *Blackmore v Butler* [1954] 2 QB 171, CA.
4 See above Ch 2 p 21 ff for a detailed discussion.
5 See *Short v Greeves* [1988] 1 EGLR 1, CA.
6 See s 23 Landlord and Tenant Act 1954, *Court v Robinson* [1951] 2 KB 60, CA.
7 Section 30(1)(f) and (g) Landlord and Tenant Act 1954.
8 Sch 2, para 1(2) Agricultural Holdings Act 1986.
9 Sch 2, para 1(2)(b) Agricultural Holdings Act 1986.

can, however, be little doubt that grant moneys would be relevant under the general clause in the rent formula (ie Schedule 2, paragraph 1(1)) which directs the arbitrator to have regard to all the relevant factors 'including' productive and related earning capacity. Entry into set aside could therefore have an influence on rent at the next review after entry, which fact will have to be considered by a tenant prior to entry into the scheme.

7.   Planning permission – non-agricultural use option

Where set aside is pursuant to the non-agricultural use option, it should be appreciated that, even if the use is one not prohibited by the Set Aside Regulations 1988, it may well require planning permission under the Town and Country Planning Act 1990. As has already been noted[10] the *use* of land for agriculture, and the use of any buildings for agricultural purposes if occupied with agricultural land, will not constitute development, and so will not require permission. Further, the General Development Order 1988[11] deems the grant of permission for the carrying out of building or engineering operations 'reasonably necessary' for the purposes of agriculture on agricultural land of more than 0.4 hectares. Planning permission will be required before land can be set aside if the proposed change of use does not fall within the permitted categories of development under the terms of General Development Order and the Town and Country Planning Act 1990.

8.   Change of occupation and/or ownership

Provision is made for the transfer of set aside undertakings whenever there is a change of occupation of a holding. Undertakings pursuant to the set aside scheme are, however, personal to the individual beneficiary and do not take effect *in rem*. Participation in the scheme, and undertakings given in association therewith, are transferred to a new occupant or owner who *voluntarily* takes on the former occupier's set aside obligations. The Set Aside regulations provide[12] that where there is a change of occupation of the whole or part of a holding, the new occupier must give notice in writing of that fact to the Minister, and can give an undertaking to comply with the set aside obligations for the holding for the remainder of the set aside period. Notice of a change of occupation must be given within three months of its having taken effect. It is further provided[13] that the Minister cannot accept an undertaking from a new occupier to comply with set aside obligations unless satisfied that he occupies the holding as an owner, tenant or the personal representative of the original occupier.

It follows that the transfer of set aside obligations is limited to changes of occupation consequent upon either the transfer of freehold ownership of set aside land, the grant of a tenancy, the assignment of an existing tenancy, or the grant of a succession tenancy to a survivor pursuant to Part IV of the

10 Above p 256 ff.
11 Sch 2, Part 6 General Development Order 1988 above, p 261 ff.
12 Reg 12 Set Aside Regs 1988 SI 1988/1352.
13 See reg 12(3) *ibid*.

Agricultural Holdings Act 1986. A transferee whose undertakings are accepted by the Minister is deemed to be an eligible person within the meaning of the set aside regulations, and entitled to grant payments. Where the transferee is a tenant, his eligibility is not qualified by reference to minimum occupation for twelve months, or by the requirement that a fixed term tenancy have at least five years to run. These exceptions are necessary, in that the transferee will normally assume set aside obligations for the residue of the unexpired set aside period. The unexpired residue will, naturally, be of less than five years' duration. Note however that it would appear that a tenant with a *Gladstone v Bower* tenancy of more than one year but less than two *may* be entitled to participate in set aside if the land were already set aside prior to grant, notwithstanding that his interest attracts no security of tenure and may be insufficient to guarantee the performance of the undertaking during the rest of the set aside period. An applicant with such an interest would not, in any event, be entitled to participate if applying in his own right *ab initio*.

If the transferee fails, within three months, to give undertakings to comply with his existing set aside obligations relating to the land transferred, the Minister can withhold the whole or part of any payments due to the original occupier, and (moreover) can recover from the latter the whole or any part of any payments previously made to him.[14] It is further provided that recovery of grant aid cannot be demanded if the change of occupation results from compulsory purchase or the death of the original occupier, where the latter were tenants. Where a transfer of occupation follows the death of a sitting tenant, the disallowance of recovery only applies if the tenancy was terminated by the landlord ie by notice to quit given pursuant to case G, or where the consent of an agricultural land tribunal to the operation of a notice to quit has been given, pursuant to section 26(1) and 27(3) of the Agricultural Holdings Act 1986. Repayment of grant aid cannot, similarly, be demanded where the tenancy is terminated following notice to quit given pursuant to cases A, B or H, to Schedule 3 of the Agricultural Holdings Act 1986.[15]

B Diversification

The non-agricultural user option under the set aside scheme (above) provides for a limited form of diversification, applicable only to arable holdings. Additionally, grant aid is now generally available to encourage diversification into ancillary forms of businesses, whatever the nature of the farming enterprise. The Farm Diversification Grant Scheme 1987[16] makes provision for grant aid for capital expenditure incurred in diversifying agricultural businesses, aid being available at the rate of 25% of qualifying expenditure. The Farm Business Non Capital Grant Scheme 1988[17], on the

---

14 Reg 12(6) *ibid*.
15 See reg 12(7), amended by SI 1990/1716.
16 SI 1987/1949.
17 SI 1988/1125.

other hand, makes provision for grant aid in respect of non-capital expenditure incurred in diversifying and marketing ancillary agricultural products and services.

1. Eligibility for grant aid

The same qualifying conditions for grant aid are imposed by both the farm diversification grant scheme, in respect of capital aid, and the farm business and non-capital grant scheme. Grant aid is limited to 'eligible persons' within the following categories of agricultural occupier:[18]

(i) An individual carrying on an agicultural business, provided the Minister is satisfied that either he, or the farm manager through whom the business is carried on, derives more than half his annual income from the business. He must, moreover, spend not less than 1,100 hours per year in agricultural activities related to that business and possess sufficient agricultural skill and competence.[19]

(ii) Any person representing a body, such as a farming company, provided the Minister is satisfied that the main purpose of that business is the pursuit of agriculture. The manager or other person through whom the business is carried on must, moreover, satisfy the requirements as to income and time spent in agricultural activities specified in (i).

(iii) A farming partnership, provided the farm manager or other person through whom the business is carried on satisfies (i) above.

(iv) The owner of land occupied for purposes of agriculture can submit a farm diversification plan relating to that land or adjacent land jointly with persons qualifying under (i) to (iii) above eg a landlord whose tenant qualifies under (i) above or who farms land adjacent to the latter.

(v) In the case of applications for non-capital grant only, provision is made for group applications by eligible persons.[20] A group application can be made by a group consisting of three or more members, each carrying on an agricultural business, provided that at least 75% of the members thereof are 'eligible persons' for grant (above) and that those members who are not do not include a company or co-operative. A group application cannot be entertained where the members of the group *each* also carry on a business involving food processing or the purification, carbonisation or bottling of spring water, and the membership of the group numbers ten or more.

The applicant for grant must either submit a farm diversification plan (in the case of a diversification grant application), or feasibility study plan or marketing plan (in the case of a non-capital grant application). For the purpose of assessing eligibility a person's income is calculated by

18 See SI 1987/1949 reg 3, SI 1988/1125 reg 3.
19 Skill and competence can be proved by the holding of a certificate issued by a recognised teaching establishment or by proof of engagement in agriculture for 5 years or more.
20 SI 1988/1125 reg 4.

reference to such year or years within the three years preceding the application as the Minister may determine.[1] If an individual claiming farm diversification grant is a contractor, there is a further requirement that he enter into a written contract with the occupier of the land which is expressed to continue for at least seven years following submission of the diversification plan.[2] This additional requirement does not apply to applications for non-capital grant.

2. Specified ancillary farm businesses

Grant aid under the Farm Diversification Scheme 1987 can only be given for the carrying on or establishment of 'an ancillary farm business'. The expenditure must be of a capital nature and incurred in respect of work, or a facility or transaction, of a kind specified in the schedule to the 1987 scheme.[3] Farm business grants under the Farm Non-capital Grant Scheme 1988 are, on the other hand, available for the purpose of carrying out a feasibility study which has been approved by the Minister, and for the purposes of carrying out a marketing plan by means of employing persons to promote a 'specified farm business'. Grant is available under the 1988 scheme to market any produce or supplies arising in the course of running a specified farm business and to design or print material, the object of which is to promote the business or products, or services connected therewith.[4] The following ancillary farm businesses qualify for grant aid under both schemes:[5]

(i) Farm based industry. This is defined to include the manufacture of craft items, food processing and purification of spring water, processing of timber, processing agricultural produce other than for human consumption and the repair and/or renovation of agricultural machinery.[6]

(ii) Farm shops eg a shop primarily, but not necessarily exclusively, used for the sale of the produce of the agricultural business.

(iii) Direct sales to customers of fruit and vegetables.

(iv) Provision of food, accommodation or drink. Accommodation which will qualify for grant under the Farm Diversification Scheme has now been limited to the provision of simple overnight shelter or hostel-style self catering accommodation in traditional farm buildings.[7]

(v) Provision of facilities for sports and recreation. This is defined to include any sport other than field sports, horse riding and sports involving the use of motor vehicles, firearms or cross bows.

(vi) Provision of educational facilities. The education provided must,

1 Reg 3(2) SI 1987/1949, reg 3(2) SI 1988/1125.
2 SI 1987/1949 reg 3(3).
3 SI 1987/1949 reg 8(1).
4 Reg 8 SI 1988/1125.
5 See Sch SI 1987/1949, Sch SI 1988/1125. Qualifying ancillary farm businesses are identical under both schemes.
6 See reg 1 SI 1987/1949.
7 Farm Diversification Grant (Variation) Scheme 1991, SI 1991/2.

moreover, relate to farming in the countryside or farm based industries.

(vii)   Provision of livery eg accommodation for the care of horses and ponies.

(viii) Provision of horses and ponies for hire. Grant aid is only available for this purpose in less favoured areas.

(ix)   The letting of land or buildings for the purpose of carrying on any of the businesses listed above. If the applicant is a tenant, care should be taken to ensure that the proposed letting will not be in breach of alienation covenant in the tenancy by which the land is held.[8]

(x)   The carrying on of any *business* of a type qualifying under (i) to (ix) above.

In the case of farm diversification grant applications, the kind of work or transaction for which grant may be paid is specified by the Regulations.[9]

Where the occupier holds under a contract of tenancy, the terms of the latter should be carefully considered before diversifying pursuant to either the farm diversification scheme or the farm non-capital grant scheme (above). Diversification into a non-agricultural activity pursuant to either scheme may constitute a breach of tenancy where, as is common, the tenancy limits user of the land to agricultural use. Further, it should be appreciated that diversification on a substantial scale may change the character of the holding, such that a question may arise whether it continues to be the tenancy of an 'agricultural holding' within the protection of the Agricultural Holdings Act 1986. The rules as to cesser of agricultural use and statutory protection may, therefore, need to be carefully considered.[10] Compensation for improvements made on the holding is probably only available for those of an agricultural nature, listed in Sch 7 to the 1986 Act which enhance the letting value of the holding *as a holding*,[11] and not eg for non-agricultural works flowing from diversification. Whether the land is tenanted or freehold, planning permission may be required prior to diversification into agricultural activities which fall outside the terms of the General Development Order 1988.[12]

8 As to which see ch 3 p 53 ff above.
9 See sch Col 2 SI 1987/1949.
10 See ch 2 above p 21. Similar problems arise with regard to Set Aside see p 301 above.
11 See s 66(1) Agricultural Holdings Act 1986 (italics added).
12 As to which see p 261 ff.

Chapter 14
Public control of land use III: quotas

A   Quotas on dairy production

1.   Introduction

Implementation of the common agricultural policy of the EEC has resulted in quantative controls being placed on the production of milk and other dairy products.[1] A target price[2] for milk is fixed annually. In an attempt to control structural surpluses in the dairy sector, a guarantee threshhold was introduced in 1982.[3] This threshold having been passed, production quotas were introduced in 1984, based upon a super levy of a confiscatory nature payable on deliveries and sales of milk. Council regulation (EEC) 804/68, as amended,[4] entitles each member state to produce milk and dairy products up to a fixed threshhold (termed 'a reference quantity'),[5] based on actual production in 1981 plus 1%. If this figure is exceeded additional levy becomes payable to the Community on the member state's over production. This will in turn be recouped by the latter from individual producers. The quota system was initially expressed to be operative for five years commencing on 1st April 1984, but this has now been extended to eight years by Council Regulation (EEC) 1109/88.[6]

The EEC provisions[7] require member states to collect the super levy in accordance with one of two formulas. Under formula A, levy is payable by every milk producer on the quantities of milk delivered by him to a purchaser, and which for the twelve months concerned exceeds the

1 The common organisation of the European Market in Milk was established in 1968 and is regulated by EC Council Regulation 804/68 (OJ L148,286 68 p 13). Consideration of the wider implications of the common agricultural policy of the European communities is beyond the scope of the present work. See further Usher, *Legal Aspects of Agriculture in the European Community* (1988) esp pages 72 ff, also Snyder, *The Law of the Common Agricultural Policy* (1986) page 142 ff. Also *Halsburys Laws of England*, Vol 1 (Agriculture) 4th re-issue 1990 para 1079 ff (Snyder).
2 This is not a guaranteed price. The target price is the price which it is hoped will be realised by the community for producers' sales.
3 See EC Council Regulation 183/82 (OJ L140, 2.5.82 p 1), amending EC Council Regulation 804/68.
4 Ie Council Regulation 804/68 article 5C (added by EC Council Regulation 857/84).
5 See EC Council Regulation 857/84 article 1 (OJ L90, 1.4.84 p 13).
6 Council Regulation 1109/88 (OJ L110, 29488 p 27).
7 EC Council Regulation 856/84 (OJ L90, 1.4.84 p 10) article 1, amending EC Council Regulation 804/68.

reference quantity determined. Under formula B, the levy is payable by the purchaser (in most cases the Milk Marketing Board) on milk delivered to it by producers which exceeds the reference quantity for the twelve months concerned. The purchaser is then under a duty to recover the levy from producers, proportionately to their contributions to the reference quantity being exceeded. The levy will be recovered through the price paid to producers. The quota system is administered in the United Kingdom using formula B, with levy being paid initially by the Milk Marketing Board and then recouped from individual producers.[8] Each purchaser has a purchaser quota, which is the quantity of dairy produce which may be delivered by wholesale deliveries to that purchaser, from holdings in a region during a quota year, without the purchaser being liable to pay levy.[9] Where formula B is used, as in the United Kingdom, the additional levy is fixed by community legislation at 100% of the target price for milk.[10] United Kingdom producers were allocated individual quotas in 1984 and will be liable to contribute to the super levy if their production exceeds this figure, as subsequently amended.

2. Categories of dairy quota

The Dairy Produce Quotas Regulations 1989[11] make provision for the following categories of quota:

(i)   *Direct sales quota, viz* the quantity of dairy produce which may be sold by direct sale from a holding in a quota year without the seller being liable to pay levy. Direct sales quota is not to include, however, any element in respect of milk bought in by a producer with a view to re-sale,[12] and

(ii)   *Wholesale quota, viz* the quantity of dairy produce which may be delivered by wholesale delivery to a purchaser, from a holding, in a quota year, without the producer in occupation being liable to pay levy.[13]

(iii)   *Regional wholesale quota* This is defined as the allocation made by the Minister from the national wholesale quota, of a regional wholesale quota for each region.[14]

(iv)   *Special quota* The Dairy Produce Quotas (Amendment) Regulations 1990[15] make special provision for the implementation of EEC legislation to enable qualifying producers who participated in the Non Marketing of milk or Dairy Herd Conversion schemes,

---

8 Dairy Produce Quotas Regulations 1989, SI 1989/380, reg 4.
9 *Ibid*, Reg 2 (1).
10 Ie by EC Council Regulation 857/84, art 1.1.
11 Ie the Dairy Produce Quotas Regulations 1989, SI 1989/380 (amended by SI 1990/132, SI 1990/664 and SI 1990/784).
12 See *R. v Dairy Produce Quota Tribunal for England and Wales, ex p Hall & Sons (Dairy Farmers) Ltd* (1990) *Times*, 15 June (ECJ). The European Court here ruled that EC Council Regulation 857/84, art 6(1), was to be interpreted so that the reference quantity assigned to each producer in respect of direct sales was to be calculated by reference only to milk sold by that producer from his own herd.
13 Dairy Produce Quotas Regulations 1989, reg 2(1).
14 For Regional Wholesale Quota see *ibid* reg 7(1).
15 SI 1990/132. Special quota is discussed further below, p 320 ff.

to apply for the allocation of 'special' quota.[16] Where a special quota has been allocated, the additional regional wholesale quota so allocated as special quota does not create, or add to, the running regional wholesale reserve for that region.[17] The normal transfer rules are excluded[18] in that upon a transfer of a holding special quota must be returned to the Community reserve, or if part of the holding is sold or leased to another producer the relevant proportion of that special quota must be returned to the Community reserve.[19] This provision does not apply, however, in relation to a licence to occupy land or to a tenancy of land under which a holding or part of a holding in England and Wales is occupied for a period of less than ten months.[20]

(v) *Wholesale development quota* In order to comply with Community legislation, the Minister must make awards of quota to producers who receive a wholesale development award,[1] and who held wholesale quota on the 1st April 1989 in respect of which they made deliveries of milk or milk products between that date and 28th February 1990, so that each producer has his wholesale development quota[2] increased to the same percentage of an amount determined with regard to him by the further examination body or by the Dairy Produce Quotas Tribunal.[3] Awards must also be made to producers who occupy a 'family type holding'[4] for whom milk production is a significant activity and who made deliveries of milk or milk products between the two dates above mentioned.[5] The Minister must also make awards to producers who held wholesale quota on the 1st April 1989 or were allocated special quota, and whose holdings are situated on specified remote islands.[6]

Levies are calculated by reference to a quota year ending on 31st March in each calendar year.

---

16 See the Dairy Produce Quotas Regulations 1989, SI 1989/380, as amended by SI 1990/132. The relevant community legislation is EC Council Regulation 764/89 (OJ L84, 29.3.89 p 2).
17 Dairy Produce Quotas Regulations 1989, reg 7 (2A) (added by SI 1990/132).
18 *Ibid*, reg 9(8), (9) (as added by SI 1990/132).
19 *Ibid*, reg 9A(1) as added. Note that the proportion of special quota to be returned to the Community reserve must be the same proportion which the agricultural area of the holding sold or leased bears to the total agricultural area farmed by the producer; *ibid* reg 9A (2) (as added).
20 *Ibid*, reg 9A (3) (A), (B) (as added by SI 1990/132).
 1 For the meaning of 'wholesale development award', see the Dairy Produce Quotas Regulations 1989, reg 2(1). For the meaning of 'wholesale' quota see *ibid* reg 2(1).
 2 For the meaning of 'wholesale development quota' see *ibid* reg 2(1) (definition added by SI 1990/664 and subsequently amended by SI 1990/784).
 3 Dairy Produce Quotas Regulations 1989, reg 20A, Sch 8B, para 1 (both added by SI 1990/664). Detailed provision as to these awards is made by Sch 8B, paras 2 to 6 (as so added).
 4 A 'family type holding' is one in respect of which less than two hundred thousand litres of quota was identified on the registers maintained under the Dairy Produce Quotas Regulations 1990, reg 25 on 1st April 1989 or, in the case of a producer to whom special quota was awarded as wholesale quota, on the date on which such quota was awarded to him; reg 2(1)(A), Sch 9A, para 2.
 5 *Ibid*, Sch 9A, para 1 (as added). Detailed provision as to these awards is made by Sch 9A, paras 3 to 7 (as added).
 6 *Ibid*, reg 21B, Sch 9B, para 1 (as added).

3.   Registration and apportionment of quotas

Dairy quotas were originally introduced into United Kingdom law in 1984.[7]
In order to administer the quota system the Minister is required to divide the
United Kingdom into regions and to make provision for the allocation from
the national wholesale quota of a regional wholesale quota for each region.[8]
The Minister is also required to keep a direct sales register and a wholesale
register in which are entered details of each individual producer's quota,
identification of the holding for which it is registered, and, in the case of the
wholesale register, details of the relevant wholesale purchasers.[9] He must
also keep a register of purchasers, in which there must be set out the name of
each purchaser, a description of his undertaking, his purchaser quota and his
purchaser special quota.[10] Quota is registered in relation to a producer's
'holding', which is defined by reference to the European Community
provisions as 'all of the production units operated by the producer and
located within the geographical territory of the community'.[11] The 'holding'
thus defined may include both freehold and tenanted land, and is not to be
confused with an 'agricultural holding' as understood in United Kingdom
domestic law, *viz* tenanted land within the meaning of the Agricultural
Holdings Act 1986.[12] The categories of producer eligible for registration are
also wide. Registration is open to any 'producer'. This is defined by the
relevant EEC provisions to mean 'a natural or legal person or group of
natural or legal persons farming a holding located within the geographical
territory of the community' who sells milk directly to customers or supplies it

7 Ie by the Dairy Produce Quotas Regulations 1984, SI 1984/1047 (revoked: see now the
Dairy Produce Quotas Regulations 1989, SI 1989/380 as amended). The domestic legisla-
tion has stimulated a limited, and highly specialist, literature on the law of milk quotas. See,
in particular, *Milk Quotas: Law and Practice* (Farmgate Communications Ltd, 1986), by
Wood, Priday, Moss & Carter. There are also, now, useful sections in Scammell and
Densham's *Law of Agricultural Holdings* (8th ed) p 318 ff and Muir Watt *Agricultural
Holdings* (13th ed) p 225 ff. Discussion in the latter is, however, of necessity confined to
consideration of tenants' compensation for milk quota. Useful discussion, of a more general
tenor, will also be found in Hill and Redman's *Law of Landlord and Tenant* (28th ed) paras
F214 ff (Moss).
8 Dairy Produce Quotas Regulations 1989 (SI 1989/380) reg 7 (amended by SI 1990/132). This
obligation arises as a result of EC Council Regulations 857/84, art 1(2) (OJ L90, 1.4.84,
p 13). Any change in the regions must be announced in the London, Edinburgh, or Belfast
Gazette (whichever applies) and in the Farming Press: Dairy Produce Quotas Regulations
1989 regs 7(1), 21.
9 *Ibid*, reg 25 (amended by SI 1990/132). Also recorded in the register must be the total
amount of direct sales quota or wholesale quota transferred to the producer as special
quota: see reg 25(2) (iiA), 3 (iiA) (added by SI 1990/132). The registers are kept through the
agency of the Milk Marketing Board.
10 *Ibid*, reg 25(3)(A). The Minister must also maintain a register of purchaser notices and a
register of particulars of wholesale deliveries to each purchaser: reg 25(3) 3(b)B. Each
purchaser must maintain a wholesale register of the producers who have given details of that
purchaser in the wholesale register maintained by the Minister under reg 25(3) 3(b)B. The
purchaser's register must also contain details of wholesale deliveries: reg 27(1) 'purchaser
special quota' is the quantity of dairy produce which may be delivered by wholesale deliveries
against producers' special quotas to a purchaser, from holdings in the region, during the
quota year without that purchaser being liable to pay levy; reg 2(1) (definition added by
SI 1990/132).
11 *Ibid* reg 2(1). And see EC Council Regulation 857/84, art 12 (D). In relation to any region,
'holding' is the division of the holding in the region: Dairy Produce Quotas Regulations
1989, reg 21. In this context 'quota' refers to direct sales quota or to wholesale quota but not
purchaser quota; see reg 2(1).
12 See above p 16 ff, s 1(1) Agricultural Holdings Act 1986.

to a purchaser.[13] It follows that registration is open not only to individuals but also to farming companies and partnerships.[14]

Whenever an undertaking is sold, leased, or transferred by inheritance, all or part of the corresponding reference quantity must be transferred to the purchaser, tenant or heir (whichever applies), according to procedures which are to be laid down by individual member states.[15] Accordingly, the Dairy Produce Quotas Regulations 1989 make provision for an apportionment of quota to be made whenever a relevant transfer of part of a 'holding' takes place.[16] In default of agreement, apportionment is made by way of arbitration.[17] Where no transfer has yet taken place, a prospective apportionment of quota may also be made.[18] In the latter case, notice must be given to the Minister identifying the part of the holding to which the prospective apportionment is to relate, and requesting an apportionment either according to the areas used for milk production at the date of the statement or by way of arbitration.[19] A prospective apportionment can be revoked by notice in writing to the Minister, accompanied by a consent or sole interest notice in respect of that holding.[20] Where a prospective apportionment is made it must be recorded in a record maintained by the Minister[1] and will govern any change of occupation of the relevant parts of the holding which takes place in the following six months.[2] The facility of prospective apportionment is of utility, especially, where a change of occupation is in prospect but has not yet taken place.

4. Transfer of quota and re-registration

The relevant EEC legislation requiring apportionment of quota following a sale, lease or inheritance of part (or all) of an undertaking is implemented by regulation 9 of the Dairy Produce Quota Regulations 1989.[3] It is there

13 See EC Council Regulation 857/84, art 12(C), Dairy Produce Quotas Regulations 1989, reg 2(1).
14 See, eg *R v Dairy Produce Quota Tribunal for England and Wales ex p Atkinson* (1985) 276 Estates Gazette 1158. It was here held that farmers who were part of a partnership, the main occupation of which was dairy farming, were arguably each a producer within the meaning of the Dairy Produce Quota Regulations 1984.
15 EC Council Regulations 857/84, art 7.
16 Dairy Produce Quotas Regulations 1989, regs 10, 10A (reg 10 amended and reg 10A added by SI 1990/132).
17 Arbitration is to be conducted in accordance with the Dairy Produce Quotas Regulations 1989 regs 9 to 12, Sch 4 (England and Wales), Sch 5 (Scotland) and Sch 6 (Northern Ireland): reg 10(B).
18 See the Dairy Produce Quotas Regulations 1989 reg 11.
19 *Ibid*, reg 11 1(A), (C) the statement submitted to the Minister must contain certain information relating to the holding as the Minister may reasonably require; reg 11(1)(B).
20 *Ibid*, reg 11(3).
1 *Ibid*, reg 11(5).
2 *Ibid*, reg 11(4)(I). If there is a change of occupation and there is no prospective apportionment, but a prospective apportionment is in the process of being made, then the apportionment of quota must be carried out in accordance with the prospective apportionment which is being made: reg 11(4)(II). It is suggested that in this event, the process of making a prospective apportionment would have to have been commenced in the six months preceding the change of occupation. Where there is a change of occupation but no prospective apportionment has been made, or is in the process of being made, the apportionment of quota is carried out in accordance with reg 9: see reg 11(4)(iii).
3 See the Dairy Produce Quotas Regulations 1989, SI 1989/380, reg 9.

provided that, whenever there is a transfer of any holding, or part of a holding, then within two months of a change of occupation pursuant to such transfer taking place, the prescribed form and such other evidence of transfer as may be required must be submitted to the Minister.[4] Special quota is exempt from the transfer rules and is separately dealt with (see below).[5]

Where a transfer of a holding (or part) in any quota year has not been notified to the Minister by the date determined by the latter in the following quota year, then the Minister is empowered to decide, for the purposes of any levy calculation, that the unused quota transferred with such a transfer is to be treated not as part of the transferee's entitlement for the year in which the transfer took place, but as unused quota available for reallocation. The transferee is not entitled in this event to demand an amendment to the amount of quota so reallocated to him.[6]

If the entirety of a holding is transferred, it is to be presumed that the transferee intends to deliver dairy produce from the holding by wholesale delivery to the purchasers named, and in the proportions listed, in the transferee's entry in the wholesale register.[7] The transferee will be registered accordingly. Where *part* of a holding is transferred, however, an apportionment of quota has to be carried out.[8] Dairy produce sold or delivered from the holding will, in the latter event, be deemed (for the purposes of the levy) to have been sold or delivered from each part of the holding proportionately in accordance with that apportionment.[9]

(a)   Transfer of quota: general principles

Any transaction which involves both (1) the 'transfer' and (2) a 'change in occupation' of a holding, or part, will require a re-registration of quota *unless* the transfer is one of a limited category excluded from the operation of the transfer rules by regulation 9(7) of the Dairy Produce Quotas Regulations 1989.[10] For a transfer and re-registration of quota to be effected, therefore, two conditions must be satisfied: there must be a 'transfer' of a holding or part, and as a consequence there must also be a 'change of occupation'. It should be noted, however, that neither a 'transfer' nor 'change of occupation' are defined with precision in the Regulations. The latter define the 'transferor' and 'transferee' of milk quota as, respectively, the person replaced, and the person becoming, the 'occupier' of a holding or part. The 'occupier' of a holding is in turn defined as including the person entitled to grant occupation of that land to another person.[11] It would seem to follow, therefore, that a

---

4 *Ibid*, reg 9(9), (1).

5 The transfer provisions described here do not apply to special quotas: *ibid* reg 9(8) (added by SI 1990/132). For the rules applicable to special quota see below p 320 ff).

6 *Ibid*, reg 9(2). Any decision made by the Minister, and any date determined by him under this provision, must be announced in the relevant Gazette and in the Farming Press at least two months before that date or where such publication is not possible, by such other means of publication as the Minister considers likely to come to the attention of producers: reg 9(3) *ibid* reg 9(4) *ibid* reg 9(5)(a). A prospective apportionment can be made: reg 9(6).

7 *Ibid*, reg 9(4).

8 *Ibid*, reg 9(5)(a).

9 *Ibid*, reg 9(5)(b).

10 This provision does not apply to special quotas – see below p 320 ff. For the exempt categories of transaction see below p 315 ff.

11 Dairy Produce Quotas Regulations 1989, SI 1989/380, reg 2(1).

'transfer' requiring adjustment of quota must be limited to a transaction involving the creation of, or a dealing in, an estate in the land concerned, eg the freehold sale of part of a holding or the grant of a tenancy. This implication is supported by reference to regulation 9(7) itself, which excludes from the operation of the transfer provisions any *licence* to occupy the land.[12]

(b) Transactions not carrying quota

The provisions requiring re-registration of quota following a transfer and change of occupation (above), do *not* apply to the following categories of transaction, specified in regulation 9(7) of the 1989 Regulations:[13]

(1) A licence to occupy land.[14] This exception is of limited significance. For re-registration to be applicable in the first place, there must be a change of occupation, which latter connotes the grant of a right of exclusive occupation to the transferee. As a consequence of the decision in *Street v Mountford*,[15] however, an agreement which confers exclusive possession for a term will, with limited exceptions, be construed as a tenancy and not a licence. Furthermore, a licence conferring exclusive possession of agricultural land will be converted under the terms of the Agricultural Holdings Act 1986[16] into an annual tenancy with security of tenure. The exemption for licences not carrying quota in the Dairy Produce Regulations 1989 would thus appear to be limited to licences *stricto sensu* of a non-exclusive nature, and exclusive licences granted in special circumstances where there is no intention to create legal relations, eg between family members.[17] It would seem, also, that no apportionment to quota would be required where a licence to occupy land is entirely gratuitous, as the Agricultural Holdings Act 1986 only operates to convert into a tenancy those licences which are granted for valuable consideration.[18] *Quaere* in any event, where there is no right to exclusive occupation vested in the transferee under a non-exclusive licence, there may be no 'change of occupation' as required by Regulation 9 of the 1989 Regulations, triggering a possible transfer of quota.

(2) The tenancy of any land under which a holding (or part) is occupied for a period of less than ten months.

(3) The lease of any land under which a holding (or part) in Scotland is occupied for less than eight months

(4) The tenancy of any land under which a holding (or part) in Northern Ireland is occupied for a period of less than 12 months and

(5) The *termination* of a tenancy or lease to which head (2), (3) or (4) above applies.

12 *Ibid*, reg 9(7)(a).
13 See *ibid* reg 9(7)(a)–(e) as amended, for the exceptions outlined here.
14 *Ibid*, reg 9(7)(a). This provision does not apply to special quotas.
15 [1985] AC 809 (HL).
16 See Agricultural Holdings Act 1986, section 2(1), section 2(2)(b).
17 See *Errington v Errington and Woods* [1952] 1 KB 290, CA 57.
18 *Goldsack v Shore* [1950] 1 KB 708 and also, as to the requirement of exclusivity, *Harrison – Broadly v Smith* [964] 1 All ER 867 and *Bahamas International Trust Co Ltd v Threadgold* [1974] 3 All ER 881. And see Chapter 2 p 27 ff above.

Prior to the introduction of the Dairy Produce Quotas Regulations 1989, a further exemption excluded from the transfer rules a 'minor change in occupation' of land used for dairy production. This exemption no longer applies and any non-exempt change of occupation of a holding must be notified to the Minister, whatever the area of land transferred.[19]

(c)   Transactions requiring transfer of quota

Transactions which are not within the limitations set out above will require an apportionment and re-registration of quota in the name of the transferee. Short-term arrangements, such as grazing agreements and *Gladstone and Bower* lets, are commonly used to effect transfers of quota. Whichever mode of transfer is utilised, the land must not be used by the purchaser of quota for the purpose of milk production during the period of the letting if the land is to revert to the vendor *without* quota at the end of the agreed period. To this end a clause is commonly inserted in the contract of sale and letting agreement, prohibiting the use of the land for any purpose connected with dairy production during the period of the letting. A question may arise as to the unlawful user of transferred land for dairy production in breach of contract. It is suggested that, in directing an arbitrator to apportion quota by reference to 'areas used for milk production' in the five years preceding the change of occupation (as to which see below), the 1989 Regulations require lawful user for dairy production. In any event, a producer so acting would prejudice his position and lose quota on reverter of the land to the grantor, as a transfer and re-registation would under regulation 9 be triggered on reversion of the land to the original grantor. It may also be important, when considering granting temporary occupation rights over land, to avoid an unwanted call on quota. To this end the apportionment rules in Schedule 4 of the Dairy Produce Quota Regulations 1989 (discussed below)[20] should be borne in mind, unless an exempt form of transfer is used. A change of occupation pursuant to any of the forms of transfer below may lead to a call on quota if the land transferred (or part) has been used for dairy production at any time during the previous five years.

The categories of transaction requiring a transfer of quota include the following:

(1)   All lettings protected under the Agricultural Holdings Act 1986. This will include, for instance, any licence conferring exclusive possession which is converted by section 2 of that Act into a protected tenancy, as also a grazing let which is outside the ambit of the proviso to section 2, eg because it is not limited to a period of less than one year. Transactions of this kind will not only require a transfer of quota, but will also confer full security of tenure on the purchaser.

(2)   Lettings for more than one year and less than two (ie *Gladstone v*

---

19   For the rule as to minor changes in occupation, formerly applicable, see Dairy Produce Quotas Regulations 1986, SI 1986/470, reg 8(5). This provision formerly exempted from the transfer rules any transfer involving a minor change of occupation of part of a holding where the area, occupation of which changed, was less than one quarter of the area of the remainder of the holding (and also no larger than five hectares). This exemption only applied, furthermore, if the interest of the occupier coming into possession was a tenancy or licence for a duration of less than one year.

20   See p 317 ff below.

Bower agreements)[1] will require a transfer of quota, albeit they confer no security of tenure upon the purchaser. The rules introduced by the Dairy Produce Quotas Regulations 1989 effected a restriction on the use of grazing agreements for quota transfer (see below), and so *Gladstone v Bower* agreements may now provide a more attractive vehicle for quota transfer. They certainly offer the safest avenue for transferring quota without creating a protected tenancy.

(3) A fixed-term tenancy for two years or more, protected by section 3 of the Agricultural Holdings Act 1986, *will* require a transfer of quota. Security of tenure will also be conferred at the end of the agreed term, pursuant to the 1986 Act.[2]

(4) Short-term arrangements with Ministry consent, whether under section 2 or section 5 of the 1986 Act,[3] will involve a transfer of quota. However, security of tenure will be excluded by virtue of the Ministry consent. Ministry consent will not be obtainable for the purpose of tranferring quota *per se*. The main import of this type of arrangement, therefore, is that when applying for Ministry consent for a short-term arrangement, eg a trial tenancy, care must be taken to ensure that land used for dairy production is not included in the proposed letting. If it is there may be an unwanted call on quota. In the case of a short-term letting with Ministry consent under section 2[4] it should also be noted that a *licence* will not transfer quota under the new rules, and a tenancy with Ministry consent will only do so if the period of let is for more than ten months. A letting will also have to be for less than one year in order to obtain consent.

(5) Grazing and/or mowing agreement for a specified period of the year which is not less than the minimum period laid down in the 1989 Regulations (ie not less than ten consecutive months or a grazing season) will carry quota. Grazing lets have hitherto been a common mode for transferring milk quota. It should be noted that the let must be for less than 365 days to avoid the creation of a secure tenancy, and for more than ten consecutive months to carry quota. Greater care is now required, therefore, when using grazing agreements to transfer quota.

(d) Sham transactions; dangers

The 1989 Regulations, it should be noted, require a 'change of occupation' of land in order to effect a transfer of quota. A transaction purportedly transferring quota may be 'sham' in either or both of two senses:

(i) *Amount of quota transferred.* The quota purportedly transferred must not be disproportionate to the area of land involved. Ministry guidance indicates that the Agriculture Departments will ensure that unduly large amounts of quota are not transferred with small parcels of land. Official guidance indicates that the Ministry will

---

1 See *Gladstone v Bower* [1960] 2 QB 384 and further, p 37 ff above.
2 See sections 3 and 5 Agricultural Holdings Act 1986, and further chapter 2 p 34 ff above.
3 As to Ministry consent, and the grounds on which it is available, see chapter 2 p 34 ff above.
4 See p 35 above.

not in general look at transfers of less than 20,000 litres per hectare. It should be noted, also, that the area to be grazed by the purchaser must generally be enough to support the number of dairy cows whose average output is enough to produce the quota being sold.[5]

(ii)   *Nature of transaction.* Where a grazing agreement is used as a vehicle to transfer quota, the creation of a secure tenancy within the Agricultural Holdings Act 1986 will only be avoided if the conditions for the grant of a bona fide grazing let are adhered to. There is in some cases a danger that one may not only transfer quota, but also confer security of tenure upon the transferee, *viz* if the transaction is 'sham' in the sense that it is not within the grazing let proviso to section 2(3) of the 1986 Act. To this end there must be a genuine intention, at the time of letting, that the transferee is to graze the land for a specified period of less than one year. Moreover, to transfer quota this must also be for at least ten months or a grazing season, pursuant to Regulation 9(7) of the 1989 Regulations. The latter prevent short 'artificial' grazing agreements being used to transfer quota. To avoid any implication of 'sham' the vendor should not keep stock on the land (unless, possibly, under a contractor arrangement with the occupier). It is also advisable that the purchaser graze the land concerned. Both the relevant Community legislation and the Dairy Produce Quotas Regulations 1989 are unclear as to the extent to which the transferee needs to *exercise* his rights over the land transferred to him. Ministry guidance, however, indicates that the transferee should have, at the very least, an exclusive right of occupation.[6] Where no *de facto* change of occupation has taken place, it is likely that the Ministry will require a full explanation of the circumstances surrounding the transaction. The more clearly it can be shown that the transferee has exercised his rights over the land acquired, the easier it will be to justify the transfer of quota claimed. *Sed quaere*; in the case of a grazing agreement it may also be possible to claim there was no bona fide grazing let, where no grazing rights are subsequently exercised by the purchaser, the implication being that there was no intention at the time of contract to graze the land for a fixed period of the year.

(iii)   Increased surveillance by the Ministry is intended to secure that quota transfers take place in accordance with the European and domestic transfer rules, ie to ensure that a genuine transaction involving an appropriate area of land has actually taken place. Ministry guidance indicates that this will normally be satisfied if a copy of the lease or other agreement can be produced, or, if there is none, that there has been an actual change of occupation of the land concerned. The Ministry have, further, indicated that where quota is transferred on the basis of a temporary transfer of land, it will be important to demonstrate positively a *change of use* away from dairying during the life of the lease, if a further apportionment of quota is to be avoided when it expires.[7]

5 'Changes in the rules for milk quota transfers' (Ministry of Agriculture Fisheries and Food, March, 1988), para 8.
6 'Changes in the rules for milk quota transfers' (*ibid*) para 9.
7 *Ibid*, para 11.

5. Apportionment of quota on transfer

Following transfer, apportionment may be carried out either by agreement or by arbitration.[8] If the parties agree the apportionment of quota they must, within two months of the relevant change of occupation, submit to the Ministry (i) a duly completed prescribed form recording the transfer, together with (ii) a signed statement that they have agreed that quota shall be apportioned according to specified areas used for milk production, and (iii) a consent or sole interest notice provided by the transferor or his personal representatives in respect of the entirety of the holding. If this is done the Minister must make the apportionment in accordance with that agreement.[9] In all other cases, apportionment must be carried out by arbitration.[10] An arbitrator may be appointed by agreement within the two months following the change of occupation. Alternatively, either party may apply within that period to the President of the Royal Institution of Chartered Surveyors for an appointment. In default of application or agreement within the time allowed, the Minister must make an application for an arbitrator to be appointed.[11]

Once an arbitrator has been appointed the matter will proceed along similar lines to an arbitration under the Agricultural Holdings Act 1986.[12] Thus, the parties have thirty-five days from the appointment in which to submit their statement of case to the arbitrator, and the award must be made within 56 days of appointment.[13] As is the case in arbitrations between landlord and tenant, references on points of law may be made to the County Court by case stated, and the Court has power to set aside an award where the arbitrator is guilty of misconduct, or where there is an error of law on the face of the award.[14] One major difference, however, is that in an arbitration under the 1989 Regulations, any person having an interest in a holding to which the arbitration relates is entitled to make representations to the arbitrator.[15] Appearance is not limited to landlord and tenant; indeed the 'holding' in this context will often comprise both freehold and tenanted land.

6. Basis of apportionment

The arbitrator must base his award on findings made by him as to areas used for milk production in the five years preceding the change of occupation (or in the case of prospective apportionment in the five years preceding the

---

8 Dairy Produce Quota Regulations 1989, reg 9(5)(A). This provides that apportionment is to be conducted in accordance with reg 10. This provision does not apply to special quotas.
9 *Ibid*, reg 10A (amended by SI 1990/1321).
10 *Ibid*, reg 10B. Arbitration is carried out in accordance with Sch 4, *ibid*.
11 *Ibid*, Sch 4, paras 1(1)–(3). The Minister must also apply to the President to appoint an arbitrator where he is given notice under reg 12, to the effect that he has reasonable grounds for believing that areas used for milk production are not as specified in the statements of agreed apportionment submitted by the parties. In this event an apportionment or prospective apportionment must be carried out (see *ibid* reg 12) (amended by SI 1990/132).
12 See chapter 16, p 358 ff.
13 Dairy Produce Quota Regulations 1989, SI 1989/380, Sch 4, paras 13 to 91. For the detailed rules as to conduct of milk quota arbitrations see Sch 4, *ibid* paras 13 to 20.
14 *Ibid*, Sch 4, paras 28 and 29. If there is an error of law on the face of the award the Court may also vary the award: Sch 4, para 30(2).
15 *Ibid*, reg 15.

arbitrator's appointment).[16] The definition of 'areas used for milk production' is central to an understanding of the law of milk quotas, for it is to this land only that quota attaches. In *Puncknowle Farms Ltd v Kane*,[17] decided under the Dairy Produce Quotas Regulations 1984, this phrase was given a wide meaning. It was there held that areas used for 'milk production' include not only areas used from week to week to support the dairy herd, but also 'areas which are used to support the dairy herd by the maintenance of animals between one lactation and another, and to support the animals which are destined for inclusion in the dairy herd on any holding'.[18] The following will therefore be included:

(a)   buildings and yards of a dairy unit
(b)   land used for dairy or dual purpose animals if bred for the herd and not resale
(c)   land used for dry cows between lactations and
(d)   land used for heifers if they are necessary for continuance of the herd, and also land used to produce forage.

A transfer of land used at any time, within the prior five years, for dairy production in this wide sense, could therefore necessitate a re-registration of quota. Similarly, it should be noted that as the apportionment is based on the user of land over the five-year period prior to transfer, it is possible for a producer to 'move' quota from one part of a holding to another by re-arranging the balance of his farming activities over a period of time. This may give rise to problems of estate management if the 'holding' (in the EEC law sense) comprises both tenanted and freehold land owned by the tenant.[19]

7.   Juridical nature of dairy quota

As a result of the operation of the transfer and apportionment provisions described above, quota can only be transferred by means of a transfer of land used for milk production. Quota therefore attaches to land, but in a peculiar way. Quota attaches not to land *per se*, but rather to a producer's 'holding'; and within that holding only to areas used for milk production. In this it differs from quota imposed under a domestic marketing scheme, eg potato quota within the potato marketing scheme.[20] Nevertheless, milk quota is not an interest in land and cannot be equated with an incorporeal hereditament, though it may have similarities. It cannot, for instance, lie in

16 *Ibid*, Sch 4, para 3.
17 [1985] 3 All ER 79.
18 [1985] 3 All ER 79, esp at 94.
19 The tenant/producer could concentrate dairy activities on freehold land, over a period of years, thus removing any claim for quota from the tenanted portion of the holding. Unless the lease of the latter contained special covenants dealing with milk, there is little a landlord can do to prevent this. A covenant against assignment or subletting will prevent a transfer of quota, in that it will prevent a change of occupation within reg 9 (above) taking place, but it will not prevent a change in the identity of the tenant's land within the EEC holding to which quota attaches by reason of the balance of his activities having changed over a period of time. Quota covenants are discussed above, Ch 3 pp 65–6.
20 See p 336 ff below. Also *Lee v Heaton* [1987] 2 EGLR 12 (covenant affecting basic quota under marketing scheme not applicable to milk quota registered under the Dairy Produce Quotas Regulations).

grant in the required sense. Neither is it 'land' or an 'interest in land' within the meaning of section 205 of the Law of Property Act 1925. It cannot, therefore, be assimilated within the existing categories of interest in land recognised in English law. It is, rather, in the nature of a permissive right to produce dairy products without financial penalty, up to a stated maximum reflected in the quota registered for each producer's holding. Its peculiarities as a quasi-property right arise largely as a by-product of the rules governing transfer of quota.

8.   Exchange, management and temporary re-allocation of quota

Except in relation to special quota,[1] any person in a quota region may exchange direct sales quota for wholesale quota with any other person with a holding in the same region, on such terms as the producers and Minister may agree,[2] having regard to the provisions of the relevant EEC legislation.[3] A producer may, furthermore, make a transfer within one region of *part* of the wholesale quota registered as his to another producer for a period of one quota year, but not to a producer who makes deliveries to a different purchaser.[4] Where there is a temporary transfer of quota the transferee must, before 31st July in the quota year in question, give notification to the Ministry of the agreement and of such particulars as the Minister may reasonably require.[5] For the purposes of operating formula B, under which levy is administered in the United Kingdom,[6] the Minister may in any quota year award to certain categories of producer a temporary re-allocation of unused quota, from the purchaser quota of purchasers to whom that producer makes wholesale deliveries of dairy produce.[7] This facility applies to three categories of producer:

(i)   those who have received an award of quota which has been mistakenly entered in the register maintained by the Minister as an amount of quota more than one hundred litres in excess of the amount of the award or allocation,

(ii)   those who have quota registered in relation to a holding which is in whole or part subject to a notice prohibiting or regulating the movement of dairy cows[8], and

---

1 For special quota see below p 322 ff.
2 Ie in relation to England and Wales alone, the Minister of Agriculture Fisheries and Food and the Secretary of State for Wales acting jointly. In relation to Scotland alone, the Secretary of State for Scotland and in relation to Northern Ireland the Department of Agriculture for Northern Ireland. In relation to the United Kingdom as a whole, the 'Minister' means these Ministers acting jointly: Dairy Produce Quotas Regulations 1989, reg 2(1), (3).
3 Dairy Produce Quota Regulations 1989, SI 1989/302 reg 14 (amended by SI 1990/132). The relevant community provisions are EC Commission Regulation 1546/88 art 5(5), (6) (OJ L139. 4.6.88 p 12).
4 *Ibid*, reg 15(1) (amended by SI 1990/132).
5 *Ibid*, reg 15(2).
6 As to which see above pp 307–8.
7 Dairy Produce Quotas Regulations 1989, reg 16(1).
8 Ie a notice pursuant to an order under the Animal Health Act 1981 or the Diseases of Animals (Northern Ireland) Order 1981, SI 1981/1115.

(iii)   those who have quota registered in relation to a holding which is situated wholly or partly within an area which at any time during that quota year has been designated by an emergency order.[9]

The quota in each case must be calculated in accordance with statutory provisions and will be subject to certain specified conditions.[10]

In making an award or a temporary re-allocation of unused quota the Minister must give priority to producers falling within head (i) above, then to those falling within head (ii) *ibid*, and finally to those falling within head (iii).[11]

A producer may apply to have such of his direct sales quota or wholesale quota, as the case may be, which is unused in a given quota year converted into wholeale or direct sales quota.[12] An application must be submitted to the Minister by a date determined by him in respect of the quota year in question.[13] The Minister must calculate the amount of unused quota which the applicant has available for conversion.[14] He must then:

(i)   in each purchaser area convert into wholesale quota so much of the unused direct sales quota as will not exceed the amount by which wholesale deliveries to that purchaser exceed the wholesale quota of that purchaser[15] or

(ii)   convert into direct sales quota so much of the unused wholesale quota as will not exceed the amount by which the aggregate direct sales of direct sellers exceed the aggregate direct sales quota.[16]

The conversion of direct sales quota into wholesale quota is effected by taking the quota and adding it to the national direct sales reserve. An equivalent quantity is then transferred from that reserve to the appropriate running regional wholesale reserve, and allocated from that reserve to the applicant's wholesale quota.[17] The conversion of wholesale quota into direct sales quota is achieved by a reverse procedure.[18]

9.   Special quota

Provision was made by the Dairy Produce Quotas (Amendment) Regulations 1990[19] for the implementation in the United Kingdom of council regulation (EEC) No 764/89. The latter enabled qualifying producers who participated in the Non-Marketing of Milk or Dairy Herd Conversion schemes to apply for the allocation of special quota. If special quota is allocated under these provisions, the additional regional wholesale quota so

9 Dairy Produce Quota Regulations 1989, reg 16(2) (amended by SI 1990/664).
10 *Ibid*, regs 16(3) to (8). The method of calculation in relation to producers falling within head (1) is specified in reg 16(3).
11 *Ibid*, reg 16(8) (amended by SI 1990/664).
12 *Ibid*, reg 18, Sch 7. The relevant Community provision is EC Council Regulation 857/84 art 6A (OJ L90, 1.4.84 p 13).
13 Dairy Produce Quotas Regulations 1989, Sch 7, para 1.
14 *Ibid*, Sch 7, para 3.
15 *Ibid*, Sch 7, para 4.
16 *Ibid*, Sch 7, para 5.
17 *Ibid*, Sch 7, para 61.
18 *Ibid*, Sch 7, para 62.
19 See the Dairy Produce Quotas (Amendment) Regulations 1990, SI 1990/132.

allocated (in the form of special quota) does not create or add to the running regional wholesale reserve for that region.[20] The transfer rules (above)[1] are excluded, and upon a transfer of the holding the special quota must be returned to the Community reserve. If part of a holding is sold or leased by the producer, a proportion of that special quota must be returned to the Community reserve.[2] A return of quota to Community reserve does not take place, however, where the holding (or part) is transferred pursuant to a *licence* to occupy land, or to a tenancy under which it is occupied for a period of less than ten months.[3] It is further provided that no part of a special quota is to be returned where a holding (or part) is transferred:

(1)   on inheritance.
(2)   By gift for which no consideration is given.
(3)   By the grant of a tenancy to a successor on death or retirement of a previous tenant under the Agricultural Holdings Act 1986.
(4)   By the grant, to a qualifying successor, of a succession tenancy under section 39 or 45(6) Agricultural Holdings Act 1986, or the grant of a tenancy (following a direction under section 39 of the 1986 Act for the grant of a tenancy to a successor on death) in circumstances where the new tenancy has been granted by agreement to the person entitled to a new tenancy under that direction.
(5)   By the agreed grant of a tenancy to close relatives who would otherwise qualify for succession rights.
(6)   By the grant of a tenancy, in other circumstances, to a successor of a tenant who has died or retired.

In each case the exemption from retransfer to Community reserve is conditional upon the transferee undertaking to comply with the undertakings of his predecessor under the relevant community legislation.[4]

Where a producer has special quota and intends to transfer the whole or part of his holding he must, prior to transfer, submit to the Minister the form prescribed for the purpose, and such other evidence relating to the proposed transfer as the Minister may reasonably require.[5] Where an exempt transfer[6] of a holding or part takes place, further, the transferee must submit to the Minister a duly completed form prescribed for this purpose and such other evidence relating to the proposed transfer as the Minister may reasonably require.[7] Where an exempt transfer of part of a holding occurs, it will be

---

20 Dairy Produce Quota Regulations 1989, reg 7(2A) (added by SI 1990/132).
1 *Ibid*, reg 9 (8), (9) (added by SI 1990/132).
2 *Ibid*, reg 9A (1) (as added). The proportion of the special quota to be returned to the Community reserve must be the same proportion which the agricultural area of the holding sold or leased bears to the total agricultural area farmed by the producer: reg 9A (2).
3 *Ibid*, reg 9A(3)(a), (b). (England and Wales only). Special rules apply to Scotland and Northern Ireland.
4 *Ibid*, reg 9B. The relevant Community provision is EC Council Regulation 857/84, art 3a (OJ L90, 1.4.84 p 13).
5 *Ibid*, reg 9C(1) (as added).
6 Ie a transfer under *ibid* reg 9B, described above.
7 *Ibid*, reg 9C(2) *quaere* where the requirement of documentation is imposed in relation to a transfer under reg 9B which has already taken place, or to the proposed subsequent transfer by a person who is a transferee under that regulation; contrast the wording of reg 9C(1) and (2) respectively.

necessary to apportion special quota in the usual manner. Apportionment of the special quota relating to that part of the holding will be by arbitration, unless within two months of transfer the transferee submits, in duly completed prescribed form, (i) a statement by both parties that they have agreed the apportionment of special quota according to areas used for milk production, and (ii) a consent of sole interest notice.[8] Where the Minister has reasonable grounds to believe that the areas used for milk production will not be as specified in the submitted documentation, or are not as agreed between the parties at the time of apportionment, he must give written notice of that fact to the person who made the statement or (in other cases) to the transferee, and an apportionment by arbitation must then be carried out.[9]

Special quota is also exempted from the rules relating to quota exchange.[10] Special entries in the quota register are required for special quota in addition to its inclusion in the entries for total wholesale quota and total direct sales quota.[11]

10. Payment of levy

In general terms, the levy payable by producers in respect of dairy produce quotas is calculated by reference to the quota allocated to the producer in respect of wholesale and direct sales, to the actual amount of sales made by that producer, and to the relevant community legislation.[12] Levy is payable by the producer if the amount of sales (whether direct or wholesale) exceeds the quota allocated to him in the relevant quota year,[13] and by a purchaser if the quantity of dairy produce delivered to him by wholesale delivery from holdings in the region exceeds the quota allocated to him in a quota year.[14] Levy must be paid within four months of the end of the quota year to which it relates and is recoverable by the Intervention Board for Agricultural Produce.[15]

Where in any quota year a producer makes sales or deliveries of milk or milk products from milk from any cows, and subsequently another producer makes sales or deliveries of milk or other milk products from milk from the same cows, the second producer is deemed to have acted in the capacity of agent for the first producer.[16] This does not apply, however, where the first producer has entered into an agreement for the sale or lease of the cows in

---

8 *Ibid*, reg 10A (as added). Arbitration is carried out under Sch 4 (as to which see p 317 ff above).

9 *Ibid*, reg 10 (amended by SI 1990/132).

10 *Ibid*, reg 14 (as amended).

11 *Ibid*, reg 25 (as amended).

12 *Ibid*, reg 19, Sch 8. The relevant Community provisions are EC Commission Regulation 1546/88 arts 12, 15, 16 (OJ L139 4.6.88 p 12), EC Council Regulation 857/84 arts 1, 4a, 9 (OJ L90 1.4.84 p 13) and EC Council Regulation 804/68 art 5c (OJ L148, 27.6.68 p 13).

13 See the Dairy Produce Quotas Regs 1989, SI 1989/380, reg 2(1) definitions of 'direct sales quota', 'wholesale quota' and 'total wholesale quota'.

14 See *ibid*, reg 21, definition of 'purchaser quota'.

15 *Ibid*, reg 20.

16 *Ibid*, reg 19a(1) (added by SI 1990/132). It follows that as the first producer's agent, the second producer will not be liable to the payment of levy on sales and/or deliveries made by him while he was deemed to have been acting in that capacity.

question, or the second producer has inherited them from the first producer, and the cows are kept on the second producer's holding.[17]

B   Landlord and tenant: compensation for dairy quota

1.   Principles of compensation

Registered quota has a tangible value, in that a holding with registered dairy quota will have a higher value (freehold or rental) than if no quota were present. Section 13 and Schedule I to the Agriculture Act 1986 introduced provisions intended to compensate the tenant of an agricultural holding for the increased value accruing to the land as a result of the presence of registered quota on a holding. The compensation provisions of the 1986 Act are based upon the principle of betterment and enhancement, ie that the tenant should be entitled to a proportion of the value of the quota allocated to the holding on the introduction of dairy quotas in 1984, such proportion to reflect his contribution to the allocation of quota measured by reference to a tenant's dairy improvements to the holding, and any associated increase in rental value.[18]

The tenant's entitlement to compensation is set out in Schedule I, para 1 of the 1986 Act. This provides that where, on the termination of the tenancy of any land, the tenant has milk quota *registered as his* in relation to a holding, then he should be entitled on quitting to obtain from the landlord a payment in compensation:

(a)   if the tenant had milk quota allocated to him, in respect of so much of the 'relevant quota'[19] as consists of allocated quota; and

(b)   if the tenant had milk quota allocated to him, or was in occupation of the land as a tenant on 2nd April 1984, in respect of so much of the 'relevant quota' as consists of quota transferred to him by virtue of a transaction, the cost of which was borne wholly or partly by him.

The provisions are intended to reward a tenant who had milk quota allocated on the 2nd April 1984 by giving him a proportion of that quota (the 'tenant's fraction') to reflect his contribution to the award of quota. In addition the tenant will receive the full value of transferred quota, ie quota he has purchased or acquired for valuable consideration. He will also receive, in compensation, the value of any excess quota *over and above* the level of quota which is deemed to be standard for the particular holding.[20] Schedule 1 to the 1986 Act attempts to achieve these relatively straightforward aims in a series of highly technical provisions.

---

17   See, *ibid*, reg 19A(2) (as added).
18   Parl. deb. (HC) vol 95, col 1047 ff and 1076. For a specialist work on milk quota compensation, with worked examples, see 'A Handbook of Milk Quota Compensation' by Woods, Priday, Moss and Carter (Farmgate Communications Ltd, 1987). The relevance of registered quota on rent review is considered separately, Ch 5 p 96 ff above.
19   For relevant quota see p 325 ff below.
20   For standard quota see p 325 ff below.

2.   The compensation provisions

(a)   Definitions for compensation purposes

The following definitions are central to an understanding of the detailed compensation provisions:

'Holding': this is defined by reference to the European provisions and means, not the agricultural holding itself (ie the land tenanted by the claimant) but all the production units used for dairy production in the occupation of the registered dairy producer. The tenant may have freehold land in addition to the land which is the subject of the compensation claim, in which event the EEC holding will be larger than the agricultural holding as defined by the Agricultural Holdings Act 1986. In this situation it will be necessary, in the first instance, for an apportionment of quota to be made between the agricultural holding (in respect of which the compensation claim is made) and the remainder of the EEC holding, ie the freehold land owned by the tenant or subject to tenancies with other landlords. This apportionment will be carried out under the provisions of the Dairy Produce Quotas Regulations 1989.[1]

'Relevant quota': Relevant quota means, (i) in a case where the holding consists *only* of the land subject to the tenancy, the milk quota registered in relation to the holding, and (ii) in any other case, such part of that milk quota as falls to be apportioned to that land on the termination of the tenancy. It is in relation to 'relevant quota' that compensation can be claimed.[2]

'Transferred quota': This means milk quota transferred to the tenant by virtue of the transfer to him of the whole or part of a holding.[3]

'Standard quota': Standard quota is ascertained by multiplying the relevant number of hectares by the prescribed quota per hectare. For this purpose a prescribed quota per hectare, based on the average yield per hectare of various classifications of land, is laid down by statutory instrument.[4] The relevant number of hectares, by which the prescribed quota must be multiplied, means the average number of hectares of the land in question used during the relevant period for the feeding of dairy cows kept on the land. Alternatively, it means the average number of hectares of the land that could reasonably be expected to have been so used (having regard to the number of grazed animals other than dairy cows kept on the land during that period).[5]

There is provision whereby if the relevant quota includes milk quota allocated pursuant to an award by the Dairy Produce Quota Tribunal, and the award has not been allocated in full, the standard quota for the land is to be reduced by the amount by which the milk quota allocated falls short of the amount awarded.[6] Note that for the purpose of calculating 'standard quota' it is the land used for *feeding* dairy cows which is relevant and not 'land used

1 See above p 317.
2 Agriculture Act 1986, Sch 1, para 2(a) and (b). See generally *ibid* Sch 1, para 2.
3 See Sch 1 pra 1(2) *ibid*.
4 The relevant regulations are the Milk Quota (Calculation of Standard Quota) Regulations 1986, SI 1986/1530, as amended by the Milk Quota (Calculation of Standard Quota) (Amendment) Order 1990, SI 1990/48.
5 Agriculture Act 1986, Sch 1, para 6(1) and (2).
6 *Ibid*, Sch 1, para 6(3).

for dairy production', the relevant concept for the purpose of apportioning quota under the Dairy Produce Quotas Regulations 1989.[7]

'Allocated quota': This is milk quota allocated to the tenant in relation to land comprised in the holding. In the majority of cases primary quota will have been allocated on 2nd April 1984 based upon levels of production during 1983 (for wholesale quota). In addition the tenant may have had secondary quota allocated pursuant to an award of the Dairy Produce Quota Tribunal. The latter could, for instance, include an award of quota for reasons such as exceptional hardship or in respect of a development claim where substantial capital investment prior to the introduction of quotas had taken place, but milk production had not commenced until some time subsequent to the initial allocation of primary quotas in 1984.[8] This quota will also rank as allocated quota within the meaning of the 1986 Act, qualifying for compensation.

'Relevant period': This means the period in relation to which the allocated quota was determined, ie in the case of most primary wholesale quota 1983, and in relation to direct sales quota 1981. Where quota was determined in relation to more than one period, the relevant period is the period in relation to which the majority was determined or, if equal amounts were determined in relation to different periods, the later of those periods. Ascertaining the relevant period is important, in that the tenant's proportion of allocated quota is ascertained by reference to the standard quota (above), which in turn is ascertained by reference to the average number of hectares used during the relevant period for feeding dairy cows, ie during (in most cases) 1983.

(b)   Calculation of compensation

The potential claims for compensation by a qualifying tenant fall under three heads:

   (i)   *Excess of allocated quota over registered quota.* By virtue of Schedule 1 para 5(2) where the allocated quota exceeds the standard quota for the land (calculated as above), then the tenant will be entitled to the value of the amount of the excess.

  (ii)   *Tenant's fraction of allocated quota.*
      Where the quota allocated was equal to the standard quota, then the tenant will be entitled to the 'tenant's fraction' of the allocated quota.[9] The 'tenant's fraction' is calculated in accordance with Schedule 1, para 7, and is the mechanism whereby the 1986 Act seeks to compensate the tenant for his contribution to the allocation of quota by means of dairy improvements. The 'tenant's fraction' can be expressed in the following formula:

'Tenant's fraction'

Schedule 1 para 7

$$\frac{\text{Annual rental value of tenant's improvements}}{\text{Annual rental value of tenant's improvements} + \text{rental value of land.}}$$

---

7 See above p 317 ff.
8 Agriculture Act 1986 Sch 1, para 11A.
9 *Ibid*, Sch 1, para 5(2)(b).

The annual rental value of tenant's improvements, for this purpose, is the rental value at the end of the relevant period, ie in relation to wholesale quota, commonly 1983. The rental value of land, for the purposes of calculating the denominator, is such part of the rent payable by the tenant in respect of the 'relevant period' as is attributable to the land used in that period for the 'feeding, accommodation or milking of dairy cows kept on the land'. This factor is included in the calculation to reflect the landlord's contribution to the registration of quota by means of having contributed the land on which the dairy enterprise was carried out prior to the registration of quota. Note that the relevant rent is that paid by the tenant in respect of the relevant period, eg in many cases 1983.

Where the allocated quota is *less* than the standard quota, the tenant's claim will be reduced and will represent such proportion of the tenant's fraction of the allocated quota, as the allocated quota bears to the standard quota.[10]

For the purpose of calculating the 'tenant's fraction' the annual rental value of tenant's dairy improvements is defined as the amount which would fall to be disregarded under Schedule 2, para 2 of the Agricultural Holdings Act 1986, on rent review, 'so far as that amount is attributable to tenant's improvements to, or tenants fixed equipment on, land used for the feeding, accommodation or milking of dairy cows kept on the land in question'.[11] Note that the relevant annual rental value is that obtaining at the end of the relevant period (commonly 1983), and not the current rental value of dairy improvements.[12] It should be appreciated that this is different to the position appertaining under the Agricultural Holdings Act compensation provisions, where the rental value at the end of the tenancy is at issue. If a landlord purchases a dairy improvement after the end of the 'relevant period' this would normally be brought into account, for compensation purposes, under the Agricultural Holding Act 1986. However, because Schedule 1, para 7(4) of the Agriculture Act 1986 specifies that any allowances given by the landlord between the relevant period and the end of the tenancy must be disregarded, it follows that a landlord could pay for improvements and still have to pay compensation for milk quota. It follows that there is no incentive for a landlord to make any allowance after 1984 for dairy improvements; indeed he may be penalised in compensation for doing so. A further effect of these provisions is, it should be noted, to give the tenant credit for an improvement which may well have no rental value at the termination of the tenancy, having been completely discounted by the latter date.

10 *Ibid*, Sch 1, para 5(2)(c).
11 *Ibid*, Sch 1, para 7(2).
12 See *ibid*, Sch 1, para 7(4).

For the purpose of calculating the 'tenant's fraction' provision is made by Schedule 1, para 10 for either landlord or tenant, at any time before the termination of the tenancy, by notice in writing to demand that the determination of the standard quota for the land, or the 'tenant's fraction', shall be referred to arbitration. Note that, for the purposes of ascertaining the standard quota, attention is directed to the average number of hectares of land used during the relevant period for the feeding of dairy cows – a different question to that relevant to apportionment of quota under the Dairy Produce Quotas Regulations, *viz* the areas of land used for dairy production. Similarly, for the purpose of calculating the tenant's fraction the relevant element in the denominator is the rental value of land used for the 'feeding, accommodation or milking of dairy cows' kept on the land.[13] For the purpose of these calculations it is specifically provided[14] that references to land used for the feeding of dairy cows kept on the land *do not* include land used for growing cereal crops for feeding to dairy cows 'in the form of loose grain'. References to dairy cows are to cows kept for milk production (other than uncalved heifers). These provisions were considered in *Grounds v Attorney General of the Duchy of Lancaster*.[15] It was there held that an arbitrator is entitled to take into account, when calculating standard quota, the actual practice of reasonably skilled and successful farmers in normally feeding concentrated foodstuffs to their cattle, whether such concentrates are made from grain grown on the land or brought in from outside. Moreover, it was there indicated[16] that references to 'land used for growing cereal crops for feeding to dairy cows in the form of loose grain' actually refer to land which is used to grow grain which is then processed on the holding and fed to the cattle. This is the only permissible inference, in that dairy cows are not fed loose grain in the manner suggested by the terms of Schedule 1 to the 1986 Act. The effect of the inclusion of these matters is to increase the standard quota for the land concerned, thus reducing the excess claimable *in toto* by the tenant and enlarging that part of allocated quota to which the tenant will only have a claim for the tenant's fraction.

(iii) *Transferred quota.*

By virtue of Schedule 1, para 1(1)(b) the tenant will have a claim for the value of so much of the relevant quota as consists of 'transferred quota' transferred to him by virtue of a transaction *the cost of which was borne wholly or partly by him.* It is a prerequisite to this head of claim that the tenant had milk quota allocated to him in relation to land comprised in the holding *or* was in occupation of the land as a tenant on 2nd April 1984 (whether or not under the tenancy which has now terminated). Further, the amount of compensation, to which the tenant is entitled will be –

---

13 See *ibid*, Sch 1, para 6(1) and 7(1)(b).
14 *Ibid*, Sch 1, para 6(5).
15 [1989] 1 EGLR 6.
16 See [1989] 1 EGLR 6, 9 per Glidewell LJ.

(a)   in a case where the tenant bore the whole of the cost of the transaction, by virtue of which the transferred quota was transferred to him, to the value of the transferred quota itself, and

(b)   in a case where the tenant bore only *part* of that cost, the value of the corresponding part of the transferred quota.[17]

The principle underlying this provision is to compensate the tenant fully for quota which he has brought onto the land at his own expense. This aim is, regrettably, imperfectly realised in the relevant provisions. The definition of a 'transaction' at the tenant's expense, triggering the compensation provisions, is itself problematical. There is a question, for instance, as to the compensation entitlement of a tenant who is the registered producer, but who farms in partnership with others and himself contributes part (only) of the purchase price of acquired quota. The logical corollary of the statutory provisions is that the claimant would only be entitled to partial compensation, giving the landlord an uncovenanted-for benefit. Whether the tenant, in such circumstances, could claim to hold quota on trust for his co-partners is open to doubt, as their interest will not be noted on the Milk Marketing Board register of producers. It should also be noted that the statutory definition refers to a 'transaction, the cost of which was borne wholly or partly by' the tenant. This definition focuses on the cost, to the claimant tenant, of acquiring quota. It is therefore possible that allocated quota could be converted into transferred quota if one tenant sells quota to another, both having the same landlord. If the lease of the first tenant has a covenant against assignment or subletting, the landlord will be able to prevent a transfer of quota in these circumstances, and should therefore ensure that he is paid an allowance for, or extracts an agreement as to compensation from, the second tenant.

(iv)   *Miscellaneous.*

The compensation provisions have attracted considerable criticism.[18] They to some extent penalise low input farming, in that the absence of extensive dairy improvements will depress the tenant's fraction and lead to a correspondingly smaller claim for compensation. The provisions also, to some extent, penalise dairy farming on marginal land, although there are now special rules for calculating standard quota in marginal areas, by reference to differential yields per hectare according to land classification.[19] A further criticism, which retains its force, is that the provisions confer substantial benefits on a special class of occupier, *viz* tenants who were in occupation of their holdings on 2nd April 1984, upon the introduction of dairy quotas. It is also perfectly possible for there to be 'relevant quota' registered in relation to a holding which is *neither* allocated quota or transferred quota as statutorily defined. Quota acquired by purchase by a tenant who

17 Agriculture Act 1986, Sch 1, para 5(3).
18 For cogent criticism of the compensation provisions see an article at (1986) 280 Estates Gazette 1212 (E Pinfold).
19 Differential yields from marginal land are to some extent catered for, in that the Milk Quotas (Calculation of Standard Quota) Order 1986, SI 1986/1530 prescribe different yields per hectare for disadvantaged and severely disadvantaged land.

entered into occupation after 2nd April 1984 would, for instance, fall in this category.

(c)   Valuation of quota

By virtue of Schedule 1, para 9 the value of milk quota to be taken into account for the purposes of calculating compensation, in accordance with the above rules, is the value of the milk quota at the time of the *termination of the tenancy* in question. In order to determine that value the Act directs that there should be taken into account such evidence as is available, including (in particular) evidence as to the sums being paid for interests in land where milk quota is registered in relation to the land concerned, and cases where no such milk quota is registered. The value of quota is, therefore, the enhanced value the presence of quota contributes to the holding at the date of termination of the tenancy. This is to be ascertained by reference to comparables of transactions carrying quota and those not carrying quota.

3.   Tenancies in respect of which compensation payable

Compensation is only payable on termination of a tenancy (defined in the following manner). Termination need not be by notice to quit, and compensation will be payable upon, for instance, a surrender of the tenancy, *cf* the tenant's entitlement to compensation for disturbance, improvements, etc under the Agricultural Holdings Act 1986.[20] For the purposes of the milk quota provisions, compensation is payable on termination of any tenancy which constitutes:

(i)   a tenancy from year to year; *or*

(ii)   a tenancy which would have effect as if it were a tenancy from year to year by virtue of section 2 of the Agricultural Holdings Act 1986 if it had not been approved by the Minister. Note that tenancies granted for grazing and/or mowing for a specified period of the year do not carry the right to compensation for milk quota; *or*

(iii)   a fixed term of two years or more to which section 3 of the Agricultural Holdings Act 1986 applies; *or*

(iv)   a fixed term of two years or more which would confer security of tenure had Ministry consent not been obtained prior to grant.[1]

Note that a *Gladstone v Bower* tenancy for a fixed term of between one and two years is not a 'tenancy' carrying entitlement to compensation for milk quota, *cf* the position as to general compensation under the Agricultural Holdings Act 1986 where the entitlement to compensation for improvements, disturbance, etc is still unclear.[2] Special provision is made for the following classes of tenancy:

(a)   *Tenancies by succession.*
Where, after 2nd April, 1984, a new tenancy has been granted by way of succession following termination of a qualifying tenancy, then any

---

20 See chapter 9, p 191 ff.

1 Agriculture Act 1986 Sch 1, para 18(1).

2 As to which see Scammel and Densham's *Law of Agricultural Holdings* (7th ed), p 37, Muir Watt, *Agricultural Holdings* (13th ed) pp 21 and 22 ff.

milk quota allocated or transferred to the former tenant in respect of the land which is subject to the new tenancy is to be treated as if it had, instead, been allocated or transferred to the new tenant. The new tenant is treated as if he had paid so much of the cost of the transaction by virtue of which any transferred quota of the former tenant was acquired and as if he hadbeen in occupation of the land on 2nd April 1984.[3] The claim for compensation on termination of the tenancy is accordingly transferred to, and maintainable by, the tenant by succession, and not his predecessor. This provision applies to tenancies by way of succession granted in three circumstances:

(i)   where the succession tenancy was obtained by virtue of a tribunal direction under the Agricultural Holdings Act 1986[4] following the death or retirement of the previous tenant;

(ii) where the succession tenancy was granted by agreement to persons entitled to a tenancy under a tribunal direction for succession;[5] *or*

(iii) where a succession tenancy was granted by agreement to a close relative of the former tenant.[6]

It follows from the above that no compensation will be payable until termination of the new tenancy, without further transmission taking place by way of succession.

(b)   *Assignment of tenancy.*

The claim for quota compensation is similarly 'rolled over' where a tenancy has been assigned after 2nd April 1984 (whether such assignment be effected by deed or operation of law). Where assignment takes place after 2nd April 1984 any milk quota allocated or transferred to the assignor in respect of the land shall be treated as if it had instead been allocated or transferred to the assignee. The latter will be treated as if he had paid so much of the cost of the transaction by virtue of which transferred milk quota was transferred to the assignor and as if he was in occupation of the land himself on 2nd April 1984.[7]

(c)   *Sub-tenancies.*

Where there is sub-tenancy of land to which quota attaches which terminates after 2nd April 1984, the 1986 Act contains special provision to protect the claim for compensation of the mesne tenant;[8]

(i)   any milk quota allocated or transferred to the sub-tenant in respect of the land is to be treated as if it had *instead* been transferred to the 'sub-landlord' (ie the mesne tenant); and

(ii) in such a case the sub-landlord (mesne tenant) is to be treated for the purposes of any claim in respect of quota as if he had

---

3 Agriculture Act 1986, Sch 1, para 22.
4 Ie under sections 39 or 53 Agriculture Holdings Act 1986.
5 Ie in circumstances covered by section 45(6) Agricultural Holdings Act 1986 see chapter 8 p 167 ff above.
6 See section 37(1)(b) and 37(2) Agricultural Holdings Act 1986, and further chapter 8 p 156 ff above.
7 Agriculture Act 1986, Sch 1, para 3.
8 *Ibid*, Sch 1, para 4.

paid so much of the cost of the transaction by virtue of which the transferred milk quota was obtained for the sub-tenant as the sub-tenant bore, and as if he were in occupation of the holding on 2nd April 1984; and

(iii) if the sub-landlord (mesne tenant) does not occupy the land after the sub-tenancy has terminated, and the sub-tenant has quit the land, the sub-landlord is to be taken to have quit the land when the sub-tenant quit it, thus triggering his entitlement to claim compensation on termination.

4. Tenants to whom compensation payable

To qualify for compensation the tenant's interest in the land must be within the categories outlined above. In addition, however, the following qualifying conditions must be satisfied:

(i) The tenant must have milk quota 'registered as his' in relation to a holding consisting of, or including, the land which he has quit;[9] and

(ii) *Claim for allocated quota or excess*; the tenant must have had milk quota allocated to him in relation to land comprised in the holding upon the imposition of milk quotas on 2nd April 1984 and

(iii) *Claim for the value of transferred quota* (above); this will only arise if the tenant had milk quota allocated to him (as outlined above) *or* was in occupation of the land as a tenant on 2nd April 1984 (whether or not under the tenancy which is now terminating).

Where there has been succession to a tenancy, assignment, or termination of a sub-tenancy, these conditions must be satisfied by the claimant's predecessor.[10]

The requirement that the tenant must have 'milk quota registered *as his*' can cause problems where the identity of the registered producer and the tenant claiming compensation are not one and the same. The tenant claiming compensation may hold the tenancy of land in respect of which quota is 'registered' but it may, for instance, be farmed by a farming company which is *itself* the registered producer. Unless the Court is willing to lift the veil of incorporation, the tenant in this instance will not have quota 'registered as his' and will not, therefore, have a claim for compensation on termination of his tenancy. Similarly, quota may be registered with the Milk Marketing Board in the name of two tenants, one of whom (only) holds the tenancy of the land in question. Here the tenants would have a claim for compensation, but difficult questions may arise as to entitlement to the proceeds of any compensation claim. A more unlikely situation would be for quota to be registered in the name of one tenant, where the tenancy terminating is in the name of more than one, eg there may be a sleeping partner/tenant who does not participate in the day to day running of the dairy business. The question will arise whether the former can himself claim compensation for quota. As he is the only one who has quota 'registered as his' it must be assumed that he can, but further questions will arise as to his

9 *Ibid*, Sch 1, para 11.
10 As to which see above pp 330–31.

ability to serve notices claiming compensation without the concurrence of the sleeping partner/tenant. In this situation, it is suggested that the concurrence of the joint tenant can be dispensed with in service of the relevant notices.[11] *Quaere* it is open to question whether implied partnership authority would extend to the service of notices claiming compensation for quota on termination, as the service of such notice is not necessary for the carrying on of the farming business in the same manner as, for instance, the service of notices claiming security of tenure.[12]

5.   Apportionment of quota for compensation purposes

The compensation provisions clearly envisage the tenant having quota registered in relation to a composite holding of mixed tenure.[13] Before calculating the tenant's entitlement to compensation it may therefore be necessary to apportion the tenant's registered quota between land in his ownership and land subject to tenancy. There is no direction in the Agriculture Act 1986 as to how quota is to be allocated or apportioned in such circumstances. It is suggested, however, that apportionment should be in accordance with the rules in Schedule 4 to the Dairy Produce Quotas Regulations 1989. These regulate all other quota apportionments and require apportionment by reference to the areas of land used for dairy production during the preceding five years.[14] Where there is a composite holding, it follows that two arbitrations will be necessary to ascertain the tenant's entitlement to compensation; firstly an arbitration under the Dairy Produce Quotas Regulations to apportion quota between freehold and tenanted land, followed by an arbitation under the Agriculture Act 1986 to assess the tenant's entitlement to compensation on termination of the tenancy.

6.   Settlement of claims on termination

Any claim for milk quota arising under the 1986 Act is to be determined by arbitration under the Agricultural Holdings Act 1986. It is expressly provided[15] that no claim for compensation in respect of quota shall be enforceable *unless*, before the expiry of the period of two months from the termination of the tenancy, the tenant serves notice in writing on his landlord of his intention to make the claim. Landlord and tenant then have a period of eight months following termination of the tenancy to settle the claim by agreement in writing. If the claim has not been so settled then it is determined by arbitration under the Agricultural Holdings Act 1986.[16] The period for service of notice of claim is extended in certain circumstances

11 See *Howson v Buxton* [1928] All ER Rep 434.
12 *Cf Featherstone v Staples* [1986] 2 All ER 461.
13 See Agriculture Act 1986, Sch 1, para 1: quota compensation payable where tenant has quota registered as his in relation to a holding consisting of *or including* the land, etc'.
14 See above p 317 ff, also *Punknowle Farms Ltd v Kane* [1985] 3 All ER 790.
15 Agriculture Act 1986, Sch 1, para 11(1). The rules governing service of notices are the same as those in the Agricultural Holdings Act 1986: see Sch 1 *ibid*, para 16.
16 *Ibid*, Sch 1, para 11(2).

where an application for succession is made, or the tenant lawfully remains in occupation of part of the land subject to the tenancy after termination.[17] The arbitration will proceed along the same lines as any other arbitration on termination under the 1986 Act. There are some minor modifications to the arbitration procedure in the case of milk quota arbitations, however:

(i)   The arbitrator has power to fix the date for payment of compensation to be not less than three months from the date of his award (in the case of other claims for compensation, payment must normally be not later than one month after award).[18]

(ii) If, before the termination of the tenancy, the landlord and tenant have 'agreed in writing' the amount of the standard quota for the land or the tenant's fraction, or the value of milk quota which is to be used for the purpose of calculating the compensation payment, then the arbitrator is directed to award payment in accordance with the parties' agreement.[19] There is a question whether, in doing so, the parties must adhere to the statutory standard for determining standard quota and the tenant's fraction. The proper inference is that they must, if only because the 'tenant's fraction' is itself a statutory concept defined with precision by Schedule 1 para 7 of the Agriculture Act 1986, as indeed is the concept of 'standard quota', defined in Schedule 1, para 6 *ibid.*

(iii) The arbitrator is, similarly, directed to comply with a determination of standard quota and/or tenant's fraction which has been made before the end of the tenancy by arbitration.

(iv) Where the standard quota and/or tenant's fraction has been ascertained (either by agreement or arbitration prior to termination of the tenancy), the arbitrator is empowered to depart from that agreement/arbitration award if the circumstances are 'materially different' at the time of termination of the tenancy from those obtaining at the time the agreement or award was made.[20] In this event he is entitled to disregard so much of the agreement or award as appears to him affected by the changed circumstances.

The provisions of the Agricultural Holdings Act 1986 as to enforcement of payment of the award of compensation, and the obtaining of a charge on the holding, are applied for the purposes of obtaining compensation under the Agriculture Act 1986.[1]

7.   Termination of tenancy of part

Special provision is made for the case where the landlord resumes possession of part of the land subject to the tenancy.[2] Where the landlord gives notice to

---

17 *Ibid*, Sch 1, para 11(3) and 11(4).
18 *Ibid*, Sch 1, para 11(5). This provision applies section 84 Agricultural Holdings Act 1986 to claims under the Agriculture Act 1986 as to milk quota.
19 *Ibid*, Sch 1, para 11(6).
20 *Ibid*, Sch 1, para 11(7).
1   *Ibid*, Sch 1, para 12.
2   *Ibid*, Sch 1, para 13.

quit part under the terms of the Agricultural Holdings Act 1986[3] or resumes possession pursuant to a provision in the contract of tenancy, or serves notice to quit part by virtue of section 140 of the Law of Property Act 1925, then the tenant is entitled to claim termination as if the tenancy of the whole had been terminated. For this purpose it will be necessary to apportion quota between not only the freehold and other land occupied by the tenant, but also between the land the tenancy of which has been terminated, and that which is still subject to tenancy.

8.   Severance of reversionary estate

Where the reversionary estate in the land has been vested in more than one person in several parts, the 1986 Act makes provision for the tenant to be entitled on quitting all the land to require that any amount payable to him by way of compensation shall be determined as if the reversionary estate had not been so severed.[4] This will entitle the tenant to any additional value accruing to the registered quota by virtue of its being marketable as one unit, rather than in several lots attached to the severed parts of the reversionary estate. The arbitrator must, where necessary, apportion the amount of compensation awarded between the reversionary owners who *together* constitute the 'landlord' of the land. Any additional costs of his award caused by the necessity of making such apportionment are to be awarded by the arbitrator as he may determine.[5]

9.   Limited owner's powers

Special provision is made for the position where the landlord or (if appropriate) mesne tenant is not an absolute owner, eg where the landlord is the tenant for life under a settlement. In such a case then, notwithstanding that the landlord is not the owner of the fee simple estate in the land, or is not absolutely entitled to the immediate leasehold reversion, he may for the purposes of the compensation provisions do anything which he might do if he were such an owner or as the case may be, were he absolutely entitled to the mesne leasehold estate.[6]

10.   Crown land, etc

The compensation provisions apply to land which belongs to the Crown or to the Duchy of Lancaster, the Duchy of Cornwall or a Government Department, as also to land held in trust for Her Majesty for the purposes of a Government Department.[7]

---

3 See section 31 Agricultural Holdings Act 1986, and further chapter 6 p 110 ff above.
4 Agriculture Act 1986, Sch 1, para 14.
5 *Ibid*, Sch 1, para 14(2).
6 *Ibid*, Sch 1, para 15.
7 *Ibid*, Sch 1, para 16.

C   Agricultural marketing quotas

Dairy quotas are unique in that they are a quota on *production*. Moreover, as we have seen they attach to land in the sense that they can only be transferred by means of the transfer of an interest in land. Agricultural marketing quotas differ, on the other hand, in that they do not impose a quota on production *per se*; rather they are intended to control the quantity of agricultural produce of a particular kind released onto the internal domestic or European market. Prior to the abolition of the Hops Marketing Scheme in 1982,[8] marketing quotas were imposed on domestic producers as regards both hops and potatoes. Domestic marketing quotas are now imposed only under the terms of the Potato Marketing Scheme, there being no common organisation of the internal market within the European community for potatoes. The introduction of the common agricultural policy of the EEC, and the common organisation of the European market in various agricultural products, has led to the imposition by European legislation of marketing quotas on production of certain products, notably grain and sugar.

1.   Potatoes

Under the terms of the Potato Marketing Scheme[9] the Potato Marketing Board enjoys extensive powers to control the buying, selling, grading and packing, storing, advertising and transportation of potatoes. It also has power to levy payment of contributions by registered potato producers.[10] Each registered producer has allocated to him a basic area for potato production, commonly the average area of the preceding year's crop. Having reviewed the trend of potato production, and after consultation with the Potato Marketing Board, the Minister determines a desirable acreage to be planted by producers, the objective being to promote and maintain production of main crop varieties of potato at the level of self sufficiency. The Potato Marketing Board exercises its power to determine basic areas and quotas so as to ensure that the areas planted by producers are as close as possible to the declared quota or desirable acreage, thus determined. To this end, the Board prescribes how much of an individual producer's basic area is to be planted each year ('the quota'). The quota is enforced using the Board's powers to levy contributions from producers. Each producer is required to pay a contribution based on a rate per hectare,[11] but where the

8 The Hops Marketing Act 1982, section 1, revoked the Hops Marketing Scheme 1932 (SR and O 1932/505). Section 4 of the 1982 Act provided for the dissolution of the Hop Marketing Board; section 2 *ibid* made arrangements for a poll of producers to be held to determine the distribution of the property rights and liabilities of the Board.
9 See the Potato Marketing Scheme (Approval) Order 1955. SI 1955/690 Sch, para 84 as amended (successively) by SI 1962/883, SI 1971/711, SI 1976/133, SI 1985/312, SI 1987/282 and SI 1990/1626.
10 *Ibid*, Sch, para 84 (amended by SI 1962/883, 1971/711, 1976/133, 1855/312 and 1987/282).
11 The 'ordinary contribution' is calculated by reference to a 'formula rate', which takes account of yields and guaranteed prices. The formula rate is calculated using a formula based on the returns per hectare of the previous three calendar years: see the Potato Marketing Scheme (Approval) Order 1955, Sch, para 84(3)C (as substituted by SI 1985/312). The ordinary contribution must not exceed the formula rate for that calendar year.

quota area is exceeded the producer is obliged to pay the Board an 'excess area contribution'. The excess area contribution is currently fixed at ten times the formula rate, and represents a punitive disincentive to over-production.[12] The payment of compensation to registered producers suffering damage through unfair discrimination by the Board is also provided for by the terms of the Potato Marketing Scheme 1955.[13]

2.　Cereals co-responsibility levy

The Cereals Co-responsibility Levy Regulations 1988[14] implement in domestic law the EEC provisions on the administration and collection of the Cereals Co-responsibility levy. The Cereals Co-responsibility levy was introduced in 1986[15] in an attempt to remove the structural surplus of cereals produced by a continuing imbalance between the supply of, and demand for, cereals covered by the common organisation of the European cereal market.[16] The community legislation imposes a co-responsibility levy, to be fixed annually by the European Commission, which is to be collected on cereals that undergo first processing, intervention buying or export in the form of grain. The levy is then passed on to the producer.[17] For the purpose of administering, collecting and enforcing the levy,[18] the Cereals Co-Responsibility Regulations 1988[19] require the Intervention Board for Agriculture Produce to keep a register of traders, and to make provision for inspection of the particulars registered.[20] Both seed merchants and any other person engaged in purchasing, processing or selling cereals, may be required to supply information relative to their activities.[1]

12 The Potato Marketing Scheme Approval Order 1955, Sch, para 84(2)B (amended by SI 1987/282). The excess area contribution was increased from five times the formula rate, successively (i) to seven times the formula rate with effect from 1st March 1957 and (ii) to ten times the formula rate with effect from 1st January 1989. This two-stage increase was effected by SI 1987/282.
13 *Ibid*, Sch, para 87.
14 See the Cereals Co-Responsibility Levy Regulations 1988, SI 1988/1001 (amended by SI 1989/576 and SI 1989/1823). Also the Cereals Co-responsibility Levy (Certified Seed Exemption) Regulations 1988, SI 1988/1207, made under the European Communities Act 1972, section 2.
15 See EC Council regulation 1579/86 (OJ L139, 23586, p 29).
16 As to the common organisation of the market in cereals see EC Council Regulation 2727/75 (OJ L281, 1175 p 1), successively amended by EC Council Regulations 3808/81, 1579/86 and 1097/88; and see EC Commission Regulation 1432/88.
17 EC Council Regulation 1597/86, art 4, amending EC Council Regulation 2727/75.
18 As to the levy see Cereals Co-responsibility Levy Regulations 1988, SO 1988/1001 note 7 above.
19 Cereals Co-responsibility Levy Regulations 1988, reg 3. The levy is recoverable as civil debt and provision is made for the payment of interest on the levy in accordance with Community legislation: *ibid* reg 10 (substituted by SI 1989/1823).
20 A 'trader' is defined as any person who purchases from producers cereals other than cereals placed on the market in the framework of a forward transaction, or who places on the market cereals produced by him (i) by way of direct export from the United Kingdom, (ii) in the form of cereals products, or (iii) in the framework of forward transaction: see the Cereals Co-responsibility Levy Regulations 1988, reg 21 for the requirement of seed merchants, etc to supply information see further *ibid* regs 4, 5 Sch.
1 Cereals Co-responsibility Levy Regulations 1988, regs 6 and 7.

Provision has now been made[2] for the exemption from the cereals co-responsibility levy of 84% of cereal seed delivered to seed merchants under multiplication contracts.[3] For this exemption to apply at least 75% of the seed purchased must be certified as seed and sold as such.[4]

3. Sugar

The common organisation of the market within the EEC in sugar has, for some time, been subject to structural surpluses necessitating the introduction of quotas. Originally introduced in 1967[5] the quota system applicable to sugar has been successively extended.[6] Under the European provisions sugar quota is divided into three classifications and allocated to each undertaking for each marketing year:

Quota A – basic quota allocated to each undertaking for each marketing year

Quota B – maximum quota calculated from quota A

Quota C – surplus production.

A levy will be imposed on production in excess of A and B quota in a marketing year, in order to help meet the costs of disposing of any surplus. Additional levies may, however, be imposed on A and B production to assist in disposing of over-production within the A and B quotas.

The European Court of Justice has, in considering the legal basis of the sugar quota system, ruled that it is legitimate to base quotas on historical production rather than levels of current consumption.[7]

It is currently proposed, subject to the approval of the European Council, to continue the sugar quota system until the end of the 1992/3 season, maintaining A and B quotas intact.

2 Ie by the Cereals Co-responsibility Levy (Certified Seed Exemption) Regulations 1988, SI 1988/1267, implementing EC Commission Regulation 1432/88.
3 Cereals Co-responsibility Levy (Certified Seed Exemption) Regulations 1988, reg 31.
4 *Ibid*, reg 32.
5 See Council Regulation (EEC) 1967/1009 (OJ L1967 308/1).
6 The quota system was extended to marketing year 1990/1 by Council reg 934/86 (OJ L1986 87/1).
7 See *The Eridania* [1986] ECR 117, Case 250/84 (ECJ).

Chapter 15

Market Gardens, Smallholdings and Allotments

Special provisions apply to certain types of agricultural holding – notably Market Gardens, Smallholdings and Allotments – for instance as regards compensation on termination of tenancy.

A Market gardens

1. Market gardens – definition

The Agricultural Holdings Act 1986 confers special rights as to compensation and removal of fixtures on the tenant of a market garden, in addition to rights enjoyed in common with other tenants of agricultural holdings. A market garden does not qualify for enhanced compensation, however, unless it is a 'market garden' within the narrow terms of the 1986 Act. This requires one of two things:

(a) *Agreement in writing.* The parties can agree in writing that the holding shall be let or treated as a market garden, or that part of it shall.[1] If part only is agreed to be so let, then the compensation provisions apply to that part as if it were a separate holding.

(b) *Direction of agricultural land tribunal.* The tenant may wish to make one or more of the improvements for which special compensation is provided by Sch 10. If this is the case, and the landlord refuses, or fails within a reasonable time to agree in writing that the holding be treated as a market garden, then the tenant can apply to the tribunal for a *direction* that the holding be treated as a market garden.[2] If the tribunal are satisfied that the holding (or part) is suitable for market gardening, they can direct that the enhanced rights to compensation, etc shall apply to all or some of the proposed improvements.[3] The direction can be given subject to such conditions as the tribunal think fit for the protection of the landlord.[4] In particular, section 80(7) gives the tribunal power to direct that the direction will only become operative if the tenant agrees to the division of the holding into two parts, only one of

1 Section 79(1) Agricultural Holdings Act 1986.
2 Section 80(1) *ibid.*
3 Section 80(2) *ibid.*
4 Section 80(6) *ibid.*

340

which is to be treated as a market garden. A new tenancy accepted by the tenant in accordance with a tribunal direction is not treated as a new tenancy for rent review purposes, and will not restart the three year review cycle.[5]

2. Special rights of tenant

The tenant of a market garden has five distinct and additional rights:

(a) Compensation on termination

Section 79(2) provides that improvements of a kind specified in Sch 10, carried out on a market garden, shall be treated as if included in Sch 8, Part I. If they were begun on or before 1st March 1948 they are treated as if included in Sch 9, Part II. The practical import is that the landlord's consent is not required prior to execution of the improvement, and compensation is available irrespective of its grant or refusal. A further consequence is that the *amount* of compensation will be the value of the improvement to an incoming tenant.[6] Compensation is payable on this basis for the following matters, listed in Sch 10:

  (i)   Planting of standard or other fruit trees permanently set out.
 (ii)   Planting of fruit bushes permanently set out.
(iii)   Planting of strawberry plants.
 (iv)   Planting of asparagus, rhubarb and other vegetable crops which continue productive for two or more years.
  (v)   Erection, alteration or enlargement of buildings for the purpose of the trade or business of a market gardener. Improvements of this kind would require consent if the holding were other than a market garden.[7]

If the tribunal have given a direction under s 80, and the tenancy is terminated by reason of the tenant becoming insolvent or *himself* giving notice to quit, special rules apply. The tenant will not be entitled to compensation unless, not later than one month after the notice to quit or insolvency, he produces to the landlord a written offer by 'a substantial and otherwise suitable person' to take over the tenancy and pay compensation due under the 1986 Act to the outgoing tenant. The offer must be framed so as to hold good for a period of three months from the date when it is produced. The landlord then has three months in which to consider the offer. If he fails to accept, compensation is payable to the outgoing tenant in the normal manner. If the offer is accepted, the incoming tenant must pay to the landlord any sums paid by the latter to the outgoing tenant in respect of rent, breach of tenancy or otherwise. Having done so, the incomer can deduct this from any compensation payable by him to the outgoing tenant. These special provisions are usually referred to as the 'Evesham custom', the

5 Section 80(8) *ibid*.
6 See s 66(2) *ibid*.
7 See Sch 7, para 9 *ibid*.

intent being to prevent the landlord becoming liable for substantial claims for market garden improvements which he has not himself sanctioned.[8]

(b)　Removal of fixtures

By virtue of s 79(3) the tenant can exercise his statutory right to remove fixtures and buildings irrespective of whether they are buildings for which he could claim compensation under the Act. They must, however, have been erected or acquired by him specifically for the purposes of his trade or business as a market gardener. Buildings to which this right attaches can, therefore, be removed even if the landlord consented to their erection, and so conferred compensation rights on the tenant.

The tenant's right of removal also attaches to *both* fixtures and fittings erected or affixed prior to 1st January 1884, and acquired subsequently for the purposes of his market garden business.[9]

(c)　Removal of fruit trees and bushes

Section 79(4) gives the tenant the right to remove all fruit trees and fruit bushes planted by him on the holding and *not* permanently set out. If, however, the tenant does not remove them before the termination of the tenancy, they then remain the property of the landlord and the tenant cannot claim compensation in respect of them.

(d)　Incoming tenant compensation

By virtue of s 79(5) an incoming tenant can claim compensation in respect of the whole or part of an improvement which he has purchased even if the landlord has not consented in writing to its purchase.

(e)　Contracting out

The parties are free to contract out of the statutory compensation for market gardens (above).[10] They cannot, however, contract out of the general compensation provisions of the 1986 Act, eg as to improvements and disturbance. Section 81 limits the right to contract out to cases:

  (i)　where this is effected by agreement in writing and
  (ii)　where that agreement secures to the tenant 'fair and reasonable compensation' for improvements for which compensation would otherwise be payable under ss 79 or 80. This is a question of fact, to be decided by reference to the circumstances of each case.

Note also that, although the 'Evesham Custom' normally only applies where a tribunal direction designates a holding a market garden, the parties can *agree* to substitute its provisions for the compensation otherwise payable in cases where the holding is designated as such by agreement. The agreement by which the 'Evesham Custom' is applied must itself be in writing.[11]

8　See s 80(3)–(5) of the 1986 Act.
9　*Cf* generally the restrictions on removal contained in s 10(2)(c) and (d) of the 1986 Act, inapplicable to market gardens.
10　Section 81(1) *ibid*.
11　Section 81(2) *ibid*.

B   Smallholdings

1.   Smallholdings authorities

Section 38 of the Agriculture Act 1970 designates county councils 'smallholdings authorities' for the purposes of Part III of the 1970 Act. Smallholdings authorities are required by s 39 to make it their general aim, having regard to the interests of agriculture and good estate management, to provide opportunities for persons to be farmers on their own account by making holdings available for letting. The upper limit of land which can be so let in an individual case is fixed by s 39(2), being an amount which (in the opinion of the Minister) is capable when farmed under reasonably skilled management of providing full time employment for not more than two men (including the tenant), with or without additional part-time employment for another man.

The 1970 Act gives smallholdings authorities power to make loans to provide working capital for tenants of smallholdings provided by them, and to guarantee the repayment of loans taken by tenants from third parties.[12] The authority cannot, however, make loans in excess of three-quarters of the aggregate working capital required for the proper working of the smallholding concerned. The 1970 Act also requires smallholdings authorities to keep separate accounts of receipts and expenses incurred with respect to smallholdings, and a record of all land which has been held by the authority for smallholding purposes and by whom it is (or has been) occupied.[13] Each smallholdings authority must make an annual report to the Minister, and the latter lays before Parliament an annual report summarising for that year the activities of smallholdings authorities in England and Wales.[14] If the Minister is satisfied that the functions of any smallholdings authority are not being satisfactorily performed, he has default powers to perform its functions in a prescribed manner, or by order to transfer its functions to himself. Where the latter occurs, the Minister is to perform the functions transferred to him as if he were an agent of the smallholdings authority.[15] There is provision for an authority to make application for revocation of the Minister's order, such application to be made at not less than 12 monthly intervals.[16]

2.   Tenancies of smallholdings

A smallholding can only be let to a person who is himself going to farm the holding. By virtue of s 44(2) the proposed tenant must also be a person who is either:

  (i)   regarded by the authority as being qualified by reason of his agricultural experience to farm the holding on his own account; *or*

12 Section 53 *ibid*.
13 Section 58 *ibid*.
14 Section 59 *ibid*.
15 Section 56(1)(2) and (4) *ibid*.
16 Section 56(3) *ibid*.

(ii) is a person in respect of whom the authority are satisfied that within a reasonably short time he will become eligible to be so regarded.

Land can be let to two or more persons, as one or more smallholdings, if they are proposing to farm the land together on a co-operative basis.[17] Lettings must, in general, be made in accordance with the authority's proposals submitted to, and approved by the Minister, and for the time being in force.

Smallholdings tenancies possess a number of features, distinct from other agricultural tenancies, of which the following might be noted.

(a) General powers of management

Section 47 of the 1970 Act gives the smallholding authorities such general powers as are required for the management of land held by them for the purposes of smallholdings. They have specific power to further the formation of corporate or unincorporated bodies, with the object of enhancing the efficiency of smallholdings through the use of co-operative methods, and particularly through co-operative purchasing arrangements and co-operative sale and marketing of smallholding produce.[18] Authorities also have power to purchase or hire machinery and equipment, stock, fertiliser, seeds and other requisites, and to sell or let them to smallholders so as to assist in the conduct of farming of smallholdings held by the authority.[19]

(b) Rent

A smallholdings authority, when determining the rent at which a holding is initially to be let, must have regard to the rent which it might be reasonably expected would obtain were the land already let as an agricultural holding under the 1986 Act.[20] The authority must assume the terms of that letting to be the same as those on which they propose to let, and that the level of rent payable for the holding has been determined by arbitration under the 1986 Act.[1] The authority must, therefore, have regard to s 12 and Sch 2 to the 1986 Act and determine the rent payable on review for a comparable agricultural holding (and not a first letting rent). Section 45(2) further directs them to assume that there would be no improvements, dilapidation, deterioration or damage of which special account would otherwise be taken in fixing the rent. Three-yearly reviews will subsequently be available under s 12 and Sch 2 to the Agricultural Holdings Act 1986. If the rent is to be varied by *agreement*, however, the authority must still have regard to the level of rent obtainable on review under the 1986 Act.[2]

(c) Fixed equipment

Section 46 of the 1970 Act gives the authority power to equip smallholdings properly by providing, improving and repairing fixed equipment, and carrying out other improvements on or for the benefit of its smallholding land.

---

17 Section 44(3) *ibid.*
18 Section 47(2) *ibid.*
19 See s 47(3) *ibid.*
20 Section 45 of the 1970 Act.
 1 Section 45(1) *ibid.*
 2 Section 45(3) of the 1970 Act.

This general power specifically includes power to enter into an agreement with a smallholding tenant for the provision, maintenance, improvement or repair by him of fixed equipment on the holding, *or* the carrying out of other improvements by him of benefit to the holding.[3] The parties are free to agree the terms on which such improvements, or provision, etc of fixed equipment, are to be carried out.

(d)   Freedom of cropping

The tenant's statutory right of freedom of cropping and disposal of produce, conferred by section 15 of the 1986 Act, is expressly removed if the tenancy is one of a smallholding let as such by a smallholdings authority.[4] This right is also removed if the land is let pursuant to a scheme, approved by the Minister, for the purpose of providing holdings on a co-operative basis, with centralised services for the use of tenants or agreed provision for the disposal of the produce of the holdings concerned.[5]

(e)   Variation of other statutory rights

If a smallholding fulfills the requirements of section 1 of the 1986 Act it will be an agricultural holding with the statutory rights conferred by the 1986 Act.

Note, however, that statutory succession under Part IV of the 1986 Act is not available to a smallholding tenant.[6] Special provision is made in Sch 3, Case A for notice to quit to be served on a tenant of a statutory smallholding on attaining the age of 65. *Cf.* the voluntary retirement provisions applicable to the tenant of an agricultural holding *simpliciter*.[7] Special rules also apply where the landlord serves notice to quit under Sch 3, Case E to the 1986 Act, alleging an irremediable breach of tenancy by the tenant. These enable the necessary material prejudice to the landlord's interest to be established not simply by looking at the effect of the breach in question, but by looking also at its effect on the arrangements made by the landlord (or Minister) for the letting and conduct of smallholdings.[8]

C   Allotments

1.   Allotments and allotment gardens: definition

The Allotments Act 1922 distinguishes between two principal types of allotment, the statutory rights accruing to which vary:

---

3 Section 46(2) *ibid.*
4 See s 82 Agricultural Holdings Act 1986.
5 See s 82(2) and (3) *ibid.*
6 See s 38(4) of the 1986 Act cf *Saul v Norfolk County Council* [1984] 2 All ER 489; [1984] 2 All ER 489, CA.
7 Sections 49 ff of the 1986 Act, Chapter 8 p 169 ff above.
8 See Sch 3, para 11(1) of the 1986 Act.

(i)   *Allotment gardens.* These are defined by s 22(1) of the 1922 Act to mean an allotment not exceeding forty poles in extent which is wholly or mainly cultivated by the occupier for the production of vegetable or fruit crops for consumption by himself or his family.

(ii) *Allotment simpliciter.* An 'allotment' *simpliciter* means any parcel of land, whether attached to a cottage or not, of not more than two acres in extent held by a tenant and cultivated as a farm or garden, or partly as a garden and partly as a farm.[9] *Cf* Statutory rights accruing to allotment gardens do not apply if the land is let with a cottage.[10] Such an allotment may, of course, also qualify as an agricultural holding within the meaning of the Agricultural Holdings Act 1986.

Section 10 of the 1922 Act gives local authorities power to enter on unoccupied land, and adopt it for letting as allotments or allotment gardens. Borough, urban district and parish councils are, further, under a general statutory duty to provide and let to residents within their area an adequate number of allotments (see s 23 Smallholdings and Allotments Act 1908).

2.   Compensation on termination

(a)   Allotments

On termination of his tenancy, whether by effluxion of time or other cause, the tenant of an allotment is entitled to compensation from his landlord for:

(i)   crops, including fruit, growing upon the land in the ordinary course of cultivation, and for labour expended upon and manure applied to the land; and

(ii) for fruit bushes or trees provided and planted by the tenant with the previous consent in writing of the landlord, and for drains, outbuildings, pigsties, fowl-houses or other structural improvements made or erected by, and at the expense of, the tenant on the land with the landlord's consent.[11]

The parties cannot contract out of these compensation provisions. Deductions can be made, however, for sums due to the landlord for breach of tenancy, wilful or negligent damage caused by the tenant, and rent arrears due to the landlord.[12]

By virtue of s 22(3) *ibid* compensation must be based on the value of the crops, etc to an incoming tenant.

(b)   Allotment gardens

The compensation available to the tenant of an allotment garden is more restricted. Such holdings cannot qualify as agricultural holdings within the 1986 Act (no trade or business is involved) and so compensation will be exclusively based on the 1922 Act. Compensation on quitting is only

---

9 Section 3(7) of the 1922 Act.
10 Section 3(1) *ibid.*
11 Section 3(2) of the 1922 Act.
12 See s 3(3) *ibid.*

recoverable if the tenancy is terminated by the landlord by notice to quit or by re-entry under s 1 of the 1922 Act, but not where re-entry is for breach of tenancy or the insolvency of the tenant.[13] By virtue of s 2(3) the tenant will be entitled to compensation for crops growing on the land in the ordinary course of cultivation of the land as an allotment garden, and for manure applied to the land. 'Contracting out' is effectively allowed, in that s 2(8) provides that compensation is not recoverable except as provided by the Act, *or by the contract of tenancy*. The latter may, clearly, vary the tenant's statutory entitlement.

If the tenancy is terminated on or between 9th September and 11th October in any year, the tenant has the additional right to remove crops growing on the land, provided he does so within 21 days after termination of the tenancy.[14]

Section 3 of the Allotments Act 1950 entitles the tenant to compensation for disturbance, but only if the tenancy is terminated:

(i) by re-entry (other than for breach of tenancy) under the Allotments Act 1922; *or*

(ii) where the landlord is himself a tenant, by termination of his tenancy; *or*

(iii) where the landlord is a local authority, where the authority's rights of occupation have been terminated.

The tenant is entitled to one year's rent of the land by way of disturbance compensation, or a rateable amount if part only of the land is repossessed.

The landlord has, by virtue of section 4 of the 1950 Act, a claim for compensation for any deterioration of the land caused by the failure of the tenant to leave it clean and in a good state of cultivation and fertility. The quantum of compensation in this instance is the cost, at the date of the tenant's quitting, of making good the deterioration complained of.[15]

(c) Determination and recovery of compensation

Compensation under the Allotments Act is, in default of agreement, to be determined by a valuation made by a person appointed by the county court judge with jurisdiction where the land is situate, on a written application made for that purpose by either landlord or tenant. If not paid within 14 days of being agreed or determined it is recoverable in the county court as money ordered to be paid by the court.[16]

In the case of an allotment *simpliciter*, if compensation is also available under the Agricultural Holdings Act 1986 for the matters at issue, the claim can be made either under the 1922 Act or under the 1986 Act. In the latter event, the quantum will be referable to arbitration under Sch 11 to the 1986 Act in the normal way. Compensation is recoverable from a mortgagee exercising his right to possession, subject to a deduction for any rent or other sums owing from the tenant.[17]

13 Section 2(2).
14 Section 2(9).
15 Section 4(2).
16 Section 6 of the 1922 Act.
17 Section 4(2) of the 1922 Act.

3.   Allotment gardens: notice to quit

By virtue of section 1 of the 1922 Act (extended by section 1 of the 1950 Act) the tenancy of an allotment garden cannot generally be terminated except by twelve months or longer notice to quit, expiring on or before 6th April, or on or after 29th September in any year. There are several exceptions allowing for shorter notice in limited cases:

(i)   termination by re-entry is permitted provided the tenancy contains a power of re-entry on account of the land being needed for building, mining or other industrial uses, or for roads and sewers. Repossession must be for one or more of the non-agricultural purposes specified, and at least three months' notice of the entry given in writing to the tenant.[18]

(ii)   where land is let by a corporation or company which owns or leases docks, railways or other public undertakings, re-entry under a leasehold power in that behalf is permitted if the land is required for the landlord's statutory functions. Three months notice of re-entry must be given.[19]

(iii)   re-entry is permitted under a power in the lease, if the landlord is a local authority and the land is required by the latter for its housing or other statutory functions.[20]

(iv)   re-entry for non-payment of rent or breach of any term or condition of the tenancy, or on account of the tenant becoming insolvent or entering into liquidation, is permitted.[1] No rights to compensation arise in this instance.[2]

4.   Removal of fruit trees, bushes, etc

Section 4(1) of the 1922 Act gives the tenant of either an allotment or allotment garden the right, before termination of the tenancy, to remove any fruit trees or bushes provided and planted by him. He can also remove any erection, fencing or other improvement made at his expense, provided he makes good any injury caused by its removal. If, however, the tenant has paid compensation to a previous outgoing tenant for any fruit trees or bushes left *in situ*, or improvements, he has the same right to compensation under the 1922 Act as if the trees or bushes had been planted, and the improvements made, by him at his own expense.[3]

---

18 Section 1(1)(b).
19 Section 1(1)(c).
20 Section 1(1)(d).
 1 Section 1(1)(e).
 2 Above p 346, n 13.
 3 Section 5 *ibid.*

Chapter 16

Jurisdiction in agricultural disputes

A   Introduction

The policy of much of the legislation appertaining to agriculture favours the assignment of dispute resolution to specialist tribunals and arbitration. Thus, first instance jurisdiction in questions of security of tenure and succession to agricultural holdings is vested in Agricultural Land Tribunals. Similarly many questions arising during the currency of a tenancy (rent review, liability for repairs etc) are determinable by arbitration under Schedule 11 to the Agricultural Holdings Act 1986. Disputes arising from the allocation of direct sale and wholesale milk quotas are determinable by the Dairy Produce Quota Tribunal, established initially under the Dairy Produce Quotas Regulations 1984.[1] In addition, some agricultural matters may fall within the jurisdiction of non-specialist tribunals; principal among these is the jurisdiction of the Rent Assessment Committee to determine the rent and terms of assured agricultural occupancies under the Housing Act 1988.

The civil courts retain an important supervisory role over the exercise of these specialist jurisdictions. Appeal on points of law lies from the agricultural land tribunal to the High Court by case stated, and to the county court from the findings of an agricultural arbitrator. Additionally, tribunal proceedings may be subject to proceedings for judicial review. First instance jurisdiction in the civil courts is preserved only for matters not specifically assigned to tribunals or arbitration. Section 97 of the 1986 Act provides that, except where the Act otherwise expressly provides, nothing in the Agricultural Holdings Act shall prejudicially affect any pre-existing right or remedy of a landlord or tenant vested in him by any Act, common law or custom. The principal jurisdictions preserved by this provision include:

(a)   actions for forfeiture, pursuant to a proviso for re-entry in the lease.
(b)   any question as to the applicability of sections 2 and 3 of the 1986 Act, so as to create a protected tenancy.[2]
(c)   actions for damages for breach of repairing covenant, if brought during the continuance of the tenancy.[3]
(d)   any question appertaining to the construction of notices to quit[3a], and of contracts of tenancy.

1 SI 1984/1047.
2 See *Goldsack v Shore* [1950] 1 KB 708, CA.
3 See *Kent v Conniff* [1953] 1 QB 361, CA.
3a See generally *Rous v Mitchell* [1991] 1 All ER 676, CA.

(e)   proceedings for possession of agricultural land (for instance following termination of tenancy, with tribunal consent, by notice to quit).

The remainder of this chapter will deal with the specialist agricultural jurisdictions of importance – principally tribunals and agricultural arbitration.

B   Tribunal jurisdictions

1.   Agricultural land tribunals

The Agricultural Land Tribunals, of which there are currently eight, were set up by section 73 of the Agriculture Act 1947. Since 1958 they have had first instance jurisdiction under the agricultural holdings legislation for a wide range of matters. The principal of these are:

Security of tenure. Applications for consent to the operation of a notice to quit,[4] and applications for succession tenancies following a tenant's death or retirement,[5] must be made to the ALT for the area in which the holding is situated. This jurisdiction provides the greater part of the tribunals' workload.

Fixed equipment and improvements. Applications by a tenant for the provision of fixed equipment, and for consent to the carrying out of long-term improvements, are to be made to the relevant ALT.[6]

Market gardens. Failing agreement between the parties, the tribunal has jurisdiction to declare a holding to be a market garden, for the purposes of the compensation provisions of the 1986 Act.[7]

Land drainage. ALTs also have jurisdiction to determine applications for directions under the Land Drainage Act 1961 for the conduct of drainage work.

The country is divided into eight areas by the Agricultural Land Tribunals (Areas) Order 1982,[8] allowing for eight tribunals each with an area assigned to it by the Order. If land lies partly within the jurisdiction of one tribunal and partly within the jurisdiction of another, an application can be made to the Lord Chancellor for an order that the land be treated as wholly within the jurisdiction of one or other of the tribunals concerned.[9] The tribunals are under the supervision of the Council on Tribunals.

(a)   Constitution of tribunals

The chairman, who is appointed by the Lord Chancellor, must be a barrister or solicitor of not less than seven years' standing, and holds office for three years. If he wishes to resign, he must do so by notice in writing to the Lord Chancellor. If, however, the Lord Chancellor is satisfied that the chairman is

---

4 Section 26 of the 1986 Act.
5 Sections 39 and 50 *ibid.*
6 Sections 11 and 67(3).
7 Section 80.
8 SI 1982/97.
9 See section 75 Agriculture Act 1947; Sch 1, para 4 Agriculture Act 1958.

incapacitated by infirmity of mind or body from discharging the duties of his office, or if he is adjudged bankrupt or makes a composition or arrangement with his creditors, then the chancellor can revoke his appointment.[10] The Lord Chancellor must also draw up and maintain for each Agricultural Land Tribunal a panel of deputy chairmen, who must also be barristers or solicitors of at least seven years' standing.[11] He is also required to draw up for each tribunal a panel of persons appearing to him to represent the interests of owners and tenants of agricultural land. The persons placed on these panels by the Lord Chancellor are selected from nominations made, at his request, by 'persons appearing to him to represent the interests of farmers or of owners of agricultural land', as the case may be,[12] ie by the National Farmers Union on behalf of farmers, and the Country Landowners Association on behalf of owners. If insufficient nominations are made, or the nominations made appear to the Lord Chancellor to include unsuitable persons, he can supplement either panel by appointing persons of his own choice not formally nominated by either body.

An Agricultural Land Tribunal is specially constituted for each hearing and consists of three members: (a) the chairman, or a person nominated by the chairman either from the panel of deputy chairmen, or from among the chairmen of other Agricultural Land Tribunals, and (b) one person nominated by the chairman from each of the panels for that tribunal, drawn up from farmers' and owners' representatives.

If he considers it expedient to do so, the chairman can nominate two assessors to be added to the tribunal in order to assist it at the hearing. The assessors must be selected from a panel of persons nominated by the President of the Royal Institution of Chartered Surveyors.[13] If the chairman is prevented by sickness, or any other reason, from nominating the lay members of the tribunal or the assessors (if required), the nominations can be made by a person appointed by the chairman from the panel of deputy chairmen for that tribunal.

A technical defect in the appointment of any member of a tribunal, or a subsequently discovered disqualification, has no effect on the validity of tribunal proceedings.[14] The tribunals are staffed with civil servants attached to them, and paid by the Ministry.

(b)   *Tribunal procedure*

Detailed procedural rules governing the conduct of Agricultural Land Tribunal proceedings are laid down by the Agricultural Land Tribunals (Rules) Order 1978.[15] In addition to laying down prescribed forms for applications, the 1978 Order makes provision for the conduct of the tribunal hearing, the manner in which evidence can be submitted, and the form and manner of the tribunal's decision.

---

10 Sch 9, para 13 Agriculture Act 1947.
11 *Ibid* Sch 9, para 14.
12 Sch 9, para 15.
13 Sch 9, para 16.
14 Sch 9, para 20.
15 SI 1978/259.

(c)   Pre-hearing procedure; forms of application and reply

The Appendix to the 1978 Order sets out fourteen forms of Application and Reply to be used in making the relevant applications or replies to the tribunal. These are:

Form   1 – application by the landlord for consent to the operation of a notice to quit, and Reply (Form 1R).

Form   2 – application by tenant to postpone operation of notice to quit, and Reply (Form 2R).

Form   3 – application for Certificate of Bad Husbandry, and Reply (Form 3R).

Form   4 – application for the variation or revocation of a condition imposed by the Tribunal.

Form   5 – application by tenant for a direction to provide fixed equipment, and Reply (Form 5R).

Form   6 – application by tenant for approval of long term improvement, and Reply (Form 6R).

Form   7 – application by tenant for determination that the landlord has failed to carry out an improvement within a reasonable time, and Reply (Form 7R).

Form   8 – application for a direction to treat an agricultural holding as a market garden, and Reply (Form 8R).

Form   9 – application by tenant for a direction to avoid or relax a covenant against the burning of heather or grass, and Reply (Form 9R).

Form 10 – application for determination that a person be treated as owner of land, and Reply (Form 10R).

Form 11 – application under the Land Drainage Act 1961 for an order to carry out ditching or drainage work, and Reply (Form 11R).

Form 12 – notice by applicant for order under Land Drainage Act 1961, following receipt of ministry report.

Form 13 – notice of hearing.

Form 14 – application for variation of order made under the Land Drainage Act 1961.

In addition the following forms, prescribed by the Agricultural Land Tribunals (Succession etc.) Order 1984, must be used when making applications for statutory succession:

Form 1 – application for Direction giving entitlement to Tenancy of Agricultural Holding, and Reply (Form 1R).

Form 2 – application by landlord for consent to operation of notice to quit, and Reply (Form 2R).

Form 3 – notice of application for entitlement to tenancy.

Form 4 – reply to application for direction giving entitlement to tenancy of agricultural holding, and Reply (Form 5R).

Form 5 – (Retirement) application for Direction giving entitlement to tenancy of agricultural holding, and Reply (Form 5R).

Form 6 – notice of application for entitlement to tenancy under Schedule 2 to the Agricultural Holdings Act 1984.

Applications must be made in the forms prescribed, or in forms 'substantially to the same effect'. If the provisions of the 1978 Rules are not complied with, however, the proceedings will not be invalid unless the chairman of the tribunal so directs.[16]

Every application and reply must be signed by the party making it, or by some person authorised to do so on his behalf (such as his solicitor), and must be delivered to the secretary of the tribunal in duplicate accompanied by two copies of a map of the land which is the subject of the application.[17] If there are more than two parties to the proceedings, additional copies of the application or reply, and maps, must be supplied for each additional party.

Applications, replies, and other documents required to be served by the Rules are deemed to be served on any person when they are delivered to him or left at his proper address, or sent to him by post in a registered letter or by recorded delivery.[18] Any document served on a company or other incorporated body is deemed to be duly served if given to or served on the company secretary. The proper address for service in the case of a company or other corporate body is its registered or principal office. In the case of an individual, it is that person's last known address. Substituted service can be ordered by the chairman of the tribunal, on such terms and in such form as he may think fit, if the person on whom service is to be made cannot be found, or has died with no known personal representatives, or is out of the United Kingdom, or if for any other reason service cannot be readily effected on him.[19]

The Rules also provide for interlocutory applications for directions, and for the disclosure by the parties (at the secretary's request) of any document or information that the tribunal may require.[20] Documents disclosed prior to hearing can be inspected and copied by all parties to the proceedings.

Any person against whom relief is sought on an application is a party to that application, as is any sub-tenant where the holding concerned has been sublet in whole or in part.[1] Where an application is made to the tribunal for a fixed equipment direction, any public authority which has power to enforce the statutory requirement specified in the application must be served with copies of the application and reply, and can be heard on the application.[2] Any other person may be joined as a party if the chairman or tribunal consider it to be desirable to do so.[3]

(d)   The hearing

Rule 23 provides that the secretary must fix a date, place and time for the hearing 'as soon as practicable' after receipt of the reply to the application. The tribunal must sit in public unless it appears to them that there are exceptional reasons which make it desirable that the hearing, or part of it, should be in private.[4] Any party may appear either in person, or by counsel

---

16 SI 1978/259, Rule 38.
17 *Ibid* Rule 16.
18 Rule 35.
19 Rule 17.
20 Rules 19 and 20.
 1 Rules 12 and 13.
 2 Rule 12(2).
 3 Rule 14.
 4 Rule 24.

or solicitor, or by any other representative if that other has been appointed in writing.[5] At the hearing, the party making the application is heard first, but the procedure to be followed is otherwise as the tribunal may direct. If a party fails to appear at the hearing, despite having had an adequate opportunity of doing so, his application can be dismissed, or (if he is the respondent) the tribunal can proceed to decide the application in his absence.[6]

(e)   Evidence

The tribunal is specifically empowered to admit evidence notwithstanding that it would not be admissable in a court of law.[7] Evidence can be given orally – whether on oath, or on affirmation, or otherwise – or by means of unsworn statements produced by the maker when giving oral evidence. If the tribunal consent, written statements by a witness not giving oral evidence can be admitted. Affidavit evidence, however, can only be admitted if the parties consent.[8] The tribunal can, at any stage in the proceedings, order the attendance of a deponent or the maker of a written statement for examination and cross-examination. The tribunal can, moreover, call witnesses of its own motion, who can then be cross-examined by any party to the proceedings. The attendance of witnesses can be compelled by the issue of witness summonses under the County Court Rules. The tribunal have a right to inspect the land concerned provided that notice of their intention to inspect the holding is given to all the parties either orally at the hearing itself, or in writing at least twenty-four hours before the intended entry.[9] The parties, their representatives and expert witnesses, have a right to attend the inspection if they so desire.[10]

(f)   Tribunal decision

The decision of the tribunal must be given in writing, and state the reasons for the decision made. The latter can be arrived at by a majority, and need not be unanimous. The secretary must send a certified copy of the decision and reasons to all parties, which copy will then provide prima facie evidence of the matters stated therein.[11]

(g)   Time limits and extension of time

The 1978 Order lays down time limits for the service of applications, replies and other documents. So, for instance, the landlord's application for consent to the operation of a notice to quit must be made within one month after the service of the tenant's counter notice under section 26 of the 1986 Act.[12] Similarly any party intending to oppose any application to the tribunal, of whatever nature, must within one month of the application being served on him reply in the form of Reply appended to the application

5 Rule 25.
6 Rules 26 and 27.
7 Rule 28(1).
8 Rule 28(2)(b).
9 Rule 20.
10 Rule 30(3).
11 Rule 31.
12 Rule 2(2).

served on him.[13] Time limits are also specified for the service of documents in proceedings before the tribunal for statutory succession.[14]

The time limits laid down are mandatory, and must be strictly complied with. If, for instance, no reply is received within the period allowed, the tribunal can make an order in terms of the application without a formal hearing.[15] Rule 37 provides, however, that the time limit for the doing of any act, or taking of any step in connection with any proceedings, can be extended by the chairman of the tribunal 'on such terms and conditions, if any, as appear to him just'. The discretion of the chairman to grant or refuse an extension of time is absolute, and can only be challenged if he can be shown to have erred in law in exercising his discretion to allow or refuse an extension of time. It was held in *Moss v National Coal Board*[16] that natural justice requires the chairman to allow the parties to make *written* representations when considering whether to exercise his discretion. He is under no duty, however, to permit an applicant to make oral representations in support of an application for an extension of time.

(h) Appeal on a point of law

Section 6 of the Agriculture (Miscellaneous Provisions) Act 1954 and Rule 33 of the 1978 Order provide for points of law arising during tribunal proceedings to be referred to the High Court for decision, by way of the case stated procedure. A case stated by the tribunal for the decision of the High Court must set out the question of law and the facts found by the Tribunal, and must be signed by the chairman. Furthermore it must be sent to the party who requested the reference within two months after the date of his request, or within two months of the making of an order by the High Court directing the reference, whichever applies.[17]

A point of law can be referred to the High Court by case stated in one of two ways:

(a) A party to the tribunal proceedings can request that any question of law arising during those proceedings be referred by the tribunal to the High Court for decision. The request can be made either during the course of the proceedings, or after the tribunal's decision has been given.[18] The request must either be made at the hearing or, if the decision has been made, not later than fourteen days from the date on which a copy of the tribunal's decision was sent to the party making the request.[19] If made after the proceedings have terminated, the request must be made in writing to the secretary of the tribunal and be accompanied by as many copies of the request as there are other parties. If the tribunal agree to the request, the case stated must be sent to the party requesting it within two months after the date of his request.[20]

---

13 Rule 15.
14 See Rule 6, SI 1984/1301.
15 Rule 15(2), SI 1978/259, Rule 11(2), SI 1984/1301.
16 (1982) 264 EG 52.
17 SI 1978/259 Rule 33(3).
18 See section 6(1) of the 1954 Act.
19 SI 1978/259, Rule 33(1).
20 Above.

Proceedings for determination of the case stated must be begun by way of originating motion in the High Court by the party requesting the reference, and are governed by R.S.C. Order 56. Jurisdiction to hear and determine the case stated is exercised by a Divisional Court of the Queen's Bench Division. Notice of motion must be served by the applicant on the secretary of the tribunal and any other party to the proceedings in which the question of law arose, and it must be entered for hearing (and notice thereof served) within fourteen days after the case stated was served on the applicant.[1]

(b) If the tribunal refuse to refer a point of law to the High Court for decision, section 6(2) of the 1954 Act empowers a party aggrieved thereby to apply to the High Court for an order *directing* the tribunal to state a case. He must, within seven days after receiving notice of the refusal, serve on the secretary notice in writing of his intended application.[2] The application is then made by originating motion to a Divisional Court of the Queen's Bench Division. The motion must be entered for hearing, and notice served, within fourteen days after receipt by the applicant of notice of the tribunal's refusal of his request to state a case.[3]

If the High Court orders a case to be stated, the matter then proceeds as if the tribunal had acceded to the applicant's request at the outset.[4]

During the proceedings in the High Court the tribunal proceedings and decision (if one has been made) are suspended. Following the High Court's ruling the tribunal must, where necessary, modify their decision to give effect to the court's decision. In any case involving a notice to quit they can further postpone the date on which it is to take effect, if necessary. The power of the tribunal to modify its decision can be exercised by the chairman in any case where he does not consider it necessary to reconvene the tribunal.[5]

It may happen that a party aggrieved may wish to make a reference on a point of law, but is unable to formulate a case sufficiently clearly from the reasons given by the tribunal for its decision. The court has power[6] in this situation to amend the case stated or return it to the tribunal for amendment and clarification. When the matter is reconsidered by the tribunal no further evidence should be called, but the parties can, if they wish, elaborate their contentions based on the evidence already given. The tribunal must record any further submissions, and may make any relevant findings of fact in relation to them. The tribunal is under an overriding duty to provide both parties with the materials which will enable them to know whether it made an error of law in reaching its findings of fact.[7]

---

1 RSC Order 56, Rule 10.
2 SI 1978/259, Rule 33(2).
3 RSC Order 56, Rule 8.
4 Ie as outlined in (a) above.
5 *Ibid* Rule 34.
6 Under RSC Order 56(1).
7 See *Moses v Hurst* (1983) 269 EG 853.

(I) JUDICIAL REVIEW OF TRIBUNAL DECISION

Control of the tribunal's conduct and decision can in some circumstances be exercised using the prerogative orders of certiorari, mandamus and prohibition. Certiorari is available to quash a tribunal decision where the tribunal has acted without jurisdiction, while mandamus will issue to compel the tribunal to exercise a jurisdiction they have wrongly refused. Prohibition is available to prevent the tribunal assuming a jurisdiction which is not rightfully theirs. An application for one or more of the prerogative orders must be made in the first instance by way of an application for judicial review, in accordance with Rule 53 of the Rules of the Supreme Court. Leave of the court must be obtained before an application for judicial review can be brought.[8]

Certiorari will lie to quash a tribunal decision in two situations:

(i)   Where the tribunal has acted without jurisdiction. This head of review applies not only where the tribunal lacks jurisdiction, but also where the decision was obtained by fraud or by the bias of members of the tribunal, or where there has been some breach of the principles of natural justice, eg the tribunal has considered evidence from one party but not from the other.

(ii) Where there is a 'speaking' order and, although the tribunal has acted within its jurisdiction, an error of law is manifest on the face of the record. Certiorari will therefore lie where it is clear from the record that the tribunal took no evidence into account when reaching its decision, or took into account evidence which should have been rejected. It will not lie, however, where the tribunal has merely attributed the wrong weight to conflicting evidence, as this is a mistake of fact, not law. Where want of jurisdiction is invoked, the court can admit affidavit evidence to see whether or not there was jurisdiction. Where an error of law is alleged and the tribunal is acting within its jurisdiction, affidavit evidence is not admissable, and the error must appear on the face of the record itself.[9] The 'record' for these purposes consists of the document which initiates the tribunal proceedings, the pleadings (if any) and the tribunal's decision – but not the evidence or the tribunal's reasons unless it chooses to incorporate them in the decision.[10] Agricultural Land Tribunals are required by Rule 31 of the 1978 Order to give reasons for their decisions and these will thereupon become a matter of record. If an error of law does not appear on the face of the record, the only remedy is to request a case stated under Section 6 of the 1954 Act.[11]

By reason of its nature, the remedy by way of application for judicial review is rarely invoked in practice.

---

8 RSC Order 53(3).
9 *R v Agricultural Land Tribunal for South Eastern Area, ex p Bracey* [1960] 2 All ER 518.
10 See *R v Northumberland Compensation Appeal Tribunal, ex p Shaw* [1952] 1 KB 338 at p 352, CA.
11 *Cf Davies v Price* [1958] 1 All ER 671, CA and *Moses v Hurst* (1983) 269 EG 853.

(j)   Issue estoppel and costs

Agricultural Land Tribunals have no general power to award costs to one party or the other. Section 5 of the Agriculture (Miscellaneous Provisions) Act 1954, however, gives the tribunal a limited power to award costs against a party who has 'acted frivolously, vexatiously or oppressively' in prosecuting an application. The object of this limited power to award costs is inter alia, to discourage the landlord from abusing the tribunal procedure by serving successive notices to quit on the same, or similar, grounds in order to harrass a tenant.

Where the tribunal have decided a matter once and for all, the doctrine of issue estoppel will apply to prevent a landlord making a fresh application on substantially the same grounds. The doctrine does not apply, however, to prevent a landlord requesting consent to the operation of successive notices to quit, even where consent is sought on the same grounds as in earlier (unsuccessful) applications. Where consent is sought, for instance on grounds of good husbandry or greater hardship, and an earlier application on these same grounds has been turned down, there is clearly potential for a change in the relevant facts which the tribunal must assess from the evidence adduced. Although the landlord is not estopped from making a further application in such circumstances, he runs the risk of being penalised in costs if he alienates the tribunal by serving successive applications asking for what is, in substance, the same thing.[12]

2.   Dairy produce quota tribunals

The initial allocation of milk quotas to producers was made by reference to direct sales and wholesale deliveries during the 'base year' of 1983, and is now of historical significance only. The Dairy Produce Quotas Regulations 1984, in establishing the scheme, made provision for the establishment of Dairy Produce Quota Tribunals to consider appeals against allocation of quota by the Minister.[13] The 1984 regulations have been superseded, but reg 32 of the (now) Dairy Produce Quota Regulations 1989 provides for the continuance of the tribunals initially established in 1984. Their principal functions are, in relation to:

(i)   *Direct Sales Quota*; to consider objections to the allocation of direct sales quota,[14] to consider special case claims and award 'secondary' direct sales quota[15] and to consider exceptional hardship claims and award gross 'additional' direct sales quota.[16] The tribunal notify the Minister in each case of the primary direct sales quota awarded, and any secondary direct sales quota so awarded.[17]

(ii)   *Wholesale Quota*; to consider appeals against the allocation of primary wholesale quota[18] and secondary wholesale quota,[19] and to

12 See *Wickington v Bonney* (1982) 47 P & CR 655, especially per Stephen Brown J. Also *Burman v Woods* [1948] 1 KB 111, CA; *Mills v Cooper* [1967] 2 QB 459.
13 SI 1984/1074, para 6.
14 SI 1984/1074, reg 7(4).
15 *Ibid* Sch 1 paras 9, 10 and 11.
16 *Ibid* Sch 1 para 17.
17 Sch 1, para 12.
18 SI 1984/1047, Sch 2, reg 4.
19 *Ibid* Sch 2, reg 10.

consider exceptional hardship claims and award gross 'additional' wholesale quota.[20]

The Constitution of Dairy Produce Quota Tribunals is governed by Schedule 10 of the Dairy Produce Quota Regulations 1989. Each Tribunal consists of up to ninety members appointed by the Minister, including a chairman appointed by him.[1] Its quorum will be three, and decisions are reached on a majority verdict.[2] The terms of appointment and remuneration of the members of the tribunals, its secretary and staff, are as determined by the Minister.[3] The 1989 regulations make no provision for tribunal procedure – in most cases, where the regulations do not otherwise provide, the procedure of each Dairy Produce Quota Tribunal is such as its chairman in his discretion determines.[4] Any document purporting to be a determination of the Tribunal and signed by the Chairman or Secretary as such, shall be taken in proceedings to be evidence of such determination.[5]

The tribunal's functions are as an appellate forum from ministerial decisions. The 1989 regulations make no provision for appeals on points of law, eg to the High Court. Tribunal proceedings are, however, open to judicial review in the normal manner, and the prerogative writs of mandamus, certiorari and prohibition will lie in appropriate circumstances.

C Arbitration in agricultural disputes

1. Arbitration under the Agricultural Holdings Act

Schedule 11 to the Agricultural Holdings Act 1986 makes detailed provision for arbitration in agricultural disputes by a single arbitrator. While Agricultural Land Tribunals deal chiefly with termination of tenancies following notice to quit, and with succession rights, the matters referred to arbitration by the 1986 Act are, rather, those which can more readily be settled by a valuer, surveyor or land agent with expertise in agricultural valuations. They principally include disputes as to the terms of the written tenancy agreement, and disputes arising on termination of a tenancy as to the quantum of compensation payable by the parties. The matters for which arbitration is available to resolve disputes between the parties are set out in Table 1 on p 269.

By virtue of Section 84 of the 1986 Act, any matter which is required to be determined by arbitration under the Act or its subordinate regulations *must* be determined by arbitration under the provisions of the Eleventh Schedule. The Arbitration Act 1950 does not apply. This does not, of course, prevent the parties settling their differences by agreement, without recourse to arbitration under the 1986 Act. The jurisdiction of the statutory arbitrator cannot be *extended* by agreement, however. Neither can it be conferred by agreement, or by an estoppel, if no jurisdiction exists *ab initio*.

20 Sch 2, para 17.
 1 SI 1989/370, Sch 10, para 1.
 2 *Ibid* paras 2 and 3.
 3 Para 6.
 4 Para 7.
 5 Para 5.

(a)   Appointment of arbitrator

The arbitrator appointed will be either a person appointed by the agreement of the parties, or a person appointed by the President of the RICS on the application of either of the parties.[6] The Lord Chancellor maintains a panel of valuers, surveyors and land agents with expertise in agricultural matters, from which appointments are made. Where the arbitration relates to holdings in Wales, the arbitrator appointed must be a person who possesses a knowledge of Welsh agricultural conditions, and if either party so requires, a knowledge of the Welsh language.[7] The appointment must be made by the President as soon as possible after receiving the application. Where arbitration is demanded on a rent review, however, the appointment must be made not *earlier* than *four* months before the next termination date of the tenancy following the date of demand ie within four months before the date on which the rent variation is to take effect.[8] If the arbitrator, once appointed, dies or is incapable of acting, or for seven days after notice from either party requiring him to act fails to do so, a new arbitrator may be appointed. In the case of a rent arbitration, the date of the appointment of the original arbitrator is taken as the date of reference, as at which the rent properly payable must be assessed.[9] Neither party has power to revoke the appointment without the consent of the other, and the arbitrator's appointment is not revoked by the death of either party.[10]

The renumeration of the arbitrator is to be fixed by agreement of the parties in cases where he is appointed by agreement, or is in default by the registrar of the county court. Where the arbitrator is appointed by the President of the RICS it will be fixed by the President.[11]

(b)   Arbitration or valuation?

Schedule 11 applies where there is an *arbitration* between the parties. It is important to distinguish an arbitration from proceedings which amount to a mere valuation, and to which the provisions of Schedule 11 therefore have no application.

Arbitration is a judicial process involving the reference of an existing difference or dispute to the decision of a third party, and must be contrasted with a valuation, which merely precludes a dispute from arising and does not settle one that has already arisen.[12] The arbitrator is bound to hear the parties, take evidence, and to determine judicially between the competing claims on the basis of the evidence that has been put before him. If, on the other hand, an expert is appointed by agreement merely to mediate between the parties, and to decide solely by the use of his own eyes, knowledge and skill, he will be conducting a valuation.[13] A valuation will be binding on the

---

6 Sch 11, para 1 of the 1986 Act.
7 Sch 11, para 1(4).
8 Sch 11, para 1(3). There is not, however, a time limit on appointments made *after* the review date, other than the general injunction to appoint 'as soon as possible' after an application (Sch 11 para 1(3)). This has implications, for instance, for the tenants right to serve short notice to quit following a rent increase (see s 25(3) of the 1986 Act).
9 Sch 11, para 3.
10 Sch 11, para 4.
11 Sch 11, para 6.
12 *Arenson v Casson Beckman Rutley & Co* [1975] 3 All ER 901 at 915–16, HL.
13 See *Re Dawdy and Hartcup* (1885) 15 QBD 426, CA; *Palacath Ltd v Flanagan* [1985] 2 All ER 161.

parties even though the formal requirements applying to arbitrations under the 1986 Act have not been fully complied with.

One further distinction should be noted. If a valuer is negligent in making a valuation he can be sued in tort by either party – landlord or tenant – who is injured by his wrong valuation. An arbitrator, however, is immune from suit and cannot be sued by either party to the dispute, even if negligent. Where an arbitrator has been negligent the only remedy is to have the award set aside, and this can only be done where he has been guilty of misconduct or there is an error of law on the face of the award. The arbitrator himself has personal immunity from suit, provided that at the time of the reference to him there was a formulated dispute between the parties which his decision was needed to resolve.[14]

(c) Initiating arbitration proceedings

Those provisions of the 1986 Act referring matters to arbitration invariably require that one of the parties initially serve a notice in writing, demanding arbitration under the Act. Having done so, each party must then submit a statement of case to the arbitrator within thirty-five days following the date of his appointment.

(I) PRELIMINARY NOTICES

Where arbitration is required during the continuance of a tenancy, the aggrieved party must first serve notice in writing demanding arbitration. In several instances time limits within which this must be done are laid down by the legislation. Where the tenant wishes to challenge any of the reasons stated in a notice to quit given under Case A, Case B, Case D, or Case E to Schedule 3 of the Agricultural Holdings Act 1986, he must demand arbitration within one month following service of the landlord's notice to quit.[15] Where arbitration is demanded on a rent review, notice demanding arbitration must be served giving the same period of notice as that required for a notice to quit. Where other matters are referred to arbitration during the currency of the tenancy (for instance the reduction of the tenancy agreement into writing) no time limits are laid down for service of the preliminary demand for arbitration. The form and content of the preliminary notice will depend upon the nature of the dispute in question, but it must in all cases be clear and unambiguous.

Where arbitration is demanded to settle monetary claims arising on termination of a tenancy, the landlord and tenant must within two months of the end of the tenancy serve notice of intention to claim on the other party.[16] This need only specify the statutory provision, custom or term of the agreement under which the claim is made. The parties have eight months following termination in which to agree the sums payable, in default of which the matter is compulsorily referable to arbitration. Where the tenant wishes to claim two years' rent as compensation for disturbance, and/or to make a claim for 'high' farming, he must additionally serve notice of his

14 See inter alia *Arenson v Casson Beckman Rutley & Co; Campbell v Edwards* [1976] 1 All ER 785, CA; *Palacath Ltd v Flanagan* [1985] 2 All ER 161. And see *Wallshire Ltd v Aarons* [1989] 1 EGLR 147 for difficulties in engaging liability for negligent valuation.
15 See Article 9, Agricultural Holdings (Arbitration on Notices) Order 1987.
16 See Section 83 of the 1986 Act.

intention to do so at least one month before termination of the tenancy.[17] If the landlord wishes to make a claim for general deterioration he must similarly serve notice of claim not less than one month before termination of the tenancy.[18]

If the time limit for service of a preliminary notice is not complied with, or the notice given is for some reason void, then an arbitrator subsequently appointed will not have jurisdiction to decide the dispute referred to him.[19]

(II) STATEMENT OF CASE FOR ARBITRATOR

Schedule 11, para 7 requires that the parties to the arbitration must, within thirty-five days of the arbitrator's appointment, deliver to him a statement of their respective cases 'with all necessary particulars'. The arbitrator's appointment is completed for this purpose when the President of the RICS executes the instrument of appointment, and time runs from that date.[20] No amendment or addition to the statement or particulars delivered is permitted after the expiration of thirty-five days, except with the consent of the arbitrator.

It was decided in *Cooke Bourne (Farms) Ltd v Mellows*[1] that amendments and additions to the statement of case can be allowed by the arbitrator after that time, even where they are of a fundamental nature. On an application by one of the parties to amend, the amendment or addition requested should ordinarily be allowed if, after amendment, the respondent will know sufficiently the particulars of the case he has to meet. The mere fact of the absence of all necessary particulars in the original statement of case cannot itself be a ground for refusing consent to an attempt to remedy the deficiency.[2] As a result, a party who has submitted his statement of case can amend at will during the thirty-five day period following the arbitrator's appointment, and can further add to or amend his particulars after that time with the consent of the arbitrator. The arbitrator should ordinarily grant consent, but can refuse to do so if he finds that the respondent will be in a worse position, as a result of the amendment, than he would have been if the matters added had originally been in the statement of case. If the arbitrator finds that since the original statement of case whether by lapse of time, or because he has altered his position, or for some other reason, it would be unfair to impose the amendment on the respondent, then consent can be refused. If the respondent is no worse off than he would have been had the amendments been in the original statement of case, then they should be allowed. Note however that a statement of case, even if inadequate, has to be filed within the thirty-five day limit before the power of addition/amendment becomes exercisable. If no statement of case is served then there is nothing to amend. The thirty-five day period within which the statement of case must be served is itself inflexible, and cannot be extended.[3]

No statutory form is prescribed for the statement of case. The particulars must give an indication of the nature of the particular claims made, rather

17 Sections 60(6) and 70(2) *ibid*.
18 Section 72(4) *ibid*.
19 For an example see *French v Elliott* [1959] 3 All ER 866.
20 See Sch 11, para 31.
 1 [1983] QB 104, CA.
 2 See *ibid* at 118–20, per Cumming-Bruce LJ.
 3 See *Church Comrs for England v Mathews* (1979) 251 EG 1074.

than simply the class of claim, *viz* they must give an indication to the respondent of the particular kind of claim that is to be made, in order that he may have an opportunity of himself examining the subject matter to see what evidence he will have to adduce in his defence, and what information he will have to give the arbitrator.[4] Particulars of this nature must be given in order to limit the other part in his inquiries, and to show the particular issues between the parties. They must be informative as to the extent and nature of the claim, as opposed to the class of claim, and must be more than mere generalities or a mere statement that there is to be a claim.[5] So, for instance, where a second year's rent is claimed as compensation for disturbance the tenant must specify the loss he has suffered, so as to enable the landlord to investigate the facts satisfactorily and prepare his case.[6] It follows that the statement of case should always include a statement of all the substantive issues on which the party serving it is relying.

Each party to the arbitration is confined at the hearing to the matters alleged in the statement and particulars delivered by him, and any additions or amendments duly made.[7] If a party fails to deliver his statement of case within the time limit he is precluded from setting up an affirmative case, or counter claim. *Semble*, however, he will still be entitled to cross examine the other party and his witnesses, with the object of destroying his case.[8]

(d)   Conduct of arbitration proceedings

The arbitrator is required to make and sign his award within 56 days of his appointment.[9] Application can however be made to the President to extend the time for delivery of the arbitrator's award.[10] Although the parties' statements of case must give information as to the nature and extent of the particular claims made, they need not give precise details on all matters incidental thereto. The parties may, therefore, wish to supplement their statements of case with further and better particulars of the claims made. It is legitimate for the arbitrator to ask them to do so, although Schedule 11 does not give him power to *require* that this be done. It should also be noted that the statement of case will itself normally only contain details of the *claims* made by each party. As both parties must serve their statements of case within the same time limit after the arbitrator's appointment, it follows that each will often have only a vague idea of the claims to be made by the other party when drafting his own statement of case. In this situation, a defending party can request alterations and additions to his own statement of case so as to incorporate his defence to the claims of the other party.

---

4 See for instance *Jones v Evans* [1923] 1 KB 12, 20, CA; *Re O'Connor and Brewin's Arbitration* [1933] 1 KB 20, CA; *Spreckley v Leicestershire County Council* [1934] 1 KB 366, CA.
5 *Church Comrs for England v Mathews*, supra.
6 See *Re O'Connors and Brewin's Arbitration*, supra – 'Disturbance two years rent £514' insufficient.
7 Sch 11, para 7(b).
8 See *Collett v Deeley* (1949) 100 L JO 108 (a county court decision).
9 Sch 11, para 14.
10 Sch 11, para 14(2). The parties may, as in common, give the arbitrator their written consent to a delayed award, for the purpose of obtaining the President's approval to an extension of time. This will be necessary for instance, where legal issues arising require resolution (by way of a case stated or otherwise) before the arbitration can proceed.

Although the arbitration hearing will normally be fairly informal, it should be remembered that it should be carried out in a judicial manner. The arbitrator must make his award after hearing the evidence of both parties. The hearing must be conducted in an impartial manner, according to the ordinary rules of evidence applied in a court action. In particular the arbitrator must not refuse to admit evidence, take evidence in the absence of both parties, or take evidence from one party in the absence of the other. If the rules of evidence are not complied with, or the arbitrator fails to conduct himself in a manner appropriate to a judicial inquiry, his award can be set aside for misconduct.

The parties to the arbitration must submit to be examined by the arbitrator, on oath or affirmation, in relation to the matters in dispute. They must also, subject to any legal objection, produce before the arbitrator any samples or documents in their possession or power which may be required and called for, and do all other things which during the proceedings the arbitrator may require.[11] The parties can call witnesses, and if the arbitrator thinks fit he can administer the oath or affirmation to both the parties and any witnesses appearing, and take evidence on oath.[12] The attendance of witnesses can be compelled by the issue of a witness summons by the county court.[13] The rules of civil evidence as to the admissibility of evidence apply, and so hearsay evidence will be inadmissible.

In principle an arbitrator acting under the 1986 Act must base his decision exclusively on the evidence adduced by the parties, and is not entitled to carry out a valuation based on his own views and expertise. Although the proceedings are judicial in nature it may in some circumstances be legitimate for him to supplement the evidence adduced by the parties with his own expert knowledge and experience. The arbitrator's professional opinion, based on his own experience acquired in both transactions and arbitrations he has been involved in, and from other sources within his range of competence, can be relied upon in addition to the evidence produced by the parties. When using factual evidence outside that adduced by the parties more care must be shown. If the arbitrator has first-hand knowledge of a transaction he can bring this knowledge into account. He cannot, however, rely on his recollection of transactions of which he has no direct knowledge, as this will amount to hearsay evidence and be inadmissible.[14] In particular, he must not make use of personal knowledge acquired in any capacity other than arbitrator.[15] Neither can he make use of his own personal experience if it is contrary to the evidence that has actually been submitted by the parties to the arbitration.

(e) Inspection of holding

The arbitrator will commonly wish to make an inspection of the holding to assess the facts for himself. This will often be the case, for instance, in

---

11 Sch 11, para 8.
12 Sch 11, para 9.
13 Sch 11, para 10.
14 See *English Exporters (London) Ltd v Eldonwall Ltd* [1973] Ch 415, 420.
15 See, eg *Owen v Nicholl* [1948] 1 All ER 707, CA.

arbitrations on a notice to do work or to remedy breaches of tenancy; here the arbitrator will need to assess whether a reasonable period has been allowed to remedy the breaches complained of, or whether the tenant has substantially complied with the notice. When carrying out an inspection the arbitrator should remember that he is acting in a quasi-judicial capacity, and so must not use the occasion as an opportunity to take evidence in the absence of the parties, eg by taking an expert valuer or architect with him, on whose evidence he subsequently relies.[16] Neither can he make an inspection in the presence of one party only, from whom he will inevitably take evidence in the absence of the other.[17] To avoid these problems a date should be fixed in advance for the inspection, and both parties given notice so that they can attend in the presence of the arbitrator, together with their advisers if they so wish.

(f) The arbitrator's award

This is governed by Schedule 11, paragraphs 14–22 of the 1986 Act. The arbitrator must normally make and sign his award within fifty-six days of his appointment.[18] The arbitrator can apply to the President for an extension of the time allowed for making the award. If the arbitrator thinks fit he can make an interim award for the payment of any sum on account of the sum to be finally awarded.[19]

The final award must be made in prescribed form provided for by the Agricultural Holdings (Form of Award in Arbitration Proceedings) Order 1990.[20] The use of this form, or one substantially to the like effect, is compulsory.[1] The award must state separately the amounts awarded in respect of the individual claims referred to arbitration, and if either party so applies the amount awarded in respect of any particular improvement or other matter included in the award.[2] The arbitrator has no jurisdiction to refuse to itemise the amount awarded for particular items of improvements etc if either party applies for a detailed award containing this information.

The award must fix a day not later than one month after its delivery for the payment of the money awarded as compensation, and costs.[3] The award is final and binding on the parties, and so a conditional award will be void.[4] So, for instance, in *Public Trustee v Randag*[5] it was held that an award cast in the form of a consultative case for the court, with a proviso that if the case was withdrawn or not proceeded with it should take effect as an award, was void as being conditional. In other words, Schedule 11 contemplates a single, complete and final award being made by the arbitrator, subject only to the

---

16 See *Ellis v Lewin* (1963) 107 Sol Jo 851, CA.
17 *Re O'Conor and Whitlaw's Arbitration* (1919) 88 LJKB 1242, CA.
18 Sch 11, para 14(1).
19 Sch 11, para 15.
20 SI 1990/1472, made under 1986 Act, s 84(2), (3)(c).
 1 *Ibid* SI 1990/1472.
 2 Sch 11, para 16 *ibid*.
 3 Sch 11, para 18.
 4 Sch 11, para 19.
 5 [1966] Ch 649.

possibility of interim payments being awarded, or consultative cases submitted to the court at an interlocutory stage for its opinion. The arbitrator has power to correct any clerical mistake or error in the award arising from an accidental slip or omission, but alterations of a more substantial nature cannot be made once the award has been given.[6]

By virtue of section 12 of the Tribunals and Inquiries Act 1971 the arbitrator must furnish a statement (either oral or written) of the reasons for his decision, if requested to do so by one or both of the parties. A request for a statement of reasons must be made before the giving of the award, and the reasons themselves must be given by the arbitrator 'on or before' the making of the award. A statement of reasons, once given, forms part of the award, and is an item of record which can be relied upon in later proceedings to have the award set aside.[7] Since 12th September 1984, a statement of reasons can be required both where the arbitrator is appointed under Schedule 11 and where he is appointed by the agreement of the parties.[8] It was held in *Re Poyser and Mills Arbitration*[9] that the reasons given must not only be proper, adequate and intelligible, but must also deal with the substantial points that have been raised by the parties during the arbitration. If there is something substantially wrong or inadequate in the reasons given this will amount to an error of law on the face of the award, which can be set aside.

Any sum directed to be paid by the award shall, unless the award itself otherwise directs, carry interest as from the date of the award, and at the same rate as a judgment debt.[10] The award can be enforced by proceedings in the county court, and if the latter so orders, it is recoverable in the same way as money ordered to be paid by the county court in the exercise of its ordinary jurisdiction.[11]

(g)   Costs of the arbitration

Schedule 11, para 23 provides that 'the costs of, and incidental to, the arbitration and award' are in the discretion of the arbitrator, who may direct to and by whom, and in what manner, the costs are to be paid. On the application of either party, the costs awarded by the arbitrator shall be taxable in the county court according to such of the county court scales of costs as the arbitrator has directed. If the arbitrator's award has not specified the county court scale which is to apply, the county court can itself direct the scale according to which the costs are to be taxed.[12]

The arbitrator's discretion as to costs is absolute. He is, however, directed by Schedule 11, para 25 to take into account the reasonableness or unreasonableness of the claim of either party, any unreasonable demand for particulars or refusal to supply particulars, and generally all the circumstances of the case. He may disallow the costs of any witness whom he considers to have been called unnecessarily, and any other costs which he

---

6 See Sch 11, para 20.
7 *Ibid* s 12(5).
8 Sch 11, para 21 *ibid* and Sch 3, para 28(7) of the 1984 Act.
9 [1964] 2 QB 467.
10 Sch 11, para 22.
11 See s 85(1) of the 1986 Act.
12 Sch 11, para 24.

considers to have been unnecessarily incurred. As a general rule, costs usually follow the issue. The arbitrator's discretion is general, however, and in the absence of proof of misconduct, abuse of discretion or want of jurisdiction, his award as to costs cannot be upset. Hence, where a landlord made an excessive claim for dilapidations and, on being successful, was awarded only a proportion of the compensation claimed, it was held that the arbitrator had acted lawfully in directing that the landlord should pay the costs of the arbitration and award.[13] Where a party to the arbitration is successful, however, the arbitrator should only award costs against him in exceptional circumstances. The parties are free to agree as to how the costs of an arbitration should be borne as between themselves, notwithstanding the arbitrator's award as to costs.

(h) Judicial supervision of arbitration proceedings

Arbitration proceedings under the 1986 Act are subject to judicial supervision by the county court.

(I) INTERLOCUTORY PROCEEDINGS

Schedule 11, para 26 provides that the arbitrator can, at any stage during the proceedings, state in the form of a special case for the opinion of the county court any question of law arising during the course of the arbitration. The arbitrator *must* state a case for the opinion of the court if the court so directs following an application in that behalf by either party. The arbitrator can also state a case for the opinion of the court as to whether he has jurisdiction to conduct the arbitration.[14] He might lack jurisdiction because, for instance, preliminary notices were not served within the prescribed time limits, because his appointment was not made within the time allowed, or if the appointment is void for some other technical irregularity.

The case stated is an interlocutory matter.[15] It follows that the arbitrator can state a case as soon as he is appointed, and before he hears evidence, but cannot do so once the final award has been made. The normal procedure is for the arbitrator to state a consultative case to the county court, and for the county court judge (after hearing the parties) to state his opinion before sending the matter back for the hearing to continue. The arbitrator's award cannot itself be cast in the form of a consultative case. The opinion of the court on the case stated is binding on the arbitrator, who would be guilty of misconduct if he ignored it.

The procedure for stating a case is laid down by Order 44 of the County Court Rules 1981. An application for an order *directing* an arbitrator to state a case must be made by originating application, and must include a concise statement of the question of law on which a case stated is sought. The arbitrator himself is not a respondent to the application, but if the county court judge grants the application a copy of the order must be served on the arbitrator.[16] The arbitrator can state a case either of his own volition, or following a direction to do so from the county court. The case itself must be signed by the arbitrator and lodged by him in the court office together with a

---

13 See *Gray v Lord Ashburton* [1917] AC 26, HL.
14 Sch 11, para 26.
15 See generally *Public Trustee v Randag* [1966] Ch 649.
16 CCR O44, r 2.

copy for the judge. The judge has power to remit the case to the arbitrator for restatement, or further statement, if he finds it inadequate.[17] Only questions of law can be referred on a case stated, and the parties cannot dictate what questions of law the arbitrator refers for an opinion. It should be remembered that the question whether there is any evidence on which to support a finding of fact is itself a question of law, and a matter on which the opinion of the court can therefore be sought. Right of appeal lies from the 'opinion' of the county court judge to the Court of Appeal,[18] and if necessary, to the House of Lords.

(II)   MISCONDUCT BY ARBITRATOR

Schedule 11, para 27 provides that where an arbitrator has misconducted himself the county court can set aside the award. It can also remove the arbitrator, although this will normally only be done where the misconduct is serious. The county court can also set aside the award if it has been improperly procured. The county court has power to remit the award or any part of it to the reconsideration of the arbitrator.[19]

Whether the extent of the irregularity is sufficient to justify interference by the court to set aside the award depends upon whether the court is satisfied that there *may* have been, or that the irregularity *may* have caused, a substantial miscarriage of justice that would justify the setting aside or remitting of the award. The award will not normally be set aside if it can be shown that no other award could properly have been made than that which was in fact made, notwithstanding the irregularity.[20] Personal misconduct by the arbitrator which throws doubt on his impartiality, or leads to a suspicion of bias, will therefore usually be sufficient to have the award set aside. So, for instance, the arbitrator should avoid accepting hospitality from either party prior to the making of the award, as this might impugn his impartiality. If it is shown that the object of one of the parties in providing hospitality was to corrupt the arbitrator, or if the court discerns that hospitality so given has in any way influenced the award, then the award can be set aside for misconduct.[1]

Quite apart from personal misconduct, an award can also be set aside for misconduct of a technical nature. If an arbitrator refuses to adjudicate upon the issues before him or rejects material evidence, this will be misconduct entitling the person against whom the award was made to have it set aside.[2] *Semble*, however, mere failure to resolve a conflict of evidence may not amount to misconduct.[3] It will be misconduct for an arbitrator, in the absence of the parties and after the conclusion of the hearing, to obtain additional evidence which the parties have no opportunity to challenge by cross-examination.[4] Likewise, the arbitrator must take evidence in the presence of both parties. He is only entitled to proceed *ex parte* where notice of the hearing has been given to one of the parties, who has then failed to

17 *Ibid* O44, r 2.
18 County Court Act 1984, s 77.
19 Sch 11, para 28. Agricultural Holdings Act 1986.
20 See eg *Rotheray & Sons Ltd v Carlo Bedarida & Co* [1961] 1 Lloyds Rep 220, 224.
 1 *Re Hopper* (1867) LR 2, QB 367.
 2 *Williams v Wallis and Cox* [1914] 2 KB 478.
 3 *Burton v Timmis* [1987] 1 EGLR 1 at 3, CA per Kerr LJ.
 4 See *Ellis v Lewin* (1963) 107 So Jo 851, CA.

attend. The award can also be set aside for misconduct if the arbitrator admits inadmissible evidence, or fails in some other respect to comply with the rules of evidence, or if he fails to deliver his award within the permitted time. It has also been held to amount to misconduct if the arbitrator refuses to adjourn the hearing to enable one of the parties to arrange legal representation.[5]

An award can be set aside as having been 'improperly procured'[6] *viz* if it has been obtained by fraud, bribery, corruption or other improper devices.

An application to the county court for the removal of an arbitrator, or for an order setting aside his award for misconduct, must be made within twenty-one days after the date of the award.[7] It should be made by originating application in accordance with Order 3 rule 4 of the County Court Rules.

(III) ERROR OF LAW ON THE FACE OF THE AWARD

Schedule 11, para 28(2) additionally gives the county court power to set aside an award where there is an error of law on the face of the award. High Court jurisdiction is thus in general excluded,[8] although proceedings for judicial review of an arbitrators findings can in principle be sought if the statutory remedies prove inadequate.

An error on the face of the award will often arise from misconduct, in which case the court can in any event set aside the award on the latter ground. The error may not always arise from misconduct, however. An award can be set aside under this head where it is obvious on its face that the arbitrator has wrongly interpreted the relevant statutory provisions, or the terms of the contract of tenancy. As we have seen, section 12 of the Tribunals and Enquiries Act 1971 requires that the arbitrator must give reasons for his decision when requested to do so by the parties on or before the giving of his decision. If the reasons given are incomplete or inadequate, in that they fail to deal with the substantial points raised at the hearing, then this may be an error of law on the face of the record entitling the court to set it aside. A failure to adequately state the reasons for the award will only have this consequence, it seems, if the aggrieved party can demonstrate that the decision is itself vitiated by reason of having been reached by an erroneous process of legal reasoning.[9] Insufficiency of reasons may give rise to an implication that this is so.[10] The reasons given by the arbitrator are incorporated into the award and form part of it, so that it becomes a 'speaking' order.[11] The arbitrator is not bound to itemise in his award, however, the exact extent of the tenant's failure to remedy breaches of tenancy, or his reasons for small findings of fact.[12]

The scope of the remedy is narrow in that it is confined to errors of law *appearing on the face of the award itself*. The court is not entitled to look at affidavit evidence in order to establish whether an error of law has been

5 *Thomas v Official Solicitor* (1982) 265 EG 601, CA.
6 Sch 11, para 27(2). Agricultural Holdings Act 1986.
7 CCR, O44, r 3.
8 See *Jones v Pembrokeshire County Council* [1967] 1 QB 181.
9 *Mountview Court Properties Ltd v Devlin* (1970) 21 P & CR 689, 695.
10 See *Crake v Supplementary Benefits Commission* [1982] 1 All ER 498.
11 1971 Act, s 12(5).
12 See on this point *Horsnell v Alliance Assurance Co Ltd* (1967) 205 EG 319.

made, neither can it look at the statements of case submitted to the arbitrator by the parties. If the latter wish to challenge the conduct of the arbitration at any time prior to the award, the proper course is for them to state a case for the opinion of the court before the award is actually made.

An application to set aside the award for error of law must be made by originating application within twenty-one days after the date of the award.[13] If it appears to the county court that there is an error of law on the face of the award it can, instead of remitting the award to the arbitrator, vary the award by substituting for so much of it as is affected by the error such award as the court considers that it would have been proper for the arbitrator to make in the circumstances.[14] The award will then take effect as varied. If, on the other hand, the court remits the award to the arbitrator, then when the court otherwise directs he must make and sign his award within thirty days of the making of the order.[15]

2.   Milk quota arbitrations

(a)   Compensation on termination of tenancy

By virtue of Schedule 1, para 11(1) to the Agriculture Act 1986, any claim for compensation for milk quota arising on termination of a tenancy is compulsorily referable to arbitration. Arbitration in this instance takes place under the provisions of Sch 11 to the Agricultural Holdings Act 1986. No claim for compensation will be enforceable unless the tenant serves notice in writing of his intention to claim, and (moreover) does so before the expiry of two months from the termination of the tenancy. The parties have eight months following termination in which to settle the claim, but if it is not settled within that period it *must* be decided by arbitration under the Agricultural Holdings Act. If the tenant lawfully remains in occupation following termination, the two-month period for notice commences on termination of his occupation.[16] The enforcement provisions of the Agricultural Holdings Act apply as to other claims on termination.[17]

The arbitration provisions applicable to quotas differ in minor respects to those in Sch 11 of the 1986 Act. By virtue of Sch 1, para 11(5) to the Agriculture Act 1986 the arbitrator can allow a longer period for payment of the award, up to a maximum of three months from the date of the award. Furthermore, if the parties have *agreed* (in writing) the amount of the standard quota for the land, the tenant's fraction *or* the value of milk quota to be used in calculating the compensation under Sch 1, then the arbitrator *must* make this award in accordance with that agreement.[18] It is by no means clear whether, in reaching agreement, the parties must base themselves on the statutory formulae. The better view is probably that they must, if only

---

13 CCR O44, r 3.
14 Sch 11, para 28(2). Agricultural Holdings Act 1986.
15 Sch 11, para 28(3) *ibid*.
16 Sch 1, paras 11(2)–(5), Agriculture Act 1986.
17 Sch 1, para 12 *ibid*.
18 Sch 1, para 11(6), Agriculture Act 1986.

**TABLE I.   Agricultural holdings: matters compulsorily
referable to arbitration**

Matter:	*Provision*
Securing a Written Tenancy Agreement, and settling terms in Sch 1.	1986 Act, s 6(1)
Dispute as to effect on agreement of operation of Section 2.	1986 Act, s 2(4)
Varying repairing obligations, where lease at variance with SI 1973/1473 ('model clauses').	1986 Act, s 8(2)
Valuing rent payable on review.	1986 Act, s 12(1)
Increase of rent following landlord's improvements.	1986 Act, s 13(7)
Maintenance of land as permanent pasture.	1986 Act, s 14(2)
Freedom of cropping – whether tenant exercising right so as to cause damage etc.	1986 Act, s 15(6)
Fair value of tenant's fixtures purchased by landlord on termination of tenancy.	1986 Act, s 10(6)
Valuation of damage by game.	1986 Act, s 20(4)
Notices to Remedy breach of tenancy – liability to repair etc.	SI 1987/710, Art 3
Notice to Quit under Sch 3, Cases A, B, D or E of the 1986 Act.	SI 1987/710, Art 9. 1986 Act s 28(4) (case D only)
Availability of Alternative Accommodation (*ibid* Case A)	SI 1987/710, Art 9
Any claim by landlord or tenant, arising on or out of termination of tenancy, under the 1986 Act, custom or agreement, eg compensation for disturbance, improvements, tenant-right.	1986 Act, s 83(1)
Milk Quotas: determination of compensation to tenant on termination of tenancy.	Agriculture Act 1986, Sch 1, para 11(1)
Milk Quotas: determination of Standard Quota and Tenant's Fraction during tenancy.	*Ibid* Sch 1, para 10(1)

because para 11(7) enables the arbitrator to disregard the agreement if the 'circumstances relevant' to the latter were materially different at the time it was made, and have since changed. It should also be noted that Schedule 1, para 10 enables the parties to require arbitration during the tenancy to ascertain standard quota or the tenant's fraction. Arbitration is initiated by notice in writing served on the other party, demanding a reference, no time limit for service being in this instance stipulated. Where standard quota and/or tenant's fraction have been determined by arbitration this binds the (later) arbitration on the compensation claim, unless there has been a material change of circumstances.[19]

(b)   Apportionment of Milk Quota

Apportionment of milk quota following a change in occupation of a holding is directed by reg 10 of the Dairy Produce Quotas Regulations 1989[20] to be carried out by arbitration, in the absence of agreement. Arbitration in this instance is carried out in accordance with Sch 4 to the 1989 Regulations, and not under Sch 11 to the Agricultural Holdings Act 1986. The occupier can, additionally, require a prospective apportionment of quota to be made by arbitration under the 1989 Regulations if necessary.[1] In carrying out an apportionment or prospective apportionment the arbitrator must base his award on his findings as to the areas used for milk production in the five years immediately preceding the change of occupation, or (in the case of a prospective apportionment) the five years preceding his appointment.[2]

Arbitration will usually follow a sale or other transfer of quota. There may, however, be situations where simultaneous arbitrations under both the 1986 Act *and* the 1989 Regulations are required. Quota attaches to a 'holding' in the European community law sense, and not simply to a holding as understood in English law (*viz* tenanted land). It therefore attaches to all the production units operated by the milk producer.[3] Some of the holding thus defined may be freehold and some tenanted. On termination of the tenancy of land within a larger 'Euro-holding' it will be necessary to apportion quota between the tenanted and freehold portions of the holding[4] *and then* having done so, to calculate the compensation payable to the outgoing tenant of the tenanted portion by arbitration under the Agricultural Holdings Act 1986.

Prior to 1989 simultaneous arbitrations could cause considerable problems, not least because arbitrations under the Dairy Produce Quotas Regulations 1986 were governed by the Arbitration Act 1950, which latter does not apply to those under the agricultural holdings legislation. The position has now been simplified by the Dairy Produce Quotas Regulations 1989, which introduced new arbitration procedures approximating more closely to those under the agricultural holdings legislation, and statutory time limits within which steps in the arbitration procedure must be taken. Arbitration under the regulations is to be carried out in accordance with Sch 4 thereof, and the Arbitration Act 1950 does not apply.[5] Like Agricultural Holdings Act arbitrations, dairy quota arbitrations are now subject to the supervision of the county court.[6]

Schedule 4 provides for the following procedure in dairy quota arbitrations for apportionment of quota:

---

19 Sch 1, para 11(6)(b).
20 SI 1989/380.
 1 SI 1989/380, reg 11(2).
 2 SI 1989/380, Sch 4, para 3.
 3 Council Regulation (EEC) No 857/84, Art 12.
 4 Under SI 1989/380.
 5 Sch 4, para 34, SI 1989/380.
 6 Sch 4, paras 28–30.

(I)   APPOINTMENT AND RENUMERATION OF ARBITRATOR

The arbitrator is to be appointed by agreement of the parties within two months following a change in occupation of the holding. The transferee must notify the Minister in writing of the appointment within 14 days of the latter.[7] If agreement cannot be reached, either party may apply to the President of the RICS for the appointment of an arbitrator, provided this is done within the two-month period following a change of occupation. In default of agreement, or application, within the allowed period, the Minister shall apply to the President for an appointment to be made, in which event he is made a party to the proceedings.[8] Where an arbitration is to make a *prospective* apportionment, the arbitrator is appointed,[9]

(1)   by the President in cases where the Minister has notified the parties that he is not satisfied that the areas used for milk production are as stated in a declaration submitted by the parties under the regulations;[10] *or*

(2)   in all other cases by agreement between the occupier and any other interested party or, in default, by the President on an application by the occupier. The occupier must notify the Minister within 14 days after an agreed appointment, or of the date of application to the President (whichever applies).

An application to the President must be accompanied by the prescribed fee, which latter is the same as that prescribed from time to time for applications under Sch 11 to the Agricultural Holdings Act.[11] Where the application is made by the Minister the fee is recoverable from the parties to the arbitration as a civil debt, either jointly or severally.[12] Once an application has been made, the President is under a duty to make an appointment 'as soon as possible after receiving the application'.[13] The appointment will be made from the panel of arbitrators maintained by the Lord Chancellor for the purposes of the Agricultural Holdings Act.[14] Once an arbitrator is appointed, his appointment cannot be revoked by one party without the consent of the other; neither will it be revoked by the death of either party.[15] If the arbitrator dies, or is incapable of acting, or for seven days after notice from either party requiring him to act fails to do so, a new arbitrator can be appointed as if no arbitrator had originally been appointed.[16]

Renumeration. By virtue of Schedule 4, para 12 the arbitrator's renumeration is:

– where he is appointed by agreement, such amount as is agreed upon by him and the parties or (in default of agreement) an amount fixed by the registrar of the county court; *or*

---

7 SI 1989/380, Sch 4, para 1(1).
8 Sch 4, para 1(3) and (4).
9 See Sch 4, para 2.
10 Ie reg 10 or 11.
11 Sch 4, para 4.
12 Sch 4, para 5.
13 Sch 4, para 6.
14 Sch 4, para 8.
15 Sch 4, para 10.
16 Sch 4, para 9.

– where he is appointed by the President such amount as is agreed upon by him and the parties or (in default of agreement) fixed by the President.

The renumeration so fixed is recoverable by the arbitrator as a civil debt due from any one of the parties to the arbitration.

(II)   CONDUCT OF ARBITRATION PROCEEDINGS

The procedural rules, set out in Schedule 4, paras 13–20, closely mirror those in agricultural holdings arbitrations. Thus the parties have 35 days from the appointment of the arbitrator in which to deliver their statement of case.[17] No amendment or addition is allowed after the expiry of the 35 day period, except with the consent of the arbitrator. *Semble* the principles enunciated in *Cooke Bourne (Farms) Ltd v Mellows*[18] would apply here, as to amendments to the statement of case in an Agricultural Holdings Act arbitration.

Both the parties themselves, and witnesses, can be examined on oath or affirmation by the arbitrator. Parties to the arbitration must also, subject to legal objection, produce to the arbitrator all samples and documents in their power which may be called for by the latter.[19] The provisions of the county court rules as to witness summonses apply, as in Agricultural Holdings Act arbitrations.[20]

One difference in milk quota arbitrations is that the parties will commonly be more numerous, and not confined to landlord and tenant. Schedule 4, para 15 provides that any person having an interest in the holding to which the arbitration relates is entitled to make representations to the arbitrator. 'Holding' here bears its European meaning *viz* land, held by whatever tenure, and comprised in the producer's unit of production.

(III)   AWARD AND COSTS

The award must be made within 56 days of the arbitrator's appointment, and is final and binding on the parties to the arbitration.[1] The President of the RICS can enlarge the time limited for making the award. Although the award is final and binding, the arbitrator has power to make amendments, but *only* to correct any clerical mistake or 'error arising from any accidental slip or omission'.[2] The arbitrator must make either a written or oral statement of the reasons for the award if so requested, provided the party requesting the statement does so prior to the award being made.[3]

Costs of the arbitration are at the discretion of the arbitrator.[4] In awarding costs the arbitrator must take into consideration the reasonableness or otherwise of the claims of the parties, any unreasonable demand for (or refusal of) particulars, and (generally) all the circumstances of the case.[5] The parties can apply for costs to be taxed in the county court.

17 Sch 4, para 13.
18 [1983] QB 104, CA (above p 361).
19 Sch 4, paras 14 and 16.
20 Sch 4, paras 17 and 18.
 1 Sch 4, paras 21 and 22.
 2 Sch 4, para 24.
 3 Sch 4, para 24. *Cf* the more stringent requirements of Sch 11, para 21 Agricultural Holdings Act 1986.
 4 Sch 4, para 25.
 5 Sch 4, para 27.

(IV) UPSETTING THE ARBITRATOR'S AWARD

The 1989 Regulations also bring quota arbitrations more into conformity with Agricultural Holdings Act arbitrations by subjecting the proceedings to the supervision of the county court. Thus:

– at the interlocutory stage, the arbitrator can state a case for the opinion of the county court on any question of law arising in the course of the proceedings, or on any jurisdictional question.[6] He *must* state a case if directed to do so by the court on application by either party.

– where the arbitrator has misconducted himself, or there is an error of law on the face of the award, the county court can set the award aside.[7] The arbitrator can also be removed for misconduct. Similar considerations will apply here as in agricultural holdings arbitrations.[8] Where there is an error of law on the face of the award, the court can vary the award by substituting what it considers it would have been proper for the arbitrator to award in the circumstances.[9] The county court, notwithstanding, has general power to remit the whole or part of the award to the arbitrator for reconsideration. In this event the latter has 30 days, following the order remitting the matter to him, in which to make his award.[10]

D Agricultural holdings: service of notices

Frequent reference has been made in the earlier parts of this book to the service of notices, and to the strict time limits within which notices must be served if substantive rights are to be exercised under the Agricultural Holdings Act. Because of the highly procedural nature of the law of agricultural holdings, it is important in many cases to be able to prove service, and to ascertain *when* service took place. Section 93 of the 1986 Act contains a number of general rules governing the service of any 'notice, request or demand, or other instrument' required by the Act.[11]

A notice is to be treated as duly served if it is delivered to the person on whom it is to be served or given, or left at his proper address, or sent to him by post in a registered letter or by the recorded delivery service.[12] Where the postal service is used, the following is the result:

(a) a notice sent by the ordinary post is duly served if it can be shown to have been actually received. The postal service is deemed to be the agent of the sender for the purpose of effecting service;

(b) if it is sent by registered post or recorded delivery service there is a rebuttable presumption that due service has been effected if the notice was correctly addressed, pre-paid and posted.[13] By virtue of section 7 of the Interpretation Act 1978 service is deemed to be

6 Sch 4, para 28.
7 Sch 4, para 29(2).
8 See p 367 ff.
9 Sch 4, para 30(2).
10 See Sch 4, paras 30(1) and (3).
11 These rules clearly apply to notices to quit, as well as to those notices and requests expressly required by the Act itself.
12 Section 93(1) of the 1986 Act.
13 As to points (a) and (b) see *Re Poyner and Mills Arbitration* [1964] 2 QB 467, [1963] 1 All ER 612, per Megaw J.

effected at the time at which the letter would be delivered in the ordinary course of post, ie the day after posting in the case of first class post. If it can be proved that the notice was not in fact received on this date, or at all, this presumption can be rebutted.

Service by physical delivery can be effected by leaving a notice at the recipient's proper address. If served in this way, the notice must be left at the recipient's proper address in a manner which a reasonable person, minded to bring the notice to the attention of the person to whom it is addressed, would adopt.[14] In the case of notices served on a tenant, good service will therefore be effected by leaving a notice at the farmhouse in such a way as to reasonably bring it to the tenant's attention.

Where an agent or servant is responsible for the control of the management or farming of an agricultural holding, notice is duly given or served on the tenant if given or served on the agent or servant.[15] The persons carrying on the management of the farm for the time being are constituted agents of the tenant for the purpose of receiving notices.[16] Where the tenant dies intestate, his estate vests in the President of the Family Division of the High Court by virtue of the Administration of Estates Act 1925.[17] The person carrying on the farming of the holding is deemed to be the agent of the President, however, and notice to quit will be duly served on the President if served on the person having management of the farm.[18] Notice to quit on the death of the sole surviving tenant should also be served on the President himself[19] where the tenant has died intestate. If the tenant has left a will, service on his executors is good service, even if they have not taken out a grant of probate, as the grant once obtained relates back to the death.[20] The landlord then has three months following service of a notice in writing by the executors or administrators of the tenant's estate, informing him of the tenant's death, in which to serve notice to quit.[1]

If either landlord or tenant is a company or other incorporated body, notice is duly served if served on the secretary or clerk of that company or body.[2] The proper address for service, in the case of the secretary or clerk to a company or other incorporated body, is its registered or principal office.[3] Where service is to be effected on any other person, the proper address for service is the last known address of the person in question. When the landlord has sold his freehold interest, the tenant can continue to effect due service by serving notices on the original landlord, until he has been

---

14 *Lord Newborough v Jones* [1974] 3 All ER 17, CA, per Russell LJ (good service where notice to quit put under door of farmhouse, but hidden under linoleum inside the door).
15 Section 93(3) of the 1986 Act.
16 *Egerton v Rutter* [1951] 1 KB 472.
17 Administration of Estates Act 1925, s 9.
18 *Egerton v Rutter* [1951] 1 KB 472; s 93(3) of the 1986 Act.
19 C/o the Treasury Solicitor, Queen Anne's Chambers, 28 Broadway, London SW1H 9JS (Practice Direction (Fam. Div.) [1985] 1 All ER 832).
20 *Cf* letters of administration, which do not take effect retrospectively.
1 Case G to Sch 3 of the 1986 Act. Time also starts to run where the landlord is served with notice of an application for succession. See generally Sch 3, para 12(b) *ibid* and ch 7, p 141 ff above.
2 Section 93(2) of the 1986 Act.
3 Section 93(4) of the 1986 Act.

informed, by notice, of the name and address of the person who has become entitled to receive the rents and profits of the holding.[4] Note, however, that notice of change of landlord need not be in writing, and can be effected orally. For the avoidance of doubt, however, written notice is to be preferred.

4 Section 93(5) *ibid*.

Appendix 1

Agricultural holdings: table of time limits for service of notices, etc

The exercise of various rights under the Agricultural Holdings legislation depends upon service by the parties of the appropriate notices within strict time limits. The following Table is intended to provide a checklist of the more important notice periods, collated for ease of reference.

Matter		*Notice or application period*	*Authority*
Matters arising during the tenancy			
Liability to carry out work under the 'model clauses'	Landlord's counter-notice contesting liability and requesting arbitration.	Within one month following service of notice to repair by tenant.	SI 1973/1473, Pt II, para 12(3).
	Tenant's counter-notice requesting arbitration.	Within one month following service of landlord's notice to repair.	*Ibid*, Pt I, para 4.
Provision of fixed equipment	Landlord's reply to request for provision.	'Within a reasonable time'.	Agricultural Holdings Act 1986, s 11(3)(b).
	Landlord's reply to tribunal application for fixed equipment directions.	Within one month of service of tenant's application.	SI 1978/259, r 15.
Fixtures	Right of removal.	Notice to landlord at least one month before both termination and exercise of right of removal. Removal to be not later than 2 months after termination of tenancy.	1986 Act, s 10(1), 10(3)(b)

378

Matter	Notice or application period	Authority

Matters arising during the tenancy – *contd*

Matter	Notice or application period	Authority
Compensation for damage by game	Notice to landlord to inspect damage.	Notice to landlord within one month of becoming aware etc. of damage.	*Ibid*, s 20(2).
	Written notice of claim for game damage.	Within one month after expiry of the year in respect of which claim made.	*Ibid*, s 20(2)(c).
Rent review	Notice demanding arbitration.	At least 12 months before termination date from which review sought, ending on said termination date of the tenancy.	*Ibid*, s 12(4), 25(1).
	Application to RICS for appointment of arbitrator.	Before the next termination date following demand for arbitration.	*Ibid*, s 12(3).

Notices to quit

Matter	Notice or application period	Authority
Notice to quit	Minimum length of notice to quit.	Twelve months from the end of the current year of tenancy. NB Exceptions listed in s 25(2) (See Chapter 6 of the text).	1986 Act, s 25(1).
	Tenant's counter-notice requiring tribunal consent to notice to quit.	Not later than one month from giving of notice to quit.	*Ibid*, s 26(1)(b).
	Landlord's application to tribunal for consent.	Within one month following service of tenant's counter-notice.	SI 1978/259, r 2(2).
	Tenant's counter-notice after unsuccessful arbitration.	Within one month after termination of arbitration.	SI 1987/710, art 11.

Matter		Notice or application period	Authority

Cases for Possession

Matter		Notice or application period	Authority
Cases B, D, E and I	Notice requiring arbitration as to reasons stated in notice to quit.	Within one month after service of notice to quit.	SI 1987/710, art 9.
	Application to RICS for appointment of arbitrator.	Before expiry of three months following service of tenant's notice demanding arbitration.	*Ibid*, art 10.
	Postponement of operation of notice to quit – tenant's application.	Not later than 14 days following termination of arbitration or tribunal consent.	*Ibid*, art 13.
	Counter-notice following arbitration (where notice to quit in alternative).	Within one month following termination of arbitration.	*Ibid*, art 11.
Case C	Notice to quit following Certificate of Bad Husbandry.	To be served within six months of grant of certificate.	1986 Act, s 26(2) and Sch 3, Case C.
Case D(b)	Notice demanding arbitration on liability to comply with notice to do work in Form 2.	Within one month following service of notice to do work.	SI 1987/710, art 3(2).
	Application to arbitrator to fix a termination date for tenancy, following extension of time for doing work.	Not later than 14 days after termination of arbitration.	SI 1987/710, art 7(1).
	Notice to quit following extended period for work.	Within one month after expiry of extended period.	*Ibid*, art 7(4).
	Demand for arbitration on notice to quit.	Within one month after service of notice to quit.	*Ibid*, art 9.

Matter		Notice or application period	Authority

Cases for Possession – *contd*

Matter		Notice or application period	Authority
Case D(b) – *contd*	Counter-notice by tenant following arbitration, requiring tribunal consent.	Within one month following delivery of arbitrator's award.	1986 Act, s 28(4).
	Application for tribunal consent by landlord.	Within one month of service of tenant's notice referring notice to quit to tribunal.	SI 1978/259, r 2.
	Application to arbitrator or tribunal for postponement of operation of notice to quit.	Within 14 days after termination of arbitration or grant of tribunal consent.	SI 1987/710, art 13.
Case G	Notice to quit following death of sole surviving tenant.	Within 3 months of either (i) service of written notice of tenant's death from personal representatives, or (ii) notice of application for succession to the holding (whichever first occurs).	1986 Act, Sch 3 Case G and Sch 3 para 12(b).

Statutory succession

Matter		Notice or application period	Authority
Succession on death	Successor's application for a direction entitling him to a tenancy.	Within 3 months, beginning with day after date of tenant's death.	1986 Act, s 39(1).
	Successor's application to be 'treated' as eligible for succession.	Within 3 months of tenant's death, in same form as application for succession.	1986 Act, s 41, SI 1984/1301, r 3.
	Landlord's application for consent to the operation of notice to quit.	Within 4 months of service of application for succession.	SI 1984/1301, r 4(3).

Matter	Notice or application period	Authority

Statutory succession – *contd*

Matter	Notice or application period	Authority
Succession on death – *contd*	Landlord's application for consent where multiple applications for succession.	Within (1) one month after number of applications reduced to one or (2) four months after service of first application on him, whichever is later.	*Ibid*, r 4(4).
	Landlord's reply to application for succession.	Within one month after service of application.	*Ibid*, r 6.
	Where multiple applications for succession, applicant's reply to other applications.	Within one month of end of the 'relevant period', ie the period of three months following tenant's death.	*Ibid*, r 8.
	Applicant's reply to landlord's application for consent to operation of notice to quit.	Within one month of service of landlord's application.	*Ibid*, r 7.

Succession on retirement

	Nominated successor's application to tribunal for direction entitling him/her to tenancy.	Within period of one month beginning with the day after service of retirement notice. NB. Application must be signed by both successor and retiring tenant.	1986 Act, s 53(2).

Notice to quit part

	Enlargement into notice to quit whole.	Written counter-notice to be served by tenant within 28 days after (i) giving of notice to quit *or* (ii) determination that notice to quit has effect	1986 Act, s 32(2).

Matter	Notice or application period	Authority

Compensation and other claims on quitting

Compensation for improvements and *all* other claims on termination.	Written notice of *intention* to claim before the expiry of two months from the termination of tenancy.	1986 Act, s 83(2).
Compensation for disturbance – 2nd year's rent.	Written notice of claim not less than one month before termination of tenancy.	1986 Act, s 60(6)(a).
Tenant's right to remove fixtures etc.	Written notice to be at least one month before *both*: (1) exercise of right of removal and (2) termination of tenancy.	1986 Act, s 10(3)(b).
Compensation for special system of farming.	Written notice of claim not less than one month before termination of tenancy.	1986 Act, s 70(2)(a).
Tenant right – tenant's option to claim customary compensation where he entered into occupation before 1st March 1948.	Option to be exercised by notice to landlord within one month after landlord's notice to elect.	1986 Act Sch 12, para 6(2).
Landlord's claim for general deterioration of holding.	Written notice of intention to claim not less than one month before termination of tenancy.	1986 Act, s 72(4).
Settlement of compensation by agreement, in lieu of arbitration.	Within 8 months from termination of tenancy.	*Ibid*, s 83(4).

Appendix 2
Short term lettings and licences with ministry consent

'Approval of Short Term Lettings and Licences: Joint Announcement by the Agriculture Departments': 10th August 1989.*

Legal position

1. One of the main provisions of the Agricultural Holdings Act 1986, which consolidates earlier legislation, is to give security of tenure to tenant farmers to encourage them to plan ahead and farm their land well. The Act therefore limits the circumstances in which a tenancy from year to year may be terminated. Sections 2 and 3 provide that, with certain exceptions, all lettings and licences to occupy land shall, if they are capable of doing so, take effect as tenancies from year to year. Under Sections 2 and 5, the Minister of Agriculture, Fisheries and Food and the Secretary of State for Wales may, at their discretion, give prior approval to an agreement to short-term lettings or licences which will not result in a tenancy from year to year.

2. *Under Section 2* the appropriate Minister may approve (a) a letting for a period of not more than one year or (b) a licence (which may be for more than one year).

3. *Under Section 5* the appropriate Minister may give his approval to a letting for not less than two and not more than five years provided the landlord and prospective tenant make a joint application in writing to him.

4. In all cases application, with full supporting details, should be made to the appropriate Divisional Office. The provision of full details is particularly important since there is no appeal against the Ministers' decision.

5. When the appropriate Minister gives his approval to a short-term letting or licence the occupier is excluded from rights to which he would be entitled if he enjoyed a protected tenancy from year to year. It is most important therefore that consents are given only after the most careful consideration. The policy is to limit approval to those cases where it would be unreasonable to expect the landlord to let his land on a full agricultural tenancy. In general this applies to temporary situations but there are longer-term circumstances where because the over-riding use of the land is non-agricultural a full agricultural tenancy would not be appropriate. Lettings under Section 5 and licences under Section 2 may, where justified, be given for a period of up to five years, unless a shorter maximum is specified below. A series of lettings for less than a year may be granted under Section 2. At the expiry of the initial period consideration may in certain circumstances be given to a further letting or licence if the landlord can show that this is justified. The main circumstances in which short-term lettings (Section 2 or 5) and short-term licences (Section 2) would normally be granted are set out below:

* Reproduced by kind permission of the Ministry of Agriculture, Fisheries and Food.

(a) *Land for development*

Wherever possible, normal agricultural tenancies are encouraged for land on which development is pending, with the landlord's position being adequately protected by the provisions of the agricultural holdings legislation. However, when land is likely to go out of use within five to seven years, the compensation payable by the landlord on the termination of a full agricultural tenancy could exceed the amount of rent paid. In these circumstances approval of a short-term letting or licence would normally be justified.

(b) *Re-organisation and transitional arrangements*

There are a number of instances in which it is desirable to make a temporary arrangement for the cultivation of the land. Therefore, according to individual circumstances, approval may be given for a short-term letting or licence for up to five years in the situations outlined below. A further application involving the same parties on the same land can only be approved if there has been a material alteration in the circumstances:

(i) If the landowner is planning the amalgamation or re-grouping of the holding; or

(ii) If he wishes to enable a prospective purchaser to work the land before completion of sale; or

(iii) if a landlord wishes to make temporary arrangements pending a decision on the future use of the land eg sale or letting of the land, or a tenant has died and the landlord wishes to make temporary arrangements before re-letting or selling;

(iv) where the landlord wishes to give a tenant who is not an established or experienced tenant a period of trial before concluding a full tenancy; or

(v) where there is a definite intention that the landlord's son or daughter will take over a vacant holding within five years.

(c) *Specialist cropping*

Approval may be given to a short-term letting or licence in cases where a farmer wishes to let land to a specialist grower for a single crop requiring 'clean land' eg potatoes, carrots, brassicas, beans, bulbs. Consent may also be given for the growing of a crop, not normally grown on the holding, to be grown as a cleaner crop. A consent will normally be for one year only unless the specialist crop requires a longer period.

(d) *Allotments*

If allotment land is temporary surplus to requirements approval will normally be given to a short-term letting or licence.

(e) *Operational requirements on government and other land*

Approval may also be given to a short-term letting or licence where some agricultural use of the land is possible and desirable but a full agricultural tenancy is ruled out by operational or training requirements which affect the use of the land (this applies particularly, but not exclusively, to land owned by MOD).

6. Within this broad framework each case is decided according to the individual circumstances. It should be pointed out that the categories outlined above are not definitive. If a landowner has land (usually a small area) which he would like to let for a short time and he considers there are good grounds why a full agricultural tenancy would not be appropriate, he should write to his local Divisional Office, setting out his case as fully as possible.

Appendix 3
Rent review: guidance notes for valuers

'GUIDANCE NOTES For Valuers Acting in Reviews of Rent at Arbitration under the Agricultural Holdings Act 1986'. (Royal Institution of Chartered Surveyors).*

'Productive Capacity' and 'Related Earning Capacity' and 'The Current Level of Rents for Comparable Lettings'.

* Reproduced by permission of the Royal Institution of Chartered Surveyors, the copyright owners. Appendix 1, which reproduces Schedule 2 to the Agricultural Holdings Act 1986, has been omitted.

PART 1

1. Introduction

1.1 These Guidance Notes deal with two aspects of the new valuation formula introduced by the Agricultural Holdings Act 1984 and now consolidated in the Agricultural Holdings Act 1986 ('the Act') applying to agricultural holdings in England and Wales.

1.2 The formula for 'the rent properly payable' which is now in paragraphs 1 to 3 of Schedule 2 to the Act is printed as Appendix 1. [Appendix 1 omitted.]

1.3 These Notes deal with the use of budgets in the assessment of 'productive capacity' and 'related earning capacity' and the application of the comparative valuation method in the assessment of 'current level of rents for comparable lettings.' The Notes are intended to draw to the attention of the valuer points of practical significance and some of the language of the Schedule, which is set out in these Notes within quotation marks. These Notes do not deal with the remainder of the valuation formula.

1.4 Valuers should always seek to agree 'the rent properly payable' without reference to arbitration.

PART 2

2. Productive capacity and related earning capacity

2.1 The most convenient way of taking account of these two factors, which are both defined in paragraph 1(2) of the Schedule, is by means of a budget.

2.1.1 For the purpose of negotiations it may not be necessary to prepare a detailed budget. But, if there is a hearing before the arbitrator, the budget should be agreed whenever possible and submitted as part of the agreed evidence. If the budget is not agreed, it is recommended that valuers should present the arbitrator with a single budget with alternative figures identifying clearly and concisely the points of difference.

2.1.2 A budget is not in itself a valuation method and should be used only to support a rental valuation.

2.2 Gross margin budget

2.2.1 A gross margin budget is one way of expressing both 'productive capacity' and 'related earning capacity.' Appendix 2 has been prepared to assist the valuer to prepare a gross margin budget.

2.2.2 It is first necessary to identify the various enterprises which make up the farming business, and the total output for each enterprise, assessed by the valuer, will represent the 'productive capacity' of the holding.

2.2.3 The variable costs of the output of an enterprise can then be deducted and expressed in units of area or on a headage basis. The gross margin per unit multiplied by the total number of units of the enterprise provides the enterprise gross margin. The addition of the various enterprise gross margins together with any other non-farm income derived from the holding produces the farm gross margin. The deduction of fixed costs (excluding interest on borrowing, tenant's interest on capital, tenant's management and rent) from the farm gross margin produces a figure which represents the 'related earning capacity' of the holding.

2.3 Preparation of the budget

2.3.1 The valuer should inspect the holding and decide what system of farming would be practised by a competent farmer. For this purpose no distinction should be made between equipment provided by the landlord and by the tenant, because the valuer must take into account 'fixed equipment and any other available facility on the holding.'

2.3.2 If the actual tenant of the holding is a 'competent tenant,' it may be unnecessary to devise a different system of farming. Further, the tenant's records of cropping, stocking rates and the numbers of tractors, vehicles, implements, machinery and labour to maintain the system may be adopted for the budget. If available, the tenant's farm accounts *may* be of assistance where they relate only to the farming business on the subject holding or can be readily separated from another business. Farm accounts are prepared in accordance with Inland Revenue requirements and, invariably, will require adjustments to take account of the date of rental valuation, home consumption, valuation changes, depreciation, repair liability and finance costs.

2.3.3 If the valuer considers that the actual tenant is not a 'competent tenant' or is not 'practising a system of farming suitable to the holding', the valuer will have to propose a system which would be practised by a 'competent tenant,' the valuer deciding cropping and stocking rates, and the machinery and labour and other costs necessary for that system.

2.3.4 Valuers should state any assumptions made in preparing the budget.

2.3.5 The budget should not be based on extremes of cropping or stocking rates of value, yield, or costs.

2.3.6   Standard texts will provide general guidance on basic data, but they should not be relied on to produce a gross margin budget for a specific holding. Appendix 3 is a list of sources of information [Appendix 3 omitted.]

2.3.7   It is the valuer's assessment of the subject holding which is paramount when preparing a budget.

PART 3

3.   Current level of rents for comparable lettings

3.1   Comparative valuation has long been recognised as the prime valuation method and is the art of using knowledge of the value of one property at a given time to assist in the valuation of another property at the same or a different time.

3.1.1   The reference in the valuation formula to 'the current level of rents for comparable lettings' as a relevant factor to be taken into account by the arbitrator is a recognition that comparative valuation remains the principal valuation method to assist in the determination of 'the rent properly payable.'

3.1.2   If the valuer can obtain, and in the case of an arbitration hearing prove, sufficient information about a transaction in respect of a comparable holding and can properly analyse it, his analysis will provide him and the arbitrator with material of prime importance in his valuation of the subject holding.

3.1.3   The elaborate definition in paragraph 1(3) affects the scope of the valuation exercise which the valuer would ordinarily adopt. Further, the valuer is directed also to disregard certain elements which he would not ordinarily ignore. Certain phrases in the definition call for further comment.

3.1.4   'any available evidence' – these words remind the valuer that if there is a hearing he may have to prove any comparable letting on which he relies. In his initial valuation, and in negotiation, he may take account of lettings of which he has hearsay but no direct knowledge. But at the hearing he will be confined to comparable lettings which either are agreed between the parties or are strictly proved. Strict proof requires that the documents evidencing the rent are produced to the arbitrator. It may also be necessary to call as a witness a person who has direct but not hearsay knowledge of the transaction to give evidence of any special circumstances which may require analysis for the purpose of comparison.

3.1.5   'the rents (whether fixed by agreement by the parties or by arbitration under this Act) which are, or (in view of rents currently being tendered) are likely to become, payable' – the valuer and the arbitrator must consider a range of rents, those fixed by agreement, by arbitration, and those about to become payable if the comparable is being let by tender.

3.1.6   The words 'likely to become payable' appear to suggest that the valuer who knows of a range of tenderers' bids, none of which has yet been accepted, must decide which bid is likely to be accepted. It is only the successful rental bid which becomes 'payable.' Bids which are not accepted never become 'payable.' A valuer must therefore exclude the bids which he considers to be imprudently high or unacceptably low and, in so doing, he will have to pay attention to the farming ability and financial resources of the tenderers.

3.1.7   'comparable agricultural holding' – these words remind the valuer that in selecting a particular comparable the greater similarity it has to the subject holding the greater the weight which can be given to it as evidence that can reliably be applied to the subject holding. A fully equipped holding should be compared with a fully equipped subject holding. Accommodation land should be compared with a subject holding comprising accommodation land.

3.1.8   Appendix 4 contains a checklist of characteristics which should be used for the purpose of comparison of one holding with another.

3.1.9 'on terms (other than the terms fixing the rent payable) similar to those of the tenancy under consideration' – these words appear to place a limitation upon the usual process of analysis. An experienced valuer is able to adjust the rent payable under a holding let on the model clauses, so as to arrive at the rent to be payable for the subject holding let on terms under which the tenant is responsible for all repairs, maintenance and insurance. He can adjust the rent payable for a holding let on terms which give the tenant a complete freedom to assign or underlet, so as to arrive at the rent to be payable for a subject holding let on terms which prevent assignment or underletting.

3.1.10 The use of the word 'similar' appears to suggest that Parliament intended a limited process of comparison. Until the Courts have indicated the scope of the adjective 'similar' when applied to the terms of a tenancy agreement, the valuer is advised that he should study the tenancy agreement of the subject holding and decide which terms are likely to have a significant effect upon his valuation. He should examine the terms of each of his intended comparable lettings and decide whether or not the terms of that letting are sufficiently similar to enable him to analyse the rent of the comparable. If he is unable to do so, he must disregard the letting because he cannot rely on it at the hearing.

3.1.11 The valuer must apply to each of the rents for comparable lettings the three disregards specified in paragraph 1(3)(*a*), (*b*) and (*c*) of the Schedule.

3.1.12 'appreciable scarcity' – the disregard only has to be quantified if there is 'appreciable scarcity.' The word 'appreciable' must mean that the scarcity is capable of being appreciated, that is identified and therefore valued. It is not enough that the valuer has a vague notion that supply and demand are in balance or imbalance.

3.1.13 'scarcity' – this may have to be distinguished from rarity. Thus there will be always a shortage of Grade I arable farms or of well-equipped dairy farms with above average milk quota. This is rarity and is a very different matter from scarcity.

3.1.14 In quantifying the amount of the scarcity disregard the valuer must decide as a matter of skill and judgment what rent the comparable would command if there was a balance between supply and demand. The difference between that figure and the passing rent is the amount of the disregard.

3.1.15 'marriage value' – this expression is not used in the Act, but is a convenient description of the second disregard. The disregard does not cover marriage value in its widest sense. The element in the rent for the comparable holding which must be disregarded is the element in the rental bid of the tenant or tenderer because he is in occupation of 'other land in the vicinity of the comparable holding.' The valuer, therefore, must discover what other agricultural land, if any, is occupied by the tenant of, or the tenderer for, the comparable holding. The requirement that the comparable holding and the other land are in the same 'vicinity' would appear to require that no adjustment is made to a rental bid of a hill farmer for a holding which provides summer grazing a considerable distance away. The requirement that the other land 'may conveniently be occupied together with' the comparable holding suggests that although the other land of the tenant and the comparable are in the same vicinity, it may be inconvenient to farm the other land and the comparable together. In such a case the bid of the tenant for the comparable would require no adjustment.

3.1.16 In quantifying the amount of the marriage value the valuer must again decide, as a matter of skill and judgment, what rent the comparable would command if there was no marriage value. The difference between that figure and the passing rent is the amount of the disregard.

3.1.17 'premiums' – if a premium is charged by the landlord of the comparable holding, and the consideration for that premium is some allowance to the tenant or a reduction in the rent, the allowance or reduction must be quantified and disregarded.

3.1.18 Once the valuer has identified the comparable holdings let on similar terms, analysed the rents achieved, or likely to be achieved on the successful tender, and applied the disregards, he will have a number of rents which, together, constitute 'the current level of rents for comparable lettings.' It is unlikely that this process will provide an exactly similar figure for each comparable. The current level is more likely to consist of a band of figures which then, together with the other factors mentioned in paragraph 1(1) of the Schedule, must be taken into account in arriving at the rent of the subject holding upon which the 'prudent and willing landlord' and 'prudent and willing tenant' would agree, 'the rent properly payable.'

3.2   Selection of a comparable

3.2.1   In selecting a comparable it may be convenient to consider the following headings:

A   Physical characteristics
B   Terms of the tenancy
C   Timing and circumstances of the comparable transaction
D   Comparability with the subject holding.

3.3   Physical characteristics

3.3.1   *Nature and Location of an Holding*

3.3.2   There is no substitute for careful inspection of the comparable holding.

3.3.3   Preferably a comparable should be from the same vicinity, although this should not rule out the use of holdings from other areas, particularly in the case of specialist agricultural systems.

3.3.4   The size and character of the comparable holding should be as similar as possible to the subject holding. Ideally, equipped holdings should be compared with the same type of holding and accommodation land compared with similar land. As an extreme example, it would be unwise to draw comparison between a 40 acre heavy clay farm with a 400 acre light arable farm.

3.3.5   The M.A.F.F. Classification Map and the accompanying Explanatory Notes should be referred to and, if available, the Soil Survey of England and Wales Land Use Capability Map. Published information such as that from the Soil Survey Unit should be used to compare the range of soils on each holding, but the general nature of this type of published information must be recognised.

3.3.6   Site inspection will show the depth of top soil and the need and suitability for underdrainage and irrigation and the availability of access, the convenience of layout and the provision of fencing and water.

3.3.7   The suitability of the holding for the generation of non-farming income should also be noted. The valuer should consider any actual or deemed planning permissions and the prospect of future successful applications.

3.3.8   *Fixed equipment and services*

3.3.9   The fixed equipment on each comparable holding should be noted for comparison with the subject holding, in particular the age, construction, size, capacity and ease of maintenance of the farmhouse, cottages and farmbuildings. Consideration should be given to whether the number of cottages is appropriate.

3.3.10   The availability and adequacy of services, eg surface and foul drainage, irrigation and water supply, electricity and gas, should be considered.

3.3.11   *System of farming*

3.3.12   The valuer should note the actual system of farming practised by the tenant of the comparable. This is because in analysing the passing rent for the comparable it may be necessary to consider what system a competent tenant would adopt.

3.3.13   The valuer should note whether the system of farming is influenced by the availability of quota and contracts for the disposal of produce.

3.3.14 *Tenant's improvements and fixed equipment*

3.3.15   Tenant's improvements and fixed equipment should be identified so that the effect of disregarding these matters can be added back to the passing rent of the comparable.

3.3.16 *Statutory and contractual matters*

3.3.17   The valuer should note whether the holding is adversely affected by wayleaves, easements and rights of way and overhead pole or pylon lines. Consideration should be given to the effect on the comparable of the many types of planning restrictions.

3.4. Terms of the tenancy

3.4.1   As noted in paragraph 3.1.9 the valuer should ascertain whether the terms of the tenancy agreement of the comparable are similar to that of the subject holding. In particular regard should be had to the repairing and insuring obligations, restrictions on land use, permitted additional enterprises, retention of sporting rights and any obligations to preserve quotas.

3.5. The timing and circumstances of the comparable transaction

3.5.1   The valuer should note the date and circumstances of the fixing of the current rent of the comparable. The current rent may not have been settled at arm's length. The current rent may have been fixed by open market tender or a sale and lease back or on a statutory succession. The rent may have been fixed under the 1984 or 1986 Acts, in which case the disregard in paragraph 1(3) of the Schedule will have been valued out. The valuer should decide in the case of new private or tender lettings whether or not the landlord satisfied himself as to the financial and farming ability of the tenant, and whether the tenant's bid took account of commercial risks.

3.6 Comparability with the subject holding

3.6.1   If the above factors are assessed by systematic analysis, using Appendix 4, the valuer can assess the comparability of the holding in question with the subject holding. The valuer can then decide whether or not to select the holding as a suitable comparable. This selection is necessarily a matter of compromise and the valuer must take a broad view in deciding whether a holding is in essence comparable with the subject holding.

3.6.2   It is advisable to use a consistent method of analysis to assess the comparable and the subject holding.

3.6.3   Appendix 4 and Appendices 5 and 6 may also be used to analyse a transaction put forward by the other valuer as comparable in order to show that transaction's lack of comparability. Further, they can be used at the hearing to disprove an exaggerated claim by the other valuer by demonstrating that a clearly superior farm is let at a lower rent than that proposed for the subject holding or vice versa.

3.7 A suggested approach to the analysis of the rent of a comparable

3.7.1   There are different ways of analysing the known rent of a comparable holding.

3.7.2   The objective of Appendices 5 and 6 is to assist the valuer to adjust the passing rent for the comparable to the current level of rent for that comparable so that each comparable can be compared on the same basis and with the subject holding. The valuer may then analyse the current level of rent for the comparable, if he considers the analysis assists his valuation of the subject holding.

3.8   Presentation of a comparable to an arbitrator

3.8.1   Evidence produced before an arbitrator may be evidence of fact or evidence of opinion from an expert witness. Evidence of a transaction relied on as a comparable is evidence of fact. The comparability and analysis of the transaction is evidence of opinion.

3.8.2   It will reduce cost and benefit the arbitrator if the parties can agree the factual evidence prior to the hearing. If this is not possible the parties' valuers should adopt a uniform method of presentation which clearly identifies the disputed facts.

3.8.3   The facts on which an expert witness has formed his opinion may be:

A   Agreed between the parties to the arbitration
B   Proved by him
C   Proved by other witnesses.

3.8.4   The facts of the comparable letting should be presented in such a manner that they can be compared readily to the subject holding. Appendices 5 and 6 can be used. If there is no agreement, supporting documentary evidence is necessary, ie tenancy agreement with comprehensible plan and any endorsements together with other relevant documents or correspondence affecting the tenancy, eg those relating to ownership of fixtures and fittings. It is prudent to obtain the approval of a party to the comparable transaction to the production of confidential information unless a witness summons is served to compel production.

3.8.5   Evidence of comparable transactions will be of little value if neither the arbitrator nor the other party has the opportunity of inspection. The valuer must arrange that the comparable holding is available for inspection by the other parties and by the arbitrator. The arbitrator may put little or no weight on the evidence unless he is given full details of the nature of the farm, the fixed equipment and the way in which the rent was last determined and any special circumstances.

3.8.6   If the valuer is unable to produce evidence of 'the current level of rents for comparable lettings' he may have to express his expert opinion from his general experience derived from sources of which he has no first hand evidence. This material may include statistical evidence published by the Ministry or other bodies. Although the material does not comply with paragraph 1(3) of the Schedule, it may nevertheless be a 'relevant factor' which the arbitrator should take into account. If such material is used by an expert witness to support his valuation, the arbitrator will have to decide the weight to be attached to the witness's opinion.

APPENDIX 1

[*Omitted*]

APPENDIX 2

See Note 1.   STANDARD FORMS OF GROSS MARGIN BUDGET

See Note 2.   **Farm plan**

Name of Holding:

Address:

Total Acreage:

Farmable Acreage:

Cropping Year:

Summary of Enterprises

CROPS:		ACRES
Winter Wheat		
Winter Barley		
Oilseed Rape		
Sugar Beet		
Potatoes		
Other		

LIVESTOCK:	HEAD	ACRES ALLOCATED
Dairy — cows		
— replacements		
Beef — sucklers		
— stores		
Sheep — breeding		
— stores		
Pigs — sows		
— fattening		
Other —		

Total farmable acreage:

Farm gross margin budget

See Note 3.   *Crop enterprise gross margins*

                                              Acres   Gross Margin

Winter Wheat
Winter Barley
Sugar Beet

          TOTAL CROP ENTERPRISE GROSS MARGIN   £

Livestock enterprise gross margins

	Numbers	Acres	Gross Margin
Ewe Flock			
Fat Cattle			
Dairy Herd			
Dairy Replacements			
Suckler Herd			
Pigs			

TOTAL STOCK ENTERPRISE GROSS MARGINS   £

OTHER NET INCOME FROM HOLDING   £

Total Farmable Acreage

TOTAL FARM GROSS MARGINS   £

Less *fixed costs*
See Note 4.   /ac
(a) Labour   men
(b) Machinery: spares, repairs,
                            fuel, power
                            depreciation/lease
                            hire
                            unallocated
                            contract
(c) Property maintenance
      Rates
(d) Sundry fixed costs

TOTAL FIXED COSTS   £
before rent and finance

BALANCE   £
(representing related earning capacity)

See Note 2.   **Examples of enterprise gross margins**

1   Combinable crops

Output per acre   tonnes @   £/tn

Variable costs per acre
    seed   kg @   £/tn
    comp. fert   kg @   £/tn
    nitrogen   kg @   £/tn
    sprays
    contract

Total Variable Costs per acre

Gross margin per acre
Enterprise Gross Margin   acres at £/ac

2 Roots

Output per acre	tns	£/tn
Variable costs per acre		
seed	kg @	£/tn
comp. fert	kgs @	£/tn
sprays		
transport		
casual labour		
levies		

Total Variable Costs per acre
Gross margin per acre
Enterprise Gross Margin   acres at £/acre

---

3 Ewe flock

Output per ewe (lambing percentage)

fat lambs	@	£/hd
store lambs	@	£/hd
	wool	
	ewe premium	
	HLCA	

Gross output per ewe
  Less ewe depreciation   per/head
  % replacement
  Less % cull

Net Output per ewe

Variable costs per ewe

concs.	kg/ewe	
@	£/tn	
vet & med		
misc.		
Forage: Stocking at		LSU per acre
seed	/ac	/hd
comp. fert	/ac	/hd
nigrogen	/ac	/hd
spray	/ac	/hd

Total variable costs

Gross margin per ewe
Stocking Rate at   LSU per acre
Gross margin per acre

Enterprise Gross Margin   acres at £ per acre

---

4   Fattening purchased livestock

Output per head

sale of fat beast	@ kgs @	/kg
less mortality %		

Gross output per head

less purchase cost at   £ per head

Net output per head

Variable costs per head

concs.	kg/head
@	£/tn

vet & med		
misc.		
Forage: Stocking Rate		LSU per acre
seed	/ac	/hd
comp. fert	/ac	/hd
nitrogen	/ac	/hd
spray	/ac	/hd

Total Variable costs per head

Gross margin per head
Stocking Rate at   LSU per acre
Gross margin per acre

Enterprise Gross Margin   acres at £ per acre

---

5   Dairy herd

Output per cow		
litre milk	@	p/l
sale of calf	@	£/head
or transfer value		

Gross Output per cow

Less depreciation per cow:
½ cost of replacement
Less % sale of cull

Net output per cow
Variable costs per cow
conc. fed per litre		kg
kg concs.	@	£/tn
vet & med		

sundries incl. A.I. levies
forage: Stocking rate   LSU per cow
seed   /ac   /hd
comp. fert   /ac   /hd
nitrogen   /ac   /hd
sprays   /ac   /hd

Total Variable Costs per cow

Gross margin per cow
Stocking Rate at   LSU per acre
Gross margin per acre

Enterprise Gross Margin   acres at £ per acre

---

6   Dairy replacements

Output per head

  Sale/transfer of downcalving

    heifer   £/head
    Less mortality   £/head

Gross Output per head

  Less purchase/transfer of calf   £/head

Net Output per head

Variable costs per head
    concs.   kg/per head   tnne
    vet & med
    sundries
    forage: stocking rate   LSV per acre
    seed   /ac   /hd
    comp. fert   /ac   /hd
    nitrogen   /ac   /hd
    spray   /ac   /hd

Total Variable Costs per head

Gross margin per unit
Stocking Rate at   LSU per acre
Gross margin per acre

Enterprise Gross Margin   acres at £ per acre

---

7 Suckler herd

Output per head

    Sale/transfer of calf   £/head
    less mortality %   £/head

    Beef Cow Subsidy
    HLCA

Gross Output per head

Less cow and bull depreciation per head
    % cost of replacement
    less % sale cull

Net Output per head

Variable costs:

    concentrate kg/hd   @   tnne
    vet & med
    misc.
    Forage Stocking rate at   LSU per acre
    seed   /ac
    comp. fert   /ac
    nitrogen   /ac
    sprays   /ac

Total Variable Costs per head

Gross margin per cow
Stocking Rate at   LSU per acre
    Gross margin per acre

Enterprise Gross Margin   acre at £/acre

---

8 Pig breeding

Output per sow

    weaners per annum
        for sale or transfer   £/hd
    Less depreciation

Net Output per sow

Variable costs

Feed:
    Sow   kg/hd   @   tnne
    weaners   kg/hd   @   tnne

vet & med
power and water
straw/bedding
variable sundries

Total Variable Costs
Gross margin per sow

Enterprise Gross Margin

---

9   Pig finishing

Output per head

same value of pig		@ kgs	@ /kg
Less mortality %			

Gross Output per head
  Less purchase cost   @   £/hd
Net Output per head
Variable costs per head
  feed   kg/hd   @   tnne
  vet & med
  variable sundries

Total Variable Costs per head
Gross margin per head
Enterprise Gross Margin

NOTES ON GROSS MARGIN BUDGETS

Note 1:   All assumptions should be clearly stated.
             Valuers may adapt the forms as required to provide greater detail.
             Units may be expressed as imperial or metric.

Note 2:   Farm plan
             Incorporates the choice of cropping and stocking of the holding, being the
             system of farming suitable for the holding.

Note 3:   Crop enterprise gross margins
             The gross margin of an enterprise is its output less its variable costs.

        (a)   *Output* states the proceeds of sale or the value of transfer from one
              enterprise to another. It will also take account of any subsidy receiv-
              able where appropriate and stock depreciation.
        (b)   *Variable costs:* These are costs capable of allocation to an enterprise.
              The following are examples of variable costs:

Allocatable Casual Labour	Allocatable contract
Artificial Insemination	Sprays and Chemicals
Veterinary & Medicine	Recording Fees

Seed	Fertiliser
Feedstuffs	Levies
Haulage	Forage

Note 4: *Fixed costs*

These costs are those which cannot be allocated readily to a specific enterprise, or which will not vary in relation to small changes in the area of an individual enterprise.

Fixed costs are made up of:

(a) Labour
(b) Machinery, vehicles
(c) Property costs
(d) Sundry overheads

(a) *Labour* required for the system of farming including regular and part time staff. The extent to which the labour of the tenant and his family is included should be noted.

(b) *Machinery:* Standard figures may be used as the primary source of information, but should be adjusted to take account of the subject holding, and may be sub-divided into: –

(1) Spares and repairs, road tax
(2) Fuel and power
(3) Depreciation
(4) Lease-hire
(5) Non-allocated contract

(1) *Spares and repairs:* the increased use of second hand machinery will result in higher repair costs.

(2) *Fuel and power:* note the interrelationship between fixed and variable costs – a farm system with a grain drying facility on the holding will have higher fixed costs, whereas a farm without such a facility will incur increased variable costs for haulage and contract drying.

(3) *Machinery and vehicle depreciation:* the annual cost of machinery replacement should take account of a mix of old and new machinery for the subject holding. The basis on which depreciation is calculated should be stated.

(4) *Lease hire:* if thought appropriate, leasing charges for particular items may be substituted for depreciation, and stated.

(5) *Non-allocated contract:* distinguish between an allocatable charge (eg sheep shearing or sugar beet harvesting) which is a variable cost, and a non-allocatable cost (eg hedge cutting).

(c) *Property costs:* These will have regard to the tenant's repairing liabilities under the terms of his tenancy. Note that standard texts assume the farmer has a full repairing liability. The valuer should note the maintenance requirements on inspection of the holding.

(d) *Sundry Overheads:* including office expenditure, telephone and insurances – the valuer should have regard to the terms of the tenancy when including figures for insurance.

APPENDIX 3

[Omitted]

APPENDIX 4

A CHECK LIST FOR ASSESSING COMPARABLES

Investigate availability as evidence at arbitration

Nature and location of the holding

District
Size of holding
Elevation, contour or gradient
Aspect and shelter
Effect of woodland
Vermin
Rainfall
Soil type
Depth of soil
Land classification grading
Access and internal roads
Proximity to livestock and produce markets
Field size and shape
Field drainage
Water resources
Irrigation
Fragmentation

Fixed equipment and services

Quality and situation of farmhouse
Number, quality and situation of cottages
Landlord's buildings and equipment
Tenant's buildings and equipment
Permanent fencing or hedging
Mains electricity (single or three phase)
Mains gas
Water supply
Drainage

The system of farming

Range of suitable enterprises
Particular constraints

Statutory and contractual matters

Easements
Wayleaves
Rights of Way

Availability of grants
Special area status
Planning and other restrictions
Charges on land
Possible compulsory purchase
Latent value

Nature and terms of the tenancy

Corporate, joint or sole tenant
Frequency of rent payments
Rent payable in advance or in arrears
Repairing obligations of landlord and tenant
Insuring obligations
Sporting (reserved or included)
Restrictions on cropping
Restrictions on stocking
Quotas and contracts
Assignable/Non-assignable
Residence clause
Ability to generate non-farming income

Timing and circumstances of the comparable rent settlement

Current rent
Date of last rent review
Method of fixing (new letting, arbitration, succession or by agreement)

1986 Act disregards

Scarcity
Marriage value
Premiums

Note: This list is not included to be exhaustive, and, depending on particular circumstances, there may be other relevant matters to be taken into account.

APPENDIX 5

ANALYSIS OF LAND VALUATION CLASSES OF THE COMPARABLE HOLDING

NOTES [*TO TABLE OVERLEAF*]
1. Obtain and mark on plan different land valuation classes dependent on soil type, productive capacity, extent of land serviced by specialist buildings and equipment.
2. Complete Appendix 5 and express acreage totals at bottom making separate allowances for non-productive areas.
     eg   120 acres greensand serving dairy buildings
           20 acres clay serving dairy building (drained)
          200 acres greensand arable
           40 acres clay arable (undrained)
           10 acres woods, buildings and waste

ANALYSIS OF LAND VALUATION CLASSES OF THE COMPARABLE HOLDING

HOLDING.. DATE.......................

FIELD NO	ACRES	Legend as per attached plan									REMARKS
		ACRES	ACRES	ACRES	ACRES	ACRES	ACRES	ACRES	ACRES	ACRES	
											TOTAL

APPENDIX 6

ANALYSIS OF RENT OF COMPARABLE HOLDING

Line
No
1 HOLDING ....
2 ACREAGE...Gross/net...
3 PASSING RENT £...........................(£.............../acre)
4 WITH EFFECT FROM...19.......
5 TENANCY TERMS ....
   ....
   ....

6 HOW COMPARABLE RENT WAS FIXED:
   *T.L. – Tender Letting; P.L. – New private Letting;
   S.T. – Sitting Tenant Review;
   S.R. – Succession Review.

Adjustment of passing rent
to current level of rent for comparable

7   Addition back for   £......................
    improvements
8   Addition/Deduction
    for unusual features of
    comparable   £...................... £....................

9   Rent adjusted before
    statutory disregards in
    Paragraph 1(3)   £...................... (£.........../ac)
10 Adjustments for disregards
    in Paragraph 1(3)
11 Scarcity................................. £......................
12 Marriage Value....................... £......................
13 Effect of premium................... £....................

14 Total adjustments for disregards in
    Paragraph 1(3)   £....................
15 Rent after statutory deductions   £......................(£.........../ac)
16 Adjustment for different valuation
    date +/–%...............................   £....................

17 ADJUSTED CURRENT LEVEL OF
    RENT FOR COMPARABLE   £....................(£.........../ac)

Analysis of Current Level of Rent for Comparable

18 HOUSE... £......................
19 COTTAGES .... £......................
20 BUILDINGS .... £......................
21 LAND (see Schedule on Appendix 5)
22 ....Acres....................... @   £............... = £......................

23	....................Acres.....................	@	£...............	=	£......................
24	....................Acres.....................	@	£...............	=	£......................
25	....................Acres.....................	@	£...............	=	£......................
26	....................Acres.....................	@	£...............	=	£......................
27	....................Acres.....................	@	£...............	=	£......................
28	....................Acres.....................	@	£...............	=	£......................
29	....................Acres.....................	@	£...............	=	£......................
30	....................Acres.....................	@	£...............	=	£......................
31	....................Acres.....................	@	£...............	=	£......................

32   Total (gross/net)
                  ADJUSTED CURRENT LEVEL OF
                  RENT FOR COMPARABLE   £......................
         ....(line 17)   (£..../ac)

Items * delete as appropriate

NOTES

References below are to line numbers on Appendix 6.

Line 1	Name and address of comparable holding.
Line 2	Acreage either gross or net.
Line 3	Present passing rent of comparable in total and per acre.
Line 4	Date when rent of comparable was last fixed.
Line 5	Terms of tenancy which affect the analysis, eg model clauses or full repairing liability, sporting rights or ability to alienate.
Line 6	How passing rent was fixed.
Line 7	Note any increase in value in respect of improvements disregarded under Paragraph 2 of Schedule 2 and add back.
Line 8	Adjust for any unusual features of comparable.
Line 9	Total adjusted rent so far.
Line 10 to 13	State basis and amount of any adjustment for disregards if the rent is considered to incorporate any element of scarcity, marriage value or any effect due to premium.
Line 14	Total of adjustments for disregards.
Line 15	Subtract line 14 from line 9 and insert.
Line 16	Adjust for any difference between date when passing rent fixed and valuation date for the subject holding.
Line 17	Subtract or add line 16 from or to line 15 to give the adjusted current level of rent for the individual comparable being analysed.
Line 18 to 31	Note availability of houses and cottages and buildings. Either include value of house, cottages, and buildings in the acreage values in lines 21 to 31, or show them separately from Appendix 5 the acreage totals of the different land categories and apportion line 7.
Line 32	The figure in line 17.

Appendix 4
Nitrate sensitive areas

Designation

The Water Act 1989[1] empowers the Minister of Agriculture to designate an area a 'Nitrate Sensitive Area' under the terms of the 1989 Act. This power is exercisable with a view to achieving the prevention or control of the entry of nitrates into controlled waters or watercourses as a result of the use of land for agricultural purposes.[2] The provisions of the 1989 Act are novel in that, unlike designating orders under other conservation legislation (see Ch 12 above), they enable the Minister to impose *positive* obligations on landowners and farmers, as well as prohibiting or restricting agricultural activities e.g. an order may require the construction of silage and/or sewage facilities.[3] Notwithstanding the conferral of mandatory powers, the thrust of the NSA provisions remains based on the voluntary principle enshrined in existing countryside legislation. Section 112(2) of the 1989 Act gives the Minister power to conclude management agreements with landowners and farmers in designated nitrate sensitive areas, and to provide grant aid. The Nitrate Sensitive Areas (Designation) Order 1990,[4] made under these provisions, has now designated ten areas as 'nitrate sensitive areas' as part of the pilot NSA scheme.[5] Detailed proscriptions to be observed under management agreements are laid down in the order, as are fixed rates of payment thereunder.[6]

The 1989 Act also empowers the Secretary of State, by order, to designate 'water protection zones' with the intent of preventing or controlling the entry of any poisonous, noxious or polluting matter into controlled waters.[7] Regulations under the relevant provisions have yet to be made.

Management agreements

Section 112(2) of the Water Act 1989 empowers the Minister of Agriculture to enter into management agreements with the owner of the freehold interest in land within a designated NSA, or with a person having any lesser interest in such land. A management agreement concluded under these provisions will bind all persons deriving title from or under the offeree landowner/tenant etc., but only to the extent that the agreement is expressed to bind successors.[8] The Nitrate Sensitive Areas

---

1 See s 112 Water Act 1989.
2 Section 112(1) ibid.
3 Section 112(4) ibid.
4 SI 1990/1013, as amended SI 1990/1187.
5 These designated areas are: Ogbourne St. George NSA, Egford NSA, Sleaford NSA, Branston Bootens NSA, Kilham NSA, Old Chalford NSA, Wellings NSA, Tom Hill NSA, Wildmoor NSA and Boughton NSA.
6 As to which see SI 1990/1013, Sch 4.
7 See s 111 Water Act 1989.
8 Section 112(3) Water Act 1989.

(Designation) Order 1990[9] makes provision for two different classes of management agreement. A 'basic scheme agreement' will include the obligations specified in Sch 1 to the 1990 order. These restrict, for instance, the amount of inorganic nitrogen that can be applied in a single application to 120 kgs per hectare, and specify the amounts of inorganic nitrogen fertiliser which can be applied in any one year to certain crops. The obligations specified under a 'premium scheme agreement' are more onerous, and are set out in Sch 2 to the 1990 Order. The latter provides four options for the conversion of arable land to permanent grassland, and detailed proscriptions as to its maintenance and grazing. A basic scheme agreement can only be concluded in respect of *all* the land in a designated NSA occupied by a farmer, or on his behalf, for agricultural purposes.[10] This rule is subject to exceptions in the care of landlord and tenant.[11]

Differing payments per hectare for obligations entered into under 'Basic' and 'Premium' scheme agreements are proscribed in Schedule 4 of the Nitrate Sensitive Areas (Designation) Order 1990.[12]

Landlord and tenant

Being a person with an 'interest' in the land let, unlike a share farmer, a tenant will be entitled to conclude a management agreement under the NSA provisions of the Water Act 1989. The latter specifically provides,[13] however, that any participant other than a freehold owner must obtain the owner's written consent before concluding a management agreement.[14] The Nitrate Sensitive Areas (Designation) Order 1990 provides,[15] further, that the Minister can (once consent has been obtained) enter into an agreement with both a landlord and his tenant, even though the land is not occupied by the landowner (or on his behalf) for agricultural purposes. Although the landowners written consent is required before a management agreement can be offered, if consent is forthcoming a tenant can conclude an agreement even if he rents other land within the same NSA whose landlord has refused consent.[16]

It is specifically provided that the compliance of a tenant with any undertaking or obligation imposed on him under the Nitrate Sensitive Areas provisions of the Water Act 1989 *shall not* be capable of constituting a breach of tenancy.[17]

---

9 SI 1990/1013.
10 SI 1990/1013, art 5(1).
11 As to which see *ibid* art 5(3).
12 SI 1990/1013.
13 See Water Act 1989, s 112(2).
14 Cf. s 18(3) Agriculture Act 1986, which merely requires a tenant to notify the owner when entering a management agreement in an environmentally sensitive area.
15 SI 1990/1013, art 5(3).
16 Ibid art 5(4).
17 Water Act 1989, Sch 25, para 75, adding a new para 9(3), 10(3) and 11(3) to Schedule 3 of the Agricultural Holdings Act 1986.

Index

Agistment
 contract of, 99
Agricultural holdings
 Act, importance of, 1
 agricultural land. *See* AGRICULTURAL LAND
 agriculture, used for, 17, 18
 anomalies, dealing with, 7, 8
 arbitration. *See* ARBITRATION
 business premises code, and, 43–45
 definition, 16
 exclusions to statutory protection –
  agreement made before 1st March
   1948, 37
  gratuitous licences, 38
  grazing and mowing agreements, 32–34
  lettings for periods between one and
   two years, 37, 38
  limited interests, tenancy granted by
   person with, 37
  Ministry consents, 34–37, 384, 385
  office holder, tenancy granted to, 38, 39
 Housing Act, protection under, 47–49
 legal interests protected –
  annual tenancy, 25
  arbitration, disputes referred to, 31
  emblements, extension in lieu of claim
   for, 30
  statutory extension of tenure, 25–29
  two years or more, tenancy for, 29, 30
  yearly tenancy, conversion to. *See*
   TENANCY
 notices, service of, 375–377
 protective legislation, 8
 record of condition of, 79
 Rent Acts, and, 45–49
 rents. *See* RENT
 single contract of tenancy, under, 16
 substantial agricultural user, 19, 20
Agricultural land
 aggregate, holding as, 16, 17
 change of user –
  agricultural use –
   abandonment of, 21, 22
   change to, 22–24
  Code, property moving in and out of, 20
  tenancy, importance of terms of, 23
 definition, 19

Agricultural land – *continued*
 development. *See* PLANNING CONTROL
 land, meaning, 19, 259, 262
 tenancy of. *See* TENANCY
 trade or business, use in connection with,
  24
 unlawful use of, 20
Agricultural Land Tribunals
 constitution, 350, 351
 costs, award of, 357
 fixed equipment, jurisdiction. *See* FIXED
  EQUIPMENT
 High Court, appeal to, 349, 355–357
 issue estoppel, 356
 judicial review of decisions of, 349, 357
 jurisdiction, 349, 350
 notice to quit, consent to. *See* NOTICE TO
  QUIT
 procedure –
  decisions, 354
  evidence, 354
  extension of time, 355
  forms, 352, 353
  hearing, 353, 354
  interlocutory applications, 353
  pre-hearing, 352, 353
  Rules, 351
  time limits, 354, 355
 succession –
  direction for, 167
  tenancy granted by, 152
Agricultural marketing quotas
 cereals co-responsibility levy, 338
 dairy quotas, differing from, 337
 potatoes, 337, 338
 sugar, 337
Agricultural rents. *See* RENT
Agricultural research
 carrying out as ground for notice to quit,
  107
Agricultural tenants
 insecurity at common law, 2
 security of. *See* SECURITY OF TENURE
 statutory protection of, 2, 3
Agricultural tenure
 alternative forms of –
  joint ventures, 39–41

409